C000076386

GLADSTONE

Gladstone
God and Politics

Richard Shannon

Hambledon Continuum is an imprint of Continuum Books
Continuum UK, The Tower Building, 11 York Road, London SE1 7NX
Continuum US, 80 Maiden Lane, Suite 704, New York, NY 10038

www.continuumbooks.com

First published 2007

British Library Cataloguing-in-Publication Data
A catalogue record for this book is available from the British Library.

ISBN 978 1 84725 202 9

Typeset by Pindar New Zealand (Egan Reid)
Printed and bound by Biddles, Norfolk, Great Britain

Contents

In memoriam

Maurice Cowling

1926–2005

Preface

I wrote in 1982 that a comprehensive new reading of Gladstone was necessary and possible. That is still the case. Meanwhile, the mountain of materials available is augmented ever more dauntingly. Publication of the fourteen volumes of Gladstone's diaries, edited by Professor M. R. D. Foot and Professor H. C. G. Matthew, was completed in 1994. They fittingly compound the first great cache of political papers initially selected by Gladstone himself for his muniment, and then further selected and arranged by A. Tilney Bassett and deposited in the then British Museum in 1930. These 750 volumes, together with the family and estate materials in the Clwyd Record Office and St Deiniol's Library at Hawarden, remain among the largest archives of British statesmen. Published material otherwise, both by Gladstone and about Gladstone, is also dauntingly voluminous. This present offering attempts to comprehend what is essential to its purpose by reconciling mass with concision.

To my earlier expressions of gratitude for generous permissions of access, principally Sir William Gladstone KG, and for aid and assistance in innumerable ways, I must add other names. Both Martin Sheppard and Tony Morris, then of Hambledon and London publishers, have provided invaluable offices in getting the enterprise up and running. Bruce Hunter of David Higham Associates has been an indispensable presence. At Continuum, Ben Hayes is an editor both critical and sympathetic at the right times and in the right ways. Slav Todorov and Vanessa Fawcett have been most meticulous in their attentions to the text. My friends Julian Jackson and Patrick Higgins have been of crucial help in all sorts of practical matters.

I regret that I did not become aware until alerted by Professor M. R. D. Foot of Jean West's valuable work on Gladstone and Laura Thistlethwayte (*Historical Research*, vol. 80, 2007, Institute of Historical Research) in time to incorporate her matter into my text.

Richard Shannon
Marylebone, 2007

Abbreviations

BL	The British Library
CG	Catherine Gladstone
D	*The Gladstone Diaries, 1825–1896*, eds M.R.D. Foot and H.C.G. Matthew (14 vols, 1968–1994)
DDCP	*Disraeli, Derby and the Conservative Party. Journals and Memoirs of Edward Henry, Lord Stanley, 1849–1869*, ed. J. Vincent (1978)
G	W. E. Gladstone
G & G, 1	*The Political Correspondence of Mr Gladstone and Lord Granville, 1868–1876*, ed. A. Ramm (2 vols, 1952)
G & G, 2	*The Political Correspondence of Mr Gladstone and Lord Granville, 1876–1886*, ed. A. Ramm (2 vols, 1962)
GGP	The Glynne–Gladstone Papers, St Deiniol's Library, Hawarden
G & P	*Gladstone and Palmerston: Being the Correspondence of Lord Palmerston with Mr Gladstone, 1851–1865*, ed. P. Guedalla (1928)
GP	The Gladstone Papers, British Library Add. Mss.
H	*Hansard's Parliamentary Debates*
Hamilton, I, II	*The Diary of Sir Edward Walter Hamilton, 1880–1885*, ed. D. W. R. Bahlman (2 vols, 1972)
Hamilton, III	*The Diary of Sir Edward Walter Hamilton, 1885–1906*, ed. D. W. R. Bahlman (1993)
LQV	A. C. Benson, Viscount Esher and G. E. Buckle (eds), *The Letters of Queen Victoria*, 9v., 3s. (1907–32)
Morley	J. Morley, *Life of William Ewart Gladstone* (3 vols, 1903)
PMP	*The Prime Ministers' Papers: W. E. Gladstone*, eds. J. Brooke and M. Sorenson (4 vols, 1971–1981)
Q & G	*The Queen and Mr Gladstone*, ed. P. Guedalla (2 vols, 1933)

Introduction

My aim in preparing this single-volume study of W. E. Gladstone is to offer to a general readership a readily accessible account of one of the most important and consequential political careers in modern British and Irish history. It is a story of how a statesman of almost superhuman energy and forcefulness of character strove to realize God's purposes, as he saw them, in the twisting and slippery paths of public service. Striving to realize God's purposes is the theme at the centre of this reading of Gladstone's life and career. For too long his intense religious faith has been exiled to the margins of the story, denied crucial explanatory power. To Gladstone's enemies and critics it has been merely a matter of rank Tartuffian hypocrisy; to his friends and admirers an embarrassing foible, understandable enough in the early fanatical Tory, but awkwardly at odds with his later enlightenment. It has been allowed at most what one of his very distinguished biographers of recent years described as a 'supportive' role.[1] In a winningly readable recent major biography of Gladstone, that of Lord (Roy) Jenkins, the religious dimension for any practical interpretational effect simply does not exist.[2]

A second theme much in need also of being accorded its properly high explanatory power is the question of the problematic nature of the Liberalism for which Gladstone is historically most famed as related mainly to his heritage as a disciple of his political 'master and teacher', Sir Robert Peel. Within this theme, the salient features are the claims of the executive against Parliament, and the claims of party leadership against party.[3] Gladstone's Liberalism was a great problem for the Liberal party. That too needs to be better understood.

The Gladstone story revised in these terms will I trust be an accurate account of his immense career. The very immensity of that career is in its own way a difficulty both for writer and reader, for all that there was a distinct and legible line of consistency throughout it. Between 1832, his twenty-second year, and 1895, when he retired, Gladstone was a member of two Parliaments of King William IV and thirteen Parliaments of Queen Victoria. Having passed with scholarly acclaim through Eton and Oxford, he became a minister of the Crown in his twenty-fourth year, a minister again and a privy councillor in his thirty-first year, of cabinet rank in his thirty-third year. He served in five Cabinets under Sir Robert Peel, Lord Aberdeen, Lord Palmerston (twice – once very briefly) and Lord

Russell, before first forming his own in his fifty-eighth year. He was four times Prime Minister, author of eleven budgets, heroic legislator, 'People's William', 'Grand Old Man', tribune extraordinary of Ireland, immensely idiosyncratic as a statesman, in his way much more than Disraeli an exotic outsider, identified in the insight of the German sociologist Max Weber as the charismatic embodiment of the 'Caesarist plebiscitarian' spirit, dictator on the battlefield of elections, by far the biggest beast in the Victorian political jungle.

I first came to Gladstone at Cambridge under George Kitson Clark as a somewhat raw colonial boy possessed of the simple opinion that Gladstone was a hero and Disraeli a villain. My intention in studying the celebrated *Bulgarian Horrors* episode of 1876 was to subject it to close attention, clear up the details, and experiment in some primitive quantitative treatment of the incidence of popular agitation and of the significance attached to it in the political-intellectual history of the time. In the result I felt a little uneasiness. It was not that Disraeli proved not to be a villain. It was that the picture presented by Gladstone's famed biographer, John Morley, was skewed and distorted. My uneasiness was greatly compounded when I was congratulated by the notorious Maurice Cowling of Peterhouse for having exposed Gladstone as a less than heroic participant.

What I had exposed, in fact, rather in spite of myself, was Morley's less than candid treatment of the episode. Gladstone's own account was perfectly honest. He admitted his opportunism, and, for that matter, admitted that, even as opportunism, it was tardy and incompetent. Compared with Gladstone's apologetic candour, Morley's dramatic fiction of his hero responding to Byronic trumpet calls took on a decidedly false note. Morley actually excised passages in Gladstone's account that did not fit his, Morley's, distorting purpose. I have spent many a time getting undergraduates to compare Morley's text with Gladstone's text and spotting the differences as an elementary exercise in textual criticism.[4]

Though I was not aware at the time of any sensible shift in my own attitude to Gladstone in general, it came upon me gradually that what Gladstone studies were most in need of was candid treatment of Gladstone; and that Gladstone himself was the best provider of this. That is to say, attend to what Gladstone said about himself, and accept that he meant what he said. That was the lesson I learnt in writing *Gladstone and the Bulgarian Agitation, 1876*, published in 1963. I have attempted to apply that lesson ever since.

That *Horrors* matter was of course a minor historiographical incident. But, as it seems to me, it bore big indicative implications. It raised no less than the issue of Morley's general reliability as a biographer of Gladstone. This went far beyond petty questions of textual criticism. It had to do with dispositions at large as to the particular authorial tilt and with what shadings and lightings Gladstone was to be depicted for public consumption. And that implication looms even larger when consideration is given to the fact that Morley's reading remains subtly influential to this day as the *fons et origo* of what must be called the standard or orthodox tradition of how Gladstone has been and is presented to the world as politician and statesman.

To put it shortly, the Gladstone we got in three hefty volumes from Morley in 1903, and the Gladstone we have inherited since from Morley, was and is a Gladstone immensely winning but essentially skewed and distorted. The power of Morley's imprint stems from two causes. First is the sheer quality of Morley's literary handling of his purpose and his materials. Second is the way Morley's literary talents agreed with the post-Victorian spirit of his times. His *Life of W. E. Gladstone*, authorized by the Gladstone family, proved to be a classic. In certain important respects it did not reflect accurately Morley's own candid private opinions as Gladstone's colleague about Gladstone's later career.[5] But his depiction of Gladstone as a 'wonderful pilgrim' questing from Tory darkness to Liberal light was a skilfully crafted celebration that more than fulfilled its purpose as an inspiration to the distraught Liberal party in its travails at the beginning of the twentieth century. If Gladstone himself inflicted grievous wounds on the Liberal party, Morley's biography of him was as a healing balm. Morley set new standards both of literary and intellectual excellence for the Victorian 'tombstone' political-biographical genre. His *Life of Cobden* of 1881 had already shown promise of high talent. His *Gladstone* was deservedly a brilliant success, and its influence continues accordingly to permeate Gladstone studies to the present time.[6]

A notorious freethinker and 'secularist', with sympathetic attractions to the 'religion of humanity' of Auguste Comte, Morley was not the Gladstone family's first choice of biographer; and he was required to abstain from treating in any depth the religious dimension of Gladstone's life.[7] Thus was inaugurated the split between Gladstone's public life and his Christian devotional life that has bedevilled Gladstone studies ever since. Morley's reading of Gladstone was a secular one, in one sense of requirement, but in a larger sense of preference, which suited the twentieth century all too well. To that secularity Morley added a liberal-left political stance stemming partly from his early political years in journalism as champion of uncompromising Radical values and claimant to succeed John Stuart Mill as Liberalism's house philosopher; and then, after the long gap consequent on parting company with Joseph Chamberlain in order to get snugly into Gladstone's pocket, partly from the 'progressive' mood that informed Liberalism in the late nineteenth and early twentieth centuries.

The Gladstone produced in this context became the Gladstone familiar over the generations since: the quintessential, model 'Gladstonian Liberal'. The awkward paradox, however, as I hope to demonstrate, was that the Liberal Gladstone was never a Gladstonian Liberal. At the heart of the Liberal story in the later nineteenth century was an original problematic about the nature of

Gladstone's Liberalism. There were shrewd observers at the time of his leaving the Conservatives and joining with Lord Palmerston and Lord John Russell in 1859 who spoke of the 'secondary, and almost accidental character of Gladstone's Liberalism'.[8] It is not the least of the evidences of Morley's genius that he deprecated the notion that Gladstone at that juncture underwent a 'conversion', for all the 'enormous significance of the party wrench'. Gladstone remained for the time, in Morley's phrase, 'a liberal reformer of Turgot's type'.[9] This was, in its way, as shrewd an analysis as any coming from the leading lights of the Liberal intelligentsia at the time. After all, as a keen student of politics himself at the age of twenty-one, Morley was already pretty much as good a rabbi as the best of them.

For Morley, Gladstone's 'conversion' would come a little later, when 'the necessity of summoning new driving force, and amending the machinery of the constitution', would disclose itself. But was there ever, in reality, such a 'conversion'? Certainly Gladstone was converted to the idea that the political constituency in the country would need to be enlarged by a second Reform Act, an idea he had hitherto consistently resisted. He was converted, concomitantly, to the idea that a new driving force of the 'people' created by Reform would be necessary as materials to be manipulated by him for ends determined by him. Quite what 'Liberalism' had to do with this remained ever a difficulty. If Liberalism is in essence the conclusions arrived at from reasoned lay discussion as to humanity's forward progress, Gladstone remained in essence a being if not quite alien to it, then in most respects other than it.

Was the case, as many supposed, at bottom a matter of Gladstone's trimming himself from being a Conservative with dim prospects to being a Liberal with bright prospects? The Conservative party, having failed in the last four general elections to regain the country's confidence, could not be the fulcrum of great governmental leverages. The advice given him back in 1857 as to his prospects by the leader of the Peelites, Lord Aberdeen: that in this age of progress, the Liberal party must govern; and if Gladstone wanted to be at the centre of power, there he would have to go.[10]

The great lesson to be learnt from observing Gladstone's leadership of the Liberal party from the 1860s through to the 1890s is that Gladstone's Liberalism was never at home in the Liberal party in Parliament (let alone in the Reform Club, where he took care never to summon it),[11] and that Gladstone's Liberalism and what can fairly be identified as parliamentary 'Gladstonian Liberalism' steadily diverged to the point ultimately almost of incompatibility. It was a different story 'out of doors'; and indeed one of the most prominent themes of the decades of Gladstone's leadership was his use of the 'people' as a weapon against unsatisfactory parliaments, a weapon quite as much aimed – as in 1868, 1880, and 1886 – at Liberals as at Conservatives. Liberalism out of doors was much more easily manipulated from the platform than parliamentary Liberalism could be driven in the lobbies.

These are matters not attended to in Morley's reading of Gladstone. This non-attendance is where a good deal of the skewing and distorting alluded to above comes from. A particularly significant part of it comes from a reluctance to cite the name of Peel. In no respect are the benefits of attending to what Gladstone said about himself and believing that he meant what he said more evident than in his readiness all through his career to testify to his devotion to the example of Sir Robert Peel and his devotion to Peel's memory. These were far from being testimonies to mere piety. All the essential grounds upon which Gladstone set out his vision of the future of his politics after the collapse in 1855 of Aberdeen's attempt to revive Peelism were expressed in Peelite terms: that the future of politics would consist in the doings and intentions of the minister and in the corresponding conviction wrought by them in the public mind.[12] To that formula of 1856 Gladstone remained true to the end of his career. Not the least of the things that Gladstone learnt from Peel's example was the necessity of providing for himself what Peel had so disastrously lacked in 1846: a massive and supportive public opinion 'out of doors' with which to challenge a refractory party or an unsatisfactory Parliament. Gladstone had to become a Liberal in order to get a grip on such an opinion. But he did not have to be a Liberal to decide for what purpose his doings and intentions would manipulate a corresponding conviction wrought in that public mind. Gladstone put the matter with his accustomed honesty in 1865. He was a member of a Liberal government. He was in association with the Liberal party. He had never swerved from what he conceived to be those truly Conservative objects and desires with which he entered public life.[13]

It was a doctrine perfectly compatible with being an authoritarian exponent of executive prerogative. That indeed was what Gladstone had always been and ever remained, whether of Turgot's type or Peel's type. At no point in his leadership of the Liberal party did Gladstone ever consult the party about what it wanted to do. All his great legislative strokes were his exclusive texts. For all that Morley was bound to insist that 'we cannot forget that Peel and Mr. Gladstone were in the strict line of political succession',[14] Morley was ever chary of confronting stark implications of that fact of succession in all strict honesty: that if in the earlier half of the nineteenth century Peel whipped the Conservative party with whips, Gladstone in the later half whipped the Liberal party with scorpions.

Perhaps the most telling indication of Morley's abiding disposition to domesticate the Gladstone beast is to be found in his almost panic-stricken confusion of the issue when confronted with Gladstone's 'General Retrospect' of 1897, a fragment among the autobiographical pieces he was then compiling. Gladstone's notion was to encapsulate his career in one concise explanatory formula. It marched appositely with his formula of 1856 about the doings and intentions of the minister and the corresponding conviction they wrought in the public mind. In 1856 Gladstone was looking forward; in 1897 looking back.

It was a question of his considering 'upon a calm review' the possibility that he had been endowed by providence with the striking gift of insight into the facts of particular eras, and their relations one to another, that generated in his mind a conviction that the materials existed for forming a public opinion, and for directing it to a particular end. He cited four signal occasions of this insight: renewing Peel's income tax in the budget of 1853, disestablishment of the Irish Church in 1868, Irish Home Rule in 1886, and confronting the House of Lords in 1894 over its challenging the 'nation' in its cruel treatment of Liberal legislation. Gladstone wanted to make clear that this providential gift of appreciating a general situation and its result was an entirely different matter from mere opportunist acceptance of public opinion in being, discerning that it had risen to a certain height needful for a given work, like a tide.[15]

Morley perversely chose to misinterpret entirely. 'It is easy to label this with the ill-favoured name of opportunist.'[16] Certainly Morley would have disliked Gladstone's magnificently imperial authoritarian tone about 'materials' to be manipulated and directed. How unliberal can you get? Could the Grand Old Man really have meant what he said? But what put Morley into a mental panic about Gladstone's Retrospect was undoubtedly a deep disquiet about its religious tone and implications. For here arises the biggest single aspect of Morley's skewing and distorting of Gladstone.

Gladstone's diaries are for the most part arid accounts of his employment of God's precious gift of time, within a quite conventional Evangelical tradition of self-incriminating soul-searching. But they are also intermittently of unsurpassed importance in their revelations of Gladstone's intimately interior spiritual life. They give details of Gladstone's self-imposed mission to rescue and redeem prostitutes, and of his enigmatic relationships with certain particularly beautiful courtesans going far beyond the requirements of rescue and redemption. There was no question of Morley's unveiling this side of the Grand Old Man's private life to the public of 1903. That was impossible and the omissions quite understandable. But by far the most important revelation imparted in his diaries was Gladstone's growing conviction that his political career was becoming embraced within intimations of the guidance of divine providence and the bestowing of direct and personal divine inspiration. These intimations culminated amid the crisis of the Eastern question in the later 1870s in a conviction that he was summoned to service within revelations of 'marks of the will of God', and visions of the relations between his public duties and the 'primary purposes for which God made and Christ redeemed the world'.[17]

As a rule, Morley's *Gladstone* text is copious in quotations from Gladstone's speeches, correspondence, memoranda and diary entries. And indeed, while he passes over Gladstone's first bout of ruminations at the end of 1878 about God's assigning him as an instrument of his divine purposes on earth, he does not ignore Gladstone's second bout of ruminations at the end of 1879 on the divine inspiration committing him to accept a 'great and high election of God', and much else of similar solemn import.[18] As with the Retrospect, to ignore such profoundly intimate and personal affirmation on the part of his subject would be, biographically speaking, impolitic. What he does, however, is to pass on promptly without any comment on that import. When it comes shortly after to Gladstone's reflections as he went to meet the new Parliament in 1880, on his being overpowered as he thought 'by what deep and hidden agencies' he had been brought back from retirement, and how he believed that the Almighty had employed him for His purposes 'in a manner larger or more special than before', Morley quipped: 'One who approached his task in such a spirit as this was at least impregnable to ordinary mortifications.'[19]

That quip tells us much about Morley's deep unease at having to grapple with such stuff. He recounted – much to his credit – an occasion at Biarritz in the 1890s when, in a 'tremendous tussle' in a 'long morning conversation on Locke', Morley was startled to discover that Mr G. was 'of the same mind, and perhaps because of the same sort of reason', as the French clerical reactionary Joseph de Maistre, that contempt for Locke was the beginning of knowledge. The young Tory Gladstone in fact gave many testimonies to his contempt for the philosophic father of Liberalism, John Locke.[20] There had been no 'conversion' on that point. Morley was profoundly shaken by this insight into the interior values of a Peelite High Churchman. 'All very well for de Maistre, but not for a man in line with European Liberalism'.[21] What, however, is most telling about this encounter is that Morley passed quickly on, avoiding any obligation to explore the mystery of how precisely such values held by the leader of the Liberal party could be reconciled within British Liberalism, let alone the wider European scene, and what implications might emerge out of their irreconcilability. Such exploration would have led Morley into strange terrain, full of hazards to his enterprise. There lurked a Gladstone very much a great beast, little apt for domestication.

For what Morley might have come upon in such exploration was the explanatory power abiding in Gladstone's being somewhat off the line of European Liberalism. Those convictions on Gladstone's part as to his assigned role in the lower world as an instrument – however unworthy, as he invariably stipulated – of purposes from on High offer by far the most plausible and most cogent explanations of the God-driven confidence with which in 1886 he launched out on his last grand political mission, to give Dublin back with generous hand its Parliament. He had never been wanting in confidence in his earlier missions. He had always been his own man with his own text in his legislative measures. Triumph in 1880 over his party and the 1874 Parliament made him henceforth invulnerable to the kind of party recalcitrance he had had to put up with in the 1860s and 1870s. But, even so, no reading of his manipulative behaviour to his colleagues in government and his party in the years between 1880 and 1886 can adequately account for his motives in the absence of an awareness that he considered himself to be in inspired assignment to the 'disposing, guiding hand of God', biding his time accordingly for what the Lord would bid him do.

Without such awareness, what we get from Morley is pretty much as blandly domestic a scene as high politics has ever provided. He makes of Chamberlain's complaint that 'I don't see how we are to get on, if Mr Gladstone goes', the 'key to many leading incidents, both during the life of this administration and for the eventful year in Mr Gladstone's career that followed its demise'.[22] What was in reality the key to those years of his second government was Gladstone's blocking all efforts in the party to provide itself with political nutrients, not excluding notions of a fair deal for the Irish, the better to clear the way for his own notion of what the duty of the party was to be. The duty of the party within the bounds he rigorously confined it was to accept obediently that a third Reform Act, a mechanistic non-nutritional measure, was all they were going to get. (Even then, he unknowingly let Salisbury loose on the Redistribution of constituencies aspect, to his and the party's detriment.)

The reality of the eventful year of 1886 in Mr Gladstone's career was his imperious foisting upon his party without consultation of a radical policy it would never of its own initiative have undertaken; and of how he ignored those backbench Liberals who desperately tried to get him to listen to advice from the party as to how a scheme for Irish autonomy acceptable to the Irish, the Liberal party and the country at large might be achieved.[23] The names of such Liberals – Rathbone, Illingworth, Pease, Firth, Brassey, Melly, Caine, Whitbread, Maguire – simply do not appear in Morley's account.

They never have appeared in any account since, such has been the influence of Morley's example. An important part of my general aim is to retrieve these names from the historical limbo into which they have been exiled and to present them as crucial witnesses in the Gladstone case. Another name of a crucial witness which does not appear is that of George Shaw-Lefevre. He was the first Liberal within the larger tradition of guidance by John Stuart Mill and John Bright on the Irish land question to grasp the idea in an effective and practical form that the way forward was not to prop up landlordism as Gladstone attempted to do in 1870 but to promote purchase of tenancies by tenants from landlords willing to sell by means of funding provided by the state. In Dublin, in 1877, Gladstone declared his approval of this policy as beneficially applicable to Ireland. In the Commons in 1879 he endorsed the findings of Shaw-Lefevre's committee to that purpose.[24] But that was a time when, having abdicated the Liberal leadership, Gladstone was in a position, as he put it of another issue at the time, of greater freedom and less responsibility. Arriving back in office in 1880, he dumped Shaw-Lefevre. Perhaps that was why Morley ignored the entire episode. Nor have any of his followers repaired the omission. It is my conviction that had Gladstone from 1880 listened to these witnesses instead of launching out on his own inspired and self-sufficient exercises in heroic legislation on Irish land in 1881 and Irish autonomy in 1886 his story would have been a very different one from that of the sad failures that actually ensued.

Certainly, it was Gladstone's genius to appreciate that there had to be an appropriate and adequate response in Britain to the Irish revolution as manifested in the Parnellite sweep of its constituencies in 1885. It was his tragedy, and Ireland's tragedy, to be possessed of an overweening but deluded self-confidence in his own capacity in precipitate leverage of the Liberal fulcrum to provide that response. Had it been left within a frame of time allowing British opinion to digest the implications of what happened in Ireland in 1885 the story, again, might have had a happier ending. But even all that begs the big historical question. The question seriously starts being asked in Ireland about 1879 and in Britain when Gladstone stormed back into power in 1880. What the Liberal party mostly wanted to deliver was a big measure of democratic local government reform both in Britain and Ireland and a measure to begin the shift on Irish land from landlordism to smallholders. It bears repeating that the key feature of his ministry from 1880 to 1885 was that Gladstone very deliberately prevented these things from happening. This is not the place to debate his motives. But it is the place to point out that this is not the Gladstone story we have been given and still get.

A generic feature of that story is the profound misconception accredited by Morley and received since that 'Home Rule for Ireland' meant only and ever what Gladstone said it meant in his Government of Ireland Bill of 1886, or as modified in 1893. This unexamined assumption has exerted a deplorably distorting effect. Home Rule was in fact a protean concept, susceptible before 1886 of many definitions, ranging from virtual independence (the Canadian analogy) to subordinate devolutionary arrangements (the London County Council analogy). Counterfactual historical hypotheses about how alternative versions might have served in different circumstances and on different occasions before 1886 are therefore legitimate matters of speculation, just as are alternative versions as recommended by our Liberal witnesses in their efforts to sway Gladstone in and after 1886.

Unexamined assumptions remain largely the rule as one surveys the Gladstone biographical record since Morley. Nothing was published until the last decades of the twentieth century to disturb the Morleyan orthodoxy. The story held firm of a sensible, practical, moderate, benevolent far-seeing statesman thwarted by malignant, sterile obstructers – Hartington, Salisbury, Chamberlain. At the present time two major biographies of Gladstone stand formidably in the tradition inherited from Morley. The late Professor H. C. G. Matthew, editor of most of the *Diaries*, published *Gladstone, 1809–1874* (1986) and *Gladstone,1874–1898* (1995), composed for the most part from the introductory material in the *Diary* volumes, completed in 1994. A consolidated volume, *Gladstone, 1809–1898*, appeared in 1997. As with Morley, classic powers are abundantly in evidence in Professor Matthew's reading of Gladstone. The Oxford mind, the Treasury mind, the vital role of the elites of reformed universities, mastery of budgetary and administrative intricacies, all are admirably deployed. His analysis of the great themes distinctly characteristic of Gladstone's politics and personality – the way his early Church and State doctrines moved towards pluralism, his ideal of a minimalist free trade state, his flexible, executive *étatisme*, his innovative forms of political communication – earn the reader's entire confidence. The very impeccable worthiness of Professor Matthew's text in such matters seems indeed to convey a correspondingly impeccable worthiness on the part of its subject. Editing the *Diaries* was in all sorts of ways an invaluable discipline.

In all sorts of other ways, however, things not in the *Diaries* tend not to be in the story. There is a dimension of Gladstone largely unreported. Where, for example, is the testimony of one of Gladstone's colleagues and companions through many decades, the Duke of Argyll, on the unsafeness of Gladstone's judgement at times of stress, and how on critical occasions the cast of his mind could become essentially fanatical?[25] Where is the testimony of another colleague and companion over many decades, Lord Acton, on Gladstone's disconcerting capacity to live entirely in what for the moment he chose to believe?[26] As for the Treasury mind, where is the explanation of Gladstone's throwing over the tenant-purchase Irish land policy he embraced in Dublin in 1877 and at Westminster in 1879?[27] These things are not mentioned. If indeed the Treasury mind was at the back of that repudiation, it deflected British policy fatefully away at a critical moment from what proved ultimately to be the solution to the Irish land problem. Such indeed were marks of the beast.

The late Roy Jenkins' *Gladstone* appeared in 1995. Apart from its winning readability, it bears to a certain extent the unequalled authority of a front-rank statesman dealing with matters familiar both to Gladstone and to Morley and himself. What emerges is a story of how Gladstone played the high political game in the same upright and wholly above-board manner as did Lord Jenkins himself. It was Gladstone's high-mindedness, Lord Jenkins had no doubt, that made him incomprehensible to the Conservatives in 1886. That was not, however, John Morley's private conviction as to Gladstone's playing his deviously high game.[28]

Lord Jenkins saluted Professor Matthew as the 'doyen' of 'Gladstone experts'. They were both of liberal-left political persuasion. Professor Matthew was a keen Labour party member; Lord Jenkins, of course, was for many years a prominent frontbench spokesman and minister for that party, until breaking away to help found what eventually transmuted into the Liberal Democrat party. Their readings of Gladstone, it has to be said, without being in any way simply or crudely derivative, are both consistent with their politics. Neither, however, it equally must be said, is uncritical of Morley. For Lord Jenkins he is 'over-respectful in content'. Gladstone's 'departures' from the highest standards of progressive politics Professor Matthew allows to be 'far from the simple nobility' found in Morley's biography.[29]

Thus Professor Matthew comments scoldingly on the 'insufficient education' Gladstone bestowed on his party prior to his great Irish initiative. He is severe also on Gladstone's failure to provide any coherent plan for the Liberal party in relation to local government; and is especially severe on Gladstone's 'ducking' the question of Irish local government. He finds the disappearance of the promising devolutionary Grand Committee initiative in 1883 'something of a mystery'. He finds the absence of any serious 'forward planning' curious to the modern eye. He is uneasy at Max Weber's Germanically sociological insights into Gladstone's charismatically Caesarist otherness. He is uneasy also at the tone of Gladstone's Retrospect for rather similar reasons, and inclines to adopt Morley's obfuscation.[30] Above all, Professor Matthew is quite shocked at Gladstone's unabashedly 'inequalitarian' opinion that the political value of the newly enfranchised masses was for morals and ethics, not for intellect.[31] This glimpse of a deplorably 'very non-Liberal view', like Morley's glimpse about contemptible Locke, leads on, however, to no exploration of strange and hazardous terrain.

It does not occur to Professor Matthew to consider whether these are significant explanatory instances telling us something about the real Gladstone rather than occasions of pained rebuke at the unwonted lapses of a modern 'progressive' Gladstone. Much of this, I suspect, comes from muddled thinking. Thus, on the Home Rule matter, Professor Matthew asserts, absolutely correctly, that Gladstone followed 'a thoroughly Peelite interpretation of the right and duty of government to propose legislation and policy unencumbered by mandate'.[32] At the same time, however, he laments that Gladstone's explanation of his failure to get it through – 'the people do not know the case' – was 'an appalling admission' for the 'leading exponent of government by argument to make'.[33] He seems to want to have it both ways.

Like Morley, Professor Matthew quotes Gladstone's conviction of a great and high election of God; but all the explanation he is willing to allow is that Gladstone must have felt 'supported'.[34] The 'powerful impulses' of the 'personal commitment the Eastern Question called forth' he allows to be 'of a new order'.[35] But of quite what is not clear. Beyond that he dared not go. He found the 'dualism' of a 'retired gentleman-scholar and God-driven statesman' 'at least curious, even bizarre'.[36] This is a respectful version of Morley's quip about mortifications. Indeed, 'bizarre' becomes something of a leitmotiv for Professor Matthew's wonderment on occasion at Gladstone's strangely errant behaviour. There are moments when one feels that Professor Matthew is almost on the brink of a breakthrough into a really new explanatory order. 'Only an astonishingly bold, robust, and self-confident politician', he points out, 'would have forced the pace the way Gladstone did between January and June 1886.'[37] Quite. What particularly impresses Professor Matthew about Gladstone at that hectic time is 'absence of self-doubt'. But where it all might have come from remains in discreet obscurity. Again, when he makes the very accurate comment that the 'address of September 1885 was the only moment in Gladstone's career when he acted as a party leader in the normal modern mould, integrative, cautious, holding the centre ground',[38] he might have drawn attention to the circumstance that the G. O. M. was engaging in an operation of deliberately not telling the nation what he was planning to do, of being what many later held against him, deceitful. There were many faces of the big beast; here they are kept decently concealed.

Lord Jenkins quotes the 'high election' extract without venturing a word of comment. On the other hand, Professor Matthew grapples with it. He discounts and marginalizes it into a supportive role in a process whereby Gladstone allegedly reconstructs a 'moral unity' through the 'humanitarianism of the party of progress', transmuting the earlier 'religious objectives' of his politics into a 'tacit acceptance of secularism' and a 'more explicitly political ideology of a progressive citizenship'. Explanatory notions Gladstone himself might have put forward about his devoted discipleship to the doctrines of Bishop Joseph Butler about the way the inner and higher prescriptions of religion are made applicable to the outer and lower world of affairs and politics are simply not admitted into consideration. This clears the way conveniently. 'Tacit' acceptance of secularism and an explicitly political ideology of progressivism Professor Matthew sees as the means of Gladstone's 'reformation of Liberalism without serious schism and with eventual success'.[39]

Quite apart from the rabbit-out-of-a-hat nature of this reformation, it has to be remarked that 'tacit' is a wonderfully convenient word. Probably the best comment apropos of it is to point out that Gladstone remained anything but taciturn in his continuing invocations of the Almighty and his convictions of providential guidance, even, on occasion and to public scandal, in public. But perhaps what is most needed is an awareness of a sub-text informing the pages both of Professor Matthew and Lord Jenkins, suggested by the extrapolation of Liberalism as the 'party of progress' to an ampler context of 'the parties of progress'. We have here, I suspect, a version of Gladstone as prophet and forerunner not only of New Liberalism but of New Labour also. Lord Jenkins contributes a disarmingly Asquithian touch.

It has to be said that Lord Jenkins, for all his own prowess as a maker of budgets and a liver of the grand life at the political centre, contributes little else. For him Professor Matthew is 'the unmatched cicerone of Gladstone's life and *oeuvre*'. Where Professor Matthew dares not venture, neither goes he. Explanation is not his forte. From time to time he exposes what can only be called a certain shallowness of understanding. Gladstone sets off to Lancashire, the Tyne, Midlothian, to embrace the 'million'. Why? Because he became, 'to put it vulgarly, hooked on crowds'.[40] For Lord Jenkins, Gladstone's visit to the 'uncompromising Tory' Lord Salisbury at Hatfield in December 1868 while in the throes of forming his first Liberal Cabinet was simply inexplicably 'bizarre' behaviour. All he can suggest by way of explanation is the occasional quirky oddity of public men. It 'foreshadowed almost exactly similar behaviour by Asquith thirty-seven years later during the making of the next major reforming government'. Gladstone, in fact, had perfectly sound reasons for consulting his fellow churchman and Disraeli-hater at that critical juncture.[41] With the same kind of shallowness of understanding Lord Jenkins accounts for Gladstone's behaviour in 1880–85 merely as a consequence of the 'improvisatory character' of his situation stemming from resignations. He explains the 'barrenness' of that ministry by Gladstone's 'failure of generalship', allowing 'issues to pass over his head'.[42] He states incorrectly that Gladstone was never a member of the Reform Club. In 1869 Gladstone had indeed to be shoehorned in by party managers embarrassed at the scandal of the Liberal Prime Minister's not being a member, and resigned with indecent promptitude after six years of pretty much ignoring the place. To this day there are people puzzled at the absence there of a grand portrait of Liberalism's Grand Old Man. What really is puzzling is the absence of any speculation as to whether this absence might bear significant comment on the nature of the Grand Old Man's Liberalism. For all his bold words about Gladstone's being the biggest beast in the Victorian political jungle, Lord Jenkins ended up with a sadly domesticated animal.

From all this it can readily be appreciated that I became dissatisfied at what seemed to me the gross disparity between Gladstone's own explanations of himself, which I had learned to trust, and these domesticatingly tacit ideological progressive explanations. They left Gladstone's accounts of the higher visions that inspired him as a difficulty unacknowledged and left dangling in a kind of interpretational void. I felt that a challenge to Morley and all that his inheritors stood for needed to be made. Gladstone, I feel I have to insist, was highly problematical precisely because he was so undomesticated. In a curious way, I felt an affinity with those sceptical Liberals like Goldwin Smith and Walter Bagehot who in 1859 pondered on what seemed to them the secondary and almost accidental 'otherness' of Gladstone's Liberalism.

Accordingly, at the invitation of Messrs Hamish Hamilton, I attempted what

I hoped would be a corrective contribution in two volumes of a biography of Gladstone, *Gladstone: Peel's Inheritor, 1809–1865*, in 1982, and *Gladstone: Heroic Minister, 1865–1898*, in 1999. (The awkward gap was a consequence of my having to wait for completion of publication of the *Diaries*.) They made, I trust, an honourable challenge. 'Dense, informative and controversial', in Lord Jenkins' words about the first volume, they indeed were too dense for their own good. The controversy rather got lost in the density. Content dulled contentiousness. All this I have attempted to avoid in the present volume. It gives also an opportunity to reinforce, improve and distinctly sharpen the focus of the argument.

The argument, it seems to me, is ultimately most revealingly and valuably focused on how Professor Matthew ultimately read the meaning of the most consequential of all Gladstone's legacies, his Home Rule for Ireland plans of 1886 and 1893. The case for Gladstone as heroic but thwarted exponent of a great missed opportunity to reconcile Ireland with the British Crown is at the heart of that reading. It might be remarked parenthetically apropos of the devolutionary principle in Home Rule that one's confidence in Professor Matthew's historical judgement is decidedly dented when he insists that the principle was neither strange nor singular at the time, as witness the 'improved and settled relations' of the Sweden–Norway example.[43] There was nothing strange in Gladstone's refusal to believe the Foreign Office reports that that exercise in home rule was falling apart amid bitter recrimination; but to find Professor Matthew seemingly unaware of it 91 years after its dissolution one can only describe as bizarre. 'Many people might also be uneasy at Professor Matthew's apparent enthusiasm on the grounds of the Gladstonian 'European idea' for what he regards as the home rule for the United Kingdom implications of Britain's adherence to the Treaty of Rome.[44] However: 'Gladstone's proposals still hold the field', he insisted in 1995, 'as the means of constitutional reorganisation of the United Kingdom.' Indeed and alas, Gladstone's proposals do still hold the field, as the embarrassments of the present 'party of progress' on the 'West Lothian' issue testify.

Morley himself, as a former Irish Chief Secretary, proposed to Gladstone in 1889 a sensible pragmatic solution to the conundrum of Irish legislative privilege and British legislative penalty: if Ireland were to have both its own Parliament in Dublin and representation at Westminster, as was to be provided for in the second Home Rule Bill eventually introduced in 1893, it would be equitable that the former should be much curtailed in competence, and the latter much reduced in numbers. It would not be possible to get this past the Irish, as Gladstone well knew. In 1886 Gladstone had offered the Irish a version of a 'Canadian' constitution, as makeweight for there being no further Irish representation at Westminster. And Gladstone was under pressure from others of his colleagues, that Irish representation at Westminster be restricted neither in numbers nor in voting; the Liberal party would need them for future majorities.[45]

Morley's pragmatically equitable proposal might well have worked. (It worked for the Northern Irish contingent at Westminster after the setting up of the Stormont Parliament in 1920.) Needless to say, Morley says not a word about it in his biography of the man who in effect vetoed it. But in any case, that kind of pragmatism will almost certainly not be allowed to work within the current dilemma of the 'West Lothian' conundrum because of the Labour party's need of future majorities provided by Scottish and Welsh representatives at Westminster. It must also be remarked that the validity of Professor Matthew's case depends on the historical skewing of the Home Rule question: the great unexamined assumption that there could have been no other version and no other way. The prevailing strength both in popular and political memory of this assumption lies undoubtedly in the fact that, given the sheer grandeur of Gladstone's statesmanship, imbued manically with overweening self-confidence, none other than the Grand Old Man could have pushed it as far as he did. Which brings me back to my backbench Liberal witnesses in the Gladstone case in 1886. They warned Gladstone that he would not get away with the Home Rule Bill he had foisted on the Liberal party. In doing so, they represented no less the noble tradition that it was to the Liberal party that throughout the nineteenth century the Irish looked for remedy of their grievances. These witnesses represented a counterfactual possibility of an alternative response to the Irish electoral revolution of 1885. This, in turn, raises the counterfactual question of how, in the hypothetical contingency of Gladstone's absence in 1886, would a Liberal government and the Liberal party have eventually muddled through to a resolution of the question. Gladstone, after all, had been announcing his imminent retirement ever since 1875. Was the cruel fact of the matter, in the end, that it was Gladstone's abiding presence on the scene, a vigorous septuagenarian, and his eagerness to play the heroic role, with all the fanaticism in the cast of his mind that had long before been identified, that led Professor Matthew to conclude that it is 'not difficult to see the latter part of Gladstone's public life as a failure'.[46] If a great historical opportunity was missed in 1886, was it Gladstone who missed it?

1

Early Years, 1809–1831

'Politics are fascinating to me. Perhaps too fascinating.'

Diary entry by Gladstone, 29 December 1831

William Ewart Gladstone was born in Liverpool, on 29 December 1809, in what was then and is now 62 Rodney Street, a handsome house in a new development in the south-east quarter of the city in which his father had made extensive investments. Although he never lived in Liverpool after his father John moved out in 1831, the city remained for William Gladstone, as one born in the purple of its commerce, a lifelong presence. From time to critical time throughout his long career, he would make of Liverpool a rostrum from which he addressed the nation on matters of high public concern.[1] An 'old Whig' was said to have remarked, 'with a touch of bitterness', on one of Gladstone's budgets, 'Ah, Oxford on top, but Liverpool below'; to which John Morley's riposte remains apt: 'no bad combination'.[2]

By the time of the birth of his youngest son, John Gladstone was well on his way to becoming one of the merchant princes of a city celebrated already as a considerable port of world commerce. He traded in the transatlantic and Baltic corn and tobacco markets. William Ewart was at that time his principal business partner. The Gladstones or Gladstanes or Gledstanes were of purely Scottish descent and Presbyterian confession. John's father Thomas had migrated from Biggar to establish himself at Leith as a modestly successful merchant. An advantageous marriage to Nelly Neilson, daughter of a Springfield merchant, proved fruitful: John, born in 1764, was the eldest of seventeen siblings, the most talented and forward of their eight sons. Tall, strong, ambitious, craggy-visaged, John Gladstones migrated in 1787 to England's second port and mercantile metropolis. There his drive and abilities would enjoy a more ample scope. He dropped the 's' at the end of his surname as being commercially ambiguous. Marriage in 1792 to Jane Hall, of a Liverpool merchant family, brought John Gladstone into connection with a wider world of established Anglican religion. It was for Jane that the fine Rodney Street house was prepared. Jane, however, was sickly and left him in 1798 a childless widower. By that time John was worth something in the order of £40,000.[3]

In 1800, 29 April, at St Peter's church, Liverpool, John took as his second wife Anne Robertson, daughter of Andrew Robertson, Provost of Dingwall in Ross-shire. Though in one way John had thus reverted to his Scottish roots, in other ways the Robertsons opened up vistas even more spacious than those offered by the Halls. The Robertsons were a family in genteel circumstances, mixing land-owning, local politics, and the law in laird-like degrees. Though worth nothing like John Gladstone in realisable cash, they possessed qualities John recognized as not merely desirable but essential for promoting the way of life and career he had in mind for himself as a rising merchant prince and potential political eminence in his adopted city.

The Robertsons were Episcopalian. When in 1815 John came to build an imposing country house, in an estate on the Mersey estuary between Bootle and Crosby, he named it Seaforth House after his wife's connections with the earl of that title. John accordingly relinquished his family links with the Kirk and with Unitarian manifestations in Liverpool, and adopted his wife's denominational colouring, which was not merely Episcopalian but pronouncedly Evangelical in tone. Evangelicalism of the kind relished by Mrs John Gladstone was not available in Liverpool, whose Anglicanism was unregenerate and unenthusiastic. John attested his commitment to his new ecclesiastical loyalty by building his own churches and installing his own incumbents in both Liverpool and Seaforth. To the latter he added a school, where his children could be given their preparatory education under immediate parental supervision.

Anne, frail and delicate like John's first wife, proved more fruitful. She bore him six children: Anne Mackenzie in 1802, Thomas in 1804, Robertson in 1805, John Neilson in 1807, William Ewart in 1809, and Helen Jane in 1814. By the time of the birth of his last child, John was 50, with patriarchal habits and manners. Mrs John, wholly self-effacing, found the duties in an alien land of running two large houses and the obligations of being hostess for a rising business and political luminary intimidating. She asked only to set the domestic religious tone of the family at a fanatical level of intellectually undemanding piety, and to guide her husband and immerse herself in a suitable variety of pious charities.

By 1820 John Gladstone was worth more than a third of a million. He dominated his business concern, choking off rival partners and clustering his dependent brothers about him. He crowned his Liverpool career by stabilizing and rationalizing grain provision for the Lancashire of the early industrial revolution by the mechanism of the Liverpool Corn Exchange. Nearly a third of his fortune by now came from investments in estates in Demerara worked by slave labour. This was perfectly in accordance with the habits and traditions of Liverpool, but it caused problems for the Gladstones. Evangelicalism was the prime ingredient of the anti-slavery movement. This domestic and political tension long remained unresolved.

Politics was now at the centre of family concerns. Having made his pile, John nursed ambitions for a correspondingly successful career in the House of Commons. Originally a Whig, he shifted his ground towards support for Pitt's war policy, and in 1812 was foremost among the citizens of Liverpool who invited the illustrious George Canning, Pitt's political heir, to be one of the members for the city. One of William's earliest memories was as a child in a red frock being set on a table in 1812 before the great man and instructed to say 'Ladies and gentlemen' to divert the company.

Canning was an inspiring image for John Gladstone of what he would like to have been, but could not be. But Canning was a feasible model for what John Gladstone's sons might emulate. Canning's genius transcended his modest origins and mastered the intensely aristocratic social and political world of his day. He exemplified what innate talent combined with the processing offered by Eton and Christ Church, Oxford, could achieve. The Gladstone children were bred up in an atmosphere heavy with devotion for that image and that model. The glories of Canning's time after having succeeded Castlereagh at the Foreign Office in 1822 as challenger of the Metternichian order in Europe, patron of South American freedom, and as partner of Byron in the movement for liberating Greece, permeated Rodney Street and Seaforth.

Then came his ultimate if tragically short-lived triumph in succeeding Lord Liverpool as Prime Minister in 1827. Canning's championing of Catholic Emancipation and resistance to wholesale parliamentary reform accorded well enough with Rodney Street. William Gladstone would frequently punctuate his politics with fond reminiscences of Canning and stirring appeals to the glorious examples set by Canning.[4] Meanwhile, resonances of the great metropolitan world of affairs and the ideal of the pagan polish of classical education pervaded the Gladstone household, mingling uneasily with the native values of provincialism and sanctimony.

The tensions thus besetting the family afflicted them in a way that William, the only one who surmounted the problem successfully, half-sensed but could not, in the nature of such things, accurately explain. They set John Gladstone off on his painful and futile quest for political eminence. They reduced Mrs Gladstone to feeble nullity. Their eldest child, Anne, had the wit to cope but not the strength. As soon as she was of years of discretion she effectively replaced her mother as the domestic linchpin. As William's godmother she played an important role in his early intellectual and religious formation.

From his cosy family school hapless Tom was thrust into the rude and boisterous world of Eton, his task being to show the way to the making of a young Canning and winning the world's acclaim. Tom was not up to it. He thus commenced a long career of mediocrity by failing to make a mark at Eton and then failing to make a mark in the House of Commons. Robertson, the next brother, was a more robust character. Destined by his father to take over the business, he was removed from Eton and sent to Glasgow for a sound commercial education. Robertson alone stayed in adult life in Liverpool, asserting his independence by marrying (particularly to William's horror) a Unitarian lady and later professing that creed. He moved also in a distinctly Radical political direction. The third son, John Neilson, escaped into the Navy. That ended in a commandership (captaincy on retirement) and in following Tom in ineffectual mediocrity as occasional backbench Member of Parliament. Helen was the only one of the children who could be said to have reacted strongly against her family. There was no other way of escape for a young female 'of family'. Much of her later bizarre career, from her conversion to Roman Catholicism to her financial scandals and bouts of alcoholism and drug addiction, had about it something of a mode of revenge. Fifteen years of age when her elder sister Anne died in 1829, Helen became her mother's companion in her life of ill-health, cures, spas, doctors and medicines, taking on much of her mother's habits of invalidism. When Mrs Gladstone died in 1835 Helen became in turn her father's domestic prop. Frustrated and unhappy in that role, she gravitated out of the family orbit, spinning erratically, until her father's death in 1851 allowed her to settle into pious retirement.

This leaves Willy, who succeeded his sister Anne as the darling and favourite of the family. Everything, indeed, rather conspired in his favour. He was the youngest son of fairly elderly parents. His father was 45 when he was born, nearly 60 when he started at Eton, nearly 70 when he graduated at Oxford. His elder brothers stood as buffers between him and the full impact of John Gladstone's formidable personality. Unlike Tom, Willy did not have to be the first of the family to brave the outside world. Indeed, Tom was there at Eton to ease Willy's early terms. Willy had Robertson to stand between himself and his father's wish to have a son go into the family firm. Moreover, Willy had the benefit of the ripening maturity of the mind and character of his sister Anne, much the acutest brain, apart from his own, in the family. It was Anne who first made Willy aware of the deeper and wider spiritual and intellectual values of their religion, a feat quite beyond the capacity of their mother and quite outside the interests of their father.

Certainly there was little, other than Anne, that might have given Willy that first, vital impulse to transcend his family's values. Willy had a way of getting on and not causing his parents anxiety or making difficulties. He gratified his father with early evidences of determination to succeed. Gladstone himself remarked on his early tendencies to 'priggish love of argument'.[5] This paternal characteristic of disputatiousness, which was to remain with him all through his long career, gave him a distinct advantage in his father's estimation. It is significant that Gladstone's earliest abiding memory of his infancy was of 'struggling or fighting' his way up a staircase, urged on by his nurse. The infant struggler or fighter up the ladder of success was very much the father of the man as well as being the son most like his father.

~

Such a son would certainly be encouraged to follow Canning's path. Willy went on to Eton in 1821, slotting into the place vacated by Robertson and having the luck to have Tom as his fagmaster. As Oppidans not on the Scholars' foundation, they lodged in a Dame's house. Tom departed in the following year without having attained to the dignity of the Sixth Form. It soon became clear that such would not be Willy's lot. He adapted himself readily, though taken aback by the entire absence of the devotional atmosphere cultivated at home. He enjoyed the advantages of being both personally prepossessing and inconspicuous. His parvenu background was not unusual in the Eton of those days. One of his fags later described him as 'a good-looking, rather delicate youth, with a pale face and brown, curly hair, always tidy and well-dressed'.[6] Sartorial niceties would continue to exercise Gladstone's attention well into his middling years. Sculling on the river and serious walking became his preferred physical exercises rather than team sports of football or cricket. 'Scrambling & leaping' expeditions are recorded. Wine parties were a regular feature of social life. Willy became known among his fellows as 'Mr Tipple'.

In most casual respects Willy was a not uncommon type of adolescent schoolboy. He became an expert on coaches and coaching, an expertise necessitated by the nomadic way of life now beginning to be imposed upon the family by his restless father. He was flogged by the notoriously prone-to-flog Headmaster, Keate. Gladstone later recalled of his Eton life that the 'plank' between himself and 'all the sins' was 'so very thin'. 'I did not love or habitually practise falsehood, meanness or indecency: but I could be drawn into them by occasion and temptation.'[7]

In certain important respects, however, Willy proved to be decidedly an uncommon type of schoolboy. Command of classical Greek and Latin came readily to him. Excellence in the scholastic exercises most esteemed in the College drew the attention of Keate's assistant, Hawtrey, later himself a reforming Headmaster and then Provost. Hawtrey 'sent Gladstone up for good', in the Etonian formula, to the diminutive but awesome Keate. 'It was an event in my life', Gladstone later recalled, and it 'for the first time inspired me with a desire to learn and to do.'[8]

Willy never lost the momentum thus gained. He was 'sent up' to Keate in all three times, establishing a reputation at Eton for exceptional scholarship. He was made Captain of the Fifth Form in 1826 and Keate promoted him to the elite Sixth Form in 1827. Beyond his classical distinction Willy gave abundant evidence in these early years of that taxonomic passion for systematizing, classifying, ordering, arranging and allocating that was one of the abiding characteristics of both the private and public spheres of his life. Significant also in this respect was his memory as a child of having 'a great affinity with the trades of joiners and bricklayers'.[9]

Another important distinctive attribute of the Etonian Gladstone was his response to the opportunities offered by Eton's latitude in allowing for activities outside the formal courses of studies. Canning's example in making Eton a training ground both for oratory and literature set a compelling precedent. Canning's fame and glory as Foreign Secretary and then Prime Minister coincided with Willy's Eton years. Though Canning had exchanged his Liverpool seat for the less exacting one of Harwich, his career was still the staple of Gladstone family attention and the focus especially of Willy's ardent hero-worship. He gained election to the Eton debating society in 1825, and thereafter the society's affairs became one of his most absorbing concerns. Keate forbade debate on contemporary political issues but there were ingenious ways of construing the past for the purposes of the present. The weekly paper of entertainment and amusement produced by Canning and his circle at Eton, the *Microcosm*, was the model aspired to by Gladstone and his circle in producing, 40 years later, the *Eton Miscellany*.

Gladstone was aware of a weight of paternal expectation that he prepare for a career in politics. Already he was calculating the matter of entering Christ Church, the grandest Oxford collegiate nursery of statecraft. The Eton debating society activities, in which Gladstone emerged as a leading figure, mark a crucial stage in the development of his self-awareness, both by providing him with a forum for expression in speech and print and by linking him in friendship with fellow-Etonians at a critical point in his adolescent emotional life. Among these were George Selwyn, later Bishop of New Zealand and Lichfield and inspiration of a Cambridge college, Gerald Wellesley (later Dean of Windsor and Gladstone's principal adviser on ecclesiastical patronage), Francis Hastings Doyle, James Milnes-Gaskell, Charles Canning, and above all Arthur Hallam, son of the historian, a youth of exceptional attractiveness.

The intense friendship which developed between Gladstone and Hallam became for Gladstone the great landmark of his Eton years, much in the way that for Tennyson shortly afterwards Hallam transfigured his time at Cambridge. *In Memoriam* testified to Tennyson's sense of desolation at Hallam's tragically untimely death in 1833, and of the spiritual solace attainable by poetic retrieval of the ideal moral quality of their friendship. In Gladstone's case the intensity of their relationship became a powerful element in his effort in the Eton years to construct the beginnings of a moral system adequate to control the pressures and urges bearing on him as he grew into adulthood. Though more than a year junior to Gladstone, Hallam's immersion in his family's easily latitudinarian and gracefully Whiggish culture more than made up for that disparity. A good part of the attraction of Hallam for Gladstone was that he embodied values quite different from those Rodney Street or Seaforth House stood for. There was nothing about Hallam of struggling and fighting up the ladder of success. Gladstone later summed him up as one of those to whom it was more given 'to *be* rather than to *do*'.[10]

Their intimacy had much about it of schoolboy romances. It was certainly quite proper and indeed in some respects quite formal. They were always 'my dear Gladstone' and 'my dear Hallam' in their correspondence. They disputed as reforming Whig versus resistant Tory, but agreed as to Canning's 'Liberal Tory' politics of emancipating Catholics, espousing commercial freedom, and challenging the Holy Alliance in Europe. They did not dispute about religion. Gladstone at Eton made no attempts to proselytize. To Gladstone Hallam admitted a wholesome fear of being called to account for himself 'at the bar of your severe morality'. At that bar Gladstone declared Hallam's Eton life an 'ideal life', without 'deviation from the ideal, in temper, word, or act'.[11]

To Hallam's example of an 'ideal life' Gladstone added the beginnings of what he later defined as the ideal of a 'severe life'.[12] This was by far the most important of the aspects that made Gladstone an uncommon type of schoolboy. There had always been a tension between the absolute values represented by his mother's and his sister Anne's loving doctrinal severity and the worldly values engendered by his father's ambitions for him. But it is perhaps the most telling evidence of the unproblematic ease of Gladstone's passage through Eton that this tension never imposed itself as a disabling burden. Willy carried over into Eton the religious exercises drilled into him at Seaforth. Nightly prayers and Bible-readings were routine. In 1825 he commenced a record of his daily expenditure of God's precious gift of time. Such journals or diaries were a common feature of the Evangelical tradition of soul-searching and testing for spiritual seriousness. That such a record would inevitably and necessarily be a basis for self-indictment was an integral feature of the discipline.

As a good Calvinist young Willy was doctrinally well aware of his hopelessly sinful nature and his unregenerate helplessness in the absence of divine grace. Willy enjoyed cards, billiards, above all the theatre, that *bête noire* of Evangelicalism. Theatre would eventually become something of a passion for Gladstone. But the moral code being instilled by his sister Anne permitted cards and alcohol but frowned upon the stage. From 1826 Gladstone began to use his birthday as an occasion of stringent self-examination, arriving invariably at dismal conclusions as to his desperate and incorrigible wickedness. Confirmation in February 1827 came to him as a plenary *rite de passage*, for all that it was administered to near-200 Etonians as the merest matter of form by the worldly Bishop Pelham of Lincoln. Gladstone became, and remained for the rest of his life, a diligent communicant. That vicious winter of 1827 had killed the Duke of

York. It was attendance at his funeral at Windsor on freezing flagstones that then killed Pelham. Another victim of those flagstones was Canning. But he managed to survive into the summer.

That was Gladstone's last golden Etonian summer. Hallam set off in July for Trinity, Cambridge. Gladstone had a year to fill in until a place at Christ Church would become available. Bulletins from his father at Seaforth about Anne's declining health troubled him. Canning's death in August, after a mere three months as Prime Minister, made the poignant void of Eton even more poignant. Gladstone paid a visit of homage to Canning's grave in Westminster Abbey on his way back from Seaforth to Eton in September, composed elegiac verses, and purchased a portrait and a bust. He departed Eton finally in December 1827, 'foolishly full of melancholy' that 'the happiest period of my life is now past'. Through all his long life Gladstone's fond devotion to the 'Queen of schools' never slackened. 'But oh! if any mortal thing is sweet, my Eton years, excepting anxieties at home, have been so!'[13]

~

The spires and towers and domes of Oxford that so enticed Gladstone as he commenced his first term in 1828 were those of a university on the way to being redeemed from its eighteenth-century torpor. Though still in the full panoply of its majestically unreformed devotion to the Church of England, new life of the intellect was beginning to stir. The statute setting up in 1800 the Honours Schools of *Literae Humaniores* and Mathematics and Physics proved successful in attracting the best minds among the undergraduates to test their wits against the examiners. Robert Peel's double first-class in 1807 was a signal public event.

Peel was by no means a political hero to Gladstone in 1828. He had refused to serve under Canning in 1827 and was the leader of die-hard Protestant resistance to Catholic Emancipation. Even after Peel's capitulation on this issue in 1829 (and the sacrifice of his seat for Oxford University), Gladstone inclined to reservations. He was distinctly unenthusiastic when in 1830 his father suggested that Peel might be the best man to replace Canning's colleague and promoter of commercial reform, William Huskisson, accidentally killed by a railway locomotive, as MP for Liverpool. As John Gladstone well appreciated, Peel was a conspicuous public specimen of an expanding manufacturing and commercial middle-class now beginning to make its mark in first-rank politics. For all Gladstone's political reservations, Peel's brilliant example in the Oxford Schools stood before him in 1828 with an irresistible academic cogency.

That example Gladstone emulated with gratifying brilliance in the Schools in 1831, emerging as one of the two candidates awarded a first class in *Literae Humaniores*. Despite intensive coaching in mathematics before going up, Gladstone wavered as to whether he should ultimately take on the Mathematical School.

Having been permitted by his father to withdraw, Gladstone characteristically determined after all to brave the trial. His first class was all the more gratifying; and it permitted him to insist thereafter that mathematics was not 'part of the indispensable discipline of a highly educated mind'.[14]

As at Eton, Gladstone's scholarly prowess in the classical literatures had been duly noticed. He tried himself in 1829 in two of the University's most coveted awards, the Ireland and Craven scholarships. Though he failed in both he advertised his merits. He won the Fell exhibition. Dean Smith promoted him to a junior studentship. He read steadily and voraciously. Aristotle became an important reinforcing influence on his already well-developed systematizing turn of mind. As at Eton, he lamented the stagnant condition of religion in the University. As at Eton he cultivated political interests and ambitions. A letter from an Etonian friend, Pickering, in August 1829, is covered by Gladstone with exquisitely penned doodles: lists of ministers, many facsimiles of Palmerston's signature (Palmerston being claimant as Canning's principal disciple), many facsimilies also of the Marquess of Clanricarde (Charles Canning's brother-in-law); and two lists of his friends bearing the honorific dignity of privy councillors: the Right Honourable Members of Parliament included Milnes Gaskell, A. H. Hallam (twice), Sir P. A. Pickering (twice), F. H. Doyle, G. A. Selwyn, C. J. Canning (twice), A. C. Wood, W. W. Farr and, modestly but decisively there, the Rt. Hon. W. E. Gladstone.[15]

Given that interest and ambition, and also in the Eton pattern, Gladstone became a keen participant in the recently established debating club, the Oxford Union. He made his maiden speech there in February 1830, and was elected to the committee. Hallam came over with members of the Cambridge Union to debate the merits of Byron versus Shelley. Hallam assured Gladstone that the future great poetic genius of the era was one Alfred Tennyson, at Trinity. It was word from Hallam also that had stimulated Gladstone in 1829 to form an essay-reading group on the model of the Cambridge Conversazione Society or 'Apostles'. The 'Weg', as it was called after his initials, appointed him secretary and met usually in his set at Christ Church.

At Oxford, as at Eton, Gladstone found time for a wide range of agreeable social occasions. There were wine parties, teas, dinners, walks, 'romping at night', outings such as the 'exceedingly pleasant' visit to Henley in June 1829 to witness the first Oxford and Cambridge boat race. Although never noted as a dandy, he remained always an admirer of high sartorial tone. Being a junior student meant wearing a gown fuller and more flowing than the 'scanty and odious concern' on a commoner's shoulders.

In certain important respects, however, Gladstone's Oxford life differed from the Eton pattern. Religious activity became more open and pronounced. Under his sister Anne's tutelage he tested his Evangelical faith. He sampled what

Oxford city could offer in the way of Dissenting or otherwise irregular pulpits. It so happened that Gladstone found himself adrift on the theological issue of baptismal regeneration, repudiated generally among Evangelicals as priestly and popish but pointed to by Anne as a blessed matter of sacramental efficacy with all manner of patristic testimonies – including, most tellingly, that of St Augustine – in its favour. Anne won her brother over. At Oxford the implications thus set going fermented quietly.

The general integrity of Gladstone's Evangelicalism survived the Oxford years intact. In his father's library he read Hooker, the founding father of national Anglican theology, but his doctrines remained as yet a 'mere abstraction'. He found the future eminences of the catholicizing 'Oxford Movement' more repellent than attractive. He respected Edward Pusey but had serious doubts about J. H. Newman. Were all of John Keble's opinions 'those of Scripture & of the Church?' Henry Wilberforce and Vaughan Thomas scandalized him with their radical contempt for many of the heroes of the Reformation. Likewise did their critics, exponents of loose 'liberal' or 'broad' doctrine, influenced by Thomas Arnold, such as Richard Whately and Renn Hampden and F. D. Maurice. Even Bishop Butler, the great ornament of eighteenth-century Anglican theology, recently come into vogue in Oxford divinity, and later to become the object of Gladstone's fervently obsessed discipleship, shocked him by his lax doctrine on human nature.

Unsurprisingly in such circumstances Gladstone found it distressing that he seemed to be losing touch with Hallam. Meanwhile he appointed himself spiritual guide and mentor to his friends. Possibly they were not as grateful for or as edified by his vigilant solicitude as he hoped. When, as prickbill, or chapel attendance monitor, he presumed to apply his ministrations to the undergraduates at large, he found himself being given a humiliating beating in his rooms by enraged young men who thought him an intolerable prig.[16]

Gladstone transferred much of his local philanthropy from Seaforth to Oxford. A new departure marked his first night in residence. He recorded meeting a woman, and having a 'long conversation' with her. The following night he 'met the poor creature again, who is determined to go home'. This is probably the first instance of Gladstone's particular philanthropic exercise in redeeming prostitutes by persuading them to give up their abandoned way of life. This became and remained an important aspect of Gladstone's private life, a vocation later to be codified and integrated into a formal system of social hygiene; but at this stage he was taking only tentative steps.

In that office of redemption it seems that Gladstone found a means of sublimating sexual urges by channelling energies into exciting but morally controllable charitable activity. During these years he candidly recorded agonies about masturbation. He mentioned 'rankling passions' that disturbed him profoundly, 'passions which I dare not name – shame forbids it & duty does not seem to require it'.[17] Accosting and attempting to 'rescue' attractive prostitutes – Gladstone never disguised that such alone were the objects of his attentions – became a means of maintaining an equilibrium between the urgent demands of what he called his 'natural (& vigorous) tendencies' and the peremptory duties both of Christian celibacy and of Christian matrimony.

At that time, Gladstone's knowledge of females, apart from his immediate relations and servants, was practically nil.[18] He idealized his mother and sisters as creatures hardly on a merely human plane. The problem of polite feminine society presented itself to him as bristling with difficulty, anxiety and embarrassment. He was shy, ill at ease and painfully aware of his social clumsiness and lack of poise and emollient small talk. He unhappily knew that his manner 'tends to turn every conversation into a debate'. He knew that his opinions were those of 'a censorious and fastidious man'. He knew also that his letters had not seldom the 'air of memoranda intended to clear his own mind'.[19] This worked well enough in the company of his family and of male adolescent companions well aware that they represented the coming generation of great men in Church and State. He concluded that it seemed to him 'that female society, whatever the disadvantages may be, has just & manifold uses attendant upon it turning the mind away from some of its most dangerous and degrading temptations', perhaps of the kind too shameful even to name.[20]

In February 1829 came stunning news from his father at Seaforth that Anne had died suddenly on the 19th. Gladstone set off for home in a state of shock, 'much dismayed: but afterwards unable to *persuade* myself of the truth of the news'. He tried to fill the gap by proposing a solemn pact with his sister Helen that they should henceforth collaborate and monitor one another's religious and spiritual development in memory of the dearest departed. This proved more distressing than edifying for Helen, a rather 'difficult' fifteen-year-old, now oppressed by her parents' increasing dependence on her domestic presence.

For the time being, Gladstone's immersion in his Oxford 'business', his reading, his prize-hunting, the Weg, the Union, held at bay any marked psychic reaction to Anne's death. But that reaction came in full force in the summer vacation of 1830. In August he wrote to his father a formidably long letter in the form of a memorandum purporting to clear his own mind. He declared his desire to devote his life to the Church and to seek ordination. There was nothing unexpectedly new about this. From time to time since entering Oxford Gladstone had indicated that he was sensing a call from religion. By the end of 1829 he recorded that his mind was 'strongly inclined to the Church'.

What was new now was the intensity of his feeling that Anne had pointed the way to a higher life of sanctity and religious devotion, far different from what he well knew was his father's desire that he profess a career of secularity and public honours. But having thus 'cleared his mind', Gladstone wrote again a few days later allowing that upon such an 'awful subject' he was as yet too immature to decide, and that he must act not upon his own 'uncorrected impressions', but 'under the guidance of others'. This was a clear invitation to John Gladstone to manoeuvre his son with soothing advice that nothing be done rashly, and that he avail himself of all advantages placed within his reach. The father knew the son well enough to rely on the certainty that in the absence of a paternal veto on ordination William would supply one himself. Given William's devotional cast of mind, his insistence on being the 'chief of sinners', his cult of the sainted Anne, it was impossible for him to admit that, in a free choice of careers, he deliberately chose secularity and political ambition. That was a responsibility he preferred his father to bear.

It was later to be a feature of Gladstone's own mythology about himself that it was ever the desire of his youth to have taken Holy Orders. 'My mental life (ill-represented in the moral being) was concentrated in the Church'; and that the 'change in the professional direction' of his life 'took place in deference to my father's wish'.[21] It was a case in fact rather of his own peculiar and complexly pious kind of collusion and complicity with what he knew his father's wish to be. Perhaps that was at the bottom of his ritual but ferocious self-condemnation on 24 December 1830, 'dearest Anne's date of birth in the human state': 'I, the hypocrite, and the essence of sin, am indeed deceitful above all things and desperately wicked, desperately wicked.'

Still, the deed was done. His perplexity as to ordination resolved, Gladstone could confront his final academic year with his way tolerably clear. In any case a political vocation in itself by no means necessarily ruled out a life of devotion to the Church. There were of course the Final Schools to bear in mind. For that ultimate test he was planning a programme of intensive twelve-hour reading days. But meanwhile pressing matters of politics intervened. The great question of the reform of the constituencies electing the House of Commons had now emerged as the capital issue of the time. It happened also that John Gladstone was managing a particularly unpleasant and corrupt by-election campaign to replace the late Huskisson in Liverpool against the son of his old friend William Ewart. 'Politics are fascinating to me', Gladstone recorded. 'Perhaps too fascinating.'[22]

The Duke of Wellington's ministry, with Peel leading in the Commons, held that existing arrangements had proved their worth and that schemes of reform on offer were both unnecessary and possibly perilous to the public interest. Gladstone took Canning's view that wholesale schemes on first principles such as were being promoted by most reformers were indeed dangerous, and that piecemeal ameliorations to the electoral system such as Pitt had earlier advocated were vastly preferable. In November 1830 Gladstone carried the Union with a powerful oration to a vote of no-confidence in Wellington's government. This was the occasion on which he was elected president. A few days later, Wellington, having failed to convince either the country or the Commons, resigned, and Lord Grey came in at the head of a Whig-led coalition pledged to comprehensive electoral reform.

Confronted now with Lord John Russell in charge of a Reform Bill providing for expanded and uniform electoral rolls and with long schedules of doomed constituencies, Gladstone took fright. He remembered Canning's arguments against the folly of attempting to replace the organic creation of centuries with the paltry contrivances of presumptuous schemers. He read Canning's anti-Reform speeches at Liverpool and made extracts. He read Canning's great 1822 speech against Reform. He went back to the source of wisdom and read Burke.

In March 1831 he trusted to God that the Reform Bill would not be carried in the Commons. It scraped through by one vote. The Lords rejected it by a majority of eight a month later. There would be another general election. By April Gladstone found the 'excitement of politics' too much for his reading. He was working himself up into a panic about Reform. He threw himself frantically into the Oxford University and City elections in May 1831. On 17 May he spoke in the Union for nearly an hour, declaiming with passionate urgency his conviction that Reform threatened 'not only to change the form of our government, but ultimately to break up the very foundations of social order'. He made a startling and profound impression on his audience. There was uproar afterwards and adjournment; and two days later Gladstone carried the division by 94 to 38. The result he thought 'delightful'.

Less delightful, however, was the handsome majority in the country won by the government, including both Oxford City and Oxfordshire. Undeterred, Gladstone launched himself into a campaign in the University against the second Reform Bill, introduced in the Commons in June. He noted in July an 'excellent speech' by Peel. That leader of the anti-Reformers in the Commons was beginning now to take on in Gladstone's view an enhanced stature.

Availing himself of useful contacts at Christ Church, Gladstone gained the entrée to the Lords and was present in a fever of excitement at the five-night debate, October 3 to 8, sitting precariously on a transverse rail for nine or ten hours. He judged the orations on both sides 'most wonderful'. It was a week of intoxication and enchantment. He slept at the Albany chambers of his brother Tom. The Lords' rejection of the Bill by 199 not contents to 158 contents oppressed Gladstone with grave thoughts of hostile reactions in the country. 'God avert them – but it was an honourable & manly decision, & so may God avert them!'[23]

Hostile reactions there were indeed. Riots abounded. But Gladstone stood firm by the honourable and manly decision. The Final Schools now loomed. Far from being an academically injurious distraction, the political excitements and the adrenalin they pumped into his system more than likely helped propel Gladstone in his storming the Honours examinations in November.

The first class in *Literae Humaniores* was posted on 23 November. Saline draughts were prescribed to quieten Gladstone down. Congratulations came from Cambridge. Pickering invited Gladstone to attend Hallam's reciting his Prize Declamation in Trinity chapel on 16 December. The Mathematical first class was posted on the 14th. Gladstone felt an inexpressible 'joy of release'. It was 'an hour of thrilling happiness, between the past & the future, for the future I hope was not excluded'. The bustle of packing for Cambridge made a last round of visits pleasantly hectic.

On 15 December Gladstone found himself 'excellently lodged and most kindly received by the Master of Trinity', the father of his Christ Church friend Charles Wordsworth. He listened to Hallam's declamation and dined with him in Trinity Hall. To his '*very* great joy' Hallam – 'the *old* Hallam' – invited a renewal of their lapsed correspondence. By 21 December he was back in Liverpool, receiving a hero's welcome. Then to Seaforth with more 'great joy' to complete the round of family salutations. The Oxford test had been triumphantly surmounted. And the future was very definitely not excluded.

2

Church and State, 1832–1841

'Politics would become an utter blank to me, were I to make the discovery that we were mistaken in maintaining their association with religion.'

Gladstone to H. E. Manning, 15 March 1838

At Seaforth there were loose threads to be tidied up and finishing touches to be added to the education of William Gladstone. As to the latter, a European grand tour was planned. First, however, the career vocation had to be sorted out. How exactly to replace the discarded option of ordination? How to ensure that the future as promised in the triumph of the Oxford Schools be indeed not excluded? On 17 January Gladstone handed to his father an elaborate memorandum on his future profession. He argued that the present political crisis put all established attitudes and ideas in doubt. Parliamentary reform would lead to an attack on the Church Establishment. It was his duty to prepare himself to assist in responding to the coming formidable vicissitudes in public life rather than to withdraw into a cloistered vocation. He felt himself now 'free and happy to own, that my own desires as to my future destination are exactly coincident with yours', believing them to be 'profession of the law with a view substantially to studying the constitutional branch of it, and on experiment as time and circumstances might offer on what is called public life'.[1]

There were yet to be bouts of mental and emotional restlessness about this decision. Had Gladstone 'veiled' to himself under 'specious names' a 'desertion of the most High God'? A 'harrowing fear' would come to him that he had betrayed the cause of God to his worldly ambition, 'and sold even the cross of Christ for the love of earth and the things of earth'.[2] His sister Helen made no secret of her opinion that she thought so; and in Gladstone's eyes Helen still stood as something of a surrogate for the sainted Anne.

Fortunately, given Gladstone's capacities for devotional self-indictment, there was now little time for introspection. He was in the thick of much bustle and packing. The family were in the process of abandoning and letting out the Seaforth and Rodney Street establishments. John Gladstone, having failed to attain his ambition of representing Liverpool in the House of Commons together with Canning or Huskisson, spurned his adopted city. All he had achieved politically had been to represent, with various degrees of exorbitant expense, vexation and brevity, the dim boroughs of Lancaster, Woodstock and Berwick. As his son William summed it up, for all his father's success as a merchant, 'considering his long life and means of accumulation the result represents a success secondary in comparison with that of others whom in native talent and energy he much surpassed'.[3]

In 1829 John Gladstone prepared the way for a return to his Scottish roots by purchasing the estate of Fasque, with a large new castle-like house, in Kincardineshire. It would not be until 1833 that the family moved in and the Gladstones could think of it as their home. In the meantime John Gladstone was content to escort his invalid wife and manage his business concerns from spas and resorts in the south – Malvern, Gloucester, Bath, Torquay, Leamington. It all came to a sense of sad retreat from high hopes and expectations of earlier years: 'snatched', as Gladstone put it, 'from a position when we were what is called entering society, & sent to comparative seclusion, as regards family establishment'.

But now he himself was bustling and packing. He took melancholy leave of the house of his boyhood on 20 January. First, he had to return to Oxford to take his degree and settle his accounts and remove his effects. (The opening leg of this journey, from Liverpool to Manchester, was his first and much enjoyed experience of the new invention of the railway.) Then there was the grand tour to prepare for. He and John Neilson (Lieutenant, RN, but at present without a ship), accompanied by a factotum, Luigi Lamonica, set off at the beginning of February 1832 for six months touring in the Netherlands, France, Switzerland, Italy and southern Germany.

~

Gladstone embarked to Ostend with his Evangelicalism substantially intact. He arrived back in London at the end of July in a much more indeterminate condition. Naturally he had been fascinated by what he observed of religion in the Catholic lands of Europe. Much of what he observed shocked his Protestant sensibilities and reinforced his anti-Roman prejudices. Shameless Mariolatry seemed everywhere rampant. He was scandalized by the indecent slovenliness of many services and offices. He was offended by direct confrontation with the provocative arrogance of Roman doctrinal claims. The physical pomp and spiritual pride of Rome itself stirred his most Protestant emotions. Half the time he was appalled at the fearful threat to religious truth and liberty posed by a Roman Church flushed in its triumph over the spirit of Revolution and in the confidence of Ultramontane reinvigoration of the worst and most reactionary Tridentine traditions. The other half was his being appalled at what he saw as manifest evidences of Rome's hopeless decadence and imminent collapse.

Nevertheless, confronted with the imposing magnificence of Rome, Gladstone felt himself stirred by new and less negative emotions. Attending Easter benediction at St Peter's, he was overwhelmed by an historical vision of what such an occasion, sublime as it was, must have been in the 'palmy days' of the papacy. 'Nothing could be finer than this scene to the eye – even now it has too many claims on the mind – but admit the assumptions of Rome and its grandeur transcends everything.'[4] That Gladstone could speak already of 'claims of the mind' signified that something portentous was taking shape.

The more conventional aspects of grand tourism were by no means neglected. Gladstone was an assiduous inspector of monuments and galleries. He responded to art for the most part through a filter of religion. No famed landscape went unremarked. (The Protestant descendants of Milton's slaughtered saints of the Vaudois proved disappointing.)

Politics were also never far from his secular observations. The old Canningite attitudes to Europe tended now to be dimmed by strongly Conservative sentiments. Lord Palmerston had receded from Gladstone's undergraduate admiration. As Lord Grey's Foreign Secretary, his policies seemed to Gladstone highly objectionable. In the quarrel between the Dutch and the newly created Belgian state, Gladstone's sympathies were wholly with the Dutch. In the Pantheon in Paris the inscription to Voltaire as a teacher of freedom to the human spirit provoked a sharp retort that 'another kind of freedom was taught before him, and will live after him'. In Italy his austrophile observations were positively Metternichean.

Most insistently, in the background, was deplorable news of politics at home. In Rome, at the end of May, Gladstone read, 'with many a thrill of horror', the debates in the Lords on the new Reform Bill. So uniformly depressing were the reports that by his last day in Rome, on the 4 June, he declared that 'even terrible news is becoming dull & commonplace'. It was in Venice on June 16, while admiring the Austrian naval arsenal, that Gladstone read the 'disastrous but expected news' that the Reform Bill had passed in the Lords.

Two signal events marked for Gladstone indelibly those grand tour months of 1832. The first occurred in the unlikely ambience of Naples. Gladstone, knowing not quite why, began examining the Occasional Offices of the Church in the Prayer Book. He was struck particularly by the Order of Baptism. This linked back to his earlier introduction by Anne to the doctrinal implications of baptismal regeneration. Now Gladstone felt 'glimpses' of the 'nature of the Church', which 'involve an idea very much higher & more important' of it than he had previously conceived. This sudden revelation of the Church as a teacher of divine truth through its doctors and traditions and sacraments made on the Protestant, scriptural Gladstone a mark never to be effaced.[5]

While absorbing this profound inward revelation, Gladstone, nearly two months later, in Milan, was recalled to awareness of the secular world by a letter from his Christ Church friend Lord Lincoln, offering him the influence and interest of his father the Duke of Newcastle at Newark in the impending general election. Lincoln had been in the audience at the Oxford Union when Gladstone eloquently denounced Reform. It was on the strength of the impression then made on him that Lincoln advised his father that Gladstone was political material well worth investing in. John Gladstone consented promptly. If ever there was an advantage placed within William's reach for him to avail himself of, this was it. The two brothers arrived back in England on 29 July.

~

The Duke's influence and interest in Newark meant a fair probability of success. The Reform Act, however, had changed the borough from a little over 500 'scot and lot' voters to a constituency of 1600. There was a new and unpredictable popular spirit abroad in the political atmosphere. The Act did not touch the traditional allotment of two members. But, given that heightened stir of tension, there would be no old-fashioned deal between parties to divide the spoils and save expense. The Tory interest would field two candidates. There would be a Whig challenger. Gladstone would have to fight for his prize. That he was well used to doing. Storming Newark would not be all that different from storming the Oxford Schools.

The 1830 Parliament was not dissolved until 3 December; but Gladstone had his Address ready early in August, within a week of his arrival back from the Continent. 'Induced by the most flattering assurances of powerful support', he ventured to offer himself to the suffrages of Newark as a professor of 'warm and conscientious attachment to our Government as a limited monarchy', to the union of Church and State, and an unswerving determination to 'admit facts, and abstract principles only in subservience to facts', as the true foundations of commercial, agricultural, and financial legislation'. He cited as objects of his solicitude the defence 'in particular' of the Anglican ecclesiastical establishment in Ireland, the 'amelioration of the condition of the labouring classes', 'measures for the moral advancement of our fellow-subjects in slavery', and 'observance of a dignified and impartial foreign policy'.[6]

Canvassing began in September. Gladstone dashed to the fray from Torquay, the family's current nomadic camp. Gladstone paid his respects to the Duke in a visit, in some trepidation, to Clumber Park on 9 October. Long conversations with His Grace in following days centred on events 'so awful that the tongue fears to utter them' in preparation for the 'grand struggle between good and evil', a principal feature of which would be the downfall of the papacy. Patron and protégé were well pleased with one another, the protégé especially being reassured as to the 'virtues of an ancient aristocracy, than which the world never saw one more powerful or more pure'.

Powerful the Duke indeed proved, as Gladstone soon had cause to rejoice. Purity was another matter. Between them the Duke's agent and John Gladstone disbursed money in Newark in lavish style. Gladstone's only problem in the campaign was his family's being implicated in the slavery question. This the supporters of the Whig candidate, Serjeant Wilde (later Lord Chancellor Truro), made much of. Gladstone responded with accounts of his father's enlightened estate practices and the importance of preparing the way to emancipation by gradual stages. He did not neglect to draw attention to the plight of factory children in Britain. As regards 'abstract lawfulness', slavery was recognized in Scripture, and thus was not 'absolutely and necessarily *sinful*'.[7]

Nominations at the Newark hustings were made on 11 December. The poll was declared on the 14th. Gladstone came top with 887 votes. His Tory colleague came second; the Whig challenger failed. Gladstone was now to be a Member of Parliament a few days before his twenty-third birthday. Newark was thus a triumph for the anti-Reform cause. But it soon became clear that the results overall in the country were 'melancholy enough' for what was shortly to become known as the Conservative party. Gladstone would enter the Commons when the first session of the 1832 Parliament opened in January 1833 as one of a party of 172 opposing 486 supporters of Lord Grey's government.

Back with the family – by now encamped in Leamington – Gladstone, looking at those dismal figures, indulged himself in doom-laden pathos. Christmas Day evoked reflections that 'before many years, we may not be permitted to celebrate this festival as now'. Doom stalked also on the Continent ('Antwerp gone! God help the poor oppressed Hollanders').

On his birthday William took stock. 'I have now familiarised myself with maxims sanctioning and encouraging a degree of intercourse with society perhaps attended with much risk, nay perhaps only rendered acceptable to my understanding by cowardice and a carnal heart.' Yet still did he trust that 'mirth may be encouraged, provided it have a purpose higher than itself'; and nor did he think himself 'warranted in withdrawing from the practices of my fellow men except when they really *involve* the encouragement of sin': in which class Gladstone certainly did rank 'races and theatres'. He avoided the opera and especially the ballet. He hoped to lead 'a severe life'.

~

Gladstone moved to London on 24 January to take his seat. He entered Lincoln's Inn and ate dinners there in conformity with his former plan to take up the legal profession; but in the new circumstances this faded into redundancy. He moved into L2 Albany Chambers at Piccadilly, the lease of which his father had already purchased. John Gladstone, as he had done with Tom and the others, set up his youngest son generously by transferring to his account £10,000 of capital stock in

Messrs Gladstone and Co. of Liverpool, to which he added £300 for furnishings. William swore his oath and took his seat on the 29th, 'provided', as he recalled, 'unquestionably with a large store of schoolboy bashfulness' in the presence of the Keate-like Speaker, Manners-Sutton. He observed that the 'corporeal conveniences' of the House were 'marvellously small'. Hayter's portrait of the first reformed House of Commons depicts the darkly handsome young Gladstone crowded next to his brother Tom on the Opposition backbenches. They would have to endure the inconveniences of the former Chapel of St Stephen as it happened for only two sessions: fire destroyed it on the night of 16 October 1834. Away at Fasque, Gladstone missed the furious spectacle. Until the Commons could move into their new Barry and Pugin chamber in 1852 they put up in the old Lords' chamber, while the Lords repaired to the royal robing room until their new chamber was ready in 1847. Having already been proposed for the United Universities Club, Gladstone now added the finishing touch to the accoutrements of his status by being elected to the Carlton Club, recently established as the Conservative response to the Reform Club.

Gladstone, however, was not a man to hang back from making his maiden speech at the earliest opportunity in the old House in the first session of the new Parliament. Particularly was this so when the two brothers jointly intervened in a matter touching their father's honour. In the debates in 1833 on the bill abolishing slavery in British dominions, that 'solemn and awful question' allowed Gladstone a chance on 3 June to plead sympathy for the maligned West Indian planters. As it happened, a planter specifically maligned was John Gladstone, subject to allegations of cruelty in his management of a Demerara estate. In his 50-minute speech, Gladstone had the satisfaction of nettling ministers and being well received by the House at large, full of gentlemen who regarded family loyalty as akin to a cardinal virtue.[8] Gladstone relaxed after the ordeal with tea at the Carlton; and two days later he was gratified to hear himself, at Harrow, praised 'most kindly' by that eminent Harrovian Robert Peel. The awkwardness of the family's Evangelicalism in relation to its slaveholding was nicely reflected in Gladstone's rejoicing in the 'joy and privilege' of breakfasting with old Wilberforce and observing him leading his family in prayer – a few days, as it happened, before the Saint's death – and then, with wry appreciation of the irony involved, going on to the Commons to vote against an amendment to the Abolition of Slavery Bill injurious to the slaveholders.

Gladstone had decidedly made himself a noteworthy presence on the Opposition backbenches. His position in the House, as one whose electoral success ran against the political tide, was much more conspicuous as part of an attenuated and embattled minority than it would have been obscured in the mass of a triumphant majority. An invitation from Peel to dine soon came. Gladstone consolidated these early good impressions by delivering on 8 July a short but vigorously bigoted defence of the Church of Ireland against cogent Whig accusations that, as the confession of a small minority of the Irish, it was over-endowed and over-bishoped.

Behind and beyond such matters of occasion and circumstance, however, remained the larger matter of Gladstone's being and doing in politics. The question now presented itself squarely to him as to the grounds and principles on which he was to assemble his parliamentary vocation. The broad outlines were tolerably clear. 'Restrict the sphere of politics to earth', he observed in 1832, 'and it becomes a secondary science.'[9] He was in politics to serve religion. Of all the attitudes and ideas put into doubt in the present crisis of humanity the old authority of religion was foremost. And, in logical and almost inevitable sequence from the horrendous Reform Act, foremost among the coming formidable vicissitudes of public life would be an attack upon the religious establishment of the Church of England and Ireland. Erastian Whiggery and infidel Utilitarianism stalked the land. A general temper of grievance and impatience with the traditional order of things infected the people.

With all the confidence of vigorous youth Gladstone set out to equip himself with the political means to offer a salutary rebuff to such secular contagions. His aim – and indeed in those early heady days, his expectation – was that alongside a renewal of the Church, the State would undertake to revive its sense of obligation to the religious establishment. Thereby the Church of England and Ireland as by law established would best be defended and preserved.

This was for the times a decidedly eccentric ambition. Before long Gladstone would find himself denounced for 'the most zealous adherence to the most antiquated and obnoxious principles of his party' as one questing to unfold the ways and means by which the English State should be obliged by its Christian conscience to enter into a renewed and revised joint partnership with the Anglican Church.

In formulating the ideals and principles of thus being 'a witness for the principles of the Church in the councils of the State' Gladstone leaned heavily on the help of two friendships that ripened from 1833 onwards. Henry Manning, Rector of Woolavington in Sussex and from 1840 Archdeacon of Chichester, was at that time moving from an Evangelical stance towards a more Catholicising position much like Gladstone himself. James Hope, a barrister, dedicated his life and career to a lay apostolate, considering himself to have taken the 'first tonsure'. Gladstone would always remember Hope as the 'most winning man of his day'. The essence of their intellectual stance was that a worthy ideal of Church–State partnership could be served only by 'high' rather than 'low' notions of the Church's claims and prerogatives. With Manning and Hope assisting, Gladstone worked his way systematically out of what remained of his Evangelicalism into High Churchmanship.

'Politics', Gladstone told Manning in 1835, 'would become an utter blank to me, were I to make the discovery that we were mistaken in maintaining their association with religion.'[10] Gladstone saw his personal vocation as fulfilling a mission to influence the general sentiments of the nation with the proposition that the State had a conscience capable of distinguishing between truth and error in religion, and that as it realized by means of its conscience that religion was the indispensable foundation of the ethical welfare of society, the State was bound to promote true religion and discountenance false religion. This was to be ultimately the nub of his argument in his book published in 1838, *The State in its Relations with the Church*. In working through the intellectual and theological implications and problems inherent in this rather severe argument his friendships with Manning and Hope were decisive. He needed the stimulation of powerful and pious intellects in full cry after 'a most blessed calling' to apply 'the searching test of Christian Catholic principles to those numerous measures of the time which are in form or substance or both calculated to bear powerfully on religion.'[11]

~

Much as Gladstone had worked his way through a series of intensive theological memoranda into High Churchmanship, so he worked his way through masses of mind-clearing memoranda into a more assured if idiosyncratic Conservatism. He concluded that while the Whig–Liberal principle of self-government was 'necessary', it was '*less* necessary' than the Tory 'principle of obedience'.[12] He could reassure himself that the Benthamite 'mechanical philosophy' now prevalent and the general disposition to see 'God the creator of all things diminished', and the averseness of the genius of the times to the 'pursuit of moral philosophy', would not be the end of the story. More abiding within the contemporary frame of romantic reaction against Enlightenment rationalism was the beginning in 1834, inspired posthumously by Hallam, of Gladstone's literary love affair with Dante, who became the most important 'symbol of a high Catholic faith'. Gladstone felt he had much occasion to lament the 'emancipation of philosophy' that 'gave us Lockes and Paleys, instead of Dantes and Lord Bacons'.[13]

But there were encouraging signs of hope. Gladstone found now in Coleridge[14] very heartening evidence of a better frame of mind indeed influencing the general sentiments of the nation. Coleridge alone, 'the man of our day who has stood pre-eminent for the powers of speculative thought, far above all others of his generation in this country', had laboured 'to re-establish the natural relation between theology and all other science', by offering a true notion of the reciprocal ends of Church and State and by counteracting philosophic materialism. There, Gladstone discerned, was the fulfilment of Burke's insight that the age of economists, sophisters and calculators had arrived. There was the 'twin sister

of that degraded system of ethics or individual morality, the injurious legacy of Locke, which received its full popular development from Paley, and was reduced to forms of greater accuracy by Bentham'.[15]

In copious memoranda he cleared his mind as to the practical rules of social engagement in living a severe life. But, undoubtedly, constant proximity to the great worked its insensibly insidious effect. At a reception at Peel's in 1834 he recorded having done 'a very absurd thing in speaking to him: as usual'.[16] He was introduced to the insidiously charming Whig Lord Melbourne, on the verge of succeeding Grey as Prime Minister. He was on his guard when it came to discourse with the Irish tribune Daniel O'Connell on the ills of Ireland. On reading Tom Paine's *Rights of Man* he offered the blasé comment: 'They do not startle me now.' He was developing in social and political poise.

It was encouraging also to observe defections from the Whig camp. As each major legislative measure passed into law – the Reform Act itself, Abolition of Slavery, the Factory Act, the New Poor Law, the Municipal Corporations Act – so another group of ministerial supporters in gaining a particular end lost a general motive for keeping longer in power a government seemingly at a loss to cope with economic distress and popular unrest, increasingly prone, with Palmerston at the Foreign Office, to be meddlesome and quarrelsome in Europe, and, above all, displaying disturbing tendencies to appease its Irish Catholic supporters with measures inimical to the vulnerable Irish branch of the Church Establishment. Both Edward Stanley (later Lord Derby, thrice Prime Minister) and Sir James Graham resigned from the Cabinet in 1834 in protest against the policy of appropriating Irish Church revenues for secular purposes. They came over to the Conservative Opposition in 1835.

Popular unrest, and the organized manifestations of it in trade unions, Chartism and the Anti-Corn Law League, presented a formidable aspect. Gladstone agreed with Manning's diagnosis that civil government was becoming 'the expression of popular will', yet took comfort in the resistant toughness of the 'strange medley' of Gothic and modern elements in the constitution.[17] He was at pains to clear his mind on 'the true position of will in government', with particular reference for democratic assumptions about the plenary claims of the notion of popular sovereignty. It was, he insisted, 'our duty … firmly to grasp by the understanding the truth that human will as will, though it has power has not authority, in the fundamental matters of government'.[18]

Undoubtedly, however, the most telling consideration bearing on Gladstone's disposition in these years not to despair was his faith in the ultimately benevolent purposes of divine Providence, and of his own humble appointed role within that providential order. 'Unless I altogether delude myself', he confided to his journal on his twenty-fourth birthday, 'I still continue to read in the habitual occurrences of my life the sure marks of Providential care and love: I see all things great and small fitted into a discipline.' He convinced himself that he was, at moments of 'sharp pressure or trial', in receipt of angelically borne scriptural visitations.[19]

Gladstone felt himself very much aware of the need of a skill in reading the meaning of events. 'Why have I not come by this time', he demanded of himself in 1841, 'habitually to recognise *my* proper & peculiar exercise? So far from this I hardly begin to perceive the truth: I faint and murmur continually: & have not yet got that higher natural theology, which reads & applies to practice *design* in all the forms of incident that beset & accompany our daily course.'[20] 'Design' was a key Gladstonian word. It was his pertinacity in this quest, together with his immense natural energy and talents, that made Gladstone so formidable. Nothing was more confidence-inducing than a sense of the divinely intimate embrace of Providence. And nothing was to prove more consequential in Gladstone's life and career in the decades to come than his assurance of this embrace.

~

Being summoned by Peel to join his administration was naturally a highly morale-raising incident besetting Gladstone's daily course in December 1834. Calling a halt to further organic reform, King William IV dismissed his Whig ministers and summoned Peel from vacation in Rome to undertake the government. Peel, on the look-out for promising talent among the younger Conservative members, could hardly fail to mark Gladstone. He was among those immediately summoned to attend the new Prime Minister designate. His father advised him to 'take anything with work and responsibility'. Peel received him 'very kindly' on the 20th with the offer of a junior lordship of the Treasury where he would be close to Peel as First Lord and Goulburn as Chancellor of the Exchequer.

Peel advised a dissolution of Parliament and a general election in January 1835. He had earlier set out his case in a speech at his Tamworth constituency. He appealed to that 'great and intelligent class of society' who were 'much less interested in the contentions of party than in the maintenance of order and the cause of good government'. He accepted the Reform Act as 'final and irrevocable' and pledged a pragmatic policy of 'careful review of institutions, civil and ecclesiastical, undertaken in a friendly temper', 'not actuated by any illiberal or intolerant spirit towards the Dissenting body'. In 1834 Gladstone made no public complaint against the adequacy of the accommodating temper of the 'Tamworth Manifesto' for present purposes, for all that on many an issue of the day he had made it clear that his temper was far from accommodating. As one who relied on 'the details of Revealed truth' as the founding principle of his politics, he seemed clearly not, so to speak, Tamworth material. On the other hand, the author of that Manifesto had made him a minister.

In any case, though the elections reduced the Whig majority from something over 300 to a little over 100 (Gladstone had the gratification of being unchallenged at Newark), Peel's government would meet the new Parliament with a short life ahead of it. King William, his *coup* of prerogative having miscarried, would be obliged to recall Melbourne.

Meanwhile, Peel and his colleagues had an opportunity to show their mettle and enhance their political credit. Hardly had Gladstone settled in at the Treasury than he was offered, as Peel had been in his time, the under-secretaryship of the Colonial Office. Lord Aberdeen was the Secretary of State; and so Gladstone would answer for the department in the Commons. Peel also confided to Gladstone that it was Lord Aberdeen's 'particular wish' that he should have the place. Gladstone went to meet his new chief, who hitherto had figured in his mind as 'Athenian Aberdeen', disciple of Castlereagh, object of Byron's invective and Canningite prejudice. Now he was to commence a special personal relationship with a man he would soon describe as pre-eminent for his 'statesmanlike mind, calmness of temper, warmth of benevolence, high principle, and capacity for business'.[21]

By the time defeat in the Commons in April led to Peel's resignation, Gladstone had time and opportunity to reassure Peel and Aberdeen that they had not miscalculated on him as an investment. His parliamentary duties were not heavy. Otherwise he made himself conspicuous by invective against the impiety of Whig ecclesiastical policy in Ireland.

That policy had lately aroused the Rev. John Keble to stir up what soon became known as the 'Oxford Movement' or the 'Tractarian Movement' (a series of *Tracts for the Times* set out its doctrinal arguments) to assert the Apostolic dignity of the Church of England and Ireland, and specifically its Catholic status of independence from meddling laymen in general and politicians in particular. As a layman and a politician, it would take some time for Gladstone to become attuned to the Tractarian ethos. Meanwhile, the abiding circumstance that Ireland was where the Church was exposed in circumstances of manifest peril, struggling since the Reformation to fulfil its mission in a land overwhelmingly given over to Roman error and idolatry, was for Gladstone the crucial testing ground. He found the going very hard. 'How few people', he would later remark, 'care for a *naked* principle.'[22]

~

When it came to resignation in April Gladstone regretted especially dissolving his official connection with the 'equity and gentleness' of the earnestly benevolent Aberdeen. He could feel for himself something of the satisfaction he had given to his leader. Another citadel in his path had been stormed. The outlook had broadened. He defended the Conservative leaders from Manning's accusation that they were failing to take up the cause of the Church. Gladstone pointed out that what the 'study and cloister' had revealed only within the past few years to 'personal piety' was a very different thing from the form of Christian feeling 'as applicable to statesmanship', which required 'time to spread over and tinge the general sentiments of the nation'.[23]

The family, now settled in Fasque, was more comfortably situated. Gladstone delighted in the place, though it never quite displaced the memory of Seaforth in his affections. He was too mediocre a rider and shooter to engage much in the conventional country pursuits. His first visit there, in 1833, was rendered sadly memorable by the news of Arthur Hallam's sudden death in Vienna on 15 September. Then a second loss came with his mother's death in September 1835. This evoked consoling records of her last hours as she departed 'in seraphic peace, like the gentleness of her own disposition'. His mother had never been for Gladstone more than a dimly benign figure in the background of his life. John Gladstone, however, a patriarchal 70, remained as busy and active as ever. Widowerhood gave him more freedom. He invested in a London house, 6 Carlton Gardens, to underpin the family's new domiciliary stability. He even revived old ambitions of a seat in the Commons. William, never one to devote himself to an ideal of bachelor independence, abandoned Albany in 1837 to share Carlton Gardens. It would be time to set himself up in an independent establishment when he married.

In the meantime there was much to occupy him in the interstices of a rising young politician's life. The House and society filled as much of his time as he cared to allot. In the spirit of his resolution in 1833 to fulfil decently his obligations to the 'primary social duties' Gladstone entertained and was entertained on principles of rational enjoyment. He was to be seen in fashionable and reputable salons. Peel received him at a grand house party at Drayton in January 1836, where he had much interesting talk with the eminent churchman Lord Harrowby, observed the Duke of Wellington closely, and heard Peel speak edifyingly on religion and the Church. He recorded as a joy and a privilege receiving Wordsworth at a breakfast, being particularly touched when the future Laureate, arriving early and finding Gladstone directing his servants at prayer, insisted on participating.

Two particular social occasions in 1835 took on a curious retrospective significance. Dining with Lord Chancellor Lyndhurst and the 'flower of the bench' in January the young Junior Lord of the Treasury noted the 'singularity' of the dress of the rather disreputable Lyndhurst's rather disreputable protégé Benjamin Disraeli. The dandy novelist, five years Gladstone's senior and failed contender at parliamentary elections, certainly noted 'young Gladstone', probably from motives of envy more than anything else.[24]

A caller at Carlton Gardens was Alfred Tennyson, the lamented Arthur Hallam's friend at Cambridge. Gladstone's decidedly cool comment on this 'unexpected honour' being due to no other tie than his 'having been in earlier life the friend of his friend', testified quite probably to an 'odd undercurrent of jealousy' between the two men who both preened themselves as enjoying primary place in Hallam's affections.[25] They met again, in 1839, at a breakfast at the poetical banker Samuel Rogers'; but anything in the way of amicable and regular acquaintance lay more than two decades distant.

In the matter of the long contemplated book, Gladstone found himself at last goaded into action by discovering the dismaying inadequacies of rival contenders in the field. Thus provoked, Gladstone summoned Manning and Hope to his aid and set to grappling with his complex and intricate materials. One of the issues presently troubling him was the controverted question of what the State should do about the subsidy given since Pitt's time to the Roman Catholic seminary at Maynooth, near Dublin, for training Irish priests, who from Reformation to Revolutionary times had trained in Continental seminaries. Hitherto it had been a routine matter for the Committee of Supply. Now the Whig ministers wanted to augment it and put it on a recurrent rather than an annual basis. To Gladstone such a policy was irreconcilable with the doctrine he was now in the process of assembling. In a brief and aggressive statement in the Commons on 30 July 1838 he objected to the proposal to renew the grant 'because it contravened and stultified the main principle on which the Established Church of England and Ireland was founded'.[26]

That style of aggression would be at the heart of his book. By August 1838 he felt sufficiently confident to send the manuscript on to Murray's. The title, much debated, was in the end formulated by Hope, who also corrected the final proofs and saw it through the press. Dedicated to the University of Oxford, *The Church in its Relations with the State* came into the public's hands before the end of 1838.

~

By that time Gladstone had departed for a second extensive Continental tour that took him through much of Germany and pretty well all of Italy, including Sicily. He looked forward to restoring his spirits amid the solemn delights of Rome. Exhaustion was only partly a consequence of grappling with an intellectually demanding book. It was a consequence also of the intense emotional frustrations of two failed matrimonial quests.

That he should record turning again to accosting prostitutes in the interval between these quests no doubt tells its own highly relevant story. Neither the banking and baronetical Farquhars nor the Earl and Countess of Morton could see in Gladstone the kind of son-in-law they had in mind. His evidently hypergamic matrimonial policy was not assisted by any talent in the arts of courtship. Caroline Farquhar, sister of an Etonian friend, allegedly told her mother of Gladstone, observed walking across the Polesden Lacy park after a hitch in transport arrangements: 'Mama, I cannot marry a man who carries his bag like that.'[27] Emily Eden said of him that there was 'something in the tone of his voice and his way of coming into a room that is not aristocratic'.[28] Such comment on something ineradicably unaristocratic about Gladstone would accompany him all his life. It was to be a problem also with the third object of his matrimonial questing, Catherine Glynne, sister of yet another Eton and Oxford friend, Sir Stephen Glynne, 9th Baronet, of Hawarden Castle, near Chester.

Gladstone was not entirely a stranger to Hawarden. He had taken refuge there back in 1836 to smooth his ruffled feathers after attendance enforced by his exasperated father at what William held to be Robertson's *mésalliance* with a Unitarian lady in Liverpool. Choosing to ignore the fact that the Gladstones had earlier been prominent among the Liverpool Unitarian community, William chose now to exhibit on a personal and intimate level a version of that studied public intolerance he was currently commending to his revitalized State and Church partnership. On that rather flustered occasion at Hawarden there is no evidence that Gladstone particularly noticed Catherine Glynne or her younger sister Mary. Both parties, moreover, had other objectives in mind at that juncture. It was at a breakfast at Samuel Rogers' in July 1838 that Gladstone noted the presence of the 'Miss Glynnes'. That was probably the occasion when, as Catherine later recalled, the austere young man was pointed out to her as a future prime minister. By 1838 both parties, disappointed in their hopes or expectations, were in a more receptive frame of mind.

It happened that the Glynnes also had a Continental tour in view. It was arranged that Gladstone would join forces with their party in Rome. The party consisted of Sir Stephen, a gentle, amiable, unworldly bachelor antiquarian, at that time a silent MP for Flintshire, his brother the Rev. Henry, bachelor Rector of Hawarden (one of the most lucrative cures in the Church), his invalid widowed mother and his two sisters Catherine and Mary.

Gladstone's initial task was to cope with his sister Helen's insistence on escaping from her stifling life at Fasque. It was decided that the quiet resort of Bad Ems would be a suitable refuge; and William and John Neilson arranged to settle Helen and her companion there before William resumed his travels. Accompanied by Arthur Kinnaird, Liberal MP for Perth, Gladstone then set off once more through the Tyrol to Milan, and on to Florence; as ever his sightseeing was indefatigable. The bright Italian sunshine hurt his already weary eyes. He felt guilty of leaving poor Helen bereft in remote Germany. He felt guilty at leaving his poor father bereft of Helen. Nevertheless he pressed on to his rendezvous with the Glynnes at Rome. Thence they travelled together to Naples in October. Gladstone and Kinnaird departed for their tour of Sicily. By now Gladstone was captivated by Catherine. The 1000-mile tour taxed even Gladstone's superb powers as an enduring traveller. He recorded parting company with the mule which had served him uncomplainingly throughout without being able to feel the slightest affection for the brute.[29]

No doubt it was refreshing also to be back with the Glynnes, who lodged in the same hotel. Leaving the Glynnes in Naples, Gladstone returned to Rome, where the solemn delights were now enhanced by Manning's presence. Lord and Lady Lincoln were there, among many other ornaments of English society. The Glynnes soon rejoined them. Gladstone frequented artists' studios. One of them, Joseph Severn, Gladstone valued for his friendship with his admired and lamented Keats. Severn recalled riding with Gladstone in the Campagna, and Gladstone's throwing his cap into the air on leaving papal territory, crying 'Long Live Liberty!'[30] This was perhaps the earliest indication that the primary impulse in Gladstone's ultimate fame as a friend of free Italy was hostility to the papacy.[31]

Another eminent tourist in Rome at that time, T. B. Macaulay, would certainly have applauded such a gesture had he known of it. At St Peter's on Christmas Eve, as the Pope attended Vespers, Gladstone was accosted by his fellow MP. Macaulay was as yet unaware that he would be reviewing Gladstone's book. 'We had a good deal of pleasant talk', Macaulay recorded in his journal.[32] Parcels of the book itself had already arrived, distributed by the proud author among the company, including Catherine Glynne.

By now the Glynnes were at the centre of Gladstone's preoccupations. He went about everywhere in their company. The attraction of '*Giá*' – their nickname for Gladstone, 'quite', or 'just so' – to Catherine was obvious enough, though there was tacit agreement to pretend that nothing was afoot. Catherine was beautiful, vivacious, pious and much the most spirited member of her otherwise rather effete if well-connected family. But even a visit to the Colosseum by moonlight on 3 January failed to elicit for Gladstone a positive response from his intended. He put voluminously on paper that his heart and hand were at her disposal, only to be told that she would need time to make her feelings warmer. Gladstone had to depart for home in Henry Glynne's company still uncertain of his fate.

The Glynnes were, it may be surmised, in some quandary about his suit. He was not of the aristocratic cousinhood among whom they were accustomed to give or be given in marriage. On the other hand, Catherine had already been jilted by just such a member of the cousinhood. How many more chances would she get? William Gladstone was promising and available. While not strictly handsome (he had too much of his father's nose), he was prepossessing: slight of figure, a little above middle height, of upright carriage, complexion pale, with a slight tinge of olive, 'and his dark hair sets off both that and the brilliance of his intellectual eye'. His provincial accent would not at that time have made him ineligible.[33] There would be no problem about money. But his background was raw, and it would be a 'high' match for him when 'new men did not then easily make such matches'.[34]

The capitulation did not come until 8 June at Lady Shelley's house near Fulham. There would be no more vexatious delay. The wedding was fixed for 25 July at Hawarden. It would be a double affair. Mary Glynne was betrothed to George, 4th Lord Lyttelton. Francis Hastings Doyle was Gladstone's best man. 'Uncle George', the Rev. G. Neville Grenville, Master of Magdalene College, Cambridge, officiated impressively. Old John Gladstone beamed about him in a haze of pride in this brilliant new connection for his clan. There was one awkward exception to the general gush of delight: Lady Glynne remained alone in 'uneasy depression' in the Castle.

Gladstone revelled in 'this glory & poetry of life' as he and Catherine honeymooned for a fortnight at Norton Priory, Cheshire, the seat of Catherine's cousin Sir Richard Brooke. They inaugurated a daily practice of Bible reading together. The Lytteltons came back up from Hagley in Worcestershire and Gladstone conducted the party on an extensive tour of the Scottish Highlands, centring on Fasque. The Gladstones moved into 13 Carlton House Terrace in February 1840. Catherine gave birth to their first child, a son, on 3 June. He was christened William Henry, and declared to be very like his father, with his mother's mouth. Soon Gladstone was drawing up the first of a series of genealogical sketches he would make in the coming years showing Willy's maternal descent from Sir William Temple and his links with the Dukes of Buckingham, and thereby with Grenvilles, Wyndhams and Pitts.[35] Yet another citadel, so to speak, had been stormed.

~

Marriage heightened Gladstone's status in society and politics. Election to the parliamentary dining club, Grillions, reflected this. But the reception of his book was the other big thing at the forefront of his mind in the early months of 1839.

As publications go, it was far from being a failure. Gladstone reported to Manning at the beginning of February that it had gone to the press for a third printing. Intended as a controversial polemic, aimed against the 'proud, ungodly spirit, which brands the forehead of the age', a mixed reception, to say the least, was to be expected. A mixed reception there was. But Macaulay's cleverly destructive review in the April *Edinburgh* garnered such repute that Gladstone's book was soon, and has been ever since, remembered only by virtue of that demolition. As Macaulay allowed, Gladstone made himself an easy target: 'a capital shrove-tide cock to throw at. Almost too good a mark.' All that Macaulay needed to do was to present Gladstone's careful arguments for Anglican monopoly and disqualification and discountenancing of non-Anglicans, stretch them to absurd limits, and exhibit those absurdities as veritable atrocities of superstitious medievalism. His hit at Gladstone as the 'rising hope' of those 'stern and unbending' Tories who chafed under Peel's moderate leadership was a plausible invention; and it took notorious purchase.

There were other, and better, critiques. Keble, in *The British Critic*, edited by Newman, found Gladstone's hostility to 'Voluntaryism' disturbing. Gladstone's solicitude to define the proper role of the State, Keble thought, put him in danger of neglecting those autonomous and divinely ordained essences within the Church upon which alone its highest spiritual fulfilment depended.[36] These acute words gave Gladstone pause. He allowed that he thought his Church and State principles 'within one stage of becoming hopeless as regards success in this generation'.[37] But the most that Gladstone for the present would concede was revision and improvement of his text and a further book – eventually to be entitled *Church Principles Considered in their Results* – realigning his ideals on more amenable historical grounds rather than on aggressive first principles.

Manning had earlier raised the question whether Gladstone might opt for a conventional political career. Gladstone replied that there was no danger of his being 'seduced by ambition'. Indeed, so far as he knew himself, he felt that his 'personal danger' lay 'another way'.[38] Quite what this portended remained opaque. There was the possibility of a more directly comprehensive mode of substituting for the abandoned vocation to Orders. Gladstone often turned his restless mind to schemes of religious fraternities and works of private charity for lay activists. He served on multifarious committees engaged in God's work. He listed in September 1840 'ten plans at present in view', including the 'Scotch college' that would revitalize Anglicanism there, at Glenalmond. In 1840 he joined together with Hope a lay brotherhood founded by the elder Thomas Dyke Acland devoted to works of mercy and charity. There would never lack ample scope for that kind of calling.

But for all Gladstone's assurances about 'another way', the question of being 'seduced by ambition' never quite faded away. That would be the pattern for the next few years. For the present the issue was to a large extent obscured by the routine obligations of Gladstone's frontbench position. As a former Colonial minister he had to be to the fore on West Indian matters. The great question what to do about the two Canadas took up much time. Gladstone criticized what he took to be feeble Whig appeasement of colonial interests. Lord Durham's report advocating the concept of 'responsible government' for colonies of settlement by no means satisfied Gladstone's metropolitan instinct. In high and resistant temper he unapologetically asserted the prerogatives of metropolitan authority: all colonies were to be regarded as 'children of the parent country'; and coercion was never to be renounced as an option of policy.[39]

~

All that sort of thing was encompassed in a wider world of high politics. The death of William IV in 1837 and accession of Princess Victoria of Kent involved dissolution of the 1835 Parliament and new elections. Melbourne's Whig majority was already crumbling. The Conservatives under Peel gained nearly 50 seats, leaving Melbourne tenuously in office but without real power. Once again Gladstone was spared a contest at Newark; but Tom's being dumped at the bottom of the poll at Leicester and John Gladstone's humiliating rejection by the electors of Dundee were distressing incidents. Gladstone dutifully attended the triumphal dinner in May 1838 at the Merchant Taylors' when Peel, Stanley and Graham harangued 300 Conservative MPs, confident that the party was once more on the brink of office, but unaware of how awkward an obstacle the young Queen was going to prove herself. Victoria's determination in 1839 to keep congenial and fatherly Melbourne in office and at her side gave Peel another two years grace before the trial of office had to be faced.

There were already premonitory indications of the difficulties Peel was going to have in keeping together a party ranging in spectrum from deep-dyed Ultras to palely-converted ex-Whigs. His 'Tamworth Manifesto' had become widely interpreted as an exercise in abandoning stiff Tory principle in favour of easy Conservative accommodation. Benjamin Disraeli, now elected in 1837, was to make his reputation in the Commons as excoriator of Peel's adaptiveness to what was identified as 'the spirit of the age'.

Such adaptiveness seemed not to be a foible of the former under-secretary of the Colonial Office. He distributed copies of his book among his colleagues, hopeful of praise and admiration for a signal contribution to the Conservative intellectual arsenal. Response was dismal. Peel himself thought it deplorable. At Drayton Manor he was observed turning over the pages of the book 'with somewhat scornful curiosity, and, after a hasty survey of its contents, threw the volume on the floor, exclaiming as he did so: 'That young man will ruin his fine political career if he persists in writing trash like this.' Unnerved by Peel's distancing himself, Gladstone begged for an explanation. Peel told him bluntly that the publication was regrettable.[40] A two-year interval was the least Gladstone needed for time to allow Peel to get over his disgust and to resuscitate Gladstone's fine political career in 1841, when the constituencies returned at last a solid Conservative majority. After all, Gladstone had been famously dubbed the rising hope of those stern and unbending Tories who chafed mutinously under Peel's moderate leadership. This of course was Macaulay's Whig mischief. But would the rising hope's fine career survive such notoriety? It was all very well for John Stuart Mill, in many respects the chief expositor of the 'spirit of the age', to estimate him as 'the only rising man among the Tories', 'the man who will probably succeed Peel as the Tory leader'.[41] But what did Mill know of the inwardness of Toryism?

Gladstone dined at Peel's early in February 1840, when there was 'much rumination on the probable course of politics and party'. He was unhappily aware that he was being pointed to as one of the '*respectable* bigots' whom Peel unwisely allowed to share the councils of his party. Gladstone certainly signalled a major new initiative in his political development in April 1840 when he launched a virulent assault on Palmerston's 'Opium War' against the Chinese Empire. 'If I have differences with my leader', Gladstone studiously claimed, 'they are as I am convinced not political but religious.'[42] It was within that frame of a need to mitigate differences that *Church Principles Considered in their Results* came out in August 1840. For the time being, Gladstone could only hope, for the benefit of his fine career, that it was indeed the case that his differences with his leader were indeed religious and not political.

As for politics, Gladstone was not without shrewd insights. If he had made no complaint in 1834 about the accommodating nature of Peel's Tamworth Manifesto, he was aware of its larger future implications. To a grumble in 1840 by Henry Philpotts, the notoriously Ultra Bishop of Exeter, that Peel was feeble and Wellington obstinate, Gladstone responded: 'There is a manifest and peculiar adaptation in Peel's mind to the age in which he lives and to its exigencies and to the position he holds as a public man. What the ultimate and general effect of his policy may be is a question too subtle and remote for one strongly to presume upon.'[43]

3

Politician and Churchman, 1841–1846

'The lower ends of a State ought to be fulfilled even when the higher ones become impractical.'

Gladstone to Edward Stanley, 4 March 1844

Melbourne's moribund administration finally succumbed in June 1841 in the course of a budgetary effort to plug the gap in the revenues that had long plagued the Whigs. Peel defeated ministers on 5 June by a single vote. The 1837 Parliament was dissolved and a general election by mid-July gave the Conservatives a majority of near 80. At Newark Gladstone and his colleague Lord John Manners were contested but carried the poll handsomely. The new Parliament met in August. Ministers were duly defeated and Queen Victoria, now married to her adored cousin Albert of Saxe-Coburg, summoned Peel to undertake the government.

That Gladstone would be a member of the new government was not in doubt. He was one of an inner group constantly consulted by Peel as to policy and tactics. He had purged the offence of his 1838 book. Members of this group were in effect a shadow administration, indeed had reason to see themselves as a shadow Cabinet. This certainly was the case with Gladstone. He had done service as an under-secretary. He recorded on 2 August that 'since the Address meetings the idea of the Irish secretaryship had nestled in my mind'. That would be to walk precisely in Peel's own official footsteps of 1812. Bonham, Peel's manager, indeed had Gladstone twice listed in his ministerial appointments file as a possible Irish Chief Secretary, though not necessarily in Cabinet.

When Peel summoned him on 31 August to offer the vice-presidency of the Board of Trade Gladstone was decidedly crestfallen. Bonham listed him as '(if not Ireland) V P of the Board of Trade'.[1] Bonham's emphatic underlining might have signified that Gladstone was to get no more than his deserts; or equally might have drawn attention to an element of anomaly in a place below what might reasonably have been expected. Peel covered his offer by pointing out that, since the President was to be Lord Ripon, erstwhile 'Prosperity' Robinson and failed Prime Minister (as Lord Goderich), Gladstone would answer for the department in the Commons. Wanting to govern men, he was set to governing casks and packages.

For one who had given assurance that there was no danger of his being 'seduced by ambition', and that his 'personal danger' lay 'another way', this was, on the face of it, errant behaviour. Not only had he accepted office; he had complained that the office was not grand enough. Gladstone brooded, convinced that he had been the victim of a late change of mind. Casks and packages were Peel's way of bringing Gladstone down to earth. He now featured in Protestant prints as the 'lay leader of the Puseyites, or Oxford Tract party'.[2] There may well have been a touch of satire in the appointment. Gladstone soon persuaded himself that it was 'easy to recognise the mercy and wisdom of God in the arrangement as it stands'. And, to sweeten the pill, there was at last the privy councillorship. Gladstone became right honourable and magnificently gold-braided on 3 September 1841, along with a duke, a duke's eldest son, a marquess's son, an earl and a baron.

Gladstone had already pondered the problems attendant on the contingency of his being offered office, and the propriety of his accepting it. He assured himself that he could 'digest the crippled action of the State'. All his reflections brought him 'more and more to the conclusion that if the principle of National Religion (a principle, which is my bond to parliamentary life) is to be upheld, or saved from utter overthrow, it must be by the united action of the Conservative party'. This shift of stance required an adjustment to his line about Peel. Gladstone now persuaded himself that both the cast of Peel's sentiments and his abilities were such as to be 'a great Providential gift to his country, wonderfully suited to her need'. His duty therefore to support Peel, regardless of Peel's unresponsiveness to the ideal of the 'Catholic Church historical and visible', remained paramount.[3]

That duty commended itself all the more as Gladstone became increasingly sensitive to the problems of social order. The progress of the 'democratic principle' worried him more than the 'dark and dubious prospects of the connection between Church and State'.[4] To Manning he wrote in 1843: 'You ask me, when will our Bishops govern the Church? My answer is by another query – when will anybody govern anything?'[5]

In a Lenten rumination in March 1842 he conceded that the point had been passed and would not return where the action of the Church could be 'harmonised' with the law of the State. But it would be 'much' if the State would 'honestly aim at enabling the Church to develop her own intrinsic means'.[6] This was an echo of Keble. Gladstone had turned his original plan inside out.

In his birthday retrospect in December 1843, after more than six months in Peel's Cabinet, Gladstone avowed: 'Of public life I must certainly say every year shows me more and more that the idea of Christian politics cannot be realised in the State according to its present conditions of existence.' For purposes Gladstone believed 'sufficient', he was 'more than content' to stay where he was. But it seemed to him that 'the perfect freedom of the new covenant' could only be 'breathed in other air'; and the day might yet come when God would grant him 'the application of this conviction'. 'Dim and distant' indeed were the 'purposes' which must take their form as God wills 'from the course of events under His Providential guidance'.

That course of events led Gladstone on a path of retreat toward a 'prospective object' of an 'unfolding the Catholic system' within the Church in some 'establishment or machinery', 'looking both towards the higher life, and towards the eternal warfare against ignorance and depravity'.[7] The ideal of a group of pious laymen bound together in a fraternity both of contemplative devotion and practical good works took an increasing hold on Gladstone's imagination in these years.

There had always been a side to Gladstone's inner emotional life that leaned in the direction of the 'cloister'. In this way some essence of the abandoned vocation to orders could be retrieved. In this way politics might not become an utter blank. Hope's 'tonsured' status in a kind of lay apostolate especially appealed to him. But he hankered as well for some kind of institutional corset. He joined a group of Catholic High Anglicans who congregated at the Chapel of All Saints, Margaret Street, whose leading spirits were the Aclands and whose spiritual mentor was Keble.[8] 'Certainly an atmosphere of devotion, a reality of earnest concurrence in the work of holy worship pervades the place, which I know not where else to look for.' A feature of this devotion that appealed particularly to Gladstone was a version of the confessional, not as a sacrament administered by a priest, but a mutually supportive private aid or boon. Sharing in the life of some such spiritual 'cell' in the Church promised for Gladstone rich private edification and blessed consolations and compensations in the way of philanthropic activity.

~

Meanwhile as a minister of the Conservative government and a member of the Conservative party Gladstone served a prime minister he judged a providential gift wonderfully suited to the country's needs. His best answer to perplexity was 'active work'. His capacity in that respect soon became noticed. Graham, the new Home Secretary, observed that 'Gladstone could do in four hours what it took any other man sixteen to do, and he worked sixteen hours a day.' One of his secretaries in later years calculated that if an ordinary man were measured for 'internal force' in units of horse power as 100, and an exceptionally energetic man to be 200, 'then Mr Gladstone's horse power was at least 1,000'. And this 'tremendous force' could be turned 'in any direction and for any purposes great or small'. Like a steam hammer, it could 'break a bar of steel or crack a nut'.[9]

In these years government groped its way towards coping with unprecedented transformations in society. Ripon, having made his reputation back in the 1820s as Chancellor of the Exchequer, was content to let his voracious subaltern have all the work he wanted. As Robinson he had been the minister who in 1816 repealed Pitt's income tax and boosted the existing duties on imported wheat – the 'Corn Law' of 1815. The Board of Trade that Gladstone came to have effective responsibility for was dominated by officials schooled in the traditions of Huskisson's commercial Liberalism and with ambitions to press beyond. Its officials conducted a propaganda campaign for dismantling the existing mercantilist apparatus strong on *a priori* free trade and utilitarian ideology but weak on reliable information and statistics. Peel distrusted the Board and looked to Ripon to call it to order. Gladstone was left to educate himself in its business. 'I learned the cause of the different trades', as he later recalled, 'out of the mouths of the deputations which were sent up to remit our proposals.' In the process he soon felt the 'stones' on which his protectionism was built 'get uncomfortably loose'. By the end of the 1842 session his faith in protection as a general economic principle, 'except as a matter of transition', was crumbling rapidly away.[10] Gladstone moved towards free trade along a path of investigation essentially independent of the Board's official ideologues.

While Ripon attended to the administrative side, Gladstone put his analytic and systematizing intellectual powers to work on the policies operated by the Board. By November 1841 he was compiling memoranda advising Peel on the conclusions he had drawn from his initial labours. His schoolman's mind was offended by the untidy clutter into which the tariff system had got, replete with anomalies and confusions, and endless occasions of lobbying, wire pulling, petitioning and litigating by commercial interests vying for advantage at the interface where mercantilist government and governmentalized commerce abraded against one another. John Gladstone had proved himself a ruthless practitioner in the arts of manipulating this world. His son was to prove himself ruthless in another direction. Gladstone's method was precisely that which he had applied to the equally anomalous and confused relations between State and Church. His rigorous logic in that earlier case had caused offence as being at odds with the spirit of the times. Now his no less rigorous logic in the present case would gain approval. He dealt with 750 delinquent tariffs in the same mood of Oxonian Aristotelianism in which he had castigated the slipshod morality of the State and the Erastian frailty of the Church.

Peel did not come into office with a preconceived plan to implement a free trade policy as understood by the Board of Trade ideologues or the Anti-Corn Law League agitators. His starting point was a much more empirical position of curing the budget deficit inherited from the Whigs. This led him to shaping government response to social distress and unrest. Peel's economic experience and judgement was leading him to the conclusion that the enormous new importance of Britain's industrial and manufacturing sector, and the social instability threatened by a 'regression in manufactures', made expedient a critical revision of the existing apparatus of restrictive, discriminative and prohibitive tariffs that inhibited industrial growth and made imported raw materials and semi-finished products dearer. Tariff barriers being erected by foreign governments against British industry could be reasonably counteracted only by removal or lowering of British tariffs on foreign produce. The political conundrum for Peel was to find the optimum point of equilibrium between the conflicting interests involved.

Peel faced two great difficulties. Agriculture remained as yet the largest component of the British economy. And it was by far the largest interest on the Conservative parliamentary benches. The Corn Law protected not only British farmers but also masses of agricultural labourers. But for Peel the issue of 'regression in manufactures' remained the pivotal point in his search for the optimum point of equilibrium in reconciling conflicting interests. Peel's leading idea for 1842 was to shift the greatest burden of revenue-raising away from duties on imported staple foodstuffs and raw materials for industry. To compensate for the temporary (as he anticipated) loss of revenue thus incurred, he needed a sure and flexible source of direct taxation. The precedent of Pitt's income tax naturally suggested itself. Pitt had forced it through in 1798 and 1800 as a desperate measure to fight a desperate war. It had subsidized the coalitions and beaten the French. Were not circumstances now as dire in their own way as they had been desperate then?

Peel's senior colleagues were amenable. Gladstone, indoctrinated in his youth by his father's inveterate dislike of the income tax as an inquisition and incentive to fraud, proposed as an alternative renewing the old house tax, repealed in 1834, 'mitigated by a careful graduation'.[11] This was rejected. His tariff proposals, on the other hand, fitted perfectly with Peel's needs. The crucial role the Board of Trade would play in such a policy consisted in the fact that, out of a total tax revenue (in 1840) of £47 million, £35 million was supplied by customs and excise duties, with sugar, tea, tobacco, spirits, wine, timber and coffee the principal items. Even allowing for the relatively restricted proportion of national wealth tapped by a mid-nineteenth-century government, a fiscal shift of such dimensions as Peel envisaged could reasonably be calculated to make ultimately a significant contribution towards alleviating what was becoming known as the 'Condition of England question'.

Peel planned a threefold approach. First, a budget early in 1842 to revive the income tax at 7d. in the pound (a little over 3 per cent.); second, a revised Corn Law later in the 1842 session to reduce substantially the existing scale against foreign importation; third, as soon as practicable later, measures to tackle the vexed problems connected with the largest single item on the customs returns, sugar. The problem of the sugar duty was the vested interest of the West Indian producers entangled with the moral problem that the cheapest sugar on the world markets was slave-grown.

The plan got off to a good start in the 1842 budget. Peel made high drama out of invoking the memory of Pitt and displaying his mastery of the intricacies. Gladstone ever after looked to it as the epochal model of budget-making. There were Conservative murmurs at the obvious implications: that Robinson's reversal of 1816 was in the process of being re-reversed. Murmurs grew louder with the Corn Bill revision that reduced import duties by half. Conservative benches became restive and resentful at the sacrifices being demanded of the landed interest by a government held by the great majority of its supporters to be properly the defender of that interest.

Peel's ascendancy and prestige held the party in line. There was a sticky moment in 1842 when Gladstone had to be held in line. The young Vice-President felt that the revision in the sliding scale of duties proposed for the Corn Bill did not go far enough, and in his finicky way thought it right to indicate that his resignation was available. To Gladstone's distress, Peel, instead of humouring him with a few paternal words, fell into a passion. Gladstone was left in great dumps before Peel recovered his equanimity.[12] As things turned out, this episode was premonitory of much more expansive passions and scenes. But for the time being Peel managed publicly to keep his temper. He fended off Whig efforts to exploit the corn issue in the 1843 session. Britain's commercial policy, after all, remained protective in form and intent. At the opening of the 1844 session he seemed to have things in hand.

As Peel's subaltern and spokesman on the tariff aspect of these grand transactions Gladstone played a conspicuous part, handing up papers to his chief as Peel expounded his strokes of fiscal mastery. At the beginning of 1843 Gladstone published anonymously in the *Foreign and Colonial Quarterly Review* a comprehensive and authoritative treatment of the government's 'Course of Commercial Policy at Home and Abroad'. His analysis identified the crucial weakness of the British economy, and the fundamental cause of much of the social distress and penury, as the 'paralysis of our foreign trade'. Because of Britain's expansion as a manufacturing economy she was more dependent than ever on reciprocity and interdependence. She must lead the way by example to foreign countries now tending to protectionism. Britain had not been innocent. 'We shall not here inquire whether the acts of our commercial policy have been defensible: we shall not examine, for example, whether the Corn Law of 1815 was or was not in error.'

Just as well. Protectionist hackles were roused. Gladstone was teaching himself to follow the line that would lead him to free trade; but equally he was learning the lesson of reconciling his preoccupation with the conscience of the state with an awareness of the moral dimension of political economy. He made no comment on his reading in the summer of 1843 of the prime text of the 'Condition of England' question, Thomas Carlyle's *Past and Present*; nor is there any reason to suppose that he was vulnerable to its hectoring rhetoric. But he could not have avoided recognizing it as a 'sign of the times'. 'This is a time', he told Catherine in August 1842, 'when we may reflect on the thorough rottenness socially speaking of the system which gathers together huge masses of population having no other tie to the classes above them than that of employment, of high money payment constituting a great moral temptation in times of prosperity, and the reductions in adversity which seem like robberies, and which the poor people have no discipline of training to endure.'[13]

~

John Gladstone had the pleasure of receiving from Peel in June 1842 a tribute to his son: 'At no time in the annals of Parliament has there been exhibited a more admirable combination of ability, extensive knowledge, temper and discretion.'[14] Much of those talents were devoted to expounding to the Commons policies which Gladstone increasingly found himself disbelieving. He early exhibited the calloused temper of confident executive power ('Copper, Tin, Zinc, Salmon, Timber, Oil, Saltmeat, all are to be ruined, & all in arms').[15] But behind Gladstone's triumphant affirmations of purposive government lay the problematic relationship of Conservative leadership and Conservative party.

Right from the start of his taking office in 1841, Peel made it clear that he did so 'on his own terms'. Painful memories of the obloquy that was visited on him after his 'ratting' on the question of Catholic Emancipation in 1829 made him adopt a severe attitude in the matter of what the duty of ministers to the public interest would be 'against the claims of party interest and personal consistency'. The long and short of it was that party interest and personal consistency would, if push came to shove, be thrown over. Peel candidly explained to the Commons that he assumed 'the right to propose such measures as he thought in the national interest'; and he declared 'disdain for considerations of "mere political support" which would make him the instrument of carrying other men's opinions into effect'.[16] Having been bred up in the school of 'the friends of the late Mr Pitt' and the tradition of carrying on the King's government, Peel 'took a high, almost high-handed, view of the position of the executive' as against Parliament and party as the major component of the House of Commons. Peel wanted contradictory things of party. He needed his party to be strong, energetic and effective in the constituencies so as to provide him with a solid majority in the Commons as the fulcrum upon which he could then lever executive potency; but, once thus empowered, Peel required his party in the Commons to be docile and obedient. Confronted with grossly contradictory demands, the Conservative party under his leadership soon began to show signs of neurosis.

Peel's rationale was that only a strong executive could cope with financial deficit, economic depression, social dislocation and the challenges to public order being made 'out of doors' by the burgeoning Chartist and Anti-Corn

Law agitations. He insisted that the executive was in an incomparably better position to form a judgement on issues of public policy than any body of backbench parliamentarians. He refused to contemplate abdicating any degree of responsibility founded on that decisive advantage. His consistent pattern of response to party refractoriness was to exploit his immense personal ascendancy and face down disaffection by sheer weight of reputation and authority. Peel was too proud and too shy to stoop to ingratiation or treat for popularity with his backbenchers. Any notion of sharing authority with his party Peel regarded as betraying his trust with the Crown, and therefore unconstitutional.

Ministerial changes in 1843 brought Gladstone into much more immediate official responsibility for that programme. The Indian Board of Control became vacant. Ripon was slotted in. On 13 May Gladstone received Peel's offer of the presidency of the Board of Trade with a place in Cabinet. Characteristically, Gladstone raised difficulties, on this occasion especially about the government's attitude to the Church. 'I have to consider with God's help by Monday whether to enter the Cabinet, or to retire altogether: at least such is probably the second alternative.' A conference with Hope and Manning sent him back to Peel with a settled mind to accept. Remember, he adjured Manning, 'my perils are increased'.

Among those perils, as he impressed upon Peel, was the possibility of 'the evil of hostility between the Govt. & the Church'. If such a calamity were to strike, Gladstone was sure his battle would not be such as to be fought in Parliament. 'I told him in evidence of the strength of my feeling upon that subject, that I had in my own mind contemplated the resignation of my seat as well as my office, in case the misfortune should happen to me of separating from him on a question of that sort.'[17]

Peel assuaged Gladstone with flattering reassurances. For much of that session Gladstone tried to appease the rightly distrustful Tory rank and file with his own flattering assurances that ministers were to be trusted on the Corn Law. He waxed indignant on the 'fertile theme' of the 'supposed intention of the Government to abandon the present law, and be guilty of double-dealing with the farmers'.[18] That, and a kind of specimen Christian political measure, a Coal Whippers Bill to emancipate the colliers of the Port of London from the system of being employed casually in gangs recruited by publicans, was about the sum of Gladstone's contributions for the remainder of the session.

Later in 1843 Peel outlined his formidable agenda. He spoke out 'very freely about commercial matters', declaring that unless the revenues improved, another great fiscal operation would be necessary, with income tax raised to five per cent and collateral relief to consumers. Were he not 'hampered by party considerations', he would propose a new Corn Law uniting the fixed with the sliding principle at a much lower rate. Party considerations were indeed in their own way formidable. Gladstone had earlier conversed at the Carlton with Philip Pusey, who told him 'that the county members had gone with Sir R. Peel to the very utmost point they could go with respect to corn: and that to speak plainly, if Sir R. Peel should become convinced that a further change was requisite, they considered that he ought to leave it to the Whigs to carry it, & resign accordingly'. Peel declared 'obiter' in 1844 in private conversation with Aberdeen and Gladstone his 'strong opinion that the next change in the Corn Laws would be total repeal'.[19] Conservative backbenchers nursed shrewd suspicions on that score. Disraeli's fictional creatures, Tadpole and Taper, memorably defined 'a sound Conservative government' in *Coningsby* in 1844: 'Tory men and Whig measures'.

The measure that provoked the first seriously mutinous backbench revolt against Peel was the Factory Bill in February. The essence of the problem, left over from earlier sessions, was hours to be worked in the vast textile industry by women and children. Ashley, the later Lord Shaftesbury, was pushing for restrictions on both. Ministers wanted restriction only for children. The issue opened up an opportunity for the resentment building up in the party at the style of Peel's leadership and the tone of his policies to vent itself. Ninety Conservative malcontents voted with Ashley and, with Whig assistance, defeated the government. Gladstone was again astonished at the passion with which Peel responded. Instead of cajoling his refractory following with some tactful awareness of their fears and insecurities, Peel and Graham harangued them with threats and set about booting the bill through. Peel whipped his sulking party into reversing its vote.

With Conservative morale shaken, Gladstone occupied himself in the 1844 session with a second great batch of tariff abatements. He immersed himself also in the new question of railway regulation. Given the unavoidably monopolistic nature of railway transportation, it was deemed proper that government should intervene in the public interest. His Railways Bill became Gladstone's pet project, and his initiation into ways of providing for state purchase in certain circumstances. This was Gladstone's introduction to 'statist' ideas linkable to Christian principles. Cheap 'parliamentary' trains were his legacy to the mass of rail travellers. A move to oblige railway companies to run such trains on Sundays, however, perturbed him. He did not know how to reconcile it to himself, he informed Peel, 'to be responsible either for the enactment or the execution of a law containing a provision so dangerous in its immediate and ultimate results to public morality'.[20] Next on Peel's agenda was a provision Gladstone found entirely irreconcilable with his bond to parliamentary life.

~

Peel wanted to do something substantial about the condition of Ireland. Daniel O'Connell was running a campaign to repeal Pitt's Act of Union of 1800. Peel's plan was to face down the Repeal agitation in 1842 and 1843, and then initiate a series of appeasing concessions calculated to take the steam out of Irish disaffection. Peel, after all, had vivid memories of how O'Connell had extorted Catholic Emancipation out of panic-stricken Tory ministers in 1828–29. That must not happen again. Peel envisaged, as Pitt had in 1800, a reconciled Irish Catholic propertied class acting as a stabilizing social ballast. There were to be concessions in the parliamentary and municipal franchises. A Commission would for the first time investigate tenure of land as a question of policy. There would be reforms and provisions in educational matters, with undenominational colleges founded in Cork, Galway and Belfast. There would be an enquiry into Roman Catholic endowments, including that of St Patrick's College, Maynooth.

Gladstone read the 'devastating dialect' of Peel's circular paper on Maynooth in February 1844,[21] almost coincidentally with the Factory Bill fracas. Peel's argument was that the British state and the Irish Catholic priesthood needed to come into a new relationship of co-operation and mutual goodwill; and that a preliminary foundation of such a relationship would be adequate financial provision on the part of the state. After two Cabinets and failure to persuade his colleagues not to proceed, Gladstone made it clear that his conscience, as embodied in his words in *The State in its Relations with the Church* of 1838, would oblige him to resign. Gladstone's case was that such a new departure in the State's relationship with Roman Catholicism would be a 'great shock to the religious feelings of the country', and would 'weaken confidence'. He was sure his colleagues 'deluded themselves' with 'visionary hopes of improvement, of control, of conciliation', all of which by the means proposed were 'entirely beyond reasonable expectation'.[22]

A riposte from Peel came promptly, provoking Gladstone into anxious reflection on 'the very serious question not whether I shall assume or avoid responsibility but whether I shall choose on the one hand the responsibility of participating in that endeavour, or on the other hand by retiring of giving a signal for disunion suspicion & even conflict in that political party by which alone as I firmly believe the religious institutions & laws of this country are under God maintained'. He saw with dismay in Peel's proposals an 'acknowledgement of the priests as instructors of the Irish people', and an acceleration of demands that the wealth of the minority Church of Ireland be largely transferred to those instructors. And he could plainly foresee also a 'further declension in the religious character of the State of these realms'. After what he had published, even if he had changed his mind – which he had not – resignation would have the merit of paying 'just tribute to public character and consistency'. The 'path of duty' was clear.[23]

Peel would not be deflected. There was no time to spare; 'we could not remain as we were'. Desperation inspired Gladstone to hit upon the delaying tactic of urging that diplomatic links with the Vatican would be an essential preliminary to any such policy as was contemplated on Maynooth. In a pre-Cabinet interview with Peel, Gladstone was put out by his chief's robust comment that, after all, 'no one could remember' any words Gladstone felt pledged to. This was the tenor generally of his colleagues, who pressed him with arguments that resignation was quite unnecessary and plied him with ingenious compromises.

Heaviest pressure came from Edward Stanley, a veteran in the Irish political wars. He tried to curdle Gladstone's blood by painting a lurid picture of the Maynooth policy as the last chance of saving the Church of Ireland from despoliation, for a policy of disestablishment and disendowment might well have to come unless something decisive to head it off by reconciling the mass of the Irish to the Established Church and the Union were not done in good time. And, Stanley added for good measure, he himself 'might so act' in such circumstances.[24]

Meanwhile, as incipient drama gathered pace behind the scenes, the humdrum business of the session had to be attended to. Gladstone found himself on 12 March rebutting Richard Cobden, the leading spirit, along with John Bright, of the Anti-Corn Law League. As he put it to Hope, five-sixths of Cobden's speech 'I should have been glad to have spoken'. In fact Gladstone was finding it increasingly difficult to keep the Commons in a straight face when he spoke in defence of the revised Corn Law. Then the first premonitions of trouble about the sugar duties disclosed themselves. And there was always Stanley on hand to press upon him unsubtle reminders calculated to give him pause about resigning. Stanley discoursed on the theme of 'the dearth of young men of decided political promise'. This was by way of prelude to Stanley's telling Gladstone that 'you are as certain to be prime minister as any man can be, if you live – the way is clear before you'. Gladstone replied primly that he 'dared not speculate on the future'.[25] Trying another tack, Stanley expatiated on the difficult position of poor overworked Peel, harassed by all the insubordinate young men.

Gladstone could indeed agree that Peel did the work of three or four men already; and Stanley's remarks on insubordination were now much to the point. By mid-June the Conservative party was embroiled, by way of the sugar duties, in an even more savage and damaging quarrel than the one it had suffered over the Factory Bill in February. Being by far the most lucrative item of the customs revenue, sugar offered the government a supremely manipulable fiscal resource. Despite two bravura speeches from Gladstone defending the government's policy of encouraging free-grown sugar and maintaining a reasonable margin of advantage for the West India growers, the link between Peel's fiscal requirements and freer trade gave impulse to the protectionist reflex of the party rank and file; and loyalty to the West Indies added extra inducement for grievance at Peel's style and tone of leadership. Peel sensed apprehensively a repetition of the Factory Bill turmoil. Determined not to be taken by surprise, he summoned a party meeting at his house on 13 June. It was a disaster. Instead of nipping mutiny in the bud, Peel provoked even more resentment and resistance. The government was again defeated by a combination of mutineers and Whigs. Gladstone wrote grimly of 'the *Crisis*'.

At a Cabinet on the 15th Peel spoke of resignation. He reluctantly allowed himself to be persuaded into a token concession. Then he almost wrecked that compromise by a speech in a tone deplored by Gladstone as 'hard, reserved, introspective'. Peel's colleagues felt they were out. Gladstone was convinced that 'a deep wound had been inflicted upon the spirit & harmony of the party: that a great man had made a great error'. Stanley saved the situation with a brilliantly 'rattling' oration, employing a moderate tone, as a member observed, 'with the sort of advantage that an ill-tempered man has when he chooses to be good-humoured; the House was flattered that Stanley thought it worthwhile to be conciliating'.[26] In such an unresolved manner the Conservative party and the Conservative government cobbled themselves back together again.

Two things were notable about Gladstone's response to the crisis. As he explained to Hope, he remained convinced that 'our course in these matters has been generally right'; but it involved 'progression', and there was a high probability that a bad harvest or two would 'break up the Corn Law and with it the party'.[27] And for all his criticisms of Peel's heavy style, Gladstone remained sure that 'Peel's final inclination must and ought to guide the Government'. The other and most revealing clue about the movement of Gladstone's mind in these fraught months, however, was his deduction from the lamentable but now undeniable fact that the 'higher theory' of the 'forms and principles of government' bore no meaningful relationship to the 'inward tone and life' of the 'wills and forces' constituting society. 'That Government has a mind, or is the presiding mind of the community is a doctrine which when the idea of mind and spirit become thoroughly dissociated one should perhaps wish extinct.'[28] The peculiar agony of the Maynooth issue for Gladstone derived not so much from his steadfastness to true principles as from a despairing conviction that he was committed to steadfastness on grounds that he could now admit to himself he wished might no longer exist.

Peel's final inclination on Maynooth remained immovable. With obstinate tenacity Gladstone urged the reopening of diplomatic relations with the Holy See, offering himself as plenipotentiary. Peel ignored him. Later, listing this episode among his 'Recorded Errors', Gladstone owned that he had tried Peel by 'a most indiscreet proceeding'.[29] Peel must have blenched at the prospect of so ingenuous a Puseyite earnestly pursuing along the mazy corridors of the Vatican 'opportunities that might be afforded' for 'bringing about in Latin quarters a more just estimate of the English Church'.

In July 1844 Gladstone accepted that the game was up. His resignation was now inevitable. He made a distinction between unwillingness to be an 'author' of such a measure, and readiness on the other hand to recognize that it proceeded from a government which he knew 'adopted it as being on the whole the best means of defence for the Church of Ireland'.[30] Peel could thus be assured that Gladstone would not vote against it, and might well vote for it. It was agreed that resignation would best be effected at the commencement of the 1845 session when the policy would be formally initiated.

~

Behind all this public drama domestic arrangements at Hawarden settled in. Given Sir Stephen's confirmed bachelorhood, and his widowed mother's seclusion, it was agreed that Catherine should continue to be chatelaine of Hawarden Castle. Gladstone thus had at his disposal a fine country seat, handsomely designed in the Regency Gothick style, ostensibly as the guest of his brother-in-law. He liked the place immensely, and he and Catherine made a winningly devoted couple. A mutual friend observed that marriage had 'improved' Gladstone 'very materially'. His manner was not so 'ascetic' as it had been; 'he really seems to enjoy life independent of the consideration that it is a sphere for the exercise of duties'.[31]

Temperamentally they complemented one another. Whereas he was prone to impose method, order and punctuality in his immediate vicinity, she was vague, untidy, unpunctual, carrying about with her an air of inimitably breezy disorder. Through the decades of their marriage, friends and guests would observe wonderingly at the way they contentedly endured a 'hugger-mugger' style of domestic life, compounded of Catherine's relaxed management style and William's habits ingrained from the nomadic family encampments of his youth. A problem for Gladstone was that Catherine never cared for formal entertaining. He found offering informal breakfasts at Carlton House Terrace a convenient substitute. Communication at Hawarden tended to be conducted in 'Glynnese', a code vocabulary combining comical, witty and slangy elements. Gladstone never mastered it.[32] It was at Hawarden, in September 1842, while shooting partridge, that Gladstone's unorthodox method of reloading one barrel while the other was at full cock led to the shattering of the forefinger of his left hand. Ever after he covered the stump with a black leather stall. (It was notable that in all the innumerable cartoon depictions of Gladstone in his career, the stall never featured. Gladstone carefully preserved the remains of the finger to be ready at the Resurrection.)

Lady Glynne eased the situation by deciding that she preferred life with her daughter Mary Lyttelton at Hagley. For all its oddness, the Hawarden arrangement worked well. It gave Catherine an independent standing, helping her to cope with being married to a formidable man. The two sisters soon made an animated axis of extended families between Hawarden and Hagley. William Henry's birth in 1840, however, raised a delicate problem. In the presumed future absence of male Glynnes, he, as Catherine's heir, became indiscreetly talked about as the eventual inheritor of the estate. There was widespread public misapprehension already that Hawarden belonged to the Gladstones.[33] Stephen's brother, the Rev. Henry, decided it was his duty to produce a male Glynne heir for Hawarden. He married Lyttelton's sister Lavinia in 1843. That situation made for an awkwardness in the domestic atmosphere. The Gladstones had to accept the possibility of a Glynne heir.

The background problem was that the Glynnes did not have enough money to keep the Hawarden estate afloat. Sir Stephen had invested most of his available fortune in a coal, brick and ironworks concern, Oak Farm, near Stourbridge. Badly managed, it soon became a heavy liability, and by 1847 bankrupt. For a time the Glynnes and the Gladstones had to abandon the Castle and retreat to the Rectory. Neither of the Glynne brothers were capable of dealing with the crisis. It fell to Gladstone, backed by his father, to take things in hand.

The Glynnes and Hawarden thus were to become a problem. For the present, as Lavinia relentlessly presented Henry at the Rectory with daughter after daughter, it was a matter of hanging on. Catherine, for her part, presented William with a daughter, Agnes, in 1842, a second son, Stephen, in 1844, another daughter, Catherine Jessy, in 1845, and then Mary in 1847, Helen in 1849, Henry Neville in 1852 and lastly Herbert in 1854. It all made for Gladstone whether in London, Hawarden or Fasque, a happy, bustling family life.

Hawarden was thus, at best, kept on hold. Gladstone was in love with the idea of a country estate. If Hawarden looked doubtful, there was always Fasque. Tom was of course the heir, but his wife Louisa, like Lavinia Glynne, kept supplying her husband with daughters. In any case, William convinced himself that neither Tom nor Louisa took pleasure or interest in Fasque. Robertson, recently Mayor of Liverpool, had his own place, Court Hey. John Neilson had his naval career to look to. Tom, already resentful at being overshadowed by his younger brother, was not at all pleased at William's proposing that, if Tom wished it and their father consented, 'one of us' – by which William meant himself – might take over Fasque.[34] Tom's only weapon against William was to stick resolutely to a stiff Toryism; and, while William shifted towards a very Catholic Anglicanism, Tom stuck to the family's Evangelical tradition.

William was greatly embarrassed, as one much under public suspicion as a crypto-papist, when in 1842 Helen was received into the Roman Church by the head of the English Catholic community, Dr Wiseman. Tom blamed William for Helen's perversion. Long returned from her German escapade, Helen remained unrivalled as the family problem, keeping the households at Fasque or Carlton Gardens in a state of barely repressed hysteria. Helen had been extricated from an engagement to a Polish count. She was not extricated from addiction to opium and alcohol. Robertson, also, could be difficult, expressing loud, excited Radical opinions about politics and religion. William had to endure long diatribes from his father against the 'corn repeal mania'.

The Disruption of the Kirk of Scotland in 1843 over patronage and the breakaway third of its ministers in the Free Kirk was a lively issue at Fasque. John Gladstone took a sternly feudal line with his tenantry in defence of the Establishment; William, following Keble's lead in sympathy with 'Voluntaryism', rather approved the anti-Erastian tone of the dissident Kirk.[35] William, often in straits to find access to Episcopal services and recoiling from having to endure the grim Calvinism of the local kirk at Fettercairn, was gratified when his father agreed to found a chapel at Fasque. And his father was a generous benefactor to the Glenalmond college project, calculated to provide Scotland with Episcopalian seminarians. In 1843 John Gladstone was worth £600,000. William and the other younger sons received an ample annual allowance of £2000, and in 1843 a further £15,000 was added to the trust managed by Robertson.

Compared, then, with the Oak Farm disaster that was steadily engulfing the Glynnes, Fasque was on a sound footing. The Gladstones were certainly also in better shape than the Pelham-Clintons. The Duke of Newcastle, bankrupted by injudicious land purchases on borrowed money, had to put his affairs in the hands of trustees. Then his heir, the Earl of Lincoln, fell into marital disaster. His wife, a daughter of the Duke of Hamilton but perhaps more relevantly a grand-daughter of Beckford of Fonthill, started in 1843 on the wayward career that would lead to pregnancy by Lord Walpole in 1849, divorce in 1850, and remarriage in 1860 to Monsieur Opdebeck, of Brussels. Apart from his natural distress at all this, Gladstone was intimately involved, not only as trustee and as guardian for Lincoln's children, but eventually in 1849 as a kind of knight-errant, pursuing the guilty Lady Lincoln up and down Italy in quest of materials for Lincoln's divorce action.[36]

Equally distressing was news from Oxford of the University's persecution of the Catholicizing Tractarian party, with particular reference to the censure of *Tract for the Times*, no. 90, of 1841, by J. H. Newman, demonstrating ingeniously that the Thirty-Nine Articles of the Church of England could bear a thoroughly Catholic interpretation. This stirred immense scandal. Newman resigned his cure at St Mary's, the University church, and withdrew from Oxford. Professor Pusey was banned from preaching. Worse was to come. Newman made known his conviction, held since the summer of 1839, that the Church of Rome was the Catholic Church, and the Church of England not a branch of the Catholic Church, because not in communion with Rome. Gladstone was appalled. The threat of Newman's defection Gladstone counted as 'the greatest crisis & and the sharpest that the Church has known since the Reformation'.[37]

~

As with Newman, so with Gladstone. It seemed to Gladstone as he confronted the unavoidability of resignation that the time was 'drawing near for a change of scenes and parts', and that it was indeed the commencement of 'a great transition'.[38] During the last months of 1844 Peel brought the Maynooth question formally before a series of Cabinets. Gladstone felt he had 'to *do the deed* all over again'. Peel commented to Graham: 'I really have great difficulty sometimes in exactly comprehending what Gladstone means.'[39] Gladstone explained himself to the Duke of Newcastle, stressing that there was no blame to Peel in 'the character of the times and of the religious and political sentiments which prevail'.[40] On 4 February Gladstone explained his resignation in the Commons. Like Peel, members had great difficulty comprehending his meaning. They were too puzzled by the intricacies of Gladstone's position to grasp why, meaning to support the policy, he felt it necessary to disturb the public mind by quitting office.[41]

Lincoln and Aberdeen both spoke to Gladstone of a short separation. Indeed, Gladstone made no indication that he would follow the logic he had outlined to Peel back in May 1843 on joining the Cabinet, when he specified that in the event of the evil of hostility between the government and the Church he would contemplate resigning his seat as well as his office. As he told Stanley on 4 March 1844, 'The lower ends of the State ought to be fulfilled even when the higher ones become impractical.'[42] He had admitted to himself that his steadfastness on public display was on grounds he might privately wish extinct. No push was to come, it seemed, from providential authority. God granted no 'application' to his conviction that the perfect freedom of a new covenant was to breathed in other air. In truth, Gladstone at this time was deploying a schoolman's casuistry to avoid the logic of his own deepest avowals. His agility in this ritual intellectual dance verged in its later stages somewhere between frenzy and farce.

By 1846, after the shock of Maynooth and resignation, after Newman's despairing abandonment of Anglicanism for Rome, when both Manning and Hope were being pushed towards the same resolution, Gladstone had come to the pass of expressing to Manning a wish that he could get a 'synodical decision' in favour of his 'retirement from public life'.[43] For he professed to remain there 'for the service of the Church'; and his views on the mode of serving her were getting 'so fearfully wide of those generally current that even if they be sound they may become wholly unavailable'.

How 'unavailable' do modes of service have to be before logical consequences are deduced? How threadbare does a garment of principles have to get before intellectual decency requires its replacement? For Gladstone to talk of needing so bizarrely unattainable an 'application of conviction' as a 'synodical decision' to do for him what he was evidently unwilling to do for himself was tantamount to a decision to set unfulfillable terms for his so oft-repeated undertakings as to his life's priorities. Gladstone, in short, was indeed being guided, as he himself feared, by a 'determined bias' which quite possibly impaired his powers of moral judgement; and quite possibly his sins were so persistent as to benumb his spiritual instincts and his faculty for discerning the will of God. At all events, he was never to intuit that the political game was up.

Why? That he was possessed of a healthy allowance of worldly ambition was sufficiently attested. The child struggling up the stairs at Rodney Street was still very much the father of the man. Gladstone undoubtedly found his 'public acts' a comfort in a rather uncomfortable world. Did Catherine's influence at this time help to hold him to politics? More than anyone else she would have been aware of his need for business and official occupation to keep him steady. Yet Gladstone's protestations that the 'general objects of political life' were not his objects still held good. On the other hand, his duty to support Peel, regardless of Peel's unresponsiveness to the ideal of a historical and visible Church Catholic, remained paramount.

Undoubtedly it was Peel's example and Peel's renown that exerted most influence on Gladstone's deciding his course at this juncture. The whole of Gladstone's subsequent career testifies to the ineffaceable impact made upon him by these years of service under Peel. He learned from Peel the lessons of how confident executive power exerts itself for purposes higher than party or sectional considerations. Like Peel, Gladstone would become a man of government, jealous of its prerogatives. He learned from Peel the lesson of how political leadership must be ready and willing at critical moments to drive a recalcitrant Commons and to overbear an unwilling Parliament. From Peel he learned the grand lesson that political party is a means to an end defined by executive necessity. From Peel he learned the lesson that the good sense of the people, as Peel himself put it, was 'a powerful instrument on which the Executive government may rely for neutralizing the mischievous energies of the House of Commons'.[44]

~

Having possession of these exemplary values of Peel was to be Gladstone's greatest long-term asset as he began to adjust and adapt himself to the great transition and its changed scenes and parts. With resignation he had cut a kind of Gordian knot. A decidedly self-sacrificial act had authorized him to put behind him all that he could wish extinct in his words of 1838. And abandoning office noisily was a way of quietly not abandoning politics. It was 'a grave practical question' whether persons such as himself 'entertaining a dark view' of the 'conditions and prospects of government' should continue to 'meddle with public affairs'. He allowed candidly that his motive for so continuing was 'egotism'.[45]

The immediate ground of his meddling would be the current critical situation within the Conservative party. Forbearance from all sides and giving credit for good motives and readiness 'to adopt favourable constructions and allow for difficulties unseen and therefore not accurately measured', would be of the essence. Gladstone contributed splendidly to party morale with a virulent drubbing of Palmerston. Gladstone enjoyed the particular pleasure of earning from Peel – 'the most conscientious man I ever knew in spareness of eulogium' – the tribute, 'that was a wonderful speech, Gladstone'.[46] Certainly Peel was in need of all the help he could get as the aftermath of Maynooth.

Free though he was now of responsibility for public business, Gladstone found himself far from free of the tax imposed on available time. In the Commons he spoke from the frontbench half way between the Treasury bench and the bar of the House with all the authority of a privy councillor on railways and sugar. Cobden's persistent and tasteless charges of bad faith on the part of the landlord class irritated him, and he had sharp words for that 'very peremptory' body, the Anti-Corn Law League. He voted bravely for the Maynooth measure in defiance of his Newark constituents. He consoled himself with the 'inward relief' provided by the discipline of the Engagement, the group of lay Anglo-Catholics formed by the Aclands under the patronage of St Barnabas, whose Rule was framed by Keble.[47] Gladstone's major initiative within the framework of the Engagement was to convert his notions of retrieving prostitutes from sinful ways into an office of charity laid down as one of its twelve rules. He started tentative accostings in the summer of 1845. He did not undertake any such direct rescue work between August 1845 and July 1849, when it could be said to have started in earnest.

Then there was talk with Hope and Philip Pusey of an autumn 'walking tour' of Ireland. 'Ireland is likely to find this country and Parliament so much employment for years to come', Gladstone told Hope, 'that I feel rather oppressively an obligation to try and see it with my own eyes instead of using those of other people.'[48] But the opportunity, ungrasped, slipped away. And in any case, it became clear that, if Gladstone were to tour that autumn, it would be to Germany on yet another mission to rescue Helen.

Before that drear family crisis imposed itself Gladstone busied himself during the spring and summer of 1845 with Dante and devoured theology and Church history. He needed to find firm underpinnings for his new basis of operation. He needed redrawn mappings of spiritual terrain. He needed to have his public credentials reaccredited. He needed new resources both of attack and defence for a workable Christian idea of politics. Where to find them? In relating State to Church Gladstone had found Coleridge his most suggestive teacher. He was looking now for doctrine that more comprehensively applied Christianity to the world. Formerly he had seen himself as a churchman seeking political accreditation. Now he was a politician seeking religious accreditation.

His duty was to turn to Anglican authority. His instinct was to seek something resonant and revered yet readily adaptable for his practical purposes. By July Gladstone was deep in the great eighteenth-century Doctor of Anglicanism, Bishop Joseph Butler, whom he had first tasted in Oxford but in whom then found little to his purpose. Now, gratified at Butler's following St Augustine's doctrines on human nature, Gladstone found Butler answering his needs in a manner he took to be, in itself, providential. A great teacher of the moral government of the world, of God as 'Almighty Maker, Governor, and Judge', Butler was to be for Gladstone a lifelong obsession. *The Analogy of Religion, Natural and Revealed, to the Constitution and Course of Nature* of 1736 offered a means of deducing a moral politics within a Christian providential scheme. In Butler's doctrine of probability as the key to life and of actions in life, Gladstone could see especially a very practical means of making the inner and higher prescriptions of religion applicable to the outer and lower world of affairs.

In an 'Exercisus Butleriani' of 1845 Gladstone began his wrestle with the Bishop.[49] 'Sad letters from Fasque', however, interrupted. Helen, gone to Baden-Baden for treatment, seemed again out of control in Munich. Armed with a letter from Dr Wiseman, Gladstone was dispatched to return her to her family. On his swift passage he called at Passy outside Paris to deliver a message from Aberdeen to Guizot, former ambassador in London and now the strong man of Louis Philippe's regime, concerning international copyright. Guizot (a Protestant) congratulated Gladstone on Peel's Maynooth policy, assuring him that England would have the 'sympathies of Europe in the work of giving Ireland justice'. Gladstone, as he later reminded Guizot, 'saved and pondered' this remark as opening to him an insight into a European view of the Irish question.[50]

Then at Munich Gladstone found that Helen had skipped out of his way back to Baden-Baden. At a loss, he found himself in the company of Bavarian scholars and divines, among whom was a Professor of Ecclesiastical History of 'liberal' tendency, Dr Ignaz von Döllinger,[51] whom Hope had urged him to seek out. They took to one another instantly. Gladstone had enough German to cope. Döllinger was to mark an epoch in Gladstone's intellectual and religious life.

The serendipity of missing Helen and finding Döllinger could not long delay Gladstone's family mission. The business was immensely distressing. On top of everything the lamentable news of Newman's submission to Rome reached Gladstone amid the incongruous promenades of the grand-ducal watering-place. In any case, he failed in his mission. He got Helen as far as Cologne, but there she stuck and had to be abandoned.

~

The personal frightfulness of Helen's case mingled with what Gladstone saw as the political frightfulness of his own. He found Catherine and the children well and happy at Hagley. But once more in London he was soon caught up with the quickening pace of the fall of Peel's ministry. Lord John Russell announced that, in view of famine impending in Ireland in consequence of failure of the potato crop, he was a convert to the total repeal of the Corn Law, and advocated public agitation to encourage the government to take the plunge. Gladstone, out of the loop of official information, remained for long unaware of the inwardness of the situation. He was jolted by revelations from Lincoln. 'It is manifest that something is in the wind – and something serious.'[52]

On 16 December, immersed congenially in refuting Newman's *Essay on the Development of Doctrine*, Gladstone was called away to politics. 'Devoured the newspapers: I do not yet understand why the crisis came now & not later.' Peel, with both party and now Cabinet hopelessly divided, resigned. Russell undertook on the 18th to form a ministry. However, though bold enough to urge Peel to take the plunge, he shrank himself from the task. He returned the 'poisoned chalice' to the Queen, who perforce handed it back to Peel. Exasperated, Peel determined on one last stroke of decisive ruthlessness.

Gladstone quailed at the prospect. Repeal could not be done, he insisted, 'in conformity with the due relation between the constituent body and without convicting us either of folly or fraud either now or in 1841' – 'unless upon the special facts of the Irish case which I do not yet know'.[53] And then: 'Upon what are we to rally as a party? Were we to be a party, separate from the Whigs?' Gladstone feared above all that these processes should run into a series: a pattern of resistance in defence of some great interest or institution followed by abandonment. He could even conceive such 'factious baseness' applying, for example, to the Irish Church. 'This must not be.'[54]

Stanley, among others, had resigned. Peel summoned Gladstone to his side at his supreme hour of need. Gladstone prayed that God would 'exclude the pest ambition'. 'I have been & am still in a great whirl', he wrote to Catherine. 'Both private & public affairs are such as to defy repose & even my nervous system has lost a little of its steadiness ...'[55] On Sunday 21st Peel asked Gladstone to fill the Colonial Office left vacant by Stanley. On the following day Gladstone read the Irish Scarcity and Crisis papers. He learned of the plight of three million in need of relief. Later on the 22nd he saw Peel and accepted, 'in opposition', he had the consolation of feeling, to his 'leanings & desires: & with the most precarious prospects'. Peel was 'most kind, nay, fatherly – we held hands instinctively & I could not but reciprocate with emphasis his "God bless you"'. Gladstone was now a secretary of state. He had accepted office in August 1841 to serve the Church; he accepted office in December 1845 to serve the State. He excused himself awkwardly to Hope. 'I have sought for the best alternative, honestly, so far as that term is applicable to any of the operations of my mind.'[56]

Not the least awkward explanation Gladstone would have to make was that to his Newark constituents. Taking office required re-election. His Grace was not best pleased. Between settling in at the Colonial Office and seeing the New Year in as a guest at Windsor of the Queen and the Prince, Gladstone barely had time for a scrambled Christmas at Hawarden. To his surprise and indignation, he was defeated at Newark. Gladstone thus was fated to conduct his transient and embarrassed tenure as Colonial Secretary for the remaining precarious months of Peel's administration outside the House of Commons.

That tenure Gladstone found to be an exasperating task. It was expressive of his sense of futility that he referred to the 'thirteen noblemen and gentlemen who have in such unhappily rapid succession flitted through this Office to which, in the penury of the times, I have been brought'.[57] The one aspect he attended to with pleasure was that concerning Church arrangements and missionary efforts. For that purpose he appointed his wife's brother-in-law, George Lyttelton, as his Under-secretary. Lyttelton was chairman of the Canterbury Association, a body dedicated to planting churchly colonists in New Zealand. Gladstone was later to complain eloquently about the difficulties peculiar to the Colonial department: problems of distance and delay, problems of partial information, interventions invariably too late, an immense mass of business of which nine out of ten cases bored the Commons and the tenth was decided on an unintelligently partisan basis.

But in any case Gladstone was in a great muddle about colonies. He indulged himself with the same delusion in 1846 as he had as Under-secretary in 1835: that it was possible to draw 'the broadest and most marked distinction between questions of a local and imperial character', and that upon the foundation thus securely laid could be erected 'a general doctrine of the necessary supremacy of the mother country over a colonial dependency'. He tried to deal with colonies in the same Oxonian schoolman manner in which he had dealt with tariffs.

One dimension of his muddle was impeccably 'liberal'. The colonies must be fostered on 'principles that are sound and pure – on the principle of self-government'.[58] But for all that he conceded that as far as the 'free settlers' of the Canadas were concerned 'we cannot mould colonial destinies against colonial will',[59] he remained in practice an exponent of imperial destinies. The most revealing instance of Gladstone's schoolman confidence that he could draw a marked distinction between questions of local or imperial character was his policy in the Australian colonies of fostering on the one hand local self-government and on the other of not only maintaining transportation of convicts but of extending the system. Such was his notion of the necessary metropolitan supremacy of the mother country that he was quite clear that this was to be done despite the 'ill odour' into which the transportation system had fallen among the Australian colonists.[60] The major incident of Gladstone's tenure at the Colonial Office was his controversial sacking of the Governor of Van Diemen's Land, Sir

Eardley Wilmot, for failing to clear away intractable problems in the colony that were hindering expansion of convict transportation.[61]

~

At the end of March 1846 Gladstone tried, with confessed lack of conviction, to convert his involuntary absence from the Commons into something to be grateful for: 'A most gracious purpose of God has spared me the most wearing part of the labours that my resumption of office should have brought: the bitter feuds of Parliament: but my heart does not answer as it should in lively thankfulness.' Peel's Irish relief measures were answering well. But at Westminster the feuds were certainly bitter. Gladstone noted after Disraeli's great philippic against Peel on January 22nd: 'Read last night's debate. The skies are dark enough.' It was vexing not to be able to be at Peel's side when he most needed help. When Peel presented his Corn Law Repeal measure to the House on the 27th Gladstone was loyally in attendance in the gallery. Gladstone was not present on 28 February when a devastating two-thirds of his party turned against their leader. He was indisposed on 15 May, the occasion of Disraeli's most virulently brilliant invective.

By June, as Graham mordantly put it, the country gentlemen could not be more ready to deal the death blow than ministers were to receive it. 'The political sky is quite impenetrable', Gladstone informed his Oxford contemporary Governor Harris of Trinidad on 15 June. What clearly attracted Gladstone was the assessment that upon the whole 'the chances, so to speak, are that the relation between us will be dissolved by my disappearance from the desk at which I write'.[62]

The Whigs duly gave Peel a majority for his Repeal Bill; but, having given, they prepared to take away. Gladstone was gratified by a by-product of imminent defeat. Peel commissioned him on 20 June to convey the Queen's offer of a baronetcy to his father. There was to be a division on a measure of coercive legislation for Ireland. On this the Whigs would pounce. Defeat for ministers was sure. Should they resign or recommend a dissolution and new elections? Wellington, rightly in Gladstone's view, was strong for fighting on and dissolving. On 26 June Peel held the shortest Cabinet Gladstone had ever known: merely announcing that, as a consequence of defeat on the second reading of the Protection of Life (Ireland) Bill, he intended to resign forthwith. So evidently weary and eager for release was the prime minister that his colleagues did not have the heart to resist.

As for himself, Gladstone quitted the Colonial Office with almost schoolboyish glee. On 6 July he went to the Palace to hand in his seals. 'And now goodbye Council, goodbye representative institutions, goodbye Emigration & Immigration except the Emigration out of office and out of Parliament [of] men in this frying season, and their immigration into the country.'[63]

4

A New Vocation, 1846–1852

'To know what kinds and degrees of evidence to expect or ask in matters of belief or conduct, and to be in possession of an habitual presence of mind built upon that knowledge, is, in my view, the master gift which the works of Butler are calculated to impart.'

Gladstone, Studies Subsidiary to the Works of Bishop Butler *(1896)*

Emigrating from the Colonial Office in the 'frying time' of summer 1846 led Gladstone into a world of incoherences. He no longer had official employment to arrange his timetable and discipline his activity. He remained an exile from the Commons. He was happy to leave office but not at all happy with the way Peel had left his office, basking in the applause of his erstwhile enemies. Gladstone's hopeful assumption was that, once the dust had settled, Peel's mighty presence would of itself become an attraction about which Conservatives could move towards reunion. He was disconcerted to hear how Aberdeen interpreted Peel's behaviour.

Aberdeen read Peel's taunting the greater part of his own party and embarrassing his loyal followers as signifying his determination to make it 'impossible that he should ever again be placed in connection with the Conservative party as a party'; that Peel had made up his mind never again to lead it, never again to take office; that he was 'fixed to the idea to maintain his independent and separate position – taking part in public questions as his view of public interests might from time to time seem to require'. Gladstone was convinced that such an attempt on Peel's part to abdicate his leadership while remaining in the Commons was impossible. With all his 'greatness', Peel could not remain there, Gladstone felt sure, 'overshadowing and eclipsing all governments and yet have to do with no government'; that 'acts for such a man' could not be isolated, but must be in series and in relation to one body of men rather than another.[1] If no one denounced more polemically than Disraeli Peel's breaking of his party, no one denounced more vehemently than Gladstone Peel's neglect to mend it.

Russell would soon have to dissolve the by now rather elderly 1841 Parliament and call a general election. The point pressed now on Gladstone was that he needed to find himself a winnable constituency. It would be too absurd if, after everything, he were to fulfil his oft-proposed intention of breathing freedom in 'other air' in so banal an involuntary manner. It happened that one of the seats for Oxford University became available. Gladstone 'desired it', as he was later 'not ashamed to own' publicly, 'with an almost passionate fondness'.[2] Representing the University of Oxford meant representing the largest body of clergymen in the Church of England. It meant for Gladstone a kind of substitute for his forsaken vocation. He knew that his repute as a crypto-papist would be a problem. He was prompt therefore to relieve his feelings about the Roman Church and its fraudulent inducements to Anglican defectors by fulminating in the *Quarterly* for June 1847, asserting his faith that the English character, with its 'energetic love of freedom', made impossible any widespread acceptance of the 'rankness of the Papal system'.[3]

Attempts were made to block the way of the 'mystified, slippery, uncertain, politico-Churchman, a non-Romanist Jesuit' as Ashley described Gladstone.[4] He would be contested: a rare event in sedate University seats. Tom declared his intention of voting as a Protestant and a Tory against William; but the wretched Tom was sternly brought to heel by Sir John. His reluctant vote helped William to the second seat at the polls in August. Gladstone's intense anguish as to success made the election 'harrowing'; 'I never can forget', he later recalled, 'my anxiety not to lose the battle in 1847'.[5]

~

The Whigs scraped a bare majority in the general election and Russell would need Peel and his 'Peelites' to sustain his ministry. It soon became clear that Peel's one settled purpose was to assist the Whigs in rounding off the free trade policy. Peel's followers, 119 at the time of the break in 1846, now numbered only a little less. They included by far the largest part of the frontbench talent of Peel's late administration. But, as Gladstone never ceased to complain, little did Peel do to answer Gladstone's earlier query: on what now were Conservatives to rally as a party? Were they to be a party separate from the Whigs?

To Gladstone the great danger was that without Peel's gravitational pull many of his followers would drift into 'some other section' of Parliament.[6] Any strengthening of the 'rump' Conservative party, led by Stanley in the Lords and a Commons collective including Lord George Bentinck and Disraeli, was to be deplored, on the grounds of protectionism of course, but now especially if it threatened the stability of Russell's ministry. And there were not a few Peelites who felt that the political logic of the future lay in a junction with the Whigs, perhaps under the 'Liberal' label that was to be adopted in 1848. Gladstone equally deplored that course. He began to set himself up as a kind of Conservative conscience among the Peelites, insisting that while 'Peel does not seem to allow himself to realise his position', power nonetheless was 'surely coming to him, & likely to be forced upon him'.[7]

Given this disposition on Gladstone's part, Peel's obstinate withdrawal became in itself a major contribution to the incoherences besetting Gladstone. Left to his own devices, he veered into strange courses. One such was his decision to support the Whig ministers in removing Jewish parliamentary disabilities, following the precedents of 1828 for Protestant Dissenters and 1829 for Roman Catholics. This was an awkward stance for an MP for Oxford University in 1847, especially as his senior colleague, Sir Robert Inglis, was a leading advocate of the argument for keeping Parliament Christian if it could not be kept Anglican. Back in 1841, on the issue of Jewish municipal disabilities, Gladstone had upheld the principle of non-Anglican disqualification in the purest vein of his doctrines of 1838; and it was entirely appropriate that he should then have clashed on the issue with Macaulay. (Gladstone was not a member of Peel's government when the matter was resolved in 1845, much in the spirit of the Maynooth policy.)

The extraordinary feature of Gladstone's response to the Jewish parliamentary disabilities issue was the extent to which his urging in favour of dispensing with them, for all that he pleaded 'pain' and 'deep regret' to Oxford, was an effusion of 'march-of-minding' which Macaulay himself might have been proud to own. The arguments for a 'Church Parliament', Gladstone told the House in tones of one who had been through it all, and knew well the lesson of inevitable defeat, then arguments for a 'Protestant Parliament', and now for a 'Christian Parliament', were all hopelessly vulnerable 'owing to profound and uniform tendencies, associated with the movement of the human mind – with the general course of events, perhaps I should say with the providential government of the world'.[8]

It was, however, typical of the incoherences attaching to Gladstone at this time that he should sing quite a different song in 1850 when it came to the matter of the threat to Oxford's Anglican exclusivity implied in Russell's plan for Commissions to inquire into the ancient English universities. There was no logical pattern to Gladstone's adaptiveness or non-adaptiveness to the times in these years. He was much more relaxed over the church rates issue in 1849, for instance, than he previously was. But when later it came to the question of Liberal divorce reform in 1857, he was as ferociously resistant as he had ever been, brandishing Leviticus and Deuteronomy at the Commons.

Free trade in itself should not be accorded a decisively significant measure of Gladstone's vulnerability to profound and uniform tendencies. As a Canningite, he was of a tradition that could see the party of Pitt as the party of freer trade, who could see himself as one needing no lessons from the Manchester School. Gladstone always had reservations as to Cobdenite ideology. While agreeing with Cobden 'in entertaining a sanguine hope that the commercial legislation of this country, with its benign contagion, so to speak', would become the rule in general legislation among the nations, he could not concur in Cobden's 'sanguine prophecy' and anticipate that 'universal peace' would immediately follow.[9] Apart from the tradition of Canning, Gladstone had a healthy respect for the efficacy of the doctrine of original sin and the natural depravity of mankind.

It was indeed amid the turmoils, domestic and Continental, of 1848 that Gladstone drew up a memorandum on the subject. 'Those who have denied the doctrine of original sin have been hard pressed to account for all the evil and misery in the world.'[10] No zealous counter-revolutionary in 1848 and 1849 exceeded Gladstone in his admiring evocation of the greatest of all counter-revolutionaries, the Emperor Nicholas of Russia, 'a grand sight in form and bearing', as Gladstone recalled of the Emperor's visit to negotiate with Aberdeen in 1844, and then of his 'towering form', the 'lightning of his eye', his 'imperial, almost superhuman presence', and above all the grandeur of his role as the 'immovable stay and pillar of continental Europe' during 'the disastrous disclosure and miserable regression' of 1848.[11] Of such disclosures and regressions Gladstone doubtless heard much in March 1848 when dining at Aberdeen's with the eminent refugees Guizot and Jarnac; and again with Guizot at Peel's.

Gladstone himself was sworn in as a special constable in March 1848 in view of the contingency of possible counter-revolutionary action against the Chartists. He was gratified to observe that the Thames coal whippers, whom he had been instrumental at the Board of Trade in rescuing from the thrall of publicans, had offered their services as special constables. He made a point of extolling them in the Commons as evidence that the government's trust in the people would be rewarded by the people's trust in government.[12] On duty as a constable on 10 April Gladstone was relieved profoundly at the collapse of the Chartist challenge. At his parish church, St Martin-in-the-Fields, he arranged an Address to the Queen thanking God for baffling the 'attempt of some misguided persons to overawe the established Authorities'.

~

Talk with Guizot might well have reminded Gladstone of his call at Passy in 1845, when Guizot praised Peel's Maynooth policy. For of all the incoherences manifest in the public world confronting Gladstone at this time none was more striking than the subversion of the Irish question. Back in 1845 he groaned under the burden of Maynooth. 'The Irish Church question is on me like a nightmare.' If the Irish Church could not be defended on grounds of truth and duty to truth, could it be defended on grounds of the poverty and numbers of Irish Roman Catholics? The dire implications of Peel's Irish policy, and particularly its Maynooth aspect, were manifest. 'It is a Trojan horse, full of armed men.' And how to separate it from 'the general question in Ireland?'[13]

At Baden-Baden, amid the frightfulness of Helen's case as she was being forcibly leeched, Gladstone had written feverishly to Catherine about his growing belief that he would never be able to do much good for the Church in Parliament 'except after having seemed first a traitor to it and being reviled as such'. Here Gladstone had a vision of himself in a kind of self-sacrificial Peel role, heroically pulling down upon him the pillars of Establishment, as Peel had crushed himself under the pillars of Protection. It was now, Gladstone discerned, in the 'highest interest of the Church to give gold for freedom'. Here Gladstone envisioned a role for himself as disestablisher and disendower, presumably of the Church of Ireland; or perhaps the Church of Ireland as a preliminary exercise for the larger event of setting Anglicanism free to imbue and revive itself with autonomous apostolic essences. 'Ireland, Ireland! That cloud in the west, that coming storm, the minister of God's retribution upon cruel and inveterate and but half-atoned injustice! Ireland forces upon us these great social and religious questions – God grant that we may have courage – to look them in the face and to work through them.'[14]

The 'general question in Ireland', especially as regards the poverty and numbers of Irish Roman Catholics, indeed forced itself upon the British political establishment in 1846 and 1847 with stormy insistence. The potato crop failure in 1846 proved much more severe than it had been in 1845. Government, both in Dublin and London, complacent after the largely successful holding operation in 1845, was overwhelmed. Gladstone wrote to Manning of the famine, this 'greatest horror of modern times', as a 'calamity most legibly divine'.[15] Whatever the legibility of the purposes of the Divinity, their practical consequence was that the demographic catastrophe obliterated the familiar Irish political landscape. The clouds in the west dissolved. The storm of the famine passed over, leaving a wasteland with O'Connell's Repeal agitation in ruins and Peel's (and Russell's) Irish reform and reconciliation programmes utterly redundant. The Irish Church question ceased to be on Gladstone like a nightmare. Gladstone's fevered vision of being a traitor to it could be set aside – as it happened, for twenty years.

~

Thus, though freedom was not yet to be granted to the Irish Church, in a way it was now conferred on Gladstone. He was relieved of an oppressive dimension of his concerns and anxieties. Of course, other concerns and anxieties quickly filled the space available. But the new circumstances did mean that his work on the underpinnings of a new vocation would be to that extent simplified. With his 'Exercisus Butleriani' in 1845 he had advanced considerably towards providing himself with resources for a workable Christian idea of politics and doctrine for applying Christianity to the world.

Gladstone interrogated Butler for his purposes as a Christian politician most searchingly in the *Analogy*. By arguing that the difficulties of understanding Revelation were no greater than the difficulties of understanding the natural order of creation, Butler offered a means of deducing moral politics within a Christian providential scheme. In the opening up of this argument, which in Gladstone's judgement stood out among the masterpieces of the human mind, Butler set forth the method of the government of God and the 'provision supplied to us for the discharge of our several offices under that government'. The evidential links between the governing agencies of the higher and lower worlds were grounded on the fact that Butler 'chose for his whole argument the sure and immovable basis of human experience'.

A theory of probability and presumptive evidence was indeed well calculated for the purposes of men of affairs. 'To know what kinds and degrees of evidence to expect or ask in matters of belief or conduct, and to be in possession of an habitual presence of mind built upon that knowledge, is, in my view, the master gift which the works of Butler are calculated to impart.' By thus providing a method of interpreting 'the dealings of God with men in the kingdoms of Nature, Providence, and Grace', men could reliably deduce that 'the intelligent Author of nature is also moral, for He takes sides in that conflict between virtue and vice, which incessantly prevails in the world'. The evidences of this providential scheme of moral government were a system of 'moral desert and punishment for sin', and 'marks of distributive justice in the world'.[16]

Equipped with this mental apparatus, and habituated increasingly with the required presence of mind to interpret and apply it as a political man trying to see his way clear in the twisting paths of public duty in the lower world of Nature, and to refer it to the higher world of Providence and Grace, Gladstone might indeed feel that he had found the right materials for building a golden bridge enabling him to cross over from being an abdicated political servant of the Church to being a renovated Christian servant of the State. As he put it to Manning, his 'four "doctors"', Aristotle, Augustine, Dante, and Butler, 'are doctors to the speculative men; would that they were to the practical too!'

No doubt it was for Gladstone a potent recommendation of Butler's doctrine, as applicable to the moral author of nature's taking sides in the incessant battle between virtue and vice prevailing in the world, that the Butlerian politician's weaponry was so amply provided in his function as an agent of virtue against vice, as an adept in detection of moral desert and punishable sin, and as awarder of marks of distributive justice. As such an agent, adept and awarder, Gladstone was to impress himself upon the body politic in future decades with a singular power of impact.

~

Work on Butler was done mainly amid the shades of Fasque or Hawarden. In those ample retreats Gladstone also pored over the copious memoranda with which he had recorded his memorable hours with Döllinger in Munich. At a time when Catholicity in the Church of England seemed to tremble on the brink of discredit and ruin, when the kind of Italianate-Irish Romanism represented by Wiseman was raising its head in anticipation of an era of advances and triumphs, it was immensely reassuring for Gladstone to find an entirely different face of Roman Catholicism. Eminently learned, Döllinger was theologically sympathetic and intellectually congenial, leaning liberally towards the Reformation as Gladstone leaned conservatively towards Rome.

Döllinger moved, much as Gladstone was moving, ecumenically toward an idea of a national Catholic Church in Germany free of state control. Döllinger's historical approach to theology and the Church Gladstone found particularly sympathetic.[17] When they bade farewell Döllinger said: 'Well, we are in one Church by water – upon that I shall rest.' Gladstone responded that it was his happiness 'to be allowed to go further'.[18] Döllinger became 'by water' a constant mental companion for Gladstone. And Gladstone let miss no chances in future to include Munich in his travels. And now, having time and space available, Gladstone found himself drawn into another expansive literary pursuit. Already Dante and Bishop Butler were grand figures in his literary pantheon. Homer would join this select group in the winter months of 1846–47 at Fasque. The attraction for Gladstone seems to have been an instinctive sense of spiritual nutrition secreted in the pagan text.

He quarried an enormous mass of Homeric notation in 1846 primarily to combat Karl Lachmann's theory that the Homeric epics had been cobbled together out of isolated fragments. A convinced 'unitarian', Gladstone argued also that Homer lived near to the time of the events he related. This case for one man describing a real world came out in the *Quarterly* for September 1847. His motive, as became clear in later publications, was a sense that Homer played a kind of presaging role in the Christian providential scheme. Gladstone's literary enthusiasms always had a practical, if often idiosyncratic, bearing. Dante's anti-papalism was not the least of his merits. Butler would in due course be put to many odd uses. The Christian uses, or abuses, to which Gladstone would put Homer became a scandal of classical scholarship.

Both Fasque and Hawarden were places thus of delightful intellectual repose. But they were at the same time places of tension and strain. At Fasque old Sir John began to fade into senile decay. Helen, hitherto notable recently for cataleptic fits curable only by the knuckle bone of some female saint and for her habit of employing the pages of Protestant divines for lavatory paper, seemed to respond by blooming into life again. Such was the reconciliation with William that his new daughter, born in 1849, was named after her aunt.

But in April of 1850 William and Catherine were shattered by the agonized death from cerebral meningitis of their four-year-old daughter Jessy. Gladstone, who had assiduously been gathering family coffins for interment in the Chapel of St Andrew, now added that of the first loss within his own household.

The complex task of dividing up Sir John's estate had already begun in 1849. William had Sir Stephen Glynne's bond of £30,000 transferred to him, together with much property and stock. In the final division after Sir John's death in 1851 Tom, the heir, got the largest share, including Fasque; but the younger sons each received in total something worth £151,000.[19] The big change was that Sir Thomas Gladstone, 2nd Baronet, by no means welcomed William's further presence at Fasque. This chilly relationship lasted until a reconciliation in 1856. Gladstone did not see Fasque again until 1858. Thus, though he had lost Fasque, Gladstone had gained wealth. This put him in a strong position in relation to Hawarden. He now had Sir Stephen's bond for £30,000. Gladstone money had largely bailed out the huge Glynne losses at the Oak Farm concern. (Gladstone calculated his own personal loss at £12,834.) Much Glynne land passed over to Gladstone. Backed up by his father, Gladstone had devoted immense amounts of time and energy to staving off the commercial disgrace of bankruptcy and by 1852 could remark on Stephen's affairs as 'materially improved'. Lavinia Glynne died in 1850 after presenting Henry with yet another daughter. That ended an awkward period for the Gladstones, providing, of course, that Henry remained unmarried. Arrangements could go ahead for young William Henry to inherit. It was a delicate and somewhat embarrassing situation, and Gladstone was sensitive to misconceived sentiments or whispers on the theme of a Gladstone appropriation of the Glynne heritage.

To the dismal burden of the Oak Farm affair was added for Gladstone a feeling that his 'rescue' work within the Engagement was not proving as satisfying as he had hoped. A St Barnabas House of Charity in Soho, established in 1847[20] as a refuge for the homeless, and a House of Mercy at Clewer near Windsor, provided refuge for penitents, but it did not provide Gladstone with the direct accosting that he needed. Catherine's many pregnancies, and the even more numerous pregnancies of Mary Lyttelton involving Catherine in long absences, Gladstone found frustrating. The 'natural and vigorous' tendencies of his youth were now no less vigorous.

Church affairs in 1847 began to take on a threatening aspect. Bishop Phillpotts of Exeter refused to institute a clergyman to a living on the grounds of his doctrinal heterodoxy in the matter of baptismal regeneration. The Rev. Charles Gorham prepared to fight his case through the sequence of appeal courts, ecclesiastical and lay. The possible sting in the tail of this process was that the end of the sequence was the Judicial Committee of the Privy Council, a body of laymen but competent, as the law stood, to pronounce on matters of doctrine and belief in the Church of England. It might well come about that the state's claim to interfere would compromise the apostolicity of the Church: for Gladstone, and for Manning and Hope, a truly horrid prospect.

That very thing eventually happened, in March 1850. Newman prepared opportune lectures 'On the Difficulties of Anglicans'. Gladstone despairingly put his trust in the bishops to rescue the Church. They did not even try. Manning and Hope deduced the obvious deductions.

There were the frustrations also of 'being a member of a sort of a wreck of a political party'. Before the end of the 1848 session Gladstone desponded that communications among the Peelites had 'dropped oddly'.[21] In 1849 he told Aberdeen that Peel's behaviour was 'false and in the abstract almost immoral – as he, and still more Graham, sit on the opposition side of the House professing thereby to be independent members of Parliament but in every critical vote are governed by the intention to keep ministers in office and sacrifice everything to that intention'.[22]

Meanwhile, Gladstone dutifully played his role as public man. He attended the dinner at Mansion House to launch the Great Exhibition project for 1851, admiring Prince Albert's speech as a '5th Gospel, a New Evangel'. There he met Lord Granville, whom he greatly liked: the beginning of a lifelong friendship. At the Royal Academy dinner he sat next to Disraeli, who was 'very easy & agreeable'.[23] He attempted in 1850, indeed in collaboration with Disraeli, to instil some bite into Opposition in another of his assaults on Palmerston, this time over the Foreign Secretary's shameless bullying of the Greek government for its allegedly harsh treatment of a Gibraltar-born money-lender, Don Pacifico.

In two passionate speeches Gladstone lauded the Conservative concert ideal embodied in Aberdeen's policy of conciliating peace with dignity in conformity with the sentiments of the civilized world. Palmerston's brazen appeal to chauvinistic sentiment with his *civis Romanus sum* tag let him escape the retribution Gladstone passionately hoped for. Gladstone thought the division 'disgusting' particularly for the number of Peelites who allowed themselves to be seduced.[24] Then Peel's tragic death in a riding accident a few days later made the void of his absence even more poignant.

This malaise of spirit and circumstances led Gladstone to his 'principal besetting sin', 'impurity', or prurient curiosity.[25] It led also to bouts of prophylactic questing in the streets to ward off the appalling temptations of 'allowing and entertaining of positive desire'.[26] In January 1849 he began experiment in flagellation as a 'principle of discipline'. Possibly he found encouragement or precedent for the use of a small whip or scourge among members of the Engagement. In any case mortifications of this kind were by no means unknown. He found himself 'trusting unduly' to it, with declining efficacy. 'Man as God made him is wonderfully made: I as I have made myself am strangely constituted. An ideal above the ordinary married state is commonly before me & ever returns upon me: while the very perils from which it commonly delivers still beset me as snares and pitfalls among which I walk.'[27]

~

With Jessy's atrocious death in 1850 on top of everything, Gladstone determined to flee the domestic scene. He would take a family party off to Italy's sunny clime. He had, after all, done that very thing for himself in 1849, when, indefatigably, he had dogged Lady Lincoln's steps in aid of Lincoln's divorce suit. That brisk escapade had had a decidedly tonic effect. The same would apply to this tour. Gladstone, Catherine and Agnes by November were settling in at Naples. Gladstone specialized in collecting from liberal but not irreligious or republican Italians items of evidence tending to the discredit of the papacy.

The Italian excursion was intended as an escape from scenes of sorrow and circumstances of malaise and frustration. Gladstone badly needed to regain his equilibrium, and his instincts were all for the tonic soothings of tourism, art-purchasing, book-hunting, sermonology, theatre, light society. The last thing he expected would be to get involved in Neapolitan politics. Had he not recently delivered a powerful critique of Lord Palmerston's deplorable penchant for meddling in the affairs of other states? Had he not objected decidedly to 'propagandism of even moderate reform' in absolutist European powers? Had he not denounced passionately Palmerston's 'spirit of interference', the 'insular temper' and 'self-glorifying tendency' he encouraged among his countrymen? Had he not ridiculed Palmerston's setting the British up as 'universal schoolmasters' to the rest of Europe? Had he not, above all, mocked Lord Minto's mission of 1847 to urge reforms in the Italian states, like unto 'nothing but the fabulous influence of the dim eclipse, which shed over the nations through which it travelled disastrous twilight', perplexing rulers and ruled alike?[28] If anyone was to be seen as an embodiment of Lord Aberdeen's policy of forbearance to foreign states grappling with difficult problems in the messy aftermath of the disastrous disclosures and miserable regressions of 1848, it was Gladstone.

News from home did nothing to ease the peevish humour in which Gladstone had set off. Russell's opportunist exploitation of the 'Papal Aggression' scare after Pius IX proclaimed the restoration of the Roman Catholic hierarchy in Britain involved a side-swipe at the Anglo-Catholic 'enemies within the gate, indulging in their mummeries of superstition'. Gladstone groaned in despair.[29] For here at last was the episcopate of England, in full fig of truculent unity, boldly setting out to do battle with the Pope on an issue of marginal significance, having but a matter of some weeks earlier, on the issue raised by the Gorham case, as Gladstone saw it, of life or death for the truly Catholic and Apostolic status of the Church, exposing themselves as lackeys of Erastianism.

Amid such morbid broodings Gladstone was astonished on 3 January 1851 to hear of the imprisonment of 'our friend Lacaita', the legal adviser to the British embassy, 'a very accomplished man', who had known one of Gladstone's current literary obsessions, the poet Leopardi, and who was at the time invaluable as a cicerone for art-purchasing and sight-seeing expeditions. Thus Gladstone was introduced to the counter-revolutionary proceedings of the Neapolitan authorities. The case of the political dissident Lacaita, connected with the case of the political dissident Poerio; and then to Settembrini, and so on. The embassy people no doubt would do their best for Lacaita. Besides, Gladstone and his party were due soon to leave for Rome, where he looked forward to more solemn delights. But Catherine, pregnant again, had suffered a miscarriage. Rest was prescribed. The Rome project had to be abandoned.

So Gladstone was stuck in Naples, with frustration and irritation about Rome now added to the baggage of frustrations and irritations he had imported with him. What had been intended as a cure for his problems of emotional instability and repressed aggression began instead to aggravate his symptoms. With reckless liberality, the authorities permitted Gladstone to visit the bagno at Nisida, where most of the prisoners were held in conditions of overcrowding and squalor. He inspected other prisons, interviewing and taking copious notes without hindrance, a distinguished and privileged guest of the Kingdom of the Two Sicilies. He arrived at the conclusion that this 'illegal government' was 'struggling to protect its utter illegality by a tyranny unparalleled at this moment, and almost without a rival amidst the annals of older atrocities'.

Each item in this indictment was a nonsense. The Neapolitan regime, however illiberal, was as legal as any other established government in Europe. To talk of an 'unparalleled tyranny' which permitted visitors to examine its prisons and interview its prisoners was absurd, particularly in view of what had happened elsewhere in the counter-revolutionary clean-up. Celebrator of the imperial presence of Emperor Nicholas, Gladstone had been aware of stern and salutary measures to restore legitimate authority in the 'June days' in Paris or in Hungary or in Lombardy and Venice. The stern French suppression of the Roman Republic in 1849 evoked no shocked comment as he passed through Rome on Lady Lincoln's heels. There was no lack of Irish efforts to solicit explosions of moral outrage. Perhaps Gladstone might have obliged had he gone on his planned Irish walking tour in 1845. The incoherences of his life in these years made pretty well anything possible.

It would equally be nonsensical, on the other hand, to read into the Neapolitan episode simply Gladstone's making the authorities there pay for his grievances: for what had happened to Jessy; for the loss of Peel and, in another sense, the impending loss of Manning and Hope; for being a member of a sort of a wreck of a political party; for Palmerston's outrageousness; for the Gorham judgment and the feebleness of the bishops; for Oak Farm; for the Marriage Bill and the University Commissions; for the sad fact that the Engagement had lost much of its early vitality;[30] or, for that matter, impurity and flagellations. Some such accumulation of emotional pressures, however, undoubtedly played a crucial part in generating the pent-up energy released by the trigger of the Nisida bagno.

And to that accumulation could be added two further aggravating elements. One was Gladstone's animus against the 'rankness' of the Roman system in Italy. Gladstone's relish for the anti-Roman testimonies of a class of intelligent Italians, not willingly republicans or unbelievers, had built up by the time of the Naples visit to a critical mass. His growing friendship with the Modenese refugee and former Carbonaro Antonio Panizzi at the British Museum contributed crucially to this animus against the Roman Church specifically as a prop for a regime such as that of the Two Sicilies.

The other aggravation was Gladstone's shock on witnessing the treatment as common felons of persons he could identify with himself as gentlemen. 'The class persecuted as a whole is … the middle class in its widest acceptation, but particularly in that upper part of the middle class which may be said embraces the professions, the most cultivated and progressive part of the nation.' These were the first 'Liberals' with whom Gladstone had come into sympathetic political connection. And there they were, sometimes actually in chains. It was not long before Gladstone (whose Italian was well found) was deep in reading C. L. Farini, the liberal Catholic historian of *Lo Stato Romano, 1815–1850* (1850), a kind of Italian Döllinger, highly critical of the Pope's temporal power.

Accordingly, Gladstone composed memoranda designed to remove common English misapprehensions that Italian Liberalism was a conspiracy of republicans and atheists.[31] He was equally assured that these victims of 'wholesale persecution of virtue when united with intelligence' were Liberals in a sense by default. To Gladstone they were men prevented from being Conservative because their government forced on them the choice only of tyranny or revolt. His sympathies were for them rather than with them. Gladstone accused the Neapolitan regime of doing the work of republicanism. As 'a member of the Conservative party in one of the great family of European nations', he was 'compelled to remember that that party stands in virtual and real, though perhaps unconscious alliance with the established Governments of Europe as such'. The pith of Gladstone's indictment of the Neapolitan government was that it disgraced the cause of European Conservatism.

~

News of his father's failing health and of the state of politics in Britain called Gladstone away in February 1851. As he travelled back from Naples Gladstone could see in the problems Lord John was having in patching up his tottering ministry little prospect of himself being comprehended comfortably in any new combination. Lord Stanley prepared for the eventuality of being asked to take office by drawing up a distribution of offices 'on the two suppositions that Aberdeen and Gladstone do, and do not, join us'. Disraeli declared his willingness to serve under Gladstone's leadership of the Commons. Stanley was 'despondent and depressed' by Aberdeen's refusal. And for all that he could see that Gladstone would be 'obnoxious to both Protestants and Protectionists', Stanley would not persevere 'unless strengthened by the accession of Gladstone'.[32]

On arriving at London Bridge Station Gladstone was greeted with the news that Stanley desired to consult him about the possibility of joining a new Conservative ministry. Gladstone could not see in the Conservative rump the makings of an active government. Stanley offered him '*any* office', subject to Canning's having first refusal of the Foreign Office and without any mention being made as to the leadership of the Commons. But as Stanley stipulated for a fixed duty on corn, Gladstone found no difficulty in joining Aberdeen and Newcastle (erstwhile Lincoln) in refusing.[33] The dismayed Protectionist Conservatives thus had their first taste of the perplexing problem of dealing with the Peelites, who seemed 'only to be had by the lot'.

For Gladstone it was in a way satisfying thus to push conventional political matters aside for the time being. They were far from the head of his agenda. He planned of course to acquit himself of the Naples affair with what eventually became the *Letter to the Earl of Aberdeen*, much to the Earl of Aberdeen's distress. Indeed, he spent an evening at Lady Granville's discoursing on 'Neapolitan horrors'. Much to Gladstone's distress, he found on the Gorham matter that the bishops were unwilling to press for amending the law of appeal. Even more distressing were matters with Manning and Hope, on the brink of submission to Rome. By the end of March Gladstone saw them slipping out of his wrestlings to stay them. On 6 April the blow fell. 'A day of pain! Manning and Hope!' 'They were my two props. Their going may be to me a sign that my work is gone with them … One blessing I have: total freedom from doubts. These dismal events have smitten but not shaken.'[34]

~

Manning's and Hope's 'going' was not in fact a 'sign' that Gladstone's 'work' would go with them. That was rhetoric from which the substance had long departed. Gladstone's pain, however, was not the less acute for it. He wrote to Hope expressing an 'unaltered affection' and a wish that separation would not mean estrangement.[35] He told Hope that what was in Hope's view 'finding a sure anchorage is in mine one of the most deplorable errors ever committed by men in perfect good faith, from pure motives, and at heavy cost'.[36] The threads of a social relationship with Hope were soon picked up again; but Manning remained a stranger for a decade. A heavy cost there was for Gladstone also. The 'sad recent events' 'not only over-set & depress me', he recorded, 'but I fear also demoralise me'. He found himself 'unmanned & unnerved', incapable out of 'sheer cowardice' of employing the discipline. The shock he underwent jolted him into admitting to himself that his rescue interests were 'Carnal, or the withdrawal of them would not leave such a void'. With one woman who came with him to his house twice he confessed he was 'certainly wrong in some things & trod the path of danger'.[37]

The crucial case that overbalanced him was Elizabeth Collins, who 'much interested' him on their first meeting on 11 June 1851. During the following year Gladstone met her on twenty occasions and sought for her in vain on five. Early in July 1851 he urged her to make a day visit to Carlton Gardens and appeal to Catherine for advice.[38] On 13 July there was a 'strange & humbling scene' of two hours which led to Gladstone's flagellating himself.[39] And then two more hours on 23 July, 'strange, questionable, or more', with another flagellation.

Thus carnality invaded charity. The sexuality that had always been a part, however firmly repressed, of Gladstone's philanthropic office, now broke through the surface. His doctrine of the 'substantive character of beauty', insisting that it was to metaphysics what pleasure was to ethics, was now given a curious new twist. Gladstone was both smitten and shaken by Elizabeth Collins' beauty. After their seventeenth meeting Gladstone told himself it was 'bad: & there must be a change'. A few days later he groaned: 'I am surely self-bewildered.'[40] It was a real struggle for him to regain his emotional composure. His rescue mission could no longer bear its former even ostensibly unalloyed character as a charitable office of his membership of the Engagement. Clearly Gladstone had crossed a crucial psychological threshold. In his smitten and unnerved state he allowed two very sensitive areas of his private life to break bounds and mix together. 'These misfortunes', Gladstone feared, might 'yet succeed in bringing about my ruin, body and soul.'[41]

These questions stayed with Gladstone as he gradually recovered his equanimity. As ever, his 'work' was therapeutic. That 'work' now was in substance as he had defined it to Stanley back in 1844: the lower ends of the State needed to be fulfilled when the higher ones became impractical. There was no question about where to start. As if defiantly hitting back at fell circumstance, Gladstone dated his letter to Lord Aberdeen on the Neapolitan horrors 7 April, the day following the catastrophe of Manning and Hope. In the void of displacement and instability compounded by his membership of a 'sort of a wreck of a political party' and the bankruptcy of his politico-religious programme, the letter represented the two solid and familiar reassuring things Gladstone could cling to: his Peel-substitute leader and a cause embracing politics and morality in a dramatic and compelling degree.

Aberdeen was by no means anxious to fit into Gladstone's requirements by intervening to restrain and correct the Neapolitan government. His permission to Gladstone to address the letter to him was a calculation reluctantly arrived at: possibly he might in some measure tone down Gladstone's obsessive excitement. The letter addressed to him on 7 April was ostensibly a private communication, and Aberdeen hoped to keep it that way. The supposition was that Aberdeen would secure Gladstone's purpose through his special and authoritative contacts with the conservative leaderships of Europe. As Gladstone put it in tones not far short of polite blackmail, he trusted that 'mitigation of these great offences to the eye of Heaven might be effected through your Lordship's aid ... without the mischiefs and inconveniences which I am fully sensible might, nay in some degree must, attend the process, were I thrown back on my own unaided resources'.

Thus the hapless Aberdeen had to balance the chances of his swaying the policy of counter-revolutionary Europe against the likely consequences of Gladstone's running amuck with his own unaided resources. Aberdeen's problem was that he was dealing with a different kind of European conservatism from that with which he was familiar in the gentler times of Metternich and Guizot. The fulcrum for leverage at Naples would have to be Vienna; and in place of Metternich was Felix Schwarzenberg, the hard man of the Austrian counter-revolution. Schwarzenberg agreed, however, to set inquiries in train in Naples. His reply to Aberdeen's carefully researched letter of 2 May was despatched at the end of June. But before it was received Gladstone, to Aberdeen's consternation, bolted. He went ahead and published on 11 July, on his own unaided resources and with their attendant mischiefs and inconveniences, *A Letter to the Earl of Aberdeen on the State Prosecutions of the Neapolitan Government*.

Clearly, Gladstone was too excited and impatient to heed Aberdeen's plea that he was in decency bound to wait for the Prince's answer. It is conceivable that he deliberately pre-empted that answer on the ground that it would very possibly steal or at least muffle his thunder. However that may have been, Gladstone got the result he wanted. As Aberdeen ruefully put it, 'Gladstone's ill-advised publication has produced the most extraordinary sensation here, amongst persons of all parties, and given a great practical triumph to the Foreign Office.'[42]

The impact of the *Letter* owed much to the incongruousness of the writer in relation to his theme. Here was dramatically gross contradiction of Gladstone's own Don Pacifico doctrine. Palmerston, astonished and delighted, seized eagerly on this opportunity, all the more apt for his purposes as coming from the pen seemingly of a converted sinner, and addressed to a disciple of Lord Castlereagh. He made a great point of applauding Gladstone in the Commons and arranging to have copies of the pamphlet distributed by British diplomatic representatives for the edification of the European courts. Gladstone found Palmerston's exploitation of him almost as embarrassing as his exploitation of Aberdeen had been to Aberdeen; which was but poor consolation to Aberdeen. 'This Gladstone affair', as Aberdeen lamented, 'has caused me a good deal of vexation; for I have been open to much misrepresentation; and although I would not, on any account, quarrel with a man I love and esteem as much as Gladstone, he knows perfectly well that I think I have great reason to complain of his proceeding.'[43]

Gladstone warned Aberdeen that he would find the matter of the Neapolitan case 'painful, nay revolting, to the last degree'. But Aberdeen would not have been the less impressed by the dangerous power of Gladstone's insistent rhetoric on outrages 'upon religion, upon civilization, upon humanity, and upon decency'; and especially for Gladstone's propagandist instinct for exploiting someone else's winged phrase, 'the negation of God erected into a system of Government'.[44] Amid this excited rhetoric Gladstone's insistence availed little that he wrote as a Conservative for Conservative purposes. To the general public viewpoint he looked to be so evidently aligning himself with the cause of liberty. This appearance persisted as Gladstone despatched a second, augmented, letter to Aberdeen on 15 July.

But the reality at the time was rather different. It is curious to observe that on 9 July, two days before bolting with his first letter to Aberdeen and six days before despatching his second letter, Gladstone had gone to the Guildhall on the mistaken assumption that he would see there the Emperor Nicholas of Russia, 'as I reckon him a sight worth much'. Did he imagine the Emperor as a guest at the Great Exhibition? Did it not occur to him that such a visit would be the occasion of public scandal, possibly riots? Was he entirely oblivious of Nicholas's gross notoriety in his dealings with the Hungarian revolutionaries in 1849, let alone the Poles back in the 1830s? Is it possible that this bizarre episode of conservative hero-worship is to be counted among the incoherences characteristic of Gladstone's life in these days, along with, say, his feverish quests for Elizabeth Collins?

However that may have been, the immediate significance of the *Letter* was what Aberdeen himself diagnosed: impulsiveness and inconsequentiality. It owed much more to Gladstone's having lost a past than to any strivings to find a future. If anything, his embarrassment at being hailed as a recruit for the cause of liberty led him to quite excessive stickiness and purism over the next few years in asserting the Conservative integrity of the Peelite group. Displaced and unstable, bereft of his props and the old familiar bearings of his political ways, he was indeed being powered, as he put it to the dismayed Aberdeen, by 'his own unaided resources'.

~

In the interval of addressing his first letter to Aberdeen and the notoriety of its publication, Gladstone resumed his bedraggled public career. On the Church front the rude jolt of displacement led him to formulate a much more severely Keblean view of the Establishment. Reverence for the episcopate was dimmed to the point of extinction. 'If we can', he noted rather ruthlessly at this time, 'we are bound to have Faith, Church, and Establishment together. If one must be parted with, however, it must be the Establishment of Religion. And if a second must be dispensed with, it must be the Church of England.'[45] Such was the sour fruit of much bitterness of soul.

Equally distressing was the fading by now of the Peelites as a considerable parliamentary party. The mass of backbenchers drifted back to the Conservatives or faded away at the next elections. All that was left was little more than a frontbench rump, over which Gladstone appointed himself a kind of unofficial whip.

Of much more moment was Gladstone's response to Disraeli's criticisms of Whig financial proposals in April 1851. Protection or free trade had held the stage as the dominant political issue since 1844. Now finance was coming back to the fore, much in the manner of the early and great days of Peel's ministry, as the crux of the relationship between government and public. Russell, to bolster his position, wanted to link finance with a second Reform Bill, recurring thus to the issue upon which he had made his name in 1831–32. Chancellor Wood's budget plan for an unreconstructed and undifferentiated income tax failed; and thus was created an immediate and obvious ground of conflict as to by whom and on what terms the issues would be resolved.

Though marginal in terms of gross national product, mid-nineteenth-century budgets were coming to create a state of 'psychological expectation', and to be thereby crucial in forming grounds of social balance, equity, and political stability.[46] A rising power of 'opinion' in the country, schooled in such pressure groups as the Parliamentary and Financial Reform Association of 1849, gave popular voice to matters of currency and incidence of taxation. Peel's posthumous fame gave to budget-making a new aura of public grandeur. As Peel's disciple, Gladstone was acutely sensitive to this dimension of politics. But, far from seeing budgets in natural tandem with the issue of franchise extension, Gladstone saw financial policy as the means of a sovereign remedy for social discontents, thus removing any need for parliamentary reform. Bad finance, he was convinced, was the mainspring for Reform agitation.

It was as Peel's disciple also that Gladstone could see Disraeli as the obvious rival for filling Wood's place and commanding the possibilities on the central ground of political credit and reputation. He soon decided that Disraeli's financial plan contradicted the principles laid down by Peel for reducing taxes on consumption of articles of industry.[47] Disraeli begins at this point indeed to take on something of the character of a moral target recently sustained by the Neapolitan regime. If Gladstone needed for the reassembling of his political vocation some such office as Butler had enjoined, as agent of virtue against vice, detector of punishable sin, and awarder of marks of distributive justice, Disraeli offered himself opportunely. (Palmerston, of course, was already marked for salutary treatment.) Gladstone had written to his father in 1849 that it was 'a very unsatisfactory state of things to have to deal with a man whose objects appear to be those of personal ambition and who is not thought to have any strong convictions of any kind upon public matters'.[48]

Gladstone's genius was to discern the lesson of Peel's ultimate failure. Peel, the most potent wielder of executive power, had no recourse beyond the walls of Parliament when challenged within those walls by a mere brute majority in the House of Commons. All that Peel ever asked of public 'mind' was that it would, as 'the quiet good sense and good feeling of the people of this Country', be 'a powerful instrument on which Executive government may rely for neutralizing the mischievous energies of the House of Commons'.[49] Gladstone's insight was to realize that a restoration of Peel's mode of government and the great things potentially to be achieved by such a mode of government would require recourse to some power external to the House of Commons far beyond merely a means of neutralizing its mischievous energies. It would need to be a power capable of overcoming those energies, by means, if necessary, of replacing a mischievously energetic Commons with a Commons imbued with a conviction corresponding to the doings and intentions of the executive minister.[50] The great decades to come of Gladstone's political ascendancy would be precisely a series of grand exercises of that insight.

In 1851 only one element of that insight was in place. If Gladstone was to arrive at a renewed vocation of politics it would inevitably take a form in some essential way as a renewal of Peel's wielding of executive power. That was never in doubt, never in question. The element remaining in question was the element of public mind. In his early days in politics Gladstone feared 'opinion'. Now he was not so afraid. Peel's mighty works of fiscal and commercial reform were in the process of reconciling governed with government. Their fruits of prosperity were now manifest in the land. That there existed a public mind of good faith could not be doubted. In time Gladstone could begin to see in the public reception of his Neapolitan initiative a new kind of beneficial energy, perhaps potentially manipulable, perhaps potentially gearable to executive government. Ultimately, Gladstone would talk of 'public opinion' as something he would 'form' and 'direct' towards ends divined by himself.[51]

But these were yet early days. The question was where to find it, how to approach it. His initiatives were necessarily tentative and exploratory. Gladstone's first exercise in exploring the phenomenon of what he would soon be describing excitedly as 'the *people*' took place at Shadwell, 14 May 1851, when he addressed a meeting of Thames coal whippers. This group of workers had become a hobby for Gladstone since his Board of Trade days, something of a proletarian version of his 'rescue' work. 'These men were delightful to see and hear', he recorded, 'apart from the excess of their grateful feelings towards me – which made me feel much ashamed.' That gratitude was in the coal whippers' minds when they invited Gladstone was natural. But what was in Gladstone's mind as he accepted and went off to so incongruous a locale as Shadwell?

~

The early weeks of 1852 were dominated by the disintegration of Russell's ramshackle Whig–Liberal government. In the previous December Palmerston, having recognised Louis Napoleon's *coup d'état* against the Second Republic in France without consulting either the Prime Minister or the Queen, was dismissed. He was already at odds with Russell in his resistance to another Reform measure. In his extremity Russell tried to shore up his crumbling position by bringing in some Peelites. He conveyed to Gladstone that the India Board was available.[52] But Gladstone was just as much opposed to Reform as Palmerston. The Peelites themselves had dwindled and were no longer in a position to prop Russell up, even had they wanted to. Their problem, indeed, was that they were not agreed as to their course ahead.

Lord Derby (erstwhile Stanley) was summoned to undertake the government. He made no approach to the Peelites, preferring to try to recruit the ex-Canningite Palmerston. He failed in this, but such was the confusion in the Commons, with disaffected Palmerstonians, disillusioned Radicals, resentful Irish, dithering Peelites, and the sharp decline in Russell's credit, that Derby had very reasonable prospects of forming a minority Conservative ministry that might well coast along and gather support on the way. Since the Peelites still constituted much the greater part of frontbench Conservative talent, Derby was at shifts to make up a plausible Cabinet. Most of his ministers had no previous official experience. Derby put Disraeli in the Exchequer, encouraging him with assurances that he knew as much finance as Mr Canning did, and that, anyway, 'they give you the figures'. Disraeli would also be Leader of the House of Commons.

The Peelites looked upon this 'Who, Who?' Cabinet (so called because of the deaf old Duke of Wellington's incredulous questions as Derby read through the list of its members) with condescension and contempt. Gladstone was particularly withering about the Exchequer. 'Disraeli', he wrote to Catherine, 'could not have been worse placed.'[53] Given the forming lines of his new vocation, the Exchequer presented itself to Gladstone as the grand desideratum of politics. Disraeli's possession of it was a provocation. But condescension and contempt did not resolve the Peelites' problem of how to respond to the new situation. Gladstone by this time was well into his lurch away from Neapolitan excesses and towards a severely Tory notion of the duty of the friends of the late Sir Robert. A junction with the Liberals, he insisted, was 'our least natural position'.[54]

He lost the fight, however, about what benches to occupy in the House. He wanted to shift with the Conservatives to the government side, on the ground that it was a dispute within a party, not between parties. The Peelite rump elected, however, to remain on the Opposition benches and sit with the Whigs and Liberals. Gladstone could reconcile himself to this as reflecting the circumstance that as yet free trade versus protection was the formal dividing line of politics. He could still assure himself that as soon as that was settled, politics could get back to 'normal'. His view was that a Derby government must bring protection 'to a speedy issue'; it would inevitably be defeated, must resign, and the battle between free trade and protection thus having been finally resolved, the way would be open for a return of the Peelites to a chastened Conservatism, and then the formation of a government 'mainly Conservative in its personal composition, connections, and traditions'.[55]

5

Peace and War, 1852–1855

> 'War has hitherto been to us Englishmen but a remote and abstract idea: and when we say we are going to War ... we do not know what we mean. It will dawn upon us by degrees, and in forms for the most part eminently disagreeable.'
>
> *Gladstone to Robertson Gladstone, 29 March 1854*

There was a general disposition among the Peelites that in all decency the Conservative government be allowed its chance to prove itself. It soon became clear that Derby and Disraeli were in any case wary of any notion of directly challenging free trade. This afforded the Peelites even more grounds for condescension and contempt, but no grounds for hostility. They fended off Russell's eager urgings to confront and remove Derby. In return for their forbearance, the Peelites stipulated that Derby must dissolve the 1847 Parliament and call a general election in the summer of 1852. They stipulated also that, upon meeting the new Parliament in a November session, ministers must bring forward their financial proposals.

Disraeli accepted these stipulations readily enough, but in doing so he deprived himself of the time he needed to calculate his financial plan with care and finesse. He had to produce an interim budget in April using materials adapted from the previous Whig Chancellor, Wood. Privately convinced that protectionism was 'not only dead, but damned', Disraeli used this budget to shift the Conservative party away from Derby's disposition to retain an element of protectionism. Even then, Derby had to admit that he did not expect a majority in the new Parliament sufficient to restore a duty on imported corn. Conservative election addresses on this issue would be studiously equivocal.

Gladstone meanwhile found the first session of 1852 very restorative of his morale. The Peelite policy of circumspect forbearance to the government suited him temperamentally at this stage, especially in contrast to Peel's deplorably rigid commitment to the Whigs. He was freer now for all manner of congenial activities. There was still much ado with Antonio Panizzi about revises and rebuttals in the Neapolitan affair. He relieved his feelings about the papacy ('a foul blot upon the face of creation, an offence to Christendom and mankind') in a review of his own translation of Farini's *Stato Romano* in the April *Edinburgh*. Church interest in such matters as the revived powers of Convocation and colonial bishoprics gave evidence of recuperation. There was the Report of the Oxford University Commission to be digested. He dabbled mildly in the new craze for phrenology.[1] And having money in fairly ample quantity led to purchases and patronage of art.[2]

But above and beyond all was the great question of his political future and the new 'work' that would be at its head and front. That Gladstone was adjusting himself to such a call is suggested in a quotation from Suetonius at the commencement of a new volume of his diaries on 1 March 1852: 'he had a longing for immortality and perpetual fame – but an ill-considered longing'.[3] His 'work' was going to be the putting of the finances of the country on a proper footing. Given that Disraeli was now Chancellor of the Exchequer, it was problematic as to how a commitment to ultimate Conservative reunion was to be reconciled with Gladstone's financial vocation. It is in these months that Gladstone began seriously to bring Disraeli into focus as a target; as a symbol and symptom of something he could persuade himself was fundamentally morally objectionable. Gladstone decided that Disraeli had failed to secure a proper balance between direct and indirect taxation by his neglect of tariff policy. By July he was remarking ominously that he found each successive financial speech by Disraeli 'more quackish in its flavour than its predecessor'.[4]

The elections were held that month. The ministerial Conservatives gained some ground but failed to clinch a majority. The Peelites, reduced by retirements and defections, came back 40 strong. Despite being vexed yet again by the 'rascalities' of a 'Protestant' challenge, Gladstone carried his Oxford seat handsomely. Russell's rag-bag of Whigs, Liberals, Radicals, and Irish were still not able to oust Derby without Peelite help; thus the Peelites could continue to fend Russell off and wait to savour the spectacle of the Derby-Disraeli ministry making their submission to Sir Robert Peel's fiscal and commercial principles.

~

Derby's government returned to face the new Parliament in November. The recent death of the Duke of Wellington cast an august gloom over the occasion. The solemn obsequies deeply impressed Gladstone. But soon he was eager to celebrate the obsequies of protection. He pressed Disraeli to declare whether the government had 'definitively, unequivocally, and finally abandoned the idea of proposing a return to protective policy'.[5] Disraeli, desperate to stay in office and produce another budget, was willing to go to any lengths short of a definitive, unequivocal and final renunciation. Russell let slip his dogs of free trade, with Villiers, Cobden's henchman, leading the pack. Disraeli had to be saved by Palmerston's good offices and by swallowing further doses of Peelite contempt, flavoured, in Herbert's case, with anti-semitism. Gladstone expressed himself as 'especially warm and indignant' at the government's evasive shuffling. His opinion of Mr Disraeli's political character, 'indifferent before, had become worse since he made his speech on Mr Villiers' motion'.[6] No doubt feeling that Herbert had said quite enough, he insisted that he was '*glad* I had not to say out what was in me about Disraeli's speech'. Nervous excitement kept him awake for the first time in many years.[7]

Nervous excitement suggests clearly that Gladstone was building up, as before the Neapolitan explosion, to something big. And clearly 'personal considerations' had come publicly to the fore with startling force. Was not the applicability of Butler's doctrines about the struggle of virtue against vice, the detection of punishable sin, the distribution of marks of justice, now manifest? All this vexed Derby. He innocently assumed that, now that the government had in all but name surrendered its ground on protection, the way would become clear for the great object of Conservative reunion. But Gladstone insisted that from Disraeli there had been 'provocation'; and that the Peelites still demanded satisfaction.[8] Possibly on the next occasion, Gladstone might well 'say out' what was in him about Disraeli.

Disraeli sustained a minority government by skilful prevarication and offering deals to anyone who would listen: Palmerston, the Irish, even John Bright the Quaker, scandalized but also amused by Disraeli's candid avowals that he was in politics to seek fame. Gladstone was ready to admit shamefacedly to himself but to no one else that he was ambitious and sought fame.

The extent to which in these years Gladstone was fitting Disraeli as a demonic element into his general interpretation of the shape of politics is illustrated by an unpublished article of 1855, 'Party as it was and as it is. A sketch of the political history of twenty years.'[9] By that time dire circumstances persuaded Gladstone that the character and morale of the political culture had suffered conspicuous decline. The plot of this curiously febrile piece is the dramatic story of how a 'normal' and beneficent party system that had developed in the epoch of reform was destroyed by the 'great and massive' but tragically flawed figure of Peel, like some doomed hero of Aeschylus or Shakespeare.

What was new was the now greatly enhanced role played by Disraeli not merely as an opportunist exploiter but as a contributory principal in the grand tragedy. His 'attacks and invectives', actuated by restless ambition, complemented with evil precision Peel's noble flaws. The 'subtle self-seeking which History will probably impute to Mr Disraeli' fed like a devourer of carrion on the stricken field of political disaster. 'It is needless', commented Gladstone quite undisarmingly, '... to enter into the moral of his singular career: and no one would gratuitously enter upon a task, which it would be so difficult to execute with fairness, at once to him, to the country, and to public virtue.'[10]

Disraeli's being constructed into a principal component of Gladstone's explanation of what had gone wrong with politics made him inevitably an equivalent component of any formulation of the role Gladstone would envisage himself playing in setting politics to rights. All the factors in the equation were beginning to assemble themselves with compelling cogency. Finance as the core of his new vocation followed naturally on his lieutenancy in Peel's great fiscal transactions. Gladstone needed urgently to make a strike. He needed to make it with precision, for his prime necessity was to establish a convincing claim to the Exchequer in succession to Disraeli. Quite how that was to come about was not immediately clear. It would not be likely to happen in any proximate future in a reunited Conservative government, since the conventions and manners of the time would require Derby to respect Disraeli's official precedence. Was Gladstone perhaps already beginning to think that a junction with Russell was no longer the Peelites' least natural position?

At all events, here now was Disraeli producing his second budget on 3 December. He was in an awkward position. He had to offer something to the interests that felt themselves the victims of Peel's betrayal over the Corn Law. On the other hand, he could not avow protectionism as his guiding principle. He was, moreover, severely hampered by constrictions of the time limit imposed by the Peelites. This meant hurry and improvisation. He did not have up-to-date returns of the figures. In the circumstances Disraeli's performance was impressive.[11]

The budget of 1852 became the focus of a quite disproportionate furore. It meant the term of the self-denying ordinance that the Peelites had imposed on the majority of the Commons. The Conservative government had been granted leave to live until it brought forward its financial proposals. Now the option of pronouncing its death sentence was available for use. This added fortuitously to the occasion a doom-laden atmosphere. Sitting on Opposition benches, as things were turning out, seemed for Gladstone entirely appropriate. He was excited. (There was another flagellation on 9 December after 'a conversation not as it should have been'.)

During the invective of Disraeli's concluding vindication on the night of 16–17 December an observer described the 'remarkable appearance' presented by the Opposition benches: 'not speaking to each other, pale in the gaslight, it reminded one of the scenes of the National Convention of the French Revolution. To complete the effect, a loud thunderstorm raged; the peals were heard and the flashes of lightning could be seen in the Chamber itself.'[12] Disraeli sat down at 1 a.m. on the morning of 17 December after what Gladstone described as a 'grand' and 'powerful' oration adorned with his famous peroration about being confronted by a coalition whose triumph would be brief, for 'England does not love coalitions'.[13] As Leader of the House, Disraeli thus concluded the debate amid a storm of cheers and counter-cheers and members began to shift themselves toward the division lobbies. Suddenly, amid a revived storm of cheers and counter-cheers, Gladstone projected himself to the table and insisted that Disraeli's speech demanded a reply, and 'that, too, on the moment'.[14]

It was a moment of inspired opportunism. By a combination of instinct and calculation, Gladstone struck precisely the point of optimum dramatic impact. His intervention intensified the already highly charged atmosphere with an unprecedentedly immediate element of gladiatorial challenge. At first he had to fight hard to gain a hearing against furious ministerial resentment at his presumption and at his embodying what they felt to be an ultimately unforgiving Peelite vindictiveness. Derby's son Stanley saw Gladstone rise 'choked with passion, for which he could find no vent in words, and his first utterances were the signal for fresh explosions from each side of the House alternately'. 'Gladstone's look when he rose to reply will never be forgotten by me: his usually calm features were livid and distorted with passion, his voice shook, and those who watched him feared an outbreak incompatible with parliamentary rules. So strong a scene I have never witnessed.'[15]

Ostensibly impromptu, provoked by what he considered the 'shameless personalities and otherwise' with which Disraeli disgraced his speech, Gladstone's strike had in fact long been 'fermenting' in him, and he 'made notes for speaking' on the 16th. He had already acquitted himself of his part in the debate with two speeches attacking Disraeli's proposals, on 6 and 10 December. But his bid on the 17th to cap Disraeli was of an entirely different order of rhetoric. Gladstone was bidding far beyond the budget. He was asserting himself as the bearer of credentials conferring legitimate authority to fulfil the purpose of his new vocation. He also released long pent-up aggressive energy. His excitement was that of a hunter closing in on his quarry. It was like 'a fox chase'.[16] 'To smash an antagonist across the House of Commons', as he later remarked to Lady Mildred Hope, 'is sometimes not disagreeable ...'[17]

In his onslaught Gladstone passed from strictures on Disraeli's bad manners to strictures on Disraeli's bad policy. Disraeli did not, in fact, threaten the national credit; nor was he 'guilty of high offence against the public' for providing no surplus in the canonical manner of Peel. Though the dazzling technical virtuosity ostentatiously displayed in the speech inaugurated the mythology of Gladstone as the great master of Victorian financial policy, it was more significant for its implicit revelations of Gladstone's view of Gladstone. The point of the speech really was in itself as a bravura performance, a kind of theatricalized politics, a melodrama of finance, with Gladstone offering himself to the public as heroic rescuer of public virtue from the clutches of a villain presented explicitly as the angel of the hosts of evil 'enchanters and magicians'.

Not only was Gladstone's intervention on the moment an inspired opportunism; his mode of exploiting the opportunity he thus created was an achievement of genius. At one decisive stroke he established himself on an entirely new and higher eminence of public reputation. Even more importantly, he signalled the onset of both a new political style and a new rhetorical method, an experimental model providing an enormous potential for future development and enhancement.

Two features of that experimental model stand out prominently. The first was Gladstone's conspicuously draping the mantle of Sir Robert Peel about his shoulders. Most of Gladstone's technical critique had to do with demonstrating that Disraeli had failed to conform to the principles of Sir Robert's financial system, of which Gladstone now proclaimed himself spokesman and keeper. 'Long associated with a recollection that will ever be dear to me, and sharing in the first struggles that he made for that great object, I must necessarily have had many opportunities of observing the workings of his mind upon the subject.' He made a special point of appealing in Peel's name to the Conservatives opposite him to repudiate Disraeli's dishonesty and trickery and return to their former and proper obedience. 'Are you not the party of 1842? Are you not the party who, in times of difficulty, chose to cover a deficit and to provide a large surplus? ... I appeal to you by what you then were.'

The second feature was Gladstone's implied claim to the Exchequer in view of the almost certain fall of Derby's government. This was done mainly by underlining at every opportunity Disraeli's lack of experience as contrasted with his own rich maturity as a man of government and high office. The theme was that Disraeli did not 'know business'; he had learned a little, but still had much to learn.

Gladstone's intervention postponed the division on the budget for a little more than two hours. Ministers were defeated by 385 to 286. It is very doubtful that Gladstone made any difference. He certainly failed to persuade the ministerial Conservatives to return to 'the party of 1842'. His indictment had the effect of making the government's defeat seem more resounding than it would otherwise have been. He did not 'destroy the administration' as myth later had it; but he gave a good impression of doing so.[18]

After adjournment, Gladstone, the Opposition hero of the hour, went off to the Carlton Club where he wrote to Stafford Northcote, his former secretary at the Board of Trade, enquiring whether Northcote would be available for employment. Going to the Carlton was perhaps a foolhardy thing to do. Stanley went there also, noting that those who had voted with Gladstone 'prudently kept away: they would not have escaped insult'.[19] Most Conservatives were puzzled at the lengths to which Gladstone, hitherto noted as the most ministerially-leaning of the Peelites, went to make any future co-operation with Disraeli unlikely or even impossible. Having no inkling of the inward necessities imposed on Gladstone by the exigencies of crossing his golden bridge and justifying his new vocation, they could only interpret his behaviour as of the same order of over-excited aberration as his Neapolitan outburst. The inwardness of his situation indeed made it difficult for Gladstone to explain himself. He made lame excuses to the effect that it was in fact Disraeli who had determined to make Conservative reunion impossible.[20]

Ministers decided to resign forthwith, and Derby went off to Osborne. Announcing his resignation in the Lords on 20 December, Derby made clear his vexation at finding all his efforts at peacemaking and reconciliation come to nought. That night, after dining with Herbert and Newcastle, Gladstone found himself in the newspaper room at the Carlton in a 'lions' den' of tipsy and indignant Conservatives, who threatened to toss him across Carlton Gardens into the Reform Club. Gladstone prudently retreated, fearing 'actual ill-usage'.[21]

~

Promptly, on 18 December, Gladstone composed a memorandum which he read that afternoon to Aberdeen, who was poised to go to Osborne the following day. In this Gladstone had a two-fold purpose. His first, practical, motive was to impress upon Aberdeen's mind that a 'great and palpable exigency of State' existed most visibly and immediately 'with regard to a subject on which the public mind is always accessible, ready, and receptive; with reference namely to finance'. No doubt Aberdeen took the hint: Gladstone wanted the Exchequer. For, despite the brilliance and resonance of his performance against Disraeli, his getting his hands on the Treasury levers was by no means a foregone conclusion.

Gladstone's second purpose was to define what seemed to him the most desirable available form of government. He urged a 'mixed government', by which he meant a coalition, as against a 'fusion of parties'. Since they were 'agreed in principle upon all the great questions of public policy immediately emergent', it followed that only a Liberal–Peelite mixture satisfied the essential criteria.

As to the Exchequer, Gladstone knew there would be no difficulty with Aberdeen. The problem would be Russell. It was fortunate for Gladstone that Russell's bargaining position was weak and Aberdeen's strong, despite the vast disparity in the respective numbers of their adherents in the Commons. Russell had damaged his standing with his own party. He was in ill-favour at the Court. In any case, Palmerston, who carried weight in the Commons, had made it clear he would not serve again under Russell. Aberdeen was the Court's clear favourite to be Prime Minister. It took all the weight of Lansdowne's seniority and prestige to convince Russell that he had no alternative but to serve under Aberdeen – to be a subaltern, as Disraeli cruelly put it, of a former subaltern of Sir Robert Peel. Mollified by an informal understanding that in due course, once the coalition was on a firm and confident footing, Aberdeen would withdraw and make way for him, Russell allowed himself to be persuaded; and thus a ministry could be formed.

When it came to distributing the offices, Aberdeen played a canny game.

Rather than brandish Gladstone's claim and provoke resistance, he led off slyly by suggesting him for either the Colonial Office or the Exchequer. He well understood with what disgust Gladstone would view the former. Russell wanted Graham for the Exchequer and Gladstone for the Colonial Office. Graham knew well enough that he had no business getting in Gladstone's way. A coalition Cabinet was constructed in which the Peelites secured six out of thirteen places. Gladstone duly took the Exchequer. Graham went to the Admiralty, Herbert to the War Office. Newcastle and Argyll joined Aberdeen to handle government business in the Lords. Otherwise, Palmerston, barred from the Foreign Office, took the Home department, where he lurked in a kind of semi-independent role of watching and waiting. Russell himself soon turned the Foreign Office over to Clarendon, and adopted also a rival posture of watching and waiting.

Gladstone only just managed to scramble up through a hurricane to Hawarden for Christmas. The tension was marked by another scourging on 30 December. There was an unpleasantly narrow squeak in his re-election at Oxford, where Low Church and anti-'Jew Bill' forces again challenged him. Not only did Gladstone display at this time wilful self-confidence. He displayed formidable powers of work. He had remarked at the time of his term at the Colonial Office: 'What a mercy that my strength, in appearance not remarkable, so little fails me.'[22] The abiding impression his son Henry had of his father in the 1850s was 'a vivid sense of his great physical strength'.[23] Gladstone himself commented at the end of 1853 on the 'singular blessing' of '*health*'.[24] He drove his secretaries as hard as he drove himself. As one of them later put it, he was an appreciative rather than a considerate master.[25] In his early forties, he embarked on the building of his new vocation certainly at the height of his physical maturity, and very nearly at the height of his intellectual powers. Gladstone, moreover, seized his moment at the Treasury in the spirit of zeal of one who felt himself, politically speaking, regenerate. He planned to produce a budget to replace Disraeli's defeated version by April 1853. Nor would it merely be a budget; it would be his evangel, his new *State and Church*.

~

In his early preparations Gladstone found in Edward Cardwell, as yet outside the Cabinet in the Board of Trade, an invaluable collaborator. He consulted his brother Robertson, a leading member in Liverpool of the Financial Reform Association, which pressed for direct taxation. There was little chance of reductions in education and defence. More congenial was contemplating the question of wine duties. He indulged himself in a lyrical passage on the possibility of decreasing the duty on 'one of the great gifts of Providence to man', dilating on the 'many useful and wholesome ends it subserved in connection with his physical temperament'.[26]

One of his minutes at this time was to bear a signal reputation: the Treasury Minute of 12 April 1853 commissioning an enquiry into the Civil Service with a view to reducing its costs and improving its efficiency. When Stafford Northcote replied to Gladstone's invitation to return to service, he asked for a place on the Treasury Committee examining the organization of the Board of Trade. A series of such committees under the direction of Sir Charles Trevelyan, Assistant Under-secretary at the Treasury, had since 1849 been investigating various departments to economize in numbers and expense and improve performance. Trevelyan wanted to expand his frame of reference and consider broad questions of principle and policy about recruitment and training for the Civil Service. He was convinced that the time was ripe for replacing the prevailing system of recruitment by patronage by a system founded on some objective criterion such as public examination. The ripeness of the time for Trevelyan, an old India hand, had much to do with the legislation being prepared at the India Board by Charles Wood to renew the charter of the East India Company and incidentally reform the system of recruitment and training of the Indian Civil Service.[27] Northcote quickly established a good working relationship with Trevelyan.

Northcote in turn soon interested Gladstone in the potential importance of Civil Service reform. Gladstone, after all, had long been attuned to Coleridge's clerisy ideal. The principle of the morality of merit would fit perfectly with his notions of a new political evangel; and from his angle, also, such reform might fit advantageously into current ideas about Oxford University reform. Gladstone was in the process of persuading himself that Oxford could not avoid a large dose of reform, and that it would best be reformed by its friends rather than its enemies. One of the most prominent reformers in Oxford was the Rev. Benjamin Jowett, intent on transforming the university from a mixed aristocratic finishing school and Anglican seminary into a serious secular institution that would prepare undergraduates for positions of responsibility in government, politics and the empire. Jowett had got himself involved in the Indian Civil Service question with a view to providing jobs for a new generation of Oxford graduates. Gladstone's role as one of the MPs for the University naturally put him often across Jowett's path; a circumstance Jowett expertly exploited. Gladstone found Jowett in some ways 'unsettling' (he was in 1855 to be denounced for heresy); but he could appreciate the cogency of the links between Jowett and Trevelyan (and Trevelyan's brother-in-law, another old India hand, Macaulay), and thence to Northcote.

So attuned to ideas of Civil Service reform did Gladstone become that, when Northcote and Trevelyan produced their draft Report, Gladstone found it wanting in rigour and set about stiffening it. There was much in this of the schoolman's logic he had ruthlessly applied in earlier days at the Board of Trade to untidy and expensive clutters of anomalies and deficiencies. As well as shifting recruitment from patronage to public examination, the Service was to be freed from all manner of restrictive practices in matters of offices, appointments, seniority and promotion. Above all, in order that the best minds be attracted to it, a strict demarcation would be established in the Service between a higher gentlemanly administrative division and a lower other-ranks executive division, where all the drudgery of copying would be done.

Immediately at hand in April 1853 was the matter of the budget. Many among Gladstone's colleagues were concerned about what they felt to be the riskiness of his proposals, especially integrating Ireland into the British tax structure. The 'corner stone' of his plan was renewal of the income tax, previously renewed three times since 1842, but now within a scheme whereby it would be progressively reduced by stages until it would expire on 5 April 1860. To cover his costs Gladstone proposed to lower the income limit from £150 to £100 and apply it to Ireland. In his view £100 was the 'equatorial line of British incomes', whereby the whole of the 'educated' part of the community was brought in and the 'labouring part' left out. By thus imposing a special tax burden on the electorate, Gladstone hoped to impose a sense of responsibility for the mass of the unenfranchised, a fiscal doctrine of 'trusteeship'.[28] And by making the burden one of fixed limits, Gladstone combined responsibility with the prospect of a reward of eventual relief. In return, to balance his policy on the indirect taxation side, he would offer remissions on tariff duties on thirteen articles of food and 123 other items to stimulate consumption.

Doubts persisted. Gladstone held fast. Doubts cancelled each other out. On Sunday 17 April, the eve of his budget statement, Gladstone prepared himself spiritually with Holy Communion and other, private, offices of devotion. Afterwards he felt obliged to tear himself away from Dante's *Paradiso* and 'give several hours to my figures'. At Holy Communion that morning at St James's, Piccadilly, he was edified by an extraordinary spiritual visitation which he was coming to recognize as a type concomitant with 'occasions of very sharp pressure or trial'. Some inspiring words of Scripture, usually from the 'great storehouse' of the Psalms, would 'come home' to him. On this fraught occasion it was from Psalm 86, verse 16: 'O turn thee then unto me, & have mercy upon me: give thy strength unto thy servant, and help the son of thine handmaid.'

On the 18th, after driving and walking with Catherine, Gladstone spoke for nearly five hours, to immense acclaim. Stanley recorded: 'It was said that for three nights before this display he was unable to sleep from excitement, but the success was worth the suffering.'[29] Again, as in December, it was the symbolism and evangelistic rhetoric which mattered more than the technical issues. His rhetorical technique consisted first in projecting himself as a third in a heroic series after Pitt and Peel. Pitt had created the income tax, 'this colossal engine of finance', as the key to victory in the French wars. Then Peel 'called forth from repose this giant, who had shielded us in war, to come and assist our industrious toils in peace'. If the first income tax produced 'enduring and memorable results', the second 'has been the instrument by which you have introduced, and by which … ere long you may perfect, the reform, the effective reform, of your commercial and fiscal system'. Now, 'if we rightly use the income tax' it would be the means of 'achieving a great good immediately for England, and ultimately for mankind'. To Peel's widow Gladstone avowed that he was 'inspired by the thought of treading, however unequally, in the steps of my great teacher and master in public affairs'.[30]

The second aspect of Gladstone's technique was the rhetoric of courage, urgency and decisiveness. The House must not 'nibble at this great question'. Gladstone assured the Commons that he, for his part, would not seek 'to evade the difficulties of our position'; there would be no 'narrow or flimsy expedients'. No one could suppose that ministers were 'paltering' or that Gladstone was not presenting a plan to 'bring to completion the noble work of commercial reform which is so far advanced'.

The third, and most important, feature of Gladstone's rhetoric dissociated him from Pitt and Peel rather than linking him to them. Gladstone saw himself as being in a position to point towards a future golden era. His scheme to extinguish the income tax by 1860 he offered as a token or augury of good omen, an auspicious sign of the good times at hand when the noble work of commercial reform should begin to show forth bountiful fruits of prosperity. The logic of his argument implied that the end of the income tax marked the end of an era of struggles and toils. This he underlined with his plan for 'a great and beneficial remission of taxes' of two millions which fulfilled Peel's principles of unleashing productivity and stimulating consumption. His imagery of the promised land – 'now I have the downward path before me and the plains of Italy are in my view' – Gladstone linked with the theme of reconciling classes and interests.[31]

~

At the end of his life, in a fragmentary memorandum entitled 'General Retrospect' composed in 1896 or 1897 among notes for a projected autobiography, Gladstone offered a most suggestive formulation of a theory of his political career, highly tendentious but at the same time valuable as an effort at an objective estimate of himself. He proposed (subject to reservations of humility) that if Providence had entrusted to him a 'striking gift', it had been shown, 'at certain political junctures', in what might be termed 'appreciation of the general situation and its result'. This was quite different, he insisted, from a 'simple acceptance of public opinion, founded upon the discernment that it had risen to a certain height needful for a given work, like a tide'. Rather it was 'an insight into the facts of particular eras, and their relations one to another, which generates in the mind a conviction that the materials exist for forming a public opinion, and for directing it to a particular end'. Gladstone identified four occasions, or 'junctures', during his career to which he considered this general formulation applicable. The first of these was his 'renewal of the income tax in 1853'.[32]

This general retrospect thus raises the possibility of credentials providentially conferred authorizing political prerogatives on a grand scale. Gladstone was scrupulous not to make any positive claim specifically in such terms: he could 'by no means' be sure 'upon a calm review'; but the practical strength of his self-assurance is thereby hardly diminished. What most signally projects itself in that document is a supreme self-confidence, an awesome power of self-persuasion. It offers a revealing insight into the entire absence in Gladstone's view of himself as an exponent of politics in any substantial sense stemming from popular authority. In this crucial sense the core of Gladstone's political sensibility remained consistent throughout his movement from Conservatism to Liberalism. By distinguishing carefully between a lower opportunism founded merely upon exploiting an existing and rising public opinion and a higher intuitive power of creative statesmanship which forms and directs public opinion, Gladstone provided himself with a most formidable means of providing legitimacy for his peculiar method of relating to popular politics and the power provided by popular politics strictly on his own terms.

~

For the present, it was a matter of digesting immense acclaim. With his first budget Gladstone had launched his reputation as the keeper of the Victorian financial conscience. Lord Aberdeen was in no doubt that as finance minister Gladstone had placed himself 'fully at the level of Sir Robert Peel'. Greville judged that he had given the country assurance of a *man* equal to great political necessities, and fit to lead parties and direct governments'.[33]

Despite some restiveness on the part of the Irish and the landed interest, Gladstone got his proposals through early in May. He was now in a state of exhaustion, having recourse to 'blue pills' and taking to riding for exercise and distraction. A distressing little episode reminded Gladstone of the vulnerability to public scandal he exposed himself to by his rescue work. An attempt at blackmail after an incident in Leicester Square led Gladstone to decide to press charges to deter others of the same mind. Committal proceedings at Marlborough Street Court on 11 and 13 May figured in the press. Greville noted on 15 May that the incident 'created for the moment great surprise, curiosity, and interest, but has almost entirely passed away already, not having been taken up politically, and there being a general disposition to believe his story and to give him credit for having had no improper motive or purpose. Nevertheless it is a very strange affair, and has not yet been satisfactorily explained.'[34] Gladstone became the butt of many a sly witticism, such as Clarendon's quip to the Duchess of Manchester about 'our Jesuit', with his 'benevolent nocturnal rambles'.[35] Gladstone confessed to his diary: 'These talkings of mine are certainly not within the rules of worldly prudence: I am not sure that Christian prudence sanctions them for such a one as me; but my aim & intention did not warrant the charge wh. doubtless has been sent to teach me wisdom & which I therefore welcome.'[36] Neither variety of prudence persuaded Gladstone against resuming the good work, which he did, rather more actively than usual, in June.

The session continued busy enough. Far in the background lurked the faintly nagging anxiety aroused by the shadow of impending conflict in the Near East, as Russia's quarrel with the Turks dragged in Britain and France, who sent fleets to the Dardanelles to bolster the Ottoman Empire as a barrier against Russian expansion. The Russians, in turn, crossed the Pruth and occupied Moldavia and Wallachia, offering to withdraw if the British and French fleets did likewise. An excited russophobe public opinion began to fester in Britain.

For post-sessional recuperation Gladstone repaired with his family to the western Highlands. In September he stayed with the Sutherlands at Dunrobin. Gladstone was laid up with a serious bout of erysipelas and out of reach when Aberdeen wanted to consult him on the question of making way for Russell, in the spirit of the understanding of December 1852. There would have been no doubt as to Gladstone's advice. He found Russell increasingly tiresome. He was becoming embroiled in an absurd quarrel in the Department of Woods and Forests involving the Commissioner, one Kennedy, a particular friend and protégé of Russell's. In any case, Aberdeen decided that pressures of affairs in the East made his continuing in office desirable. Russell could not see it that way. Serious turmoils for the coalition were in train.

Russell vexed Gladstone also with stubborn resistance to the Civil Service reform proposals of the Northcote-Trevelyan Report. Russell led most of his colleagues in sticking on the principle that the indispensable criterion for appointment as a civil servant of the Crown must be the status of a gentleman, and the code of honour inseparable from such. Patronage alone was the means of assuring that the Service be reliably recruited. In vain did Gladstone argue that the whole point of linking Civil Service reform with reform of the universities was to ensure that recruitment of the proposed administrative level would in effect be restricted exclusively to clever young gentlemen; that the tendency of the reforms would 'strengthen and multiply the ties between the higher classes and the possession of administrative power'.[37] In the end he gave up the unequal struggle, and the Northcote-Trevelyan Report was put aside to await better times.

Vexing too for Gladstone was Russell's incessant pushing for a new Reform measure. Gladstone took the view that a reformed machinery of the state would serve the interests of the people much better than extended franchises. As he put it to Graham, 'This is *my* contribution to parliamentary reform.'[38]

A second consequence of Gladstone's bout of illness at Dunrobin was that his nurse there was Duchess Harriet, a formidable, intelligent and pious woman with whose mind Gladstone could join in matters of religion, intellect, art and politics in a way quite impossible with Catherine. Their friendship became of capital importance to Gladstone in the coming years. She eased his entrée into the grand Whig salons. Stafford House in London and Cliveden at Taplow especially became for Gladstone – almost invariably in Catherine's absence – retreats of delight and repose.[39]

Hawarden now also, as Sir Stephen's financial problems materially improved, offered more settled promise of delight and repose. A joint residence of Gladstones with Sir Stephen now seemed the natural foundation of domestic life. This was just as well, for relations with Tom, for all that he was now blessed with a son and heir, were worse than ever. By October 1853 Gladstone was arranging his books and papers in the 'north room'. He fussed congenially over new bookcases. By 1855 he could note: 'Our room is growing characteristic; & I think of having our own furniture.' Lady Glynne's death in 1854 eased the way of dispositions. In 1855 the legal arrangement providing for Willy's inheriting at the demise of the last male Glynne was effected. Gladstone busied himself in the park, planning and laying out the path from the Castle to Hawarden church, which was to become over the years a *via sacra*. In October 1853 he noted the felling of three beeches in the park: the beginnings of his most famous and characteristic exercise, prompted by the very practical motive of realizing the assets of the estate.[40] Soon Gladstone was speaking on Sir Stephen's behalf at the Estate Rent Dinner. The irruption of many young Gladstones would eventually necessitate, in the early 1860s, large additions on the north-west corner of the Castle. Meanwhile, despite the rather makeshift character of these arrangements, Gladstone found in 'this sweet place' the solace he needed. He thus inaugurated his new domestic life 'with auspices somewhat less unhopeful for the family'.[41]

~

The most significant immediate consequence of Gladstone's budgetary renown took the shape of an invitation from the corporation of Manchester to inaugurate on 12 October 1853 the grand monument to Sir Robert Peel. This would be Gladstone's first big public exercise in engaging politically with popular opinion upon a national stage. The Manchester affair was his first step along the road to his becoming by repute 'the people's William'; or, to put it from his own point of view, his first step along the road where he began to learn 'out of doors' the arts of the striking gift conceivably vouchsafed to him of forming a public opinion that he would direct toward a particular end.

Manchester for its part certainly received Gladstone very much in a spirit appropriate to his greatly enhanced public stature. He was the 'eminent statesman' whose 'comprehensive and consistent financial scheme', with its 'admirable commercial measures', had marked him out as deserving well of the interests that Manchester saw itself as representing. Avowing himself Peel's 'pupil and his follower', Gladstone for his part paid tribute to the capital of free trade's 'advanced intelligence' and to the 'prominent part' it played in influencing the fortunes and destinies of the country; and to the exhibition it offered of the elevation through industry and art of all classes, not only the 'educated classes', but the whole feeling of the community. This certainly was the aspect of Manchester that most impressed itself on Gladstone. The audience at the Peel dedication, he observed, was 'of *men* almost exclusively, & working men. There I spoke, to the cracking of my voice.'[42]

At the foundation-laying of a new school the following day, Gladstone, with a novel *frisson* of sensibility, 'had again to speak to an assembly of the *people*'. Something of a sense of thrill at adventuring into strange new reaches of political experience had been evident earlier at the first of such exotic occasions, the coal whippers' meeting at Shadwell. But this was something on a much bigger and more exciting and public scale. Gladstone was starting to enrich the texture of his new vocation with an ingredient of the virtuous masses. He was beginning to provide for himself a preliminary measure of that public and popular recourse which Peel had lacked.

It was provoking indeed that at such an occasion Gladstone could not indulge himself to the hilt at Manchester with issues appropriate to the moral qualities of advanced intelligence and moral elevation that its people so eminently manifested: financial questions, vindication of Aberdeen's administration, abolition of the duties on paper as a further, and vital, measure of exempting great manufactures from costs and contributing to the wider education of the people through cheaper literature and a cheaper newspaper press. Instead, circumstances obliged him to divert valuable time and energy to the unrewarding Eastern question.

The Turks, emboldened by British and French encouragement, had declared war on Russia on 4 October. Aberdeen resisted the pressures of the anti-Russian faction in the Cabinet, led by Palmerston, to challenge the Russians in the Black Sea. But the warlike currents of opinion threatened to overbear the Prime Minister. The British 'national' public was spoiling for war against Russia in defence of the liberties of Europe. They saw the gallant Turks as resisters to the grim Muscovite despotism that had enslaved the Poles and delivered the Hungarians into servitude. Napoleon III in France was eager to inaugurate the Second Empire with a glorious war against the greatest pillar of the system of 1815. Nicholas himself felt under threat, and stiffened his responses accordingly.

At Manchester, Gladstone ranged himself ostentatiously behind Aberdeen. He warned against the 'glare of glory', and denounced war as the enemy of freedom and of the 'real moral and social advancement of man'. He extolled Aberdeen's policy of 'peace and negotiation'. Like the philhellene 'Athenian' Aberdeen, Gladstone could not take the Turks seriously as defenders of liberty. He saw the Ottoman Empire as 'full of anomaly, full of misery and full of difficulty'.[43] But no more than Aberdeen could Gladstone stem the tide for war. This was especially the case when Palmerston in December resigned, ostensibly in opposition to Russell's Reform policy, but in reality, as bellicose public opinion well appreciated, because of his dissatisfaction with what he held to be Aberdeen's feeble appeasement of the Russians.

At this point Gladstone began to panic. He faced having to decide whether the collapse of the coalition government would be more of a disaster than a war in alliance with Turkey against Russia. His political investment in the coalition was total. Everything his budget stood for would be lost if Aberdeen's Cabinet cracked under the strain. There was no recourse elsewhere. Soon Gladstone eagerly endorsed Aberdeen's taking Palmerston back into the Cabinet in order to keep it afloat. This crucially undermined the influence of the peace faction. In effect, Gladstone accepted war as the lesser evil. His conscience allowed him to abandon his Manchester doctrine on the ground that Nicholas was indeed responding arrogantly to European efforts at mediation, but that in any case there were fair chances that the war might well be closed down by diplomacy and cause no lasting damage to the finances.

When on 6 March 1854, Gladstone came to present his second financial statement he did so in a political atmosphere entirely different from that of the previous year. Then it had been a matter of beckoning to a promised land of peace and plenty. Now it was a matter of mere days before the formal declaration of war on Russia. Gladstone's mood was appropriately subdued. He did not hide the bitterness of his regrets at losing the opportunity of the planned tax remissions; nor did he disguise his regret at the all but declared war itself. At a time when patriotic uplift might have been thought in order, Gladstone chose instead to characterize the expenses of war as a 'moral check' which it had pleased the Almighty to impose upon 'ambition and lust of conquest'; and to warn against the 'pomp and circumstance' and 'glory and excitement' about war that blinds men to its evils and miseries.

He urged strongly a policy of paying for the war by increased direct taxation rather than by recourse to loans and increased indirect taxation. This he advocated partly as a moral check and partly on his interpretation of Pitt's war finance. War would be waged as by 'rational and intelligent beings', attending not only to the necessities of war but to the 'first and earliest prospects of concluding an honourable peace'.[44] He observed to his brother Robertson that war had 'hitherto been to us Englishmen but a remote and abstract idea: and when we say we are going to War … we do not know what we mean. It will dawn upon us by degrees, and in forms for the most part eminently disagreeable.'[45]

These first and earliest prospects of peace were Gladstone's measure of the financial necessities of the war. Their consequences for him were indeed eminently disagreeable. He increased the income tax for six months from 7d. to 10½d. He asked for a sum of about £50 per head of the forces to be embarked to the east and estimated for a deficit of £2.8 million. Essentially he saw himself directing a holding operation to keep the general position of 1853 as intact as the exigencies of war would allow. Thus he made himself a hostage to fortune; and events decreed that not only would there be no early and honourable peace, and that the war would be waged not by rational and intelligent beings but in a manner that made it a byword for incompetence and blundering. The hysterical public expected new Wellingtons and Nelsons and the liberation of Poland. It had to make do with Florence Nightingale and the charge of the Light Brigade.

Gladstone, moreover, was in dispute with the Bank of England over financial arrangements. He was determined to end time-honoured conventions lucrative to the Bank but in his opinion detrimental to the public interest. His larger purpose was to subordinate the Bank decisively to a responsible 'Ministry of Finance', an aggressively French 'statist' style of designation he was now prone to apply. He exposed himself to effective attack from Disraeli. With more than a touch of paranoia, Gladstone assured Robertson that the truth was 'that it is common to periods of this kind to be disturbed by panic and we now have for the first time a man calling himself a party leader and not unwilling to gain notoriety by inflaming apprehensions mischievous only to the Country'.[46]

Solaces and mitigations were few. With the loving care and devotion he applied to all his dealings with Oxford, Gladstone drew up and piloted through his University Bill embodying the reforms recommended by the Royal Commission. 'The governing and teaching powers shall remain entire and intact with the Established Church', he reassured the Provost of Oriel; 'but Dissenters shall have all that does not interfere with this governing and teaching power.'[47] The Bill went on to pass smoothly through the Lords, despite resistance from the University's Chancellor, Derby. Much in the same spirit of offering sensible concessions Gladstone took the opportunity in the 1854 session to put into practice his doctrine of the Church's advantage in giving 'gold for freedom' by proposing a compromise solution to the perennial church rates question. He did not succeed, but he signalled his willingness to deal with moderate Dissent.

On the day before his supplementary budget on 8 May 'in the agony of my work' of 'labour and turmoil', he was visited by another of those angelically borne presentiments of Scripture that he marked as moments of high revelation amid his intercourse with the Almighty. But the real damage had been done. In such circumstances of crisis Gladstone groaned about a 'tumult of business'. On 19 March he recorded: 'I have been more overcome & undone by this day than by any day's *labour* for a long time, and cannot describe the end of it otherwise than as being stunned by God's mercy.'[48] It was as well, in fact, for Gladstone's reputation that Aberdeen's government fell at the beginning of 1855, for by then the discrepancy between his doctrine and his policy was of embarrassing proportions. He was contemplating a loan of £12 million and a hefty increase in indirect taxation, responsibility for which, in the event, he was happy to pin on to Lewis.

~

The war aims of the allies boiled down in 1854 to mounting a swift raiding operation to reduce the Russian port and arsenal of Sebastopol in the Crimea. All alternative theatres had proved ineffectual. A raid on Sebastopol imposed itself from sheer want of anything more plausible. With the failure of the Vienna negotiations Aberdeen's authority waned and Palmerston's waxed. Gladstone made no move to challenge the decision to go for Sebastopol. His overriding motive remained the survival of the coalition. For that he needed Palmerston now as he had needed him earlier. Aberdeen grew increasingly vulnerable to public dissatisfaction. Palmerston waited for a national call for strong leadership to prosecute the kind of war originally envisaged. Russell, terrified at being trumped by Palmerston after having been eclipsed by Aberdeen, grew restless, demanding to get control of war policy and insisting that Aberdeen hand over to him as provided for in the initial arrangements for the coalition.

Under these stresses the Whig-Peelite fault line widened ominously. Disraeli divined this line of weakness in a notable speech in March 1854, when he drew an invidious contrast between the 'two systems of policy' contending for direction of Britain's response to the Eastern question. There was 'that school of opinions which I call British opinions', advocated by Palmerston and Russell, believing in the vitality of Turkey, and in Turkey's future as an independent and progressive country, forming a powerful and sufficient barrier against Russian expansion. Against this was the 'other school, which I call the school of Russian politics', believing that Turkey was exhausted, and that nothing could be done to prevent anarchy, but by 'gradually enfranchising the Christian population', and which 'contemplates the possibility of Russia occupying the Bosphorus'. Aberdeen, during his 'long and consistent career', had pursued this policy: in 1829, in 1844, when he 'entered into a virtual agreement with the Emperor Nicholas' for 'ultimate partition and intermediate interference'; and as soon as Aberdeen became first minister in 1852 Nicholas renewed his efforts.[49]

Disraeli's lead was followed in July in debates that damaged the government and wounded Aberdeen, both by the extent to which Palmerston emerged as the available alternative war leader, and by what he considered a lack of support from his Peelite friends, Gladstone the most conspicuous among them. Demoralized by having to ask for a special vote of credit and extra expenditure, Gladstone felt quite unequal to the task.

The swift raiding operation on Sebastopol was bungled. The dismayed government had to contemplate the likelihood of the campaign being bogged down over a winter for which no preparations had been made. The British administration and its military authorities failed to redeem the situation. Gallant victories were won at Alma and Inkerman but no strategic purpose was achieved. Scandals of incompetence piled up. The 'national' public, bitterly disillusioned, clamoured for heads to roll. Newcastle, having taken over the War Office, was vulnerable. A thunderous campaign by *The Times* marked a new power of the newspaper press. To his consternation Gladstone found himself being accused of having 'starved' the war.[50] He was particularly incensed by demands in the Commons led by the Radical Roebuck for a select committee to inquire into the scandals of mismanagement. His executive hackles instantly on the rise, Gladstone condemned it furiously as an illegitimate invasion by Parliament into the executive sphere.[51]

By the end of 1854 Aberdeen's coalition was on its last legs. By threatening resignation Russell tried to pressure Aberdeen into giving way to him. No doubt Russell was intolerable as a Cabinet colleague, but what he was arguing for – a new drive and energy – was what was needed; and, when the crash came, it was Russell rather than Aberdeen's friends whom the Commons, rightly, preferred to believe. For all his animus against Russell, Gladstone had to admit that, when he made his exculpatory statement after resigning in January 1855, Russell carried the House. Attempts to patch things up by replacing Newcastle by Palmerston were to no avail. Russell's 'powder magazine blew the whole fabric into the air'.[52]

Aberdeen's Cabinet met for the last time on 30 January. Aberdeen proceeded to Windsor under doleful winter skies. The Queen sent for Derby, who proposed that Palmerston, Gladstone and Herbert should join him. Gladstone insisted that Graham be included, and insisted also on retaining the Exchequer. As Stanley commented, on this 'Disraeli could not in honour or consistency surrender'.[53] Palmerston aimed at manoeuvring Derby out of the way to make his own path clear. In any case, at this juncture, as Derby soon came to realize, Gladstone's distaste for the Conservative party was as nothing to the Conservative party's distaste for Gladstone.[54] Gladstone hoped that by blocking all alternative combinations, Aberdeen would be recalled. When he in effect blocked Lansdowne he made what he was to rue as the greatest blunder of his career.[55]

The dismaying prospect began to take shape for Gladstone of Palmerston as first minister. So convinced was Gladstone that Palmerston was 'not fit for the duties of the office of Prime Minister' that, obsessed by his hopes for Aberdeen, he helped unwittingly to allow Palmerston to slip through.[56] A dismaying notion began to seep into Gladstone's mind that he was witnessing the ultimate and degrading consequences of Peel's destruction of the old party system. Russell's negative capacities for damage thus let loose were bad enough. But what of Palmerston's positive powers for evil?

At Aberdeen's insistence, Gladstone agreed to face the 'irksome and painful task' of resuming office under Palmerston. The great issue of war and peace must take precedence over every other question. Gladstone was determined that the 'moral union and association' with Aberdeen must continue and be publicly known to continue. In Cabinet, in a thoroughly sulky humour, he found fault with everything. Palmerston 'tossed among us' notions 'without any clear broad or strong views of his own, as for what chance might bring'.[57] The one clear and strong notion that Palmerston tossed among his colleagues was his glum report that the Commons were set on having their select committee inquiry. The backbenchers were naturally determined to maintain their unwonted advantage over the arrogant Treasury Bench. Gladstone, its most arrogant occupant, 'went so far as to say that if the inquiry into the state of the army were allowed by this government it neither could nor ought to enjoy a week's credit or authority in the House of Commons'; and intimated that he 'could not see any way to this concession under any circumstances'.[58]

The Queen and the Prince sensibly urged submission. At a Cabinet on 20 February a majority, equally sensible, decided that a determined House of Commons could not be opposed and to resign after a fortnight would reduce ministers to a laughing stock. Gladstone's frenzy conversely intensified. Behind and inside it was much more than constitutional objections to unwarrantable invasion of executive privilege. There was welling bitterness about the treatment of Aberdeen. Above all there was awareness that his financial programme of 1854, as subsuming the crucial landmark budget of 1853, was now bankrupt. To carry on would mean confessing failure.

Along with Herbert and Graham, and despite entreaties from Prince Albert, Gladstone resigned on 21 February. Gladstone's explanatory speech on the 23rd dwelt pathetically on the fate of the 'trusted', 'admired', 'eulogized' colleague of Sir Robert Peel, Lord Aberdeen, 'dismissed by a blow darkly aimed'. He denied passionately that he was a 'deserter'; the government, in submitting to invasion by the legislature, had made a 'fatal choice'.[59] Yet the awkward fact remained that Gladstone was receding from his earlier position that the great issue of war and peace took precedence over every other question. His sense of proportion, never very secure at the best of times, evaporated in the intense heat of his fanatical insistence that the political crisis had been subsumed and therefore somehow cancelled by the constitutional monstrosity of the Roebuck committee. 'However tainted we may be, I aver with confidence that we have resigned our offices in resistance to the most revolutionary proceeding of our day.'[60] Gladstone would find that his 'taint' – especially the accusation that he had 'starved' the war – was not so easily washed away. On the 25 February he handed over the Treasury to Cornewall Lewis. On the 28th he handed back his seals of office at the Palace, discoursing on the demoralized state of politics. As for the Palmerston government, he assured the Prince with some asperity that it would 'not last a twelvemonth'.[61]

6

Becoming a Kind of Liberal, 1855–1859

'... adequate strength for the purposes of Government is not now to be drawn from the names & reputations of men, but must rest upon the doings & practical intentions of the Minister, and by a corresponding conviction wrought by them in the public mind.'

Gladstone to Aberdeen, 13 March 1856

These four years out of office were for Gladstone largely a time of distressing frustration. They differed entirely in that respect from his previous spell out of official employment, during the years of Russell's ministry between 1846 and 1852. Then he had needed time and space to renew his credentials and to reassemble his vocation. Now he found himself in circumstances more eminently disagreeable even than he could have envisaged when he used those words to Robertson. The fund of political credit he had amassed in 1853 was dispersed. Palmerston as prime minister embodied a mockery of every ideal that the Peelites in the coalition government had attempted to resuscitate. Gladstone's painfully gained and yet more painfully and reluctantly postponed vocational mission required the restoration of what he saw as the capacities of a ministry: to govern to grand effect. The dismal prospect now in view was that in the hands of Palmerston instability would conspire with negation and sterility in domestic policy and, in all probability, with yet more recklessness and bluster in foreign affairs.

Gladstone promptly set about relieving his rage and frustration in his 'Party as it was and as it is' piece.[1] The high culture and morale to which politics had attained under the beneficent order of for the most part firmly defined party lines under Grey, Melbourne and Peel was now, Gladstone lamented, in decay. As he had assured the Queen and the Prince, the Court would find 'little peace or comfort' until 'Parliament should have returned to its old organisation in two political parties: that at present we were in a false position, and that both sides of the House were demoralised'.[2] To the damage caused by the great but tragically flawed figure of Peel, together with the insidious machinations of Disraeli, was now added the damage inflicted by a war gone badly wrong. The prime beneficiary of national disaster, Palmerston, would exacerbate the evils now prevalent in public affairs. Without some 'firmness of texture' given to public affairs by the 'tissue of political party' properly constituted, there could be no effective resistance to popular pressures. Now, one party in the Commons is 'too weak for its work, and the other has its strength so ill-adapted that it is neutralised by inward disorder'. The Russell government, 'half-smitten with feebleness from the beginning', had become the type of the new dispensation, with Palmerston as its 'great illustration'.[3]

The most vivid aspect discernible in Gladstone at this juncture was a peculiarly Peelite resentment at disinheritance. Resentment took oddly plaintive forms. There was, of course, the giant figure of Peel himself, showing 'too much of the front of Pride', pulling down the Temple of 'strict party order and organization', like another Samson Agonistes. Peel's role indeed, Gladstone could see, was 'perhaps even a determining influence over the present positions of leading men, and the actual forms and relations of party'. His proud indifference of a wounded spirit to spend labour in soothing passion and conciliating support left its baleful legacy. Then his conduct in 1846 to 1850 was 'a mistake'. He was blameable for not fighting to recover the soul of the Conservative party. More: his 'great and massive figure' stood in the way of any alternative recourse. Why did he not advise his followers to join the 'Whig or rather Liberal' party? Why did he leave his particular friends and followers as 'superfluous baggage of the world', 'very inconvenient and even dangerous personages'? 'Why did he leave them hanging between earth and heaven, between wind and water?' 'Did he mean them to be eternally divorced from their old friends and eternally prohibited from making new? Did he contemplate the dying out of a party connection altogether and the substitution of philosophical for Parliamentary Government?'[4]

Was Gladstone seriously blaming Peel for his own predicament? Or merely conferring upon his own sense of frustration and inability to move decisively in either direction a spurious dignity it could not otherwise have claimed? Or was he, more subtly, starting to shift his position in such a way as to allow himself more latitude for manoeuvre in the matter of possible alternative recourses in whatever circumstances or contingencies the future might produce?

Meanwhile, it took a long time for Gladstone's bile to subside. Argyll, visiting at Hawarden in 1855, was disturbed at evidences of frustration and violent impulses under uncertain control. 'I saw how unsafe was his judgement.'[5] 'Puss' Granville, with that instinct for soothing tact that would make him Gladstone's favourite confidant, confided: 'I think you are well out of it.'[6] Gladstone tried his best to be consoled. 'I have been deeply interested in the business of my office, but now that we are out I rather feel myself in the way except as to finance and I propose to keep myself as little in politics at present as I can well contrive.'[7]

For all his proposing, Gladstone failed to contrive keeping himself in political restraint. He had credit to restore, and renown to keep polished. He gave notice on 19 March of his determination 'completely to set free the press', whether cheap or dear, from the taxation that inhibited 'the handling of public events and news of all kinds, and apply to this subject those principles of free commerce which have been extended with such efficacy to the general mercantile transactions of the country'.[8] High principle joined conveniently with an opportunity to assist in taking revenge on *The Times* for the damage it had done to Aberdeen's government. The Newspaper Duties Bill replaced with a postage duty by weight the old flat rate stamp duty that had given *The Times* an advantage over its competitors. This became the charter of a new radical and provincial press. For many years to come Gladstone would suffer under *The Times*'s displeasure. Moreover, the newspaper issue as linked to the agitation of the pressure group of 'strong and advanced Liberals' such as Cobden and Milner Gibson for Promoting the Repeal of Taxes on Knowledge raised the concomitant issue of the paper duties, which had been on Gladstone's agenda for reduction or abolition both as customs and excise since 1853.

~

The war unavoidably was still much with Gladstone. The one aspect of it at all tending to mitigate Gladstone's distress was the Piedmontese intervention on the side of France and Britain. The military convention of March 1855 called from Gladstone a statement as to the Kingdom of Sardinia's claims to sympathy and respect as a country that, 'amidst difficulties almost unprecedented, has succeeded in establishing for herself the blessings of a free government'.[9] The inwardness of this was declared in an important article Gladstone published in the June 1855 *Quarterly*, 'Sardinia and Rome', an account of the resistance being mounted by the Vatican to legislation designed in Turin to reduce the temporal privileges of the Roman Church in the Piedmontese state. Here Gladstone avowed that the 'doom of the Pope's temporal power is in all appearance sealed', and that in its example of 'tempered liberty', avoiding either absolutism or anarchy, the Turin government offered a model to Italy and thus made Piedmont's position and policy 'pregnant … with important results'.[10]

That article inaugurated a journalistic campaign by Gladstone to find relief by venting his frustration and distress through a medium that allowed a manner less inhibited than parliamentary convention permitted to a resigned minister and privy councillor. Aberdeen cautioned him that his anonymity was a polite fiction. For Gladstone that was rather the point of the exercise. And it was very much to that point that he should lead off with a fulmination against the Church of Rome. His old anti-Romanism, now excited anew by such reactionary manifestations as the Austrian concordat of 1855 and the promulgation of the dogma of the Immaculate Conception of the Virgin, merged with the implications he had unwittingly set in train at Naples.

Ever since the Neapolitan affair Gladstone had been marked by the *Risorgimentisti* as a promising object of cultivation. Piedmontese policy in intervening in the war aimed at making the Italian question a feature of the peace. Clarendon at the Foreign Office was eager to help effect this. He and Gladstone had been since 1854 engaged in a kind of conspiracy to find ways of alleviating the plight or indeed of liberating victims of the Neapolitan regime. By the summer of 1855 Gladstone was coolly ready to abet, 'in flagrant violation of the canons of conduct between civilized states',[11] a desperate plan by Panizzi to release by force prisoners on the island of San Stefano by advising him to apply to Palmerston and Clarendon for a grant from the Secret Service Fund. Palmerston and Clarendon were perfectly willing to connive. Eminent diplomatists at Italian courts were implicated also. But unlucky shipwreck in the end aborted the project.[12]

Resignation had made Gladstone freer to pursue his own policy for peace. He revived the argument he had first put forward at Manchester in 1853 in support of Aberdeen's hopes for negotiation and in opposition to the war policy associated with Palmerston. In the big debate on the prosecution of the war in May 1855 Gladstone insisted that the legitimate objects of the war had been substantially gained. Russia's overweening notions of her prerogatives had been sharply repudiated by Europe, and now the Russians were displaying 'a different language and a different spirit'. Gladstone argued that the great need now was to come quickly to reasonable terms and abandon all ideas of imposing a punitive and humiliating peace on the Russians – particularly if the real origin of the trouble, the 'internal state or institutions of Turkey', was ignored. Gladstone despaired of any contrivances to hobble Russian power permanently being imposed: 'the more I feel the extreme indignity which, if so forced, it inflicts upon her; and there is no policy, I think, which is so false and dangerous as to inflict upon Russia indignity without taking away strength'. The proposed stipulation that Russian ships of war be banned from the Black Sea Gladstone denounced as an 'imperfect remedy for the past, imperfect justice as between the parties, and an imperfect security or guarantee for the future'.[13] No power of the first order could be permanently coerced; and there was no further point in persevering in the siege of Sebastopol, the capture of which would mean nothing and achieve nothing.[14]

These were golden words of wisdom, extraordinarily perspicacious. Their effect was spoiled by a note of dogmatic zealotry, especially in a tendency toward uncritical russophilism that alienated potential support. 'Gladstone, as usual, overdid his part', noted Argyll. This he would continue to do for the next several years. Argyll remarked that Gladstone 'could always argue in private life with perfect temper'; but 'upon any question on which he was keenly interested, and on which his mind was irrevocably made up, he could not even entertain an opposing thought'. Under such circumstances 'his mind was essentially fanatical'.[15]

~

Naturally during these months Gladstone awaited impatiently signs of the much-desired collapse of Palmerston's ministry. Quite how such a contingency would place Gladstone remained a matter of speculation. On 1 February, coming across Disraeli, Gladstone offered his hand, 'wh. was very kindly accepted'. Perhaps a little startled, Disraeli might well have entertained speculations. There was much talk at the time of a 'Gladstone-Dizzy coalition', or a 'Treaty of Alliance' and 'compact upon the Peace Principle'.[16] Derby vetoed any schemes Disraeli may have nursed; and in any case Gladstone's counter-productive rage made his pursuit of Palmerston as vain as his pursuit of the Turks. For Gladstone the painful fact abided that he lived in political limbo. 'I greatly felt being turned out of office', he later explained to Bishop Wilberforce of Oxford. 'I saw great things to do. I longed to do them. I am losing the best years of my life out of my natural service ...'[17]

Frustration helped to drive Gladstone towards a diversion. At Hawarden he noted on 6 August: 'Began the *Iliad*: with serious intentions of working out something on old Homer if I can.' His intentions were to expand the thesis he had urged against Lachmann in 1847 that the Homeric epics were indeed by Homer and not stitched together out of fragmentary lays, and that their author composed them at no great distance in time and place from the events described. But added to that was now a much deeper purpose. Gladstone had convinced himself that Homer's stature as by far the greatest poet in the pre-Christian world pointed to his being the medium of a divine legation. God's revelation as vouchsafed to the Jews had been transmitted by them in what Gladstone considered a narrow and inadequate manner: theologically correct, but wanting in wisdom and guidance about human nature and human society.

As a politician with a vocation to order human affairs in conformity with God's purposes, Gladstone increasingly became dissatisfied with the Hebrew Scriptures as a statesman's manual. He came to see Homer as the provider of the kind of illuminations and insights about man, society and politics he was looking for. The logic was impeccable: if Gladstone was convinced of the Christian validity of his vocation, and if in reading Homer he felt himself to be a recipient of insights bearing directly on the purposes and directions of that vocation, it followed that those insights must have been provided as an essential item of God's providential economy.

Imbued with this somewhat crack-brained religio-politico-literary enthusiasm, Gladstone set off with the family early in September for a vacation at Penmaenmawr on the coast of North Wales. It was a convenient spot to reach from Hawarden, combining the charms both of sea and mountain. The resort suited the Gladstones well, and this was to be the first of many happy stays.[18] The

Homer project took root. On departing, Gladstone accused himself of having 'lived too happily for one who thinks as I do about the course of events and the responsibilities of needless war'.[19] He read the detailed accounts from Sebastopol: 'wh. were for England grievous'.[20] Not so for the French, who in any case were now carrying the burden of the war. Their storming the Malakov redoubt put the imminent taking of Sebastopol in sight. Peace, of a kind, was in view. Given that, Gladstone's major preoccupation was to prepare the way for a return to office when Palmerston had been got rid of and politics restored to a proper footing.

In February 1856 Gladstone drew up an outline of a comprehensive financial policy. He listed 21 projects.[21] His guiding notions were to set in train the creation of what amounted to a Ministry of Finance, with all public accounts under the effective control of the Treasury. He thus signalled the revitalizing of his second vocation. He was picking up the threads of the aborted mission of 1853 and forming them into the sinews of a grand strategy for a financial policy big enough and bold enough to remoralize politics by the sheer pull of its gravitational mass. It was a highly characteristic expression of his amalgam of Peelism, 'statism' and aggression.

In many ways the 'statist' aspect was the most interesting feature of Gladstone's outlook at this juncture. Much of it of course descended from his earlier 'high' notions of the State in its relations with the Church, forming the basis of a new and revitalized public morality. But the curiously French flavour of his vision of a Finance Ministry suggests an affinity with certain aspects of Parisian authoritarianism. Entertaining such an affinity was in no respect for Gladstone an alien affectation. He had ever been, and would remain, a seriously authoritarian exponent of the prerogatives of executive power.

As to aggression, most of it was directed at the Bank of England, which Gladstone never forgave for obstructing him in 1854. He determined also to 'make further provision for the custody & management of monies in the hands of the public: & for security of depositors in Savings Banks & the like'.[22] This was the germ of his later project for popular savings banks operated by the Post Office network. In this way he calculated that he could strike a blow not only for small depositors but also at the Bank: for ready access by government to such a mass of deposits would help to spare the Treasury from having to go begging in Threadneedle Street.

All this was by way of preparing another of his grand missives to Aberdeen. On 13 March Gladstone elaborated his strategy for the benefit of the leader of the Peelites. The war was coming to an end. A time for new departures was at hand. Care must be taken not to be caught unawares by the new circumstances of the 'great civil juncture' of the peace. The disorganization of political parties over the previous decade was a 'capital evil', which 'discredits government, retards legislation, diminishes the respect necessary for the efficiency of Parliament, and is thus unfavourable, by a sure though circuitous process, to the stability of our institutions'. This 'chronic evil of executive weakness' could not be overcome by the mere willingness of political men to form a government 'with a policy to seek'. Any such willingness would be more than counterbalanced by 'less of compactness among their followers, more of feeble and half-hearted support'. Gladstone concluded that no strong government was possible 'unless it be in a marked manner founded upon a policy'. Thus the needs of public affairs and the peculiar state of parties and Parliament 'lead up to the same point'.

Yet a strong government with a programme of strong measures was in itself no longer enough. There was a new and powerful element in public life: public opinion. This public opinion had been 'irritated and wounded'; and the public mind would 'not be at rest unless under the consciousness that those who are to govern recognise the nature and magnitude of the work they will have to perform'. Political men will be estimated 'chiefly with reference to measures'. For himself, Gladstone was 'inclined to resolve to enter no government, actual or possible, without an adequate assurance, that it will take its stand upon such a policy as I have generally indicated'. It would be better 'to decline taking any part in public affairs upon such an occasion as the next turn of the wheel is likely to present', and to wait for an opportunity 'when arrangements more advantageous to the nation could be made', rather than 'to enter a weak government in the rather presumptuous hope of making it by personal adhesion one degree less weak'. Adequate strength for the purposes of government, Gladstone concluded, 'is not now to be drawn from the names & reputations of men, but must rest upon the doings & practical intentions of the minister, and by a corresponding conviction wrought by them in the public mind'.[23]

~

To this decidedly authoritarian formula Gladstone remained faithful to the end of his career. In it he combined the inheritance of his devotion to the example of Peel as the strong minister of executive power with the benefit of his analysis of what Peel ultimately had lacked in being without recourse to opinion in the country imbued with convictions as to his doings and intentions and available for manipulation against recalcitrance in Parliament. The financial programme and the strategic *modus operandi* were crucially important steps in his feeling his way towards a more mature relationship between his sense of vocation and his sense of 'insight' into the means whereby that vocation could be realized in politics by masterful invocation and manipulation of the 'public mind'. The immediate problem was to get a government not only strong in itself but one in which Gladstone could take command of finance and which could elicit a sufficient response from public opinion.

The Peelites set about making it known that neither Palmerston nor Russell would be satisfactory 'as ministers with reference to the administrative work to be done'. It would be best if both could somehow 'disappear', with perhaps Clarendon being allowed to come to the top as a sop to Whig feeling.[24] Gladstone arranged that his letter of 13 March be conveyed in substance to Lord Derby and his friends to make them aware of 'our idea of the dangers impending and to be avoided'. Derby, sensibly cautious, confined himself to enquiring about the intentions of the Peelites as to acting together and pointing out that he could not summarily discard his own people to make room for them *en bloc*. Perhaps the Peelites, if unwilling to join him in office, might grant the Conservatives the same friendly countenance that he and Graham had given Peel in 1835, which later grew into political identification? Gladstone was willing to concede that this case was a 'possible one'; and indeed might 'be the best of the alternatives before us'. With the detested Palmerston in power Gladstone was prone to lean in this direction, a revived version of his insistence in 1852 that junction with the Whigs and Liberals was the Peelites' 'least natural position'.

As far as sessional activity in 1856 gave clues as to his intentions, Gladstone offered little encouragement to those Liberals. He dealt with Russell's resolutions pressing for a policy to put education 'within the reach of every child' in a manner that a later Liberal admirer wonderingly described as 'almost incredibly reactionary'.[25] His main concern in the session was to augment his critique of the terms of peace concluded at Paris. The great benefit of the war had been the 'moral demonstration on the part of Europe' impressing itself on the mind of Russia; and that what was 'remarkable' was the 'purity in the origin of the war' as an expression of the moral community of the concert. The terms neutralizing the Black Sea he denounced as a 'series of pitfalls'. The real problem, untouched by the treaty, was the condition of the Christians in Turkey, with immense danger of 'future complications'. He complained especially of the government's 'niggardliness' over the appeal for freedom and independence of the Danubian Principalities of Moldavia and Wallachia. This was an issue he was beginning to build up as a personal cause.[26]

This strong emphasis on foreign affairs distinguished even Gladstone's intervention in the budget debate, where he left Lewis alone and took the opportunity yet again to extol the Piedmontese and to stress his sense of the utmost importance of maintaining abroad a conviction of 'our sense of duty' of lending the Piedmontese 'every support that the moral influence of England can give'. This led to a rare and brief gleam of courtesy to Palmerston as a fellow admirer of Piedmont's role of exhibiting a 'right example to Italy'.[27]

A good deal of bile was released in the 'Declining Efficiency of Parliament' piece in the September *Quarterly*, dilating on the 'decay of zeal and abeyance of political duty' in Parliament. The defects of the Prime Minister, it was clear to Gladstone, 'must inevitably prevent his ever taking rank among the great prime ministers of England'. Compared with the 'immense energies of Peel', Palmerston's conceptions were 'vague, flat, bald, and shallow, in an unprecedented degree'.[28] Gladstone was beginning to see himself in some significant measure an embodiment of Peel's immense and beneficent potency as against Palmerston's negativism and shallowness. Would it be reserved for him to replace 'Palmerstonism' with a political system expressive of Peel's values? 'There is a policy going a-begging', as he put it in December 1856; 'the general policy that Sir Robert Peel in 1841 took office to support – the policy of peace abroad, of economy, of financial equilibrium, of steady resistance to abuses, and promotion of practical improvements at home, with a disinclination to questions of reform, gratuitously raised.'[29]

~

The domestic dimension was now serene. With Herbert's difficult birth in 1854 Catherine's child-bearing days were over. The marital adjustments required of Gladstone were, in a manner of speaking, already in place. Willy and Stephy were getting on well at Eton. Hawarden that summer and autumn fulfilled its promise. 'The new walk called mine gives a road to Church a very little longer & opens the park delightfully.' The Thomas Gladstones together with Helen came down in July in a warm atmosphere of family reconciliation. Above all Gladstone observed with satisfaction the climb back to prosperity of the estate. The coal leases looked well. The Homer book progressed. He found much to be thankful for in his end-of year self-adjurations. Into politics he felt himself 'drawn deeper every year'. In the 'growing anxieties & struggles of the Church' he had 'no less share than heretofore'. On Boxing Day Gladstone assessed the value of his personal goods and estate at upwards of £187,000. On his forty-seventh birthday he allowed that 'blessings have abounded more than usual'. And 'seven children growing up around us' were 'each the object of deeper thoughts & feelings & of higher hopes'.

He planned to launch himself into 1857 with another *Quarterly* philippic, 'Prospects Political and Financial'. Palmerston was the target of its invective. Derby was the target of its purpose. Gladstone had in mind the 'expediency' of a 'conference on the state of public affairs',[30] with a view to 'ascertain whether there would be any chance 'of an 'understanding as to the course to be pursued during the coming session' that might 'not only lead to greater harmony' but also 'possibly tend hereafter to the reunion of the now discordant Conservative elements'.[31] Bishop Wilberforce of Oxford, visiting Hawarden in November, noted how 'very strong against Palmerston' Gladstone was, and how 'manifestly' he leaned to 'a Conservative alliance'.[32]

The Peelite seniors were quite divided in their prognostications. Graham did not doubt that Gladstone would seat himself with the Conservative opposition come the 1857 session. Aberdeen was not so sure. He was concerned to protect Gladstone from impulsiveness and from a rather unbalanced detestation of Palmerston. Aberdeen candidly warned Gladstone that 'much prudence and circumspection' would be required of him before he arrived at a decision to join Derby. He pointed out that Gladstone's position in the Commons was 'very peculiar'. With an admitted superiority of character and intellectual power above any other member, Gladstone did not 'really possess the sympathy of the House at large'.[33] No doubt this gave Gladstone pause; though it did little to allay the Palmerstonophobic spleen of the new *Quarterly* tirade. 'Prospects Political and Financial' rebuked the Prime Minister for failing to rise to the occasion as defined by Gladstone's earlier 'Declining Efficiency of Parliament'.

He offered a model of an alternative government. This would take as its primary duty a policy of real retrenchment and economy. Gladstone laid heavy stress on the sacredness of the policy of 1853: that 'covenant' must be kept, and Lord Aberdeen and his political friends were its guardians and guarantors.[34] As an exercise in providing an encouraging atmosphere for negotiations with Derby, the *Quarterly* piece left something to be desired. The Peelite emphasis on heroic energy was not in accord with the disposition of the bulk of Lord Derby's friends; and would tend to make them all the more aware of the benefits of Palmerston's keeping Russell out and hobbling the Liberals. Already there was an awareness coming into being among many observers of public affairs that the epoch that began with Peel's fall and continued under Russell and Palmerston was in its own way commendable precisely for the negative qualities so lamented by Gladstone. Setting aside the accident of the war, a quiet, rather pedestrian public life had much to be said for it.

When it came eventually to their three-hour conference at St James's Square on the state of public affairs on 4 February, Derby found Gladstone elusive. For all that Gladstone declared himself anxious to end the Peelite isolation, denouncing himself as a 'public nuisance', and for all that he declared his desire that Lord Palmerston be displaced was so strong that he was 'content to act thus without enquiring what was to follow', being convinced 'that anyone who might follow would govern with less prejudice to the public interests', Derby could not pin Gladstone down to any specific undertaking independent of his Peelite brethren.

In the matter of a joint attitude to the budget Gladstone made sure negotiations were conducted as between two parties. There was the awkward question as to whether Disraeli or Gladstone should take the lead in moving the joint resolution. To his Peelite friends urging him to take charge as the standard-bearer of the principles of 1853, Gladstone explained that 'from motives which I could neither describe nor conquer I was quite unable to enter into any squabble or competition with him for the possession of a post of prominence'. Disraeli tended to obtrude awkwardly into Peelite calculations. Graham wished to see Gladstone lead the Commons under Russell in the Lords; but admitted that 'the same thing would do under Derby but for Disraeli, who could not be thrown away like a sucked orange'.[35]

After all these bold exercises in Peelite integrity, it was humiliating that they split over the issue of matching the county franchise with that in the boroughs. Gladstone and Herbert voted with the government to stop the bill; Graham and Cardwell followed Russell and the more 'advanced' Liberals: 'a bad night for Peelism'.[36]

Gladstone did his best to repair the damage on the following day, 20 February, with a fierce attack on Lewis's budget. But the fierceness of his attack went far beyond the necessities of the case as between Peelites and Derbyites. It was an assault so brutal as to recall Argyll's observations at Hawarden on how 'unsafe' was Gladstone's judgement. Argyll now declared Gladstone's performance 'very overstrained, and unfair in argument in the highest degree'. Lewis himself spoke of it as so personally bitter that he was quite amazed.[37] To the equally astonished Stanley the occasion remained a vivid memory ever after: he would measure evidences of Gladstone's 'excessive irritability' 'rarely equalled in Parliament' against it as a fixed point of reference.[38] He observed Gladstone's manner of speaking with 'that peculiar vehemence, like that of a man under personal provocation, which has marked his displays during this session'.[39] Greville likewise observed Gladstone 'so inflamed by spite and ill-humour that all prudence and discretion forsook him; he appears ready to say and do anything and to act with everybody if he can only contribute to upset the Government, though it is not easy to discover the cause of the bitterness, or what schemes of future conduct he has devised for himself'.[40]

These readings of Gladstone quite lacked – understandably and indeed necessarily – any awareness of the turmoil within Gladstone stemming from frustration at his thwarted vocation. Given such awareness, the cause of the bitterness and the schemes of future conduct are readily decipherable. Gladstone's assault on Disraeli's budget in 1852 was of much the same brutality and of much the same purpose. Other than frustration and aggression, the salient feature of this version was Gladstone's intense concern to revive and enhance the buoyancy of his credit of 1853. It was of the essence that he be in an unchallengeably strong position to claim the Exchequer when the opportunity arrived to take office in a strong ministry 'in a marked manner founded upon a policy', as he had stipulated to Aberdeen in March 1856. This was the indispensable condition of his resuming and fulfilling his new vocation as in fact (if not necessarily in form) the practitioner of the 'doings and intentions of the minister' with respect to the measures called for by the times and as the demiurge and focus of the 'corresponding conviction wrought by them in the public mind'.

For this grand purpose Gladstone had to project himself anew as the custodian and tutelary genius of the tradition of Peel. His mode was to assert the principles of 1853 as the sacred repository of financial truth and virtue, the touchstone upon which all subsequent policies had to be tested. Gladstone larded his indictments of Lewis's many sins with allusions calculated to burnish his personal myth: 'I remember periods – for instance, 1842 …'; 'the rule by which I had to abide in 1853 …'; 'well do I recollect the day when Sir Robert Peel …'[41] In the same spirit of resuscitating the spirit of 1853 Gladstone converted his 'Memorandum of Finance' of February 1856 into official published form as *Memorandum on Financial Control* in April 1857. This documented Gladstone's anticipations of an early end to Palmerston's ministry and his own imminent return to office.

~

Almost immediately on top of the budget another chance of striking at Palmerston presented itself in the matter of the gunboat diplomacy practised by the government against China. The Chinese authorities in Canton had arrested on a charge of piracy a *lorcha* registered in Hong Kong as *Arrow* and flying the British flag. For Palmerston it was another case of *civis Romanus sum*. Cobden, who led the attack, despairingly predicted that yet again Palmerston would escape deserved retribution. It is possible that Gladstone's immensely eloquent and passionate intervention on the fourth and last night of the debate, on 3 March, may have turned a few crucial votes. To his surprise, Palmerston was beaten by 263 to 274, with Disraeli, Russell and Roebuck among the majority alongside Cobden and Gladstone.

Gladstone went home that night 'being excited which is rare for me'. The Commons had wiped the stain of 1850 from its escutcheon. It had righted the wrong done to China in 1840. Above all, it had administered a stinging rebuff to the 'great illustration' of the demoralized politics of the time. Palmerston had contrived to stay on twice the twelvemonth Gladstone had disgustedly allotted to him in February 1855. The Prime Minister announced on 5 March that the 1852 Parliament would be dissolved. Gladstone immediately settled down to another piece for the *Quarterly* in anticipation of Palmerston's being repudiated by the electorate.[42] He had in view a new *Letter to the Earl of Aberdeen*, with Palmerston as the target instead of 'King Bomba'.[43]

Not even an imminent general election, however, could coagulate the Derbyite and Peelite Conservatives. Gladstone conferred again with Derby on 5 March and discussed the expediency of not 'knocking our heads against one another at every election as we did in 1852'.[44] But Gladstone evaded anything like a treaty of co-operation. What he did do on 6 March, was, in effect, to wag an admonitory finger at Derby. He put it candidly thus: 'It seemed to me it was high time for them to consider whether they would or would not endeavour to attract towards themselves such a strength of public opinion as would really put them in a condition to undertake the government of the country: without which they could not be a real opposition according to the spirit of our parliamentary system.'[45]

This point about the 'strength of public opinion' was the lodestone that would guide Gladstone to his eventual political destination, whatever that might be. It was, after all, a whole dimension of the prerequisites as outlined in 1856 to Aberdeen for re-accrediting his vocation. At a seemingly hopeful position of vantage Gladstone could now review his prospects. Palmerston presumably was as good as out. Gladstone might reasonably assume he was as good as in. If the electorate were to return a new Commons that would consummate the process begun in the old House of emancipating politics from the degenerate Palmerstonian thraldom, a prospect would be opened up of a wholesale and wholesome recasting of old combinations into new and much superior forms. Not only would there be Russell's men, and Cobden's men, and for that matter Roebuck's men; there would be the newcomers outside the Commons campaigning to get in. In the light of such a vision unreconstructed Derbyite Conservatism did not look all that impressive.

Unchallenged at Oxford, Gladstone campaigned hard for Stephen Glynne in Flintshire as well as assisting further afield in Chester and Liverpool. His excitement was manifest. Argyll observed a 'campaign of oratory, all over the country, for the purpose of influencing its decision'. He told Aberdeen: 'Gladstone has been making a speech in every town – every village – every cottage – everywhere he had room to stand, and at Liverpool it was an avowed canvass for Derby'.[46] This was in fact Gladstone's second thrilling excursion among 'the *people*'. But by the end of March and the early days of April all the indications were grievous. A surge of support for Palmerston in the country unseated Cobden, Bright and Milner Gibson. Russell remained in eclipse. Sir Stephen was rejected as a 'Liberal Conservative' by the Flintshire voters; John Neilson was dismissed at Devizes. Palmerston improved his parliamentary position handsomely to the tune of the best part of 50 seats, leaving the Derbyite Conservatives ever more a minority and the Peelites shattered.

As early as 31 March, when the horrid shape of things to come was sufficiently outlined, Gladstone addressed 'dismal ruminations' to Aberdeen, consisting mainly of an analysis of the hopeless condition of 'Peelism'. What sort of figure was it to cut? He feared that it should be 'extinguished', and even more, 'lest it should have gone out, as is said, with a stench'. A 'creditable exit' seemed 'peculiarly needful' in the new Parliament. But whither? Every argument of honour and consistency pointed to reunion with the Derbyites. Would not any other course 'bear the marks both of duplicity & of an undying hatred?' Not only did protection not now stand in the way. On every question of the hour, foreign policy, expenditure, taxation, the Peelites were 'in general agreement with Lord Derby & the bulk of his party'.

The argument was equally cogent against union with Liberalism. That option, Gladstone now argued, had been and gone. The circumstances that had made possible the coalition of 1852 no longer obtained When Aberdeen formed his government 'the act was done, which would probably have led to a real & final amalgamation with the Liberal party: but which had not produced any such amalgamation at the time when, the mortar being still wet, Lord John Russell's powder magazine blew the whole fabric into the air'. On all the great questions of the hour the bulk of the Liberal party, 'in consequence of taking Lord Palmerston as its leader', had 'placed itself in almost continual, at least in very frequent, antagonism with us'. There was, indeed, the possible alternative of Lord John Russell, unreconciled with Palmerston and, even in eclipse, potentially formidable if only because of his itch for franchise reform and educational meddling. How could the Peelites become parties 'to such tampering with our institutions'? That Graham, Cardwell and now Herbert were moving in this direction Gladstone deplored as unwarrantable pre-emption of events; and could not bring himself to believe that Graham 'in his heart' was persuaded that franchise reform was a present want of the country. 'Our whole safety, for ultimate vindication', Gladstone insisted, could be found only 'in our following with perfect good faith the guidance which events afford.'

The crucial point here, behind the camouflage of the pathos, was, embedded in the verbiage, one small remark that outweighed all the rest. It was the only item in his analysis that told against Derby: 'Lord Derby is much weaker than he was in 1852.' Within the terms of Gladstone's new criteria for determining the optimum shape of future politics, that was a decisive verdict. Combined with the equally brief but pregnant remark that Russell, for all his faults, offered a possible alternative recourse, it was a damning verdict.[47]

Aberdeen responded with perfect tact by taking the cue to draw the moral from Gladstone's tale – a moral Gladstone was unable or unwilling to draw for himself. 'It is clear that we must accustom ourselves to the conviction that there is no such thing as a distinctive Peelite party in existence.' Aberdeen indeed considered 'the amalgamation of Peel's friends with the liberal party to have practically taken place'; and he believed too that 'in this age of progress the liberal party must ultimately govern the country'. In all this, Aberdeen pointed out, Gladstone would be 'free to act as your conscience may dictate; and there can be no doubt that until the moment for decision shall arrive, your true place is at the side of Graham and Herbert, both from political affinity & private friendship'. Constituted as the new Parliament was, 'and situated as political parties actually are', Aberdeen believed that 'the future, & indeed the early future, is big with great events; but that you will do well to preserve your present position until you find yourself in the face of a real emergency'.[48]

~

'Situated as political parties actually are' could be read by Gladstone two ways. The first was as an echo of his own conclusion as to the debility of the Derbyite Conservatives. 'With a shrug or a sigh, they fold their arms, and provisionally accept Lord Palmerston as for the moment a necessity'. The second was that Palmerston in 1857, for all his triumph in the country, had at his behest no real 'homogeneous band'. The 'ground is mined beneath his feet'. And there was still Lord John to be contended with as a likely agent of instability in a 'miscellaneous and confused' Commons. These were notions garnered by Gladstone in another of his series of expostulations in the *Quarterly*, 'The New Parliament and its Work'.

This was the abortive letter to Aberdeen adjusted to the painful reversal of electoral expectations. The prevalent note was a sullen petulance. But, of gleams of hope discernible amid the gloom, Gladstone could indeed identify the bigness of great events in the early future as the outcome of what he called an incomprehensible election of 'great and general insincerity' bringing forth a Commons accordingly of a 'mass of motley materials'. And, notwithstanding Palmerston's being an unworthy minister, he might yet die 'a martyr to the Constitution'. He might refuse to countenance a democratic measure of franchise reform. In which case, Gladstone trusted that, 'irrespective of general confidence', he would 'receive from the independent portions of the House a warm support'.[49]

Parliamentary convalescence was little aided otherwise. Gladstone took it hard that 'Peelism, that repository of political virtue, that peculiar guardian of the models of financial policy of 1842, 1845, and 1853, was now unhappily extinct'. As the wounds healed he picked up the threads of legislative concerns. On the Divorce issue he resisted with a pertinacious tenacity that established a new record for parliamentary obstruction; a resistance rather compromised, however, by ripostes as to his conspicuous part in assisting Lincoln to get his divorce.[50] But Gladstone's big point was the horror of bringing divorce to the doors of all classes. His resistance to 'great expenditure' was almost equally unshakable.[51] Nor did he fail to identify the nefarious link between great expenditure and the deplorable 'spirit of our foreign policy'. He harried Palmerston over the French Suez Canal project, which he vindicated against Foreign Office jealousy and extolled as a 'great stroke for the benefit of mankind'. He also opened up again the question of the Danubian Principalities of Moldavia and Wallachia, rejoicing that the elections rigged by the Turks and the Austrians with British connivance to keep them separate and thus obstruct the forming of a Romanian national state had been quashed at the insistence of the Emperor Napoleon III.[52]

Outside the House occasions were mixed. Election to The Club, the famous convivial dining club founded by Dr Johnson, was gratifying. But rescue work continued in a desultory and unsatisfactory manner. Gladstone complained of 'half-heartedness' on 29 May and administered the discipline as self-mortification. He dined with Graham and the Herberts 'as if Peelism were not dead'. He kept up his Italian links. He saw much of Panizzi. At the end of May he met Felice Orsini, exponent of Mazzinian propaganda and refugee from Austrian dungeons. It was gratifying also that Willy, now entered at Christ Church, should have been selected as one of a group to accompany the Prince of Wales for an educational excursion that summer to the Rhineland and Switzerland. There was a refreshing break early in July at Glenalmond to examine for prizes and meet the new Warden, Hannah, *vice* Charles Wordsworth, now Bishop of St Andrews.

That summer, however, became memorably tragic for the death of Mary Lyttelton. After eleven pregnancies, her physician had warned her that a twelfth would be likely to prove fatal. A dutiful Victorian wife, she kept the prognosis to herself. The birth of a twelfth child in February was fraught with severe complications. While Gladstone wrestled with the Divorce Bill, Catherine watched over her fading sister at Hagley. Gladstone managed to extricate himself to be present when Mary died, serenely, on 18 August. George Lyttelton was prostrate. 'He fully accepts the will of God', Gladstone noted, '& to see his behaviour is most edifying.'[53] Back at Hawarden Gladstone solaced himself with Homer leavened with Döllinger. Homer, on the whole, predominated. Gladstone finished the text on 10 February 1858. 'If it were even tolerably done, it would be a good service to religion as well as to literature: and I mistrustfully offer it up to God.'

~

Placid times ended abruptly in the new year, when on 14 January 1858 an attempt was made by a group of Italian exiles to assassinate Napoleon III by means of bombs. Among the perpetrators was Gladstone's acquaintance Orsini. The operation was planned in the vicinity of Leicester Square and the bombs were manufactured in Birmingham. Walewski for the French government made stiff representations about Britain's giving irresponsible latitude to international criminals. Orsini among others was tried in France in February and executed in March. The Orsini connection embarrassed Gladstone. Palmerston took Count Walewski's point about giving asylum to assassins to the extent of agreeing that it would be appropriate to convert conspiracy to murder from a misdemeanour to a felony. Palmerston's careless complaisance to Walewski cost him dear. The patriotic claptrap of the 'national' public that normally sustained him now turned against him as a truckler to Bonapartism. As Palmerston faltered, Gladstone pounced. Ministers were astonishingly beaten on 19 February by 215 to 234. The only really promising indication before the division, Gladstone reported to Catherine, was that Palmerston was 'actually rabid'.[54] Some 80 disgruntled patriots deserted their chief. The ground was indeed mined beneath his feet. Palmerston tendered his resignation to the Queen on the 20th. There was no question of another dissolution. Lord Derby was sent for.

Gladstone was ecstatic. 'It almost revived the China night.'[55] His excitement at the fall of the 'great fustian Ministry' was almost disturbing in its intensity. Later, in yet another *Quarterly* piece, he allowed his wish to father his thoughts to a highly incautious degree: Palmerston could not 'under any ordinary circumstances, whatever be his longings, resume the station he has lost'.[56] At Aberdeen's a message from Lord Derby caught up with him, offering an unspecified place in a Conservative Cabinet. Herbert and Graham both arrived and a negative reply was drafted and despatched. 'The case though grave was not doubtful.' Gladstone went off into the night with Herbert; and they parted 'with the fervent wish that in public life we would never part'.[57]

The argument of 13 March 1856 applied decisively.[58] It was important that Palmerston had gone out, but not necessarily important that the 'next turn of the wheel' had put Derby in. And, apart from anything else, Gladstone's plans presupposed an unchallenged claim to the Exchequer. His disinclination to compete with Disraeli remained as strong as ever. We could not, as he had put it in 1856, 'bargain Disraeli out of the saddle'.[59] Yet the very coolness and briskness of Gladstone's refusal marked a stage in his emancipation from one of the main practical principles by which his political understanding had been anchored. Of the analogies borne by his shedding his purely Conservative identity and loyalty in the late 1850s to the manner of his dismantling his State and Church programme in the late 1840s, not least was his profound unwillingness to admit to himself or anyone else that the process was under way. He was never more studiously a Conservative than at the time of his coming to the conclusion that actually existing Conservatism would be most unlikely to be an adequate vehicle for his renewed vocation.

But as the party actually in office again in 1858 the Conservatives could count on Gladstone's forbearance. He was content to sustain what he later described as the 'regular, the undisputed, let us add the generally successful administration of public affairs by a Government which is, or is supposed to be, politically opposed to the large majority of the House of Commons'.[60] What a relief that 'new actors are upon the stage!'[61]

To crown all, the Homer book, published by Parker's, came out at the end of March. *Studies on Homer and the Homeric World*, in three bulky volumes, made no serious impression on the scholarly community of the time. Gladstone was distinctly out of his depth in most of the abstruse reaches of the technicalities. It was his insistence, however, that the Homeric religion contained elements of divine truth and that those elements therefore reflect the 'authority of a providential order' and amount to a species of 'supplementary revelation', that startled his readers. Jowett dismissed it as 'mere nonsense'. Others compared it to Bishop Warburton's *Divine Legation of Moses*, one of the grand oddities of misdirected eighteenth-century erudition. Karl Marx, himself no mean classical scholar, thought it 'extremely typical of the incompetence of the English to achieve anything in classical scholarship'.[62] Gladstone noted a review in the *National Review* 'which ought to humble me'.[63] That review, by the Oxford scholar and historian Edward Freeman, demolished Gladstone's ethnology, lacerated his mythology, mocked his 'strange mixture of timidity and daring', and concluded that at bottom Gladstone's argument was 'simply unintelligible'.[64] Gladstone remained imperturbably unhumbled. His power of persuading himself was immune to such mundane critiques.

In a spirit of indulgence to the new actors on the stage Gladstone offered a very friendly response in April to Disraeli's budgetary proposals, expressing hopes that the policy of extinguishing the income tax would be adhered to and that the present scandalous rate of expenditure would be decently reduced. Likewise on Compulsory Church Rates Abolition he was co-operative with ministers, asking only delay to mitigate the Church's being severed from its traditional mode of local financing. He was rather more critical of their plans to recast the government of India in the aftermath of the Mutiny, objecting especially to the wide powers of the proposed new office of secretary of state as inimical to Treasury control over expenditure. Gladstone's general indulgence to the Conservative government in the 1858 session worried those Liberals who looked to him as the greatest potential recruit to their cause.[65]

~

Gladstone's *chef d'oeuvre* in the 1858 session was his great speech on 4 May to his motion urging the Commons and the government to uphold the cause of the Romanians against the Turks and the Austrians. He had raised the question before unavailingly in the face of Palmerston's resistance. The Foreign Office and the embassy in Constantinople colluded with the Turks and Austrians to strangle the Romanian state at birth. Gladstone had already rejoiced that France, together with Russia, had secured the quashing of the elections rigged to produce a vote against the union of Moldavia and Wallachia. The question was now poised. A conference would soon meet in Paris. It was vital to give support to the French. Gladstone trusted that the new Conservative ministry, which had no motive for sticking to Palmerston's 'Crimean' policy, could be persuaded to take a fresh look at the matter in concert with the French to patronise Romanian unity and independence as one of the few positive achievements of an otherwise largely barren war.

The 1858 Romanian speech provided the positive dimension of his negative critiques of what by now was becoming identifiable as the 'Crimean' aspect of Palmerstonism, as offered in his Manchester speech of 1853 and his speeches against the continuance of the war in 1855 and the spuriousness of the peace in 1856. Though he rehearsed his russophile prejudices, the 1858 speech was a model of restraint and good sense. He argued that there was no chance of the British or French peoples being always ready to pay £50 or £100 millions to prop up the Turks; and that therefore the logical, sensible and rational, as well as humane, liberal and generous course was to promote emancipation of Christian subject peoples under the anyway rotting Ottoman yoke. If Russian aggression was the principal fear then 'surely the best resistance to be offered to Russia is by the strength and freedom of those countries that will have to resist her. You want to place a living barrier between her and Turkey. There is no barrier, then, like the breasts of free men.'[66]

That Palmerston should oppose Gladstone's Romanian initiative was to be expected. The Crimean War had been fought to preserve the independence and integrity of the Ottoman Empire. It would be absurd to set about undermining that integrity and independence in the peace. The crucial disappointment for Gladstone was that Disraeli, speaking authoritatively for Malmesbury at the Foreign Office, echoed Palmerston's argument and placed the Conservative government firmly on the side of the Crimean policy. Disraeli spoke equally for his own notions of what 'British politics' in the East should be.

Gladstone had now a disposition to feel aggrieved against the Conservative government. This was an immediate consequence of importance: first, it was another jolt that helped to loosen his political understanding from its old anchorage; second, it confronted him for the first time with the realization that on a major issue of policy there was nothing to choose between Palmerston and Derby. His grievance over the Romanian affair assisted Gladstone shortly afterward in refusing Derby's offer of either the Indian Board of Control or the Colonial Office. Gladstone's general forebearance encouraged Derby to make another effort to entice his 'only half-regained Eurydice'. To facilitate the transaction, it was made clear that Disraeli was willing to surrender the leadership of the Commons to Graham. For Gladstone nothing had happened to make him feel that the criteria of March 1856 as applied to February 1858 applied any more promisingly now. A great matter like the reshaping of India was naturally tempting; and it was indeed 'handsome' of Disraeli to waive his claims. But, as he reported to Aberdeen and Graham, Gladstone's 'clear opinion' was that joining the Conservative government would 'shock the public sentiment', while doing nothing materially to 'enlarge and strengthen its hold upon public opinion, and change in its favour the present distribution of political strength throughout the country'. He added pointedly the complaint that the government was falling into 'the groove of Lord Palmerston's eastern policy'.[67]

Graham, the most Liberal-leaning of the Peelites, advised Gladstone nonetheless to go with Derby. His point was the passing of time and opportunities. His advice comprehended every consideration except the one at the centre. Aberdeen had already put his finger accurately on it with his simple doctrine that in this age of progress Liberalism must command politics. Gladstone was not prepared merely to be the leaven of an unreconstructed Derbyite lump. Disraeli's dramatic intervention in aid of Derby, while indeed handsome, missed the point. Keenly aware of the widely held view that 'our mutual relations have caused the great difficulty', Disraeli begged Gladstone to observe without prejudice the various offers he had made to surrender the leadership of the Commons to ease Gladstone's way back to the Conservatives. Did not Gladstone think that the time had come when he 'might deign to be magnanimous?' Gladstone's response in the circumstances might have been less nonchalant; but in assuring Disraeli that their relationship was not the 'main difficulty' in the way, and that the difficulties were 'broader than you may have supposed', he acted in perfect good faith. It was a question, he told Disraeli, not only of connections which make harmonious and effective Cabinet co-operation possible; it was a question also of 'what connections can be made with public approval'.[68]

~

The last act of Gladstone's part in the fortunes of Derby's minority government – a government that, as he acknowledged, existed with 'pretty general approval, with nearly universal acquiescence' – involved him in two dramatic scenes, in one of which a comical element predominated, in the other of which irony was the keynote.

An autumn tour of the Scottish Highlands in 1858, taking in the Sutherlands at Dunrobin and Aberdeen at Haddo, climaxed for the Gladstones with a return to Fasque, with Sir Thomas and Louisa now all graciousness. At Haddo a curious letter had caught up with Gladstone at the beginning of October: an invitation from Edward Bulwer-Lytton, the Colonial Secretary, to go to the Ionian Islands Protectorate as High Commissioner Extraordinary to investigate the situation there and advise the government as to remedies for its problems. Doubtless ministers calculated that acceptance by Gladstone might open a chink of possibility of his ultimate return among them.

Faced with increasing unrest amid a population overwhelmingly desirous of *enosis* with Greece, the High Commissioner, Sir John Young, at the end of his tether in 1857, had recommended either handing the Islands over to Greece, or annexing the northern group including Corfu as a crown colony and leaving the remainder to join with Greece. The European Concert, in whose name Britain since 1815 had administered the Protectorate, would have to be consulted; and particularly the power with the nearest interest, Austria.

Aberdeen and his other friends did their best to persuade Gladstone not to get entangled in a petty matter that would expose him to mockery for further Homeric eccentricity. Armoured, however, in his self-sufficiency compounded of innocence and assurance, Gladstone decided in the end to accept Bulwer's commission. He would take Catherine and Agnes and Lacaita along with him. Travel would be, as usual, a tonic. Doing a service for Derby's ministry at a safe distance would be a harmless substitute for serious commitment. An opportunity to escape the sterile parliamentary scene had much attraction. Undoubtedly the Homeric aspect was tempting. Gladstone quite accepted that it was a petty affair; but he saw 'the complexity of the case' as inversely related to the 'extent of the sphere': a *magnum in parvo*.[69] And was he not equipped with very clear principles about the correct relationship between metropolitan power and outlying dependency?

Gladstone tried to pacify Aberdeen by making Arthur Gordon, Aberdeen's son, his secretary. Gordon viewed the Ionian excursion as 'a political drama alternately tragical and comical, not unmixed with occasional scenes of the broadest farce, but always picturesque'.[70] This was a partial opinion, not unconnected with the facts that Gordon fell in love with Agnes and fell out with both her parents.

Gladstone saw himself as 'labouring for truth and justice'. He stopped by at Vienna on his way to assure the Austrians that his mission would do no harm to their interests. Indeed, his 'work', as he saw it, was to put a decisive stop to all ideas in the Islands of union with Greece. For this thoroughly Peelite interpretation of 'justice and mercy' he sacked Young and took over as Acting High Commissioner and set about curing disaffection in the manner of his dealing with refractory tariffs and delinquent budgets. His sacking of Young was reminiscent of his sacking of Eardley Wilmot in Van Diemen's Land. He expected that Ionians 'of station and intelligence' would see the necessity of submitting to metropolitan policy, and that a deferential Ionian electorate would reinforce their position after having received concessions to certain 'popular principles of government'. Being not absolutely disqualified from 'discharging the duties political freedom must entail', they could surely see the need to subordinate their dream of *enosis* to the 'dictates of other and larger interests', particularly as connected with the present state of Eastern Europe.

Gladstone lived thus in a world of fantasy and absurdity. He stopped over briefly in Athens to assure himself that *enosis* was not greatly in demand among the Hellenic official elite. Nor indeed was it. The punitive Anglo-French occupation of Piraeus in 1857 helped to inculcate that sentiment. But that had little bearing on Greek popular opinion in general and Ionian opinion in particular. The Ionian Senate and Assembly ignored him other than to present petitions demanding *enosis*. Back in London Herbert exploded and Graham fretted at Gladstone's bold takeover. Aberdeen, a connoisseur of Gladstone's penchant for getting things somewhat out of proportion, offered reassurance: *'Ah! But he is terrible on the rebound.'*[71]

For a while Gladstone himself worried about his chances of rebound. To his horror he discovered that by taking on the high commission he automatically vacated his Oxford seat. This put him in a panic to reverse the procedure. A replacement commissioner, Sir Henry Storks, a military man with experience in Mauritius, was hastily shipped out. By the time he arrived, it was as if on a rescue mission, with Gladstone in what amounted to besieged predicament. It is unlikely that Gladstone's final transactions had any official legal status. It hardly mattered. He took solace in a course of rescue work among the Corfiote *hetaerae.*

Gladstone was no more successful in persuading the Ionians to renounce *enosis* than he would have been in persuading Australians that they would have to accept the continuance and expansion of penal transportation. His three massive and elaborate reports, printed for use of the Cabinet, faded into obscurity. It was felt that, in the circumstances of the Italian war, it would be inexpedient to lay documents before Parliament bearing on the question of the rights of subject peoples within the jurisdiction of the public law of Europe. As things turned out, non-publication proved immensely convenient for Gladstone's later Liberal reputation.

In fact, Gladstone's return journey in February 1859 through Italy and France was of much more import than his Ionian misadventure. A war atmosphere infected Venice as the Gladstones dined as guests of the Viceroy of the Lombardo-Venetian kingdom, the Archduke Ferdinand Maximilian, younger brother of the Emperor Francis Joseph. Gladstone found the Archduke 'kind, intelligent, ingenuous & earnest'.[72] Sardinia-Piedmont, with France behind, was in the process of goading the Austrians into a belligerent false step. By the time the Gladstones reached Turin 'dark omens' abounded. The Piedmontese politicians would hardly fail to mark the passage of so distinguished a friend of their country. Gladstone spent an hour alone with Cavour, who was 'confidential down to a certain date'; which was presumably his meeting at Plombières in July 1858 with the Emperor Napoleon, when it was agreed in principle that Austrian power should be driven from Italy. As the party diligenced, sledged and entrained their way across the Alps and France, Gladstone noted: 'Much rumination'.[73]

~

Back at Carlton House Terrace in early March the Italian theme remained in the ascendant. On 9 April Gladstone met the young disciple of Döllinger and rising intellectual leader in England of liberal Roman Catholicism, Sir John Acton.[74] All this was accruing into a critical mass. But now a new element was added. What was emerging of capital significance in the Italian question was the government's disposition to take a pro-Austrian attitude as tensions mounted between

Piedmont and Austria. This was perfectly in accordance with Conservative tradition in the nineteenth century. It was the policy Aberdeen would have adopted. But the point was that it presented Gladstone for the first time with a major issue of policy on which Derby was at odds with Palmerston.

This was decidedly not the case with the other issue that had now come into prominence, that of Reform. Derby and Disraeli had decided that some serious domestic initiative had to be undertaken by the Conservatives. The 1857 election had been a serious setback. If ever they were to establish credentials to govern, they needed to expand their support in the country beyond the existing bounds of Conservative voters in the constituencies. Extending the parliamentary franchise as settled in 1832 was beginning to become one of the questions of the time. Ever since Russell had tried to rescue his reputation by starting it up in 1850 it had gathered considerable support out of doors but as yet little purchase in the Commons.

Gladstone notoriously was not enthusiastic. His line was that agitation for Reform was a symptom of the degenerate state of politics ensuing since Peel's crash. He had recently made it clear that one of the very few things he was ready to give Palmerston credit for was that Palmerston could be relied on to block any measure of democratic Reform. Derby and Disraeli were exactly of the same mind. They had in view a measure that would redound to their credit as reformers but that would pose no threat to the system established since 1832. Disraeli's Reform Bill was thus an unconvincing affair, the lowest common denominator between Derby's willingness to offer and Palmerston's willingness to accept. Its public reputation was damaged by Bright's sneer at 'fancy franchises'. Gladstone recorded himself 'sorely puzzled' by the question, and read both J. S. Mill and Walter Bagehot unavailingly for enlightenment. In the Commons on 29 March he defended Disraeli's bill against a hostile amendment from Russell advocating a greater extension of the borough franchise. But he could see in the issue 'no substantial difference of opinion traceable to differences in this House between political parties'. He agreed with Bright that Parliament should settle Reform 'in a spirit of trust towards the people'. He agreed with Russell that the 'lowering of the suffrage in the boroughs was the main purpose in having a Reform bill', and, unless that was done, 'it would be better that we do not waste our time on this subject'. Like Disraeli, Russell was not strong enough to command a strong bill. Given a choice of weak, unsatisfactory schemes, Gladstone would choose the government's as the more likely to put an end to the unwholesome agitation in the country.

The criteria determining Gladstone's judgement on Reform were clearly those set out in March 1856. It was not an issue sufficiently dividing parties; and it was not an issue proposed by a strong government as a means of fulfilling ends proposed by a strong government. Gladstone's consequent lack of interest and candid advocacy of the expediency of a quick settlement so that Parliament could get on to 'the many other demands on our time' shocked the more earnest Reformers. In later years, when he had a reputation as a reformer to cherish, he was embarrassed and querulous at revelations of this insensibility.[75] But at the time he made no bones about his principal stipulations that a good Reform Bill would preserve the beneficial interests of property as the foundation of the county franchise, and that a plentiful supply of nomination boroughs should be available to nurture promising young parliamentary talent. 'Gladstone seems', as Sir John Trelawny commented, 'to have been as singular as people expected he would be.'[76]

On the division on 31 March Russell and Bright defeated Disraeli and Gladstone by 330 to 291. The Queen was quite amenable to Derby's advice that the 1857 Parliament be dissolved. The general election brought foreign affairs to the fore. Reform was largely ignored. So was finance. Gladstone signalled the restoration of the ascendancy of the Italian question by making his last appearance in the session on 18 April a sharp rebuke to Disraeli for endorsing Austrian policy. Gladstone contended that, without accepting the extreme thesis of Austria's expulsion from Italy and a great breach of the treaties of 1815, nevertheless Lord Palmerston was to be supported in championing Piedmont's right to a place in any conference of the powers and should not be obliged to disarm.[77]

A friend remarked after meeting Gladstone in May 1859 that 'Foreign politics seemed to have the chief place in his mind'.[78] Now, with the Italian matter, the delinquencies of Malmesbury contrasted with the virtues of the italophile Clarendon. Gladstone set out his case in a piece in the April *Quarterly*, 'The War in Italy'. Austria's determination to reduce Piedmont to the status of a compliant satellite exposed her to the hitherto uncertain British public as the villain of the case. The crux of the matter was that Gladstone was moving, willy-nilly, closer to Palmerston. Much as Gladstone might deplore the painful irony of this circumstance, he could not evade its logic. Any residual notions of wriggling out of it were stilled when, in an election speech in his constituency at Tiverton at the end of April, Palmerston launched into an open avowal that he hoped the coming war would end with the Germans being driven out of Italy. Aberdeen, who of all his contemporaries knew Gladstone best, remarked to Graham that Palmerston's 'brilliant stroke' at Tiverton had 'secured Gladstone, who is ready to act with him, or under him, notwithstanding the three articles of the *Quarterly* and the thousand imprecations of late years'.[79]

The Conservatives did well in the elections, but not well enough to break out of their minority situation. The pressures bearing on Gladstone to align himself with the new majority were insistent. How much longer could he afford to spend the best years of his life out of his natural service? The Conservatives had failed, seemingly conclusively, to get themselves in a condition really to undertake the government. Financial policy remained for Gladstone the lodestar of politics. But as yet no substantial public opinion on it was formed to be directed by his insights. He would have to accept what rescue from limbo was available to him. Much of his later insistence on the crucial role for him in 1859 of the 'overwhelming interest and weight of the Italian question' bore the 'character and flavour of self-justification'.[80] It remains, after all, a piquant consideration that in the matter of the Ionian people, Gladstone had been perfectly ready to give satisfaction to the Conservative government, and, for that matter, to the absolutist regime of Vienna.

What forms and combinations would reveal themselves in the new Commons majority was as yet unclear. In some respects prospects were encouraging. It would not be the old Palmerstonian conglomeration stemming from the defunct coalition and the 1857 election. It was likely that Russell would return. He was problematic in many ways, but his pro-Italian credentials were unimpeachable; and, above all, he was not Palmerston. In any case Gladstone was determined to strike one last stroke for honour and consistency: he saw Palmerston on 28 May and stipulated that when the government met the new Parliament he would vote on the motion of confidence for Derby and Disraeli, as he had voted for their Reform Bill. At the beginning of June he confessed himself 'much harassed and distressed at his position relative to the government and opposition'.[81] A new bout of rescue work led to an application of the discipline.

On 6 June, the eve of the new session, the Liberal party gathered in Willis's Rooms. Herbert attended as a token of the goodwill of the former Peelite group. Palmerston and Russell announced their reconciliation and their reciprocal willingness to serve under the other. Herbert and Bright made encouraging utterances. The calculation was that there was now a certain majority to beat Derby and Disraeli. The motion of no-confidence was moved on 7 June by the young Lord Hartington.[82] Through several nights of debate all the eminences of the House gave forth except Gladstone, who registered his silent vote for Derby and Disraeli in the division on 10 June. Ministers failed narrowly to hold their own, by 310 to 323.

The Queen, confronted with the dire prospect of 'those two dreadful old men', Palmerston and Russell, tried to dodge by inserting Granville as an acceptable alternative. Granville himself dodged out as quickly as he decently could. Palmerston was confident that, confronted with the necessity of a decision, the Queen would not choose 'selfish, peevish Johnny'. Accordingly, on 13 June Gladstone received his summons to attend on Palmerston. 'Went to Ld P. by his desire at night: & accepted my old office.'[83]

7

A Peelite in Liberal Guise, 1859–1862

> 'The horizon enlarges, the sky shifts, around me. It is an age of shocks: a discipline so strong, so manifold, so rapid and whirling, that only when it is at an end, can I hope to comprehend it.'
>
> *Gladstone, diary entry, 29 December 1860*

By joining with Palmerston and Russell in June 1859 Gladstone saw himself as having become a member of 'the only administration that could be formed, in concert with all the friends (setting aside those whom age excluded) with whom I joined and acted in the government of Lord Aberdeen'.[1] He thus awarded himself a kind of legitimacy of consistency. It suited him to designate himself a 'Liberal-Conservative'. He got around to resigning from the Carlton Club in March 1860. He did not join the Reform.

His point about 'my old office' was of the essence. He told Herbert next day that 'he would not have joined the Government otherwise'.[2] Palmerston had hoped to resume with Cornewall Lewis, who had served him well at the Exchequer when Gladstone deserted him in 1855. Gladstone's ability in 1859 to oblige Palmerston to shunt Lewis aside derived from a relationship with the 'country' cultivated since 1853 with which Lewis could not compete. It was thus an appointment distasteful to Palmerston and painful to Lewis. And to many who had observed Gladstone's ferocious impugning of Palmerston since 1855 there was something indecent about it, especially when contrasted with the example of Cobden, who disdained Palmerston's offer of the Board of Trade.

Shaftesbury, Palmerston's stepson-in-law and confidant, recorded that Palmerston feared Gladstone's 'character, his views, and his temperament, greatly. He rarely spoke severely of anyone. Bright and Gladstone were the only two of whom he used strong language.' Shaftesbury recounted that when Parliament was dissolved in 1859 Palmerston urged him to do all in his power 'to secure Gladstone's seat for the University', as tending to act as a brake on his restless movement.[3] Which point came immediately home: for to Gladstone's great – and, in the circumstances, totally unreasonable – irritation, he found his re-election on taking office contested.

It was one thing for Gladstone to get his 'old office' back; it was quite another to get back the old sense of rapport that had sustained and inspired him in the good days of the Peel and Aberdeen administrations. Political life with Palmerston in the coming years was likely to be at best difficult, at worst stormy. Gladstone could take comfort in calculating that, at 75, Palmerston could not have many years left to him. Gladstone had the comfort also of old Peelite colleagues: Herbert went to the War Office; Newcastle to the Colonial Office. Argyll sustained business in the Lords with Granville's assistance. Graham now had joined Aberdeen in elder statesmanship. Russell insisted on the Foreign Office. He also stipulated that the price for his reconciliation was to be a new Reform Bill. Milner Gibson was slotted into the Board of Trade. Ominously for Gladstone, however, was the knot of Old Whigs clustered around Palmerston: Lewis at the Home Office, Wood at the India Office, Somerset at the Admiralty, Grey at the Duchy of Lancaster. Clarendon hovered outside behind them.

Gladstone wrote to John Stuart Mill, now established as Liberalism's house philosopher: 'My office indeed is at this time not a pleasant one: for on every side the prospect of it is dark with increased charges and increased burdens, while the distance is worse than the foreground.'[4] What did Mill and the other luminaries of the intelligentsia make of this decidedly eccentric recruit to the Liberal cause? Mill himself seems at the time not to have taken any account of Gladstone individually. He saw 'no prospect of any thing but mischief from the change of ministry', and he saw no likely benefit to the cause of Reform. It was simply another turn of the old-fashioned party-political wheel.[5] Walter Bagehot, the most prominent financial journalist of the time, proposed a thesis of Gladstone's 'adaptive mind': 'Mr Gladstone is essentially a man who cannot impose his creed *on* his time, but must learn his creed *of* his time.'[6] Bagehot cited testimony by Gladstone himself, writing on the role of the orator in *Studies on Homer*: 'his choice is, to be what his age will have him, or else not to be at all'.[7] At the same time, however, Bagehot understood the profoundly unliberal implications of Gladstone's executive predisposition and his manipulative relationship to opinion: he 'has the same sort of control over the minds of those he is addressing that a good driver has over the animals he guides: he feels the minds of his hearers as the driver the mouths of his horses'.[8]

Others in the 'movement' stressed the 'secondary, and almost accidental, character of Gladstone's liberalism'.[9] It was a commonly expressed opinion of him among Liberalism's rabbis that 'as a Liberal he had no clearly thought-out political philosophy'.[10] There was always a sense of Gladstone's being an artificially contrived Liberal. A candid observer with a cynical turn might see it as a case of an ambitious man trimming himself from being a Conservative with dim prospects to being a Liberal with bright prospects. That he did not join the Reform Club was widely held to be a telling indication. The ambiguities of his position were well attested by his friend Robert Phillimore's regrets at his taking his name off the Carlton. 'It is a marked and significant act of entire separation from the *whole* party and will strengthen Disraeli's hands.'[11]

All that the radical Oxford University reformer and 'philosophical' politician Goldwin Smith could make out, was that Gladstone had 'apparently, no notion of any system of government other than party, which he seemed to treat as though it had been immemorial and universal'. All that Gladstone could supply to fill the gap noted by Smith in political science or the absence of any clear perception of the polity he was seeking to produce, was a 'guiding idea, when once he had broken loose from his early Toryism', of 'liberty, which he appeared to think would of itself be the parent of all good'. Smith's ultimate pragmatic diagnosis of the essential Gladstone boiled down to the fact that he was 'ambitious, happily for the country; he wanted to recover the means of doing great things. His admirers need not shrink from that avowal.'[12]

Smith was certainly on the right track in that ultimate diagnosis. But Gladstone in fact had no want of a clearly thought-out political philosophy. By 1859 the problem was that the core of it was not a Liberal one. That, however, was to be Liberalism's problem, not Gladstone's. Morley himself thought it 'a mistake to treat the acceptance of office under Lord Palmerston as a chief landmark in Mr Gladstone's protracted journey from tory to liberal'. The example that occurred to Morley was that of 'a liberal reformer of Turgot's type'; that is, grand practitioner of executive power, aiming to do great things.[13] There is a case to be made for Peel as the 'progenitor of Gladstonian Liberalism'.[14] There is a convincing case to be made for Peel as progenitor of Gladstone's Liberalism. As Gladstonian Liberals were going to find to their cost, the two concepts were far from being identical. In due course and time's smoothing of angularities, Gladstone would declare that the first Liberal government of which he was a member was that of Lord Aberdeen.[15] As Gladstone himself put it to the voters of South Lancashire in 1865: 'I am a member of a Liberal Government. I am in association with the Liberal party. I have never swerved from what I conceived to be those truly Conservative objects and desires with which I entered life.'[16] Liberalism's rabbis were quite justified in their suspicions that Gladstone, for all that he had hoisted Liberal colours, was likely to prove a highly idiosyncratic and problematic Liberal.

~

The first whiff of the long six years of conflict between Gladstone and his chief came before the end of June with a brush over the issue of the Suez Canal. But Italy promised for the present welcome occasions of collegiality. Gladstone was in hopes that England might assist in bringing the question to a 'happy settlement'.[17] Battles between the Franco-Piedmontese and Austrian armies at Magenta and Solferino led to the Austrians yielding Milan and entrenching themselves in their

Quadrilateral of fortresses.[18] The Emperor Napoleon had no stomach to take on the Quadrilateral. An armistice was arranged.

Gladstone's Cabinet memorandum of 30 June was in many respects not entirely remote from the spirit of the negotiations between the Emperor Napoleon and the Emperor Francis Joseph that took place a few days later after the armistice of Villafranca. Gladstone was anxious at Piedmontese ambitions to 'domineer' and be a bad neighbour to Austria in the future. Her ambitions must be kept within bounds. Gladstone's one *nostrum* for Italy was 'local freedom'. He deprecated unification. His two main desiderata now were the cessation of Austrian direct dominion in Italy and an 'essential change' in the temporal prerogatives of the papacy. Any lasting settlement would need Austrian consent; so perhaps Lombardy-Venetia could be given in sovereignty to that Archduke Ferdinand Maximilian who had impressed Gladstone so favourably earlier in Venice? The Pope should be given guarantees as to dignity, independence, security, wealth; but his sovereignty must be reduced to a 'suzerainty'. Britain should play a 'European' role in strengthening the hand of the Emperor Napoleon in coming to a co-operative policy with Austria to secure these ends.[19]

The deal closed by Napoleon and Francis Joseph at Villafranca was that, apart from Austria's ceding most of Lombardy to France for retrocession to Piedmont, all the Italian princes would be restored to their sovereignties and the Pope would preside over an Italian Confederation of which Austria's Venetian territories would be part. Piedmont's ambition to be the nucleus of a Kingdom of North Italy stretching from the Tyrrhenian to the Adriatic seas thus received apparently a decisive check. This was to be formalized in a Treaty of Zurich. Diplomacy seemed to have ended the Italian War in contrast to the way it had not ended the Crimean War.

~

Gladstone's official life reverted to its own domestic wars. Conflict with Palmerston devolved initially into a pattern of fiscal wrangling on two main fronts that often interpenetrated. On one front was the knot of issues comprehending Gladstone's determination to get public expenditure under control by dealing faithfully with the wine duties and the paper duties, and the way these became complicated with plans for a commercial treaty with France. On the other front was Palmerston's determination to put the country on a secure footing of defence against an alleged threat from France, involving massive expenditure, especially on fortifications and naval construction.

For Gladstone the primary concern was the need to get up a provisional budget by 18 July. A deficit of five millions had to be coped with. There were no obstacles in Cabinet. His principal contrivance was a sharp hoist of the income tax from 5d. to 9d. To Robertson he defended this augmentation of the income tax 'regardless of charges of inconsistency', because it was unavoidable for the public service 'on its present enormous scale'. It bedevilled ideals of getting a proper balance between direct and indirect taxation. Gladstone saw it as a 'grand instrument for war, and for special occasions, and for fixed reforms. But I shall rejoice to see the day when it may be dispensed with as an ordinary instrument of finance.'[20]

After this stop-gap Gladstone had leisure to meditate on 'the future of our finance'. There was the vital question of re-accrediting his vocation. There were the principles and projects of 1856 to be set into beneficent motion. In hot dispute with Disraeli, Gladstone insisted on his 1853 budget as the crucial benchmark of financial 'principles of high policy': 'I demur ... entirely to the doctrine of the right hon. Gentleman that this growth in the civil expenditure is a thing natural, normal, and proportioned to the state of the country'.[21] In the new situation of 1859 it was necessary for Gladstone to readjust the resentments and targets he seemed in need of. Palmerston was now (publicly at any rate) out of range. The indulgence to Disraeli of 1858–59 would thus be withdrawn. 'I am afraid that the truce between us is over and that we shall have to pitch in as before.'[22]

There was Reform also to attend to; and, if possible, be set aside. Gladstone guardedly explained to the veteran Reformer Brougham that the question contained 'all the elements of a false position'. On the one hand, the 'good sense and practical turn' of the English people suggested confidence in a 'tolerable solution'; but on the other, 'what ministries it will scatter on its road may be very uncertain'. Security for the 'good use of the present franchise' lay, he thought, 'not so much in the competency of the voter as in his willingness to defer to others more competent & in his respect for the established order'. Gladstone humoured Brougham by allowing that the same security might be hoped for 'on a lower & broader basis'; but had to apologize for the government's having 'made no progress whatever' on the issue; and that, for himself, 'sordid considerations compounded of alarm at the state and prospects of our expenditure' made him 'inapt to embrace any constitutional question'.[23]

Among concerns in the private sphere of life theatre remained close to Gladstone's heart. He presided at a dinner given by fellow-Etonians to Charles Kean, whom he praised for raising the moral tone of the stage. Theatre-land of course was always convenient for expeditions of rescue in the West End. Gladstone first met Maria Summerhayes at the end of July, 'full in the highest degree both of interest and beauty'. He was 'long' with her on 4 August and soon he was proposing that she sit for William Dyce, one of Gladstone's most approved artists, for a portrait commissioned by him. (She now appears demurely in the Aberdeen Art Gallery as 'Lady with a Coronet of Jasmine'.) He warned himself on 1 September:

'My thoughts of S require to be limited & purged.' By the 16th he was reading Tennyson's 'Princess' with her ('much & variously moved').[24]

Tennyson had in fact replaced Homer for the time as Gladstone's intense literary obsession. Very little of Gladstone's Homeric mania was of interest to anyone but Gladstone. But with Tennyson Gladstone engaged critically with a contemporary poet popular beyond precedent, already an icon of the Victorian age. He read 'Idylls' on 14 July; noting in the very midst of his budget preparations: 'Tennyson: who has grasped me with a strong hand.' An urge to acquit himself with a comprehensive statement including the earlier 'In Memoriam', 'Maud', and 'The Princess' asserted itself irresistibly. He wrote to the *Quarterly* editor proposing a review of Tennyson. 'I have never felt fanatical about him; but his late work has laid hold of me with a power that I have not felt, I ought to say not suffered, for many years.'[25]

From the evidence of his article in the October *Quarterly* Gladstone seems to have been gripped by a sense of dual vocation, an intersection of Tennyson the seasoned Liberal Laureate with himself as the new Liberal statesman in alliance as prophet and practitioner of a better age. His ideal was of Literature and Politics in moral harmony; but his main purpose was to enrol Tennyson, somewhat as he himself had been enrolled, in the ranks of the progressive movement of the day. His rebukes to Tennyson for behaviour unbecoming to this role, such as the warlike conclusion to 'Maud', or for aggressive postures to the French, or for patches of hysteria and morbidity, were all the more strict.[26] He defined Tennyson's 'business' in terms he would employ increasingly to define his own. 'Mr Tennyson is too intimately and essentially the poet of the nineteenth century to separate himself from its leading characteristics, the progress of physical science, and a vast commercial, mechanical, and industrial development.' He could not long 'either cross or lose its sympathies; for while he elevates, as well as adorns it, he is flesh of its flesh and bone of its bone'. Gladstone believed that it was Tennyson's 'business to do much towards the solution of that problem, so fearful in its magnitude, how to harmonise this new draught of external power and activity with the old and more mellow wine of faith, self-devotion, loyalty, reverence, and discipline'.[27]

For Gladstone the Arthurian romance in the 'Idylls' had 'every recommendation' for this purpose. 'It is national: it is Christian. It is also human in the largest and deepest sense …' Tennyson's poetry had 'raised the character and hopes of the age and the country which produced it'. Gladstone's obsessive and almost hysterical love-affair during these years with the Arthurian symbolism of the *Idylls* seems to have been a kind of emotional compensation for undergoing the dark night of Palmerstonism. On the way back to London on 14 October Gladstone was 'getting Guinevere by heart', partly as a personal testimony to an intimate sense of his own guilt in relation to Catherine,[28] but also as a kind of testimony of his own sense of vocation to raise the character and hopes of his age and his country.[29]

~

Much depended for Gladstone in the matter of raising the character and hopes of his age and country on the activities at that time of Richard Cobden. Primed by the Saint-Simonian free trader Michel Chevalier, Cobden planned to pull off a great stroke of international commercial concord by preparing the way for abolition of protective tariffs between France and Britain. Cobden saw in Gladstone his co-operative agent within the government. Gladstone would embody the elements of the commercial treaty in his budget for 1860. On 12 September Cobden arrived at Hawarden when there was 'further conv. with Mr Cobden on Tariffs & relations with France. We are closely and warmly agreed.' Their notion was to give an example to the world of the pacifying influence of free trade in a situation of tension between Britain and France.

There was no chance of legislating the project through the protectionist French chambers. It would have to be done by diplomatic treaty. The Emperor Napoleon was prone to sympathize with Saint-Simonian notions (the Suez Canal was another) and if he could be persuaded, he possessed the necessary constitutional powers. For Cobden it was an opportunity to pull off something grand outside the government he had proudly refused to join. There would be objections from purists that free trade was incompatible with commercial treaties; but that would be no serious impediment. For Gladstone it was the kind of grand exploit that marched well with his predisposition for heroic acts of beneficent executive power.

At Paris and then with the Emperor at Saint-Cloud Cobden began his negotiations. To the Emperor again at the Tuileries in December, Cobden explained that Mr Gladstone was 'anxious to prepare his Budget for the ensuing session of Parliament and it would be a convenience for him to be informed as soon as possible whether the French Government had decided to agree to a commercial treaty, as in that case he would make arrangements accordingly'. The Emperor returned assurances as to the principle of reciprocal free trade; it was a matter of settling questions of detail.[30]

As Cobden grappled in Paris with the questions of detail, Gladstone grappled with his own awkward questions. China was again on the agenda. Efforts by the powers to oblige the Chinese to renounce their isolation of assumed superiority and come within the comity of nations by establishing diplomatic relations, opening ports, and making arrangements about tariffs and trade, had led to conflict. Gladstone could not object in principle to the objects of the imposed Treaty of Tientsin. Besides, having swallowed the camel of Palmerston, he would not strain at the gnat of a coercive China policy.[31]

There were discussions on the Reform question with Lewis ('my great wish is to promote in a liberal spirit to get it to a settlement but a departmental instinct leads me towards preferring ceteris paribus a rating franchise').[32] There was Summerhayes, 'for whom I wish to exert myself'. There was a trip to Holyhead to witness the trials of Brunel's 12,000-ton *Great Eastern* and to attend a public dinner on board: 'the ship of an overpowering vastness'. Back in London he missed Summerhayes after a play at the Haymarket ('Rem in T[rafalgar] Square from 11½ to one.'). After dining at Herbert's on the 19th he met her at eleven and took her to Downing Street, 'espy. to see the pictures'. Back at Hawarden he discussed this congenial theme with Catherine, along with 'the State of the departed'.[33]

A gratifying interlude at Cambridge for an honorary degree marked a return to serious business with Cabinets preparing for the 1860 session. In the matter of the commercial treaty Cobden had laid the ground for diplomacy. Gladstone was copious with official instructions for the negotiators. Russell's persisting with his Reform Bill was an annoying distraction. Sweeping the remaining protective duties from the tariff would leave large holes in the revenue. Gladstone nonetheless felt sure this was the opportunity to clear away the biggest restrictive item, the paper duties. Thus he would redeem the implied pledge he had given in Manchester in 1853 and the pledge he had given to himself in 1856. There would need to be some nimble manoeuvring in the new estimates.

All such innocent estimations came abruptly to an end when Palmerston, flanked by Somerset and Herbert, demanded huge outlays on naval construction and fortifications in the face of an apprehended threat of invasion by France. (The French had constructed the first iron-clad warship, *La Gloire*.) Palmerston made clear that he would be neither denied nor deflected. Given the options of extra taxation or a loan to fund the biggest item in the charges, fortifications, Gladstone opted for a loan. That way his immediate exigencies would get some relief.

On this menacing note the political year closed. At a time of crucial consequence, when Gladstone particularly needed as much remissive capacity in the revenue as he could get, he was being burdened with huge extra demands that, moreover, in a kind of surreal way, contradicted the dimension of peace that was at the foundations of the commercial treaty project. He retreated with Argyll for repose with the Sutherlands at Trentham. Duchess Harriet had become a kind of Egeria for Gladstone, wise, soothing, knowledgeable (in 1859 she resumed the office of Mistress of the Robes for the Queen). It was not likely, however, that Gladstone was soothed there by reading the much talked-of book by Charles Darwin, *On the Origin of Species by Natural Selection*, that offered evolutionary explanations of natural phenomena incompatible with orthodox Christian readings of Holy Writ.

But the close of 1859 confronted Gladstone above all with the fact that he had passed his fiftieth year 'in this wayward world!' 'Grace & glory, sin & shame, fears, joys, pains, emotions, labours, efforts, what a marvel is this life, what a miracle the construction of it for our discipline?' On 29 December, his birthday, 'came into my room my wife and seven children'. 'Yet there is in me a resistance to the passage of Time as if I could lay hands on it & stop it: as if youth were yet in me & life & youth were one.'

~

To start the new year of 1860 on the right foot, and relieve his feelings on the naval and fortifications issues, Gladstone launched an attack on the education estimates. Government provision of *per capita* grants to schools claiming them on the basis of complying with the Education Department's Code now amounted to nearly a fifth of the entire civil expenditure of the state. In Robert Lowe, the new head of the Education Department, Gladstone had an eager collaborator. They had had earlier dealings in the areas of university and Civil Service reform, and Lowe's zeal both for economy and examinations was the key to the controversial Revised Code of 1861 whereby government grants were tied strictly to a retrospective principle of 'payment by results'.

It was also an alleviation of strained feelings for Gladstone to recur to the 'very first' motive that had guided him into his relationship with Palmerston. As one linked with Palmerston and Russell as the 'Italian party' in Cabinet, Gladstone gave Russell the benefit of his updated thinking. His earlier fears about the 'domineering' tendencies of Piedmont were now eclipsed by fears that Austria would intervene to ensure that the Villafranca arrangements as formalized at Zurich be not subverted by the surge of events threatening to topple the old order. He now argued that since Britain and France could never unite 'for any European purpose which is radically unjust', it followed that they represented the spirit of Europe's moral community; and their duty was to ensure that the free choice of the peoples of Tuscany, Parma, Modena, the Romagna, the Marches and Umbria as to the future of Italy be not nullified by Austrian intervention.

Gladstone's other main point was that British opinion had moved 'rapidly and steadily in favour of the Italians'. The government would have public support if it moved with the French to exclude Austria; and 'we ought cheerfully to stake in so noble a cause the existence of an administration'.[34] More than that: in conference with Russell Gladstone made it clear that in the 'improbable event of a war' should Austria defy the Anglo-French initiative, he would not reckon 'on confining our share of it within narrow bounds'. It was certainly a testimony to Gladstone's strength of italophile feeling that he should contemplate the contingency of war with such nonchalance. His combativeness owed much to his readiness to show a bold front to fulminations from Rome, which he thought constituted 'something of a challenge to all governments as such'.[35] Clarendon, much more shrewdly suspicious of Napoleon's plans that France should supplant Austria as the dominant power in Italy, was indignant at the 'present intention of Pam., J. R. and Gladstone' to 'cram this policy down the throats of their twelve colleagues'.[36]

The great fact of the Italian situation as Gladstone composed his glowing francophile and italophile sentiments was that the Piedmontese were managing with French connivance their takeover of the central Italian regions at the price of ceding Savoy and Nice to France, and giving the French a free hand to prop up the Pope in Rome and settle the future of Naples and Sicily. Given, however, Gladstone's strong predisposition, reinforced powerfully by the commercial treaty issue, to make the rosiest interpretation of French motives, he was in no position to react very convincingly against the consummation of Franco-Piedmontese connivance in March 1860 when Turin got its votes for union and Napoleon got Savoy and Nice. And though as far away as ever from any idea of the desirability of Italian unification, Gladstone was in an equally weak position to object when in May 1860 Cavour's connivance with Garibaldi's expedition to Sicily resolved the matter at the expense of the French as well as the Neapolitan governments. In due course, as the question faded as a primary concern, Gladstone marked the proclamation of the Kingdom of Italy in 1861 by apologizing for his tardy conversion to 'the yearning of Italians for political unity' and by lauding Palmerston and Russell as tutelary geniuses of a redeemed Italy.[37]

~

The immediate task in 1860 was securing the commercial treaty with France and then wrapping it protectively in his budget. Russell maddeningly got in the way by insisting on prior leeway for his Reform Bill.[38] To sceptics about the treaty such as Graham Gladstone extolled it as 'the operation for which I have been living. I have seen in it not merely the increase of influence for a peaceful solution of the Italian question, not merely the extension almost to consummation of the Tariff Reforms begun in 1842, but also the means of allaying the passions that menace danger, and of stemming the fears which in my opinion have done us so much discredit.'[39] His admiration for the Emperor Napoleon's statesmanlike sagacity continued undimmed. There was a curious mixture of predisposition to statist executive potency, excited perhaps by memories of the overpowering impression of the *Great Eastern*, that led Gladstone to remark of Napoleon to Brougham: 'For my own part at this moment, and on the given conditions of the case, I really desire no more than to live in the same boat with him, a stoker or sub-stoker on his engine.'[40] Sure enough, there was a gossipy echo of this remark in a letter from Argyll shortly after. 'There is a story going about town which has been repeated to me – "that Gladstone now expresses unbounded confidence in the Emperor, even to acting stoker in his train" – a weak invention of the enemy, but showing the direction of the attack ...'[41]

Of enemies there was no stint. Gladstone kept Cobden posted about resistance, insisting however that he was not 'desponding or indifferent'. 'But give us a Treaty carrying *bona fides* on its face (I do not doubt its being in the heart) and I have no fear of its fate.'[42] At a Cabinet on the 21 January Gladstone saw the treaty through. It was signed in Paris on the 23rd. 'My mind is relieved', he noted. 'I have now a standing ground & weapons in my hand.' 'The ascendancy of Gladstone', Trelawny observed, 'is daily more conspicuous.'[43] In other quarters there was lively speculation about Gladstone's intentions as to the paper duties. Monteagle, his old enemy at the Bank, assured Clarendon that, though Gladstone was 'audacious enough for many things', he would bet Clarendon 'any money' that Gladstone had 'not dared to think of *that*'.[44]

In fact Gladstone had dared to think of that. He pressed his plan for the big remissions on paper and wine in Cabinet. His audacity over the paper duties provoked stiff resistance. Then on the evening prior to his budget statement, Gladstone succumbed to congested lungs and a croaking throat. There was to be a postponement for four days. It was testimony to the drama of the occasion, and also a measure of Gladstone's public reputation, that *The Times* looked back to England's waiting in suspense for Peel's arrival from Rome in 1834 as the only comparable moment. Now, 'the most conspicuous disciple of that great statesman has his moment of concentrated attention'. The world was agog. What was to be the 'great secret of the impending Budget?' The bitter 9d. on the 1859 income tax? And what had the French Emperor 'given to Mr Gladstone to put in his bag'?[45]

From his sick-bed Gladstone conducted hectic last-minute negotiations with Palmerston for delay on the fortifications loan. The Prime Minister chose to be entirely amenable and soothingly arranged a convenient Cabinet at Gladstone's house. Palmerston's priority was for another Gladstonian budgetary triumph that would reflect well on the government. Unpicking Gladstone's more audacious projects could await the subsequent legislation.

Gladstonian budgetary triumph there was. The rhetoric was of the same theatricalized politics and the same morality play of finance as in the mythology launched in 1852. Thus the familiar pattern: 1853 the model and benchmark; the means and ends as defined by the catalogue of February and the doctrine of March 1856. In place of Disraeli the angel of the hosts of enchanters and magicians was now a disgraceful septennate of regression and feckless loss of control over the rate of expenditure. The commercial treaty allowed much scope for uplifting rhetoric on the theme of 'new departures' and the knitting 'together in amity these two great nations'. Gladstone offered tributes to the Emperor for his benign solicitude and to Cobden for his 'great and memorable service'.

Interests that would suffer from French competition were immediate and vocal. The treaty's benefits were as yet abstract and prospective. This would matter in the long run, when budgetary items became bills. In the short run, Gladstone's winning eloquence on the benefits of cheap light French wines, as opposed to traditional fortified wines, carried the day. When it came to the paper duties, however, Gladstone adopted a challenging stance. It was one thing to deprecate them as impediments to manufacture. It was quite another to extol the immense impulse abolition of the greatest of the 'taxes on knowledge' would give to 'cheap literature'. He celebrated the way in which abolition of the paper duties would reinforce the impact of the newspaper stamp duty in stimulating further a phenomenon 'highly creditable to the conductors of what is called the cheap press'. These were provocations as much to the Palmerstonian bulk of the Commons as to the Conservative Opposition. Gladstone compounded the offence thus caused by another bitter penny on the income tax, to 10d., with flourishes on the theme of how a 'round shilling' would solve so many fiscal problems, and contribute by striking away shackles on the arms of industry – 'no small, no feeble, and no transitory part of national defence'.[46]

Early indications were that Gladstone had carried it off. Palmerston put the best face he could on it. Bright was ecstatic. Greville recorded that Gladstone had 'achieved one of the greatest triumphs that the House of Commons ever witnessed'.[47] Trelawny thought his statement to be of 'extraordinary brilliancy'; and doubted if 'Gladstone's achievement was ever surpassed by any effort on a similar occasion'.[48] Gladstone sustained momentum through the early stages of the legislation. Greville concluded that the contest was over. 'He is now *the* great man.'

Greville concluded prematurely. The commercial treaty lost much of its lustre when the announcement of the impending annexations to France of Savoy and Nice touched off a francophobic spasm in British opinion. A popular Volunteer movement burgeoned, with Tennyson providing poetic inspiration. Gladstone's line that his budget was a budget of peace, and thus ever more needed, and that the commercial treaty was a necessary 'sedation' to the war passion, failed to stem the public mood of reaction. Critics broke cover. Most telling was resentment over the 'democratic' implications. Palmerston now made no secret of his hostility. Horsman spoke for many of his fellow Liberal MPs when he accused Gladstone of exposing a new career of 'agitating class interests'.[49] Old Peelite loyalties were compromised by Herbert's unwavering support for Palmerston's view that, in the light of China operations and European dangers, 'no sane man' would throw away so vital a resource in the 'permanent revenue' as the paper duties.[50]

Close fighting in Cabinet started on 24 April. Gladstone managed to save repeal in Cabinet, but found his temper severely tested in the Commons. Part of the intensity of Gladstone's early religious struggles to form his first vocation passed by political transference in the later 1840s and the beginning of the 1850s into something akin to a secular equivalent of spiritual pride. Already this had expressed itself virulently in the executive arrogance on display in the crisis of 1855. There were similar displays in the Commons in the 1860 session. A disposition to hector and drive provoked resentment and resistance. When, speaking on the Reform Bill on 3 May to 'an adverse & difficult House', and claiming 'some credit for my desire to see this question disposed of', Gladstone should not have been surprised to be greeted with '*Ironical cheers*'. But then, being Gladstone, he was. When in retreat at one of the many Clivedens that season, his Egeria, Duchess Harriet, took the opportunity to give Gladstone 'excellent advice in a manner delicate beyond all conception' about 'sensitiveness in the H. of C.'[51] Greville observed that Gladstone was 'said to have become subject to much excitement, and more bitter in the House of Commons than was his wont. The severe working of his brain and the wonderful success he has attained may account for this, and having had his way and triumphed over all opposition in the Cabinet, it is not strange that he should brook none anywhere else.'[52]

Indeed Gladstone did triumph over opposition in Cabinet. But when on 8 May he recommended his Paper Duties Repeal Bill he found himself speaking to 'a very adverse House'. Trelawny noted Disraeli's attack as vehement and *ad hominem*. Gladstone 'lay back white with rage'.[53] The bill scraped through by only nine votes, and went up to the Lords already morally defeated. Palmerston told the Queen that the Lords would perform 'a good public Service' if they threw it out.[54] On 21 May their lordships accepted Lord Derby's advice that the needs of the revenue were paramount, and returned the bill to the Commons, 193 to 104. The conventions were well understood that the power of the purse lay with the Commons and that the Lords might not amend a money bill. There was no modern precedent for sending a bill back.

Gladstone's outrage led him to talk of a *coup d'état*. It made him, conspicuously, a Radical hero. He told Robertson: 'This is a most serious matter, 100 times as much so as would have been the mere rejection of the Bill in the House of Commons.' He would have to consider carefully 'what I should endeavour to urge upon my colleagues'.[55] On the 22nd a 'rather stiff' Cabinet failed to accede to demands by Gladstone, backed by Russell and Gibson, for something decisive by way of visiting the displeasure of the Commons on the Lords.

~

Wrangling in Cabinet long persisted about quite how to respond to the Lords. Wide differences of opinion ruled out 'decided action'. Gladstone deprecated a Radical agitation demanding that the bill be sent back up to the Lords backed by adequate menaces. A series of declaratory resolutions asserting the claims of the Commons would be put to the House. Gladstone hoped that 'we have turned the corner'. But nothing could in his eyes attenuate the magnitude of the event. 'Notwithstanding the Treaty', he wrote to Bright, 'notwithstanding the progress towards freedom & peace in Italy, it has left, for us, a great black mark on 1860; & both the H. of C. and its members are smaller than they were.'[56]

Impasse on the question of the Lords turned Gladstone aggressive on the fortifications front. Palmerston, emboldened by the turn of events, brushed him aside. By early June Gladstone noted: 'My resignation *all but* settled.'[57] Argyll mediated and Palmerston pointed out the evils and hazards that would attend on resignation. People would say, however unjustly, that Gladstone was 'afraid of the financial consequences of his budget, & running away from them'; and that, moreover, 'out of office he would be thrown into Companionship with Bright which would be Ruin to him as a Public Man'.[58] Gladstone diverted his attack by keeping his vendetta against the Bank turning over with punitive measures to deprive the Bank of a large part of the fees it charged for managing the Debt.[59] Then Russell decided to abandon his Reform Bill. Gladstone argued that the government, having come in on Reform, should resign. Palmerston interpreted this as 'to cover under a general Resignation his own failure as to Budget, & to escape from being a Party to a Fortification Loan'.[60]

Thereupon, Gladstone returned to aggression on the Lords' front. The proposed declaratory resolutions he held to be inadequate. He asked Palmerston to apprise Her Majesty that he could no longer continue to carry on the business of his department. Palmerston earnestly entreated Gladstone to reconsider. Neither Argyll nor Gibson was prepared to follow. Gladstone reconsidered, subject to a stipulation that once the matter of the resolutions was disposed of, he would have personal freedom to take such steps as might be feasible to vindicate the rights of the Commons. This effort he launched on 5 July, with an assault on the 'gigantic innovation' and 'great encroachment of the Lords, the 'most gigantic and the most dangerous that has been attempted in our times'.[61]

Gladstone's vindication fell flat. Palmerston could go ahead and settle arrangements for the Fortifications Bill. 'Impossible to say whether Gladstone will go or stay.'[62] Gladstone stayed. There were transactions through Argyll and Herbert that he was able to construe as concessions. Palmerston's construing was less flattering. 'He evidently has throughout been playing a game of Brag & trying to bully the Cabinet & finding he has failed he has given in.'[63]

Palmerston had already made contingency plans to survive the 'surgical operation' of a resignation or resignations. Derby and Disraeli conveyed an undertaking that 'if Mr Gladstone were to propose a democratic Budget making a great transfer of burthens from indirect to direct Taxation, and if, the Cabinet refusing its concurrence, Mr Gladstone were to retire, the Conservative Party would give the Government substantial support'; and that 'no step would in such case be taken to produce a change of Government'.[64] To this pledge the Queen was privy.

The Exchequer would have been offered to Lewis, and the Queen, as Clarendon assured Lewis, would have accepted Gladstone's resignation 'with satisfaction'. Lewis had the pleasure of responding to Clarendon that Gladstone had backed down on fortifications because the Cabinet took 'the measure of his foot'.[65] Palmerston assured the Queen that any future obstruction from Gladstone would follow the same pattern: 'ineffectual opposition and ultimate acquiescence'.[66]

In any case by now Gladstone was in retreat in the Commons. On 20 July he suffered on the Savings Bank Monies Bill his '*first* defeat on a measure of finance in the H. of C.' There were still to be many squabbles and testy exchanges between the Prime Minister and his Chancellor of the Exchequer, but, after a Cabinet on 25 July that settled the 'distinct basis' of the fortifications scheme, their antagonism faded with the approaching end of the session.

~

On the domestic front matters were mixed. Gladstone was gratified that Catherine finally visited Cliveden. 'Your account of the place and of its mistress are *very* interesting and I am very glad that you have at last made out the visit.' It seemed 'almost unnatural that you should not have been there'.[67] Perhaps Catherine took a different view. She responded to her husband's relationship with Duchess Harriet with what has been termed a 'pragmatic detachment'.[68] She was aware of her inability to meet her husband's intellectual demands; she was not prepared to compromise an attachment that served to the advantage of his public career. But the big family problem of the day was Henry Glynne's revived matrimonial ardour.

As so often happened with Gladstone, solemn public transactions proceeded majestically against a backdrop of domestic scuffling. There were determined females prepared to do right by Henry Glynne's brood of motherless daughters. But what agitated the Gladstones was a renewed possibility of a Glynne heir, which would undo all the expensive arrangements made to save the Hawarden estate. It was all 'a great care' to Catherine. By mobilizing lawyers a few days before his budget statement in February 1860 Gladstone gave Catherine 'more comfort and support respecting Henry's error'. A first female was repelled, but a second soon took her place. The prospect of a scandalous breach of promise case began to take shape. Papers had to be prepared for Sir Stephen's signature. At some trouble and cost Gladstone eventually steered clear.

All such scuffling was suspended on the news of the death of Aberdeen. On 21 December: '*To Ld Aberdeen's funeral: no common occasion.*' This was the biggest personal break with the political past since Peel's death more than ten years earlier. As Gladstone later put it, Aberdeen was 'the man in public life of all others whom I have *loved*. I say it emphatically, *loved*. I have *loved* others but never like him.'[69] Aberdeen's passing marked a point of disjunction, with aggravated symptoms. On completing his 51st year Gladstone declared: 'I cannot believe it. I feel within me the rebellious unspoken word. I will not be old. The horizon enlarges, the sky shifts, around me. It is an age of shocks: a discipline so strong, so manifold, so rapid and whirling, that only when it is at an end, can I hope to comprehend it.'

~

Looking back from 1897, Gladstone designated the sessions of 1860 and 1861 as 'the most trying part of my whole political life', his 'nadir in public estimation'.[70] The pattern of events in 1861 and largely in 1862 continued that set in 1860. Wrangling over charges for fortifications and iron-plated warships persisted unabated. Indeed, on Herbert's resignation from ill-health in 1861, he was succeeded at the War Office by the unforgiving Cornewall Lewis. In the matter of a meagre surplus in 1860, Palmerston, with a renewed compact with the Conservatives in his pocket, did not flinch from warning Gladstone that, were the Commons to jib as they had done in 1860, the Chancellor of the Exchequer would have to fight his own battle. In a curious twist to the constitutional conventions, the Prime Minister thought 'it right to say beforehand' that he did not intend that the fate of his government should 'depend upon the Decision which Parliament may come to on your proposal'.[71] 'But I must hang on', Gladstone confided to Catherine '– port is close at hand.'[72]

Despite a furious 'tug of war' in Cabinet, Lucy Lyttelton observed on 30 April: 'Uncle W. in rollicking spirits over his Budget'.[73] The paper duties crisis was resolved in May 1861 when Gladstone protectively wrapped around it a penny reduction back to 9d. on the income tax and dared the Lords to reject. There were not a few lords ready to take up the dare, but Derby advised the inexpediency of further resistance. Gladstone's triumph provoked a 'tirade' in the *Quarterly* from Lord Robert Cecil, MP for Stamford and rising star among the younger Tories, accusing Gladstone of playing Bright's game and of helping to undermine the limited parliamentary franchise and the House of Lords, the only barriers holding off the 'uncurbed dominion of the multitude'.[74] On the other hand, the 'cheap press' hailed Gladstone as their man. It was indeed in the *Telegraph*, the first London penny daily and the most formidable of the titles stemming from the stamp tax abolition of 1855, that its editor, Edward Levy, would promote Gladstone as 'the People's William'.

~

The new year of 1861 had been marked by a letter from John Bright. He put it to Gladstone that the 'men whose minds are full of the traditions of the last century – your *Chief* & your *Foreign Minister*' – would 'still cling to the past', and 'seek to model the present upon it'. But a 'new policy & a wiser, & a higher morality',

Bright asserted, were 'sighed for by the best of our people, & there is a prevalent feeling that *you* are destined to guide that wiser policy, & to teach that higher morality'. Bright was 'quite sure that the Towns, & our great populations, will regard the Govt. with increased favour if they see them having some regard to the pressure of taxes upon them'.[75]

In his cautiously circumspect reply Gladstone chose to dwell on the rather marginal matter of talks to reduce Anglo-French naval rivalry. Did this demureness conceal a reluctance to engage squarely and candidly with questions that bore all too directly on enlarging horizons and shifting skies? In invoking the role of guide and teacher, Bright defined with tolerable accuracy Gladstone's own sense of the purposes of his vocation. That accuracy did not make the definition the more commendable to Gladstone. It touched too bluntly on sensitive personal and political nerve-ends. Bright's theme of 'Towns, & our great populations' was all too disturbingly consequential for Gladstone not only in the hitherto rather distanced sense of what the 'advanced intelligence' of Manchester in 1853 represented for him, but also now in the very immediate and painful context of his contemplating giving up his Oxford University seat.

It would not be long, indeed, before deputations from towns and great populations waited on Gladstone with urgent requisitions that he represent them. He faced once more the same perplexity as came upon him after he comprehended that the 'work was gone' of his first vocation. 'This whirl which carries me off balance' was the forming of his new vocation in the early 1850s. Now the 'shocks' caused by subterranean shifts and pressures were again impinging upon his consciousness in a confusing and incomprehensible manner. To an alarmed consciousness of rapid and whirling movement, Gladstone instinctively imposed stasis in a recurrence of his pattern of reluctance to let go of old links of stability and safe anchorages.

Thus Gladstone's instinct would be to evade rather than embrace the more ambitious implications of Bright's appeal, for all that it addressed – it might be thought, rather helpfully – Gladstone's own professed ambition of 1856 to engage with 'opinion'. That there was an 'opinion' in being attendant on financial and taxation matters, and in sighing for guidance in a higher and wiser morality, was testified to by Bright himself. But battles over finance were fought in Cabinet, not in the press, let alone on the platform or in the streets. Paper duties repeal was, as Gladstone said, 'a great event for me'. But it remained essentially a financial event. J. A. Froude, wishing to place *Fraser's Magazine* at the disposal of 'the only statesman in whom since Sir Robert Peel's death' he had full confidence, put the case to Gladstone that he should mobilize support in the popular press.[76] Gladstone replied cautiously that 'the whole subject of working through the press for the support of the measures of the financial department is very new to me'. He would, however, he assured Froude, 'bear the subject in mind'.[77] Though

Gladstone praised 'what is called the cheap press', it is clear from his response to the advances of his prompter, Thornton Hunt of the *Daily Telegraph*, that he had not as yet fleshed out ideas of how to go about reciprocating that paper's celebration of him as 'the People's William'.[78]

~

'My life is a life from hand to mouth', Gladstone complained; 'I have always too much to do, & always a great deal undone.'[79] About Oxford reform he continued in great addlement. 'I have no business to be an Oxford Reformer', he told Thorold Rogers, the Cobdenite political economist, 'more than my butler has to amend my manners.'[80] Memories of Oxford times and Church vocation were stirred on 20 March when he met Manning for the first time since 1851. The initiative was Manning's, with a view to exchanging letters. 'Under external smoothness and conscientious kindness', Gladstone felt, 'there lay a chill indescribable.'[81] To Keble Gladstone confided his distress at the way his efforts to resolve the church rates problem were ungratefully received by his university constituents; and how 'very uneasy' he was 'at the incessant war & strife on these things'.[82] Much the same weariness with the incessant war and strife in Cabinet no doubt contributed to Gladstone's remark on an Easter visit to the ailing Herbert at Wilton 'of my hope that for different reasons we should both be "out" soon'.[83]

Already Gladstone had received requisitions from two deputations urging that he abandon Oxford for the enlarging horizons and shifting skies of the modern world – in one case the industrial West Riding of Yorkshire, in the other the new division of South Lancashire. A tempting City of London seat had been vacated by Lord John's elevation to the Lords as Earl Russell. Gladstone declined all requisitions.[84] A conclave in July 1861 with his chief Oxford supporters concluded that he 'ought not to stir'. Palmerston wanted to keep him in Oxford; and Brand, the Chief Whip, was deputed to make this clear to the Oxford people. Still, it was certainly indicative, apropos of towns and great populations, that Gladstone should have made occasion to extend his condolences to the Radical MP and Leeds journalist Edward Baines on the 'unhappy' failure of his bill to extend the borough franchise.[85] Bishop Wilberforce was struck in conversation at Cliveden on 18 March by the degree to which Gladstone was 'now strong' for an increase of the franchise.[86] It was for Gladstone a poignant consideration that the two Peelite comrades most favourable to franchise extension died that year: Herbert in August, Graham in October. A turn of interest by Gladstone in the direction of Reform would have about it at this stage a certain logic. It was no longer an irrelevance as it had been in 1859, or a nuisance, as it had been with Russell. And there were conceivable circumstances, confronting the Lords and the serried masses of Palmerstonians and Derbyites, when opinion 'out of doors' might advantageously be stimulated.

What was, however, decidedly an irrelevance and a nuisance from Gladstone's point of view at this juncture was the emergence in the Commons of the Ionian question slanted in such a way as to present it as part of the 'Eastern question' at large. Over the Principalities in 1858 Gladstone had denounced the Conservatives for 'falling into the groove of Lord Palmerston's Eastern policy'. Now he found himself slipping in to that same groove. Evaporation of Gladstone's former intense criticism of the Crimean policy was manifested eloquently in his silence on the various scandals of Turkish repression in the Balkans, and especially in the atrocious massacres of Maronite Christians in Syria and Lebanon. These registered precisely the onset of the 'convulsive volcanic disintegration' of the Ottoman Empire that he had so accurately predicted.

In tetchy justification of his not applying now to the Ionians the doctrine of liberty he had applied to the Italians, Gladstone stuck to his 'Crimean' brief that the independence and integrity of the Ottoman Empire was a capital interest of Britain and Europe. He insisted that it would be 'nothing less than a crime against the safety of Europe', as connected with the state and course of the great Eastern question, 'if England were to surrender the protectorate of the Ionian Islands for the purpose of uniting them to Free Greece'. The delicate bearings of such a move in the 'Greek provinces of Turkey' ruled out simple solutions.[87]

~

Meanwhile, another aspect of foreign affairs impinged. Abraham Lincoln's election as President of the United States in November 1860 proved to be the trigger setting off the civil war between the Union and the breakaway slave-holding southern states that formed the Confederacy. At breakfast Sir John Acton was 'most satisfactory' on the matter: that is to say, he deplored the obstinacy of President Lincoln in persisting with his hopeless project of restoring the Union by force.[88] For all that he detested the principle of slavery, as Gladstone assured Duchess Harriet, he considered the war to be 'without cause' and hence foolish and wicked.[89] The idea began to occupy his mind of the government's offering good offices to the parties in the war. The battle of Bull Run in July 1861 seemed to indicate beyond any doubt that the eleven seceded states forming the Confederacy could not be coerced back into the Union. Gladstone happened to be at Windsor when the Castle was buzzing with the news of the arrest by the United States authorities of the Confederate agents Mason and Slidell on the British ship *Trent*. 'The Queen & Prince spoke much of the American news: & in the Anti-Northern sense.'[90] Between them, the Cabinet and the Prince – now rather mysteriously ailing – softened and abridged a characteristically pugnacious draft dispatch by Russell on the matters of apologies and reparations, with Gladstone as courier shuttling between Westminster and Windsor. The Prince's emending of the Cabinet's emendation of Russell's original draft was indeed his last official act. He died of Windsor's bad drains on 13 December.

The Report of the Secretary of the Treasury of the United States in 1862 Gladstone thought 'fitter for a swindler than a Minister', as he told Russell; and surely meant to drive the Americans 'by financial terror into abandonment of the war'. This kind of consideration bore heavily on Gladstone's general appreciation of the situation in the conflict between the Union and the Confederacy. By the summer of 1862 that appreciation had expanded from advocacy of British good offices for mediation to advocacy of European intervention. 'Europe' had made Italy. Now what was needed in the American case, as Gladstone recommended to Palmerston, was Europe's applying in 1862 against the ambitions of the Washington regime the same salutary pressures as had been successfully applied in 1860 to the ambitions of the Vienna regime.

In this idea of some kind of beneficial intervention Gladstone reflected a growing sentiment in the political class. The strategic advantage of the Confederacy over the Union seemed decisive: the Union had to win the war; the Confederacy had merely to avoid defeat. Nothing since Bull Run a year before gave any convincing evidence of will or capacity in the North to undertake so enormous and necessarily lengthy and bloody a task. Lincoln's resolute intent in the face of an irresolvable stalemate seemed a kind of bloodthirsty obstinacy. Much of the Union's natural support in Britain remained mute or lukewarm so long as Lincoln resisted the drastic recourse of emancipating the Negro slaves. Hostility in Europe to the 'democratic' North and Lincoln, and worries about the potentially disturbing power of a unified United States, joined conveniently with humanitarian sentiment.

Gladstone partook, more or less, of these sentiments, to which he added anxiety about the building up of a possibly explosive situation in Lancashire, starved of cotton imports by the Union blockade of the southern states. In Manchester serious incidents of unrest and protest among unemployed cotton operatives broke out in June and again in September. On 18 July Gladstone pressed Palmerston not to commit himself against a policy of mediation. Palmerston accordingly reserved the government's freedom of action. Gladstone reported to Catherine: 'Lord P. has come exactly to my wish about some early representation of a friendly kind to America if we can get France & Russia to join'.[91]

Manchester happened at that time to be very apropos of Gladstone's wider purposes. He went up there and to Stockport in April at the invitation of the Association of Lancashire and Cheshire Mechanics' Institutes to test the waters of 'out of doors' in general and with a view to retreating possibly from Oxford in particular. Ever since his first *frisson* at talking to the '*people*' in 1853 Gladstone held Manchester in special esteem. Now it represented not only 'advanced intelligence' but a centre of 'distress and crisis' under the pressure of the cotton famine. His address on 23 April at the Free Trade Hall was distinguished for evidences of an important new stage in his view of the development of an expanding popular dimension of advanced intelligence manifesting itself in 'real political and social progress' and 'admirable patience and comprehension'. After all, he had made quite clear in the debate over Russell's Reform Bill in 1860 that he did 'not admit that the working man, regarded as an individual, is less worthy of the suffrage than any other class'; nor did he regard a £6 borough rating franchise as dangerous; and nor did he think enfranchising a quarter of adult males 'very unreasonable'.[92]

But the nature of Gladstone's relationship to this democracy would ever remain idiosyncratic. His role was that of guide and teacher. There would be no change in his assumption that advanced intelligence as popularly expanded by patience, comprehension and mental improvement would be a matter essentially of improved capacity to respond adequately and deferentially to initiatives derived from superior 'insight' and credentials issued from on high. Thus, when Gladstone informed the Mechanics of Lancashire and Cheshire that the nineteenth century was the 'age of humane and liberal laws', and the 'age of extended franchises', the 'age of free trade' and the 'age of steam and railways', he stressed also that it was the 'age of warmer loyalty and more firmly established order'; and was likewise the 'age of examinations'.[93]

Even so brief an excursion among the people on Gladstone's part could now touch nervous susceptibilities about his 'playing Bright's game'. Conflict over budgets was now replaced by conflict over platforms. To Palmerston, it seemed that Gladstone and Cobden were agitating in concert. Disraeli likewise protested that Gladstone's summoning the genius of the people was a very serious impeachment of the prerogatives of the Commons. Gladstone deprecated 'in all good humour' being 'classed with Mr Bright or even Mr Cobden'.[94] In the House he felt it expedient to disown efforts by the 'economico-radical party' to recruit him. But when, as a consequence of 'economico-radical' machinations on the Tyne, an invitation came from the Mayor of Newcastle to a tour and a grand reception early in October to pay tribute to his services to the causes of economy, peace, and social progress, Gladstone felt he could hardly decline.

~

The press of business meanwhile took its toll. There were grapplings with Palmerston about a suitable memorial to the deceased Prince Consort. Gladstone's producing a budget in 1862 without a surplus caused a '*sensation*' – 'a general buzz I have heard around me' – 'but in a most friendly House'. The French panic was over. 'Fortifications got their first blow.' This was Gladstone's most low-key statement since 1854. After the alarums and excursions of 1860 and 1861 something of an equilibrium had been attained in Cabinet. He kept the income tax at 9d. and offered no remissions. He accounted his first achievement as 'Minister of Finance' as having halted the growth of public expenditure.[95] By June of 1862 Gladstone discerned that the 'tide had turned' on fortifications.

Another project of public concern to which Gladstone gave assiduous attention (and personal investment) was the beginning of the London Metropolitan underground rail system, inaugurated in May 1862. 'Mrs Dale', alias Summerhayes, remained both a comfort and a distraction, 'in whom my interest does not flag'.[96] Catherine laid the foundation stone for the chapel of the new House of Charity ('with deep interest for C. G.: & spoke at the meeting'). The Trustees of the St Barnabas House abandoned the former workhouse in Rose Street and moved around the corner to the more commodious quarters at No. 1 Greek Street, Soho Square, recently vacated by the Metropolitan Board of Works.[97]

At Penmaenmawr Gladstone diverted himself and his brother John Neilson, lately a widower, by dabbling in spiritualism and table-turning. At Hawarden 'chill news' came of Willy's '*second* class' in Classical Moderations. Chill news of tribulations in Lancashire prompted the Gladstones to contribute to relief of distress. He devised plans for providing work for six unemployed men in the park over the winter at 12s. a week. At the Castle Catherine took in ten factory girls to be trained for service. Catherine was involved also in a scheme to set up a soup kitchen in Blackburn, where there had been riots after the sentencing of poachers. Distress was the theme also of reports from Ireland; more generally diffused, but not less thought-provoking. Gladstone discerned that 'among other objects in the distance, Ireland is again slowly growing into a political difficulty'.[98]

~

Lancashire and its distress was much on Gladstone's mind as he prepared for the Tyne visit. So was America. The whole of their present proceedings, he told Argyll, were 'an exaggeration and caricature of such follies as we of the old World have unhappily from time to time committed'. There were difficulties about mediation, problems about taking the first step; 'but I cannot subscribe to the opinion of those who think that Europe is to stand silent without limit of time and witness these horrors and absurdities'.[99] Both Palmerston and Russell were coming to the same mind that the time was fast approaching when joint mediation with France and Russia might be proposed to the Americans. To Gladstone it was clear that the 'progress of Confederate Arms' was such that, if it continued for even a short time, President Jefferson Davis might fairly be authorized 'with something like justice to ask of us prompt recognition' of the Confederacy. It was desirable not to be brought to that step without first having offered our good offices and 'made a friendly effort to induce the North to recede'.

A second material point was that the population of Lancashire had borne their sufferings with a fortitude and patience 'exceeding all example, and almost all belief'. But if such resignation should even once give way to excitement, 'our position in the face of America, and our influence for good might be seriously affected'; and it might appear that we were interfering in our own interests rather than in the 'general interests of humanity and peace'. French policy in Mexico was an awkward problem, in that, with a view to rescuing French investments from debt repudiation, they were taking advantage of the Union's being distracted to install as Emperor that Archduke Ferdinand Maximilian, baulked of his Lombardo-Venetian kingdom; hence the necessity of having Russia as a party to establish the requisite moral authority. Gladstone promised to give satisfaction at the Newcastle event, which, he explained, arose out of the French treaty, was harmless, and approved by Henry Brand.[100]

Thus Lancashire, the Tyne and America all tended to push Gladstone in a direction that was a bonus as far as his relations with Palmerston were concerned, but which in any event represented crucially for him a compelling occasion to assert himself boldly as guide and teacher, to begin reciprocation of services offered him in the press. It was no longer, as at Manchester in 1853 or even in 1862, to be a tentative exploratory reconnaissance. 'The case of Lancashire is deplorable', he wrote to Arthur Gordon, 'but even this is a trifle in the eye of humanity compared with the wholesale slaughter that is going on, and its thoroughly purposeless character, since it has long been (I think) clear enough that Secession is virtually an established fact, & that Jeff. Davis & his comrades have made a nation.'[101]

Gladstone departed with Catherine on 4 October for the Tyne tour. For all that Lancashire was but a trifle in the eye of humanity, there was much to be said about what it signified for the fellow-countrymen of the Lancastrians. As for America, he contemplated an overture to a grand gesture in the style of Canning: the calling of an Old World into being to redress the balance of the New.

8

Embracing the Millions: Lancashire and the Tyne, 1862–1864

'My life has not been inactive. But of what kind has been its activity? It seems to have been & to be a series of efforts to be and do what is beyond my natural force.'

Gladstone, diary entry, 31 December 1863

At Gilside, near Gateshead, the seat of William Hutt, MP, one of the prime movers of the scheme to devise a 'triumphant visit' to the Tyne, Gladstone 'reflected further' on 7 October on what he should say 'about Lancashire & America: for both these subjects are critical'. President Lincoln's Emancipation Proclamation had been published in *The Times* the previous day. Lincoln proclaimed freedom for all slaves in seceded states which should not have returned to the Union by 1 January. *The Times* considered that this form of blatant inducement was 'more contemptible than it is wicked'.[1] Gladstone was in perfect accord with that sentiment. By proffering such a bribe Lincoln made slavery the cement of the Union. In any case Gladstone was immune to what he called 'negrophilist' enthusiasm. He went at six 'to a crowded & enthusiastic dinner of nearly 500. I was obliged to make a long oration which was admirably borne.'

What Gladstone had to say about the French treaty and free trade was predictable and innocent. But his handling of the Lancashire cotton famine exposed a degree of moral sensitivity that his purist economic admirers later deprecated as 'excessive and impolitic indignation'.[2] Relief committees and private charities were all very well, but 'remember that it is the sacred right of the people – a lien constituted by law upon the property which is liable for the purpose of supporting them'; and Gladstone hoped that any relief given would be entirely devoid of any hint of reproach or circumstance of humiliation 'on account of misfortunes, of which they are as innocent as children, but which they have borne like heroes'.

This invocation of the duties of property had something of an accent of the old Toryism about it; and when Gladstone then got on to the delinquencies of certain mill-owners he spoke very much as a county magnate who had lately presided at the Mold agricultural dinner and who delighted in playing on Sir Stephen's behalf the benign feudal lord at Hawarden. He stigmatized men in the manufacturing class who in the name of the rights of property and mere profit and loss were so 'insensible to the solemn and sacred claims of their noble work-people' as to sell off their cotton stocks and shut down their works. Gladstone pointed to the public indignation and charges of 'moral guilt' that would be directed against 'some great landowner' who exploited the rights of property in the same manner.

After this outburst Gladstone turned to the American question in a much more restrained tone. He could not say the big things he wanted to say. He could not advocate mediation because the Cabinet had not formally decided on it. But he could usefully teach and guide public opinion by pointing out authoritatively the signal and capital fact that made mediation so logical and desirable. For the Americans he pleaded a neutral temper and an avoidance of any exultation at the patently obvious and inescapable fact that their Union was dismembered beyond all hope of repair. And as he could not mention mediation, so he could not mention diplomatic recognition of the Confederacy. But, in the spirit of the doctrine he had urged on Palmerston back on 2 May, here was a public opinion that needed to be stimulated in the right direction on a prospective issue. 'We may have our own opinions about slavery' – Gladstone's was that the Negroes would be better off dealing with their own masters than dealing with the Federal government – 'we may be for or against the South; but there is no doubt that Jefferson Davis and other leaders of the South have made an army; they are making, it appears, a navy; and they have made what is more than either, they have made a nation (*Loud cheers*).'[3]

It happened that G. J. Holyoake, the secularist campaigner and journalist, was deputising for the reporter for the Electric Telegraph Company, and appended to a condensed version of Gladstone's words, '(The announcement caused great sensation.)'[4] This he later described as 'too strong'. There was, rather, 'a general movement as of unexpectedness, and "surprise" would have been a more appropriate word'; but there was no time to wait for it, 'and the "sensational" sentence was all over London before the speech was ended', setting the 'political commentators on fire'.[5]

Gladstone caused 'surprise' at Newcastle because he seemed to be manipulating or preparing opinion for mediation or even recognition, not because he was implicitly pro-southern. Opinion in Lancashire was predominately pro-southern,[6] and it was not likely to be less so on Tyneside. Offence was taken in pro-northern circles. Bright concluded that Gladstone's mind was too unstable for him to lead a party or a nation successfully. 'He was born of a great slave-holding family', was his verdict to Cobden, '& I suppose the taint is ineradicable.'[7] Mill apologized to the American historian J. L. Motley for Gladstone's having said things 'which I very much regret'.[8] Gladstone himself later listed his words as a 'palpable error which was of a very grave description'.[9] But at the time he was under no such burden of regret. He explained to Russell that 'according to some of the newspapers, some words which I have used at Newcastle respecting America have a wider sense than I intended'.[10] Russell eagerly looked forward to leading a mediation and being a 'second Canning' – all the more so, perhaps, because of his embarrassment at having been responsible for not detaining ram No.290 at Birkenhead dockyard from slipping away and converting itself into the devastating Confederate commerce-raider, *Alabama*. *The Times* commented that Gladstone had 'only made a statement considerably within the truth'.[11] Palmerston was waiting for one more decisive Confederate victory as the cue to go ahead with the French and the Russians. The battle awaited – Antietam, 17 September 1862 – proved, however, to be the beginning of the end of the Confederacy's fortunes.

Even so, that fact was by no means obvious in October 1862. Gladstone chose to interpret Antietam as a wholesome check on the tendencies of the overconfident Confederates to produce obstacles to peace. Cobden himself countenanced the notion of mediation.[12] Robert E. Lee, the Confederate commander, would still be victorious at Fredericksburg and Chancellorsville. Palmerston, however, advised by Cornewall Lewis and Argyll, adopted a more reserved and cautious position.

That was as yet nothing to Gladstone as he prepared to play his leading part in the great Tyneside theatre of politics. To the Tynesiders Lancashire was remote and America in the dimmest distance. The man being produced for them to salute as their hero was at hand. After an address at Gateshead on 8 October the party 'embarked in the midst of a most striking scene which was prolonged & brightened as we went down the river at the head of a fleet of some 25 steamers amidst the roar of guns & with the banks lined or dotted above & below with great multitudes of people'. Holyoake recalled thousands of miners coming up from the pits of Durham and Northumberland, fired by promises that they 'would see a sight in England, which they might not soon see again – a Chancellor of the Exchequer who was known to have a conscience'. 'Great numbers' succeeded in shaking hands with Gladstone as he embarked on the *Harry Clasper* (named after a famous Tyne oarsman). Men swam before the vessel for considerable distances; 22 miles of river bank were lined with people, women holding up their children to give them a glimpse of the great man. 'The expedition ended at six, & I had as many speeches as hours. Such a pomp I probably shall never again witness: circumstances have brought upon me what I do not in any way deserve.' Gladstone admired the 'daring and comprehensive' works transforming the Tyne: the Tyne docks, Wellington Quay, Wallsend, Jarrow, South and North Shields and Tynemouth. They returned to dine at Gilside. 'C. went through everything in a wonderful manner.' Catherine indeed was enchanted. She would ever after insist that this was the first occasion on which William was accorded anything like the recognition he deserved.

From Newcastle and Sunderland on 9 October the party progressed to Middlesbrough and then to Darlington, Mr Henry Pease, MP for South Durham, in attendance. 'Middlesbrough was as warm or if possible even warmer.' More steamboat processions and an 'incessant flood' of information. 'The labour however is too much: giddiness came over me for a moment while I spoke at Sunderland, and I had to take hold of the table.' Gladstone was 'most happy to lie down for 15 minutes at Mr Vaughan's in Middlesbrough'. The couple retired to Upleatham as guests of the Lord-Lieutenant of Yorkshire North Riding, Lord Zetland.

~

By the 15th the Gladstones were back at Hawarden. There was much reflecting to be done. But none of it told in the direction of retractive caution. On the way back, at York, Gladstone dared something he had not dared on the Tyne: something that really would have stirred a 'sensation'. He invoked Canning's name and authority with a variation on Canning's famous boast of 1826: 'We may say that we turn to a country of the Old World to redress and compensate the calamities and failure of the New. (Cheers).'[13] This was as good as saying 'mediation'. All the more was Gladstone annoyed when arriving back in London he found that Lewis had circulated a memorandum arguing against Russell's plans for mediation. Gladstone immediately composed his own counterblast against Lewis, stressing the 'European' point that one of the noblest distinctions of the nineteenth century had been a 'gradual and sensible growth of what might be rudely called an international opinion' analogous to public opinion. It was the 'moral force' of that international opinion that had nullified the Treaty of Zurich of 1859; now it could be mobilized to bring the Washington government to its senses as it had brought the Vienna government. Further delay would make loss 'more probable than gain'. Public peace might well be compromised by the distress in Lancashire. As the people of England were being 'rapidly drawn into Southern sympathies' the more difficult it would be for the British government to appear to maintain a 'friendly and impartial aspect in any proceeding'. And as to the question of slavery: any mediation from which the South would ostensibly, 'though perhaps not really', be the gainer should involve 'every moral influence with a view to the mitigation, or, if possible, the removal, of slavery'; and the later mediation was left, and the more the south saw the result in terms of its own 'daring and tenacity', the less easy would this be to achieve.[14]

In society Gladstone made no secret of his views as to the *fait accompli* of secession. He made himself knowledgeable about the most suitable new border between the Union and the Confederacy once Lincoln had come to his senses.[15] Stanley observed his holding forth at the Cowpers': 'He thought Virginia must be divided, and probably Tennessee likewise.'[16] To remonstrators he turned a blandly unapologetic front. Harriet Sutherland, indignant at Gladstone's sentiments on the 'purposelessness' of the war, was informed that 'if Mr Lincoln's lawless proclamation[s] continue for much longer & the war with them, I am afraid that destruction, which may be but for the moment, must become permanent and final'.[17] Many Dissenters, with proud memories of the Anti-Slavery movement, were offended. To Newman Hall, the most prominent Congregationalist divine in London and often lately in Gladstone's counsels on matters such as church rates and degree subscriptions at Oxford, Gladstone insisted that 'negro emancipation cannot be effected in any sense favourable to black or white, by the bloody hand of war, especially of civil war'; and he lamented deeply 'the act of those who, not swept along like the Northern Americans by a natural & scarcely avoidable excitement, undertake from an impartial position to favour in the interests of the negro the prolongation of this dreadful conflict'.[18]

Fortunately for himself, Gladstone did not persuade the Cabinet to go for mediation. On any day of the week Palmerston would take Lewis's advice rather than Gladstone's. With Argyll in support of Lewis, and with his own lifelong ambition to suppress the slave-trade, Palmerston remained content to stand cautiously aside. But Gladstone did persuade the Cabinet, on the other hand, that there was no case for any public expenditure for relief of Lancashire's distress. The Poor Law guardians and overseers, having begun often on a most 'niggardly scale', were now amending fast. Voluntary subscriptions of over half a million testified to the advantage of private charity over 'that worst of all forms of aid', state provision. In a situation where 432,000 people, one in five of the affected population, were already in receipt of relief, Gladstone could well believe that Cobden's call for a national subscription might be in order. The superiority of the voluntary ethic was manifest. 'A public grant in my opinion', Gladstone insisted 'is not to be thought of. Indeed, I can hardly conceive the time when more than a loan could be asked from the State on behalf of the vast property of Lancashire.'[19]

There was little otherwise to detain him in the 1862 session. His budget proposals were unmolested. 'Better times now!' he exulted.[20] There were better times also in America. He was willing to concede to Argyll that Lincoln's second proclamation emancipating all slaves in the seceded states was improved in tone. 'It gives more of body and form to the idea of relieving the poor blacks: and morally it tends in some degree to set quietly aside the mischievous Proclamation of September and to become a kind of substitute for the same.'[21] Lee's victory at Fredericksburg in any case seemed to make Lincoln's improved moral tone redundant. 'Surely this will end the madness.'[22]

More significant than Gladstone's misreading of the American situation was the reading by which he chose to interpret Lancashire and the Tyne. At the Saturday Evening Assembly of the Working Men of Chester, on 27 December, Gladstone offered the first fruits of his reflecting on his recent experiences in the north of England. This took the form of a full-scale and mature mythology of the virtue of the Lancashire cotton operatives confronting the cotton famine, with reference particularly to the display of qualities worthy of the conferment of the parliamentary franchise. No 'murmuring against the dispensations of God; no complaining against man; no envious comparison of their case with the case of their employers; no discontent with the Government or the Laws; a universal and unbroken reverence for public order'. All these things presented 'a noble picture, instructive to us all'. It was a picture 'intended for us all to look upon, and to learn from; for if cotton has done this for the men of Lancashire, cotton is but the instrument in the hand of God, and He can find some other instrument with which to do it for us, when He sees that we need the lesson and can profit by it'.[23]

This 'noble picture' was a retouched and heightened version of that development of the popular dimension of 'advanced intelligence' Gladstone had saluted in April 1862 in the shape of the Lancashire and Cheshire Mechanics' Institutes. It was a picture that – like any great, characteristic Victorian work of art – bore an obliquely distanced relationship to the realities of life.

Popular life in cotton-starved Lancashire was far from being characterized by such paragons of virtue as Gladstone depicted. The point was that Gladstone made of Lancashire a stage setting for a morality drama of his own devising. He was the impresario of a curious kind of political theatre as the counterpart of his own kind of personal political theatre, first made dramatically manifest in the budget issues of 1852 and 1853. The mythology was not as yet quite in its fully matured form. Gladstone would first have to confess the fault of his own pro-southern sympathies (largely shared by the Lancashire operatives) before he could, in 1866, add to the tale of their virtue the crowning myth that they 'knew the source of their distress lay in the war yet they never uttered or entertained the wish that any effort should be made to put an end to it, as they held it to be a war for justice and freedom'.[24] If providential purpose guided and sustained the role of guide and teacher, it implied equally the eventual reciprocation of the guided and the taught. For Gladstone the hand of God now touched on the franchise question.

Divine accreditation was but the logical consummation of the unfolding providential purposes and consequences that for Gladstone had always been at the heart of the commercial and fiscal reform programmes of his second vocation. Peel's budgets, free trade, his own great series of budgets now almost at the point of fulfilment, had, as he saw it, nurtured and emancipated a new generation, appreciative of the beneficence of its immediate political inheritance, correspondingly responsive to the claims of that heritage for loyalty and deference. And now, perhaps above all, there was in being the prospect of a mass of popular energy 'out of doors' never available to Peel but promisingly available to Peel's disciple and inheritor. Gladstone could see himself on the verge of presiding over a grand synthesis of cause and effect. On 31 December he gave thanks for 'the ending well of what has been so good a year'.

The new year indeed started well. 'Made my *first* sketch of a budget for 1863–4. The figures, so far as I can judge, look very well.' He calculated a revenue of £71 million, charges of £67 million. As he looked out on the wintry Hawarden park land, Gladstone wrote to Palmerston 'outlines which I see before me dimly moving in the mist'. Gladstone discerned the shape of an income tax reduced to 7d., which would be not only an important remission 'but a considerable political measure' as well. That was where Peel had renewed it in 1842. So would be getting the sugar duty back 'to the *peace* point'.[25] On 2 January Gladstone found himself 'greatly pleased with the look of the figures – so much so it rather interfered with my sleep'.

Other shapes were discernible moving portentously in the January mists. The Chester speech had been noted by interested parties. One of the most important of them was George Wilson, Manchester cotton magnate, one of Gladstone's requisitioners for the South Lancashire seat in 1861, soon (1864) to be President of the National Reform Union, and in 1865 one of Gladstone's principal sponsors in South Lancashire. Writing with 'great frankness', Gladstone explained to Wilson that the purpose of his reference 'on two occasions in conjunction with the Lancashire distress to the question of the franchise' had been 'not in any manner to force forward the question, but to endeavour to impress the idea' that it was 'a grave and serious one', and that 'it must at some time be entertained', that it was 'desirable to dispose of it', and that the 'labouring classes' were 'worthy of a more generous treatment than was accorded to them in the House of Commons on the introduction of the Bill of 1860'.

Further: Gladstone owned that it was his opinion 'that the public mind in general' wanted 'a good deal of this preliminary manipulation' before any further parliamentary effort was made. His chief 'object of anxiety as to any effort about the franchise' was 'not that it should be early but that it should be creditable and successful: that it should not be such as those which have preceded'. But he freely added that if it could realize the conditions he had described, then the earlier it was, the better, 'for the honour of all parties & for the public good'. Gladstone emphasized carefully that Lord Russell would be his leader in that 'desire & intention'.[26]

This view of his role as manipulator of the public mind was a highly characteristic aspect of Gladstone's sense of himself as accredited political guide and teacher. His financial vocation as defined in the 1850s was now substantially fulfilled; a new vocation was taking shape. Horizons were still enlarging and skies as shifting as ever. Of Russell's 1860 Reform Bill, Gladstone had written to Brougham on the theme of a deferential electorate's being conceivably established on 'a lower and broader basis'.[27] That conceivability had now become practicality.

~

Meanwhile, as the subterranean pressures made their way, Gladstone coped with the surface phenomena. Return to London was softened by recourse to Drury Lane, where he 'laughed immoderately' at a second view of Lord Dundreary, the buffoon character in the rage of the season, Tom Taylor's *Our American Cousin*, at the Haymarket.[28] Reading Kinglake's *Invasion of the Crimea*, however, was no laughing matter. It was not at all agreeable or just to the Aberdeen government ('I am afraid that Newcastle blabbed on what took place and this blabbing was much tinged with egoism').[29] There were rescue cases to be placed at the Clewer Refuge and with milliners. Willy's third class in the Oxford Law and History schools was something of a dampener; but Stephy seemed steady in a calling to the Church. There were more frowns at worrying news from Bowden Park, where pining John Neilson seemed to be sinking. The family gathered early in February. John died on the 6th. This was the first death of a sibling since Anne's in 1829. There was much avuncular concern about John's eight-year-old only son, John Evelyn, 'little Jack', and property arrangements.[30]

Even amid the funereal gloom of Bowden Gladstone found Palmerston in pursuit in the matter of the Prince of Wales's marriage settlement. Palmerston was willing for £110,000; but Gladstone insisted that when he saw the Queen at Windsor she was quite content with the round £100,000. At the first Clivedens of the season Gladstone defended unabashedly his anti-Lincoln views on the American war. He busied himself at the Treasury with the worrying and expensive problem of venereal disease in the armed services. He was an unabashedly statist advocate of compulsory registration and examination of prostitutes in garrison, arsenal and dockyard towns, and of subjecting soldiers and sailors to stoppage of pay to meet the expenses of their treatment for disease. He was in no doubt that the government ought 'in the most circumspect manner to make an effort for effectual repression'.[31] In this way Gladstone was one of the authors of the Contagious Diseases Act, smuggled through in the most circumspect manner in the 1864 session, but soon to become notorious as the target of one of the most insistent agitations of public moral purity in the later Victorian era.[32]

Innocently unaware of all this trouble in store, Gladstone rejoiced at the budget figures still looking well. 'The sea of politics is smooth.' He was solicitous to cosset his pet Public Accounts Committee; but his submissions before it were so expressive of executive potency and expertise that the House grew cynical. It would not be long before one of its members, Sir Henry Willoughby, announced that he thought 'House should know its powers and its usefulness were extremely limited'.[33]

On 10 March the wedding of the Prince of Wales to Princess Alexandra of Denmark at St George's Chapel, Windsor, was the 'most gorgeous sight' Gladstone had ever witnessed, '& one of the most touching'. He ventured out that night into the Strand to admire the illuminations, finding the crush at Temple Bar 'dangerous to life: not made for one of my age'. Nevertheless he took the opportunity intrepidly to put in some rescue work. Then there was a slight scuffle with Palmerston over plans for the Albert Memorial. The Prime Minister was inclined to 'give way to the Queen's feelings' and find more money. Gladstone was adamant in defence of the public purse. At Cliveden on 23 March, in a debate on Scott's design for an immense canopied monument in gilt bronze, stone and marble in the Great Exhibition site in Hyde Park, Gladstone found himself 'pretty nearly alone on the hard side'.

There were matters more politically consequential. On 4 March Gladstone voted for the Abolition of Declaration Bill, removing those aspects of the Test and Corporation Act offensive to Dissenters. This was a straw in the wind. Dissent was a powerful ingredient in the Reform movement, and in the subsequent matters likely to stem from a Reform measure: one of which, for example, might well be the Irish Church. A growing rapport with Dissent was evident in Gladstone's concern later in the 1863 session with their grievances in the Burials question. Dissenters, he told the Commons, had 'some title to come before this House and ask for an alteration of the law' on the basis of 'principles of civil and religious freedom on which, for a series of years, our legislation has been based'.[34] Trelawny commented on Gladstone's words: 'Very remarkable they seemed in a speech from him, & so people thought.'[35] This marked yet another distinct movement on Gladstone's part away from strict establishmentarianism. He gained Dissenting applause; but he drew upon his head witheringly churchly rebukes from Disraeli – 'Disraeli has taken the Church of England into his care'[36] – and Lord Robert Cecil.

More to the point, he attracted the hostile attentions of the MP for Leominster, Gathorne Hardy. Resentment against Gladstone among Oxford University voters burst out again in a campaign to contest his re-election, with Hardy as their new champion. Gladstone professed himself frankly at a loss to understand the grounds that had prompted these adverse feelings.[37] Gladstone compounded his offence by his attitude to the question of Anglican subscription for all degrees other than the baccalaureate. Not the least of his offences was to extol the 'Cambridge compromise', whereby only theological degrees and membership of the Senate were thus subscribed for. No doubt it was a relief to be able to assure the Vice-Chancellor that his new proposals about club liquor licences would be no impediment to the traditional amenities of the common-room.

On 13 April Cornewall Lewis died. He was but three years older than Gladstone. For Palmerston it was a stunning blow. He had been grooming Lewis as the man to lead a future anti-Radical coalition to head Gladstone off. Delane of *The Times* was another influential player in this game. Now, all that would stand in the way of Gladstone's ascendancy was the shrivelled reputation of Russell. The immediate consequence for Gladstone of Lewis's demise was in fact the mundane but tricky problem of having to cope with Miss Florence Nightingale's determination to get her protégé Ripon (the son of Gladstone's old chief at the Board of Trade) into the vacant War Office. Gladstone thought that a head of a great spending department in the Lords would be a difficulty; but Miss Nightingale got her way.[38]

~

While the friends of the Church simmered in Oxford Gladstone delivered on 16 April his seventh financial statement. He was 'in less force than usual', Sir John Trelawny noted. Having recently suffered a bad fall from his horse in Rotten Row, he wore a black patch between his eyes and 'looked ghastly'.[39] He got income tax back to Peel's initial 7d., reduced substantially duties on both tea and sugar, and allowed himself a modest surplus. Lancashire and Ireland he identified as the two main areas of pressure in 1862 and 1863. Because of crop failures the value of agricultural produce in Ireland had declined over three years by nearly a half; and nearly as much as the established annual valuation of the country (£13.4 million): a state, Gladstone declared, 'not less remarkable than painful'.[40] Apart from the one item of the income tax, Gladstone regarded himself as having substantially completed the programme of 1856. If he had not reduced government expenditure as decisively as he could have wished, he had checked its growth and brought it under control. He caused a storm by proposing to tax charitable bequests. Mostly they cost their death-bed donors nothing; and were almost invariably inefficiently or corruptly administered. Eventually he had to admit defeat in the face of sentimental agitation. With the 1863 budget he in effect presented, as he put it to the House, 'an Account for the last four years'.[41] 'It wound up I hope a chapter in finance & in my life. Thanks to God.'[42] He registered this sense later in 1863 by publishing *The Financial Statements of 1853, 1860–63* as a kind of testament of his stewardship.

Thus the budget of 1863 marked for Gladstone the definitive end of his second vocation. What then? He noted on 17 April a 'feeling of deep unworthiness, inability to answer my vocation, & the desire of rest'. As yet Gladstone had but dim and unformed notions; a general awareness that great things were to be done when the inert mass of public opinion would be animated by the manipulatory power of his insight. Such dim and unformed notions were in fact already present in his financial statement: Lancashire and Ireland. His doctrine and its wider implications on the former was by now a well known theme: the people of Lancashire displaying signally that 'power of endurance, that self-command, that cheerful, manly resignation, that true magnanimity in humble life', giving such solemn pause for thought. Ireland was less a case of moral drama, but not less morally thought-provoking. Already, in 1862, Gladstone had discerned that Ireland was slowly growing into a political difficulty. Now he manipulated opinion to address itself to that difficulty.

~

All this was portentous enough to one imbued with the notion of a vocation to guide the wiser policy and teach the higher morality. There was the constant pressure of delicate and fraught issues. 'It is sometimes said', as Gladstone once remarked, 'that I am too apt to draw distinctions.'[43] The distinctions that would soon need to be drawn related to the condition of Ireland. Back in the 1840s Gladstone had spoken of the Irish Church question as a wooden horse full of armed men.[44] Now there were Irish members ready to drag the horse through the gates of the Church. His discussion of fiscal aspects only made more eloquent the great unmentioned question hanging in the air. Nevertheless, the implication of his conclusion was unfiscal and plain: We 'must look to the influence of good laws, liberal legislation, and thorough and hearty equality in our endeavour to apply the principles of justice and freedom to all three countries'.[45]

Opinion in Cabinet on the Irish Church problem was well reflected in the remark made by Lewis to Stanley in July 1862: it was the real difficulty of the day; while it remained there was no hope of conciliating the Irish Catholics; yet the difficulty of dealing with it was so great as to prohibit action.[46] Roundell Palmer, the Solicitor General, testified later that Gladstone told him in 1863 that he had 'made up his mind on the subject, and that he should not be able to keep himself from giving public expression to his feelings. How far or how near that might be practicable, he could not foresee; but, under the circumstances, he wanted his friends connected with the University of Oxford to consider whether or not they would desire for that reason a change in the representation of the University.' Gladstone testified for himself: 'I did not give my days and nights to the question ... yet the question continually flitted, as it were, before me.'[47] It certainly flitted as a ghostlike presence through the debate of 12 June 1863.

Given the devastation of the Irish social and political landscape in the 1840s and 1850s, it was not wonderful that continual flittings should be slow to congeal into some kind of fixed vision for Gladstone until 1863. It was a political difficulty of very slow growth. After suspension for nearly twenty years the phrases of the 1840s now began to take on a revived reality. Was he not still bound in consistency to strip the Irish Church? It was the Church, after all, of merely 700,000 of the Irish population of five million. Was it not in the highest interest of the Church to give gold for freedom? But the revived reality was far distant from the feverish fears stoked in the aftermath of Maynooth. The Irish Church question remained a heavy question, in many respects complex, and politically quite dangerous; but it no longer lay on him like a 'nightmare'. In the intervening years Gladstone witnessed the 'process' that separated the 'work of the State from the work of the Christian faith'. As a 'consenting party, in a certain sense, to that process of separation', Gladstone now took a much more relaxed view of ecclesiastical matters. He consorted now with Dissenters. He pressed the President of Maynooth to join his breakfast parties when in London in the season.[48]

The case of the Church of Ireland was that by giving gold it would gain not only freedom for itself but would emancipate the vast majority of the Irish people, Catholic and Dissenting Protestant, from subjection to an alien or unwelcome establishment of religion. It was the case also that 'Ireland forces upon us' great social along with great religious problems. The question of the Irish Church could not be separated from the 'general question of Ireland'. These were Gladstone's own phrases of the 1840s. The greatest danger of Irish Church disestablishment lay in its implications beyond the purely ecclesiastical. That was why there was much support for the expediently evasive recourse of 'concurrent' endowment of all three major Irish denominations, Roman Catholic and Presbyterian as well as Anglican. Nevertheless, from a certain viewpoint the establishment of the Irish Church stood out unmistakably as the biggest blot on the face of the British polity.

What was new and important for Gladstone in 1863 was that he needed body and work for his forming vocation. The logic that impressed itself upon him with an irresistible cogency now was that, if what he could make of Lancashire and the Tyne as representing body in terms of numbers and harnessable energy was to become available on a lower and broader basis of franchise, what would be the most appropriate work at which to set those numbers and energies?

The answer to that question had to await public declarations on Gladstone's part about both franchise and Church. These would need prudent management and timing. His eventual commitment to 'religious equality for Ireland' Gladstone would cite as one of the occasions of his career when his 'appreciation of the general situation and its result', and his 'insight into the facts of particular eras, and their relations one to another', generated a conviction that the 'materials' existed for 'forming a public opinion and directing it to a particular end'.[49] From Gladstone's own angle of perception he was subject to imperatives of quite categorical authority. The pattern of things seemed to have about it attributes quite reasonably interpretable as of a providential dispensation. The great works of 1842, 1846, 1853, and 1860 had borne their fruits; those fruits, manifested on the Mersey and the Tyne, constituted mighty new social and political materials. How could it be otherwise that he was somehow appointed to form and direct such materials to a particular end?

All would be determined by capacities and chances. As to capacities, Gladstone, now in his early fifties, stood in the optimum phase of mature mental and physical vigour. As for chances, Palmerston, the great obstacle, could not hold out much longer. Russell, hopelessly adrift at the Foreign Office, could live politically for one object only; and that, a second Reform Act, now matched precisely Gladstone's own grand prospective necessity. Gladstone seemingly stood poised to enter advantageously upon an inheritance of a promise brilliant beyond precedent in the nineteenth century.

~

The one serious defect amid Gladstone's mature mental and physical vigour was his proneness to hector and drive in the Commons. There were ominous signs in 1863 of a recurrence of the problem last provocatively evident in the 1860 session, when Harriet Sutherland had done her best to induce a better morale. A Palmerstonian Commons did not relish Peel-style leadership. In 1861 Palmerston himself had warned Gladstone that the Commons allow themselves to be led, not driven.[50] Trelawny observed 'the tendency there is to teaze him. He is, sometimes, provoking for his very crushing power & command of words, wh. is more remarkable than his command of his temper.'[51] Many Liberal members immediately subject to Gladstone's 'dictatorial manner and want of tact' began to dread the likely outcome of Palmerston's imminent decease.

Nor would the turn of events in America have improved Gladstone's temper. Lee's victory at Chancellorsville in May led to a bid at the end of June by Roebuck to push for recognition of the Confederacy and mediation, together with France and Russia. Napoleon III, already deep in Mexican schemes, was ready; but Palmerston was even more cautious than he had been in January. Gladstone himself now became aware of a 'strong counter-current of feeling' in Britain against the south's 'strict adherence to slavery'. Lincoln's second emancipation proclamation had clarified the moral issue decisively. Gladstone now shifted position: intervention would only stimulate a patriotic reaction in the north and risk 'making worse that which is already sufficiently horrible'. 'Doubt', he declared, 'ought to be ruled on the side of safety.'[52] It was expedient also that the strong counter-current of public feeling against the south should not be in any way or degree divided, diverted, or compromised as a strong current of feeling in favour of Reform. He signalled his sympathies to Dissent over Church subscription for Oxford higher degrees and allowance of halls and hostels.

The 1863 session had proved unexpectedly taxing. Probably then he did not receive with unalloyed joy Palmerston's notice on 12 August that part of the recess would have to be spent as minister-in-waiting at Balmoral. Nor was it with unmixed feelings that he directed that £50,000 be provided for Scott's Albert Memorial.[53] There were, moreover, vexing problems with artists in state employ. In the matter of the lions at the base of Nelson's column in Trafalgar Square: 'Does Sir E. Landseer mean to give us four designs of Lions or only one?'[54]

The awkward *Alabama* question caused anxiety. Gladstone reported to Argyll that, with Palmerston now much more sensitive to Union susceptibilities, a '*most private* order' had been given to forbid the ironclads in the Birkenhead yards quitting the Mersey. The problem of these Confederate rams Gladstone found 'most difficult and perplexing'.[55] As Master of the Mint he grappled with the minting of florins and half-crowns; the issue being that the latter were wearing out and there was a danger of a dearth of sixpences when florins (started up as preparation for decimalization) began to grow numerous. There was Willy to coach for his All Souls examination. Gladstone was glad to be able to rejoice with Argyll about Jefferson Davis's recent proclamation on the slavery issue: 'a great & glad event'. Although Gladstone remained convinced that it was 'highly criminal to attempt the extirpation of mere slavery as such by war', should however it please God in His wisdom 'so to overrule the passions of men as to make this war conduce to the abolition of so pernicious a system', Gladstone was most cordially ready to sympathize with Argyll's feelings of joy '& shall likewise be prepared to give you much credit as a prophet'.[56] There were still major reservations. To Charles Sumner, the American statesman and abolitionist, he explained that he disapproved of war to end slavery but would be glad if slavery ended as the consequence of war. He added that he would be very pleased should the Union be re-established; but that would be to contemplate 'a contingency which as it seems to me is wholly unattainable'.[57]

'Suit and Service' at Balmoral was enlivened by the drama of the Queen's being overset while driving in her 'sociable' at night. When Gladstone 'lectured her a little' for imprudence she insisted that 'all her habits were founded on the Prince's wishes and directions and she could not alter them'. Gladstone had, unawares, started off in the immediate aftermath of the Prince's death on a risky tack with the Widow of Windsor. He pressed on her that her 'great affliction was sent to her for good'.[58] 'Bearing up' by drawing fresh devotion out of emotional devastation was a commonplace of Gladstone's spiritual repertoire. He was a bad psychologist in supposing he could apply it in the case of the Queen.[59] As yet, no shadow passed over their relationship. The Queen was 'all as one could wish', though much distracted by the quarrel between the Danes and the Germans over the question of the 'Danish Duchies' of Schleswig and Holstein, and very prone to Albert's pro-Prussian views. Gladstone himself was more distracted by the problem of the Confederate rams, about which he thought Russell was being 'very incautious'. 'I would write and tell him so', he told Catherine, 'but that as I had made an incautious speech about America myself last year I do not feel entitled to take so much upon me ...[60]

From Balmoral Gladstone called at Glenalmond and Edinburgh for university matters on his way back to 'the old desk in the old room', as he told Catherine, 'where I have spent many a time over my work with an anxious brow'. At Cabinet on 13 October Gladstone conveyed to his colleagues the Queen's anti-Danish views on the Danish Duchies question. Then up to Hawarden for Helen's confirmation by the Bishop of Oxford. There was 'much conversation with the Bp on what might follow Ld Palmerston. He will have me hold for first place: I say no.'[61] Gladstone would be loyal to 'the little man'.

An excursion to Burslem to lay the foundation stone of the Wedgwood Memorial Institute gave Gladstone occasion to test the air for what might follow Lord Palmerston in a manipulative foray among the populace. There was little joy when Willy returned without his All Souls fellowship. 'What next?' Willy seemed strangely reluctant to be fitted into a parliamentary seat. Hopes about the 1864 session were dampened by Palmerston's reluctance to countenance tax reductions, given the American and European situations. 'This Danish business', Gladstone told Catherine, 'is a very nice one in itself & with the Queen. She is rather wild & Lord R. does not show much tact in managing her.'[62] A Cabinet on the estimates on 1 December was disappointing. 'The Estimates postponed: the sky not being clear. I mean the Cabinet sky.'

Neither was the Oxford sky clear, nor the Lancashire sky. Robertson and George Wilson found Gladstone a difficult prospect: the more doubtful Oxford became, the more reluctant was Gladstone to make a clean and convenient break. Not the least of the obstacles in the way of Gladstone's making a break was that he had Brand the Whip breathing down his neck on Palmerston's behalf. One mitigation of the Oxford problem was that it made Palmerston amenable to Gladstone's advice on ecclesiastical preferment. Looking at God as a benign but remote foreign Great Power, Palmerston had allowed Shaftesbury to cram the bench of bishops with Low Church mediocrities. Gladstone was grateful for occasional corrective opportunities among his Oxford friends.

At Hawarden the Castle was buzzing with the question, will Lucy Lyttelton become engaged to Frederick Cavendish, Hartington's younger brother? There were to be further adjustments in the matter of America. He wrote to John Stuart Mill about Britain's neutrality in a manner which that leading advocate of the Union found 'on the whole very satisfactory'.[63] There were yet further adjustments consequent on the French installation of their Emperor Maximilian of Mexico. Disraeli reported Gladstone as declaring it 'one of the greatest political blunders ever perpetrated, certainly, the greatest political blunder of his time'.[64] But always the mundane task recalled Gladstone to his duty. 'I cannot say', he informed the Commissioner of Works and Buildings, 'that I am well satisfied with Sir E. Landseer's tone in this business with the lions ...'[65]

Still, there were blessings to be counted in his end-of-year birthday reflections. There were as ever the perils of 'lurking unextracted sin'. 'My life has not been inactive. But of what kind has been its activity?' Had he adequately fulfilled his vocations? 'It seems to have been & to be a series of efforts to be and do what is beyond my natural force.' Nevertheless: 'In other quarters some better gleams of light.'

9

Embracing the Millions: Reform and Ireland, 1864–1865

'God knows I have not courted them: I hope I do not rely on them: I trust I may turn them to account for good.'

Gladstone, diary entry, 14 October 1864

Among the better gleams of light discerned by Gladstone at the beginning of 1864 was the prospect that the stifling grip of Palmerston and Derby on political movement since 1859 might be sensibly loosened. The questions as to what to do about Reform and what to do about Ireland were pushing themselves insistently towards the front of politics. Gladstone was emerging pre-eminently, if sometimes uncomfortably, as the chief spokesman for the movement and the new dynamic it was creating. Throughout all the distractions imposed upon him, Gladstone kept the crucial Reform issue steadily in view. It was now crucial because it was known that Baines, the Leeds MP, was planning to introduce another bill to lower the borough franchise from the existing £10 rateable qualification to £6. Gladstone kept Robertson abreast: 'I am not however one of those who think there is much present danger of monopoly of political power in the hands of the most numerous class & I confess I wish their share of it were *sensibly* enlarged.'[1]

All eyes were looking towards 11 May, which was when Baines would introduce his Borough Franchise Bill. Baines was casting a fly across the political waters with the hope of luring Gladstone to rise to the bait. And if Gladstone sought occasions of 'preliminary manipulation' of opinion, here was a splendid opportunity. On 10 May, almost as if to prime him on the theme of the responsible virtue of the artisan class, a deputation from the Amalgamated Society of Engineers waited on Gladstone with a request that he modify the regulations so as to allow trade unions to deposit their funds in the Post Office banks.

The House of Commons was thus 'prepared for some momentous utterance' from Gladstone when Baines's bill came up. 'Rumours had been rife' that Gladstone would speak; the House was 'fully prepared for a startling declaration'; and though it was at the very beginning of a morning sitting, 'a considerable audience was already collected to hear him'.[2] Palmerston was understandably apprehensive. 'I hope', he cautioned Gladstone that morning, 'that in what you may say about Baines's Bill you will not commit yourself and the Government to any particular amount of Borough franchise.' There was a danger of the working classes, under the control of trade unions and 'directing Agitators', swamping the classes above them.[3] Palmerston decided that his absence from the debate would be expedient.

Gladstone commenced by echoing Palmerston's point that opinion at present would not make it advisable or justifiable for the government to submit such a measure to Parliament. Why then would he not vote against Mr Baines's bill? Because the parliamentary history of Reform since 1851 had been 'a most unsatisfactory chapter'. He was convinced that discussion of the question in the Commons must, 'through that gentle process by which Parliamentary debates act upon the public mind', gradually help to bring home the conviction that it was in the interests of the country 'that the matter should be entertained; and that it ought, if we are wise, to be brought to an early settlement'. Thus far, Gladstone had shown why. He shifted his argument and challenged his opponents to show cause why not. He implied that presumption was for if there be no proof against. Hence the slipping out of the notorious words: 'And I venture to say that every man who is not presumably incapacitated by some consideration of personal fitness or of political danger is morally entitled to come within the pale of the Constitution.'

The 'advanced' Liberals 'shouted with delight'; 'a murmur of consternation ran through the rest of the House'. Seeing 'how acute was the impression he produced', Gladstone 'made a floundering attempt to retrace his steps'. In giving utterance to such a proposition, he explained, he did not of course recede from the protests he had previously made 'against sudden, or violent, or excessive, or intoxicating change'. But he did apply his proposition 'with confidence' to this effect, that fitness for the franchise when it is shown to exist 'is not repelled on sufficient grounds from the portals of the Constitution by the allegation that things are well as they are'.[4]

By thus repeating at the end of his explanation the principle of moral right, Gladstone added fuel to the flames rather than dampening them. 'He did not succeed in reassuring his astounded hearers. The rapturous cheers of his Radical allies accompanied him to the end of his speech.'[5] In an 'advertisement' to his authorized version of the speech, Gladstone apologised that his consternating phrases were not 'a deliberate and studied announcement'. They were 'drawn forth on the moment by a course of argument from the opponents of the measure', who appeared to assume that the present limitations on the franchise required no defence and were 'good and normal'. In any case, he spoke 'without reference to the present'. It was not the time to 'attempt the solution of problems of real intricacy, which belong wholly to the future, and which are little likely to become practical for another generation'.[6]

There is a curious echo here of Gladstone's old propensity to wish that he did not hold the opinions he held. That night, he recorded: 'Some sensation. It appears to me that it was due less to me than to the change in the hearers & in the public mind from the professions at least if not the principles of 1859.'[7] Was this honest puzzlement, or self-delusion, perhaps unconscious, perhaps wilful? Gladstone's celebration of close boroughs in 1859 had disgusted Bright. Gladstone's last pronouncement on Reform in the Commons in 1860, blandly demanding credit for his sincerity, had been mocked with ironical cheers.

In fact there had been a crucial shift in Gladstone's own attitude to the question, set originally in motion more by the paper duties crisis in 1860 and 1861 than by anything else; but even at that stage still a matter of tentative opportunism and contingent convenience. Behind Gladstone's spurious claims to virtuous consistency was the simple but sovereign circumstance that whereas to the vocation formed in the 1853 budget and the 1856 programme, franchise reform was at best an irrelevance and at worst an obstacle, to the vocation now shaping itself extended suffrages in the towns were of the essence.

People other than Gladstone naturally measured the velocity of impact in terms of the stark contrast between Gladstone the reformer of 1859 and 1860 and Gladstone the reformer in 1864. Trelawny judged his 'pale of the Constitution' speech 'an historical event. Rousseau is, apparently, in communication with our Chancellor thro' some medium.'[8] Stanley reported that at the Cosmopolitan Club Gladstone was the 'general subject of conversation'. There was agreement that 'he had broken with the old Whigs and placed himself at the head of the movement party'. 'It was felt on all hands that he was the inevitable leader' and yet at the same time that 'the *hauteur* of his manners, his want of skill in dealing with men', and 'his pedantic stiffness in adhering to his own opinions as rigidly in small matters as in great, will make him most unpopular in that capacity'.[9]

The Queen wrote to Palmerston 'deeply grieved at this strange and independent act of Mr Gladstone's'. He should not have made such an 'imprudent declaration' as a member of the government.[10] Palmerston very promptly made his displeasure plain. 'You lay down broadly the Doctrine of Universal Suffrage which I can never accept.' Brand, the Whip, was 'startled'. Gladstone protested unconvincingly that his words were 'neither strange nor new nor extreme'.[11] Stanley dined with the Clarendons. 'Among other things Lord C. said of Gladstone that a physician in attendance on him had declared that he would die insane.'[12] Wood thought that, after Palmerston, Gladstone was 'inevitable, but most dangerous'.

Press comment did nothing to minimize the significance of the event. *The Times* thought it a thing 'so strange and so startling' that the full importance of the event could scarcely yet be realized. The *Telegraph* exploited the event to the hilt. 'Sincerely and in the name of England, we thank Mr Gladstone for the courageous manifesto which he pronounced on Wednesday.' It had 'echoed through the land like the clarion of a leader who trusts his cause, his followers and himself, and who sounds a general advance'. A dozen 'veracious, manly, and outspoken words' had put the 'Conservative reaction' into limbo; the great Liberal party was once more a living power; the labarum of the crusade of progress had once more been unfurled. By this 'bold and wise step Mr Gladstone had advanced to the very front of the great Liberal party'.[13] Sentiments of the same style of caricature and hyperbole gushed from the *Morning Star* and other organs of the 'movement'. In response to Robertson's cordial applause Gladstone trusted that for the rest of the session he was in 'some hope of being more quiet'.[14]

~

For the rest of the 1864 session Gladstone did attempt to be more quiet. He wrote a minute for Russell's benefit on 'transport of Circassians'. These were Muslims preferring emigration from the Caucasus rather than Russian rule. The scheme was to plant them among the Bulgarian Christians of Turkey in Europe. To the British 'Crimean' public they were gallant victims of Russian tyranny. For Gladstone the matter was an issue within a wider issue of Turkish financial delinquency.

A happier diversion was the marriage in the Abbey on 7 June of Lucy Lyttelton to Frederick Cavendish. Granville's private secretary and soon to become Liberal MP for Yorkshire West Riding, Lord Frederick became Gladstone's family favourite. Less agreeable things also impinged. At one of Gladstone's breakfast parties, Stanley observed his 'evident mortification' at the sinking of *Alabama* off Cherbourg. Stanley observed also his astonishment at the eagerness of the 'negrophilists' to sacrifice three white lives in order to set free one black man, even after it was shown that there was no disposition among the blacks to rise in their own cause. 'He could have understood the American feeling of dislike to the breaking up of the Union, but not the fanaticism of English sympathisers.'[15]

When back in February Gladstone had written to Robertson about his sadness at seeing 'both Federals & Confederates in America more confident than ever', he had rejoiced to report that nothing had happened to 'damp my hopes of avoiding any share in those unhappy quarrels on the Continent'.[16] Gladstone became involved in such unhappy quarrels because, since Russell's elevation to the Lords in 1861, Palmerston was much in need of a heavyweight frontbench figure to speak in the Commons for the government's foreign policy. Brand had begun by slotting Gladstone into the groove of Lord Palmerston's Eastern policy.

It was a matter of embarrassment to Gladstone. By now he was in that groove up to his neck, rebutting accusations of barbaric Turkish proceedings in the Balkans and Lebanon. Rather as with the China affair of 1860, having swallowed the camel of Palmerston, he would not strain at the gnat of putting up a patently insincere lawyer's brief on behalf of the Foreign Office and the Constantinople

Embassy. It was like his speeches for Peel defending the revised Corn Law. Cobden, who led the attack in the Commons on Palmerston and Russell, could see that Gladstone spoke 'with evident reluctance'[17] when he expounded his line that after all, there existed a belief that the principles upon which the Crimean war had been fought were sound principles; and that 'in compliance with the faith of treaties', we must be loyal to the Turkish government, and were we prepared for 'a total reversal of British policy'?[18]

A further embarrassment for Gladstone was his being caught out in a total reversal of his own policy on the Ionian Islands. Having deposed their Bavarian King Otto in 1862, the Greeks were casting about for a replacement. Interested powers pressed forward their candidates. Palmerston and Russell, eager to detach Greece from Russian tutelage, were ready to offer the Islands as a bribe. The Greeks, for their part, were willing to humour the British. The Queen's second son, Prince Alfred (later Duke of Edinburgh), could have had the Athenian throne. It was gained by a Danish prince, brother of the affianced Alexandra, Princess of Wales to be. It was as well that only a thin House now heard Gladstone citing the dangers to the peace of Europe if Ionian *enosis* led to further Greek demands to incorporate the 'Greek provinces of Turkey', Thessaly and Epirus. Yet it was precisely those provinces that Palmerston and Russell unavailingly pressed the Turks to cede to Greece.[19]

Such ins and outs were par for the twisting political course. Gladstone was fortunate early in 1863 in not being required to defend the gunboat diplomacy of bombarding Kagashima in Japan. Perhaps unhappy memories of his perjuring himself in competent lawyer's briefs on behalf of the Turks arose when he put it to Russell that the latest information on Turkish finances disclosed 'a state of things somewhat ominous'.[20] In the matter of Garibaldi's awkward presence in Britain early in 1864, however, Gladstone was perfectly prepared to slide into the groove of Lord Palmerston's requirements.

The Italian hero had arrived in April to pay a visit of gratitude to the British people. Ministers were nervous of the presence of a man held by European governments – not least that of Italy – as little better than a revolutionary bandit. Radical elements in Britain prepared to salute the General as a genius of the democratic revolution and as a mighty stimulus to the 'movement' in Britain itself. There were plans for a triumphant provincial progress over four to six weeks. His managers had provisionally booked something over thirty engagements. Gladstone offered his services to Palmerston. 'I do not know what persons in office are to do with him: but you will lead, & we shall follow suit.'[21] Palmerston's lead was to keep Garibaldi tightly confined to London, to hobble him with a press of respectable admirers, and to be rid of him as quickly as decently possible. Among his most useful accomplices to that end was Gladstone.

Given Gladstone's predispositions, there was nothing surprising or unlikely in this spoiling role. He would have no particular sympathy for a campaign of democratic incitement conducted by Europe's most notorious anti-clerical freemason, even if that animus was directed foremost against the Roman Church. More importantly, as one who saw his vocation as former and director of public opinion, as teacher, guide and, in his own special term, manipulator, Gladstone had no motive for encouraging rival performers in the field, performers, moreover, who were likely to get both the directions and the distances wrong. Gladstone himself meditated another manipulative Lancashire tour in the recess later in 1864. He had no wish to be upstaged. There could be only one embracer of the millions at a time.

After the initial mass demonstrations on the General's arrival, the Sutherlands deftly enveloped him in their hospitable web. Gladstone observed Garibaldi's receiving ovations at the Opera. He indulged his own form of sentimental populism: 'It was good, but not like the *people*.' Gladstone reserved the *people* to himself. Palmerston's tactic was to manufacture concern about the unsustainable strain a tour would inflict on the General's health. This was publicly refuted by Garibaldi's own physician.[22] Palmerston requested Gladstone to warn Garibaldi not only that his physical well-being would be endangered, but that also in any case his reputation would lose in 'real dignity' from so many receptions frequently repeated. Garibaldi agreed reluctantly to abandon the provincial tour. The Gladstones received the now disconsolate General at Carlton House Terrace on 20 April. Garibaldi's own painful impression was that the government did consider 'the prolongation of his stay in England very embarrassing and are very anxious that he should go'. 'This simple & heroic man' departed abruptly shortly after. Amid the subsequent recriminations, Gladstone stuck shamelessly to his official brief. He denied that politics ever came into the matter.[23]

~

Getting rid of the simple and heroic Garibaldi was easy. Not so easy was getting rid of 'those unhappy quarrels on the Continent'. The two most prominent of them were the Polish quarrel with their Russian oppressors in 1863 and the quarrel between the Danes and the Germans over the future of the mainly German 'Danish Duchies' of Schleswig and Holstein in 1864. Following the demise of the former Danish Crown, these lands were disputed between various claimants in a notoriously intricate dynastic riddle. In neither case did Gladstone stick to his official brief on behalf of the government's pro-Polish and pro-Danish policies.

The Polish case was that the Poles, observing the way the western powers had helped the Italians to get out from under the Austrians, invited France and Britain to fulfil the logic of the Crimean War by helping them get out from under the Russians. Palmerston and Russell encouraged the Poles to hope for western intervention on their behalf. French reluctance to participate made any such intervention impossible. The Poles were left in the lurch. Gladstone, pressed into defending the government's scuttle, had an opportunity to go with rather than against the grain of his instincts. In a curious way, his old fixation on the imperial image of Emperor Nicholas seems not to have entirely faded. His line now was that the friends of the Poles held language of a 'sanguine and therefore of a speculative nature'. The Emperor of Russia – by now Nicholas's son Alexander II, liberator of the serfs in 1861 – 'has some claims too on our sympathy'.[24]

In the case of the Danish-German conflict, Gladstone led resistance in Cabinet to Palmerston's and Russell's reckless encouragement of the Danes. On 23 July 1863, Palmerston declared in the Commons that if Denmark found itself at war with the Germanic powers of Austria and Prussia, Denmark would not stand alone. This, together with Russell's later echoing it, made the Danes obstinate and careless, and easy meat in the end for Bismarck, lately appointed Minister-President of Prussia. Palmerston and Russell – 'those two dreadful old men', as the Queen described them to uncle Leopold of Belgium[25] – were hopelessly out of their depth.

By June 1864, the Austrians and Prussians, having cleared the Danes out of the Duchies, commenced invasion of Denmark proper. The Danes, in desperate straits, called on Britain to rescue them. A Cabinet on 11 June Gladstone found 'very stiff'. But 'all went well'. The 'war party' was held at bay. As Palmerston had thwarted Gladstone's eagerness to intervene in the American case, so Gladstone now thwarted Palmerston's eagerness to intervene in the Danish case. The country, Gladstone assured the gratified Queen, had no real wish to go to war; and pro-Danish public excitement arose from 'misapprehension of the question'.[26] By 25 June ministers fudged a compromise. Britain would not intervene unless Denmark's existence as an independent power or the security of Copenhagen were put in doubt. A wrangling government drifted into peace in 1864 as a wrangling government drifted into war in 1854.

Derby decided on a motion of censure rather than confidence. He preferred keeping Palmerston in office rather than cope with the consequences of his removal. As he had been foremost in holding off the war party, Gladstone was foremost in fending off Disraeli's indictment of what by any measure was a disreputable British diplomatic scuttle. Responding to Palmerston's plea that he be a 'great Gun', he overwhelmed Disraeli with a prancing, fencing, evasive farrago, obfuscating the substantial issues. With this effrontery he carried the Commons. The government's defeat in the Lords reflected the discredit of the episode much more accurately. Privately, Gladstone admitted as much. 'The debate ought to be an epoch in Foreign Policy: we have much to learn.'[27] In fact, the only thing that made it epochal was Lord Robert Cecil's analysis of the Polish and Danish cases as salutary lessons in how not to conduct foreign policy.

Had France and Russia been willing to collaborate, Gladstone almost certainly would have adopted a much more spacious outlook. The Germanic powers would have felt the weight of that European moral authority Gladstone had been eager to impress upon Washington. But Napoleon III stipulated too heavy a Bonapartist price for fighting a great war on the Rhine. The Russian price was a dismantling of the Crimean system. Gladstone's reputation as an advocate of non-intervention in 1864 arose essentially out of making a virtue of necessity. He was not an advocate of peace in any consistent morally principled manner. As in 1860 with Austria, he was quite prepared to conceive in 1864 the possibility or necessity of war. His position, perfectly rational in its own terms, was that neither the possibility nor the necessity presented themselves. Later, Gladstone was fertile with alternative readings of the episode, stressing his willingness to challenge the Austrians and Prussians had the French been willing to participate: which unwillingness he judged Napoleon III's greatest mistake, for had there been war in 1864, 'France, with Great Britain at her side, would never have undergone the crushing defeat which she had to encounter in 1870–71 ... That is to say, the whole course of subsequent European history would in all likelihood have been changed.'[28]

~

On 22 July an observer noted Gladstone in Pall Mall, 'walking along unnoticed and alone. He looked at me in passing, and so enabled me the better to notice his brilliant flashing eyes and the stern melancholy of his mouth. At once, I said to myself, that is by far the most powerful face I have seen today.'[29] That day, there was a Council in Osborne. The Queen, as Gladstone reported to Catherine, 'asked particularly' about Palmerston's 'health and strength, without expressing any *wish* one way or another, which seems intelligible enough'. The Prime Minister's provoking capacity for survival seemed all the more provocative as Gladstone found himself having to fend off invitation after invitation to appear out of doors 'out of regard', as he explained to George Melly apropos a projected excursion to York, 'for what I consider morbid nerves' indoors.[30]

Nor was Gladstone himself immune from the reverberations set off by his 11 May speech. Enlarging horizons and shifting skies were as alarming and unsettling as ever. The Oxford side of him remained sensitive to hostile vibrations. To a Lancashire Conservative MP and Oxford voter he declared himself 'disgusted' at being classed with the ultra-Liberals, 'says he cannot imagine what he has said or done to earn that character, declares himself Conservative in feeling: above all is perplexed at the effect produced by his speech on reform, which he meant and believed to be moderate in tone'.[31] In other moods, however, as when in conversation with a Middlesex Liberal MP, 'he thought it would not do to go to a dissolution without some proof that they really were the Liberal party (his own words)'. The two questions on which he thought 'action possible' were 'reform and the Irish Church'. 'He would not explain as to the latter – what he thought ought to be done, but talked of the establishment as a "hideous blot" and used other strong language'. He 'further expressed a personal wish that the present cabinet should fall, on the ground that it had grown indolent and feeble, and wants some years of opposition to give new life'. That might seem 'an odd speech from a minister but it is quite in Gladstone's line'.[32] These shifting moods reflected a new version of a pattern as old as Gladstone's career: the forming of each new vocation manifesting itself in painful tension between the imperatives of the 'discipline' of an 'age of shocks' and deep instincts to cling to links of stability and safe anchorages.

One of the shocks was the judgment of the Judicial Committee of the Privy Council on the *Essays and Reviews* case. This collection of liberal Anglican critiques of orthodox Church authority, published in 1860, had been converted from a minor doctrinal scandal into a major crisis of belief by the intemperate Wilberforce of Oxford. Tait, the Bishop of London, voted with the lay judges against the two Archbishops and cleared the defendants of heresy. Gladstone launched himself into a campaign to increase the episcopal element in the Committee for purposes of ecclesiastical appeal.[33] For all his ecclesiastical loosening, Gladstone remained theologically as tightly dogmatic as ever. Relaxing at Polesden Lacy he devoted himself much to the problem of eternal damnation, one of the weaker points of the Church's defences. At Cliveden he conversed with Argyll on 'Future Punishment'. 'We had a delightful evening.'[34]

Back at Hawarden in August Gladstone had the pleasure of examining the new rooms built on to the north-west corner of the Castle helping to accommodate the Gladstone family contingent, and 'especially with a view to the vast undertaking of moving my books'. For the ground-floor room in the new block was to be the definitive 'Temple of Peace'. The exterior, in a coarse 'Victorian' style, contrasted with the refined Gothick of Sir Stephen's father's reconstruction at the beginning of the century. Gladstone's study had two pairs of windows on the west side looking up to the ruins of the old castle on a knoll to the west of the new; near the left-hand window Gladstone would set his two small desks. The other group of windows looked out to the north or entrance front. A passage eventually book-lined and known to the family as the 'chapel of ease' linked the Temple to the centre of the house; and a doorway connected it with the neighbouring old great drawing room. False book-ends on the drawing-room side of the door included whimsical titles, of which perhaps the most whimsical were four volumes of *An Israelite without Guile* by Ben Disraeli, Esq. Studying the measurements of the new room was indeed a matter of high import to one who, like Gladstone, preened himself on his craft in the science of bookcase arrangement.

After Penmaenmawr (and being much taken by W. Galt's *Railway Reform*, a scheme for state purchase of the railways under the terms of Gladstone's 1844

Act), the pattern of 1863 repeated itself in another suit and service as Minister in Attendance at Balmoral. On this occasion the dramatic accident was the rending of Gladstone's pantaloons, almost making him late for dinner. He observed, by way of regaining composure, that the Queen drank her claret 'strengthened, I should have thought spoiled, with whiskey'.[35]

There were serious concerns also at Balmoral. 'I feel much pain', Gladstone wrote to Russell, 'in looking at the Irish difficulty, slowly growing up again'.[36] To George Wilson at Manchester, President of the Reform Union, he pleaded that those interested in franchise extension be thoroughly dissuaded from 'taking any step to connect my name with it, outside the walls of Parliament'.[37] Partly this was by way of avoiding pre-emption of the Lancashire tour already prepared for the October recess, and by way partly of clearing the ground for a brawl with Palmerston over the services estimates. Gladstone's logic was that, given a new epoch in foreign policy, the Army and Navy estimates might advantageously be reduced from £27 to £21 million. He pointed to the 'salutary reform' of the education charges at the ruthless hands of Robert Lowe as exemplary.

~

As an interlude in this polemic came the Lancashire tour. The novel element in it as compared with 1862 was the prominent part played by Robertson Gladstone. Massive Robertson embodied two important new links in Gladstone's public life: Dissent and Radicalism. He functioned now as Gladstone's principal impresario in Lancashire. His seat at Court Hey became Gladstone's field headquarters. Press attention was now much more efficiently invited. Throughout the circuit of Bolton, Farnworth Park, Liverpool and Manchester, Gladstone developed what were now his standard themes: the benign revolution in class relation, the great role of the legislation of the past 25 years, with special honour to Sir Robert Peel's leading the way with his 1842 budget and free trade, Gladstone's own 1853 budget, the commercial treaty, the 'moral and political consequences' of paper duty repeal in its beneficial effects on the popular press, the lessons of the cotton famine, the prospect of a 'brilliant chapter' for the future.

The warmth of the response he elicited proved rather more than Gladstone bargained for. 'Great and real enthusiasm', he noted of the Farnworth occasion; 'I was much struck with the people.' The tour 'grew to proportions', as he later described to Baines, 'that were in one point of view at least inconveniently large'.[38]

When he came to haven with the Dowager Countess of Ellesmere at Worsley on 14 October, Gladstone reflected on the brilliant ending of an 'exhausting, flattering, I hope not intoxicating circuit. God knows I have not courted them: I hope I do not rely on them: I pray I may turn them to account for good.' Gladstone thus defined adequately for his own purposes the essential distinction between demagogy and necessary manipulation. He weakened from these soundly manipulative sentiments sufficiently to add: 'It is however impossible not to love the people from whom such manifestations come, as met me in every quarter.' He retired 'somewhat haunted by dreams of halls, & lines of people, & great assemblies'.[39]

From two points of view the Lancashire tour of 1864 was entirely satisfactory. In the short term, it offered an encouraging preview of a possible recourse in the event – necessarily soon – of a general election. In the longer perspective, Gladstone could be reassured that the impetus of his campaign to form, manipulate and direct a public opinion was being sustained. He was on course to equip himself at some future critical time with resources Peel had lacked.

~

For the immediate term Lancashire was but a respite in the war of attrition he was waging with Palmerston. At Hawarden Gladstone inaugurated his new Temple of Peace by replying to Palmerston 'in a rather decisive tone, for I feel conscious of right & of necessity'.[40] In the midst of this brawl came news of Newcastle's death: 'the very last of those contemporaries who were also my political friends. How it speaks to me!'[41] Gladstone set off for Clumber to attend the funeral at Markham Clinton; then on to Worksop as executor of the embarrassed estate and trustee for its problematic heirs.

Palmerston's demands on the revenue persisted. As Gladstone explained to Catherine: 'This *sort* of controversy keeps my nerves too highly strung and makes me sensitive, fretful, and impatient. I am not by nature brave, and am always between two fears, and I am more afraid of running away than of holding my ground.'[42] He did not hold his ground. There was huge resentment among his colleagues against what they saw as yet another attempt at arrogant imposition of his single opinion against their collective judgement. The best he could do was request that the correspondence be circulated. For her part, the Queen returned the letters to her Prime Minister with 'cordial and unqualified approval of every word said by Lord Palmerston'.[43]

Agreeably less rigorous would have been an occasion in which Gladstone's developing link with Dissent began to take more defined shape. To Catherine he reported on 15 November: 'I am going to Mr Newman Hall's to meet some Dissenting Ministers at tea! What odd predicaments & situations life abounds with.'[44] There in leafy suburban Hampstead he met Robert Vaughan, Baldwin Brown, R. W. Dale of Birmingham, and other luminaries of Dissent. It was all rather reminiscent of forays into exotic parts of Shadwell to consort with the coal whippers. 'They behaved extremely well to me.'[45] Indeed they would. They had high hopes of Gladstone. He seemed to be shaping promisingly on both the Oxford and Irish disestablishment fronts, as well as the franchise question.

In November Gladstone settled in to his pre-sessional London life. He maintained rescue work at a steady pace. He was still seeing Summerhayes occasionally, but without the anguish of other days. Wrangles with Manning had become almost a routine aspect of life. By now it was over the Pope's temporal power and his Encyclical *Quanta cura* recently promulgated with its notorious appendage, the *Syllabus errorum*, anathematizing every principle of freedom cherished by nineteenth-century Liberalism.[46] The railways question also was on his mind. 'I have *promoted* the public discussion of the subject of Railways', he informed Argyll, 'as a needful preliminary, in this case, to forming a public opinion.'[47] Again there was work to be done at Clumber with other executors and other trustees and the unsatisfactory young Duke. Gladstone wished he was 'without misgivings for it or what belongs to it'.[48]

In a certain way a curious item belonging to the 'Beckford inheritance' did pass on to Gladstone from the late Duke in the form of a Mrs Thistlethwayte, née Laura, daughter of Captain Bell of Bellbrook, Co. Antrim, bailiff on the estate of Lord Hertford. After a career as a Dublin belle and as one of the more 'notorious heterae' of Hyde Park, Laura Bell married in 1852 Captain Augustus Thistlethwayte, a former military gentleman resident in Grosvenor Square. His estate was only 500 acres; 'but all lay between the Edgware and the Bayswater Roads'.[49] She was a beautiful woman, much in the favour of the late Duke; 'the greatest beauty of her age', 'half sybil, half prophetess', one of the 'sights of the town'.[50] The Opera buzzed on her appearance. Reputedly, she had been the artist Landseer's mistress, and indeed was said to have assisted in modelling the lion designed for the base of Nelson's column. She experienced some kind of ethical or spiritual regeneration about which she lectured at the London Polytechnic as 'a sinner saved by grace through faith in the hands of God'. Her appearance on the platform was a 'realization of beauty and art', her graceful hands adorned with large diamond rings. Although respectably married and a well-known equestrienne on Rotten Row, where Gladstone probably met her, Mrs Thistlethwayte's equivocal reputation, her 'past' as a courtesan in the demi-monde, gave her an air of mystery. She was not therefore a 'case' for Gladstone in the way his two previous most disturbing cases – Collins and Summerhayes – had been. But perhaps all the more because of her 'saved' condition and her profession as female evangelist, Mrs Thistlethwayte's attractiveness was to prove even more unsettling.

~

For Gladstone the end of 1864 came with a feeling that 'all the ascent seems to lie before me, none behind'. He inaugurated a sessional rescue season by dealing with a 'sort of wild case'. A Cabinet on 19 January was a sort of wild case too, 'about as rough as any of the roughest times'. He circulated stiff memoranda on Canadian defences and Navy reductions. Lords Palmerston and Russell, he assured

Catherine, 'really are our old women on these subjects'.[51] Nevertheless, they won the fight. Palmerston set about exploiting his advantage by warning Gladstone off any ideas of substantial income tax reduction. It was a tax exclusively on the upper and middle classes; and tended to be increasingly productive of revenue. Its cornucopic character was, precisely, Gladstone's complaint against it. He had to concede that abolition as he had planned in 1853 was not possible in the present state of opinion.[52]

The session of 1865 was to be the last of the 1859 Parliament. The political atmosphere was heavy with a sense of the times waxing late. There was talk of Palmerston's not meeting the Commons after the election but retiring to the Lords to manage Gladstone's assumption of the leadership of the House and to mediate in likely quarrels. Stanley recorded on 14 February of Gladstone that 'the language held on his own side is, "He must lead, for there is no one who can compete with him, and yet his temper and restlessness make him entirely unfit"'. His colleagues, 'to put it in its mildest form', were 'not his cordial friends'. He was decidedly unpopular with the Conservative Opposition. 'His strength lies in his extraordinary gift of speech, his great general ability, and the support of the mercantile class in the manufacturing towns.'[53]

One man's nervousness about Gladstone's 'temper and restlessness' was another man's hopeful anticipation. And such hopeful anticipation was likely to be expressed by the representatives of the mercantile class in the manufacturing towns. Just as the 1864 session had opened in the knowledge that Edward Baines of Leeds was to introduce his Borough Franchise Bill, so the 1865 session opened with the announcement that Lewis Llewellyn Dillwyn, Quaker MP for Swansea, would move a resolution that the Church of Ireland was in a very unsatisfactory state, and that the early attention of Her Majesty's Government to its situation was desirable. As with Baines's bill, Dillwyn's resolution was framed very much with a view to the irresistible temptation it would offer to Gladstone's temper and restlessness.

Meanwhile, as both nervousness and anticipation stewed quietly together, Gladstone had the pleasure of offering the chairmanship of the Board of Audit to Cobden, who, denied a pension by Palmerston, was in financial straits.[54] Cobden's death in April, however, made this stroke of enlightened patronage stillborn. Gladstone remained as keen as ever to do something big about railways, perhaps regulation, perhaps purchase. He told Stanley of his plans for a commission on which Bright would sit as a kind of administrative house-training. He was sure the railway companies had too much influence and were an unhealthy power in the state.[55]

The first whiff of the Irish case came before the end of February. It was one thing, to fend off Irish complaints as a notoriously economical Chancellor of the Exchequer; it was quite another to fend off the question of the Irish Church now that it was accreting politically towards a state of critical mass. By 1865 Gladstone was clear that should the matter of the Irish Church be fairly and squarely presented in the Commons, there was no way consistent with personal integrity, political decency and parliamentary honour by which he could evade it. His approach would be to speak for himself, not as a minister. Bright recorded him as thinking in 1864, 'when the Liberal party is restored to life, that question would come up for settlement, and he should regard it as one of the great purposes of the party, although it would necessarily separate him from the University of Oxford'.[56]

In such a nervous atmosphere Stanley remarked Gladstone's 'social unpopularity' increasing apace. 'His colleagues detest him, and make little scruple in saying so – Wood and Clarendon more particularly. He is complained of as overbearing and dictatorial beyond what is permitted even to men of his eminence, while his eccentricities attract ridicule.' Suspicion of Gladstone as a crypto-Roman was as much as ever a source of hostility. At a Levee on 22 March Palmerston confided anxiously to Clarendon that he had 'the best reason for knowing' that were Gladstone rejected at Oxford and 'returned for a constituency like S. Lancashire', he would 'within six months profess himself a R. Catholic'. Even Clarendon, convinced as he was of Gladstone's incipient insanity, scouted this as extravagant.[57]

Certainly, Gladstone's increasing isolation among his colleagues led to a sense of dissociation. The nearer he got to South Lancashire the more his Liverpool origins were remembered. Stanley, himself the heir to the greatest of Lancashire magnates, observed the way Gladstone's religious enthusiasm and his mercantile and popular connections distanced him from the Whigs. Isolated from their cousinhood, he 'will never consent to share power, but, like Peel, if he makes any friends, will choose them only among men young enough to be his pupils.' Yet Stanley judged that these differences, 'though fatal to friendship, may give way before the necessity of political union, at least for a time'.[58]

There were occasions when, even among his near connections, Gladstone rubbed painfully against one of the cousinhood. When George Lyttelton presumed in April 1865 to express misgivings, his brother-in-law called him tersely to order: 'Please to recollect that we have got to govern millions of hard hands; that this must be done by force, fraud, or goodwill; that the latter has been tried and is answering; that none have profited more by this change of system since the corn law and the Six Acts, than those complain of it.'[59] 'It is certain', Stanley noted on 22 March, 'that of late G. has been in an excited and irritable condition, for which nothing in the state of public business appears to account ...'[60]

It was indeed on that day that Gladstone dined with the Thistlethwaytes, staying 'till near 12: an extraordinary but interesting scene'. He had thrice written to her earlier in the month in intervals of working on 'Rudiments of a Budget'. Catherine sometimes accompanied him on his social visits to Mrs

Thistlethwayte's tea-parties, but the deeper personal and emotional relationship Gladstone formed with the lady remained an aspect of his intimate life that he did not share with his wife. For Gladstone Laura Thistlethwayte seems to have combined the womanly attractiveness of a Collins or a Summerhayes with something of an exotic version of the educated and pious Harriet Sutherland. As far as can be judged, her technique for keeping Gladstone hooked seems to have consisted in doling out episodes of her life story rather in the manner of Scheherazade's tales, never quite coming to an end.[61]

~

On the other hand, Gladstone's excitement and irritability might just as plausibly have been ascribed to the fact that the debate on the Irish Church was due to commence on 28 March, and, much as with the Reform debate of the previous year, all attention was directed at what Gladstone would have to say about it. His relationship with the Irish Church question was in one important respect markedly different from that of the franchise. Most of his colleagues in Cabinet were critical or even hostile to the Church of Ireland as a minority establishment. It was not Gladstone's opinion about the Irish Church that caused nervousness; it was that he might propose that something drastic be done about it soon. Wood told Stanley that he believed the Irish Church establishment 'an abomination', and believed that most public men felt the same way; 'but to attempt to meddle with it would be madness'. He 'should be sorry to answer for what Gladstone might say or might not say on any question (laughing)', but 'certainly no joint action would be taken by the Cabinet.'[62]

Palmerston thought a word in season would not come amiss. He wrote to Gladstone on the 27th pointing out that Gladstone's intention to state his 'personal views on the Matter, as an Individual but not a Member of the Government', might give rise to future difficulties should the issue become a matter for Cabinet decision. This gave pause. Gladstone made his statement on the 28th – for all that he felt it 'a case of lifesave: I could not say less' – as a member of the government.

He opened by saying that ministers were 'not able to concur' with the motion, though at the same time they were 'not prepared to deny the abstract truth' of that part of it which propounded that the Church of Ireland was in a very unsatisfactory state. Ministers could not support the whole motion unless they were willing now or soon to bring in 'some plan for the purpose of removing that unsatisfactory character'. It was 'not so much a question for the present as for future consideration.' Gladstone then retailed all the stock arguments: the failure of the Irish Church as a Protestant mission; the advantages to it as a missionary Church of not being an anomalous establishment; the mistake of supposing that disestablishment in Ireland would lead to disestablishment in England. All this indicated that in the present position of the Church of Ireland were 'elements which show that her difficulties cannot be surmounted by the wisdom of her rulers or by the piety and devotion of her clergy, but that they are the essential elements of a false position'. What was the remedy? The 'dictates of propriety and good sense' compel ministers not supporting the motion and not making a promise 'it would be out of their power to fulfil'.[63]

This circumspect declaration killed the debate. As Gladstone had said, it was a question for the future. He later testified that had anyone asked him in the first half of 1865, 'How soon will it come in?' he would have replied, 'Heaven knows; perhaps it will be five years, perhaps it will be ten.' There was, further, a personal consideration. By 1865, Gladstone pointed out, he had completed 33 years of a strenuous career. He had followed most of his contemporaries to their graves. It was hard to find in the whole history of the country someone permitted to reach their 40th year of labour in the House of Commons. Hence he did not have in 1865 a sense of a practical application to '*himself* personally'.[64]

That Gladstone should have been in two minds on the question was not wonderful. Disestablishing the Irish Church would be a matter of deliberately grasping a virulent nettle. But above all the crucial element that determined his assessment of the political equation in the 1850s remained in full sovereign authority: he had yet to be assured that there would be a public opinion – 'a movement of the public mind' was his later phrase – correspondingly responsive on this question to the 'insight' expressed in his 'temper and restlessness'. To adapt the formula he had applied to the railways question, Gladstone would have to promote public discussion as a needful preliminary to forming a public opinion. Such a public opinion had yet to be formed and manipulated. And for the immediate future he had no high hopes of any formative opportunities likely to be made available by the elections soon to be held. His expectation, and indeed hope, was that the government would fall.

To enquirers Gladstone stressed that the issue was 'remote, and apparently out of all bearing on the practical politics of the day'; hence he had no scheme in his mind. There was a broad distinction to be made in politics between abstract and practical views. That was the reason he had been so long silent on the question; and why probably he would be so again. But he trusted it would be understood why he was unwilling both as a minister and MP for Oxford University to allow the question to be debated an indefinite number of times and remain silent.[65] Which was as placatory an effort as was decently possible; and gave substance to Palmerston's earlier comment to Shaftesbury about the expediency of keeping Gladstone tied down to his university seat.

~

As budget day approached Gladstone calculated that the real increase of all public expenditure *per annum* compared with 1853 was 10 million. That was his measure of what he had failed to achieve against Palmerston. The very buoyancy of the revenue disturbed him; a penny of income tax used to raise a million of revenue; now it raised £1.3 million. In defiance of Palmerston he hit back by reducing income tax by 2d. to 4d., its '*proper* minimum'. There were various other remissions and a start on the malt duty, 'indulgently received as usual'. But the substantial feature of the 1865 budget was Gladstone's celebratory rhetoric. It might be given to our acts, Gladstone suggested, quoting Arthur's hopes for his Round Table in Tennyson's *Guinevere*,

> To serve as models for the mighty world,
> And be the fair beginning of a time.[66]

The tone was valedictory. Gladstone's expectation was that this would be his last budget for the present state of politics. He looked forward to release from office. He could not affect nonchalance at the coming round another time of Baines's Borough Franchise Bill. He resolutely avoided speaking 'for fear of aggravating matters', though he did vote for it in a minority of 214 to 288. Enough government supporters joined with the Conservatives to defeat it: possibly a portent of things to come. Then, even more embarrassing, came round yet again Tests Abolition (Oxford). Gladstone now found himself uncomfortably between the fire both of his dissatisfied constituents and of dissatisfied Dissenters.

Palmerston's complaisance in allowing Gladstone to mitre a new Bishop of Chester was gratifying, particularly as the bishop was chairman of Gladstone's Oxford election committee. His efforts, on the other hand, along with other heresy-hunters among the Colonial Bishoprics Trustees, to unmitre the heretical Bishop Colenso of Natal, were unsuccessful. This doctrinal conservatism was for Gladstone a necessary psychological counterpoise to an ecclesiastical Liberalism he was now starting to apply to Ireland. On both the Roman Catholic Oath Bill and on the University Education (Ireland) Bill he voted to relieve conscientious obligations impeding Roman Catholics. In the debate on the former bill the Roman Catholic MP for Co. Louth, Tristram Kennedy, used the phrase about the representatives of his co-religionists being 'muzzled'. Taken up mockingly by Derby in the Lords on 26 June, it became notorious – a kind of sessional catch-phrase.[67] On the university matter, Gladstone prepared the reshaping of Peel's undenominational 'Queen's Colleges' of the 1840s in Galway, Belfast and Cork to cater for Roman Catholic susceptibilities. Since 1852 the Catholic bishops had been hostile to enrolment of Catholic undergraduates. Those colleges, as Gladstone put it, were 'wisely devised to meet a purpose; but we must admit that the colleges were made for the people of Ireland, and not the people of Ireland for the colleges'.[68] He rejoiced that on the Irish college and university system 'we have taken a just as well as a prudent step'.

The justice and prudence of Gladstone's ecclesiastical Liberalism was becoming increasingly a subject of controversy among Oxford University voters. He was at pains to scotch rumours that his loyalties were divided between Oxford and Lancashire. His explained his attitude to Lancashire as 'simply passive'. He certainly thought by 11 July that he would get in for Lancashire if he was seen to be failing at Oxford; 'which on the whole does not seem to be expected'.[69] On 7 July he passed two hours with a rescue case. He was observed walking in the Mall. 'A slight man of moderate height, with a sprightly, tremulous gait; a face of great power; hard, yet pathetic, worn with struggles & thought: the cheeks deeply lined, the mouth set & compressed, the eyes half-closed, looking inwards.'[70]

~

The general election was at hand. 'I trust God will look mercifully on His poor overburdened creature', prayed Gladstone, 'as he trips and stumbles along the road of life.'[71] The road along which Gladstone had just passed was the familiar smooth one to Cliveden. He misjudged the elections both in general and particular. He did not expect any surge of support for the government; and he did rather expect to be returned for Oxford University. As in 1859, Palmerston urged Shaftesbury to do all he could to ensure Gladstone's return. 'He is a dangerous man,' said P.; then Palmerston added, alluding to Derby's famous usage of the previous month: 'Keep him in Oxford, and he is partially muzzled; but send him elsewhere, and he will run wild.'[72]

Gladstone conscientiously voted in Westminster for his Cheshire neighbour Lord Richard Grosvenor and for John Stuart Mill. Soon another new MP emerged in the shape of Willy, expensively returned for Chester.[73] Gladstone had made of Willy's candidature a kind of proxy campaign of the kind convention barred at Oxford and of a kind at odds with Palmerston's blandly empty appeal to the electorate at large. Gladstone's keynote was 'a sensible extension of the franchise for the working man'.[74]

Early polling at Oxford looked bad. 'Always in straits the Bible in Church supplies my need. Today it was in 1st Lesson I Jer.19: "and they shall fight against thee: but they shall not prevail against thee, for I am with thee saith the Lord, to deliver thee."' By the afternoon of 17 July it was clear that the Lord had not delivered him. Palmerston denounced the 'gross folly' of the Oxford voters in setting Gladstone loose. Gladstone, on his way to a 'short but sharp' Lancashire campaign, was entrained to Manchester before noon on the 18th, examining figures and composing addresses of farewell to Oxford and greeting to Lancashire. To Oxford he declared that he left the 'incidents of the political relation' between the University and himself 'to the judgment of the future'. To 'my native county' he extolled the legislation of 25 years, asking for 'confirmation of that verdict', and for a pronouncement 'with significance as to the direction in which you desire the wheels of the State to move'. He hoped, before his words could be read, 'to be among you, in the hives of your teeming enterprise'.[75]

At the Free Trade Hall Gladstone found 6000 people and unbounded enthusiasm. It was political theatre of a kind he relished. 'At last, my friends, I am come among you. And I am come – to use an expression which has of late become very famous, and which, if I judge the matter rightly, is not soon likely to be forgotten – I am come among you "unmuzzled".' He had loved Oxford 'with deep and passionate love'; but now, 'by no act of mine, I am free to come among you', at the 'eleventh hour', 'I make my appeal to the heart and mind of South Lancashire'. His review of the 'beneficent and blessed' process of reform, however, was anything but a prelude to a rousing promise of better to come. Rather, he stressed that he had been six weary years in office, and the political health of the Liberal party would benefit from a spell out of office. As to the franchise issue: 'Never have I spoken a word which, fairly interpreted, gave the smallest countenance to the schemes ... of any who would favour or promote the adoption of precipitate or wholesale measures ...' Would that this question be kept out of the 'vortex of party politics'.[76]

As 'unmuzzling', this was strange stuff. To launch an eleventh-hour campaign by announcing that one wished for a spell out of office and that one's party was in no fit condition to continue in government was a procedure baffling to the activists around George Wilson. Gladstone pressed on to Liverpool. His speech to the Liverpool crowd was not much more apropos. He had clung to the representation of Oxford University 'with desperate fondness'; but he strove 'to unite that which is represented by Oxford to that which is represented by Lancashire'. 'I come into South Lancashire, and I find here around me an assemblage of different phenomena. I find the development of industry; I find the growth of enterprise; I find the progress of social philanthropy; I find the prevalence of toleration; and I find an ardent desire for freedom.' Nonetheless, however, he insisted that 'if there be a duty that more than any other should be held encumbent upon the public men of England', it was 'the duty of establishing and maintaining a harmony between the past of our glorious country, and the future that is still in store for her'. For good measure, Gladstone confided that though he was a member of a Liberal government, and 'associated' with the Liberal party, he had never swerved from what he conceived as those truly Conservative objects and desires with which he entered life.[77] He later prefaced the published edition of his election speeches with the line from *King Lear*: 'He'll shape his old course in a country new.'

Thus, though unmuzzled, Gladstone hardly left any fang marks on the body politic. This was part of his general miscalculation about the elections; which in turn derived from his fundamental misreading of the pace of political movement. 'The course of the Elections has a little surprised me', he wrote to Sir Thomas (who crashed in Kincardineshire just as his father had). 'I did not expect them to be so favourable to the Government.'[78] When Gladstone and Robertson went early to the poll on 20 July there were anxious moments. Gladstone eventually scraped into third place, behind two Conservatives.

~

Palmerston, 'well-satisfied with G's moderation in S. Lancs', was ready with congratulations, 'though many Friends would have preferred seeing you still for Oxford'.[79] At a Cabinet ('All in good humour') Gladstone had to digest the amazing fact that the government had gained 26 seats. A more thoroughly Palmerstonian Commons had been returned than that of 1859. Behind the scenes all was not good-humoured. Clarendon despondently predicted 'the inevitable political future' as Russell and Gladstone, with Gladstone having 'all the real power'.[80]

At Osborne the Queen's humour was a trifle strained. For the first time Gladstone noticed a distancing. In all her conversations with him 'she is evidently hemmed in, stops at a certain point, & keeps back the thought which occurs'.[81] No doubt the Queen shared the thoughts that led Stanley to remark that 'Gladstone's speeches are watched with extreme and increasing interest: he has become the central figure in our politics, and his importance is far more likely to increase than to diminish.'[82] His charisma was increasingly evident in the market for political memorabilia. For all Gladstone's 'moderation' in Lancashire in 1865, his speeches were, in Stanley's word 'effective', not so much for what he actually said, but more for their emblematic character as gestures of recognition from manipulator to manipulated.

From the point of view of Gladstone's commitment to his new vocation, such a role was essential and inescapable. In order to manipulate – 'turning them to account for good' – one had to embrace. God knew, he had asserted in 1864, he did not court them. This was true enough; though there was more than a touch of blandishment, the flattery that coaxes. To a world not attuned to the inwardness of Gladstone's politics, however, that nuanced distinction was not readily apparent. Like the Queen, observers became puzzled and anxious. Another such was Manning. Gladstone denied his charge of 'extremism'. 'I profess myself a disciple of Butler; the greatest of all enemies to extremes. But in a cold or lukewarm period, and such is this in public affairs, everything which moves and lives is called extreme ... Your caution about self-control however I do accept – it is very valuable – I am sadly lacking in that great quality.'[83]

After a deep wound in Oxford and a close shave in Lancashire Gladstone needed all the self-control he could muster. He confessed 'gloomy surmises' about the Church. 'It is a question between gold & faith: and the gold always carries it against the faith.' And he did insist that retribution must fall on those who, though with minds and eyes, 'will not read the signs of the times'.[84] His message to Bishop Wilberforce was that in its wilful blindness Oxford and what it symbolized would suffer much hurt. He was not angry, 'only sorry, & that deeply'. For his 'revenge – which I do not desire but would battle if I could – all lies in that little word "future" in my address, which I wrote with a consciousness that is deeply charged with meaning, and that that which shall come will come'. To this already sufficiently menacing prophecy of retribution, Gladstone added sententiously: 'there have been two great deaths or transmigrations of spirit, in my political existence. One, very slow, the breaking of my ties with my original party. The other, short & sharp, the breaking of the tie with Oxford. There will probably be a third and no more.'[85] When Wilberforce enquired to know the plain meaning of this 'oracular' utterance, Gladstone thought it best left in its 'proper darkness'.[86] Was he thinking of a breaking of ties with a Church ever carried by gold rather than faith?

For the time being Gladstone was noted as being in Cabinet 'quiet and subdued'.[87] By now deprived of his last illusions on the American case, he confined himself apologetically to offering the Union 'moral support' to finish off its great task in hand.[88] Gladstone meanwhile declined all invitations for further excursions in Lancashire. His duty was to be quiet after having been so conspicuous. This new Gladstone gratified Palmerston, who persuaded himself that Reform could be fobbed off with a commission of enquiry, or perhaps even remain a dead letter. Clarendon, reported Stanley, 'tries to undeceive him'.[89]

Clarendon's instinct was the sounder. Gladstone's power of recuperation, like all his powers, was formidable. But his forming notions at this stage about a 'future' of things moving and living were occluded still by the obstinately static presence of the Prime Minister. Palmerston's departure was the next logical necessity. It happened eventually in October, as Gladstone attended the memorial service for Newcastle at Clumber on the 18th. 'The news', he told Catherine, was 'bewildering'. 'At 6½ a Telegram came announcing his death & made me giddy.' 'This is an event that has made my brain spin.'[90] Shaftesbury remembered Palmerston's warning: 'Gladstone will soon have it all his own way; and, whenever he gets my place, we shall have strange doings.'[91]

10

Reform, 1865–1868

'It is not in our power to secure the passing of the measure; that rests with you, and more with those whom you represent, and of whom you are a sample, than it does with us; still we have a great responsibility, and are conscious of it, and we do not intend to flinch from it. (Here the whole audience rose in a body and cheered for several minutes.)'

Gladstone, speaking for the government on the Reform Bill to the Liverpool Liberal Association, at the Amphitheatre, Liverpool, 6 April 1866.

The Queen had already, on 15 October, settled arrangements with Russell that he should undertake the premiership on Palmerston's demise, then expected any day. From Clumber Gladstone wrote to Russell that he was ready to serve 'in the exact capacity I now fill'. This formula allowed Russell freedom to dispose the leadership of the Commons. Gladstone's substantial point about the new government was that it could not be 'wholly a continuation, but must in some degree be a new commencement'.[1]

On the 23rd in London Gladstone conferred with Russell, who requested him to stay on at the Exchequer and pressed on him the leadership of the Commons. With misgivings, Gladstone accepted on the 24th. Gladstone now stood in relation to Russell where Graham had envisaged them back in the 1850s. Stanley judged Gladstone's leadership as 'in any case inevitable'.[2] As Bagehot had put it in 1860, 'England is a country governed mainly by labour and by speech. Mr Gladstone will work and can speak, and the result is what we see.'[3]

Palmerston's funeral on the 27th Gladstone thought a 'solemn & touching scene'. That day, at Hughenden, Disraeli 'talked a great deal about Gladstone', Stanley recorded, 'puzzled by his persistence in High Church opinions: which he cannot think affected, for where is the motive? Yet which it is hard for him to think that a man of such talent can really hold.'[4] Other people were thinking a good deal about Gladstone also. Charles Wood lamented: 'Our quiet days are over; no more peace for us.' Clarendon could only hope rather despairingly: 'Gladstone's temper and want of tact are what we all know: but he has looked into himself, he has been warned by a personal friend (a woman: no man could do it)'

– Dowager Duchess Harriet of Sutherland – 'and he is determined to conciliate the House if possible.'[5]

Gladstone now stood where Palmerston had lately stood as the great man of the House of Commons, officially second only to Russell in the governmental hierarchy, but actually, as many would have it, holding all the real power. Yet, as he surveyed the scene, Gladstone would have been aware of inhibiting circumstances. His inheritance proved not of such brilliance as once it seemed promisingly to be. After strenuous years he fervently wanted repose. The government's success at the elections both surprised and dismayed him. He had counted on another Conservative interlude. The great works lying ahead, Reform and the Irish Church, he had hitherto been able to distance himself from with fond calculations, perhaps a generation for the former, five or ten years for the latter.

The evidence is abundant over the previous years of the 1859 Parliament that Gladstone saw himself operating in unpropitious circumstances with indifferent materials. The very atmosphere of politics he felt 'cold or lukewarm'. The marked feature of these past years had been a 'truce of the parties'. No wonder, then, as Gladstone confided to a prominent Yorkshire MP, 'I scarcely venture to look forward in politics. The large gains however at the elections do not altogether tend to mere ease. We shall know better by and by what the Liberal party in the new Parliament is made of. As far as its members go, they tend to indicate a strength, which would make it highly responsible to the country for the efficient performance of its duties.'[6] That was an optimistic assessment of members returned for Palmerston in what, after all, was Palmerston's Parliament. Cheer from 'out of doors' was therefore all the more welcome. Thanking Edmond Beales, President of the Reform League, for an 'obliging letter', Gladstone trusted that their 'indulgent judgment' might 'serve as a new encouragement to the steady performance of duty during whatever may remain to me of political life'.[7]

There was much left over from the old Parliament to bear in mind. Keeping animosities in good heart was for Gladstone a Butlerian duty. With Palmerston's departure it was likely that Disraeli would emerge in sharper focus. Another matter of moment was the fact that the government of the United States had decided to press for compensation for the damages done to its maritime interests by the depredations of *Alabama* and other Confederate commerce raiders constructed in British yards.

Determined to salvage something from the wreckage of his American misconstructions, Gladstone began to envisage the possibility that a moral cause might be retrievable from the principle of international arbitration. His initial move was to deflect Russell cautiously from immediate and outright rejection of the American case. Britain's 'proper course', Gladstone urged, was 'to lead the Americans to bring out the whole of their pleas and arguments, that we might have them fully before us previously to coming to a decision of great delicacy and moment'.[8]

~

As for Russell, now at last emancipated from Palmerston's shadow and about to undertake a second tour as Prime Minister, the general assumption was that the object of his career since 1850, a second Reform Act, must be his immediate concern. 'If Johnny is the man', as Disraeli remarked, 'there will be a Reform Bill – very distasteful to the country. The truce of parties is over. I foresee tempestuous times, and great vicissitudes in public life.'[9] On the face of it, this presented no problem for Gladstone. Had he not in his proxy campaign for Willy at Chester stipulated for a 'sensible extension of the franchise to the working man'? Yet the indications were that Gladstone in these early months would have much preferred marking time with reorganization plans for the Treasury. Russell, however, ever notorious for his 'rapidity', would allow no such respite. His first act on kissing hands on undertaking the government was 'to tell the Queen that he would want to bring in a Reform Bill', and his second was to tell Gladstone that unlike all his earlier abandoned efforts 'it would be a life or death question'.[10]

Confronted thus with Russell's rapidity, Gladstone reluctantly followed suit. He later assured the Commons as evidence of bona fides that ministers, gathered in their first Cabinet after the death of their 'lamented leader', agreed that they would prepare a Reform Bill to be introduced without any arts of delay. The important point in the new relationship of the Prime Minister with the Leader of the Commons was that both men were studious to avoid any recurrence of their old quarrels. Russell's handing over the Foreign Office to Clarendon removed the one likely impediment to their entente. Russell and Gladstone were now on converging political tracks. For if Reform was to be the great thing, that convergence would consist essentially in foisting Reform on a largely unwilling Liberal party in a largely hostile House of Commons.

The Reform issue became entangled with the problem of party unity, which in turn became entangled with the problem of filling ministerial places. Clarendon had vacated the Duchy of Lancaster. If foisting was to be the order of the day, some tactful management would be requisite. As a leadership team, Russell and Gladstone needed to ensure that the 'old Whigs' and their henchmen were on side to keep Reform looking palatable to the Palmerstonian backbenches. Would it not then be politic to placate the leaders among the Liberals who had in 1865 joined with the Conservatives to defeat Baines's Borough Franchise Bill? Russell favoured Horsman; Gladstone preferred Lowe.

In this respect John Bright was a big problem. Now that 'the reign of humbug' had ended with Palmerston's death,[11] he did not have Cobden's excuse for refusing a ministerial place. The 'movement' Liberals in the House and the masses of them out of doors needed some gesture from ministers that they were in earnest. Gladstone thought Bright might be feasible for the Duchy, but was more concerned to keep his distance and deprecate public notions of a Gladstone–Bright partnership in the van of progress. In the end it was decided to leave the place vacant for the time being. Then Chichester Fortescue's promotion to the Irish Office left the Colonial under-secretaryship available. Russell was willing to accept Gladstone's advocacy of the pro-Reform 'advanced' Liberal, the Bradford worsted manufacturer W. E. Forster, as a kind of Bright-substitute.

Throughout all this Gladstone had his hands full. Not only would there be no blessed repose from office; now, piled on top of his Treasury and leadership responsibilities, was to be the responsibility of framing the Reform measure. A Cabinet on 1 December 'chiefly on Jamaican horrors & on U. S. correspondence' signalled the coming of heavy tidings. Reports told of the grisly consequences of Governor Eyre's stern repression of an alleged insurrection of former Negro slaves. To Argyll Gladstone expressed his feelings that the intelligence was 'so horrible and sickening' that 'one hopes against hope that some of it is fabulous'.[12] A few days later, dining at the sculptor Woolner's, Gladstone found himself in dispute with Tennyson. Gladstone condemned Eyre for needless and illegal brutality; Tennyson defended him for dealing faithfully with a savage mob. The intellectual fault-line opened by the shock of the Jamaica case took on a public dimension in the agitation and counter-agitation it engendered, with J. S. Mill to the fore in the name of moral absolutism on the anti-Eyre side, and Thomas Carlyle rallying opinion to his defence on grounds of the state's duty against anarchy. And the 'U. S. correspondence' was the opening round of a fraught and wearisome negotiation on the matter of the British government's liabilities for its negligence in the *Alabama* affair.

~

The fraught and wearisome negotiation immediately confronting Gladstone was trying to get the details of Reform straight. The bill, as in 1832, would be for England and Wales. Separate subsequent bills were envisaged for Scotland and Ireland. A meeting at the Home Office on 22 November on 'Reform Information' started detailed work. Reliable statistics were never to be available. There were many who thought that in these circumstances the sensible proceeding would be to adopt the simple principle of a household suffrage linked to payment of rates and length of residence: the 'thoroughly English idea', as Milner Gibson put it, 'of settled heads of families being voters'. Gibson further put it to Gladstone that 'people are tired of the rental franchise of £6, £8 and the like'.[13] Gibson enlisted Forster in a combined effort to convince Gladstone of the merits and expediency of the Household principle. They failed. Gladstone had put it to Lewis, back in 1859, that a 'departmental instinct' led him towards preferring, ceteris paribus, a 'rating franchise'.[14] From that instinct Gladstone never deviated.

At that time of 1865 the idea of household suffrage was dangerously associated with John Bright, who held it to be the ancient privilege of the English folk. When, in December, Russell abandoned his efforts to appease Whig doubters and denied their demands for an evasive commission of enquiry, he settled for a reduction of the £10 borough rateable-value level set in 1832 to the £6 level of his 1860 bill as the point of equilibrium on the franchise calibration where the resisters and the advancers would be politically balanced. There would be a measure of lateral extension of the 'beneficial property' franchise in the counties to offset the new weight of 'heads'. There would be a modest degree of redistribution of seats.

All this seemed a prudent calculation when Bright was agitating the country on Reform, appealing to that 'auguster thing' than Parliament or Crown, 'the almost voiceless millions of my countrymen'.[15] The £6 limit was transmitted to Gladstone as the datum for his consideration; and so began the long comedy of the quest for the golden lip on the rental-rating ratchet. Gladstone was already aware of difficulties about the rating figures, which varied from place to place. He soon became aware of even greater difficulties about the £6 level. Such estimates as he could fairly calculate suggested that £6 might prove dangerously democratic.

At Hawarden over Christmas Gladstone worried away at the problem. The first shock on arriving back at Carlton House Terrace ('Saw, before I reached home, not less than 5 or 6 faces of much beauty, all astray') was news that Russell, with all his old rapidity, losing patience with the tiresome negotiations about the Duchy place, had peremptorily appointed G. J. Goschen. An import from the world of banking and finance, Goschen was a backbencher of only three years' standing. It was a deliberate snub to the recalcitrant Whigs, already offended at the passing over of their candidate for promotion, Lord Hartington. Gladstone thought the Prime Minister's 'precipitancy amounts to a disease'. Such was the fuss that in the end Russell had to reshuffle the Cabinet to slot Hartington in at the War Office. To this somewhat flustered Cabinet Gladstone presented his findings on the £6 borough franchise.

Meanwhile, Gladstone became determined to ease his way by disentangling Reform from Redistribution. The practical point was that boroughs, and especially boroughs vulnerable to be redistributed, were overwhelmingly Liberal territory. '*Why* is a good enfranchisement to be condemned unless with a good redistribution?' he demanded. Given a Conservative Opposition of 290, and say Lowe and Horsman and their 'tail' to be ten, you have 300 opponents to start with. Then, if you plan to take away one member from say 30 boroughs, how is it to be supposed the 60 representatives of those boroughs would vote? 'What margin would remain for carrying a Bill?'[16] Redistribution would offer a wider target to Reform's enemies and false friends. Bright and his friends 'out of doors' mainly agreed. Redistribution would be better done by the reformed Parliament. To complainers who felt that without Redistribution the government's plan lacked a vital component, Gladstone responded robustly. 'With regard to [a] thorough general approach, I will at once say boldly the case does not admit of it. Cherubim and Seraphim, if they had to frame a bill, could not obtain it, in the present state of things. If the Government show: 1. Care. 2. Courage, and the party: 1. Forbearance. 2. Loyalty (and of these last I have little doubt) we may come through; but at the best with some wry faces, some shrugging of shoulders, and divers hairbreadth scapes.'[17] Another memorandum to the Cabinet Committee on Reform in February dealt with the counties and with a variety of refinements for the boroughs. But what was now exercising the Cabinet's attention were the stark implications seemingly emerging from the £6 level. It would appear that out of 440 boroughs in England and Wales, 260 would be materially dominated by working-class 'occupier' voters. The 'balance of the constitution' would be upset. The level was promptly raised to £7.

By this time the first session of the 1865 Parliament was well launched. Gladstone did his best to conciliate the Commons. As Leader he threaded his way through Cattle Plague and Jamaica scandals. He spoke on Irish disturbances, on the dangers of 'Fenianism' in America, and defended the suspension of habeas corpus in Ireland. He outlined further legislative ameliorations for Irish higher education and landlord-tenant relations. The Queen expressed her gratification at the accounts she had on all sides of the 'admirable manner' in which Gladstone had commenced his leadership.

The forthcoming budget was not likely to be troublesome, though a brush with Lord Clarence Paget at the Admiralty revealed an aspect of Gladstone's outlook of long-term significance. He put it to Paget that to ask for increased estimates in the present circumstances of the world would be an affirmation in substance that the present state of naval expenditure was 'really normal'. In a very early manifestation of 'arms race' anxiety, Gladstone protested that 'we shall become deeply responsible to the world' if we continue to set other countries the example which 'our enormous naval force now places before them'.[18] In sessional business otherwise Gladstone colluded with the smuggling through of a renewal of the 1864 Contagious Diseases Act. The Irish Catholic bishops, to Gladstone's indignation, snubbed as insufficient the government's effort to cater for Catholic susceptibilities in resuscitating Peel's plans back in the 1840s for universities to nurture a native Irish governing order.

~

A Cabinet on 8 March 'settled after discussion but with harmony the final form of the main points of our Bill'. Gladstone introduced the Reform Bill on 12 March to a Commons chamber 'much crowded both with members and strangers', and buzzing with curiosity.[19] Ministers had in view enfranchising some 400,000 new voters, half of them of the skilled labouring class, in order to lay the political foundations of the nation on a broader and more secure foundation. These would be added to an existing constituency of about a million. The calculations were that something like one in four of adult males would be within the pale of the constitution. The principal mechanisms would be a £7 borough occupier rating and a £14 county rating, together with 'fancy franchises' for lodgers and Post Office Bank savers. Gladstone could not avoid explaining the change from the original £6 level, since that figure featured in some earlier draft versions of the bill. He made an anti-democratic virtue of this necessity. His tone on the whole was indeed apologetic, congruent with the expectations he had sketched as to wry faces, shrugging shoulders and divers hairbreadth scapes to come. He dwelt on the wreckage of earlier bills littering the political landscape. He pleaded with the House not to see this bill as 'a Trojan horse approaching the walls of the sacred city, and filled with armed men, bent on ruin, plunder, and conflagration'. It was a bill that comprehended the 'just limits of prudence and circumspection'; it accorded with the 'beneficent process of the law of nature and of Providence'; it was a boon that would be 'reciprocated in grateful attachment' of the people to the Throne.[20]

Then followed the debates that made the 1866 session illustrious in parliamentary annals. Roundell Palmer, the Attorney-General, judged them 'remarkable as a display of intellectual power'.[21] Gladstone he thought 'magnificent'. Bright emerged as 'a great humorist as well as an orator'. Bright's sally at Horsman, one of the leading recalcitrants, as a skulker in the 'political Cave of Adullam', where gathered 'everyone that was in distress, and everyone that was discontented',[22] at once coined two new terms of readily negotiable political currency. John Stuart Mill was, in Gladstone's estimation, 'admirable'. But it was one of the most prominent of the Adullamites, Robert Lowe, who raised his reputation most conspicuously. He launched two powerful and brilliant assaults on the bill that took the Commons by storm. His central point was simple: virtue, morality, justice and right had no bearing on the question. It was consequences that mattered, not motives. In terms of beneficial political consequences, the existing franchise answered all requirements.

Gladstone noted some 'lively skirmishing' on 23 March, when he counter-attacked Lowe's notorious invective about democratic venality, ignorance, and drunkenness with admonitions that they not talking of an invading army, they were talking of 'our fellow-subjects, our fellow-Christians, our own flesh and blood'.[23] Lowe made himself vulnerable by his provocative, oligarchic ferocity; but Gladstone equally exposed himself to charges of sentimental cant and enquiries as to how it was that flesh and blood ceased to obtain below the £7 ratchet lip. Wry faces, shrugging shoulders and hairbreadth scapes were signalled in a bipartisan amendment jointly moved by Lords Grosvenor and Stanley demanding that Redistribution be included. This in purpose was cover for hostility to Reform. The salient point now established was that foisting Reform on Palmerston's House of Commons was going to be even more of a difficulty than originally envisaged.

~

The Easter recess found Gladstone among his constituents in Liverpool. (Robertson, a grieving widower since October last, was absent.) Two big events had been arranged. They gave Gladstone opportunities to speak 'out of doors' as Chancellor and Leader. Lowe's success in the Commons nettled and disconcerted him. Nor was it merely a matter of Adullamites. The Conservative party, hitherto reserved and waiting to see how things would go, was now in the field with visions of the larger possibilities suggested by a replay of the 1865 combination against Baines's bill. Disraeli, impressed by Lowe's impact on the Commons, turned away from notions of a compromise Reform settlement towards ambitions to do damage to Liberal unity and Gladstone's prospects. The Conservatives, moreover, had perfectly sound partisan reasons for wanting to block ministers' plans for the county franchise. Clearly Gladstone could no longer rely simply on the 'forbearance' and 'loyalty' of the Liberal party to see him through. Gladstone felt himself confronted with the prospect of a hairbreadth scape. He needed to strike back.

The first big event was a grand formal banquet at the Philharmonic Hall on 5 April. Flanked by Argyll and Goschen, who embodied token decorum, Gladstone spoke for the government on a wide range of current issues before coming to the Reform question. His problem was that Reform at that moment was constituted in a bill before the House of Commons. Convention required a careful discretion in a responsible minister speaking out of doors on a matter being considered indoors. He twitted and pilloried Lowe. But Gladstone's sense of his need caused him to appeal daringly to opinion out of doors to keep the Commons straight. 'It rests with that public of which you form an important part', he told his audience, 'to determine what shall be the issue.' Ministers, he concluded, 'leave the issue of the cause in the hands of the great British public'.[24] These were bold words, interpretable as intended to intimidate Parliament. Worse was to come.

The Liberal Association event at the Amphitheatre the day following was a much more rumbustious affair. Gladstone devoted his whole time to the desperate predicament in which Reform languished, like captive Andromeda in need of rescue from the dragon of Adullam. His rhetoric blazed with images of unswerving fixity of purpose. 'We have passed the Rubicon, we have broken the bridge and burned the boats behind us.' His message on behalf of ministers was unabashed. 'It is not in our power to secure the passing of the measure; that rests with you, and more with those whom you represent, and of whom you are a sample, than it does with us; still we have a great responsibility, and are conscious of it, and we do not intend to flinch from it. (Here the whole audience rose in a body and cheered for several minutes.)'[25]

By thus summoning the genius of the people to his aid, the Chancellor of the Exchequer and Leader of the House of Commons committed a scandalous offence against the protocols of political decorum. This was the first time a responsible minister had done such a thing. In another sense, Gladstone simply slotted in to the logic of his vocation. It was a premonitory anticipation of what was to become his grand formula of political action: the imposition of his will as 'leader of the nation' over the will of his parliamentary party in particular and of Parliament in general.

Back at Westminster, Gladstone protested innocence in his usual deprecatory manner. He moved the second reading of his bill with much more restrained rhetoric. He was nervous of the Conservatives. He declared his intention to avoid all issues of party or of class. Lowe rebuked him. It was absurd of Gladstone to 'pretend that the influence of agitation was not resorted to'; and it was not the fault of some of those who took part in the agitation that it did not 'develop into an influence of terrorism'.[26] Brand, the Whip, warned Gladstone of ominous instances of backsliding. Gladstone himself pleaded with the veteran Peelite Lord Ernest Bruce, invoking the shade of Sir Robert: '*every man* who shared his labours, who possessed his confidence to the end of his life, who knew his mind, has recommended and supported larger measures of extension than those which we now bring forward'.[27]

Russell ordered capitulation. Redistribution would be included. One of Gladstone's flanks was now turned. Disraeli launched his charge. He extolled the 'English spirit' of popular privileges as against the democratic rights spirit of the American constitution. He incautiously extolled Gladstone's speech as a passionate young Tory against the Reform Bill at the Oxford Union in 1831. More slyly, he extolled the late, lamented Sir George Cornewall Lewis, who, had he lived to succeed Lord Palmerston as Leader of the Commons, would not have counselled the Whigs 'to reconstruct their famous institutions on the American model'. He alluded also to Gladstone's being an alien import to Liberalism from outside. This provoked from Gladstone one of his supreme orations.

In his diary for 27 April Gladstone recorded: 'Spoke from 1 to past 3 following D. It was a toil beyond my strength: but I seemed somehow to be sustained and borne onwards I know not how.' Here Gladstone referred obliquely to his earlier commendation of the bill as integral to a 'beneficent process of the law of nature and of Providence'. Gladstone's sense of his being sustained and fortified by a higher, unworldly power, for a purpose congruent with 'that great and all-embracing plan for the rearing and training of the human children of our

Father in heaven, which we call the Providential Government of the world',[28] would become increasingly a theme of his diary commentaries and self-analysis. Certainly, at this high moment of almost desperate political crisis, it fuelled powerfully his rebarbative talents. He mocked Disraeli's 'American' extravagance. He denied the Cabinet was in thrall to Bright. He defended his Liverpool speeches. He withered Lowe. He devastated Disraeli's taunts at 'the political errors of my boyhood': he apologized for having been at that time 'bred under the shadow of the great name of Canning'. 'I grant my youthful mind and imagination were impressed with the same idle and futile fears which still bewilder and distract the mature mind of the right hon. Gentleman'.

There were touching, and in their way revealing, words comparing his relationship with the Liberal party with Russell's. 'I am too well aware of the relations which subsist between the party and myself. I have none of the claims he possesses. I came among you an outcast from those with whom I associated, driven from them, I admit, by no arbitrary act, but by the slow and resistless forces of conviction.' The classical tag from Virgil with which Gladstone illustrated this point was perhaps infelicitous: Aeneas, shipwrecked on Carthage shore, proved not a lucky find for those who succoured him. Aeneas had his own destiny to fulfil. And that Gladstone should then proceed to preface his peroration with an invocation of Peel was, if highly characteristic, yet not without its aspect of infelicity. 'Elevate your vision', was his Peelite text for the benefit of the sulky Palmerstonian ranks of his adopted party. They must understand 'the enormous and silent changes which have been going forward among the labouring population'. The working classes were not adequately represented 'in proportion to their intelligence, their virtue, or their loyalty'. He pointed to the 'magnificent moral spectacle' of their fortitude in Lancashire at the time of the cotton-famine distress. He urged the House to see that they were now 'making history', laying the foundations of much that was to come. This battle for Reform was the same battle as that for removing civil disability for religious opinions; as that for the first Reform Act; and as that for the cause of Free Trade. 'You cannot fight against the future. Time is on our side.' The 'banner which we carry in this fight' was the banner of 'the great social forces which move onwards in their might and majesty', ensuring 'a certain and not too distant victory'.[29]

It was magnificent. But the implications of Gladstone's emphasis on Parliament's duty to bow to forces outside it and greater than it were ungrateful to many parliamentarians of perfect good faith in the matter of Reform. Whigs and Palmerstonians of a sceptical turn observed uncomfortably the way Gladstone's well-known 'inclination to religious enthusiasm' became translatable through his doctrine about 'profound and uniform tendencies' associated with the providential government of the world into a kind of ungainsayable spokesmanship both for 'the future' and for 'the people'. His 'same battle' rhetoric was purely non-sequitur. Were, say, free trade and democracy compatible? The scandal of the Liverpool episode was not forgotten. Wry faces and shrugging shoulders enough in any event made a hairbreadth scape likely in the division for the second reading. 'The House was charged with electricity like a vast thundercloud; and now a spark was about to be supplied.'[30] Ministers stipulated for a majority of ten to sustain the bill's credibility. With 631 members voting (the largest division so far recorded) the majority was just five. Lord Ernest Bruce was not among them.

Frantic scenes of near delirium erupted in the chamber and the galleries. Lowe was in a kind of ecstasy, his albino colouring mantling to something like bishop's purple. There rose a 'wild, raging mad-brained shout from floor and gallery such as has never been heard in the present House of Commons'. It was a night, as one member recalled, 'long to be remembered'. The House of Commons had listened to the grandest oration by the greatest orator of the age; and then had to ask itself how it happened that the Liberal party had been disunited, and a Liberal majority of sixty 'muddled away'.[31]

~

Russell summoned the Cabinet for the following day, the 28th. He wanted to fight on, trusting to the new Redistribution Bill to turn the tide. Ministers concurred. The message Gladstone now delivered to the party was that Reform would not be conveniently abandoned. 'If the Bill falls, we fall.' Introducing his budget on 3 May, he rejoiced that it involved nothing likely to raise controversy 'after the warm debates and sharp crisis of last week'. By the same token, it could do nothing to repair party morale. Gladstone grimly introduced Redistribution on 7 May. It was prudently anodyne. A sullen mood now prevailed in the Commons. Gladstone's prestige was severely compromised. The bloom of invincibility had faded.

With the government in travail, its friends out of doors hastened to its relief. A letter from Gladstone to a pro-Reform demonstration on Primrose Hill gave Disraeli occasion to protest at the 'reign of terror' with which the Leader of the House was 'continually threatening us'.[32] Gladstone's temper no longer served any conciliatory purpose. Lord Robert Montagu complained of his 'tone of dictation'.[33] The pace of events quickened. Well-meaning amendments provoked John Bright into furious denunciation of fancy franchises and into advocacy of sound, solid household suffrage. There was nothing new or particularly important about that. What was new and important was that Roundell Palmer, the Attorney-General, intervened to declare his wholehearted approval and support. He predicted that the household criterion was 'the point to which we must ultimately advance'. 'I, for one, should be well-pleased to advance now.'[34]

Hitherto, Palmer had been looked upon wistfully by the Palmerstonians as the last hope, after the demise of Lewis, of heading off Gladstone. And in times to come Palmer would indeed distinguish himself as an obstacle to Gladstone's plans. For the moment, his urging the case of a 'definite status, and the stake of one who was or might be the head of a family in the social system', as against mere arbitrary ratal calibration, was ungraciously received by Gladstone as insubordinate and rash.

By early June, Gladstone had effectively lost control of the Commons. The House relapsed into procedural chaos. Members rushed *en masse* in and out of lobbies in a confusion of divisions. Gladstone was now limping, vulnerable. His relentlessly high-minded stiffness in refusing to bend in any detail of his proposals laid him open for blame and ambush. One particular amendment, by Lord Dunkellin, designed to restrict eligibility for the franchise, had taken on a fortuitous significance amid the general turmoil. He moved his amendment on 18 June. Ministers were incoherent in their response. Gladstone failed to give an early, decisive lead. By the time he declared that it was unacceptable it was too late to halt the slide of defectors. Gladstone recorded: 'Spoke on Lord Dunkellin's motion fully. After much anxious communication with Colleagues, & a little pressure on some, made a short declaration at the close.' One of Gladstone's critics thought it the case that 'Gladstone lost his temper sadly and bullied his party', doing himself and his cause much harm.[35] Ministers were defeated in the division, 304 to 315. Lord Ernest Bruce yet again joined the Cave, now crowded with 44 Adullamites. 'With the cheering of the adversary there was shouting, violent flourished hats & other manifestations', Gladstone observed frowningly, 'which I think novel & inappropriate.'

'If the Bill falls, we fall.' These words now came home. The Cabinet reconvened on the 19th. 'Decided to resign, not without difference and in the teeth of the Queen.' Gladstone always doubted the wisdom of this decision. He accepted it reluctantly, preferring a dissolution and an appeal to the constituencies. He put it to Russell that a general election would be the only way to 'keep faith with the people' in the matter of Reform, and the only way to redeem the honour of Parliament. Even were the Liberal party returned in reduced numbers, this would be well worth it if the reduction was also a 'purging'. The main thing was real strength 'available for great public purposes'.[36] Russell, furiously unforgiving of the treachery of the 'forty thieves' in the Cave, and infinitely reluctant to see his second longed for premiership crumble away, had only Argyll and Gibson with him and Gladstone for making a fight of it. The majority of the Cabinet held that the 'apathetic state of the people at that date' ruled out that recourse. Brand advised that to dissolve would be a 'fatal mistake'. Bright, naturally, was loud and long in demanding appeal to the country, but Gladstone's colleagues were weary of being hectored by Bright. Russell, queasy at the ungallantry of deserting the Queen with the European situation so dire as the Germanic powers quarrelled over their Danish Duchies prey, explored alternative possibilities; but none answered. Russell was obliged to press his resignation on the Queen.

Gladstone announced the government's resignation to the Commons on 26 June. 'I kept to facts without epithets; but I thought as I went on that some of the words were scorching.' The wreckage of yet another Reform Bill now littered the political landscape. Gladstone told Queen Victoria: 'from all the miscarriages attending the past history of this question, not ministers alone, & leaders of parties, nor parties alone, but Parliament itself & Parliamentary Government were discredited'.[37] On 6 July Gladstone 'finished in Downing Street. Left my keys behind me. Somehow it makes a void.'

~

Derby took over as Prime Minister and Disraeli took Gladstone's places at the Exchequer and as Leader of the Commons. For his part, Gladstone adopted the stance of one handing on the baton of Reform. He informed the Conservative frontbench on 20 July that it would be a matter of great satisfaction to himself and his colleagues if the new government should feel themselves in a position enabling them to deal with this matter in an effectual manner. Support would be offered gladly for a measure 'prudent and effectual'; but resistance would be uncompromising to anything 'illusory or reactionary'.[38] Should the Conservatives decide to take up the baton, Gladstone had two settled convictions in mind. The first was that they would be obliged to offer a larger rather than a smaller enfranchisement than the one they had helped defeat. That would be their punishment. The second was that he would be able to supervise a Conservative bill and command its salient features and produce eventually a Reform Act conformable to his own requirements. That would be his revenge.

There was a considerable disposition among Conservatives not to take up the baton. A variation on this theme was the notion of a deal with the Adullamites to concoct a minimal compromise measure. As against this there were two considerations. The first, speculative, one was that since the Conservative party had little joy of the existing franchise, a substantial change might well be for the better. Secondly, as out of doors agitation burgeoned in protest at the way the suffrages of the people had been made the plaything of parliamentary factions, there was much to be said for getting a sufficient measure through to calm the country down. On 23 July an enormous demonstration defied the feeble Home Secretary and stormed the railings of Hyde Park. Watching from a balcony on Bayswater Road, Matthew Arnold witnessed what was to be the inspiration for *Culture and Anarchy*. Gladstone, riding in the park on the 24th to view the 'field of battle' of devastated shrubberies and trampled flower beds, commented, 'Alack for the folly that made it.' More of the same was in train, with Bright rampant. In the end it was the Queen who felt that the danger of destabilizing agitation made some pacifying measure desirable. 'The Queen', Derby told Disraeli, 'wants "*us*" to settle it.'[39]

As Conservative ministers mulled over the prospect, the healing power of a sojourn in Italy was what now attracted the Liberal chiefs. The Russells set off for Florence, temporary capital of Italy, where Lady Russell's brother, Sir Henry Elliot, was Ambassador. It was in its way a piquant occasion when Gladstone conferred with Russell in the capital of the Cavourian ideal of *libera chiesa in libero stato*. Here the two statesmen, famed as pillars of the 'Italian party', came to terms on an Irish version of that ideal. Russell concluded with satisfaction that Gladstone was 'as little disposed as I to maintain Protestant ascendancy in Ireland'.[40] The Gladstones had plans for a long recuperative retreat in Rome.

The papal capital was at that time a place of unparalleled interest. With the recent Austrian withdrawal from Venetia, the Roman territory now stood out invidiously as the last gap to be filled by the Italian state. A French army alone propped up the Pope's temporal power. (Garibaldi in 1867 would make a courageously premature attempt to put an end to it.) A nervous sense of an ending pervaded the Roman atmosphere. The Cardinal Secretary of State Antonelli famously lamented that the world was turned upside down. Gladstone plunged into his usual avocations of grand society, sermonizing, sightseeing and antique hunting. There were audiences with cardinals. Nor was there stint of collegial society: Clarendon, Cardwell and Argyll were keen observers of the latter days of the temporal power. The Vatican made itself receptive to the English. Manning, since 1865 Wiseman's successor as Archbishop of Westminster, assured his agent in Rome that Gladstone was '*much* softened' from of old. He was keeping silence on the temporal power, and 'has been helping us in Ireland'. It would be well to cultivate him with a view to future benefits.[41]

It was cultivating Pius IX with a view to future benefits that Gladstone had in mind. With Catherine, Agnes and Mary, he received pontifical blessing. He was received in personal audience. Gladstone wanted various things: insights into 'Roman affairs' and preparations for the forthcoming Vatican Council; insights into areas where his theological intimacy with Döllinger would be material; above all, help on Ireland. His indignation at the behaviour of the Irish Catholic bishops over the Irish higher education question remained keen. For all His Holiness's 'exceedingly genial & simple & kindly manner' Gladstone could extract nothing of use. (There was a 'quadrilateral' joke: His Holiness liked Mr Gladstone but did not understand him; he understood Mr Cardwell but did not like him; he both liked and understood Lord Clarendon; but neither liked nor understood the Duke of Argyll.)

Gladstone lingered long in Rome. The life of London, even of Hawarden to a degree, had lost its savour. There was much of the same sense of escape from personal crisis as there had been in his previous visits in the late 1830s and 1849. His own world, in its way, had been as much turned upside down as Antonelli's. The Cardinal had made that lament on the news of the Austrian defeat at Königgrätz in July 1866. Gladstone might well have made it in the aftermath of the Dunkellin division in June. Rome was reluctantly relinquished at the beginning of the new year. He was not back in the London scene until near the end of January. It was a matter of much observation that he did not give the customary pre-sessional dinner to his Commons colleagues. Granville explained to Wood, now Lord Halifax: 'He dares not ask Bright, and funks omitting him.'[42]

~

Derby did not envisage a hasty exercise. Politic deliberation, perhaps with a preliminary commission of enquiry to feel the 'pulse of Parliament and the country', was what he had in mind. The best approach would be by the tactic of resolutions; tentative, exploratory, avoiding an immediate declaration of details. Such details as he had in mind he declared to Disraeli in December 1866: 'Of all possible hares to start, I do not know a better than the extension to household suffrage coupled with plurality of voting.'[43] Plurality of voting meant a voter casting more than one vote in a constituency. It was a standard 'safeguard' provision. Derby's willingness to entertain the household principle meant that the Conservatives started off at a great advantage. At the opening of the session on 5 February Gladstone was all guarded blandness. He welcomed the Canadian Dominion and ameliorative measures for Ireland. On Reform he merely observed that ministers' intentions were 'enigmatical'. He proposed no amendment to the Address. He remained confident that he could shepherd the minority Conservatives.

A large part of that confidence came from his feeling that with the Irish Church question in reserve he had a means of keeping the fissile Liberal party united. His Florentine discussions with Russell allowed him to announce at the end of 1866 that the time had come when religious equality might be established in Ireland. This became a persistent sub-text of his politics for the benefit of the party. Russell's willingness to take the lead relieved Gladstone from the awkwardness of having to explain away his perhaps five years, perhaps ten, reservation. He was unwilling to admit that Fenian disturbances had anything to do with it.

Guarded blandness was the keynote also of Gladstone's tactic early in 1867 of not alienating Palmerstonians on foreign policy issues. Already he had distanced himself from Romanian efforts to enlist his support in aid of their braving the Ottoman suzerainty by electing a hereditary prince.[44] Gladstone trusted also that the Ottoman authorities would not be found blameworthy in the matter of the Cretan insurrection. Emboldened by the emancipation of their Ionian brethren, the Greeks of Crete sought to overthrow their Turkish oppressors. Gladstone was hopeful a little later that the Turks would be ready to listen to friendly counsel. To carpers Gladstone was quite forthright: 'I would not venture to say one word which would have the effect of encouraging the people of Crete to throw off the Ottoman rule.'[45] Urgent representations from Lord Clarence Paget in Malta detailing the horrors of Turkish repression in Crete and the need for speedy intervention by the powers failed to animate Gladstone.[46] This was politic with a view to Liberal unity.

Meanwhile, Gladstone confronted the principal issue of the day. 'Spoke after Disraeli after his extraordinary scheme & position', he recorded on 11 February. 'It was difficult in many ways.' The essence of Gladstone's difficulty was his fixed determination to impose upon Disraeli a version of his 1866 bill, whereas Disraeli, by his resolutions, advertised to the Commons that he sought any bill precisely not of Gladstone's provenance that could catch majority acquiescence. Since the Conservatives preferred to leave the counties alone, it would be a question simply of the boroughs. Disraeli began his bidding clumsily. This was partly because of old problems about reliable statistics. It was also because Disraeli was an amateur in the game. Gladstone, unsurpassed in his intimacy with the complex minutiae, was always in a position to savage Disraeli's feckless initiatives. But not the least part of his difficulties was that, being so well versed in the intricacies, he had become inflexibly bound by them. Disraeli was made free by his ignorance and incompetence.

Nonplussed, Gladstone moved warily, declaring his wish to be helpful to ministers. 'We are here embarked upon a common cause.'[47] He kept his temper and handled his party with tact. While Bright and Lowe, at polar ends of his party, demanded that Disraeli convert his resolutions into a definitive bill to be shot at, Gladstone protested: 'I am not taking the part of an opponent of the Government.'[48] Disraeli's big difficulty was to reconcile Derby's instruction that his franchise bill be 'in no niggard spirit' with acceptance by the sceptics in his Cabinet, led by Lord Cranborne, the former Lord Robert Cecil. What gave Disraeli most scope for manoeuvre was his belated discovery of plausible figures indicating that household suffrage with personal and full payment of rates would add no more voters to the registers than Gladstone's bill would have added.

This set Disraeli loose. He conveyed his revelation on 1 March to 150 Conservative MPs, including most of the borough members. They proved to be responsive to the idea of 'finality' involved in solid bedrock. Having this support, Derby and Disraeli were immune from dangerous fall-out when Cranborne, Carnarvon, and General Peel resigned from the Cabinet on 4 March. There would be no dissident 'Cave' behind them. Moreover, it was now clear that there would be no 'fusion' with the Adullamites to secure a restrictive, minimal, compromise settlement. Lowe and his friends remained confident they could block any Reform measure. Lowe put his finger on the crux: he pointed out that for the first the Leader of the Commons had pronounced 'the fatal and ominous words, "household suffrage"'.[49]

Fatally, Gladstone misconstrued Disraeli's discomfiture at the resignations of Cranborne and the others as his opportunity to strike. He revelled all the more in the commanding ease with which he could demolish Disraeli's improvisations. On 5 March, Gladstone dug in his heels. He insisted obdurately that his £7 occupation formula must obtain. He assembled his forces for a frontal assault. 'We are near the point of our final plunge', he warned one of the leading Adullamites, Lord Elcho, on 7 March. Household suffrage, even with securities, was 'a proposal wider than we think – nay, as we know that Bright thinks, the circumstances demand or warrant'.[50] The point had been reached where Gladstone opposed Disraeli on the ground that Disraeli was being too generous to the non-enfranchised.

When Disraeli presented what he now at length concocted as his Representation of the People Bill on 18 March, he proposed 'a most popular principle', the enfranchisement of 'male occupiers of dwelling houses'. For all that some 723,000 householders not presently voters would thereby be added to the registers, Disraeli was at pains to insist that such an extension of popular privilege was quite at odds with 'democratic rights'. There were to be safeguards and securities, alternative franchises would be available, and there would be plurality of voting. He dismissed the familiar formulas of rating and rental. The essence of the matter was to urge on the House a simple, commonsensical, readily acceptable criterion.[51]

Lowe in fact put the attractions of this criterion to members most tellingly: 'they believe they find in it a new principle, going lower, perhaps, than they would themselves like to go, but still giving themselves something that would afford rest and tranquillity after the storms of the last fifteen years – something so low they cannot fall lower'. Lowe warned, of course, that it was all a deceptive mirage; household suffrage would prove rather to be a 'quicksand', a 'quagmire'.[52] It was Gladstone's absurd fate to allow himself to become a kind of adjutant spokesman for Lowe's doctrine. He expounded spacious objections to household suffrage.[53]

The simple logic of the situation nevertheless began to work its way. In 1866 Gladstone had been thwarted by a Cave of anti-Reformers. Now the threat beginning to take shape was of a kind of counter-Cave of the keen, forward Reformers mixed with frightened 'moderate' men. Liberal members, confronted with the alluring temptations of household suffrage, betrayed symptoms of being enticed. Gladstone swiftly took steps to call them sternly to order on 21 March, at Carlton House Terrace. 'Meeting of the party, 2½ – 4: the end as good as I could hope.' Disraeli, in fact, judged much more accurately the amount of 'murmuring, round robins, and scuffling of feet' in the sulky Liberal ranks directed at 'iracundus Achilles'.[54]

This was as good a cue as any for Roundell Palmer to make a second critical intervention. On 26 March he reminded the House of his intervention of 30 May 1866; and that members must be aware the he was 'not one of those who entertain any alarm at the idea of household suffrage'. Palmer defended the principle as combining a liberal element of 'large and satisfactory admission' with a conservative element of heads of families inhabiting rateable houses embodying a 'natural principle of finality'[55] In 1866, Palmer had put himself behind Bright. Now Bright, embarrassed and fast-retreating, was nowhere in sight. Palmer had helped materially to sabotage Gladstone's 1866 bill; now he was helping to sabotage Gladstone's resistance to Disraeli's 1867 bill. He challenged directly Gladstone's call to order of 21 March.

Disraeli in turn took Palmer's cue. Palmer, a soundly Oxonian High Churchman, was as good a specimen of that genus as Cranborne, and a counterweight encouragement both to doubting Whigs and Conservatives as much as to opportunist Liberals and Radicals. Disraeli candidly opened the bidding. At the end of the second night of the second reading on 26 March, in a brazenly bravura speech, Disraeli invited the House: 'Act with us cordially and candidly, assist us to carry this measure.'[56] The Commons, bemused by his effrontery, let him have his way. The following night, 27 March, saw the 'droll situation', as Gladstone watched in astonishment, of the bill's passing its second reading without a division.[57]

To Gladstone it was imperative that this absurd trend of events be summarily stopped. He commanded another party meeting for 5 April at Carlton House Terrace. He planned to lay down the law about dealing with the committee stage. But even as Gladstone stamped his foot and summoned his legions, Disraeli presented his budget on the 4th, dripping with cordial and candid signals to Liberal backbenchers, who applauded while the Conservative benches remained silent.

More bemused than ever, 250 Liberal members gathered at Carlton House Terrace to be harangued by their leader. Ominously, there were something like 70 absentees. There had been resistance to the summons by many who resented Gladstone's driving. Gladstone, as he himself recorded, 'spoke at length'. He proposed to replace Disraeli's bill with a version of his own 1866 bill by tying the hands of his party with an instruction and marching them into parliamentary battle as a manipulated phalanx. Gladstone's behaviour and demeanour were entirely characteristic. It was one of his finest Peelite moments. Members complained of dictatorial behaviour, of Gladstone's having 'always monopolised the discussion', of members never being asked to give their opinion.[58] Having been obliged to swallow the second reading, Gladstone now compensated by refusing to accept amendments to his plan. He seemed oblivious to the danger. He was loyally supported throughout by Bright; but by now Bright sounded decidedly hollow.

Some Liberals, disliking Gladstone's dictatorial manner and proposed method of procedure, conferred at the Reform Club on 7 April. A further gathering met at the Commons tea room on the 8th, giving rise to the definition of the 'Tearoom Cave', as a kind of counter-version of the Cave of Adullam. This was mutiny. Something like fifty Liberal members were prepared to defy their Whip. Brand's position had become untenable. A delegation was despatched to Gladstone with demands that he drop features of his instruction. Gladstone became aware on 6 April that the ground had begun to slip under his feet. 'Conclave on the situation & on Disraeli's foolish amendments.' It was no longer a matter of the foolishness of Disraeli's amendments. Offended and affronted, Gladstone nonetheless conceded the demands of the Tearoom mutineers: 'the retreat was effected, perhaps "as well as could be expected"'. The retreat revealed itself to be but a cunning feint. He appeared to be unteachable. His attack was a disaster. His friend Robert Phillimore observed on 9 April: 'Entire collapse of Gladstone's attack on Government yesterday ... Disraeli's insolent triumph.'[59]

The issue became critical on 12 April, when Gladstone, doggedly unwilling to yield a jot or tittle, persisted with his attack. Gladstone was more than ever a master of the intricacies; but the House was more than ever weary of them. To Gladstone's immense indignation, Disraeli abruptly refused to accept his amendments: 'a declaration of war'. Disraeli was willing to accept almost any amendment provided it was not from Gladstone. Phillimore met Gladstone and Catherine as events were moving to the brink of a division and observed his '*disgust* and *deep mortification* at the defection of his party'. Phillimore's remark, that, 'if deserted, he will abdicate, and leave them to find another leader', was 'fully responded to by him'.[60] The expectation was still, nonetheless, that Gladstone would carry the division, even if with a 'hairbreadth scape'. As Big Ben struck two in the morning, Gladstone found himself in the minority, 289 to 310. Forty-five Liberals voted or paired against their party. Given the natural Liberal majority in the Commons, revived and as it was hoped repaired after the fissure of 1866, Gladstone's rueful comment was apt: 'A smash perhaps without example.'[61]

~

If in Disraeli's opportunist reading of the House of Commons there were the fruits of long, hard and often bitter experience of the wiles of minority politics and its exigencies, Gladstone's failure to read his party with anything like accuracy either in 1866 or 1867 spoke eloquently both of his 'instrumental' view of party as such and of the problematic deeply embedded in the manner and motives of his becoming 'associated' with the Liberal party in the first place. Gladstone's uneasy relationship with the Liberal parliamentary party was to a great extent inherent in his much more comfortable relationship with 'opinion' out of doors. Echoes of Liverpool in the Easter recess of 1866 still resonated. It was a very 'Gladstonian' admirer of Gladstone, Frederick Temple, Headmaster of Rugby, who wrote supportively after the 'smash' in 'hearty admiration' of Gladstone's efforts: 'I do not feel that the present Representatives of the Liberal Party in Parliament can be taken as a fair expression of the Liberal feeling in the country.'[62] It was another eminent Rugbeian, Thomas Hughes (of *Tom Brown's Schooldays* fame), Liberal MP for Lambeth, who pleaded on behalf of the loyal majority that Gladstone should not in any way draw back or leave 'the "free lances" to get what may yet be got out of this Government'. Gladstone, and Gladstone alone, could rally the 'true Liberals'.[63]

Yet it was going to be the case that the 'free lances' were very much out to get what yet might be got from the Conservative government. The circumstances were such that Gladstone was now incapable of rallying the 'true Liberals'. The message to that effect was put to Gladstone candidly by George Denman, Palmerston's former colleague at Tiverton. Household suffrage was inevitable: 'we should recognise the fact that, so far as *this* question is concerned, there is no such thing as a Liberal Party, and that every one is at liberty to act and speak for himself without reference to the convenience of his Party'.[64]

Indignant readiness on Gladstone's part to consider abdication was no doubt a genuine emotion, but there is no evidence that he contemplated more than a marked withdrawal of his presence for a time from the frontbench. He left much of the routine business after the Easter recess to juniors such as Ayrton and Palmer. He commenced a new volume of his diaries by quoting Bunsen's resolution not again to 'enter into public life', but to devote the years yet remaining to 'great objects of eternal significance'.[65]

The remainder of the session, so far as Reform was concerned, had to do with the working out of Denman's logic. Gladstone admitted to the House: 'I have been ... definitely overruled.'[66] The 'free lances' were at large. Given that household suffrage was 'inevitable', the questions remaining had to do with the securities and safeguards of plurality of voting, personal payment and the like. So long as counties were left safely out of contention, Conservative members began to drift towards the notion that, while borough democracy was no doubt deplorable, it might do more damage to the Liberals than to themselves. This notion arose apropos of what the Liberal free lances were now aiming at: giving Disraeli a majority in return for getting rid of 'safeguards' and giving votes to 'compounders'. These were tenants who did not pay rates directly, but who 'compounded' by including them in their rent. Inclusion of compounders would enormously increase the enfranchisement by something like four times the numbers originally contemplated.

As the session wound its exhausting way into the doldrums of summer, an amendment in the name of one of the Tearoom Cave became the focus of attention in the crucial matter of the compounders. Grosvenor Hodgkinson, a provincial solicitor, 'reversed the plan of the Queen's advisers, and determined the essential character of the New Reform Act'.[67] Hodgkinson got in the way of Gladstone's own plan to take over the details of the government's household suffrage bill. This in turn pushed Gladstone, now back in something like his old contentious form, into competing with Hodgkinson on behalf of the compounders. There remained the assumption that ministers could never consent.

The atmosphere outside as well as inside now got sticky. There was another huge Hyde Park demonstration. A 'monster deputation' from the Reform Union waited on Gladstone at Carlton House Terrace on 11 May to declare confidence in his leadership. 'Spoke at some length: a quasi-manifesto.' In what was described as an 'angry speech', Gladstone weighed the implications of recourse to 'the people' in aid of his offering 'a decided resistance' to the government in Parliament. The Liverpool echoes now resonated once more. He informed the Commons on 17 May: 'I must consider what is taking place and what is likely to take place out of doors'. He could not contemplate without the greatest pain 'the probable recommencement and continuance of a most resolute opposition out of doors of a character which I cannot pronounce to be illegitimate'. Those 'agencies out of doors, which are intended to form, to develop, and to mature public opinion, are the legitimate expressions of the people, by which bad legislation is to be corrected'. Gladstone deplored 'circumstances by which the business of governing this country' would be 'taken from within the walls of this House and transferred to places beyond them'. But he could see that 'that is the state of things at which we are likely to arrive, unless some measures be adopted to prevent it'.[68]

Over the years to come this style of argument would become Gladstone's grand leitmotiv: danger to the state and the constitution came from those who resisted his proposals. The Commons at this moment had its own retort to such terrors. Gladstone was attempting to smother Hodgkinson with the warm embraces of the millions. He recommended Hodgkinson's amendment, making much of the point that his stand was 'upon our part a complete waiving of the ground upon which we have stood'.[69] It would, of course, involve equally a waiving of the ground upon which Disraeli and the government stood.

After speaking Gladstone left the chamber along with most of the members on his way to dinner. In a thin House of fewer than 100 members, Disraeli thereupon upstaged Gladstone by taking him at his word. Without prior consultation with his colleagues, Disraeli casually accepted Hodgkinson's amendment without a division as 'the quickest way out of the maze'.[70] Many a 'snug dinner party' prematurely broke up in consternation as the wire agencies sent forth the startling news. Gladstone hastened back to the chamber, stunned at Disraeli's coup. His bitterness came through in a later comment on the way a dog will love and follow his master drunk not less than his master sober, 'so the 250 Conservative gentlemen, who had hailed the measure in its narrow and reactionary form, continued to support it with equal fidelity when it had assumed its present wide, and as some would say, democratic proportions'. 'It was short, rapid, noiseless. Two hours of conversation, no debate – and all was over.'[71]

Disraeli had his bill as good as in the bag. After swallowing the multitudinous compounders, there would be no straining at the safeguard gnats. John Stuart Mill was gratified by this 'great and splendid concession', which no doubt encouraged him to attempt to tack female suffrage on to the bill. Cranborne furiously denounced a 'change of startling magnitude', which he misinterpreted as Disraeli's obsequious yielding to Gladstone's 'imperious dictation'.[72] Gladstone declaimed in futile indignation at Disraeli's 'astounding declaration of consistency'.[73] The best comment was put in despairing exasperation by Lowe: 'Was it in human foresight to have imagined such a thing?'[74]

~

Gladstone distanced himself from the final stages of the bill. He excused himself to Harriet Sutherland for withdrawing from frontbench leadership: 'for me to be present and interfere continuously, or so far continuously as I might in other circumstances, would exhibit needlessly from day to day the divisions and consequent weakness of the Liberal party'.[75] When it came to the closing debate on the third reading on 15 July he thought it best not to take part, 'for fear of doing mischief on our own side'. He left Cranborne to launch a philippic at Disraeli's treachery and Lowe to lament the coming dominion of the multitude ('I believe it will be absolutely necessary that you should prevail on our future masters to learn their letters').[76] Brand, the Whip, thought it appropriate to retire. Bright, more prosaically, expressed a sense of disillusioned anti-climax. 'It is curious that there is no exultation in the passing of the Reform Bill. The whole thing has been so unpleasant & so discreditable, that we who gain by it seem to have no satisfaction in it. It was very different in 1832 – & in 1846, when we won after great fights.'[77]

When it came to considering amendments from the Lords, where Derby avowed that the Bill was 'a leap in the dark', and where Russell talked wildly of sending it back, Gladstone detected that the Liberal party was 'more healthy than of late'.[78] Perhaps this owed something to the fact that he had meanwhile been plugging away at Irish questions. On 7 May he intervened in a debate on the Irish Church initiated precisely to lure him into the open. Gladstone concluded that 'the time is not far distant when the Parliament of England, which at present undoubtedly has its hands full of other most important business and engagements, would feel its duty to look this question fairly and fully in the face'.[79]

Thus Gladstone, after all his travails, managed in the end to leave an imprint of auspicious purpose on the 1867 session. Once back at Hawarden, in August, his primary concern was to acquit himself of an account of the last session for the *Edinburgh Review* that would adequately expose Disraeli's delinquencies. The 'good sense of the public', Gladstone did not doubt, 'has sickened at attempts alike despicable and ridiculous to claim originality and consistency in the very act of plagiarism and tergiversation'. But the central thrust of his denunciation of that whole sad episode was to point to what yet remained to the future. 'Time, as it has thus far been, so it will continue to be', the 'vindicator and avenger' of the Liberal party. There was nothing to show that it had disabled itself from resuming 'the command of public affairs and of Parliamentary legislation'. And, given that resumption of command, what then? The 'very air is full of the presage of events to come', he insisted, and to 'exigencies, duties and opportunities of the State, enlarged in proportion to the widening of its franchise'. The public was 'impressed with the belief that within these last years a real arrears of work has accumulated'. There was education, there was economy, there was the Army, there were the colonies. Above all there was Ireland. 'What is our arrear in Ireland? That word suggests a whole range of painful misgivings, and of a work which, if much longer delayed threatens to become impracticable.'[80]

The unspoken definition of the 'work' for Ireland Gladstone left eloquently suspended in the autumnal atmosphere of the last days of the old politics. Otherwise, as balm to his wounds, there was Homer. He commenced revision of his *Studies on Homer* in a work that would emerge in 1869 as *Juventus Mundi: the Gods and Men of the Heroic Age*. He was eloquent at the first Lambeth Conference of the Anglican world on the claims of the Church of England to stand 'in the very centre of all the conflicting forms of Christianity'.[81] Then came the interruption of an emergency session in November, occasioned by the decision of ministers to send an expedition to Abyssinia to rescue Consul Cameron and other British subjects being held captive by King Theodore, and to take counter-measures against the assassinations and violence of the 'Fenian' conspiracy.

The opening of the emergency session was marked by one of Gladstone's rare personal exchanges with Disraeli. Socially they were on a footing of somewhat contrived amiability, by means of reciprocal enquiry about the welfare of spouses.[82] Now Mary Anne Disraeli's serious illness prompted a truce. Disraeli wrote to Gladstone on 20 November regretting that his emotions had made it impossible on the previous day to thank Gladstone adequately for his 'considerate sympathy' in kind words in his speech on the Address. 'My wife had always a strong personal regard for you, & being of a vivid & original character, she could comprehend, & value your great gifts, & qualities.'[83]

Gladstone 'chivalrously' abstained for the time from political hostilities, though captious about the Palmerstonian style of the Abyssinian expedition. But on the whole he refrained from the minatory and avenging tone of his *Edinburgh Review* piece. He trusted that the Scottish and Irish Reform Bills would be put in hand without delay. He trusted also that the legislative responses to the Irish land question and to Fenian outrages would be equally efficacious.

These hints of big things to come hung in the air of the Christmas and New Year recess. Then in December came the most violent of the series of Fenian atrocities that had occurred throughout 1867 – in Canada, in Ireland, Chester, and Manchester. Now, in London, explosions at Clerkenwell gaol caused many deaths and injuries. It happened that Gladstone was to speak at Oldham on trade unionism, restraint of trade and strikes, in terms provoking huge offence in the trade union movement. He opportunely undertook that Irish social evils be attacked not in their manifestations but 'in their roots and in their causes.'[84] Here was Gladstone's shifting the Irish Church issue from prospective to immediate status. Battle lines were thus in essence early drawn.

Certain other dispositions shaped themselves for addressing the future and the first days of a new politics. At Christmas Russell confided his intention to retire from the Liberal leadership. Gladstone conveyed to Russell on 26 December that his 'title to repose' could not be questioned. But, rather as earlier with the leadership of the Commons, it did not come at a propitious moment. 'Nor', he confessed to Russell, 'am I sanguine as to what is to take place in the Liberal party when your decision is known.'[85] In his birthday ruminations at year's end Gladstone inaugurated a motif that was to become as insistent and as long-lived as it was to be unfulfilled: 'I long for the day of rest.'

Clarendon put the problem to Granville of their problematical new leader: he could not discover 'a germ of appreciation towards Gladstone'; but neither 'an attempt to discover how he can be done without'. There seemed 'a determination to distrust him, and to find fault with whatever he does or does not do'. 'His genius and eloquence enable him to soar high above the heads of the party, who are always suspicious of what he may devise when he gets into higher or unknown latitudes.' It would remain, Clarendon concluded, an insoluble conundrum.[86] They were stuck with him, and he with them.

Then on 25 February Gladstone heard from Stanley that Derby had resigned from ill-health, and Disraeli, having been requested by the Queen to take over, was prime minister and *ipso facto* leader of the Conservative party. This was important far beyond the point simply that the Conservatives now had in their own way as problematical a new leader as the Liberals. Disraeli would provide a much more eligible target than Derby upon which Liberal unity could be focused. Gladstone on the 28th 'considered a good deal on the personnel of our party with a view to contingencies'. Battle lines on a larger scale were now drawn.

11

Strenuous Government, 1868–1871

'The Almighty seems to sustain and spare me for some purpose of His own, deeply unworthy as I know myself to be.'

Gladstone, diary entry, 29 December 1868

With battle-lines drawn and new commanders in place, hostilities commenced promptly. This was entirely Gladstone's doing. He wanted, as he foretold amply in his *Edinburgh* piece, revenge. He was eager that Liberalism should resume forthwith its command of public affairs and legislation. He had, in the Irish Church question, the means of it. It constituted aptly an exigency, duty and opportunity of the state.

Russell's departure was important in clearing the way. Russell advocated a 'concurrent' policy with respect to Irish ecclesiastical endowments. This meant diverting funds from the ample Church resources to increase existing endowment for Presbyterians and Catholics. In this way, wholesale disendowment of the Church might be avoided as part of a policy of disestablishment. This went back to Whig ideas in the 1830s. A variant, now espoused by the Conservatives, was to make three establishments 'concurrent'. A shrewd Ulster Conservative put the case against them accurately. 'If Gladstone and his friends go for anything *like* Ld Russell's proposition they will fail signally. If they throw it over, & go for a complete disendowment of everybody, they may catch voluntaries, radicals, & anti-poperymen, & make a formidable phalanx.'[1]

That kind of formidable phalanx was very much what Gladstone had in mind when on 12 March he summoned 'a Conclave 12 – 2 on the Irish question'. Vindicating and avenging the Liberal party would not be accomplished by half-measures. A clean sweep of straightforward disestablishment and disendowment all round was in order. The Irish question, it was announced, had become the 'question of the day'; there was 'foreboding and alarm', not merely anxiety, as Parliament came to find itself 'on the eve of a great struggle'.[2] It was by now clear that Gladstone need have no fears about rallying or testing party allegiance. Although the Whigs found Gladstone disturbing in general and distasteful in many particulars, they could not deny the validity of the tradition of Whiggish animosity towards the Church of the Irish Ascendancy. Echoes recurred from the distant past. Lord Derby and Gladstone were respectively at the opposite poles of their positions in the 1830s and 1840s. In speaking for Liberal doubters Roundell Palmer echoed now the Gladstone then: 'I cannot separate myself in feeling from my fellow-churchmen in Ireland.'[3] But Granville remarked on the 'almost unanimous opinion of the Liberal party'.[4]

On 16 March Gladstone launched his attack. The government, he declared, had 'failed to realise in any degree the solemn fact that we have reached a crisis in the affairs and in the state of Ireland'. The land question and the education question needed attention; but most urgent was the Church. If any good was to be done for the Church of Ireland it must be by putting an end to its futile existence as a state establishment. This would be a 'great and formidable operation', but not beyond the courage and statesmanship of the British legislature.'[5] To Disraeli it was an 'announcement of startling importance'.[6]

On 23 March Gladstone augmented the startling importance of his general advance with notice of three resolutions. They constituted a peremptory stroke that quite unnerved Disraeli's Cabinet. He protested at the sudden and 'unseasonable' nature of Gladstone's assault, with the session well advanced, with much business to transact, on an issue that would better be left to the new Parliament.

Gladstone carried the House brilliantly on 3 April. The divisions consistently of a near 60 majority were 'wonderful'. It was at this moment of public triumph that a disturbing element intruded privately. The peremptory tone of Gladstone's resolutions offended the Queen. She visited Derby at St James's Square on that 3 April, speaking 'in the most unreserved terms of condemnation of Gladstone's motion and conduct'. She felt her prerogative being touched disrespectfully. Derby reported to Disraeli: 'I took it upon myself to say that I had strongly urged you in the event of defeat, not to think of resigning, to which H. M. answered, "quite right".'[7]

With painful memories of the 1867 session, Gladstone trusted in the Commons that the Irish Church question would not be 'degraded into a warfare of trick and contrivance'. He defended his past record with respect to the question. He denied sudden 'apostasy'. His big point now was that there was a prospect of carrying the issue to a successful conclusion: circumstances were now 'ripe'.[8] This ripeness in the time bore for Gladstone much deeper import than mere 'right-timing' or opportunism or the expediency of gathering the Liberal party back into unity. 'Religious equality for Ireland' he would later cite as the second incidence, after the 1853 budget, of his gift of 'insight' at critical junctures of appreciating the general situation and its result. The very air presaging great events to come, the exigencies, duties and opportunities of the state, enlarged in proportion to the widening of its electoral base, all conjoined with Gladstone's appointed office in the divine economy, now assumed a potent urgency in an articulation between the doings and intentions of the minister (or in this case of the minister-to-be), and a corresponding conviction to be wrought by them on the public mind.

As the pace of events quickened, voices appealed to Gladstone for a less precipitate advance. 'I should acknowledge the justice of your claim that I should pause & meditate', as he replied in one such case, 'were it not that I had paused long, meditated often, & thoroughly convinced myself by the experience & recollection of many years that I am in the path of right, & therefore doing what does honour, as far as so poor a creature may, to God, as the God of truth & justice.'[9]

Thus fortified, Gladstone pressed onward after the recess. By now ministers were in disarray. On 27 April Gladstone put his first resolution forward for formal adoption by the Commons. 'Much oppressed in *nerve*, only by the bigness of the subject, & with a great sense of giddiness.' On 30 April he carried the division with crushing decisiveness, 330 to 265. Disraeli announced that it would be necessary for Her Majesty's Government to consider its position.

Liberals assumed that, in the conventional manner, ministers, having lost the confidence of the Commons on a matter of the highest public import, would offer their resignation, whereupon Gladstone would be called upon to form a new government. Dissolution on the existing registers was not a practical option. Registers for the vastly expanded new electorate would take some time yet to be in readiness. On 4 May Disraeli announced that Her Majesty had been pleased to decline the government's proffered resignation, and that the 1865 Parliament would be dissolved 'whenever the state of public affairs would permit'. His rationale – to which presumably H. M. was agreeable – was that the Irish Church resolutions were 'unseasonable' and improperly the occasion of resignation, in that they had been forced forward with untoward suddenness, and would be dealt with much more appropriately by the new Parliament; that the government's Reform Bills for Scotland and Ireland were still in train; and that the new voter registers would take time to be in place.

Disraeli thus had available the 'trick and contrivance' of an option of a 'penal' dissolution. Any move by the Liberals to oust ministers would expose them to the charge of making a nonsense of Reform by forcing the constituencies to vote on obsolete registers. All Gladstone and his party could do was fulminate against Disraeli's clinging to office. Gathorne Hardy recorded Gladstone's being 'in a white heat with an almost diabolical expression of countenance'.[10] Disraeli was able to wither Lowe by challenging him: 'If you want to have a vote of Want of Confidence, propose a vote of Want of Confidence.'[11] Gladstone prudently declined a vote either of confidence or censure.

He got all his resolutions triumphantly passed, however, amid 'stirring scenes'. He got his Compulsory Church Rates Abolition Bill through at last, though hardly as a matter of exerting imperious mastery over cowed ministers. The government granted Gladstone sessional accommodation partly because they had to, but partly also because they wanted to. A majority of bishops in the

Lords carried amendments that in fact represented a rebuff to Gladstone's plan. Faced with ministerial unwillingness to extend their accommodation, Gladstone reluctantly settled for what he could get.[12] Rejection by the Lords of his Irish Church Suspensory Bill prohibiting any further appointments to temporalities provoked a demonstration that marched from Clerkenwell through to Hyde Park Corner, occasioning tremors of 'some excitement' within the clubhouses of Pall Mall and St James's. A deputation addressed Gladstone at Carlton House Terrace. He expressed his pleasure at this manifestation of 'real working men'.[13]

Clarendon commented that while confidence in Gladstone seemed on the increase throughout the country, it remained 'feeble and stationary in the H. of C.'[14] Thus it was that the Conservative government held on until necessary business was completed and the Parliament was prorogued on 31 July. Disraeli was able to announce that a dissolution on the new registers would be possible in November.

~

Preparations for a general election now dominated the political scene. Already, on 10 July, Gladstone had conversation with Granville, 'long & large, including possible ministerial arrangements'. 'Puss' was consolidating his place as amenably supportive confidant. Gladstone was in no doubt that Liberalism's habitual political hegemony would be confirmed and reinforced by the new electorate. He was less confident about his own prospects in Lancashire. 'Protestant' anti-Irish sentiment was strong there. It was thought prudent to provide a fall-back refuge for him in Greenwich. He expended much time in wrangling correspondence with critics who accused him of apostasy on the Irish Church, with much quotation from his writings and speeches in the 1830s and 1840s.

At Hawarden in September he commenced work on 'what may be "A Chapter of Autobiography"', in which he envisaged setting out the whole history of his personal concern with the Irish Church question in order to demonstrate his good faith. He defended himself from the two accusations being made, betrayal of his early Church and State doctrine and opportunism in springing the issue in 1868. On neither indictment was Gladstone in great difficulties in pleading innocence. He could demonstrate how the question had over the decades 'continually flitted' before him. He could demonstrate that, with Palmerston's death in 1865, the 'calm was certain to be succeeded by a breeze, if not a gale'. Within a month he had it prepared for the press. Gladstone instructed his publisher, Murray, to hold it back until after the election so as to avoid giving it a partisanly electioneering character.

Serious campaigning work began in October, with a return appearance in the Liverpool Amphitheatre as the star turn. Clarendon professed anxiety that 'Merry-pebble' would be 'worked up by his meetings to a state of excitement which Christmas will hardly cool'.[15] Certainly, 'unmuzzled', Gladstone was now leaving fang marks on the body politic that he had not left in 1865. The mood of his *Edinburgh* article of the previous October, with its themes of vindication and vengeance, of vast arrears to be overcome, of the presagements of great events in the air, of the exigencies, duties and opportunities of the state, set the tone.

With November came the elections. A welcome telegram on the 17th from Greenwich announced that Gladstone had secured a seat, if second to a Tory distiller. But defeats of prominent Liberals in formerly safe Lancashire seats – Milner Gibson, Hartington – indicated that Gladstone too was vulnerable to what the mortified Gibson called 'Murphyism or Orangeism'.[16] The poll at Liverpool for the South-Western division of South Lancashire on the 21st confirmed this. Gladstone and his fellow Liberal candidate were left trailing behind the two Conservatives. The ignominy of retreating to the second Greenwich seat was, however, more than compensated for by the decisively enhanced Liberal ascendancy in the country overall. The people 'out of doors' had made an impact of a novel kind on parliamentary politics. Gladstone could fairly see it as a 'Gladstonian' impact. His formula of 1856 foretelling a corresponding conviction wrought in the public mind by his doings and intentions now took on the character of potent reality.

Quite how that reality would shape itself in the parliamentary majority was another matter. Its likely dimensions of near 100 worried sceptical Whigs like Clarendon. It was clear that Dissent – or Nonconformity, as it was more comprehensively now known to include the Wesleyans – was a formidably augmented force in the new Commons. 'Heaven knows, however, of what materials it will be composed, and one can only feel sure that such a team will require to be driven by a more skilful Jehu than Gladstone.'[17]

~

Given the somewhat anomalous status of the Conservative government since its defeats at Gladstone's hands in April, there was a certain fitness in Disraeli's unprecedented act of immediate resignation when the electoral fact of dismissal became manifest. The conventional procedure would have been to meet the new Parliament. Disraeli's decision to resign was deplored on the grounds that it seemed to recognize the ascendancy of electoral power out of doors at the expense of the constitutional role of the House of Commons in deciding the fate of ministries. Gladstone, stickler as he was on niceties of parliamentary and constitutional usage, made no complaint at the compliment thus implicitly accorded to the judgement of the people.

In haste to set the wheels rolling, Gladstone was immediately in touch with Disraeli about immediate sessional arrangements and the new Speaker for the Commons, Denison (and with compliments also for Mary Ann Disraeli's peerage of Beaconsfield).[18] At Hawarden on 1 December he was alerted by the Queen's secretary, General Grey, as to her intention to invite him to undertake the government. Grey assumed Gladstone would come to London, but Gladstone proposed Hawarden 'as attracting less attention'. Thus it was on 2 December that Evelyn Ashley, Shaftesbury's son and Palmerston's former private secretary, attended Gladstone as he felled an ash in the park. Ashley recollected, some 30 years later, that as he held Gladstone's jacket, the telegram was delivered announcing Grey's imminent arrival that evening. Gladstone remarked: 'Very significant.' 'I said nothing, but waited while the well-directed blows resounded in regular cadence. After a few minutes the blows ceased, and Mr Gladstone, resting on the handle of the axe, looked up, and with deep earnestness in his face, exclaimed: "My mission is to pacify Ireland." He then resumed his task, and never said another word until the tree was down.'[19]

Having settled preliminaries with Grey, Gladstone found the Queen at Windsor on 3 December 'kind, cheerful, even playful'. No doubt Victoria was impressed by the need to put the best face on things. No allusion was made to the Irish Church question. Evidently, though 'perfectly kind and accessible', she was slightly flustered. He was aware of a curious constraint in her manner. It was not until 5 December, on going through the budget figures with her, that he asked 'whether I ought to kiss hands: she said yes and it was done'.

Victoria employed Granville's 'tact and conciliatoriness' to slide in 'the *Old Whigs*'. In fact Gladstone had more trouble with Bright than with all the Old Whigs. Milner Gibson, Cobden's substitute in 1859, was out of the running. Now came the task of offering a Cabinet place to a man Gladstone had been chary of offering a pre-sessional dinner place to in 1867. Bright stipulated that acceptance of office would depend on the government's taking up the secret ballot. Bright had no administrative talent. But his presence in the government as the first non-Anglican Radical was felt by Gladstone to be inescapably the seal of good faith between the new ministry and the new electorate. After a long struggle, Gladstone persuaded him to accept the Board of Trade. Some of the Old Whigs found Bright too close for comfort. Grey, Halifax and Somerset refused Gladstone's offers of places.

By late on the 6th dispositions were beginning to emerge with something like clarity. Palmer was ineligible for the lord chancellorship because of the Church issue. Gladstone took pains to cultivate Delane of *The Times* by keeping him in the picture.

> You may like certainty at a time such as this.
> The appointments actually made to the Cabinet are
>
> Mr Gladstone – First Lord has kissed hands
> Ld Justice Page Wood – Chancellor

Ld Clarendon – Foreign Secretary
Ld Granville – Colonies
Duke of Argyll – India
Mr Cardwell – War
Mr Lowe – Chancellor of the Exchequer
Mr Childers – Admiralty
Mr Bright – President Board of Trade
Mr Fortescue – Secretary for Ireland
Mr Bright has declined the rank and office of a Secretary of State.
A seat in the Cabinet has been offered to Lord Russell & declined with the most friendly assurances of his disposition towards the Government. Sir G. Grey is in the north and his intentions are not yet known.

Should there be more intelligence tonight – Mr Glyn [Brand's successor as Chief Whip] will be in a condition to let you know.[20]

There was much observation on the 'ominous absence of many supposed candidates' from among the Whigs. De Grey accepted the lord presidency to add a touch of Whig tone.[21] Fortescue, who as husband of the grand hostess Lady Waldegrave reputedly 'dined his way into the Cabinet', would keep routine Irish business out of Gladstone's way. Hugh Childers, of Australian provenance, had done well as Secretary of the Treasury in 1865–66. Gladstone, mindful of his brush with Paget in 1866, sent him to the Admiralty to cut down the estimates and assert the First Lord's prerogatives against the Sea Lords.[22] The big surprise was Lowe. Lowe himself was not surprised – 'my sins in 1866 notwithstanding'. Gladstone thought highly of Lowe's economical capacities. He admired Lowe's penchant for being 'effectively disagreeable'.[23] Lowe's appointment at the time seemed an apt stroke both of political forgiveness and administrative shrewdness. The new Home Secretary, H. A. Bruce, a Merthyr coal and ironmaster, represented something of what has been described as 'moralised commercial efficiency'.[24] Goschen at the Poor Law Board also belonged to that category. Another was W. E. Forster, who, an ex-Quaker brother-in-law to Matthew Arnold, was a controversial choice to head the Education department. Meanwhile, Bright was being house-trained at Osborne by Granville.

There were irritating distractions. A steely letter from the Liverpool feminist Josephine Butler intruded: how did Mr Gladstone propose to vote on Mr Shaw-Lefevre's proposed Married Women's Property Bill, and on admitting women to the parliamentary suffrage? Gladstone warily declined giving pledges. His attitude in 1867 to J. S. Mill's attempt to tack female suffrage on to the Reform Bill had been obscure. He did not speak directly on the question, but was understood to think it impracticable.[25] Mill's defeat in Westminster by the free-spending Palmerstonian newsagent W. H. Smith seemed now rather to diminish the issue.

What was on Gladstone's mind in these last days of 1868 was a significant preparatory visit. He devoted the first weekend of the new session to Hatfield House, seat of the newly succeeded 3rd Marquess of Salisbury, formerly Cranborne and Lord Robert Cecil. He and Gladstone were much apart in their politics but much together in their churchmanship. They were also, now, after the horror for both of them of the 1867 session, much together in their despite of Disraeli. Gladstone's immediate motive was to sound Salisbury on how the Lords would receive his planned Irish Church legislation. Dismissed in the country and confronted with Gladstone's clear mandate for Irish disestablishment, the Conservatives in the Commons were now helpless to stem or stay. The Lords would be the crucial scene. Left to themselves, the Conservative lords would have elected Salisbury their leader. This was impossible for Disraeli to accept. A harmless substitute, the Duke of Richmond, was inserted. But Salisbury's countenance would be crucial for Gladstone.

Gladstone arrived at Hatfield fresh from an audience at Windsor, where he 'stated the case of the Irish Church. It was graciously received.'[26] Doubtless this gracious reception was the gist of the overture relayed to Salisbury. Possibly compromise in the matter of disendowment might have been aired. Gladstone commenced his preparatory intercourse with the Irish ecclesiastical Establishment. To Archbishop Trench of Dublin he gave assurance, on Hatfield writing paper, that all views held by the Irish Anglican episcopate 'will at all times have my most respectful attention'.[27]

Thus did the victims in 1867 of Disraeli's treachery and his plagiarism and tergiversation come together on the eve of battle. They were curiously linked by Lowe, an habitué of Hatfield. It had been to the Dowager Lady Salisbury that Lowe had written in September: 'I wish that they would make me Chancellor of the Exchequer.' And it was with some such sense of community of spirit that Gladstone thanked Lady Salisbury for kindness and hospitality, adding some words about her husband of extraordinary, and in some ways poignant, prescience. 'I feel it the more because although in public discussion on recent events his name comes to the mind of everyone I dare not pronounce it, for fear I should not myself be satisfied to leave it without a mark, & on the other hand I do not know how much harm I might do by a word of civility to him, that is, to the interest which England has in him. In one way or another, if he is spared, his time must come'.[28]

The long-drawn-out process of administration-making was now almost complete. Hartington had to wait until 1869 to scramble back into the Commons, when he could be accommodated with nothing better than the Post Office. But, in a certain way, Gladstone's most significant appointment in December 1868 was Robert Peel's son Arthur as Parliamentary Secretary to the Poor Law Board. Gladstone wrote to Sir Robert's daughter: 'I tread the footsteps of greater men.

It is now just 34 years since yr father did for me what I have been doing for your brother Arthur ... And whatever seem the seeming changes of name or measures of this I am inwardly sure, that I am as loyal as ever to your father's principles, & that if he had been alive I will not say he wd have been with us, but we with him, in the very work & purpose we are now about.'[29]

~

The intensity and authenticity of Gladstone's evocation of Peel as the tutelary genius of the work and purpose he was now about leave no doubt as to his sense of the reality and material relevance of that filiation. It was of a piece with his *Edinburgh* manifesto of 1867. In surveying the 'merits and services' of the Parliaments between the Reform Act of 1832 and the Crimean war, Gladstone concluded unequivocally: 'It was a golden age of useful legislation, and of administrative improvement.'[30] Gladstone saw himself at the end of 1868 as the retriever and fulfiller of that golden age. The epoch that followed Peel's smash and the smash of Aberdeen's effort to resuscitate Peelism had been an epoch of political bad faith, an epoch most fittingly associated with the name of Palmerston, and fittingly also capped by that ultimate exponent of bad faith, Disraeli.

Now all the Tennysonian promise of the golden years returned. The air was full of auspicious presagements. In his prophetic *Edinburgh* manifesto Gladstone had discerned that 'more strain is wanted for the engine of the State; and, to say nothing of the counties, the profound change that has been made in the borough franchise of itself suffices to warrant the belief that the stimulus will be supplied'. The reformed Parliament 'must be an ambitious, and may be an impatient and exacting Parliament'. The strain would be supplied; the engine would be started; the drivers had been appointed. Power was now Gladstone's to control. Power was exciting. On Christmas Eve: 'At night went to work on a draft of Irish Church measure, feeling the impulse.' The head of his secretariat, Algernon West, was impressed by Gladstone's air of potent energy and high seriousness of purpose.[31] As Gladstone confided to his diary on 29 December: this birthday opened his 60th year. 'I descend the hill of life. It would be a truer figure to say I ascend a steepening path with a burden ever gathering weight. The Almighty seems to sustain and spare me for some purpose of His own deeply unworthy as I know myself to be.'

~

Hawarden provided three weeks of repose and preparations for the serious business of the new Parliament. Liberal managers, oppressed by the indecency of the Prime Minister and leader of the Liberal party being not a member of the Reform Club, arranged for Gladstone to be shoe-horned in. The signal social event of that time was the first visit of Sir John Acton, accompanied by his stepfather Granville. Unfortunately for Acton, he arrived when Gladstone was deep in what was to become *Juventus Mundi*. As editor of the liberal Catholic *Home and Foreign Review*, Acton had hoped for conversation encouraging for both Irish and English Catholicism. What he got was a 'dreadful hour' before dinner, 'listening to Gladstone's theories about Homer, and this morning I have been reading a manuscript book of his, which he is going to publish ... a hard trial'.[32] For all such trials, Acton was not deterred henceforth from a near lifetime's assiduous courtiership within the Gladstone entourage.

Gladstone himself was having hard trials with the Queen. She refused to open the Parliament ceremoniously in person. Gladstone fell back on hoping that on the occasion 'of the meeting of the Parliament of which the House of Commons has been chosen by a greatly enlarged constituency', H. M. might at least receive addresses from both Houses.[33] H. M. remained in no mood to collaborate. Her hostility to his policy was no secret. Gladstone's private language about the Church of Ireland and its partisans in the Church of England was triumphal. 'It is greatly to our interest to nurse and develop the party of "Surrender".'[34] 'As they mean to fight', he remarked to Granville of the Irish bishops, 'I am not sure that it is a bad thing for us to have so little handiness in Dublin, and so little ability in Armagh.'[35] On the English side, 'the party of concession, from amongst those who have hitherto resisted', was shepherded in Convocation by the Bishop of Peterborough and by Wilberforce of Oxford. The Bishop of Gloucester assured Gladstone early in March that the 'wiser bishops' would accept the national verdict.[36]

Gladstone launched the great centrepiece of the session in a crowded and intent Commons on 1 March, in a 'marvellous exposition'. 'The use of his intellect', as one of his backbenchers remarked, 'is evidently not merely a delight but a necessity of his nature.'[37] Gladstone was determined that his epochal Irish Church Bill would bear the personal stamp of his power and authority. He announced that the Church of Ireland, 'if not the home and the refuge, the token and symbol of ascendancy', evocative of 'painful and bitter memories', would be disestablished and disendowed as from 1 January 1871. All other endowments of religion in Ireland would likewise be extinguished. The bishops and representative clergy and laity would constitute a self-governing body for a new Church of Ireland: truly a free Church in a free State. The proceeds of disendowment, calculated at £16 million, once existing interests and obligations were fairly discharged, would be devoted to a fund (estimated by Gladstone at nearly half the total) for beneficial measures of relief not eligible under the existing Poor Law. Gladstone claimed to be acting in the spirit of Pitt's Act of Union, recognizing the incompatibility of legislative union with religious inequality. He was confident of the 'approving verdict of civilized mankind'.[38]

This was heroic government engaging in a set-piece frontal assault on a deeply entrenched historic vested interest. There was little to worry about from the Conservative Opposition in the Commons. Disraeli accepted that the election had given Gladstone a presumptive right to deal with the question, and was relying on the Lords to mitigate the consequences. It became clear that Gladstone's biggest problem would be Roundell Palmer, who offered the most effective opposition to the measure in the Commons.

Palmer's arguments centred cogently around the implications of Church disestablishment for the Act of Union of 1800. That was certainly the way the matter tended to be read in Ireland. And the question of the Union had implications relating to the question of the landed Ascendancy in Ireland. Gladstone's supreme concern was to keep an equilibrium between a sustained momentum for his measure while at the same time restraining and confining the energies radiating from that momentum from invading contiguous political tissue. Cardinal Cullen, the head of the Irish Catholic hierarchy, assured Gladstone that his Church Bill was 'very well adapted to promote the interests of Ireland', and that it would 'inaugurate an era of peace and prosperity'.[39] What, however, it was immediately inaugurating was an era of Irish agrarian agitation.

The mass of rural Irish had little direct concern with the Church of Ireland. But they had an immense concern with what the Church issue seemed to promise in relation to the land issue. A vast swell of excited and deluded hopes and expectations for the disestablishment of the alien and absentee landlords was beginning to build up. For Gladstone the danger was that this swell might get out of control. Bright gave the swell an added impulse when he let slip indiscreetly his candid opinion that there would be no peace in Ireland until far greater numbers of the population were put in possession of the soil of the country.[40] Gladstone, embarrassed, 'spoke on Irish Land, trying to cover Bright'.[41]

Bright's opinion was standard Radical doctrine, much in currency among such grand mentors of Liberalism as J. S. Mill. Gladstone conceded that the 'land question' was a 'branch of the great question of Protestant ascendancy' in Ireland. He conceded also that, in dealing with the Church question, Parliament was 'in a certain sense, dealing with the land; for it has been the maintenance of Protestant ascendancy, in the form of the religious Establishment which has been one great and permanent cause of the mode in which the power of the landlord has been used, and his relations to his tenant have been habitually and vitally affected by that which, in its first aspect, seems only to be a religious or ecclesiastical question.' Gladstone insisted, however, that nothing had shaken the general principle of property or the actual state of possession or settlement in Ireland. In this he was profoundly unconvincing. He felt himself obliged to undertake 'to cap the great task, in which we are now engaged, in respect to the Irish Church, with another equally great task', that of applying effective remedies to the grievances of the 'occupiers of the soil of Ireland'.[42]

That there would be a big Irish land measure for 1870 was not in itself surprising; but what was awkward for Gladstone was the appearance of being hustled into it. Entanglement of questions about the Union and questions about 'tenant right' and indeed 'landlordism' as such with the Church measure gave stimulus and stiffening to resistance, especially in the Lords. On seeing the third reading through on 31 May Gladstone delivered a clear threat with respect to the 'future progress of this measure in "another place"', very much in the style and spirit of his quarrels over the paper duties in 1860 and 1861. Throughout the whole course of his Church measure, Gladstone had displayed an extraordinary parliamentary mastery. Now, as he threatened the Lords, his mastery seemed all the more impressive. 'Gladstone is unusually forcible and calm', observed Trelawny. 'I never knew a speech of his more terse. He is speaking like a winning man.' At his peroration there were 'cheers and clapping of hands'. On 7 June: 'On entering the House tonight Mr Gladstone was received with a burst of cheers, which were intended as a note of warning to the Lords.'[43]

In the Lords it was Salisbury – 'young Sarum', as Granville dubbed him, aware of Gladstone's 'personal regard for him' – who helpfully led the way to an uncontroversial second reading.[44] But then, incited by a furious Lord Derby, hostile amendments flew thick and fast. 'Sad work in the Lords', Gladstone recorded on 6 July. He was already in touch with Dean Wellesley of Windsor with a view to mediation with Archbishop Tait and the Queen. When the Lords' amendments duly came back to the Commons Gladstone was in no mood to concede. As he put it indignantly to Manning, those relating to disendowment reduced the bill to an 'imposture'.[45]

Eventually Gladstone was desired by the Cabinet to see the Queen at Windsor, 'for the sake of peace and of the House of Lords', with one final concession.[46] Archbishop Tait had already been squared. Gladstone was in hopes that Palmer could be of use through Salisbury and the bishops. For Gladstone the strain became quite seriously stressful. Stanley, always a shrewd observer of Gladstone, recorded at this time: 'Gladstone's own temper is visible and audible whenever he rises to speak: but he has so far restrained the expression of it so as to have said nothing particularly offensive, though the mixture of anger and contempt in his voice and look is almost painful to witness. With all his splendid talents, and his great position, few men suffer more from the constitutional infirmity of an irritable nature: and this is a disease which hard mental work, anxiety, and the exercise of power, all tend to exacerbate.'[47]

The Lords prudently gave way on the most contentious amendments. By now Gladstone was in a state of collapse. He left Granville to negotiate the finalities. The Conservative party and the House of Lords had been overawed and overborne. The Irish ecclesiastical ascendancy had been humiliated. The engine of the state had, as Gladstone foresaw, taken and borne a tremendous strain. As Granville put it: 'Who can write history? You however can make it.'[48]

~

It was a great relief for Gladstone to get away to Walmer, where Granville, 'the most delightful of colleagues', resided as Lord Warden of the Cinque Ports.[49] September was a time of recuperative tours and visits. At Balmoral he drafted a memorandum for the Queen on improving the House of Lords with new peerages and found her 'exceedingly easy and gracious'. She was less easy and gracious in her report to her daughter, the Crown Princess of Prussia: 'I cannot find him very agreeable, and he talks so very much.'[50] Apart from his preoccupation with the Irish land problem, Gladstone's principal concern was to prepare *Juventus Mundi* for publication. As with the reception of *Studies on Homer*, learned mockery was incited: 'When William shows himself a Johnny Raw / Right honourable is the loud guffaw.'[51] Gladstone remained, as ever, serenely unperturbed by scholarly disapproval.

Behind the grandeurs of 'making history' remained the prosaic obligations of administration. Matters of patronage in the old style of rewards and inducements for party services were by no means despised by Gladstone, but he was determined to shift the bulk of official preferment in the directions he had indicated in the Northcote-Trevelyan report on the reform of the Civil Service in 1853. That report he imbued with his vision of a Coleridgean ideal of a clerisy of guardians of a higher notion of the duties and functions of the state. The Crimean war and its Palmerstonian aftermath had stifled such plans; but now the renewal of the 'golden age of useful legislation, and of administrative improvement', opened up new opportunities. In Lowe at the Exchequer Gladstone had a zealous collaborator in his old quest to 'strike a real blow at Parliamentary Patronage'. To get around resistance from Clarendon and Bright (from very different viewpoints), Gladstone set up a Cabinet committee to make them 'so insulated that their ground would be untenable'.[52]

Resuscitating the Northcote-Trevelyan reform proposals from their 1853 limbo would be one of the more pleasurable aspects of the 1870 session. He pressed ahead with his ideas of a new ethos of peerage creations. His brush with the Lords had made Gladstone sensitive to the constitutional role of the peers. He put it to the Queen that the Lords' evident tendency to become averse to the Liberal party would necessitate counteractive measures. It would not be in the best interests either of the Lords or of the country 'that their assembly should stand in marked combat with the steady and permanent judgment of the country which on every occasion since 1830 except one has returned a Liberal majority'.[53]

Gladstone urged the need for more working Liberal peers. Victoria was reluctant to approve any change in the general territorial character of peerage creations. She refused Gladstone's proposal of a Jew, Nathan Meyer Rothschild, Liberal MP for Aylesbury, as she might well have done also, had not Gladstone been dissuaded by Granville, of the infidel John Stuart Mill. On the other hand she accepted his recommendation of Sir John Acton, 8th Baronet. Roman Catholic peers had not been created since 1688. Acton was away in Rome at the time, a kind of unofficial observer for Gladstone at the Vatican Council. Quite apart from the religious aspect, Acton's peerage remained an oddity. He was certainly nothing of a working peer. Gladstone's motive for advising the creation probably had to do with honouring Döllinger through his most eminent pupil and thereby making a point to the Vatican.

Perhaps the most characteristic creation by Gladstone at this time was the Blachford peerage for Frederic Rogers of the Colonial Office. By this unprecedented honour for a civil servant, Gladstone signalled his commitment to an ideal of the higher service of the state. Otherwise, his creations in these years were conventional enough; and although he was by no means jealously restrictive in the matter of peerages, he failed, then and later, to make any marked impression on the political complexion of the House of Lords. His problem in this respect is best illustrated in the difficulties he had in distributing the higher decorative honours. The Dukes of Norfolk and Leinster and Lords Bessborough and Portsmouth declined Garters on the ground of unwillingness to offer political support; and Lord Meath declined a Patrick.

It was to ecclesiastical patronage, however, that Gladstone characteristically gave his most devoted attention. 'A vacant see', recalled one of his secretaries, 'is a great excitement to Mr Gladstone. Indeed I believe it excites him far more than a political crisis.' In 1869 he set out meticulously the seventeen qualities he considered needed attention when considering candidates for promotion to the episcopal bench.[54] His first episcopal vacancy was Exeter. His choice was Temple, Headmaster of Rugby. He knew this would be controversial. Temple had been one of the notorious *Septem contra Christum* of *Essays and Reviews*. 'When the hour comes', he told T. D. Acland, 'there will be a great outcry.'[55] Outcry there was; but Gladstone lived long enough to see Temple eventually preferred first to London and then to Canterbury. Gladstone delighted in preferring old Oxford friends. He was able to promote Wilberforce from Oxford to Winchester.

Such preferments bore on Gladstone's current quarrel with Manning in defence of 'history and reason' in general and in particular Döllinger, the leading clerical resister in Germany to Pius IX's intention to promulgate the dogma of Papal Infallibility. It would come to the point in 1870 of Döllinger's pleading that the British government intervene against the 'infatuated proceedings of the Roman Court'. Gladstone's cautious response was that the two agencies most likely to avail against a 'light-minded and hot-headed Pope' remained France and the Catholic episcopate.

Nor were these Catholic and Roman matters without their immediate and practical bearing on the question of university education aimed at assimilating

Irish Roman Catholic gentry as a native component of a reformed governing order. Gladstone had been scandalized in 1866 at the way the Liberal government's efforts in this direction had been thwarted by the Irish Catholic bishops. He had tried, ineffectually, to make a point about it in his audience with the Pope. He was determined to do something about it in the present Parliament as a coping stone on his Church measure and his planned land measure. To Acton he predicted that as with the Ultramontane contagion that caused a 'very powerful opposition' raised against the 'very moderate measure of justice which we attempted to carry in 1866', 'the storm will rise again when we come back, as we must before long, to the subject of higher education in Ireland'.[56]

~

Rather in the rear of Gladstone's concerns in 1869, but not less laden with prospective political significance, was the question of United States' claims for reparation for the depredations of the British-built Confederate privateers, especially *Alabama*. As earlier with Russell, Gladstone, for all the disconcerting 'bunkum' being produced in Washington, urged on Clarendon the expediency of giving a wide frame of reference for an arbitration so as to give it a more substantial profile as a 'very solemn proceeding of authority', and, as such, the means of converting a rather bad-tempered bilateral negotiation on to a higher international moral plane as an example to a civilized world stunned by Bismarck's 'blood and iron' in 1866.[57] That very solemn proceeding of authority would, like the Irish university issue, be a matter of some years hence.

More immediately, Gladstone planned for the major initiative on popular education in England that he had identified in 1867 as one of the country's more conspicuous arrears. The people's education, it was widely felt, needed to be transformed from historic muddle to reasoned state policy. Scandalous numbers of children were denied regular schooling. There were many observers of the Paris *Exposition Universelle* in 1867 who judged that Britain's predominance in industry and manufactures was fast fading; and that in modern times good schooling was the key to a nation's success in the international battle of life. As with arrears of schooling, so with the prevalence of public houses: the Liberalism of 1868 demanded a big initiative of social hygiene against the drink trade, for which Bruce prepared schemes for restricting licences and opening hours. Both the Education and Drink questions would expose Gladstone's uneasiness among the Gladstonian Liberals. In the former case it would be the awkwardness of his religious conscience. In the latter it would be the benefits of public houses in ministering to the comforts of the people. The 'Mr Tipple' of Eton days became a father wont to amuse his children with tipsy songs. But overwhelmingly in these latter months of 1869 Gladstone addressed his huge appetite for strenuous politics to grappling with the conundrum of Irish land.

Not the least part of the conundrum was the rising tide of Irish expectations. These expectations took on increasingly the colour of what in Britain were derided as 'Irish ideas': that is, ideas in conflict with orthodox notions of absolute property rights, individualism and classical political economy. In the context of 'Irish ideas', the fall of the Irish Church portended the return of the land to the people. Vague hopes among the peasantry attached to a great extent in practical form to the notion that the logic of the Irish situation pointed to a land policy of funding the purchase of tenancies by tenants. Nor was this merely the logic of 'Irish ideas'. Anti-landlordism in Britain stemming from Radical traditions now had John Bright in the upper levels of government as expounder of the social benefits of many small proprietors. Many Irish landlords struggling with declining agricultural returns would welcome arrangements on reasonable terms to sell up. A tenancy purchase policy, moreover, had a wide and growing range of support within both parties at Westminster who were in general not at all susceptible to the doctrines of J. S. Mill. Their logic was that the survival of any significant landlord class in Ireland would depend on there being ramparts of small proprietors to shelter estates from confiscatory impulses. Salisbury was an early adherent to this idea.

A tenant-purchase policy had the great merit of going with the grain of Irish realities on the ground. The provision in the Irish Church Disestablishment Act of funding for tenants to purchase Church tenancies gave every indication of working well. Would this not advantageously be the germ of a larger policy applicable throughout Ireland? Thus was Gladstone advised that he would do well to consult Sir John Gray, MP for Kilkenny and proprietor of the Dublin *Freeman's Journal*, the most influential organ among the Irish tenantry.

Quite without the expertise he had been able to apply to the Church question, Gladstone devoted himself to a crash course of 'three months of hectic consultation and hard political bargaining' in framing his land measure within a political landscape of shifting ground and uncertain, slippery footing.[58] The great feature of his framing was that he would have nothing to do with any extensive measure of tenant-purchase. Partly this – as things turned out, lamentable decision – is attributable to the 'Treasury mind' recoiling from the prospect of a considerable outlay of public money assumably vulnerable to 'Irish jobbery'. It can also be attributed to Gladstone's instinctive predisposition to legislative heroism. As with his Church measure, Gladstone seems to have been determined that a grand Irish Land Bill would bear also the stamp of his power and authority as one sustained and spared for the Almighty's purposes. Arranging funding for tenant purchase would be a matter of petty administration. He ignored advice to consult Gray.

Gladstone's broad approach on Irish land was to smother 'Irish ideas' with English goodwill and the warm embrace of a reformed landlordism, but yet to recognize them just sufficiently to engender Irish goodwill in return. His land policy was in fact the reverse of his Church policy. There his disestablishment and disendowment had been absolute, and he dismissed all concurrent alternatives. Now he would attempt to foster a kind of concurrence between an official establishment of compulsorily benign landlords and an unofficial establishment of assumably grateful tenants.

The mechanics of this ambitious social engineering would be concessions to 'tenant-right' in matters of compensation for improvements initiated by tenants, evictions, and fairness of rents; all to be subject to special commissioners sitting in Land Courts. Irish landlords were to surrender from one quarter to one third of the value of their estates in return for a new lease of life being given to Irish landlordism. Precisely: re-establishment purchased by part-disendowment.

Critics of Gladstone's scheme would indeed denounce it as a system of 'dual ownership', and, as such, an offence to 'English ideas'. For the economics of the market were substituted judicial proceedings about 'fairness'. Rights of property were deeply compromised by 'tenant-right'. Yet Gladstone wanted to be seen as the defender and upholder of property rights. His model was the mutually beneficial landlord-tenant relationship he knew on his own ground in Flintshire. 'If I have an ambition', he declared, 'it is to make an estate for my children.'[59] He wanted this model steadily to obtain in Ireland so as eventually to obliterate the 'inveterate mischiefs' of a 'tradition & marks of conquest, & of forfeiture'.[60]

~

Political excitements attending the drama of Irish legislation transferred themselves into Gladstone's old pattern of religio-sexuality. Laura Thistlethwayte became increasingly through 1869 an object of intense interest and concern for Gladstone. She seems to have at least partly filled the gap left by the lamented Harriet Sutherland's death in 1868. Over the period from January 1869 to June 1871 he wrote 112 letters to her and met her on 45 occasions. 'Dear Mrs Thistlethwayte' became 'Dear wounded Spirit'. He never tired of receiving instalments of her 'really marvellous and most touching tale'. Was he a gullible dupe?[61] He accepted from her the gift of a 'Mizpah' ring that he wore.[62] In his birthday retrospect for 1869: 'My review this year includes as a prominent object L T: the extraordinary history, the confiding appeal, the singular arousal.' Quite what Catherine and the family made of this is not clear. No doubt Catherine knew her husband well enough not to attempt to intervene in the inner recesses of the religio-emotional needs of his intimate life.

On the political side Gladstone's retrospect pleaded mercy for the past and 'future grace to be Thine instrument if scarcely thy child'. Seeking grace to be the Lord's instrument would pile pressures on the parliamentary session of 1870 very much in the style of 1869. Soon Disraeli was protesting at the workload demanded by these further exercises in strenuous government. Gladstone later admitted that 'blame is assignable to us for having undertaken so much business'.[63] A bill to bring in the secret ballot for elections caused Gladstone some embarrassment. He had long been known to think the ballot 'trash';[64] but now circumstances obliged a change of front. 'It is rather alarming', as an observer commented, 'to observe the agility with which he conforms his opinions to those which he had but lately opposed.'[65]

Gladstone launched his Irish Land Bill on 15 February with nothing of the *éclat* that had accompanied his Church measure the previous year. The reception in the House to Gladstone's eloquently plausible exposition reflected an underlying discomfort and unease. Once more Roundell Palmer broke from the Liberal ranks to offer what Cardwell described as a 'most dangerous opposition to important parts of the Bill'. To Gladstone it was a scandal that opposition to his measure was being 'led and officered from the Liberal party'.[66]

Amendments piled in. The Irish, looking on the bill as an alien imposition largely irrelevant to the practical issues of Irish land, provided but feeble assistance. Gladstone reluctantly allowed Bright to tack on clauses providing for tenant purchase; but made sure they were dissuadingly restrictive. He expended such tremendous quantities of his public and parliamentary credit in pushing through the Irish Land Bill that neither he nor his ministry were anything like as formidable thereafter. Gladstone himself put it with uncanny prescience when he told Clarendon that he felt about the imperativeness of his bill 'as a bee might feel if it knew it would die on its sting'.[67] To Manning he reported that he had been 'obliged to resort to something like menace' to assert his authority. *When* it was settled, Gladstone assured Manning, 'I shall begin to detach my hopes and interests, if I may, from the political future'.[68]

Bright very sensibly advised that it would be prudent to postpone the Education Bill to the next session to ease the congestion. Partly his motive was that he cordially detested the way it had been drawn up by Forster and Gladstone. Gladstone's central concern with the question was always that, directly or indirectly, education must conduce 'to the most effectual propagation of religion'.[69] Forster gave credence to the claim of the Church of England that, as the national religious confession, it should have first call on any grants in aid from the Education Department and through its inspectors. Soon Gladstone was deeply enmeshed in assisting Forster to get his bill past the large and enraged Nonconformist section of the Liberal ranks. The Nonconformists, being unable to dominate religious provision in schools, wanted religion kept out of schools. It soon became a matter of Liberals furiously fighting Liberals. The Conservatives sat back to enjoy the spectacle.

Certain valuable things were achieved in the early weeks. The Order in Council setting in place the 1853 recommendations for reform of the Civil Service was approved on 4 June. This was mainly Lowe's work. His budget likewise passed with full credit. Cardwell also had in place impressive dispositions for reform of the military system. But by mid-session Gladstone was near collapse. He escaped for an interval of retreat with Granville at Walmer. Granville even enticed him to Epsom to see the running of the Derby.

His colleagues were equally under stress. To Irish Land would have to be added a Coercion Bill to damp down Irish agrarian unrest. 'This Cabinet', Gladstone told Russell, 'is the most laborious as a whole I have ever seen.'[70] The Queen had already expressed concern for Clarendon's health. Bright broke under the strain. So nearly did Cardwell and Childers. Mrs Cardwell protested to Gladstone.[71] Lowe was quarrelsome. One junior minister, Acton Smee Ayrton, fabled for offensiveness, created a kind of permanent administrative uproar. The Liberal MP Trelawny noted as early as 31 March: 'The work of Parliament has beaten us. Its magnitude even in peace is beyond our powers ... double sittings are already to be held before Easter.'[72] Clarendon died on 27th June. Granville took his place at the Foreign Office. Halifax consented to return to plug the Whig gap.

Ministers regrouped, but failed to convince the House on Irish land and failed to hold their ground on English education. Gladstone's complex judicial apparatus of commissioners and land courts in his Land Bill evoked little confidence.[73] Disraeli's tactic was to assist ministers to limp through the Commons' stages and get the bill up to the Lords for more bracing treatment. Conservative assistance was even more in evidence on the Education Bill. The parliamentary spectacle here unfolding was of the Liberal party largely at odds with the Liberal government. The Liberalism of 1868 was little attuned to Gladstone's pushing for Anglican dogmatic vitality. Gladstone's efforts at compromise did not appease the embattled Nonconformists, who complained at being marched by their leader 'through the Valley of Humiliation'.[74] The deal they were offered was that in unschooled places ratepayers could set up rate-funded schools to be managed by elected School Boards, in which religious teaching would be strictly 'undenominational'. This invitation to 'fill in the gaps' was thought at the time a paltry concession. Gladstone was obliged to appeal to the Commons at large. The Liberal government, he declared, did not exist for the benefit of any sectional interest; 'we are the government of the Queen'. This Peelite note rang bravely. But what it came to was an invitation to the Conservatives to save 'religious education' for the nation. This they willingly did.

That the Liberal government had to get its Education Bill through the Commons by grace of the Conservative Opposition gravely compromised its prestige. The aura of invincibility of 1868 was fading. This new vulnerability was important because it was contagious and infected the Land Bill debates. The Lords were less intimidated than they had been in 1869, but they were aware that any replacement bill would be for the worse. Lords were stubborn on certain points. Argyll played something of the same candid role for the Liberal peers as Palmer had played for the Liberal commoners. Like many another, Argyll suspected shrewdly that Gladstone's Land Bill was going up an Irish dead end. Apropos of that, it was notable that Salisbury much approved the 'Bright clauses' providing for purchase by tenants and deplored Gladstone's grudging restrictions on them. The 'extraordinary' circumstance disclosed itself of 'how little good one hears of the Bill from Irishmen of any party'.[75] That its judicial complexities would be a boon to lawyers and tend to exacerbate landlord-tenant relations rather than reconcile them was readily predictable. And as Clarendon predicted, it would encourage opinion in Ireland that the British government was on the run, and that repeal of the Union was the next step. The Irish MP, Isaac Butt, disappointed with provision for the tenants, launched his 'Home Rule' movement while the Land Bill was going through the Commons.

It took time for the symptoms to manifest themselves, Gladstone's remark to Clarendon about the bee dying on its sting proved indeed uncannily prescient. More insidious maladies infected the wounds of the 1870 session. Gladstone's stipulations for reductions in the Army estimates led to a calling home of the legions from the Empire. The colonial governments complained of niggardly 'Little Englandism'. At the Colonial Office Granville prudently censored documents relating to the new Canadian dominion so as to veil the government's desire, while not wishing to change 'abruptly' Britain's relationship with the self-governing colonies, to 'gradually prepare both countries, for a friendly relaxation of them'.[76] Gladstone was imprudent enough, on the question of that relationship, to disclose in the Commons in April 1870 that it should be on such a footing that 'if separation should occur, it should be in a friendly way'.[77]

This and similar official declarations caused a stir of discomfort in British opinion at what seemed imperial abdication. Notions took root both in Britain and the self-governing colonies of movements to counteract ideas of 'friendly relaxation' as a prelude to separation and to stimulate sentiment in the direction of imperial consolidation. At Windsor in November 1869 Granville was confronted with the Queen's complaint that England was 'being reduced to the state of a second-rate power'.[78] Russell revealed himself in the 1870 session as restless on the question of defence and security of the colonies. Disraeli began to sniff the air of politics for the fragrances of what would soon be defined as reactive sentiment of 'Empire'.

With all this Gladstone was unperturbed. Although he had shown himself unwilling to challenge directly the prevalent Palmerstonian orthodoxy in either foreign or colonial policy, he was ready all the same to chip away at their financial foundations. It would naturally be a feature of his own ministry's policy that 'Palmerstonism' be discounted. Offering the Americans an international arbitration over the *Alabama* dispute was a signal case in point. In any case, as he put it in February 1870: 'In truth the period since we came into office has been one of universal and almost total silence in the H. of C. with regard to foreign affairs.'[79] Gladstone's greatest concern on the European scene was the machinations of Pius IX in the Vatican Council. Otherwise, all appeared serene. When Granville arrived at the Foreign Office in June 1870 to replace Clarendon he was assured by the permanent Under-secretary that there had never been so quiet a time in Europe's affairs.

~

That all changed with brutal suddenness when in July France, goaded by Bismarck, declared war on Prussia.[80] The swiftness and magnitude of the catastrophe of Napoleon III and the Second Empire stunned the world. Gladstone had been looking forward to the grateful possibilities of mediation such as he had been prevented from proposing to Washington. Two considerations bore upon Gladstone's thinking during these events. The first was a perfect readiness to put Britain forward as an active participant in the frame of power politics. If he had gone to war reluctantly against Russia in 1854 he would have gone to war rather eagerly against Austria in 1860. He was also ready to join with France against the Germanic powers over the Danish affair in 1864. The second, more particular, consideration was the question of Belgian neutrality as guaranteed by the Great Powers in London in 1839. That the French had designs on Belgium and Luxembourg in 1870 was not in doubt. That guarantee had been interpreted as a collective one. Though Britain could intervene unilaterally, there was no obligation so to do. Gladstone advised the Queen that the best response would be a 'new point of departure'.[81]

The new point of departure accordingly was to set Granville to the task of shifting Britain's position on to a revised foundation of international moral authority. France and Prussia were both approached with an undertaking of British belligerent alliance: Britain would prosecute war within 'the limits of Belgium' in alliance with either power should the other power invade Belgium. Gladstone pushed Granville keenly to get these treaties in place before any great battle altered the relative positions of the belligerents. All that Parliament was told before the event was that the government had 'taken into consideration the whole state of the case', and that they had 'adopted such steps as appeared to them best calculated to establish confidence and security'.[82]

Parliament was informed by Gladstone and Granville of these treaties involving possible belligerence in the last minutes of the last day of the session, 10 August. Gladstone envisaged his new departure as a preliminary stage on the way to a brilliantly expansive exercise in mediation. In which case, no doubt, the prestige and authority of his government would have been immensely enhanced. As it happened, however, the Germans thwarted Gladstone by the speed of their victorious campaign. As he put it to Laura Thistlethwayte, 'Here I am the slave of events.'

All that events now offered Gladstone by way of initiatives was the question of intervening in the matter of German intentions to annex French territory. 'I think it well deserves attention', he told Granville, 'whether we ought to make any remarks upon Bismarck's bold paper about Alsace and Lorraine.'[83] In a fractious Cabinet on 30 September Gladstone struggled hard to persuade his colleagues 'to speak with the other neutral powers against the transfer of A. & L. without reference to the populations'.[84] He failed. Granville resisted any form of intervention not substantiated by will and capacity, if necessary, to use force. Laying down the moral law without intent to enforce it would expose Britain to an even more humiliating snub than Palmerston's 'brag' over Denmark had been subjected to in 1864.

Gladstone made it clear to Granville that he found the Cabinet's refusal to follow his European lead 'rather indigestible'.[85] There were indications that, in response to the French appeal for succour from the neutrals, he was prepared to go into some form of 'armed neutrality' as earlier advocated by Disraeli, if the other neutral powers could be persuaded. He had composed a paper on Bismarck's proposed peace terms that Granville deprecated as indiscreet. Gladstone decided to counter-attack by publishing his paper in the *Edinburgh Review*.[86] He would be careful, of course, to ensure anonymity. He told the Queen in a 'much excited' manner that there would never be a cordial understanding with Germany if she took that million and a quarter people against their will, and that he 'wished they could know this'.[87]

Gladstone's authorship was soon leaked in the *Daily News*. This exposed him and his government to mockery. That the role of Britain in relation to cataclysmic European events should ultimately take the form of a furtive item of journalism added a touch of absurdity to the proceedings. The credit that would have attended mediation turned sourly into bathos. Gladstone predicted accurately to Granville that the 'violent laceration and transfer of Alsace-Lorraine is to lead us from bad to worse, and to be the *beginning* of a new series of European complications'.[88] His fulminations against 'Bismarckism, militarism, and retrograde political morality' were soon lost in the din of recrimination. The air became thick with notions – much canvassed by the unfortunate French – as to what Britain might have achieved by a forceful policy of armed neutrality at the head of a European league.

Disraeli and the Conservatives benefited from the domestic fallout of the resounding French crash. These benefits accrued when the Russians, taking their cue from the Italian occupation of Rome and the ending of the Pope's temporal power in September, took the opportunity in November to repudiate the clauses of the Treaty of Paris in 1856 forbidding a Russian war fleet in the Black Sea.

These 'Black Sea clauses', hobbling Russian power against the Ottoman Empire and the Straits, had been the jewel in the crown of Palmerston's 'Crimean system'. Anti-Russian war fever instantly ignited, with Russell, to Gladstone's disgust, 'leading the mad'.[89]

This was a particularly cruel blow to Gladstone, who had conspicuously, in 1856, decried the impolicy of Palmerston's imposing humiliating restrictions on Russian sovereignty. Now Gladstone found himself being blamed by excited 'national' opinion for failing to reimpose by threats, or if necessary war, treaty provisions he had denounced as mischievously counter-productive. All that Gladstone could do was to set Granville to covering the nakedness of *Realpolitik* with a 'European' fig leaf by persuading the Russians to go through the forms of getting their case accepted by a conference of ambassadors in London.

Even more unfortunate for Gladstone was the way this ebullience of 'national' or 'Crimean' agitation, with many evocations of how Lord Palmerston would have dealt with matters, fed into the concurrent mood of perplexity about the question of Britain's problematic relations with the self-governing colonies. Both had to do with sentiment about 'Empire' and Britain's standing in the world. There were parliamentary expressions of 'unease and uncertainty' as to those colonial relations having taken on a 'tone of irritation, dissatisfaction and distrust sadly in contrast with the spirit of mutual respect and confidence which had hitherto generally characterised that intercourse'.[90] Such expressions now mingled with questions as to the adequacy of the armed services to fulfil their functions; which mingled in turn with resentful complaints at Britain's humiliating bystander stance in Europe.

~

Maimed on Irish Land, wounded by dissension on English education, infected by unease on foreign and colonial policy, Gladstone's party and government were nonetheless to be called on by their leader for yet another gruelling exercise in legislative heroism in 1871. Again the strain would be applied to the engine of the state. There were arrears yet to be redeemed. There were entrenched interests to be worsted. The Army was going to be subjected to drastic and economic reorganization, with special attention paid to abolition of purchase of commissions in infantry and cavalry regiments. The Universities of Oxford and Cambridge would be made further conformable to progressive requirements. The drink trade would feel the stern hand of licensing restriction. Another social problem, the trade unions, would be enfolded within the law. The secret ballot would be introduced for parliamentary and municipal elections. As a propitiatory gesture to his adopted party, Gladstone arranged that in the forthcoming edition of *Dod's Parliamentary Companion* his allegiance would be listed as 'Liberal' rather than, as since 1860, 'Liberal Conservative'.

All these legislative measures promised to be contentious. For the first time he would be leading the government without a commanding legislative centrepiece to hold Parliament either in awe or terror. Bright would not bear the work, and insisted on retiring. Fortescue replaced him at the Board of Trade. Goschen went to the Admiralty to relieve the exhausted Childers. Hartington was 'bullied' into the Irish Office. There were new faces and talents in Cabinet. Forster was given the ballot to manage. James Stansfeld, old comrade of the 'Italian party', moved from the Treasury to the Poor Law Board and then the Local Government Board.

In what was now something of an annual ritual, the Gladstones were 'most kindly received' by the Salisburys at Hatfield in November 1870. Having succeeded Derby as Chancellor of Oxford in 1869, Salisbury was placed strategically in the matter of Gladstone's forthcoming bill to abolish religious tests at the ancient universities. Foreign affairs would also have been aired. Salisbury too had struck out fiercely at Bismarck in the recess; but he could share nothing of Gladstone's faith in a European moral order. In the years to come Bismarck would find them puzzlingly but differently irritating.

Another matter on Gladstone's mind in the closing months of 1870 was the 'royalty' problem. The rackety life of the Prince of Wales had led to his appearance in the witness box in a scandalous divorce case. Gladstone used his influence to shield the Prince from being cited as co-respondent. Victoria asked Gladstone to 'speak seriously' to the Prince. Gladstone wanted also to speak seriously to the Queen. He wanted to ease her out of her obstinate clinging to widowed seclusion. He had succeeded in 1869 in persuading her to open the new Blackfriars bridge. It was a splendidly successful occasion. He planned to build on that success. It was gratifying that Victoria agreed to open the 1871 session in person. He worried about the future of the monarchy. Public stirrings of republican sentiment, associated particularly with the Liberal MP for Chelsea, Sir Charles Dilke, made Gladstone increasingly anxious in 1871 to lance the boil. Much of the public stir had to do with an aggrieved sense of not getting royal value from the royal Civil List. Speaking 'in rude and general terms', as he put it to Granville, 'the Queen is invisible, and the Prince of Wales is not respected'. The fund of credit built up by the Crown was diminishing. Gladstone feared the outlook ten, 20, 30, 40 years hence 'is a very melancholy one'.[91]

Gladstone's tactic was to use Ireland as a lever. The Prince could be found some kind of official employment to keep him out of mischief in the public eye of the metropolis. And what he did best – affably meeting and greeting – would help to answer Irish complaints that Ireland was deprived of the royal presence. Gladstone nerved himself to a remedial confrontation with the Queen on 21 June at Windsor. He found her disconcertingly resistant.

~

The other, and much more decisive, side of the case of the Queen's resistance was the steep slide in Gladstone's own position. The 1871 session very quickly took a disastrous turn. After two sessions of prudently deliberate reserve, Disraeli judged the moment right for a signal intervention. His censure on the Black Sea issue was indeed well-judged. Derby (erstwhile Stanley) recalled Gladstone's being so exasperated that 'some unparliamentary violence was feared'.[92] Gladstone had cause also to be exasperated at the unforgiving attitude of the Americans over the *Alabama* negotiations. Sensitivities in Parliament needed to be sheltered from revelations in that matter. Trelawny thought that Gladstone had 'been wanting, of late, in temper, discretion & straightforwardness'. He could see the Tories soon putting the government in a minority. 'We, Liberals, are in a sad plight – under a cloud, at least.'[93]

By early March the Conservatives very nearly put the government in a minority. Disraeli had to lead his MPs out of the Commons to 'prevent a catastrophe'. He needed more time to ripen the prospect of Conservatism's return to office. Gladstone's majority was in a thoroughly distempered condition. The Nonconformists had not forgiven his Education Act. The 'Advanced Liberals' were in revolt on the expenditure issue. The publicans resented Bruce's Licensing measure. The country gentlemen resented Goschen's rating intentions. The clergy were affronted by the abolition of religious tests at Oxford and Cambridge. There was much middle-class resentment at meddling with their endowed schools. Lowe's tax on horses irritated the farmers. Believers in open and honest public politics deplored the furtiveness of the ballot. The income tax hoist irritated all direct taxpayers. The Army much disliked the implications for social integration of the officer corps involved in the abolition of purchase. The Trades Union Congress was offended at the Trade Unions and Criminal Law Amendment Bills, which the Congress thought, by treating unions as a form of social disease, like drink, made far too much of intimidating 'rattening' and unreasonably made picketing illegal.

Trelawny thought 'the course of Ministers, in every respect', seemed to be 'weak and inapposite'. Gladstone was 'falling in the estimation of his party'. He now found himself being regularly harassed by the Contagious Diseases Act abolition sect, zealots of moral purity. The government was 'going down hill'.[94] Derby noted on 3 March: 'The House is tired of Gladstone: inclined to magnify his mistakes.' Disraeli was 'in high spirits' about the problems and blunders of ministers as much as about his Black Sea success.

There were disturbing background influences. In May 1871 somewhat of a public panic was set off by the outbreak of horrific socialist violence in the Paris Commune and equally horrific suppression of it. Then an unprecedented surge of industrial unrest in the North and the Midlands stimulated the Scottish engineer Scott Russell to launch his 'New Social Alliance', aimed at bridging the gulf between the possessing and labouring classes. This raised many perturbing questions about a new ordering of social policy. Gladstone's Irish legislation itself contributed to anxiety about challenges to property rights, and a sense of general unsettlement of all opinions, social, political, and religious. Disraeli was intrigued by Russell's ideas, seeing in the Alliance 'a new method of outbidding the Whigs, or rather Gladstone'.[95] Gladstone, in his old-fashioned way, dismissed the whole affair as quackery.

With Gladstone a propensity to drive came swiftly in reaction to resistance. The Army Bill and the Ballot Bill became the nodal testing issues of the session. There were Liberal protesters at Gladstone's being a 'Bismarck', applying 'offensive' and 'unconstitutional' pressures to stifle debate.[96] Observers gave Goschen's Local Rating Bill and Bruce's Licensing Bill little chance. 'Whether Cardwell will succeed is a question by no means solved', noted Trelawny. 'The budget may not add to any good temper remaining in the Public mind.'[97]

This was precisely the point where Lowe stumbled badly. Hitherto, in his 1869 and 1870 statements, Lowe had performed solidly and sustained well the cherished reputation he had inherited from Gladstone for the financial soundness and expertise to be expected from Liberal governments. Now the spell was broken. Lowe blundered, particularly on the issue of levying a tax on matches (*ex luce lucellum*, in his learned quip – from light, lucre), which 'struck the House with some astonishment'.[98] It was seen as an imposition on the poor; and Lowe's plan had no chance once pathetic processions of 'match girls' from Messrs Bryant & May's establishment began petitioning Parliament. Formidable in advance, Lowe had no resource in retreat; and Gladstone was obliged to take over and replace the abandoned direct tax with a hoist on the income tax.

Derby recorded: 'On the whole this business is a heavy blow to the ministry – the first they have had.'[99] Within a few days there was defeat in a division. 'The state of the House is indescribable: ministers have managed to offend nearly every important interest in the country.'[100] As Gladstone, with his back to the wall, fought indomitably to save the budget, Trelawny declared himself 'really tired of hearing the Lancashire twang of our verbiose and diffusive leader'.[101] Gladstone had to abandon several bills or parts of bills. The Trade had drummed up very effective agitation in recent by-elections against Licensing. Cardwell came under Liberal ambush over the purchase issue. These 'repeated shocks are disintegrating the strength of the Government seriously'.[102] On 28 May Gladstone suffered a sharp collapse and kept to his bed for several days. He was judged as suffering in encounters with Disraeli, 'who surpasses his rival in calm & premeditation – also, in point. His allusion to Gladstone's change on the Ballot was a very palpable hit.' With the government unable to keep the House in hand, Trelawny felt it 'difficult to believe that either the Army Bill or the Ballot Bill will pass this year'.[103]

These were the bills Gladstone was determined to pass. He summoned a party meeting at Downing Street on 6 July to rally his forces. Though now, nominally at least, a member of the Reform, his instinct against meeting his party on their rather than his ground remained firm. Enough solidarity was rallied to get Cardwell's Army measure up the Lords. But the Commons soon relapsed once more into a 'very unruly state', with Gladstone's prestige waning. 'He wants several of the happy qualifications in a leader, which Palmerston had.'[104]

There was clearly going to be trouble with the Lords over both the Army and Ballot Bills. The government now lacked the confidence and authority necessary to intimidate and overcome the Lords, as it had done in 1869 and 1870. Gladstone's waning prestige invited attack. He took precautionary steps. 'We were most kindly received and very happy at Hatfield – Army Bill notwithstanding.'[105] As Chancellor of Oxford, Salisbury was helpful for Gladstone in being willing – though with misgivings – to shepherd through the University Tests Abolition Bill as an issue not between Church and Nonconformity but between Christianity and unbelief. Gladstone could not persuade Salisbury, however, to adopt the same accommodating attitude over the Army Regulation Bill.

Abolition of purchase as an aristocratic privilege was a long-desired Radical objective. It was desired also by those who criticized the 'gentleman-amateur' ethos of the officer corps in an era when Austrian and French military deficiencies had been exposed by Prussian professionalism. Gladstone had not been tactful in his quest to let the nation 'buy back its own army from its own officers', declaring that it was 'undoubtedly alleged that under the present system generals and others in high command were rather wooden-headed'.[106] At the second reading the Lords detached the purchase abolition provisions from the Army Bill. Three days later, in a very excited House of Commons on 20 July, Gladstone announced that, since the purchase system was originally installed by royal warrant, ministers had advised the Queen to exercise her prerogative to cancel the warrant.

With this stroke of retaliation against the Lords Gladstone at least recovered his Peelite poise and retrieved something from the general wreckage of the session. For all his pious insistence on due observance of constitutional usage, Gladstone in fact was very ready to defy the opinion of a Parliament that, as in 1866 and 1867, had failed to live up to the high legislative requirements he demanded of it; and nothing was more characteristic of him than to resort to high executive prerogative. He was ever ready to make a joke of the 'numerous proofs of my domineering disposition'.[107] Liberals of Palmerstonian tendency might well lament: 'How different would have been the conduct of some of the Premiers whom it has been my lot to observe &, generally, follow!'[108]

For Gladstone that was, precisely, begging the question. It was not for avoiding confrontation with the Lords or for 'having several of the happy qualifications in a leader, which Palmerston had', that Gladstone had in 1868 invoked the tutelary genius of Peel, or the potent image of the straining engine of the state.

12

Defeat and Abdication, 1871–1875

'It is not my intention to assume the functions of Leader of the Parliamentary Opposition in the House of Commons to the new Government.'

Gladstone to Arthur Peel, Chief Whip of the Liberal party, 19 February 1874

For all that with his *coup* against the House of Lords over the purchase issue Gladstone had retrieved something from the wreckage of the 1871 session, the session still remained a wreck. The Liberal government's strongest card consisted in the implausibility of a Conservative alternative. Two by-elections in 1871 indicated possibly significant shifts of opinion away from the Liberal government. At Westmeath, hitherto a steady Irish Liberal seat, the government's candidate was defeated by what Derby described as 'a "nationalist" or "home rule candidate" which means a repealer'. Were this precedent to be followed – 'and that it will be, appears probable' – a new Irish difficulty, 'more serious than any we have yet dealt with', would have arisen.[1]

At the second by-election, in East Surrey, a brewer, Watney, defeated one of Granville's Leveson-Gower Whig clan. Gladstone viewed it as a portent possibly analogous to the fading of the Grey–Melbourne majority after 1831. Or it might simply reflect the Trade's animus against Liberalism for the Licensing Bill. 'It is another matter', he told his Whip, Glyn, 'if our own bettermost friends are falling away or cooling.'[2] Derby, again prescient, asked: 'Is this the beginning of the middle-class reaction against Gladstone?'

Gladstone had his own response to that question. He and Catherine retreated to the refreshing sea breezes of Whitby, where Willy – made a Lord of the Treasury by his father in 1868 – was MP. 'I fell all to pieces, in mind more than in body', Gladstone confessed to Granville, 'but I hope that if allowed to vegetate here for a little while mental life will return to me.'[3] Return to mental life took the form at the Congress Hall on 2 September of recasting the story of the late unfortunate session in terms reminiscent of his declarations at Liverpool in April 1866. Then he had summoned the genius of the people against a recalcitrant Parliament. Now he identified the power and influence of plutocratic class interests concentrated in London with the metropolitan press as their organ and medium of animus against his government. It was to the people he now looked to 'redress the balance of the Press if the Press goes wrong'. Monckton Milnes protested that 'there is a Demon, not of Demagogism, but of Demophilism, that is tempting you sorely'. Gladstone retorted on the theme of 'plutocracy', the power of property and wealth, its 'domination in the Clubs, and in the Army'. He was sure that 'in a political view the spirit of plutocracy requires to be vigilantly watched and checked. It is a bastard aristocracy, and aristocracy shows too much disposition, in Parliament especially, to join hands with this bastard.'[4]

On his homeward progress great crowds and deputations thronged the way. At Wakefield he delivered an address on the virtues of Sir Robert Peel. If Parliament was not sound, there seemed every evidence that the people were. Then on up to Aberdeen, where he was honoured with the Freedom of the City. Much 'enthusiasm for the Government' seemed again in evidence. His speech there gained the reputation of being 'a distinct and manly repudiation' of the aims of the Home Rule agitators in Ireland. In fact it was an ambiguous statement occasioned by irritation at Irish ingratitude. The Home Rulers had no cause for grievance against the 1868 Parliament. 'There is nothing that Ireland has asked, and which this country and this Parliament have refused.'[5]

His reception at Balmoral at the beginning of October was notably chilly. 'I have felt myself in a new and different footing with her.' Possibly this chill disposed him to be discreet in his speech to a vast multitude at Blackheath in his Greenwich constituency later in the month. Here he justified his conduct of the session, adding a sideswipe to put a stop to the 'social reform' nonsense of the Social Alliance. Granville assured him that the scheme of a Conservative 'coalition with the workmen' would 'do Dizzy harm with his practical and sensible friends, and cannot have much political effect'. Scott Russell's group had put forward such ideas as 'a decent house and wholesome food at a fair price'. Gladstone thought this 'Manifesto Internationale and something more, ought to make some sport for us. Is it Dizzy?' Gladstone felt sure 'the wizard of Hughenden Manor is behind the scenes'. 'I will say they are quacks; they are deluded and beguiled by a spurious philanthropy.'[6]

~

It was a matter now of bracing oneself for the 1872 session. Gladstone set up 'a little Autumn Session of Cabinets' to prepare bills and estimates 'so that they may be thoroughly matured and early'.[7] The strategy would be to retrieve the government's programme rather than adventure in new political terrain. The lesson of 1871 was not so much to recoil from strenuous effort as to make sure that the procedural shambles be not repeated.

Ballot and Licensing would be at the front. Bruce found himself in difficulties on Licensing. 'Unfortunately Gladstone cares for nothing but "Free Trade", which the House won't have', as Bruce desponded, 'and I cannot get him really to interest himself in the subject.'[8] A subject that Gladstone found himself impelled to take an interest in was 'that plaguy ship': the *Alabama* case now began to take on a menacing and urgent immediacy. A Court of International Arbitration was now established at Geneva. The Foreign Office informed Gladstone that the US claims, 'swollen in every possible way', amounted to £4,479,463.[9]

Another subject of Gladstone's keen attention in 1871 was the disagreeableness of colonial governments in their assumptions of fiscal independence. This was a matter very much at the centre of current perplexities about Britain's imperial standing. Gladstone was shocked to discover from Kimberley, Granville's replacement at the Colonial Office, how far things had gone in this respect. Although he had spoken quite nonchalantly in the Commons in April 1870 about the possibility of colonies parting from the imperial bond, he now had to face the possibility of New Zealand's admitting shoes from Sydney tax-free, but taxing those from Northampton. That, he felt sure, 'brings us near the *reductio ad absurdum* of the colonial connection'.[10] He found Kimberley alarmingly relaxed in the matter, especially when confronted with the 'insolence' of the former Young Irelander, Mr Gavan Duffy, in Australia. Gladstone could not see his way to going along with Kimberley to concede 'everything except neutrality in war'. 'I really do not see upon what foundation any duty of military & naval protection on our part is to rest, if the foreign relations of Colonies are to pass out of our hands into theirs. Would Mr Duffy be kind enough to give us a definition of the Colonial relation, as to rights and duties, on the one side and on the other, as he would have it. *What* will be the remaining duties of the Colony towards the mother State?'[11]

This hankering after a definition of rights and duties was entirely characteristic of Gladstone. He was reluctant to accept that a colony under the British Crown could be in practice independent.[12] In the end he had to concede. There was no way of forcing colonial governments to be logical and consistent in definitions of rights and duties. After a generation of 'responsible government' for colonies of settlement that was unthinkable by the 1870s. The only sanction available to the British government was to withdraw British troops from coercive military operations conducted by colonial governments. As far as the self-governing colonies were concerned, the British Empire was in practice a voluntary operation.

Alarming news about a very serious illness of the Prince of Wales at Sandringham brought Gladstone down from Hawarden on 9 December. On the 11th the Cabinet considered the contingency of the Prince's death. But with his slow recovery, Gladstone began to see the chance to turn the affair to account in the 'royalty question'. The idea was floated of 'a public recognition say at St Paul's'. Gladstone responded enthusiastically. He was in hopes of squashing the republicans with a grand manifestation of national and popular solidarity with the monarchy. 'We have arrived at a great crisis about Royalty', he told Granville;

'the last opportunity to be given us of effecting what is requisite.' A national Thanksgiving Service would 'scatter that disagreeable movement with which the name of Sir C. Dilke has been connected'.[13] Gladstone wanted something as grand and elaborate as possible; and the precedent of the service for the recovery of George III in 1789 was examined. The Queen, averse to cathedral services, pomp and 'false and hollow' ceremonial display in the name of religion, proved difficult to convince. Gladstone relentlessly wore down her resistance to the point where she grudgingly approved a 'semi-state' ceremony to be held soon after the opening of the 1872 session of Parliament in February.

The theme of Gladstone's birthday and end-of-year meditations now began to take on a decided consistency of lament at his life's confinement in arduous public duties and his yearning for release. On parting from 1871 he hoped that 'God in his mercy may soon deliver me into a freer and purer air'.

~

Gladstone's purpose in 1872 was to rally the elements of a renewed legitimacy that would provide strength for dignity and credit as had been supplied copiously in 1869 and sufficiently in 1870 but had been lacking in 1871. He failed to persuade Bright to resume his totem role. The Parliament Gladstone met in February was from the start fractious and distempered. Speaker Denison had had enough in 1871, and Gladstone pressed his former Whip, Henry Brand, to take the chair. This was thought by many to be improper.

Other patronage improprieties exposed Gladstone's vulnerability to accusations of want of 'judgement and moderation', of proneness to 'vehemence & excitability'.[14] A rigid insistence on having his way in small things as in great was as advertised as ever. He insisted on putting a Cambridge man into a rectory reserved specifically to Oxonians. He shocked Lord Chief Justice Cockburn by chicaning his way through statutes to appoint Attorney-General Collier to the Judicial Committee of the Privy Council. He scraped through the scandalized House of Lords by one vote. This executive arrogance made Gladstone 'intensely unpopular with the House: much more so this year than the last', with his 'increasing irritability and violence, itself the effect of an overworked brain'. There was talk among Liberals of Forster's taking over the leadership of the Commons.[15]

Of the more substantial matters of government, the Ballot Bill was hashing the old mutton. On Licensing there had been placatory and appeasing retreat, but no guarantee of better fortune. It was hopeless now to expect Lowe to restore prestige on the financial front. The *Alabama* arbitration loomed over the session like a lowering cloud. Tennyson wrote cheeringly to Gladstone: 'Heaven help you fair through the Session – like enough to be a rough one – but – if you let these Yankee sharpers get anything like their way of you in the Alabama Claims, I won't pay my "ship money" any more than old Hampden.'[16] The great danger was that the Geneva Tribunal might accept the American interpretation of the Treaty of Washington and allow their claims for 'indirect' damages for such things as prolongation of the war. Gladstone assured the Queen that the conduct of the Americans was the most 'disreputable' he had ever known in his recollections of diplomacy.[17] The crux of the matter was that Gladstone could see himself confronted with the options of humiliation or, if Britain were to withdraw from the arbitration, war.

Amid all the gloom the one bright moment for Gladstone was the brilliant success of the Thanksgiving Service at St Paul's on 27 February for the recovery of the Prince of Wales. Even at 'half-state' Gladstone thought the spectacle magnificent, and the 'behaviour of the people admirable (to us very kind).' There were observers who judged the ovation given to Disraeli and Lady Beaconsfield even kinder, marking yet another point in Disraeli's emergence from the political reserve into which he had withdrawn himself since 1868. Having got some positive movement on the way to improving 'relations between the Monarchy and the Nation', Gladstone set about determinedly to exploit the occasion by 'framing a worthy and manly mode of life, *quoad* public duties, for the Prince of Wales', Ireland being once more the designated locale, linked to the project of an Irish royal residence.[18]

'It will be a calamity if we fail, either with the Queen, the Prince, or both.'[19] Fail Gladstone duly did. 'There is a manifest *twist*, in the Queen's mind', he complained to Lord Spencer, the Lord-Lieutenant, 'with respect to Ireland.' Gladstone, both exasperated and exasperating, persisted in spite of all her efforts to fend him off. She proved in the end a match for his tenacity. There simply was no way the Prince would allow himself to be exiled to Ireland. She was well aware that the balance of advantages had tilted her way. Gladstone was by no means as formidable a political force as he had been. The monarchy was becoming seen as an influence for social stability at the centre of a 'modernised national ideology' of imperialism.[20] Victoria wrote to her daughter, now German Crown Princess: 'Mr Gladstone is a very dangerous Minister – and so wonderfully unsympathetic. I have felt this very much, but find his own followers and colleagues complain fully as much.'[21]

The Queen remained stiff and assured. She made it clear to Derby that she expected 'a political crisis'. He cautioned that the Conservatives could not think of taking office while in a minority of near 100; but that they would do their best to prevent embarrassment and 'help in working the machine'.[22] Ministers got the Licensing Bill through with the machine thus being worked. The *Licensed Victuallers Gazette* proclaimed the Trade's message: 'we shall hail with delight the advent of a Conservative Ministry'.[23] There were Conservative fears still about the Ballot, but also prudent considerations that too stout a resistance might give Gladstone a handle for a Liberal rally. Gladstone threatened the Lords with an October session and a November dissolution. Glyn advised that in an election 'without a cry' the government's existing majority of 86 would decline to 32 seats.[24]

The long and short of it was that in the 1872 session the government failed to retrieve its vital power. Little could be done to bind the party's wounds on the education imbroglio. 'The education question is all wrong', as Bright put it, '– and so wrong that it now cannot be put right.'[25] For all the buoyancy of the revenue Lowe remained a depreciating asset. The estimates remained unpruned. All the evidence suggested that Gladstone's Church and Land measures in Ireland had stimulated rather than pacified agitation. The traditional influence there of the 'gentry and quality' was being undermined. Junior ministers, with the irrepressible Ayrton in their midst, brawled with each other as Gladstone remonstrated ineffectually. In the background by-election losses to the Conservatives multiplied. A Conservative gain in the West Riding suggested that 'great towns and manufacturing villages' could no longer be counted as safe Liberal terrain. The Conservatives held Preston; a notable win, as it was the first constituency to poll on the new secret ballot. In 1872 the Conservatives captured seven Liberal seats and lost none.

Disraeli chose his moment well to launch his strategic counter-attack at Manchester early in April. He pointed out the 'portentous birth' in Ireland of 'sedition rampant, treason thinly veiled'. He deplored Liberal harassment of 'every institution and every interest, every class and calling in the country'. He taunted Liberal ministers with having subjected themselves as well as the country to humiliation over the Black Sea and *Alabama*. Above all, his picture of the jaded Liberal Cabinet caught the national imagination: 'The unnatural stimulus is subsiding. Their paroxysms end in prostration. Some take refuge in melancholy, and their eminent chief alternates between a menace and a sigh. As I sit opposite the Treasury Bench, the ministers remind me of one of those marine landscapes not very unusual on the coasts of South America. You behold a range of exhausted volcanoes. Not a flame flickers on a single pallid crest. But the situation is still dangerous. There are occasional earthquakes, and ever and anon the dark rumblings of the sea'.[26]

~

All eyes now were on the Geneva arbitration. For the time being it guaranteed the survival of the government. The last thing the Conservatives wanted was to inherit it as long as it remained unsettled. The court would consider the American claims for indirect damages. The alternatives of humiliation or withdrawal and war loomed ever more starkly. 'What am I now?' asked Gladstone of 'Dear Spirit'. 'As Dizzy says an exhausted volcano ...'[27] The public mood waxed excitable. Lord Russell declared that Her Majesty's honour must not be impugned in aid of President Grant's re-election. Gladstone desired from Granville intelligence about the military and naval capacities of the United States. He was grateful to Disraeli and the bulk of the Conservatives for holding fire and disdaining to follow Russell's lead. 'Dizzy was perfect', Gladstone reported to Granville. 'I understand he was much pleased with my having called to inquire after Lady Beaconsfield a few days ago.'[28] Again, at the Crystal Palace in Dulwich on 24 June, Disraeli behaved well. He famously banged the drum of Empire and deplored Liberalism's substitution of cosmopolitan for national principles, but was notably reticent about *Alabama*.

After dire weeks of suspense, on 27 June Gladstone in the Commons and Granville in the Lords announced that the Americans had withdrawn their indirect claims. The eventual award in September to the United States of £3,250,000 Gladstone considered too punitive; yet 'as dust in the balance compared with the moral example set' of two proud nations 'going in peace and concord before a judicial tribunal' rather than resorting 'to the arbitrament of the sword'.[29] These were words Gladstone used later after the dust had settled. But at the time, once the initial feeling of relief had passed, and for long after, it left a sense of public rancour.

That rancour permeated in many directions. It reached back to the dismay at Britain's European effacement in 1870. It linked to the current fashion for Empire, much touted by Disraeli as a kind of consolation and compensation for the distempered public. All of which contributed to exposing what was increasingly being identified as an area of Liberal deficiency. The sense of general dissatisfaction with Britain's ambiguous relationship with the self-governing colonies led to parliamentary initiatives in 1872 for arrangements for colonial governments to participate in matters concerning the general interests of the Empire.[30]

Instinctively, Gladstone reacted against the 'new imperialism', just as he had reacted against the 'quackery' of the new 'social reform', of which Disraeli made much at Manchester. He intervened in an attempt to have Kimberley withdraw from a range of 'forward' colonial advances, but found himself blocked by Colonial Office insistence that 'in the present tone and temper of the public mind no abandonment of territory would ... be permitted by Parliament, or sanctioned by public opinion'.[31] Soon Gladstone found himself the official sponsor of Sir Garnet Wolseley's expedition to subdue the King of the Ashanti. He kept clear of a motion in the Commons by Henry Richard of the Peace Society extolling the principles of Cobden and international arbitration.[32] In answer to Richard's evocation of Cobden, Gladstone unblushingly made great play with the name of Palmerston.[33]

These were expedient tactical retreats from exposed positions. Seemingly there was daylight at last on the Army estimates. He could congratulate Cardwell on having accomplished a 'large, & I hope a permanent and salutary work'.[34] The

1872 session was in the end surmounted. Derby conceded that 'on the whole the Cabinet has got through its difficulties safely if not triumphantly'.[35]

There was no question of scrambling through another session in that dishevelled manner. Given his survival, Gladstone could see the prospect only in terms of a reversion to the high Peelite strenuousness of 1869 and 1870. For 1873 there would be no less than a third pod to the Irish question: a return to the higher education measure of 1866, but now in such a manner of shock assault as would jolt the government and party into revived animation.

~

While contemplating the formidable demands of the 1873 session, Gladstone found much to concern him in these times of the early 1870s in the domestic, ecclesiastical and intellectual aspects of his life. The sad domestic event was the death in July 1872 of the Rev. Henry Glynne, Catherine's and Sir Stephen's brother and Rector of Hawarden since 1834. There would be no more scufflings about possible matrimony and a Glynne male heir. The immediate question arose as to how Sir Stephen, as patron of the lucrative living, might dispose of it. Even with curacies incumbent it was a considerable place, worth nearly £3000 a year. With his sister and her husband in residence on his own ground, there was little doubt that the call would come to his nephew, the Gladstones' son Stephen, since 1868 a curate in Lambeth. The Rev. Stephen had his own doubts about returning to Hawarden to live in the shadow of the 'grand people'. But in the end, as the patron had bowed, so the son and nephew bowed. One of the early pleasures of Stephen's incumbency was to marry Agnes to the Rev. E. C. Wickham, Fellow of New College, Oxford, about to take up the headmastership of Wellington College.[36]

There were the distractions of current literature, but they had to be set aside as Gladstone became painfully absorbed in the fortunes of excommunicated Döllinger and the Old Catholics who refused submission to the Infallibility dogma. Another formidable problem confronting him in these years was to examine more closely than hitherto Darwin, with whose *Origin of Species* of 1859 he was already familiar and whose *Descent of Man* was one of the major intellectual events of 1871.

An intellectual characteristic of the times, in Gladstone's view, was a 'mental rashness' that infected mind and criticism. With respect to Darwin, he thought there was something 'truly portentous' in the 'avidity' with which the age 'leapt' to 'ulterior conclusions' at which the *Origin of Species* was thought 'scarcely to hint, & which his physiological theory did not even require'. Gladstone remained confident in any event that it had not been given to Mr Darwin 'to sweep away that fabric of belief which has stood the handling of 1800 years & of stronger men perhaps than any now alive'.[37]

There were questions about the demands of science on the state. Gladstone had misgivings. He greatly respected some scientists individually, but had 'little sense of what science or scientific method represented'.[38] He was a keen member of the Metaphysical Society, set up in 1869 by James Knowles, editor of the *Contemporary Review* and later founder of the *Nineteenth Century*. The society aimed 'to unite all shades of religious opinion against materialism'. Over the years Gladstone engaged in many controversies with men such as Tyndall, Lubbock and especially Huxley, 'Darwin's bulldog'.[39] To Friedrich Max Müller, the Oxford orientalist and philologist, Gladstone confessed that he lacked the 'physical knowledge really necessary to deal with the Darwinian question'. But he felt 'less unable to deal with the non-physical part of the subject'. Here, his 'ever-strengthening conviction' was that 'strength of belief lies in – Butler'.

The '*method of handling*' of Gladstone's supreme theological mentor was, he was sure, 'the only one known to me that is fitted to guide life, and thought bearing upon life, in the face of the nineteenth century'. But Gladstone felt he could do little 'until I abandon politics, which God in his mercy grant me before long'.[40] His fervid loyalty to Bishop Butler helped make Gladstone proof against the newer trends of thought to which many of the younger generation were turning, seeking means of revitalizing the individualism of Mill through idealist metaphysics. Gladstone was not impressed by the kind of Hegelian theory of a higher vocation of the state taking root in Oxford. 'German philosophy', he told Manning, 'has added but little to the stock of our knowledge of the mind & nature of men, if indeed it has added anything.'[41]

Of men of science in general, Gladstone could see 'nothing in their pursuits, or in their words as a body, to invest them with special authority in regard to the greatest questions of history, philosophy, & religious belief'. In answer to new lines of criticism and research Gladstone always professed himself as being a 'firm adherent of the principle of dogma, & under a strong conviction as to the central elements of the dogmatic system of Christianity'.[42] These were indeed the uncompromising doctrines of an address he delivered in December 1872 at Liverpool College, asserting that the major duty of the times was to repel threats to religious faith from speculative rationalism. He remained also, consonantly, in touch with his 'other worldly' interest in spiritualism (via, at this time, the group around Henry Sidgwick and Arthur Balfour).[43] Nor had he lost touch with the phrenologists, one of whom thought he had cause to comment on Gladstone's 'over-active mind'.[44]

A collision late in 1873 with the social evolutionist Herbert Spencer illustrates well Gladstone's rather prickly and uneasy relationship with most 'men of science'. Preparing a new edition of his *Principles of Sociology*, Spencer alluded to Gladstone as 'typical of the anti-scientific view in general', on the strength of his Liverpool College address. Gladstone challenged Spencer for misunderstanding his providentialist argument that the 'functions of the Almighty as Creator and Governor of the world' were being denied on insufficient grounds. Spencer allowed that he had interpreted Gladstone perhaps too narrowly; but insisted on his 'scientific view' that the power manifested in the universe 'from the movements of the stars to the unfolding of individual men' worked 'in ways that are absolutely uniform'.[45]

Much more agreeable to Gladstone was Stanley Jevons' treatment of scientific method in his *Principles of Science* of 1874. Gladstone welcomed it as being cautious and circumspect in its ulterior conclusions. He accorded Jevons, indeed, his supreme intellectual accolade. 'I hope you will not be shocked if I designate it by an epithet which to my mind conveys the highest commendation: it seems to me eminently *Butlerian*.' As to evolution and Darwinism: 'I must say that the doctrine of Darwin, if it be true, enhances in my judgment the proper idea of the greatness of God, for it makes every stage of creation a legible prophecy of all those which are to follow it.'

He set out a series of sceptical propositions about the claims of science.

> That there is gross ambiguity & latent fallacy in much that we hear about 'uniformity of laws'.
> That we are not warranted in predicating, of time & space themselves, that they are necessarily conditions of all existence.
> That there is real insoluble mystery in some of the formulae of mathematics.
> That we are in danger from the precipitancy & intellectual tyranny of speculation.
> That the limits of our real knowledge are (if I may use the word) infinitely narrow.
> That we are not rationally justified in passing our own inward perceptions of things inward, & confirming the sphere of knowledge & things outward.

These, Gladstone explained to Jevons, were his 'old convictions which I live in hope of doing something before I die to sustain and illustrate'.[46]

Darwinist speculation, however, impinged upon Gladstone in a manner bearing important and immediate political implications. He recorded reading in December 1872 Walter Bagehot's recently published *Physics and Politics: or Thoughts on the Application of the Principles of 'Natural Selection' and 'Inheritance' to Political Society*. This was Bagehot's speculative exercise in accounting for human prehistory in terms of the survival of the fittest, and in terms of the role of the crucial 'hereditable excellence' in national life of what he termed 'animated moderation', the key element in mankind's most successful achievement in social evolution, the 'polity of discussion'. Gladstone made no comment on Bagehot's 'ulterior conclusions', which were no less than to extol the late Lord Palmerston as the best example of the progressive and efficient quality in English statesmanship.

Very much an intellectual bellwether of his times, Bagehot had already, in his *The English Constitution* of 1867, composed in effect an elegiac lament for the passing of the collusively quiet times of Palmerston and Derby. Now, he contributed influentially to a rising new cult of the lamented Palmerston, a potent symbol of past stability and sureness to set against the present figure of the frenetic and flailing Gladstone.

~

From the metaphysical realm of speculative disturbances Gladstone returned to grapple in the real world of Irish disturbances. The central feature of the 1873 session was going to be a measure long promised and expected, to make good the gap left in Irish policy by the absence of universities and colleges designed to foster a native ruling gentry class, Catholic but pacified.

Gladstone had long been prominent in guiding the Anglican elites of Oxford and Cambridge to a better appreciation of and adaptation to the requirements of the progressive nineteenth century. The ending of religious tests in the two ancient English universities had been effected also in 1871 in Trinity College, Dublin. Thus, together with the Queen's University Colleges of Cork, Galway and Belfast, Ireland was equipped with a higher education system of 'mixed' or 'united' non-denominationalism. As the Declaration of Members of Dublin University in favour of 'United Academical Education' put it to Gladstone in 1870, 'the association of young men of different religious persuasions in the same Lecture Halls, and at the same Commons Table, is productive of the best results of religious creed, and in teaching all to tolerate and respect the conscientious opinions of others'.[47]

That principle had been acceptable to many Roman Catholics of the older Irish tradition. But what observers of the Irish scene were now becoming aware of was the blowing of chillier Irish Catholic winds. That had been made evident in the dismissal in 1866 of Liberal efforts to make reasonable provision for Catholic consciences. Paul Cullen, Archbishop of Dublin, was a severe type of prelate. In 1872 Cullen made it clear to Gladstone that the Irish hierarchy was convinced that non-denominational education was too dangerous to the faith of Irish Catholic youth. Any new initiative must be such that 'Catholics could be fully instructed in the doctrines and practices of their religion'.[48]

Behind these phrases was a mentality as Ultramontane as any in the Vatican Curia. The big problem was that by 1873 an Irish Catholic demand for higher education as defined by Cullen sat ill with the Liberal party. That party had, largely, welcomed the disestablishment of the Irish Church. It had accepted with more or less resignation the partial disestablishment of the Irish landed Ascendancy. It was decidedly uneasy at the prospect of disestablishing the principle of non-denominational higher education in Ireland by setting up Roman Catholic colleges controlled by priests. To most Liberals this profoundly contradicted the great point of Liberalism. The Roman Catholic Church had of late years flaunted its insults to Liberalism in the 1864 *Syllabus*. And it had, ultimately, in 1870, flouted the progressive nineteenth century with the dogma of Papal Infallibility. Gladstone took care to be publicly discreet. He was aware also that several of his colleagues saw the question as offering, in Granville's words, 'an admirable opportunity for an honourable defeat'.[49] Liberal opinion was decidedly attuned to the newly established 'mixed' or 'united' non-denominationalism that obtained with the ending of Anglican tests at Trinity College, University of Dublin.

~

For the challenges of the 1873 session Gladstone braced himself with his usual sojourn with the Salisburys at Hatfield. The crucial test for Gladstone was to restore his personal authority by imposing on both the British Parliament, and more particularly its Liberal component, and the Irish Roman Catholic Church a measure that neither of them liked. There were other measures aplenty. Goschen's Local Rating would be reintroduced. Roundell Palmer, now newly promoted as Lord Chancellor Selborne, would introduce his Supreme Court of Judicature Bill, aimed at conferring the benefits of more certain, cheap, expeditious and effectual administration of justice. There would be an attempt to appease the Nonconformists with an Education Act Amendment Bill. It was hoped that Lowe's fifth budget would do something to restore the government's financial reputation.

There was a moment of unaccustomed good feeling when Gladstone offered Disraeli condolences on the death of Lady Beaconsfield. Not the least of the pities of Mary Anne's passing was that it removed the last intimate personal element concerned to preserve a degree of civility in the relations of the two political rivals. Catherine Gladstone was much less disposed to see herself in that emollient role.

For Gladstone the fortunes of the 1873 session and those of his government would be determined by the fate of the Irish University Bill. Gladstone felt he had cause not to be utterly bereft of grounds for confidence. He had Archbishop Manning in support. And 'even as to Irish University education', as he put it to his brother Robertson, 'I am not without hope of obtaining fair play, which I trust is all we want'.[50] His plan was to separate Trinity College from the University of Dublin, which was to become purely an examining body to which teaching institutions would be affiliated. Three of these would be denominational: Magee in Ulster for the Presbyterians, and St Patrick's at Maynooth and a further college in Dublin for the Catholics. The teaching of religion would be separated from secular education. This was calculated to reconcile the Nonconformists. In the Catholic institutions certain areas of secular teaching would be under strict reservation, and certain 'controversial' areas would not be examinable. There would be state-aided finance so arranged as not to require the British taxpayer to subsidize Catholicism.

On 13 February Gladstone unfolded his scheme in a speech of 'prodigious length' and 'dazzling eloquence'. He argued that the well-being of Ireland depended ultimately on the 'moral and intellectual culture of her people'. But when he disclosed restrictions as to teaching and examining – there were to be no chairs in theology, philosophy, and modern history in the denominational colleges – he raised a laugh.[51] This was ominous of trouble. The restrictive 'gagging clauses', as they were dubbed, provoked the obvious response that they would precisely prove fatal to high mental culture.[52]

At first it seemed that Gladstone had pulled it off. But soon the initial spell of his potency faded. Doubts emerged as to 'whether the ultramontane priesthood in Ireland would accept it'.[53] The priests were insisting on full and entire control of publicly funded institutions. That was not what Gladstone had in mind in the matter of 'fair play'. Gladstone circulated to Cabinet a report of dire negotiations with Cullen. 'Overhead it is dark, & underfoot a chaos, but our course is perfectly clear & straight & as far as real criticism is concerned the Bill has stood it well.' The most serious danger and difficulty that Gladstone foresaw was that of mutilation in the Lords, 'as I do not see how the Government could resign on it'.[54] By 8 March defeat was expected. As a last resort Gladstone made the issue one of confidence. To Manning he declared defiantly: 'I shall fight to the last against all comers, but much against my inclination which is marvellously attuned by the vision of my liberty dawning like a sunrise from beyond the hills.'[55]

An onslaught on 10 March from that inveterate enemy of priestcraft, W. Vernon Harcourt, gave the cue to the Liberal pack. The Conservative party shared certain concerns with the Catholic Church about the benefits of denominational education, Disraeli, affronted both by the 'nonsense' in the bill and by Gladstone's vote-of-confidence procedure, preferred risking the unwelcome prospect of minority office rather than working the machine. The Irish University Bill crashed by 284 to 287 votes. Forty-eight Liberal defectors took the view that the measure was not one 'on which the existence of the Government ought to turn'. That also was Disraeli's opinion.

There was much debate about the course to take: ignore the vote (which would have suited Disraeli); revise the measure; propose another vote of confidence in general terms. But what would be the advantage of staggering on, getting nowhere? To Gladstone resignation seemed decidedly preferable to dissolving the 1868 Parliament. There was no populist cry to be made out of Irish universities. Returning to office with a much reduced majority was simply another way of going nowhere. Above all, there was in being 'a factious spirit' that debilitated the Liberal party generally. 'There is now no *cause*', Gladstone concluded. 'No great object on wh. the Liberal party are agreed & combined.'

At a Cabinet on 13 March Gladstone made clear his own preference for a 'temporary rest'. His colleagues, 'without any marked difference, or at least any positive assertion to the contrary, determined on our tendering our resignations'. On that day, having had audience of the Queen, Gladstone announced in the Commons that he had offered his government's resignation. He denounced a factious and malignant combination of Romanism and Toryism.

Now Gladstone could fairly assume that he was indeed free, and that his vision of liberty was dawning like a sunrise from beyond the hills. As he put it to Manning: 'You give no heed to the wailings and pleas of my old age: but I do, & the future of politics hardly exists for me, unless some new phase arise and, as in 1868, a special call may appear: to such call, please God I will answer; if there be breath in my body.'[56]

The immediate twist of events, however, was that Disraeli declined to accept the Queen's invitation to him to form a government. Disraeli's position was that Gladstone had been constitutionally ill-advised to make the Irish University issue one of confidence; and that the components of the adverse majority, being fortuitous, bore no responsibility for consequences. Gladstone fought tenaciously to stay out; but Disraeli foiled him. Gladstone conceded defeat and allowed himself to be 'foisted in' on 17 March.

~

Gladstone was now leader of a wounded and limping ministry without a cause. Kimberley, surveying the government's plight, concluded shrewdly: 'Our old programme is completely exhausted: and Gladstone is not the man to govern without "measures", nor is he at all suited to lead a party in difficulties. He must have a strong current of opinion in his favour.'[57] For his own part, Gladstone was eloquent to Ripon on the 'great difficulty of the loss of "*vital power*"', with problems of education and economy hanging over awkwardly. Cardwell's Army estimates were now looking much less promising than had been hoped. But if vital power was to be found anywhere, Gladstone's instinct was to look to economy as the likeliest source. There was, therefore, the presumption that, if obliged to stay in office and see the session through and then dissolve the 1868 Parliament, Gladstone would revert to the spirit of 1853 to shape a 'special call' to generate vital power out of some big issue of finance.

Meanwhile there was little enough to sustain a sense of drive and purpose. Lowe's budget did not help. Goschen's local taxation reform also failed to register any helpful impact. By-election losses continued relentlessly. There were troubling personal problems. Over the Easter recess Gladstone was at odds with Robertson over the Seaforth accounts. Hope-Scott's death later in April evoked many poignant memories. Then came distress on 8 May at J. S. Mill's death; and, in its way the greater distress of discovering that it would not be possible for Gladstone to take part in any project of a public memorial until the question of Mill's part in the 'loathsome' matter of birth control was cleared up.[58] Glyn's inheriting the Wolverton peerage deprived Gladstone of his Chief Whip. He appointed Arthur Peel; but all Peel could do was continue the glum litany of reports of by-election disasters: 'since the first Licensing Bill we have ... gained no seat from the Tories and have lost 15'. Dover was causing great anxiety.[59] Even the Conservatives were astonished at winning Dover. Derby noted: 'This really looks like winning at the next election, if we make no blunder.'[60]

There were galling defeats for the government in the Commons and losses of temper on Gladstone's part. Welcome relief in July came in another soothing Hatfield weekend. But there were more 'scrapes' with brutish Ayrton at the Board of Works and, of more moment, with Lowe over the Zanzibar contract with the Post Office. This was a project to bribe the Sultan with a regular mail service in return for his suppressing the slave trade. The government was held to have 'lost character in the transaction'.[61] Ministers seemed to be tottering in a vicious cycle of lucklessness and discredit. The death of Bishop Wilberforce of Winchester in an accident while riding with Granville left Gladstone with 'a sad sense of a great void in the world'.[62] Gladstone collapsed on 23 July. 'Gave way under great heat, hard work, & perhaps depression of fever.'

It was on that day, in fact, from his sick-bed, that Gladstone made the first initiative discernibly and definably within the frame of generating 'vital power'. He authorized Forster to declare the Prime Minister's personal approval of G. O. Trevelyan's County Franchise Bill to assimilate the county franchise with the occupier borough franchise of 1867. This declaration, for all that it involved no pledge on behalf of the government, sent a frisson through the political world. Ripon abruptly resigned. To Liberals of 'moderate' persuasion it seemed that Gladstone was striking out as a discredited politician with nothing to lose.

The occupier county franchise was a very long-term issue. It would not be of use for the coming dissolution. But it was a portent all the same. Giving votes to agricultural labourers and miners – for that was what it would come to – was seen as something of an English version of the partial disestablishment of the Irish landed Ascendancy. There were many Liberals who, like Ripon, read a large significance into it. In the background in 1873 of continued industrial strife and then in June of the 'revolt of the labourers' against the squires and farmers led by Joseph Arch of the Agricultural Labourers' Union, Gladstone's declaration of 23 July looked like part of a plan ominously deep. Derby was approached by a Liberal MP representing a group of colleagues looking to the Conservatives for a 'policy of repose'. 'The explanation: that they are alarmed by the attitude of the working men, and at the power acquired by the trade unions: and belief that Gladstone, half out of ambition and half out of sentimental sympathy, is ready to throw all the influence of the State into the scale against the employer.'[63] This was to misread Gladstone. A good part of workers' agitation at the time was trade union backlash against Gladstone's restrictive legislation. In September 1873, when the 'labourers' revolt' touched Harwarden, Gladstone assisted quite readily in reducing wages at the Aston Hall colliery nearby.

Escape from the miserably unproductive session was the immediate priority. Parliament was prorogued on 5 August until 22 October. Under cover of sessional truncation Gladstone reshuffled his pack. Post Office and Board of Works scandals meant that Lowe had to be removed from the Exchequer. Ripon's resignation in any case prompted a more general reshuffle. In deference to the magnitude of the crisis, Bright consented to return, this time at the Duchy of Lancaster. From the Home Office Bruce took the peerage of Aberdare and moved up to the Lords to replace Ripon. Gladstone put upon Cardwell the painful task of shunting the very unwilling Lowe to the Home Office. Hartington was sore at being left stranded in the Irish Office. For the Exchequer Gladstone considered Goschen and Childers; but then decided to take it himself. That was where the big strategic possibilities were likely to be available; there would be the remaking of a great hinge of state. To Gladstone it was all an immense strain He assured the Queen that he hoped 'to come through it without breaking down'.[64] Cardwell did break down.

The recess at least offered respite. Ministers could regroup, the better to face the planned October session. An irritation nagged Gladstone. Did his taking on the Exchequer mean that he had to secure re-election at Greenwich? Given the haemorrhage of Liberal by-election losses that would be a risky affair. The Law Officers gave Gladstone assurance; but certain punctilious critics were not content. It was a matter that was bound to be raised at the revived session. He found time to intervene at a Hawarden parish meeting, where his support for the voluntary denominational principle in schooling and his deprecating the setting up of a School Board caused considerable public stir.[65] This unabashed assertion of Anglican interests scandalized John Morley, Comtist editor of the freethinking *Fortnightly Review* and claimant as J. S. Mill's successor as the mentor of Liberal values. To his Radical friend, Joseph Chamberlain, screw manufacturing Mayor of Birmingham and orchestrator of Nonconformist agitation through the Education League, Morley pointed out that Gladstone's words 'commit him to Voluntary Schools & Church Supremacy for the rest of his life'.[66]

This was on Gladstone's part deliberate provocation. Since he saw no hope of reconciling the Nonconformists, he saw no point in not making clear his personal opposition to any 'repression' of religion in schools. He confided to Granville his fear that the education controversy would 'eventually either split the party, or fatally cripple it for a time in regard to Parliamentary action'. The Nonconformists, he was sure, meant 'mischief for the future'. They had the power, as he pointed out to Lord Frederick Cavendish, 'to throw us into a minority, &

they probably will use it; but they have not power to do more'. There was nothing to be done other than to 'avoid sharp issues'.[67]

~

Having thus set aside education as a problem as much as possible to be kept out of sight, for Gladstone the important thing now was to light upon an issue that would tend to override party divisions and pull Liberals and Liberalism, both in and out of doors, together. Now that he was back at the Exchequer, he was immediately in charge of a potential engine of regeneration. He wrote to 'Dear Bright' ('Let us bid farewell to *Misters*') on 14 August: 'What we want at present is a *positive* force to carry us onward as a body ... It may possibly, I think, be had out of *Finance*.' Now that the government had got over the scrapes of the last session, 'we have now before us a clear stage for the consideration of measures for the Autumn. We must, I think, have a good bill of fare or none.'

That good bill of fare would depend crucially on the services estimates. Gladstone was once more in consultation with Cardwell, 'to whom at the W.O. I told in deep secrecy my ideas of the *possible* finance of the next year: based on the abolition of the Income Tax & Sugar Duties with partial compensation from Spirits & Death Duties. This *only* might give us a chance.' Having thus sketched the elements of a reversion to the high Peelite tone of 1853, Gladstone set off for Hawarden 'with a more buoyant spirit and greater sense of relief than I have experienced for many years'. He explained to himself that 'this gush is in proportion to the measure of the late troubles & anxieties'.[68]

There was in fact little that was new in the elements Gladstone sketched. Debates throughout the 1873 session on the correct relationship between direct and indirect taxation, and the correct incidence of indirect taxation, had rehearsed them thoroughly. The question was widely canvassed both in debate and by deputation: Why not repeal the income tax? Had not that projected repeal been the very foundation of Gladstone's grand financial plan of 1853–1860? Gladstone had already taken soundings from the trade about sugar duty abolition. 'My view about finance is this', he told Bright from Balmoral. 'It is in finance *only* that I see a possibility – I will not say more – of our being able to do something that may raise us to a higher and firmer level.'[69]

At Hawarden on 13 September Gladstone convened Bright, Wolverton and Granville to help him thrash the matter out. Over four days they waded through the figures. Gladstone calculated that he would be in want of £8 million to replace his planned remissions. A revenue surplus was to be expected, but its extent as yet unknown. An October session now seemed impracticable. Estimates were not reliably formed until the last quarter. A further prorogation shifted the new session back to 16 December. Then it was postponed to 5 February 1874. Gladstone informed Speaker Brand: 'The Financial question looms large &

probably will be the hinge of the Session – possibly of the Election too.'[70]

A lull followed while the necessary revenue figures were awaited. Gladstone was enthralled by photographs of the 'Troy' excavations, sent by Heinrich Schliemann via the British Museum 'expressly for your inspection'. Gladstone was in no doubt that Schliemann's excavations provided decisive evidence justifying his faith in the 'basic historicity of the Homeric epics'. He set about making himself Schliemann's 'prophet' in England. Schliemann's offer to sell his collection to the Museum for £50,000 was 'of course not to be entertained'.[71]

~

The time was getting nearer for decisions. Should the Greenwich seat be abandoned? Gladstone informed Lord Westminster that he could not as yet accept his offer of the Grosvenor influence at Chester. He thought 'about next May' was the time 'when it is most likely, or least unlikely, that we may see our way better than at present'.[72] Gladstone envisaged at the beginning of 1874 a signal and masterful budget in April that would spearhead a dissolution and an appeal to the constituencies for renewed confidence. No other remedy for the present state of affairs seemed feasible. Resignation was ruled out by the events of 1873. Dissolution at the moment would mean coming back with a uselessly small majority. As he put it to Granville, as the 'signs of weakness' multiply upon the government, things were getting to the point of its ceasing to have the confidence of the country. What was needed was reanimation of some form of the 'vital force' of 1868. The supreme remedy was the model of 1853: to 'frame a budget large enough and palpably beneficial enough'.[73] 'It is not by a multitude of small details however well handled they may be', he told Bright, 'that we can mend the position of affairs. It wants some one issue, clear, broad, & straight.'[74]

The Treasury was by now in a position to estimate that a surplus of £5 million would be available. Gladstone could look to a clear, broad and straight path to eliminate the income tax and sugar duties and to reduce rating incidence; but only if Goschen at the Admiralty and Cardwell at the War Office could yield substantial remissions. 'Have the Govt. & party any other mode of giving their friends fair play at the elections', Gladstone asked unanswerably, 'than by such a Budget as has been sketched?'[75] He summoned Cardwell and Goschen, together with Granville and Bright, for a conference on 19 January. Cardwell and Goschen confessed themselves unable to deliver. On the 20th Gladstone took to his bed.

But already Gladstone's mind had started on a different tack. It was on Sunday the 18th that Gladstone 'thought of dissolution'. 'Told Bright of it. In evening at dinner told Granville and Wolverton. All seemed to approve. My first thought of it was as escape from a difficulty. I soon saw on reflection that it was the best thing in itself.'[76]

The great matter of reanimating vital force was thus turned by Gladstone back to front. From a big budget being the means of restoring public authority to the government prior to a dissolution, a dissolution would become the means of providing public authority needed to launch a big budget. In bed on the 20th Gladstone reflected 'on our "crisis"'. He drafted a long address setting out the case for an immediate appeal to the country. The material points bearing on his thinking were, first: 'We gain time, & avoid for the moment a ministerial crisis.' This gain would put ministers in possession of better information about estimates and 'arrest the certain drain of the single elections', now a long series of defeats impairing the government's credit and taking the heart out of the Liberal party and damaging it for the final struggle. Then a further advantage would be that the 'formidable divisions in the party would be aborted or held in suspense if we have an *immediate* Dissolution upon a question of universal & commanding interest'. Every week of a pre-dissolution session would have its dangers in the present circumstances of division and dissension.[77]

All this added up seemingly, to 'the best thing in itself'. 23 January was a 'very busy, stirring day, of incessant action'. At Cabinet Gladstone stated his motives '& recommn to Dissolve on the grounds of general advantage. Granville concurred. All agreed.' The address was considered, with revisions and deletions of passages likely to be offensive to Catholic Irish. Gladstone spoke of 'perserverance in economic efforts' in the renewed Liberal government.[78] There was talk of reshuffled placements. After carrying his budget in redemption of election pledges, Gladstone would hand over the Exchequer to Goschen.

The times indeed were busy and stirring. The news would be publicly sensational. Parliament, after all, was on the very brink of reassembling for the session. The 1868 Parliament was dissolved with effect on 25 January, with a general election forthwith. Abolition of the income tax would be its keynote. For all his later denials of 'theatrical motive' it is very likely that Gladstone relished the element of political theatre involved. The precipitancy and abruptness of the event bore a dramatic charge bespeaking masterful urgency. Something of the élan of 1868 was now surely reanimated.

The political world was stunned. The immediate impact seemed to ratify Gladstone's astonishingly bold stroke. The Conservatives were staggered and in disarray, uncertain whether to denounce income tax abolition as an unworthy bribe or to claim that they were contemplating exactly the same measure. Most Liberals agreed with Frederic Harrison that Gladstone had pulled off a 'dextrous party move'.[79] Derby was one of the few shrewd doubters. 'It is too early to judge, but on the whole I incline to think Gladstone has made a mistake.'[80]

It was not long before Gladstone himself inclined to think likewise. He spoke at Greenwich to a rain-sodden crowd on the 28th: 'An enthusiastic meeting. But the general prospects are far from clear.' The clearer they got, the worse they got. Faltering prospects made some of Gladstone's colleagues fear that, with defeat looming, he might launch out desperately on the county franchise. If income tax repeal was not attractive to the classes, might not Gladstone decide to turn to the masses? As Cardwell put it, Gladstone was the 'turning point of the people's politics'.[81]

Gladstone, however, decided to turn to the people's politics in Ireland to help to save Liberal seats there from the Home Rulers. He had included in his Greenwich address friendly remarks about the desirability in Ireland of improvement in local and subordinate levels of government. Something with more bite, he felt, was needed to fend off the Home Rulers. He selected Lord Fermoy as the recipient of a kind of Irish sub-manifesto. Now Fermoy learned from Gladstone the 'test' to be applied to the question. If Home Rule lightened the burdens of the Westminster Parliament, but yet did nothing to damage the permanence and stability of the Union, it could be sympathetically, and with due caution, entertained. Gladstone pointed out that 'with respect to Home Rule I have not yet heard an authoritative or binding definition of the phrase which appears to have been used by different persons in different senses'.[82]

The Liberal party was shedding seats everywhere, except in Ireland, where there were a few gains. Gladstone's own return at Greenwich 'after Boord the distiller' he felt 'more like a defeat than a victory'. The Liberal party lost 69 English seats, and three Welsh and twelve Scottish. Disraeli would have a majority of over 60. It was the case, as Gladstone ruefully pointed out, that more seats were transferred from one party to the other than at any election since 1831–32.[83] He allowed it was very much a 'national condemnation', 'emphatically enough pronounced'.[84] The ballot clearly had provided cover for Liberals to 'react' over to the Conservatives. From Peel he requested explanatory information. Was it 'Conservative reaction'? Was it the licensed victuallers? Dissentient Nonconformists? The Irish vote in Britain? Or any other special cause?[85] In view of his own humiliating situation at Greenwich, it was understandable that Gladstone should give the Trade pride of place in villainy. 'We have been swept away, literally', he told Spencer, 'by a torrent of beer & gin.'[86]

~

Disraeli's precedent of instant resignation in 1868 suggested itself enticingly. It deviated from 'a sound general rule', but it was justified in the circumstances. There would be no advantage to the public interest in meeting the new Parliament. The Queen was quite complaisant.[87] On the eve of going off to Windsor Gladstone gave a Cabinet dinner. 'It went well. I did something towards snapping the ties, and winding out the coil.'

What he did was to disconcert his colleagues with a statement about big changes in prospect. Aberdare reported a 'startling announcement': that he would 'no longer retain the leadership of the liberal party, nor resume it, unless the party had settled its differences'. He would no longer expose himself to insults and outrages reminiscent of 1866–67, about which he still had a lively sense of bitterness. Although possessed of a keen awareness of having again been the victim of disloyalty over the past three years, Gladstone denied that his decision was dictated by temper or sulks. The Liberal party would have to learn that all duties and responsibilities were confined not to leaders alone, but to followers as well. 'He wishes them', as Aberdare reported to Ripon, 'to enjoy the blessings of anarchy for a while in order that they may learn to appreciate the necessity of party obedience.'[88]

At Windsor Gladstone and his colleagues returned their seals of office to the Queen. Aberdare thought him 'evidently in a high-wrought state of sensitiveness'.[89] It soon became clear that Gladstone's announcement about withdrawing from the leadership was no mere evanescent whim, as in June 1867. After the Cabinet dinner he had 'walked on the flags up and down' with Granville and Wolverton, resisting their objections to anarchy. He lay awake that night for three hours with an 'overwrought brain'. But he could see that all was good. 'That which is now come is the old aim of my wishes & most unworthy prayers.' To Peel he wrote on 19 February: 'It is not my intention to assume the functions of Leader of the Parliamentary Opposition in the House of Commons to the new Government.' He further informed Peel obscurely that he could even give his opinion, 'if it were generally desired on the question', whether it be expedient that the leadership 'should be at present assumed by anyone else'. What was the Liberal party to make of this? How could it not expediently be assumed by someone else? How otherwise was the party to be managed as an Opposition?

Such questions were left hanging in the air. Gladstone, it seemed, would remain in the House of Commons, like Peel in 1846. To what purpose? Peel's purpose at least had been clear: to prop up Russell's government. Gladstone's purpose was obscure. Was this the 'breathing freedom in other air' he had prayed for at the time of Maynooth? Was this detaching his hopes and interests from the political future that he had spoken of in the aftermath of the Irish Land crisis of 1870? Was it the 'freer and purer air' he had yearned for at the end of 1871?

For the rest, Gladstone made clear to Arthur Peel that, uppermost in his mind, as it had been in 1867, was the refractoriness of the party. He denied motivation arising from 'any cause of complaint'. But he felt that public men who had given their best years were not bound 'in the absence of any strong and special cause' to spend their old age in service. After his labours since 1868 he was in need of rest; and the country knew by sad experience of public careers unduly prolonged.[90] Gladstone was willing also to allow, at this 'hour of outward discomfiture', that his colleagues had had 'much to bear with and from me'.[91]

On 20 February Gladstone had final audience of the Queen. Resignation honours included Westminster, rewarded with a dukedom, and Cardwell, shattered in health, removed to the Lords with a consolation viscountcy. It was material in relation to the ambiguity and uncertainty in which Gladstone left his party at this juncture that he should have declined the Queen's pressing offer of an earldom. He explained to Sir Thomas, head of the family: 'I do not see that I am wanted or should be of use in the House of Lords: and there would be some discrepancy between rank and fortune, which is a thing rather to be deprecated. On the other hand I know that the line I have marked out for myself in the House of Commons is one not altogether easy to hold: but I have every disposition to remain quiet there, and shall be very glad if I can do so'.[92]

13

The Question of the East, 1875–1877

'I was simply an humble collaborateur with the English people in a work which they had taken into their own hands. In the matter of humanity and justice they required no instructor. It was the nation that led the classes and leaders, and not the classes and leaders who led the nation.'

Gladstone in the House of Commons, 18 February 1877

Gladstone would remain in the House of Commons in some, as yet, unclearly defined role. Whereas Peel in 1846 had made a clean break with his party, Gladstone's abdication was anything but clear-cut. What began to emerge amid the fog of obscurity surrounding his motives in staying on in the Commons was that Gladstone's earlier yearnings about breathing freedom in other air, or passing into a freer and purer air, or detaching his hopes and interests from the political future, did not actually now quite apply. His gestures towards defining what he was now to be about reeked rather of the ambiguities of the conditional clauses he had so far advanced: in the absence of any strong and special cause; until the party had settled its differences; remaining quiet if he could do so. Aberdare was in no doubt that withdrawal was a way of punishing the party for its refractoriness. Resumption of leadership would come in due course when circumstances made an imperative call.

All this emerged gradually over the next weeks. Gladstone would have the best of both worlds: the answer to the 'old aim' of his wishes and most unworthy prayers connected conditionally to resumption of high duty when the strong and special cause should call. It was precisely from that ground of personal advantage that Gladstone's sense of entitlement to 'take counsel with himself' took the form of arrangements convenient for himself but grossly inconvenient for his colleagues and his party. He was unwilling to take on the tedious burdens of leadership of an Opposition. Yet invariably he coupled such declarations with an escape clause: as having by no means renounced 'all hope either of witnessing or taking part in' the 'future triumphs of sound & active liberalism';[1] or that his withdrawal must always be 'liable to be restrained and restricted' should there arise 'some great public cause for which to contend'.[2]

His colleagues found themselves trapped in Gladstone's warmly enveloping web of subordinate clauses. It was not for him, as Gladstone elaborated on 7 March, to prejudge or indicate in any manner the course that the Liberal party might take. 'If they shall deem it their duty to arrange in the usual manner with some other person to discharge the functions hitherto entrusted to me', such a person, 'within the limits of action which circumstances at present impose on me, will have all the support which in an independent position I can give him'.[3] Peel arranged a meeting of all old colleagues on 9 March, where it was proposed that Gladstone lead for two more sessions, until the end of 1875. Gladstone decided he would lead only occasionally in 1874, and make a final decision at the beginning of 1875. The party meanwhile was free to choose a 'provisional leader'.[4] Gladstone issued a circular to Liberal MPs on 12 March in the form of addressing explanations to Granville, as leader in the Lords.[5]

Anything more unsatisfactory from the point of view of Gladstone's colleagues or the Liberal party at large could hardly be imagined. The Liberal frontbench in the Commons declined taking up the idea of a 'provisional' leader and adopted an informal arrangement of responsibilities. The leadership in the Commons, and in some vague sense the leadership of the party as a whole, was suspended until such time as circumstances should dictate otherwise. Gladstone serenely explained himself to Döllinger: 'I have not recorded any vow on the subject of return to office, but I think it very unlikely that any adequate cause should arise to bring me back to my recent position.'[6]

The party meanwhile would have to make the best of this conditional state of being. Arthur Peel indicated his sense of the absurdity of the situation by resigning as Chief Whip.[7] Harcourt, briefly in office as Solicitor-General and never patient with Gladstone's imperial mode, informed Frank Hill of the *Daily News*: 'There is no whip, no office, no nothing. The thing is ridiculous & disgraceful.' The fate of the Liberal party depended 'on whether G. chooses to get out of the sulks'.[8]

When the 1874 session did get under way Gladstone found himself the object of resentments in his bruised and bewildered party.[9] He attempted to head off trouble with elaborately pre-emptive explanations, with the theme that it was the duty of government 'never to continue to carry on the business of the country unless it is convinced that it is possessed of the strength necessary for carrying on with dignity and credit'. It followed that with respect to the decision to dissolve, nether regret nor apology was necessary or appropriate.[10]

As to the Fermoy letter, a particular object of grievance, Gladstone did his best to extenuate his fault by reassuring his party of his Unionist orthodoxy with a vigorous assault on Isaac Butt's 'ragged scheme' of Home Rule, which he trusted 'this House will never condescend to adopt'. 'The plan is this – that exclusively Irish affairs are to be judged in Ireland, and that then the Irish Members are to come to the Imperial Parliament and to judge as they may think fit of the general affairs of the Empire, and also affairs exclusively English and Scotch ... I want to know in what portion of his plan are we guaranteed against the danger that our friends from Ireland who shall be invested with exclusive power over consideration of Irish affairs in Dublin may come here to meddle with matters exclusively English or Scotch?'[11] It was a good question.

Perhaps a 'civil talk' a few days earlier did something to make Disraeli supportive when two MPs, a Conservative and a Liberal, moved a vote of censure against Gladstone for an unconstitutionally precipitate dissolution of the late Parliament without there being an emergency. Gladstone defended the abruptness of the decision 'by the peculiar circumstances out of which it sprang'. Disraeli advised the resentful members to judge Gladstone at his best: 'I should remember the great victories which he has fought and won; I should remember his illustrious career, its continual success and splendour, not its accidental or even disastrous mistakes.'[12]

Once these storms had subsided, Gladstone settled down to a leisurely and rather detached version of sessional leadership. His interventions were sparse, mostly formalities or 'ecclesiastical evenings'. There were occasional flashes of the old Gladstone, as when he roundly denounced the annexation of the Fiji Islands[13] and 'that socialistic budget of Northcote's', giving special relief to the bottom end of income tax payers.[14] But for the most part he was reticent and discreet.

Now there was much more space for personal and domestic concerns. To Catherine's dismay, he began proceedings to sell up 11 Carlton House Terrace. There was anxious correspondence with Döllinger, whose excommunicated plight in Germany was material to Gladstone's attention to the beginnings of the *Kulturkampf* between the Reich and the Roman Catholic Church. 'Bismarck's ideas & methods are not ours', he wrote to Lord Odo Russell, the Ambassador in Berlin. But he was clear that he was more with Bismarck on this issue than against him. 'I cannot but say that the present doctrines of the Roman Church destroy the title of her obedient members to the enjoyment of civil rights.' Gladstone would 'hate to say this publicly, for I want no more storms, but it may become necessary'.[15]

He was exercised also by the dangers of 'plutocracy'. He feared that a 'great & threatening shoal if not rock' lay ahead, likely to wreck the ship of state and its people.[16] That the new wealth and ease were sapping the nation's moral fibre was a theme common among Liberals at a loss otherwise to account for an anomalous Conservative election victory. For Gladstone it was a matter of recurring to his denunciations of the metropolitan ethos in his Whitby outburst in 1871. He was much gratified when Theodore Martin sent him the first volume of his *Life of the Prince Consort*, praising it for the 'rebuke & admonition' given to idle wealth and its dangers to the aristocracy.[17] He was much less gratified by revelations of the exiguous 'religious interior of the Prince'. The capacious religious interior of his

'Dear Spirit', on the other hand, was ever a matter of attentive concern.

The amenities of that Hawarden season were sadly compromised by the sudden death, on 16 June, of Sir Stephen Glynne, while 'searching for antiquities in Shoreditch High Street'. With Catherine's two brothers now deceased, the male line of the Glynnes of Hawarden became extinct. Under the arrangements of 1865, Catherine's eldest son Willy entered into his inheritance. Gladstone always professed a 'strong repugnance to becoming the actual or the virtual master'.[18] In fact, with his and Catherine's continued residence, there was no avoiding his becoming virtual master. After the funeral on 24 June 'came the interviews and explanations'. Willy – a notably reticent MP – 'expressed his perfect readiness to act as I recommended under the new arrangements'. The Gladstones were now to be the house guests of their son. Willy Gladstone stood now in Sir Stephen's place in the Castle as Stephen Gladstone stood in the Reverend Henry's place in the Rectory.

~

Quiet times in the Commons might well have continued had not Disraeli decided to put his government behind a bill introduced in the Lords by Archbishop Tait. The Public Worship Regulation Bill aimed at giving diocesan bishops powers to criminalize the 'ritualistic' practices of certain High Church or 'Anglo-Catholic' clergy deemed to savour of popery. Gladstone objected passionately to the implications of the measure for state control of the Church. It evoked painful memories of the Gorham case in 1850. In its wholly unnecessary interference Parliament, Gladstone feared, was 'treading on the edge of a precipice'. Over that precipice might fall the Church as an establishment of religion.[19]

Disraeli's and the government's official stance at the outset was one of neutrality. Salisbury managed to get the bill down to the Commons in a less ferocious form. Even so, Gladstone counter-attacked with voluminous resolutions. Disraeli had long been spoiling to strike at the 'Rits'. It would be popular in the country and in Parliament. The Queen egged him on. Gladstone had exposed himself vulnerably in a Commons of decidedly 'Protestant' sentiment. Liberals of anti-sacerdotal leanings came out in support of the bill. Forster, Lowe, Goschen and especially Harcourt proved good enemies of priestcraft. Disraeli could not resist the temptation to put the government behind the measure to suppress 'the Mass in masquerade'. Gladstone and his resolutions were swept aside by the Protestant tide. There was a particularly bruising encounter with Harcourt, whose 'slimy, fulsome, loathsome eulogies upon Dizzy', Gladstone thought, were aimed at him. He regretted the affair '*extremely*', as he told Granville. 'It is a new scandal & a new difficulty for the party.'[20]

Tait and Disraeli got their Public Worship Regulation Act, but got little satisfaction from it. The ostentatious willingness of Anglo-Catholic clergymen to bear witness through the martyrdom of noisy trials and imprisonment soon discredited it. Heads were shaken at Gladstone's having yet again exhibited excessive excitability and want of a sense of proportion. Selborne complained that Gladstone 'can hardly be brought to interest himself at all in matters (even when they are really great matters) in which he is not carried away by some too strong attraction'. When so carried away, 'he does not sympathise with, or take counsel with' those whose point of view at all differed from his own. 'This makes it hardly possible for him to be a Minister, except when it is time for some "heroic" measures, for which he can excite public enthusiasm.'[21]

Once the sessional reverberations had died away, Gladstone put his views on the problem of Ritualism in an article for the October *Contemporary*. But even as he prepared his defence of Catholic Anglicanism, Lady Ripon stunned him with the news of Ripon's decision to submit to Rome.[22] Gladstone's response – 'may he pause' – dwelt on the seeming strangeness of such an act when the Roman Church had dealt itself such a blow in Germany.[23]

It was to Germany that Gladstone was bound in September. His sister Helen was sequestered still in Cologne. But it was to Munich and Döllinger that his mind was set. Accompanied by Willy and Helen, Gladstone found his sister 'deeply to be felt for'. Then at Munich there was much intense talk with Döllinger; and an awkward moment when in a street Döllinger and Gladstone came upon Döllinger's excommunicator, Archbishop Gregor Scherr. Perhaps it was the incitement of that encounter together with sad thoughts of the Ripons that caused Gladstone the following day to send off to Knowles of the *Contemporary* an insert for the Ritualism article. In this Gladstone asserted four propositions: that Rome had substituted for 'the proud boast of *semper eadem* a policy of violence and change of faith'; that Rome had refurbished anew every rusty tool she was fondly believed to have disused; that 'no one can become her convert without renouncing his moral and mental freedom'; and that Rome had repudiated equally 'modern thought and ancient history'.[24] This converted a defence of unpopular Ritualism into a popular attack on Romanism.

Gladstone returned to Hawarden in a state of mental excitement. Something like the Neapolitan eruption of 1851 was building up. His experiences of late were accumulating into an emotionally explosive dynamic of resentments. There was the Roman Catholic hierarchy in Ireland and their killing his University Bill. There was his sister Helen's plight. There was the Public Worship fracas. There was the Ripon bombshell. There was the *Kulturkampf*. There was Döllinger's brave struggle against Roman Curial arrogance, fighting to save his conscience from a kind of 'moral murder'.[25] There was Gladstone's interest in the Cavourian ideal of a *libera chiesa in libero stato* in Italy in its struggle against the sinister forces of 'Vaticanism'.[26] Not least was Gladstone's conviction, as he later explained to Granville, that the Ultramontanes in France were 'waiting, in one vast conspiracy, for an opportunity to direct European war to the re-establishment by force of the temporal power; or even to bring about such war for that purpose'.[27]

Before September was out, Gladstone started work on what was to be published in November as *The Vatican Decrees in their Bearing on Civil Allegiance: A Political Expostulation*. In substance, this was an extension of the insert he had sent from Munich for his *Contemporary* article. He had told Odo Russell that he wanted no more storms, but that one might be necessary. At Hawarden Acton pleaded unavailingly that the decrees had no practical bearing on the civil allegiance of Catholics. The public impact of *Vatican Decrees* was gratifyingly explosive. Murray reported 52,000 copies sold and 20,500 more printed before the end of November. If Gladstone had been on the unpopular side of the Public Worship issue he more than redeemed himself now. Both Newman and Manning were provoked into rebukes on behalf of loyal Roman Catholic subjects of the Queen. The Queen herself, for all her Protestantism, was not amused. 'What an incomprehensible old man he is!' She reminded her daughter Victoria: 'Old Lord Palmerston was not wrong when he said to me, "he is a very dangerous man"'.[28]

Detonations of Gladstone's polemic reverberated throughout Europe. Bismarck 'admired the manly courage and great lucidity' with which Gladstone exposed 'the false doctrines of Rome', and treated 'a question that has such vivid interest for Germany at this moment.'[29] Gladstone's impulse carried him far: to a critique of Pius IX's speeches for the January 1875 *Quarterly* and then on to *Vaticanism: An Answer to Replies and Reproofs* published by Murray's in March, and beyond that to 'Italy and her Church', an examination of the ways in which the Italian state and people might combine to resist and defeat the insolence of the Roman Curia, for the *Church Quarterly Review* in October 1875. Gladstone was in a position to recommend to the Italians as a model of a free church in a free state his own creation of the disestablished Church of Ireland, or, for that matter, the Free Kirk of Scotland.[30]

On receipt of *Vaticanism*, Bismarck felt a 'deep and hopeful gratification' to see the two nations, 'champions of liberty of conscience encountering the same foe', standing henceforth 'shoulder on shoulder in defending the highest interests of the human race'.[31] Gladstone was not entirely happy thus to be enrolled as a comrade in the *Kulturkampf*. Granville cautioned against becoming implicated in 'injudiciously violent actions' of the German authorities.[32] Gladstone slanted his response judiciously, avowing that 'a deep interest in the ideal of freedom, inadequately represented by our Metropolitan Press, is felt by the nation'.[33]

Judicious slanting was a feature also of his anti-Roman polemics. William Monsell, Lord Emly, an old friend from Engagement days and a 'Limerick' convert to a cultivated lay ideal of Roman Catholicism, had cautioned Gladstone that it would be a 'serious thing' to 'declare war on the religion of the Irish people'.[34]

Gladstone took his point. He avoided direct confrontation with Romanism precisely where it was a real power nearest home, in Ireland.[35] As he put it in *Vatican Decrees*, noting that the Roman Church governed five million (or one sixth) of the population of the United Kingdom, it had ever been a 'favourite purpose' of his career 'not to conjure up, but to conjure down, public alarm'.[36]

~

On his 65th birthday Gladstone found himself deprived of the mental repose he had hoped for by controversy 'which presses upon both mind & body'. Even less was mental repose now aided by the near prospect of the 1875 session. The Liberal party, disabled by the 'absence of any great positive aim (the late plan having failed) for which to co-operate', and by wounds as yet unhealed in economy and education, was in need of firm sessional leadership. Gladstone's inclination was firmly to rule himself out. This sadly compromised domestic repose. Catherine was by no means content to be removed both from Carlton House Terrace and from the centre ground of high politics.[37]

To Granville Gladstone put it that there were 'great incompatibilities' in the way of his resuming the party leadership. There was the religious question generally, with the Church of England 'on the brink of a most serious crisis'. While this question remained unresolved, Gladstone felt that any '*strapping* up' of the relations between himself and the party could only constitute a new danger, particularly when there was no public object on the pursuit of which the party was agreed. While Gladstone was sure Liberalism had been heartened by *Vatican Decrees*, he could see 'no daylight' in 'general politics'. 'Nothing will rally the party but a cause or such portentous blundering as is almost beyond hope or fear.'[38]

Granville did his best to hold Gladstone for the party. But already Gladstone was drafting a memorandum of abdication to be read to his colleagues. Granville protested: 'A great party should have a recognized leader in Parliament more especially the party favouring progress, but not unanimous as to the rate at which progress should be made.' Granville made also the very material point that Gladstone's intending to remain in the Commons would in itself create obvious practical difficulties.[39]

All such considerations Gladstone serenely ignored. It would be 'for others rather than for me to take the lead in considering what arrangements may be requisite for the regular conduct of Parliamentary business for the convenience and advantage of the Liberal party'. It would, concomitantly, be his duty 'to conduct my own proceedings with the fullest regard to such arrangements'.[40] Thus a semi-detached leadership of the party was to be converted into a semi-detached relationship with the party. Granville was the reluctant recipient of Gladstone's letter of 13 January 1875, stating that he could see 'no public advantage' in his continuing to act as leader of the Liberal party; and that at the age of 65, after

42 years of laborious public life, he thought himself 'entitled to retire on the present opportunity'. 'This retirement is dictated to me by my personal views as to the best method of spending the closing years of my life.'[41]

In many respects this simply confirmed the misgivings of many shrewdly sceptical Liberals at the problematic implications of Gladstone's hoisting Liberal colours in 1859; of his trimming, at that juncture, from being a Conservative with dim prospects to being a Liberal with bright prospects. Prospects were no longer bright. Two other things were not mentioned. Gladstone had denied 'any cause of complaint' at the time of his initial broaching of the question of the leadership in February 1874, though it was evident that he felt keenly the degree of disloyalty to him in the party, and that the element of disloyalty was by no means absent from his mind. The other point was the 'conditional' aspect of 'special call', or 'cause'. He would not now resign his seat in the Commons, but his attendance would be only 'occasional'. Deeming himself unable to hold the party together 'in a manner worthy of it', he nonetheless would be willing to aid 'with a view to arresting some great evil or procuring for the nation some great good'.[42]

~

The overwhelming testimony of the evidence available suggests that very few people who had any close personal knowledge of Gladstone believed that his retirement would stand the strain of many months, let alone years. Just as Gladstone himself back in the late 1840s had judged Peel's resumption of his natural role as the greatest man in politics 'inevitable', so now most Liberals envisaged for the most famous Liberal a fame-enhancing future public role. The Sheffield MP Anthony Mundella found it 'hard to believe that Gladstone has quite retired from politics'. Soon Mundella concluded: 'Gladstone will assuredly return some day. He cannot resist the temptation of a good fight.'[43]

The very beginning of the new order was expressive of its embarrassed and provisional character. Gladstone was possessed of the curious presumption – an odd but characteristic and revealing touch – that, by addressing his letter of abdication to Granville, he had conferred upon the Liberal leader in the Lords the leadership of the Liberal party, as if it were an office in his gift.[44] Granville found this embarrassing,[45] and declined as leader in the Lords even to summon a general meeting of the party. He left it to Arthur Peel's successor as Whip, W. P. Adam, to arrange a meeting of the Liberal MPs at the Reform Club. At this meeting, on 3 February, Bright presiding, Forster, finding himself unacceptable because of the education issue, withdrew his candidacy as leader in the Commons, and the reluctant Lord Hartington was elected. Both Whig leaders were clear that in the extraordinary circumstances, an overall party leader was not electable, partly because of the fragmented condition of the party but partly also because of Gladstone's awkward presence. The leadership of the party would be 'adjourned to the day when, a Liberal majority having been again constituted, the choice of the Sovereign created a Liberal Prime Minister'.[46]

The awkwardness of Gladstone's presence was compounded when Bright proposed that he should retain his frontbench seat in the Commons in comradely solidarity with the new leader. Granville had every reason to believe that Hartington by no means shared Bright's sentiments, and felt much the oppressiveness of 'the anomaly of his (Hartington's) rising to speak for the party, with Gladstone sitting on the same bench'.[47]

Gladstone continued his serenely untroubled course. He was observed 'in high spirits, boasting of not having felt so well for many years, and cordially anxious to be of any use he can to Hartington and his late colleagues'.[48] As Mundella noted, 'Gladstone attends the House very well and keeps a keen and watchful eye on all that is going on. His advent to power sooner or later is considered certain.'[49] Gladstone's keen and watchful eye was not confined to the Commons. He indulged himself with another outing to Newman Hall's Hampstead house, where he began mending fences with the Nonconformists. There was much ado selling off the Carlton House Terrace lease and despatching masses of things to be auctioned by Christie's and Sotheby's. Catherine was not at all pleased to find herself shifted to 73 Harley Street, Marylebone. She was never assiduous as a political hostess, but her devoted identification with her husband's fame and fortunes meant that in many ways his withdrawal would have greater consequences for her than for him. She could share little of his literary and scholarly interests or his religious enthusiasms.

~

For the most part, Gladstone kept a loyally reticent stance in the 1875 session. He contributed nothing to the debates on the government's 'social' legislation as inspired by the New Alliance, designed by Disraeli and his Home Secretary, Cross, to be a relaxing political bromide in contrast to Gladstone's strenuous excitements. Gladstone was very willing, at Hartington's request, to maul Northcote's budget, lamenting the passing of an epoch of 'generous rivalry' between the parties in the matter of economy; though conceding that his ideas on the subject might be 'antiquated and belong to the period of some 20, 30 or 40 years ago'.[50] There were other occasions of intervention, but Hartington on the whole had little cause for complaint, and in turn Gladstone could judge that 'Hartington does his work well, and he develops'. Gladstone's resignation from the Reform Club at the end of the year was taken to be 'an act of political significance', and 'engendered a somewhat bitter feeling in the Club'.[51]

Literary production continued apace. After the 'Italy and her Church' piece, Homerology in various forms revived, incorporating what Gladstone boldly interpreted as the implications of Schliemann's latest excavations. Gladstone played 'prophet' to Schliemann at the Society of Antiquaries. Max Müller was scandalized at Gladstone's twisting the evidence to suit his idiosyncratic purposes. 'So great a man, so imperfect a scholar!' To Max Müller Gladstone's abuse of the new findings was 'really painful, all the more so because it is cleverly done, and I believe *bona fide*'.[52]

There were personal and family distractions. Catherine's niece May Lyttelton, of whom there were hopes as the intended of Arthur Balfour, died in March 1875: the only loss among George Lyttelton's numerous progeny; from which the depressive father never recovered. Later in the year Gladstone's enormous and eccentric brother Robertson died, leaving the family's business affairs in a state of confusion. After the funeral at Knotty Ash on 28 September, Sir Thomas remarked in what Catherine called his 'grubous and grim' manner that Robertson's will was 'very faulty'. One of its faults certainly was its effect of leaving William's third son Harry's position in the firm a matter of dispute and uncertainty with the remaining partners. Gladstone set about remedying Harry's difficulties, costing him 'more care than any other of a temporal nature since the smash of 1847'.[53] Happier was the lot of Willy. In July he became engaged to the Hon. Gertrude Stuart, daughter of Lord and Lady Blantyre. There was for Gladstone the gratification that Lady Blantyre, sister to the Duchess of Argyll, was a daughter of the late Harriet Sutherland. Gladstone had the pleasure of signing the deed making Willy absolute owner in law of the Hawarden estate. The couple were married at St George's, Hanover Square, two days later.

~

What was of political note in the latter part of 1875 was the re-emergence of the 'Eastern question', the fate of the vast regions over which the decaying Ottoman Empire more or less held sway. Gladstone was not at all attuned to any disposition to involve himself in it. His last intervention in 'liberation' mode had been way back in 1858, over the Romanian case, and the 'breasts of free men'.[54] Back in 1863, in one of his occasional lawyer's-brief statements on Palmerston's behalf, he had asked the question: was the country prepared for a total reversal of British policy?[55] The answer then was obviously, No. Was there any reason since to suppose that opinion had to any significant degree changed? 'Palmerstonism' as a public tradition seemed indeed more solidly in being than ever before, given the reaction against the Liberal government's perceived failings to sustain Britain's world standing. It was clearly Disraeli's intention to emulate the Palmerstonian tradition and benefit from its reputation and popularity. In 1854, after all, he had extolled the 'British school of politics' of Palmerston and Russell against the 'Russian school of politics' of Aberdeen.[56] When in 1867 Gladstone, Aberdeen's heir, succeeded Russell as leader of the Liberal party, the 'national' or Palmerstonian tradition, without being positively repudiated, was at a discount. With the Black Sea and *Alabama* affairs to prompt him, Disraeli set about restoring to the disinherited national party of England the national inheritance discounted by Gladstone. It seemed a profitable manoeuvre, tricked out with Disraeli's plausible doctrine about the inherently 'national' qualities of Toryism as against the inherently 'cosmopolitan' qualities of Liberalism; and tricked out also with the new evocation of Empire.

So it was that when in August 1875 Gladstone's attention was drawn to the atrociousness of Turkish attempts to suppress a Serb insurrection in Bosnia and the Herzegovina, he responded in very much the same manner as with his refusals to concern himself with similar occurrences in Crete.[57] 'You, Sir', came an appeal, 'have before this raised your voice on behalf of freedom', and, at the sound of that voice 'the shackles fell from the limbs of Neapolitan captives. Will you not, Sir, say a word on behalf of the Christians of European Turkey, who are now fighting for their religion and their homes. Your voice will reach the Bosphorous, and the Sultan will listen.'[58] Gladstone's voice did not reach the Bosphorous. He was well aware of the crumbling Ottoman finances, but when the crash did come in November and the Sultan declared bankruptcy, dragging down with him the Khedive of Egypt, his response was cool. He thought it loomed 'very large' as 'one of the greatest political events'; but, as he remarked to Granville, he felt assured that Disraeli would handle it 'rationally'.[59]

From November onwards, however, this detached and cool response to events began to change. It was while Gladstone was staying with Hartington at Chatsworth that the news broke of Disraeli's startling coup of purchasing for £4 million the bankrupt Khedive of Egypt's 44 per cent holding in the Paris-based Suez Canal Company. Gladstone's instinctive response to the 'amazing news' was entirely critical and negative. He was captious about the money. 'If not done in concert with Europe, I fear grave consequences: and am not in the least degree moved by the storm of approval which seems to be rising.'[60] That storm of approval arose precisely because it was not done in concert with Europe. Disraeli's purpose was to assert Britain's international prowess in a manner not heard of since Palmerston's time. The Queen applauded it, particularly as a hit against Bismarck's 'insolent' pretensions that Britain had ceased to count as a European power.

When Gladstone wrote indignantly to Granville of Disraeli's stroke of *haute politique* as an 'act of folly fraught also with present danger', Granville simply pointed to the political irrelevance of such objections. Since many senior Liberals, including not least Hartington, approved of the purchase and all that it implied, Granville supposed that 'the quieter we keep about the Suez Canal at present the better'.[61] Colleagues of Disraeli such as Northcote and Derby, who echoed Gladstone's critique exactly, also had reason to keep quiet. Disraeli himself was well primed as to the difficulties of his critics. He wrote to his crony Lord

Barrington: 'Your letters – amusing. I can see G's face & could have predicted all he said.'[62]

There were Liberals, however, who found what Gladstone said not in the least amusing. For Hartington it was the first serious occasion of Gladstone's getting across his line of policy. Edward Levy of the *Telegraph* hoped that Gladstone would not pronounce himself against 'this wonderful unanimity in the public mind'. Levy suggested 'that here is an occasion absolutely unique, where maxims too rigid may betray the best Liberal into an unprofitable alienation from the spirit of his country'. 'The bargain would only be a bad one if it cost us the belief that you … and the Liberal party did not warmly support what, I suppose, has for its inspiration, the safeguard of the Empire.'[63]

This argument failed to impress Gladstone. 'I rack my brains upon the great stroke of genius', he told Granville. 'And the manner in which it was received really makes me blush for my Countrymen and for their press.'[64] But Disraeli's and Derby's next step did impress Gladstone. In December 1875 France and Italy approved the initiative of the 'Three Emperors' League' of Germany, Russia, and Austria-Hungary in the form of the Andrassy Note,[65] warning the Turks to come to terms with the Bosnian Serbs or be confronted with coercive intervention. The British government adhered. Gladstone rejoiced. Here was the Concert of Europe seemingly in beneficent reality. He was not to know that British adherence was decided with reluctance and at the pressing invitation of the Turks, glad to have a friend at court. Disraeli's natural disposition was to have snubbed the Note as a breach of the stipulations of the Treaty of Paris of 1856 forbidding interference with the internal affairs of the Ottoman Empire. It was also to have been a snub as challenge to Bismarck's presumption to run Europe.

Unaware of the true shape of things in Whitehall, Gladstone could conduct his customary reflections at the end of 1875 undismayed by any sense that the Suez affair threatened to be an overture to any consistent policy of Palmerstonian turcophile adventure. He tried to soothe Catherine, explaining to her his conviction that the welfare of mankind did not now depend on 'the state of the world of politics'. The 'real battle' was being fought in the 'world of thought', where a deadly attack was being made 'with great tenacity of purpose and over a wide field upon the greatest treasure of mankind, the belief in God and the Gospel of Christ'.[66] Gladstone hoped that his 'polemical period' of the past year was over. 'May the next be of a purer & holier Retrospect.'

~

Hopes that the end of 1876 might afford Gladstone a purer and holier retrospect were by no means implausible as Disraeli's Parliament gathered for its third session in February. It was true that Gladstone continued to deplore the Suez coup. It was true that he held the Royal Titles Bill, by which the Queen was to assume the style 'Empress of India', to be of 'evil omen'.[67] Yet it was also true that he made a particular point of praising ministers for their wise adherence to the Concert in the matter of the Andrassy Note, as witness to a 'European conscience' embodied in the 1856 Treaty of Paris.[68] To do this, indeed, he cut across Hartington's Palmerstonian damnings with faint praise. For Hartington this was the second irritating instance of Gladstone's getting across his line of policy.

Yet even when Disraeli dropped his mask in May by snubbing the next European initiative to coerce the Turks in the form of the 'Berlin Memorandum', and despatched the Mediterranean fleet to Besika Bay outside the Dardanelles in what was taken as a Palmerstonian riposte, reminiscent of 1849 and 1853, Gladstone's reaction lacked both outrage and urgency. Nor was restraint abandoned when early reports came in of Turkish massacres of Bulgarians, attempting to emulate the Serb insurrection, also in that month of May.

This circumspection on Gladstone's part came partly from a sense of prudence in not taxing Hartington's patience too rudely, and partly from an awareness that, as with the Suez affair, the government's policy was widely popular, not least among Palmerstonian Whigs and Liberals who rejoiced that something of Britain's old proud standing in the world was being restored. He was engrossed, besides, in literary matters. To Manning in April Gladstone remarked that 'great events' seemed to be 'drawing near in the East';[69] but he remained blankly detached.

Much of the Easter recess was consumed in battling on the domestic front against the Blantyres' efforts to rescue their daughter and son-in-law from what they felt was the stifling atmosphere of familial adoration cultivated by Catherine. Willy's dual role as nominal master of Hawarden and devotedly dutiful and obedient son was in its way even less grateful than Sir Stephen's had been. Then came, early in May, the stunning tragedy of George Lyttelton's suicide. At first it appeared accidental: a fall from the staircase at 18 Park Crescent, Marylebone. Then suicide became the inescapable finding. Then the Guardian Life Assurance people took an interest. Then Gladstone, after inspecting the fatal site, persuaded himself after all that it was an accident. The depressed man 'fell in too rapid a descent', while 'running away from his attendant'. 'How deep are the mysteries of God. This is horrible. But let us trust, & adore.'[70]

That horrible episode certainly diverted Gladstone's attention from the great events drawing near. But even when at the end of May Lord Stratford de Redcliffe, former 'Grand Elchi' at the Ottoman Porte, disclosed to Gladstone accounts of extraordinarily barbarous proceedings by the Turks in the Balkans, Gladstone's detachment was not dented beyond conferring with Hartington and Forster. He found neither of them disposed to pick a quarrel with the government on an issue of foreign policy. Nor yet was he. His main concern with Sir Henry Elliot, now as fervently Palmerstonian an Ambassador at the Porte as he had been in Turin and

Florence, was to solicit his good offices in aid of Schliemann's excavations.

The Ottoman authorities announced that disturbances in Rumelia had indeed broken out, but they were hardly of the order of an insurrection, and that the Imperial government had in any case taken energetic and efficacious measures. Elliot's dispatches to Derby at the Foreign Office chimed in with assurances as to journalistic exaggeration and Russian propaganda.

It was Forster who was first among the party chiefs to make a move. He prodded Hartington to question Disraeli. The Prime Minister easily eluded Hartington's half-hearted interrogation. The public success of the Besika Bay riposte to the Berlin initiative – 'popular now as a proof of vigour against Russia', as Granville pointed out to Gladstone[71] – seemed to put the matter beyond any likelihood of 'portentous blundering' that might be beneficial to the Liberal Opposition.

Soon, however, the pace of events quickened. Confirmation that extensive massacres of Bulgarians in Rumelia had indeed occurred came from newspaper correspondents for *The Times* and *Daily News*. Reliable estimates indicated some 25,000 killed, up to a hundred villages and townships destroyed, a thousand children sold as slaves, 10,000 imprisoned and undergoing torture. The principal perpetrators, it appeared, were those Circassians, known of old to Gladstone, who had fled from Russian oppression in 1864 to be planted among the Bulgarians.[72] They now largely composed the irregular bands of 'Bashi-bazouks', soon to be of ugly notoriety. Stratford, too, had received 'sad accounts' of 'Turkish atrocities in Bulgaria'. He would rejoice to be mistaken, he told Gladstone, 'but, to judge from present appearances, the cloud no bigger than a human hand appears to be spreading into a storm of infinite dimensions'.[73] Gladstone relayed to Granville Stratford's and his findings that the government had been quite wrong to exclude themselves from the Berlin initiative, that Derby's recent version of events in Rumelia as a 'civil war' misrepresented the situation, and that dispatching the fleet to Besika Bay sent an unwarrantably encouraging signal to the Turks.[74]

Stormy indications were not lacking now in domestic public opinion. Bishop Fraser of Manchester denounced the government's apparent countenance of Turkish proceedings. Other Church authorities were petitioned to address Eastern Christian ecclesiastics 'to free the Church of England from the scandal of appearing to look on unmoved at the atrocities'.[75] High Churchmen, still smarting from the iniquities of the Public Worship Regulation Act, were much to the fore. Stirrings of the 'Nonconformist conscience' were also evident.

As yet Gladstone remained little attuned to these stirrings. For most of July, while public alarm mounted at what seemed Britain's virtual complicity in horrific transactions, Gladstone dallied in desultory activities. He declined a requisition by a group of Liberal MPs to chair a protest meeting. He declined opportunities to join deputations to Derby at the Foreign Office. He declared that he would reserve any pronouncement until after the production of official papers and a ministerial statement about future Eastern policy. Shaftesbury had to be drafted in to fill the chair hopefully allotted to Gladstone by the League in Aid of the Christians of Turkey for a protest meeting in Willis's Rooms on 27 July.[76]

Gladstone was later profuse with apologies for what came to be seen as an astonishing insensibility. He had had in his possession, after all, every component material to such a case – not least 'the breasts of free men' – ever since he laid the foundations of an alternative Eastern policy back in 1858, in the Romanian episode. All he needed to do now was to dust it off and apply it to the Bulgarians. That he failed betimes to do so he explained as his shrinking 'naturally but perhaps unduly' from recognizing the claim the cruel outrages on the Bulgarians 'made on me; upon me individually'. 'I hoped that the Ministers would recognize the moral obligations to the subject races of the East, which we in honour contracted as parties in the Crimean war and to the Peace of Paris in 1856. I was slow to observe the real leanings of the Prime Minister, his strong sympathy with the Turk and his mastery over his own Cabinet.'[77] To which Gladstone might have added very reasonably a failure of prevision of an astonishing event: that the constituency he had failed to raise in 1858 over Romania would come upon him unawares in 1876 over Bulgaria.

By the end of July, pressure from Liberal MPs led by Mundella and Evelyn Ashley forced ministers to concede a debate in the Commons. By this time Gladstone was beginning to stir himself into a more receptive frame of mind. Seemingly random and contingent events began to assume an integrated, significant shape: Bosnia, Suez, the Indian title, veto of the Berlin initiative, Besika Bay, perhaps now the Bulgarian case. Insistent pressure from his Reverend High Church friends Malcolm MacColl and Canon H. P. Liddon that he 'speak on the Eastern question, and tear away the mask from the fanciful pictures of Turkey wh. the Government & a portion of the press have presented to the public',[78] pointed to the opportunity offered Gladstone by the debate fixed for 31 July. For that debate a Conservative motion, as Gladstone remarked to Granville, 'called on us *inter alia* to vote approval of the proceedings of the Government. This I for one cannot do. I can hardly suppose you or H. will do it.' Gladstone was clear that 'a very grave question' had been raised. 'I must speak my mind.'[79]

~

Gladstone did speak his mind. But speaking his mind on 31 July proved to be not at all the speech for which MacColl and Liddon had pleaded. It was not a speech that would reach the Bosphorous and make the Sultan listen. Old Lord Russell, indeed, who hankered for a return to Canning's policy of Christian emancipation, dismissed it as timid and wanting in earnest purpose. Tellingly, it was perhaps the only major speech ever made by Gladstone on foreign policy invoking no appeal to the genius of Canning. Gladstone looked back, not forward. His speech of 31 July complemented his speech of 8 February congratulating the government for adhering to the Andrassy Note. He denounced now the disruption of the Concert by vetoing the Berlin Memorandum. He deplored the giving of undue encouragement to the Turks. He regretted unworthy distrust of the good faith of Emperor Alexander II of Russia. He spoke as the only remaining member of the Commons bearing 'historical' responsibility for the Crimean war. On that ground he declared himself 'not ashamed' to insist on the principle of reconciling any notions of Christian autonomy with strict observance of Turkish territorial integrity. An independent Slav state would be too problematical to contemplate. He could but hope that the government might yet discover a solution giving 'consolatory assurance' that the Crimean war had not been fought in vain. He mentioned the rumours of extensive and atrocious massacres of Bulgarians only to declare that it was an aspect into which he did not propose to enter.[80]

The 'atrocitarians' of the time were desperately disappointed. MacColl and W. T. Stead, rampaging editor of the *Darlington Echo*, and the others had to make the best of it. The vociferous historian E. A. Freeman 'trembled' when he read the speech, shocked by the emphasis on Turkish integrity.[81] On that score Bishop Fraser did not hesitate to make his irritation public. To them and many others of what might be called an emerging 'post-Palmerstonian' cast of mind, hoping for 'consolatory assurance' that the Crimean war had not been fought in vain and that the 'wicked Treaty' of Paris should remain intact was to miss the whole point of what was happening in the Near East.

Gladstone was lucky in having Disraeli respond with a rebuke that was later elevated into a cherished accolade: 'in that debate Mr Disraeli had to describe my speech as the only one that exhibited a real hostility to the Government'.[82] Disraeli did that simply to exhibit Gladstone's estrangement from the general approval accorded to the government's policy. To Gladstone it became the one precious item of evidence he could put forward to mitigate his otherwise consistent record of unknowingness. 'It was however at that time', he confessed, 'an opposition without hope.' He thereupon 'went into the country', and 'mentally postponed all further action to the opening of the next Session'.[83]

Hence it was that Gladstone was in snug retreat at Hawarden, immersed congenially in Homer and theology, through the last days of the 1876 session. These were the days when the first sensational reports of the American journalist J. A. McGahan, describing in horrific detail the scenes of atrocity, exploded in the *Daily News*. These were the days when the Foreign Office admitted that there were grounds for concern. These were the days when public outrage ignited in earnest. These were the days when two debates in the Commons were forced by Liberal backbenchers, in default of any lead from their frontbench or even presence on the part of Gladstone.

On the last day of the session, 11 August, Disraeli, brought to bay by Evelyn Ashley, put up a vigorous defence. Briefed by the Foreign Office about exaggerations and relying on Elliot's version of events, he persisted in his earlier sceptical and deprecatory vein about 'coffee-house babble' and his 'alleged want of sympathy with the sufferers by imaginary atrocities'. Doubtless, he allowed, there had occurred deplorable excesses; but the government's duty remained nonetheless to defend and uphold the 'Empire of England'.[84] Disraeli reflected ruefully that the session had ended not a day too soon. The awkward issue would drop out of sight during the recess. Frank Hill of the *Daily News* left for his vacation on 12 August, also not foreseeing 'the clearing storm which was about to break'.[85]

Of all the lackers of foresight, it was Gladstone who lacked most unforeseeingly. He even allowed Granville to dismiss Russell's call for a return to the tradition of Canning as mere senile raving. With masses of evidence now appearing in the official government Blue Books, Gladstone began to have inklings that perhaps he had been missing the big point. There was a touch of *esprit de l'escalier* in his regrets that there were 'two subjects on which I should have *dwelt* but for the belief that the debate must last and that others would handle them: the Bulgarian atrocities and the pretended colonisation of European provinces with Circassians'. To Granville he expressed also the faint hope in a somewhat leaderish tone that the subject of the massacres might not 'slumber through the recess'. 'As a party question this affords no despicable material, but there are much higher interests involved.' He went so far as to hope that the subject of the charges against Turkey '*might* even come up in an amendment to the Address next February'.[86]

At least Gladstone had the consolation, as he put it to Döllinger, apropos of the Vatican's strongly anti-Orthodox slant on the Eastern crisis, that while Britain had played an unworthy part, it was 'not so bad, by a great deal, as the Pope's'. Of the claims of the Orthodox, Gladstone was copiously informed by Madame Olga Novikov, a kind of Russian version of 'Dear Spirit', whose salon he had on occasion frequented.[87] Meanwhile, through August, the phenomenon of what was becoming known, somewhat ambiguously, as the 'Bulgarian atrocities agitation', or, as astonished Conservative ministers dubbed it, the 'cyclone' or 'tornado out of Bulgaria', the 'rabies Bulgarica', swept on its way. The Conservative government found itself confronting an unprecedented outburst of the deepest moral energies of the Victorian age.[88]

So, in a not totally different way, did Gladstone. At a big public meeting at Manchester on 9 August Bishop Fraser rebuked him for his obsession with Turkish territorial integrity. H. P. Liddon, the eminent High Church divine, preached an electrifying sermon at St Paul's on 13 August, following it up with a letter to the *Daily News* calling on some public personage to 'meet the need of the moment'.[89] Freeman, Stead, Denton and the other 'atrocity-mongers' waited in a fever of anxious impatience for their messiah to manifest himself.

But at Hawarden the delights of theology held Gladstone in a powerful attraction. He was deep in the problem of eternal damnation. Before Gladstone's mind became excited to a pitch necessary to effect a change of mental gears and a turn in the direction of the Eastern question, he had to be convinced that the question promised the chief elements of what he had come to miss in politics ever since the last spasm in 1870 of the spirit of 1868: a 'special call'; a 'regaining of vital power'; 'some one issue, clear, broad and straight'; a '*cause*'. Until such awareness came upon him of the possibility of a rapport with a manifestation of moral excitement on a popular level and massive scale, Gladstone lacked the ultimate excitement. It had to be 'the nation, not the classes'.[90]

~

That ultimate excitement was not long in coming. The pivotal moment came on 18 August. Scanning that day's *Daily News*, Gladstone's eye fell upon an item announcing that a rally of working men was to be held in Hyde Park to condemn the government's Eastern policy and demand the recall of Sir Henry Elliot as an accessory to the crimes of the Turkish regime. As Gladstone put it later, in terms expurgated by pudic Morley, it suddenly came upon him that 'the game was afoot and the question yet alive'.[91] Gladstone's imagery of inspired opportunism was equally dramatic in his version of the crucial event to Henry Broadhurst, one of the earliest working-class Liberal MPs. The issue, recounted Gladstone, he thought 'for the moment dead', and he had '(mentally) postponed action on it', when 'tidings of an intended working men's meeting in Hyde Park altered my plan and made me at once perceive that the iron was hot and that the time to strike had arrived'.[92] Truly it was the nation, not the classes. 'So I at once wrote and published on the Bulgarian case.'[93]

These vivid images are *ex post facto* by twenty years. It was in fact not for a further ten days that Gladstone put aside his notes on 'Future Retribution'.[94] Already at Hawarden he was confronted by massive deputations of Liberal excursionists.[95] He said later of the agitation: 'I admit to me it has been an unexpected movement. I have been astonished at its commencement and progress.' It came, as Gladstone saw it, 'suddenly', at a time when the 'natural leaders of local parties' were dispersed. It commenced, survived and expanded as an affair of the people.[96]

He began to soften up Granville. 'And altogether I feel more inclined to say something, during the recess, on the Turkish policy, than I have been for any such escapade during the last four years.'[97] The opportunity of a speech was on offer from the Liberal candidate at the Buckinghamshire by-election consequent on Disraeli's elevation to the Lords as Earl of Beaconsfield. But, as Gladstone explained to Granville, he declined the opportunity, not wanting to excite speculation 'on my position in the party, and thus possibly to produce distrust

& division'. He really hoped, however, 'that on this Eastern matter the pot will be kept boiling'.[98]

Gladstone had every intention of doing what he could himself to help keep the pot boiling. But how? A speech would unavoidably have about it an official air. The precedents of the *Letter to the Earl of Aberdeen* and the *Vatican Decrees* suggested themselves as bearing a much more appropriately free lance character. Gladstone started work on a pamphlet on 28 August. Charles Wordsworth, Bishop of St Andrew's, visiting Hawarden the following day, noted the striking impression Gladstone made of being a 'busy, restless-minded man, if ever there was one'.[99] The 29th was also the day in which the preliminary report of Eugene Schuyler, the American Consul-General in Constantinople, establishing officially the facts of the atrocities, was published in the *Daily News*. Gladstone broke the news to Granville under cover of applauding his 'nursing' of the Bucks by-election. 'Good ends can rarely be attained in politics without passion: and there is now, the first time for a good many years, a virtuous passion.' He declared himself 'in half, perhaps a little more than half, a mind to write a pamphlet: mainly on the ground that Parliamentary action was all but ousted. Does this shock you?'[100]

Granville allowed that he was 'a little startled'. While he would have vetoed a speech, he could not object to a pamphlet. Hartington was scathing on Gladstone's complaint that parliamentary action had been ousted. It was Gladstone who ousted himself from the debates. The striking reference to a politics of 'virtuous passion' was indeed startling. Gladstone was clearly getting in to an excited condition. His colleagues were well versed in their analyses of his needing (in Kimberley's formula) 'a strong current of opinion in his favour', or (in Selborne's formula) needing to have public enthusiasm behind his 'heroic' politics. Such a 'change or growth' of 'public feeling', as Gladstone remarked to Elliot on 3 September, 'has been witnessed as I have not known all my life, and the only question now is how far it will go'.[101]

It seemed, thus, astonishingly, that Gladstone's rhetorical question of 1863 – was the country prepared for a total reversal of its Eastern policy? – was now being answered in a decidedly positive way. Did Gladstone have glimpses of public feeling going as far as to provide him, as the exponent of the 'future triumphs of a sound and active liberalism', with the means of 'arresting some great evil or for procuring the nation some great good'? Gladstone's urgent images of hunting and forging ('the game was afoot', 'the iron was hot, and the time to strike had arrived') are not wholly reliable witnesses in this matter as they were coined twenty years after the event. Perhaps more indicative was Gladstone's interest in the provenance of the 'quotation or proverb "Vox populi vox Dei"'. Nine references from *Notes and Queries* were extracted by Panizzi's assistant Fagan for Gladstone's solemn contemplation.[102]

That was done the day after the appearance of Gladstone's pamphlet, *Bulgarian Horrors and the Question of the East*, on 6 September.[103] Gladstone struck off his response to the virtuous passion of the people in fine frenzy. On 3 September he left for London to make checks and revises at the British Museum in a state of effervescence. He resisted Granville's objections against the principle of full autonomy for the subject Christians. He complied reluctantly with Granville's advice against attacking Lord Beaconsfield 'individually'. It was also for Gladstone an 'act of some self-denial' on his part to follow Granville's advice to 'abstain from all notice of the conduct of the Court of Rome' and its British and Irish manifestations.[104] 'Between ourselves', as he later wrote to Bright, 'I may mention that G. who received my pamphlet in proof wished me to generalize the concluding part but I thought that with the purpose I had in view it was absolutely necessary to propose something the country would understand.'[105]

That 'demophilic' purpose was already putting a strain on relations with the Liberal frontbench and the 'moderate' lump of the party. By April 1877 Gladstone could reflect that he had not a single supporter in the '*Upper* official circle' of the Liberal party. 'But had I in the first days of September asked the same body whether I ought to write any pamphlet I believe the unanimous answer would have been no.'[106]

By 5 September, after a final consultation with Granville and Hartington, printed copies of *Bulgarian Horrors and the Question of the East*, dedicated to Stratford de Redcliffe, were delivered by Murray's. Copies were dispatched widely among the higher echelons of the political world, including Lord Beaconsfield. In high good humour of intellectual and emotional release, Gladstone went off to the Haymarket theatre to see a farce. A friend of Beaconsfield's witnessed the curious spectacle of three empty stalls in front of him being occupied successively by Granville, Gladstone and then, trailing disconsolately, Hartington. Gladstone 'laughed very much' at the performance. 'Harty Tarty' 'never even smiled'.[107]

~

So was loosed what was hailed, with pardonable misapprehension, as the 'well-timed pamphlet'. MacColl was enchanted at the prospect of the 'no less glorious fruit' it would bear than the pamphlet on the 'far less heinous' atrocities of the Neapolitan regime. Philip Clayden of the *Daily News* also rejoiced to be able to announce its publication, 'as I see day by day', he told Gladstone, 'from the vast number of letters which come by every post how people are everywhere wishing for some statement from you'. Despite his qualms, Granville wished Gladstone 'joy of the receipt of *the* pamphlet'. Its 'receipt' became an instant legend. After the first day of public sales Gladstone could report proudly to Granville that it was 'alive and kicking: four and twenty thousand copies now printed, and they think it is not at an end'. Within four days, 40,000 copies were sold; within a month, 200,000.[108]

Bulgarian Horrors was a rehash of Schuyler, McGahan, the Blue Books and Gladstone's speech of 31 July, laced with virulent invective against the Turks. In it Gladstone set out the elements of a post-Palmerston politics that would find its accredited exponent in himself. Just as he had his case for the Bulgarians already formulated in the case for the Romanians in 1858, so now he had his case against the Turks. It had no particular literary merit except for the famous 'bag and baggage' phrase in the rhetorical peroration. The provenance for this was Stratford,[109] but in any case it confused the issue. It was not helpful in proposing 'something the country would understand'. Rather, it proposed something the country misunderstood. Gladstone demanded the extinction of Turkish 'administrative action'. The fame of the bag and baggage phrase led to widespread misapprehension that he had called for the expulsion of the Turks from Europe.[110] This misapprehension was very helpful to the agitation. It concealed the fact that beneath the rhetoric the substance of Gladstone's case continued moderate. Turkish territorial integrity remained the foundation, though Gladstone did not, as on 31 July, go out of his way to assert that he was not ashamed to stipulate this. His main practical point was the necessity to come to an understanding with Russia. Derby commented aptly: 'A tame conclusion for so vehement an invective!'[111]

However apt, Derby's comment missed the point. The significance of *Bulgarian Horrors* consisted in its character as a unique response to a series of stimuli that coloured its form and content and made it the supremely representative expression of a passionate moment of history. It succeeded so completely because it concentrated into a single utterance a profoundly excited public mood struggling for articulation. The essential point was that it was far less a case of Gladstone exciting popular passion than of popular passion exciting Gladstone.

This point bears centrally on Gladstone's alleged 'right-timing'.[112] *Bulgarian Horrors* was a consequence of opportunism, not of insight. Gladstone scrupulously did not list his dramatic intervention of 1876 among the grand occasions of providentially inspired conviction of an appreciation of a general situation and its result, leading to the forming of a public opinion and its application to a particular end. As he put it to Clayden at the *Daily News*, 'you have led the people of England; and I am about to walk as best I can in your steps'.[113] Disraeli's biographer Buckle's highly coloured picture of the malignant Gladstone as the 'old hunter, once more sniffing the scent', stalking his noble quarry with cunning patience, waiting for the right moment to strike and pull down his 'too successful rival', does Gladstone far too much credit for perspicacity; though, ironically, echoing unknowingly Gladstone's own image of the game being afoot.[114] And only the blurred interpretation of events later received could allow Morley to get away with his wholly mythic presentation of Gladstone's breast being agitated by a 'mighty storm', lit by the 'lurid glare' of the atrocities. Morley suppressed Gladstone's honest phrase about the game being afoot and substituted his own figment about Gladstone's heroic response to a Byronic trumpet call.[115]

Awareness that he and a great movement of a virtuous public mind had come into rapport was for Gladstone more than a little intoxicating: 'the first time for a good many years'. That that movement, in its autonomous nature – commencing, surviving, expanding without direction from 'natural leaders' – thereby contradicted Gladstone's own grand formulae defining the essential nature of his forming opinion for ends decided on by himself,[116] did not at the time seem important. It seemed less important that 'the people' had arrived at their own conclusions – unexpected and astonishing as Gladstone found it – than that those conclusions happened to coincide with Gladstone's own.

For the moment, the crucial point was Gladstone's astonishment at the unexpected nature of the movement of the public mind and his lateness in perceiving it and his tardiness in jumping on to it. 'Late it is true', as one of the more excited 'atrocity-mongers' put it of *Bulgarian Horrors*, 'but still in time to do immense good.'[117] It is only the grandeur of unforeseeable events to come that gives this statement its comically patronising air. It was perfectly accurate and legitimate in its time. Gladstone's own testimony to his slowness of observation and his natural but perhaps undue shrinking from recognizing claims made on him, rules out such suppositions that he must have 'waited for nearly two months in a mood of very dangerous calm'.[118] Gladstone was not waiting, and his calm was indeed one of desultory nonchalance, embarrassingly innocent.

Innocence was not, however, the keynote of Gladstone's proceedings thereafter. Once he realized that the game was afoot and that the iron was hot for striking, he launched himself into action of undelimited possibility. 'From that time forward', as he later wrote, 'until the final consummation in 1879–80, I made the Eastern question the main business of my life.'[119]

~

During those years, the immediate and practical aspect of Gladstone's business was trying to get the Liberal party as a whole to come to his own view of the requirements of the case. He was indeed committed now to witnessing future triumphs of a sound and active Liberalism. He did indeed intend to help arrest a great evil and procure for the nation a great good. The question at the heart of the matter was, would the party take the matter out of Gladstone's hands, and leave him to revert to a semi-detached status on the margin of events? The first phase of that quest lasted until two events in 1877 transformed the situation. The first, on 24 April, was the Russian declaration of war against the Ottoman Empire. The second, on 14 May, was the Liberal party's rejection of Gladstone's appeal.

Throughout the intervening months, Gladstone incessantly pressed Granville and Hartington to take a more 'advanced view' of the issue. At a mass demonstration at Blackheath in his Greenwich constituency on 9 September, Gladstone made solemn affirmation of his conviction that the agitation sprang, pure and undefiled by party and political motives, from the very bedrock of morality and righteousness in public affairs, the simple, undesigning conscience of the people. But the political substance of his message was deliberately temperate: he professed still to hope for satisfaction from the government. Hartington gave him answer at the Sheffield Cutlers' dinner. After consulting with Granville about the best 'line' to take, he treated the agitation and Gladstone very respectfully but yet made no outright criticism of the government's Eastern policy.

A prominent feature of the Blackheath event was, amid a popular mood of almost religious intensity, a multitude of appeals to Gladstone to take up a public role of leadership of the anti-government movement. Would he not 'hear in this great crisis the voice of God in the voice of the people?' Embarrassed by these and many other entreaties, Gladstone wrote to Adam, the Liberal Whip: 'I am a follower & not a leader of the Liberal party and nothing will induce me to do an act indicative of a desire to change my position. Any such act would be a positive breach of faith on my part towards those whom I importuned as I may say to allow me to retire, and whom I left to undertake a difficult and invidious office.'[120] This uneasy equilibrium of scruple and reluctance in relation to the party leaders and the party as a whole on the one side, and tenacity and persistence in this great crisis in hearing the voice of God in the voice of the people, set the theme of Gladstone's conduct as a 'follower and not a leader' right through to what he called its 'consummation'. Nevertheless, long-drawn out though it was, the central node of the problem was for all practical purposes resolved in the few weeks after 6 September.

That node consisted essentially in the fact that neither the Whigs and the mass of Palmerstonians and 'moderates' in the Liberal party, on the one side, nor the Conservatives on the other, would budge. That meant eventually that Gladstone was left stranded somewhere offside, with only a gaggle of 'advanced' Liberals indoors and the 'people' out of doors.

Granville quite accurately saw that Gladstone was '*much too sanguine*' as to the readiness of the party as a whole to go ahead in a policy of emancipation in collaboration with Russia. Whigs instinctively disliked 'to force the Executive in Foreign Policy'. Argyll alone approached Gladstone in the warmth of his feelings. Lowe also was warm, but the decline of his reputation made him a doubtful asset. Bright was 'far from satisfied with Gladstone, though he did not like directly to abuse him'. Bright wanted a purely Cobdenite policy of isolation. There was a general distaste, as Lord Halifax put it, for seeing 'the populace' 'running a little wild on the Bulgarian atrocities'. There were also many, like Harcourt, with a great distaste for the possible return of Gladstone to the leadership. Forster, of whom Gladstone had hopes, set off to Constantinople to see for himself. Hartington, trumping Forster's trick, did likewise. Both returned unimpressed by schemes of Christian autonomy.[121] The Jewish community, mindful of Ottoman tolerance and the anti-semitic intolerance of emancipated eastern Christians, took the cue of Levy's shifting the *Daily Telegraph* across to the Conservatives.

For their part, the Conservatives maintained a solid front. Beaconsfield took the opportunity of a speech at Aylesbury on the eve of the Bucks poll to give 'that Greenwich Tartuffe his quietus'. He defied the agitation and all its works. He denounced Gladstone's activities as 'worse than any of those Bulgarian atrocities which now occupy attention'.[122] The Queen was wholly with him.[123] The Bucks seat was held. Granville pointed out to Gladstone the abiding strength of anti-Russian feeling and the evidence of Liberal defections at the poll. He deprecated Gladstone's hopes for an autumn session: Liberal divisions would be exhibited; the Conservatives would keep an unbroken line.

Gladstone's answer was to go to the country. A series of country house visits in the north soon became a kind of popular triumphal progress. At Staindrop station, on 23 September, he allowed himself to be 'carried away' into self-vindication by the frantic importunity of the crowd. There were twinges of guilt. 'I shall soon seem a rogue and imposter.'[124] There were also preliminary indications that something in the way of mass popular adulation more portentous than the Tyneside and Merseyside episodes of the 1860s was in the making. If he had lost the Romans and the Jews, Gladstone had regained the Nonconformists. Newman Hall hailed him as the great leader of Progress, Freedom and Humanity.[125] Staindrop might well prove the first step towards having the 'leadership of the nation' pressed upon him.

Staindrop was certainly an indication that Gladstone's restraint was wearing thin. By early October, despairing of any retreat on the part of ministers, and now of any advance on the part of the Liberal leaders, he informed Granville that he no longer felt under an obligation to keep in step with the party. He would henceforth be an 'outside workman', preparing 'materials' for Granville and the party to 'manipulate' and 'build into a structure'. He was 'convinced that a virtual emancipation ought to take place', and he rather believed it would; and at any rate he felt himself 'bound to promote it as one of the public'. 'The distinction involved in these words may be fine', he concluded, 'but I think I can only observe it as well as I can.'[126]

~

By this time, however, the 'movement' had lost steam. Partly this was because of the inherent difficulty of sustaining the momentum of spontaneity at the heart of the agitation of August and September. Partly it was a consequence of Gladstone's leaving the question to the 'calm but resolute' consideration of the country in the weeks of futile effort to coax Granville into assuming the leadership Gladstone had left vacant at Blackheath. The 'atrocity-mongers' were at a loss. There was in fact little Gladstone could actually do now in the way of being an outside workman preparing materials for Granville and the party to build upon. 'What next?' enquired W. T. Stead on 16 October. Gladstone was hardly less perplexed than Stead for want of 'adequate measures'. He pottered about while his enemies and critics rejoiced in the manifestations of a 'reaction'.

Two big events rescued Gladstone from this predicament. The first was a notion stemming from Sheffield Liberals of looking to the precedents of the Anti-Slavery and the Anti-Corn Law movements as inspiration for a grand national convention. This they envisaged as a kind of out-of-doors substitute parliament, calculated to rally and consolidate the forces demanding a reversal of the government's Eastern policy. The second event was a decision by the European powers to convene a conference at Constantinople at the end of the year to persuade the Turks into supervised reforms. Lord Salisbury, Secretary of State for India, would be Britain's plenipotentiary.

For Gladstone the project of a national convention early in December immediately took on the function of aiding and sustaining Salisbury's mission. It is possible that Gladstone was aware of Salisbury's urgings on Beaconsfield that the traditional Palmerstonian policy was played out, and that something better must replace it. In any case, here was a grand opportunity for getting on terms with the Russians. Already, in 'The Hellenic Factor in the Eastern Problem', published in the December *Contemporary*, Gladstone had set out a claim for the Greek provinces still under Ottoman rule to have an equal share in the emancipation movement being claimed by the Serbs and Bulgarians. But above all, for Salisbury's benefit and inspiration, Gladstone recalled the spirit of Canning ('one of the most brilliant names in our political history' and 'one of the names dearest to the heart of Greece'), and the spirit of Byron ('a name which might yet supply a guiding light to some British statesman').[127] Salisbury's was a temperament immune to such inspirations; but Gladstone accepted that his appointment was the best thing 'in spirit' that Beaconsfield's government had so far done 'since the Eastern Question began to burn'.[128]

The fortunes of the National Conference on the Eastern Question, held in St James's Hall, Piccadilly, on Friday, 8 December, the Duke of Westminster presiding, were thus linked to those of the Conference of the powers at Constantinople, whose preliminary sessions commenced on 14 December. The difficulties Salisbury would have at Constantinople were sufficiently advertised by Beaconsfield at the Guildhall on 9 November, in a truculent speech giving what Gladstone described as 'almost incredible provocation' to the Russians. Indeed, Gladstone discerned 'some new lights about his Judaic feeling in which he is both consistent and conscientious'.[129] At St James's Hall the convenors, called by James Bryce and his committee to the 'high and glorious mission' of vindicating the 'principles of humanity' and blotting out the legacy of the 'fatal Crimean war', were invited to concern themselves with four general points: instant reparation must be made by the Turks to the injured and despoiled Bulgarians; the Muslim population must be disarmed; the Christians must be accorded autonomous government; and British policy should aim at fruitful co-operation with Russia.

The two weighty sessions at St James's Hall set the seal of a deep sense of responsibility on the passionate movement of August and September; the National Conference reaffirmed solemnly, after the heat of the initial reaction to the atrocities, the principles and purposes of the autumn agitation. Upholders of an ideal of moral absolutism in affairs of state in the tradition of the late J. S. Mill were convenors: Browning, Lecky,[130] J. R. Green,[131] Herbert Spencer, Charles Darwin, T. H. Green.[132] William Morris was the secretary. The old russophile Thomas Carlyle contributed his immortal phrase about the 'unspeakable Turk'. John Ruskin was his proxy for the occasion. The list of speakers included Trollope, the Bishop of Oxford, Henry Richard, Bryce,[133] Shaftesbury, Liddon, G. O. Trevelyan, Freeman, Fawcett[134] and, as star turn, Gladstone.

Ostentatiously escorting Madame Novikov, Gladstone spoke 'I fear 1½ hours with some exertion, far from wholly to my satisfaction'. He thought the occasion 'great, notable, almost historical'.[135] His themes were to strike back at Beaconsfield, and to urge upon Salisbury the illustrious precedent of Canning, whose good understanding with Emperor Nicholas had unlocked the freedom of Greece. The Conference, however, never quite succeeded in establishing its claim to a character distinct from a Liberal demonstration – a Liberal demonstration moreover bereft, as Beaconsfield cheerfully calculated, of fully 60 names among the 'decided anti-Russian' section of the Liberals; while Derby could take comfort in the quite 'remarkable' 'absence & silence of the Whig chiefs'.[136]

At Constantinople Salisbury's good understanding with Ignatiev, the Russian plenipotentiary, was sabotaged by Elliot at his side and Beaconsfield in London, bypassing Derby. The Turks, emboldened once more, resisted all reform proposals. The Conference broke up in failure on 22 January. A Russian declaration of war was now almost inevitable. With that failure came also the failure of the National Conference on the Eastern Question.

~

With the shadow of war darkening the political scene, Gladstone accounted his 1876 Christmas as the 'most solemn I have known for long: see the Eastern sky of storms, and of underlight!' The coming of the new session would place Gladstone unavoidably in a position of much more anomalous prominence than in 1875 or 1876. Pre-sessional preparation included a tour of Wiltshire and Somerset, centred on a gathering of Eastern sympathizers at Longleat, seat of the eccentric Conservative, Lord Bath. Gladstone's presence caused much local stir. To his 'equal surprise and satisfaction', he reported that he found 'the people of these rural & Tory counties' as 'sound and warm on the Eastern question as the men in the North & North East'.[137] He assured Consul-General Schuyler that all talk of 'reaction' in the feeling here was 'trash'. 'The people do not repent of their outburst in August. The majority of London newspapers are governed by the sentiment of the Clubs of the West End.'[138] 'The nation is sound', he assured Madame Novikov.[139]

At Gladstone's own West End club, the United Universities, A. J. Munby, the poet and civil servant, 'at a writing table there, found myself vis-à-vis to Mr Gladstone: old, eager, hurriedly writing, pen in mouth'.[140] The new Blue Books were out. Gladstone devoured them assiduously between 10 and 19 February. They offered much in the way of means of 'going further'. The gem was the soon-to-be notorious dispatch of Sir Henry Elliot to Lord Derby of 4 September 1876.

Responding to Derby's anxieties about the stirrings of public outrage at Britain's seeming complicity in atrocities, Elliot denied 'blind partisanship' on behalf of the Turks, and insisted that he was guided by a 'firm determination to uphold the interests of Great Britain'. That those interests were 'deeply engaged in preventing a disruption of the Turkish Empire' was 'a conviction' he shared in common 'with the most eminent statesmen who have directed our foreign policy, but which appears now to be abandoned by shallow politicians or persons who have allowed their feelings of revolted humanity to make them forget the capital interests involved in the question'. The necessity that existed for England to prevent changes from occurring that would be 'most detrimental to ourselves is not affected by the question whether it was 10,000 or 20,000 persons who perished in the suppression'. That 'fearful excesses' had been 'strikingly brought home to us all cannot be a sufficient reason for abandoning a policy which is the only one that can be followed with a due regard to our own interests'.[141]

With materials such as this Gladstone set out eagerly in his role as outside workman preparing materials for Granville and Hartington. His latest notion was that, on the strength of what the Blue Books disclosed, ministers might be vulnerable to a well-designed motion, '& that at all events a stroke would be struck in the country'.[142] The duumvirate were not amenable.

The soundness of the country was the nub of Gladstone's message to Parliament at the opening of the 1877 session. He now towered over the Commons as never before. Disraeli had gone, replaced by the recessive Stafford Northcote, Gladstone's former private secretary at the Board of Trade. Gladstone vindicated the 'much despised "autumn agitation"'. He deplored the Concert of Europe's being 'set at nought and repudiated'. He vindicated the National Conference. He vindicated his 'poor pamphlet'. 'I was simply an humble collaborateur with the English people in a work which they had taken into their own hands. In the matter of humanity and justice they needed no instructor. It was the nation that led the classes and leaders, and not the classes and leaders who led the nation.'[143]

Refused yet again by his leaders, Gladstone set to work with his pen over the Easter recess. An interlude in Kent gave him the opportunity to call at Down House to pay respects to Darwin for his part in the National Conference. Another ally in the cause he met at this time was John Morley, Radical author in 1874 of *On Compromise*, a critique of Gladstone's having compromised too much. It was an important moment when Gladstone recorded: 'I cannot help liking Mr John Morley.'[144]

Soon came *Lessons in Massacre* in March, accusing the government of telling the Turks, in effect, '*Do it again*'. He held back the pamphlet until definitely assured that Granville and Hartington 'actually decline a parliamentary movement'. (Hartington in fact wanted to veto the pamphlet.) They declined a parliamentary movement on the cogent ground that it was a hopeless prospect. This made Gladstone conclude that his 'duty was clear'. He loosed *Lessons*, though without any expectations that it would match the impact of *Horrors*. It was a useful overture to a statement in the House on 23 March about the urgency of a Canningite policy of working with the Russians. Duty now included joining with Liberal members who questioned Elliot's fitness to continue at Constantinople. This was an affront to the decorum embedded in the establishments of the official world generally. 'Nothing can please me so much as to walk in the rear', he assured Granville, 'but I ought to make known to you that my patience cannot stretch over this point & if nobody else objects to Elliot I must.' On 27 March in the Commons he quoted the notorious *raison d'état* passage from Elliot's dispatch of 4 September. 'What is to be the consequence to civilization and humanity ... if British interests are to be the rule of British agents all over the world, and are to be for them the measure of right or wrong?'[145]

By now Gladstone was well launched in the mode of challenging, in the name of the nation, the leadership of his own party and the House of Commons at large, and in some sense Parliament at large. He was inundated with assurances from the nation that he was indeed its leader. Granville, never convinced of the reality or efficacy of the abdication arrangements of 1875, had all but abandoned any pretence of leadership. The more Gladstone went unctuously through the forms of treating him as such, the more Granville deprecated the hollowness of the 'ephemeral honour'.

The next great exercise Gladstone fixed to get under way on 27 April, a few days after the Russian declaration of war on the Turks. 'This day I took my decision: a severe one, in face of my not having a single approver in the *Upper* official circle.' His most vociferous approvers were the Radical section led by Dilke and a new recruit to the Liberals in 1876, Joseph Chamberlain, of Birmingham municipal 'gas and water socialism' fame. Demonstrations throughout the country were at an extraordinary spate. For Gladstone they manifested the spontaneous moral instinct of the people. Matthew Arnold had other insights. 'They are in consternation at the Reform Club', he reported on 5 May, because, while most of the Liberal party want to go with Hartington, 'the Liberal constituencies are pouring in letters and telegrams to their members desiring them to vote with Gladstone. *Chamberlain has organised the thing*, with the hope, no doubt, of winning over Gladstone for future purposes; and is a great and successful organiser.'[146]

Gladstone launched his resolution urging a total reversal of Eastern policy on 7 May. It was to be a supreme effort. He confronted a largely hostile House, his own frontbench 'virtually silent'. 'Such a sense of solitary struggle I never remember.' A. J. Balfour cited his oration as 'a feat of parliamentary courage, parliamentary skill, parliamentary endurance, and parliamentary eloquence' that would, Balfour believed, always be unequalled.[147] Forster thought Gladstone an '*inspired man*' in his 'thrilling' peroration on the theme of 'other days when England was the hope of freedom'. But when the five nights' debate closed on 14 May, the division revealed the government with a comfortable margin on top of its normal majority: 354 against 223. 'These numbers are not propitious', observed Gladstone. As he put it to 'Dear Spirit': 'the people are one way and the Parliament another.'[148]

14

A Great and High Election of God, 1877–1880

> 'I profess to believe that it has been an occasion when the battle to be fought was a battle of justice humanity freedom law, all in their first elements from the very root, and on a gigantic scale. The word spoken was a word for millions, and for millions who themselves cannot speak. If I really believe this then I should regard my having been forced into this work as a great and high election of God.'
>
> *Gladstone, diary entry, 28 December 1879*

That the people were one way and the Parliament another became for Gladstone the grand theme of the 'business' of his life as events moved towards 'consummation'. The essence of the business was simple: the people would replace the bad Parliament of 1874 with a good Parliament.

From August 1876 to May 1877 Gladstone had set himself to guiding his nominal leaders in the Liberal party to accept an obligation on them to lead the party in a direction pointed to by Gladstone as conformable with that ultimate end. Their reluctance so to do was neither impractical nor immoral. Their main task and responsibility was to hold the party together. Gladstone, after all, had abdicated on the ground of his being incompetent to do that. This put him, in a phrase that later became notorious, in a position of greater freedom and less responsibility.[1] Gladstone was asking them to bow to what he was convinced was a 'great popular conviction'.[2] They had two objections to this. In principle they disliked Parliament's bowing to popular convictions out of doors. In practice they were not convinced that that particular popular conviction correctly assessed the merits of the case of the Eastern question. Nor were they prone to sentiments proposing that the voice of the people was the voice of God.

Beyond that, whatever the 'consummation' of the matter might turn out to be, no man could say before the event. After all, were there any compelling reasons for supposing that Gladstone was especially qualified as a political prophet? He was manifestly a failed political leader. He had left his government and his party in a state of dereliction. He got the dissolution and election in 1874 spectacularly wrong. Whatever the ultimate consummation of the events clustered around the 'Eastern question' was to be, it would depend just as much, at least, on Lord

Beaconsfield's arts and decisions as a prophet as on Gladstone's.

That, from May 1877 onwards, Gladstone would take a course much more independent of the party and its leaders was to be expected. Of the division of 14 May Granville ventured with a kind of despairing hope that 'the party voted pretty well'.[3] This was no longer anywhere near good enough. What was on Gladstone's mind now was the notion of some new kind of party, purged of malign influences such as plutocracy, clubland, 'society'.

In the debate that commenced on 7 May, the first member to rise in Gladstone's support was Joseph Chamberlain. Though a newcomer to the Commons, Chamberlain was already a substantial national figure out of doors. Like Gladstone, he too had notions about a new kind of Liberal party. It would be Radicalized and purged of Whigs and Whiggery, it would disestablish the Church of England, assimilate the county franchise, and it would promote on national lines something of the programme of social and financial legislation previewed in municipal initiatives in Birmingham. To those ends he was organizing a National Liberal Federation, to be centred in Birmingham with a view to consolidating and intensifying the energies of 'advanced' Liberalism out of doors as a preliminary to a takeover of parliamentary Liberalism. Chamberlain shared Nonconformity's conscientious revulsion at the Bulgarian horrors. But from them he saw a chance of extracting immediate political benefit. The Federation was due to be inaugurated at Birmingham on 31 May. Chamberlain had Gladstone in mind as a potent inaugural presence.

Chamberlain calculated that Gladstone, if not exactly usable, could not fail to be useful. He wrote to his Radical friend Dilke: 'If he were to come back for a few years (he can't continue in public life very much longer) he would probably do much for us, & pave the way for more.'[4] Dilke reported to Harcourt that Chamberlain wished Gladstone '"formally to resume the reins" – and shows profound dislike of Hartington, founded on no reasons at all'. This confirmed Harcourt's suspicions that the 'extreme crew' were exploiting the opportunity provided by the atrocities agitation to demand the deposition of Granville and Hartington and the recall of Gladstone; which consideration he passed on to Granville. Harcourt remained confident, however, that Gladstone was a spent force, and that there would be 'no return from Elba'.[5]

Chamberlain had invited Gladstone on 16 April to attend the inauguration of the Federation. He dwelt on the claims Birmingham had on Gladstone for its consistent Liberalism and its support for Gladstone's 'crusade' on the Eastern question. One of the first things Gladstone did after the division on 14 May was to reply to Chamberlain. On 16 May Chamberlain thanked Gladstone for his acceptance.

This was a shock to the duumvirate. They had not counted on Gladstone's readiness to consort with the 'Brummagem Robespierre'. Gladstone was under no misapprehension as to Chamberlain's ulterior motives and his far from disinterested concern with the Eastern question. But he calculated that a bargain with Chamberlain could be advantageous. His message on the East would go back through the delegates to the country. He assured Granville that he would stay aloof from any ideas of recasting policy. The 'vital principle' of the Liberal party, like that of Greek art, he informed Granville, was '*action*'; and he was hopeful that the spread of the Birmingham principle 'from below' of local party organization 'may prove a great stroke in the interests of the party'.[6]

The massive demonstration at Bingley Hall reflected a desire on the part of both Gladstone and Chamberlain to remake the Liberal party on their own terms. Gladstone was convinced that the Liberal party, 'as in so many other cases', was alone the 'instrument' by which a 'great work' was to be carried through.[7] If Granville and Hartington refused a policy of 'action', they rejected, in effect, what Gladstone conceived to be the essential function of the party over which they presided. To their objections that action in Gladstone's sense would break up the party, Gladstone's was an 'instrumental', implicitly Peelite answer: in certain circumstances purging or even breaking a parliamentary party was a beneficent necessity. 'What I of course regret is that the action of the party as a whole does not come up to its action and feeling in the country at large.'[8]

Chamberlain made sure that Gladstone was received royally, with flags, bands, and cheering crowds. Staying with Chamberlain at Southbourne, Gladstone observed him closely. 'He is a man worth watching and studying: of strong self-consciousness under most pleasing manners and I should think of great tenacity of purpose: expecting to play an historical part, and probably destined to it.'[9] In his speech Gladstone did what he could to apply balm to the party's wounds. He took solace in seizing the opportunity to call on Newman at the Oratory, in the somewhat incongruous company of the Unitarian Chamberlain. Gladstone hoped to steer Newman a little away from Rome's unworthy Eastern line, and to allay a little of the offence of *Vatican Decrees*. But the 'wonderful pair were nervous and constrained, and each seemed a little relieved when, after twenty minutes of commonplace conversation, they rose to part'.[10]

~

'My earnest hope', Gladstone told Granville at the beginning of June, 'is that this Eastern Question is to reach a close or resting place during the summer and that then I shall be a free man again.'[11] This was not to be. Alexander II had proclaimed that war against the Turks would enforce compliance with the 'European' terms offered to and rejected by them at the Constantinople Conference. Had the Russian campaign been swift and bloodless, such compliance would have immensely eased the Eastern crisis. But the Russians failed to pull off a quick victory and got bogged down in the Balkans. There were 'disquieting rumours' of British moves in aid of the embattled Turks that brought Gladstone into consultation with his nominal chiefs. There were hopes that Salisbury would resign. Salisbury certainly had excellent reason to resign for the way he had been connived against at Constantinople; but, having once already resigned to no effect from a Conservative government, he preferred to hang on for better times and chances. In any case, Hartington could not see that 'anyone seems prepared for a regular attack on the Govt., nor to recommend hostile measures against Turkey'. He agreed with people who 'thought it rather ridiculous' that Gladstone should 'go on struggling as he does'.[12]

Gladstone went on struggling. He loosed a letter to the *Daily News* on 3 July denouncing rumoured government intentions to intervene. He detected similar conspiracies also in Egypt, where an Anglo-French dual control of the Khedive's revenues had been established. Gladstone suspected that 'our first site in Egypt, be it by larceny or be it by emption, will be the almost certain egg of a North African empire'.[13]

A brief respite of sea-cruising along the south coast in July hardly interrupted the insistent pace of his strugglings. He had pestered Tennyson unavailingly to compose something Miltonic for the Bulgarians on the lines of his Polish sonnets of the 1830s. The inveterately russophobe Tennyson, however, would contribute nothing beyond a tribute to the freedom fighters of Montenegro.[14] Gladstone by now had become the object of appeals for his countenance to the claims of peoples themselves struggling rightly to be free. His fame as the tribune of the oppressed Bulgarians incited Greek efforts to capitalize on his 'Hellenic Factor' piece. Gladstone found himself having to tread warily between conflicting claims of Slav and Greek. There were even Turkish accusations of Russian atrocities. Treading warily was the rule also when approached by Afrikaners from the Transvaal, led by Paul Kruger, lamenting the 'evil fruits' that would come of the annexation by the British Crown of their Republic.

The 1877 session passed without incident. The Russians remained stalled in front of the Turkish defensive lines. Gladstone darkly suspected that Beaconsfield would 'like an occasion for action'. Beaconsfield certainly had no intention of letting himself be lured into Egypt. Constantinople was his line of defence, and so far it remained unthreatened. Gladstone nonetheless declared himself as 'having faith enough in the Prime Minister's patience & strength of will to be quite unable to put aside the contingencies of some *coup* during the recess'.[15] Gladstone tried an outflanking *coup* on his own account. He pressingly invited Salisbury to Hawarden. Salisbury evaded the manoeuvre. He would not spurn Beaconsfield. He would wait to get a grip on Beaconsfield's policy. The old anti-Disraeli Hatfield axis was now extinct.

At Hawarden, Gladstone reviewed his investments. Ever disappointing were the Metropolitan Railways securities. Much more lucrative was the Egyptian Tribute

Loan, now kept buoyant by the Anglo-French dual control.[16] He much deplored the efforts of Willy and Gertrude to escape to Leeswood, near Mold. His work on *Thesaurus Homerikos* was impeded by masses of Liberal excursionists who invaded the place to pay devotion to their leader. Chips from his tree-felling were greatly valued. Hawarden was becoming a kind of political pilgrimage shrine and cult-centre. Nonconformity and its conscience was a prominent component of the cult. Gladstone, hailed as the incarnation of principled political moralism, a witness for 'truth, righteousness & humanity', became 'more and more a prophet of the most high God'.[17] The big issue presented in this 'new invention in the way of public agitation' was invariably Gladstone's intentions for the future.[18] Much as he disclaimed with vehemence any hope or desire to lead again, the uncertainty could not be exorcised.

With the autumn of 1877 came Russian advances across the Balkans. What Gladstone described to Shuvalov, the Russian Ambassador, as 'inflammable material' 'rather abundant in portions of the public mind', began to take fire. Gladstone became the focus of a kind of counter-agitation. There were many who blamed him, by the part he played in the 1876 agitation, for encouraging the Russians to suppose that they could deal with the Turks without any need to apprehend British intervention. Gladstone's defence was not thought entirely convincing. 'What was I during those events? An insignificant private individual, having no official position.'[19] Every day made 'more and more strange the present Tory, plutocratic, and rowdy feeling or rather fury against Russia, when contrasted with the perfect calmness with which they looked on as she perpetrated her real misdeeds in Poland'. He identified London as the 'great focus of mischief: through money, rowdyism, and the *Daily Telegraph*'.[20]

~

In many ways this was a good time to depart for a 27-day visit to Ireland in October and November. The visit has been seen as something odd and untoward, a waste of valuable time and opportunity to 'learn' about the needs of Ireland.[21] There was speculation about his motives.[22] He invited Salisbury's nephew Arthur Balfour to accompany; but, like his uncle to the Hawarden invitation, Balfour politely declined. Ostensibly, it was an obligation to visit Catherine's old friend, Lady Meath.[23] Possibly this was as much a pretext as a reason.

However that may have been, there is little reason to suppose other than that Gladstone's political motivation had to do with helping to repair the damage being done to Liberalism in Ireland by the Home Rulers, in the context more especially now of Irish Catholicism's deliberate refusal of the moral claims Gladstone felt the Bulgarian cause exerted on Christian consciences generally. With the Bulgarian case he had made his peace with the Nonconformists of England and Wales. Gladstone went to Ireland with a view to doing something towards putting the Irish right with him as much as putting himself right with the Irish.

Gladstone had been aware in 1876 of the notably feeble incidence of agitation in Ireland.[24] The extent to which he appreciated that the commonest initial thrust of nationalist response to the atrocities was to equate the Turks and the English as alien oppressors, and to identify with the Bulgarians as a people struggling for liberation, was not clear. He would have been perfectly capable of taking the point, even if he thought the comparison with the Turks grossly inappropriate, and the accusation, after his reforms of 1869 and 1870, in any case obsolete.

Ireland tended to occur instinctively to the English mind whenever this broad issue was raised. For Gladstone the sharp point of such considerations would have been blunted by his own grievances against Irish Catholicism. The pressures of the Irish hierarchy in Ireland deprecated responses to the Bulgarian case that identified the plight of the Bulgarians with the plight of the Irish. The special Catholic twist to the matter was to keep the Irish anti-English in the West but pro-Turkish in the East. This accorded with the Roman Curia's anti-Orthodox stance. The shifts observable in the responses of the emerging challenger to Butt as the Home Rule leader, Charles Stewart Parnell, were in conformity with this twist.[25] Gladstone went to Ireland with his head full of the iniquities of the Irish bishops and the iniquities of the Home Rulers, rather than the iniquities of English rule. Earlier at Birmingham, he had in effect rehearsed his Irish foray. He could not carry the Irish with him in the recent great parliamentary struggle. He was forced to conclude that the Irish Nationalists, demanding freedom for themselves, opposed the cause of freedom in the East. It is quite beside the point to lament that he failed to 'learn' anything there. He did not go to learn. He went to teach.

Another spur was that Liddon and MacColl had toured Ireland a few weeks before Gladstone arrived. MacColl reported his impression that the Irish people on the whole were 'all right' on the Eastern question.[26] The problem was that the leaders of the Irish people were far from 'all right'. There was no enthusiasm in his reception by the Home Rulers. Given Gladstone's curious line of argument that Daniel O'Connell – 'perhaps the most vigorous, elastic, and sagacious of all popular leaders known to history' – would never have advised, joined in, or given countenance to, the policy of the Home Rule party in Parliament,[27] this was not surprising. Equally unforthcoming were the Catholic bishops. Cardinal Cullen explained to Gladstone that his reception might have been warmer but for the insults of *Vatican Decrees* and *Vaticanism*. There was to be no mending of fences here as there had been with the Nonconformists.

Nothing therefore in the way of 'the people' were presented to Gladstone in Ireland. That he confined himself to the Pale and grand houses was one reason for this. After all, this was his habit in every tour he had made to embrace the millions in England. What was lacking was preparation with some Liberal political management to manipulate opinion and present it to him. Gladstone declared himself at a loss: 'much perplexed with the number of kind invitations: the larger parts of my project gradually fade from view, and my movements must be in a small circle'. His comment after lunching with the Duke of Marlborough at Vice-Regal Lodge: 'But not enough of *Ireland*.'[28] That was not the Duke's fault, or others of Gladstone's noble hosts. He expected also that somehow the Eastern question would be presented to him. He complained to Madame Novikov that the Duke was 'the *only man* who has spoken to me on the subject since I touched these shores!'[29]

The Irish visit of 1877 was untoward not because of Gladstone's failure to learn, but because of his failure to teach. There was an additional ironic touch. The one thing Gladstone apparently did learn in Ireland was that purchase of tenancies by occupiers was the way ahead on the land question. That was, after all, the land policy of most Home Rulers. It was already the preferred route of many Conservatives. The 'Bright clauses' Gladstone had grudgingly allowed to be tacked on to his Land Act in 1870 placed so many obstacles in the way of intending purchasers that by 1877 only 900 tenants had purchased under that provision. This was widely held to be unsatisfactory. A parliamentary committee was set up in 1877 under the chairmanship of a tenant-purchase advocate, G. J. Shaw-Lefevre. He looked to the example of the very successful system of secured loans to facilitate sale of tenancies under provisions in the Irish Church Disestablishment Act of 1869. Some 6000 tenants on Church lands were purchasing their tenancies.

In his Dublin speech of 17 November, after defending his Church Act and extolling his Land Act and proclaiming the need for far-reaching reform of local government to relieve the Westminster Parliament of unsustainable burdens, Gladstone declared his support for the principle of a more efficacious system of purchase of tenancies, applauding Shaw-Lefevre's looking to the provisions in the Church Act for that purpose.[30] The landlord–tenant relationship, he declared, was natural in England, 'inseparable from our social state'. But there was a different state of things in Ireland. Purchase of tenancies by occupiers in a 'good and appreciable number of instances' would be the best cure for the 'sharp division' between the interests of Irish landlords and Irish tenants. Creating 'a class of small proprietors in Ireland' would give 'new views and new ideas' to the land problem. The object of making the same man both proprietor and cultivator was 'an object of great importance' for Ireland. Gladstone applauded Bright and looked forward to effective improvements in his provisions.[31]

Gladstone spoke not as Liberal leader but as abdicated statesman without responsibilities either for the present or the future, and simply as author of the 1870 Irish Land Act. What he said was quite extraordinary, even astonishing, in one so famously the embodiment of the 'Treasury mind' and so much a celebrator of beneficial landlordism. It was certainly a signal case of greater freedom and less responsibility. The impression he left was that the future Liberal policy on Irish land would be likely to go in the direction of occupier purchase of tenancies. That was what Shaw-Lefevre hoped and believed when he produced his report in 1879. Gladstone gave him every reason so to do. He endorsed wholeheartedly Shaw-Lefevre's urging the Conservative government to adopt the policy of Irish tenant purchase, insisting that it was more than merely an economic necessity; it was a moral, social and political necessity as well.[32]

~

The Russians were now driving down towards the Thracian plain. British policy, Gladstone told Madame Novikov, had been 'ignoble'. 'Look well to yours. I firmly hope your Emperor will not allow his eye to be diverted from that work of European liberation wh. he has undertaken.'[33] Gladstone's immediate struggle was to help preserve British neutrality. Granville warned: 'The war clique of the Carlton are moving and sounding.'[34] Gladstone marked the close of 1877 as 'a year of tumultuous life', not the purer and holier air he had hoped for. But yet the 'part assigned to me in the Eastern question has been a part great and good far beyond my measure'.

There were other notions of the part assigned to Gladstone. Thorold Rogers wrote: 'I take it for granted that your comparative retirement from political or rather party life must be, whether you like it or not, temporary, and that you will have the advantage, when you are drawn back again to public business, of a new departure.'[35] A 'new departure' in relation to party was indeed likely to be of the essence of Gladstone's advantage as things began to take shape: a kind of vindication of what he had struggled through from 1871 to 1874. 'You cannot doubt your power', as Rogers put it to him in the new year, 'and you would not debate your duty.' The great requirement was a purging of Parliament: getting rid of plutocracy, 'society' and torpidity.[36]

These themes would very likely have been aired at a new year gathering at Hawarden: Argyll, Acton, Alfred Lyttelton, with Ruskin the lion of the party.[37] To advocates of a new departure also in more boldly offensive manoeuvres against Lord Beaconsfield's assumably warlike plans Gladstone, while deploring the 'great evil & a bad precedent in foreign policy' of his interventions, found himself 'driven to suspect that Beaconsfield will despair of taking the country in front, & will try it in flank'. He warned Granville that if 'evil symptoms' manifested themselves, he would reluctantly have to become 'a Bashi-Bazouk on this question'. 'Dizzy' was of course 'looking for the weak side of the English people', on which he had thrived so long; and 'he must feel greatly encouraged by the decided way they accepted his tomfoolery in the affair of the Suez Canal'. 'We are governed on Asian principles.'[38]

Beaconsfield summoned his 1878 session for what to Gladstone seemed the ominously early date of 17 January. What schemes were brewing as ministers contemplated the general collapse of Turkish resistance? The Russians were now surging on to Adrianople, which they would enter on 20 January. Soon Constantinople would be in their view. Ministers announced a vote of credit. On 23 January the fleet was ordered through the Dardanelles to stand off Constantinople itself. The order was rescinded at the request of the Turks. They were negotiating an armistice.

In the resignation of the Colonial Secretary, Lord Carnarvon, Gladstone read the most ominous implications. He was scandalized especially at the rumours of Beaconsfield's 'perfidy' in retailing to the Queen details of Cabinet infighting. Gladstone had never mentioned to her the views, dissident or otherwise, of individual members of his Cabinet.[39] He dined at the Phillimores' with Carnarvon himself on 26 January: 'long and interesting conversation with Carnarvon on Beaconsfield himself and the policy'.[40] Carnarvon's revelations stimulated Gladstone immensely. He knew now that Derby had resigned and then withdrawn his resignation; and was on the brink. Gladstone now had also a much more accurate estimation of Beaconsfield's disinterested view of Egypt. But that made Constantinople all the more something Beaconsfield was ready to go to war for. And from Carnarvon – known to Beaconsfield as 'Twitters' – Gladstone would have learned of the Prime Minister's masterful mien, with the Queen furiously in support.

At Oxford on 30 January, Gladstone's stimulations got an unrestrained airing. He was there under the auspices of Thorold Rogers and T. H. Green to speak at the Corn Exchange to the Oxford Liberal Association. Amid denunciations as to Lord Beaconsfield's domineering over his colleagues, the abomination of the £6 million vote of credit, and the pity of the Irish party's selfish attitude, Gladstone let loose remarks deemed indiscreet to the point of scandal. 'To my great pain, and with infinite reluctance, but under the full and strong conviction, I may say, of my political old age, for the past 18 months I may be said to have played the part of an agitator.' 'My purpose, I will tell you fairly, has been with extremely inadequate means, and in a very mean and poor degree ("No, no"), but still to the best of my power for the last 18 months, day and night, week by week, month by month, to counteract as well as I could what I believe to be the purpose of Lord Beaconsfield.'[41]

That evening Gladstone, together with Cardwell, inaugurated the Palmerston Club at a dinner at the Randolph Hotel. He professed to find it odd that the Tory Club at Oxford should be named after Canning; for he believed 'that there were not two persons more nearly identical in their opinions than Mr Canning and Lord Palmerston'. This forced assimilation of his old anti-hero with the first of his political hero-figures was part of his tactic to deprive Beaconsfield of any benefit from accrediting to himself the 'national' tradition of Palmerston.

For the benefit of the 160 noblemen and gentlemen in the Randolph Hotel audience, including Benjamin Jowett, now Master of Balliol, and his prize pupil Alfred Milner, who presided at the occasion, buzzing at the shock of the Corn Exchange incident, Gladstone rehearsed another of his thematic standbys. 'Perhaps it was my fault, but I must admit that I did not learn when I was at Oxford that which I have learned since – namely, to set a due value in the imperishable and the inestimable principles of human liberty.' In moving a vote of thanks, Milner retorted 'with cool emphasis' that Gladstone had neglected a very important aspect of the Eastern question – 'the interests of the British Empire'. Jowett commented: 'Gladstone does not appear to me to have gained so much with the mob as he has lost with the upper and educated classes, who after all are still the greater part of politics.'[42]

The upper and educated classes in the House of Commons left Gladstone in no doubt that he had lost much in their estimation. Even Phillimore thought his Corn Exchange proceedings 'a mistake in point of judgement & taste. But for them the Govt. wd. have been in a great difficulty.'[43] Gladstone was in a great difficulty, provoking groans and laughter when claiming to have contributed 'towards the tranquil and concordant settlement of this great question', and offering to let 'bygones be bygones'. His Oxford words, he insisted, were in apology rather than boast. It was a misfortune that he should, after so many years of service to the Crown, have found himself 'driven to so much extra-Parliamentary action in such a time as this'. He defended himself with precedents of opposition to official foreign policy. 'I ask what is the brightest jewel in the name of Fox? Undoubtedly, the resistance he offered to the Revolutionary War.'[44]

Animosity certainly was what Gladstone now aroused, as the victorious Russians imposed armistice terms on the Turks. 'The temper of the majority is a thing hardly credible.'[45] The public temper by now was marked by the vogue for 'Jingo' – 'the burden of a music-hall song', as it was explained to the Commons, 'which had made much talk outside and had brought into politics a class-name which promised to live, and to be the first new descriptive party epithet since the days of "Whig" and "Tory"'.[46] On 24 February rowdy mobs gathered outside 73 Harley Street. 'Windows were broken and much hooting.' Mounted police intervened. 'There is strange work behind the curtain if one could but get at it.'

~

The Russians and Turks settled the terms of their armistice on 1 February. On 13 February the fleet was reordered through the Dardanelles to stand off Constantinople. On 3 March the Russians and Turks concluded the negotiations of the Treaty of San Stefano. 'Europe', it seemed, had now been vindicated and redeemed from the failed Conference at Constantinople in January 1877.

'Instinctively I feel a weight taken off my shoulders', Gladstone recorded: 'but with this I suppose on the removal of tension, an increased sense of mental exhaustion.'[47] In 'The Peace to Come' and 'The Paths of Honour and Shame' for Knowles's *Nineteenth Century*, he set out his views on what a sound European settlement would look like. He warned particularly against the influence of Metternichian Austria.

Close co-operation with Austria, however, was what ministers decided was necessary when the shape of things imposed by the Russians on the Turks at San Stefano became clear. They created a vast Bulgaria, sprawling from the Black Sea to the Aegean, and far into Macedonia in the west. It looked as though the Russians, exasperated and exhausted, had succumbed to the temptation to get away with setting up a satellite replacement of Turkey-in-Europe. This was not at all what had been envisaged at the Constantinople Conference. It contradicted Gladstone's own prescriptions for justice as between Slav and Greek. For the Serbs as well as the Greeks it was intolerable. More to the point, to the Austro-Hungarian monarchy it was unacceptable. The Austrians insisted that the San Stefano treaty must be brought before Europe for revision. Bismarck stepped in to offer Berlin as the seat of a Congress of Powers and himself as 'honest broker'.

It was the obvious and logical policy for the British government to back the Austrian demand. Tension in British opinion sharpened once more as preparations were set on foot to call out the reserves. The Cabinet debated occupying Cyprus or Alexandretta. Jingo patriots were on the march once more with their refrain, 'We've got the men, we've got the ships, we've got the money too.' The Emperor Alexander had indeed allowed his eye to be diverted from the work of European liberation. What reflected badly on the Russians reflected badly on Gladstone. His Harley Street house became again a target of mobs. On 10 March the Gladstones found themselves beset as they walked towards Oxford Street, and had to take refuge in Cavendish Square, whence they were rescued by a cab escorted by mounted constables.[48]

Derby had resigned as Foreign Secretary on the decision to call out the reservists. On the day following, 8 April, Gladstone addressed the Commons on the theme that there was 'no great emergency' to justify the government's warlike measures and there must be no notion of restoring the 'balance of power in the East' by building up again that 'fabric of iniquity – the Ottoman Empire'.[49] Let down by the Emperor Alexander, Gladstone was in a weak position. He took it out on Granville. There was, Gladstone insisted ruthlessly in answer to his leader's complaints, 'a higher duty than party allegiance'; and in any case he 'never made so great a sacrifice to party' as in May 1877 when he got no support on his resolution, especially as he was 'convinced that the negative decision of you all was a mistake in the view of party'.[50]

In such circumstances of alienation from party and Parliament, Gladstone by 18 June recorded only occasional attendance: '*now* a rare event for me'. There was much to lament about Northcote's 'painful budget'. Lamentable also was the thinning of ranks. He travelled to Lichfield to attend Bishop Selwyn's funeral. He called at Pembroke Lodge at Richmond for a last sight of Russell: 'a noble wreck'. Alienation from the Commons and his party linked naturally to a feeling of dissatisfaction with Greenwich as a constituency. The idea of a comprehensive 'new departure' suggested a new constituency, one from which the implications of Gladstone's appeal to the people out of doors could assume an explicitly imposing dimension. It was absurd to adopt grandly demophilic postures as the second member of a dim suburban borough. A general election would not be due strictly before 1881. But it was certain that Beaconsfield would dissolve the 1874 Parliament some time before that. W. P. Adam, the Whip, was made aware of Gladstone's necessity. There were moves in Leeds to invite Gladstone to accept nomination in a big populous northern industrial city. Its disadvantage was that Gladstone would be one of three candidates and, with Conservatives at present holding two seats, there was no certainty that Gladstone would top the poll.

What Gladstone was in need of was a conspicuous single-member seat, preferably held by a conspicuous Conservative, who could be conspicuously challenged in an electoral tournament, a kind of proxy battle on behalf of the masses against the classes, with prospects not too far short of guaranteed victory. On 16 May Gladstone recorded: 'Lord Rosebery *cum* Mr Adam.' The young Scottish peer and the Liberal Whip came to put the case of Midlothian (in effect Edinburghshire): a constituency of fewer than 3000 voters, hence readily readable, held with a majority of 135 by the Earl of Dalkeith, heir to the dukedom of Buccleuch. It was tempting. There were resonances of Sir Walter Scott. That it was far from the metropolitan heartland was a positive recommendation.

While Gladstone mused on Midlothian, affairs of the East continued as fraught as ever. Salisbury was now Foreign Secretary, but having gained his object by not backing Derby against Beaconsfield, he was not well placed to make much immediate difference. He would accompany Beaconsfield at Berlin, but Gladstone could no longer see in him any of the Canningite promise hoped for at Constantinople in 1876.

The obdurate unresponsiveness of the Commons provoked Gladstone into yet more agitated journalism. 'Liberty in East and West' in the June *Nineteenth Century* castigated Beaconsfield and Salisbury for their part in the Berlin Congress. They had fastened on to their country the 'odious recollection that on this great occasion she had played the part of leading counsel for the cause of servitude and barbarism'. Meanwhile, the 'prophecy of Mr Canning that the forces and hopes of freedom would rally round England in an European convulsion have been completely reversed'. The 'Great Bulgaria' of San Stefano was trisected. Part became a new autonomous Bulgarian state. Part became a semi-autonomous 'Eastern Rumelia'. The rest was restored to direct Turkish rule, linking Constantinople back to Macedonia and the Adriatic.

Offence was taken in the Commons at Gladstone's publishing these denunciations while the Congress was deliberating.[51] There would have been even greater offence taken had not Knowles, the *Nineteenth Century* editor, excised words from Gladstone's copy: a reference to Beaconsfield as '*that alien*', whose iniquitous purpose it was 'to annex England to his native East and make it the appendage of an Asiatic empire'.[52]

Then on 8 July Gladstone was stunned by the government's 'astounding announcement' of a Convention with the Turks, negotiated by Layard prior to the Congress, whereby Britain would guarantee the integrity of Turkey in Asia in return for undertakings of reform and the occupation of Cyprus. Gladstone found this 'new Asiatic Empire' 'hard to take in at once'. Barrington reported to Beaconsfield in Berlin that 'Gladstone looks like a caged tiger with his bone taken from him'.[53] Gladstone denounced the Convention as 'insane', an 'act of duplicity not surpassed and rarely equalled in the history of nations'.[54] Beaconsfield, triumphantly returned from Berlin bearing 'peace with honour', dismissed Gladstone as a 'sophistical rhetorician inebriated with the exuberance of his own verbosity'.[55]

In the debate on the Treaty of Berlin, Gladstone almost exhausted his extensive repertoire of censure. It was frustratingly difficult to encapsulate nearly two years of tenacious, intransigent and passionate crusade into one perfectly formed and articulated critique. Much of the declamation rehearsed the themes of his previous polemics in the *Nineteenth Century*. The independence of Romania and Serbia was but poor reparation for the many delinquencies of the treaty. The 'action of the British Government has not been directed to the extension of the work of liberation; but, on the contrary, to its contraction'. The Bulgarians had been treated disgracefully. The Greeks had failed to secure their claims in Thessaly, Epirus and Crete, being fobbed off with promises of boundary rectifications. The 'selfish jealousy' of England's confederate, Austria, had deprived Montenegro of justice, and, by the Austrian occupation of Bosnia and the Herzegovina, had blocked the hopes of the Serbs. Huge wrongs had been done to the prerogatives of Parliament by the 'mad undertaking' of the Cyprus Convention.[56] Gladstone found his consciousness of not having done justice to the enormity of the case such that it supplemented his fulmination with 'England's Mission' in the August *Nineteenth Century*, the pith of which was that Beaconsfield's government had 'set up the principles of Metternich and put down the principles of Canning'.[57] Knowles was delighted with it: '*now* people will not be able to say that the Liberals have no clear chart to sail by in Foreign Policy'.[58]

By now the circumstance that Hartington conspicuously took an entirely different line in the Commons was not a matter of serious consequence for Gladstone. The real battle was to be fought elsewhere. The possibility of a general election was in the air. Beaconsfield's government had ended the 1878 session on a high note. There was much speculation that he might take the opportunity to dissolve Parliament and capitalize on peace with honour. The 'forward policy' of his proconsuls in India and South Africa seemed to be going well. At the Guildhall in November he was ebullient amid the hosts of exultant Jingoism. He had a perfectly sound, non-opportunist case for this: his policy had been morally traduced; let the people judge. Had Beaconsfield seized the moment he almost certainly would have retained a majority and given the Conservative party another lease of office; and incidentally would have vindicated Granville and Hartington within the Liberal debate and left Gladstone dangling. But, old, frail, exhausted and unnerved, he let the opportunity slip. That gave Gladstone his supreme chance.

~

Autumn in 1878 at Hawarden was enlivened by another visit by Ruskin: 'health better and no diminution of charm'. Years of grappling with Tennyson's ideas had attuned Gladstone to the ways of great and simple sages. Ruskin, dismayed at Gladstone's propensity towards intercourse with the nation, accused him of being a 'leveller'. He was enchanted by Gladstone's response: 'Oh dear, no! I am nothing of the sort. I am a firm believer in the aristocratic principle – the rule of the best. I am an out-and-out *inequalitarian*.'[59]

Back in June of 1878, Gladstone began work on 'a Morceau on the Popular Judgment in Politics for Mr Knowles'. James Knowles embarked in 1877 on the *Nineteenth Century*, inspired by Matthew Arnold's prescription for 'largeness of temper and lucidity of mind' and the editorial principle of 'signed writing by eminent persons'.[60] Knowles invited a symposium of representative eminent persons to offer their thoughts on the theme: 'Is the popular judgment of politics more just than that of the higher orders?'

In his contribution Gladstone in effect updated his doctrine of 1856 about the doings and intentions of leadership and the corresponding conviction wrought by them on the public mind. As to Knowles's question Gladstone was in no doubt that in all the great controverted questions of the nineteenth century, saving only Catholic emancipation, the popular judgement was indeed more just than that of the higher orders. In 'judging the great questions of policy', those classes excel who escape the 'subtle perils of the wealthy state'. It was in the 'moral sphere' that the causes of this superiority were to be looked for. It was the unsophisticated mind, even the barbarian mind, that saw with simple clarity into the moral heart of matters. [61]

Rather more implicitly and discreetly, however, Gladstone was also making it clear that the political value of the masses was for morals and ethics, not for intellect. If they needed no instructor in the matters of humanity and justice, they needed instruction in the ways and means of attaining their ends, in deciding the when and the how. It was always, one way or another, a matter of reversion to the 1856 formula: the doings and intentions of the active agent and the conviction wrought by them on the patient public mind.

Gladstone's faithfulness to that formula was a thing rather occult, not only because of its very nature it was not something to be publicly proclaimed, but also because, in Gladstone's mind, it was part of a larger, and quite intensely private area of his concerns where the inner and higher prescriptions of religion were applicable to the outer and lower world of affairs and politics. Throughout 1878 Gladstone was moving towards a culminating point where the slow accretions of religious conviction as to his assigned role in the lower world were accruing into a critical mass.

~

Nothing in the latter months of 1878, once the peril of a snap dissolution of Parliament was past, gave Gladstone any reason to doubt the general reliability of his assessment of the boiling pot.[62] Every public appearance by Gladstone continued to excite manifestations. At Hawarden he pored over electoral statistics, especially those provided by by-elections. 'We have won *ten*', he pointed out to Granville, 'since the Eastern question has been before the public.'[63] His reading of the figures was that they augured well. 'The pot is beginning to boil', he told Granville. 'I hope it will not boil too fast.' He believed that the Tory party was heading for a 'great smash'.[64]

The first shadows were in fact beginning to pass over Beaconsfield's fortunes. The proconsular 'forward' policies of Lytton in Afghanistan and Bartle Frere in the Cape both began to show symptoms of overreach. A short session of Parliament had to be summoned in December to bail out the Afghan war. Gladstone added Afghanistan to his long list of Beaconsfield's delinquencies. 'I consider that this war is an unjust, a guilty, an unreasonable, and impolitic war – one of mischief for the fame of England – one of mischief to the future of India.'[65] Beaconsfield, observing Gladstone's oratorical progresses, asked Barrington: 'Pray continue the correspondence during the "pilgrimage of passion" & keep me au fait to the effect produced.'[66] The effect produced was pretty much what Gladstone was hoping for.

~

Gladstone felt a new sense of adventure coming on him in the last days of 1878 in his lifelong quest for the 'higher natural theology, which reads and applies to practice *design* in all the forms of incident that beset and accompany our daily course'.[67] He never doubted the profound truth of his conviction in 1832: 'Restrict the sphere of politics to earth, and it becomes a secondary science.'[68] Nor did he ever doubt his early assurance that he continued to 'read in the habitual occurrences of life the sure works of Providential care and love: I see all things great and small fitted into a discipline'.[69] No less in 1878 than in 1840 was Gladstone dependent ultimately on the 'details of Revealed truth' as the foundations of his political principles.[70] The two earlier transmigrations of Gladstone's career – his change in 1845 from being a political servant of the Church to being a churchman in the service of the state, and when in 1859 as a Peelite he took on Liberal guise – made no diminution of the 'power exerted within Gladstone's political and public existence by commitment to a concept of spiritual mission, of moral redemption of the world, of great service to mankind by means of his devotion to Christ crucified and immanent within His Church Catholic'.[71]

The applicability of the inner and higher prescriptions of religion to the outer and lower world of affairs and politics had now arrived at the culminating point where the accumulated convictions of 'Providential care and love' as to his assigned role in the great design of the providential government of the world had indeed accreted into a critical mass that in turn constituted a kind of personal inspiration or revelation.

On the matter of divine inspiration, Gladstone, as a Butlerian, had robustly untroubled opinions.

> It seems difficult to conceive why any intelligent mind should doubt the capacity of our Maker to choose, frame and regulate the modes of his communication with us.
>
> No doubt some real impediments may be created by the injudicious claims of those who have not perceived that Inspiration is not necessarily uniform and may be adjusted by the Divine Wisdom to varieties of time, character and circumstances. Among its range of variety I take to be the degree in which it includes the company of elements not inspired. Again the inspiration of one who has received special commands, in the manner of describing the execution of those commands, may differ as to any points from the general inspiration accorded to those who have worked under the general laws of duty.
>
> I lean to the belief that the comprehensive arguments of Butler are in no way tied down to the proposition he seeks to prove, and supply a master key to our obligations in respect to the problems associated with our relations to the Almighty.[72]

Gladstone had for long possessed that 'master key'. Now, on his sixty-ninth birthday, came the time to turn it.

> And now these three years last past, instead of unbinding and detaching me, have fetched me back from the larger room which I had laboriously reached and have immersed me almost more than at any time in cares which are certainly cares of this life.
>
> And this retroactive motion has appeared & yet appears to me to carry the marks of

> the will of God. For when have I seen so strongly the relation between my public duties and the primary purposes for which God made and Christ redeemed the world? Seen it to be not real only but so close and immediate that the lines of the holy and the unholy were drawn as in fire before my eyes.

For Gladstone – always as a rule very prompt to take to his bed at the first symptoms of even minor malady – not to have been confined to bed all the year past for more than a single day was indeed a cause for wonder. In the physical and mental effort of speaking, also, often to 'large auditories', he had been 'as it were upheld in an unusual manner and the free effectiveness of voice had been given me to my own astonishment'. 'Was not all this for a purpose: & has it not all come in connection with a process to which I have given myself under clear but most reluctant associations. Most reluctant: for God knoweth how true it is that my heart's desire has been for that rest from conflict and from turmoil ... I am aware that language such as I have here used is often prompted by fanaticism. But not always. It is to be tried by tests. I have striven to apply them with all the sobriety I can: and with a full recollection that God sometimes sees fit to employ as his instruments for particular purposes of good those with whom notwithstanding He has yet a sore account to settle.'[73]

~

All the indications as the new year of 1879 began to unfold were that the pot was indeed boiling away. The question of Midlothian was becoming urgent. Rosebery was confident: 'There is humanly speaking no doubt whatever of your return.' Adam calculated, accurately as it proved, a Liberal majority of about 200.[74] The Conservatives could be counted on to fight frantically. Defeat would be 'far greater as a calamity, than success as a gain'. But that would 'enhance the notoriety of the contest. It may be necessary to make a pilgrimage in the County.' All this increased the 'value of the prize'.[75] In his address of acceptance to the Midlothian committee, Gladstone, as a veteran of eleven Parliaments, renounced retirement in the face of domestic misgovernment and the fact above all that 'the faith and honour of the country have been gravely compromised in the foreign policy of the Ministry'.

Bright visited Hawarden on 30 January. 'We talked much on politics. On a crisis he said the entire Liberal party would require you to come forward: I gave him, besides the coward's reason, three strong reasons against it.' These had to do with the difficulties of a new government in relation to old colleagues and elements of trouble in the 'non-official portion of the Liberal party'. On the strength of these reasons Gladstone kept a low profile in the session. Disaster at Isandhlwana did not provoke him into intervention in the Zulu war debate. Nor did the unravelling of Lytton's campaign to establish a 'scientific frontier' in

Afghanistan exercise him unduly. He voted for Trevelyan's bill to assimilate the county and borough franchises as an earnest of his faith in the right judgement of the people. When Shaw-Lefevre moved his resolution to increase the facilities for occupiers purchasing tenancies under the Irish Land Act of 1870 Gladstone declared his entire approval.[76] But by and large Gladstone now took little interest in the parliamentary dimension of his life. Over the session hung the likelihood of a dissolution and a general election. The second 1879 session was the seventh of the 1874 Parliament, already elderly.

As the Parliament dwindled away there were distractions enough. 'My dear Mrs Th' suddenly replaced 'Dear Broken Spirit' after August. There were the embarrassments of ostentatious gifts and Mr Th's being sued for unpaid debts. There was a good deal of theatre. Phillimore, an old Christ Church friend who recalled Gladstone's puritanical Evangelical days, found it amusing to observe Gladstone 'defend plays and the Theatre – on no subject have his opinions undergone a more complete revolution. Great favour was shown to painting and music – why not the drama?'[77] It was certainly the case that few theatrical memoirs in the coming decades lacked their Gladstone anecdote.

At the Royal Academy dinner in May Gladstone had the satisfaction of observing 'Lord B. *not* warmly received by the general company.' It was gratifying that the Prince of Wales was 'just as of old: and other royalties generally free and gracious'. For indeed Millais's near full-length portrait of Gladstone was the centre-piece of the Academy's exhibition. It made Gladstone look prim, demure and innocent. At tea at Lady Derby's on 21 May Gladstone found himself 'face to face with Lord Beaconsfield; and this put all right socially between us, to my great satisfaction'. Civil social relations, however, did not spare Lord Beaconsfield from Gladstone's post-sessional fulmination, 'The Country and the Government' in the August *Nineteenth Century*. Gladstone was eloquent especially on 'the stain of blood' marked on the nation by unjust wars in Afghanistan and South Africa. Gladstone was now the recipient of persistent representations from Pretoria about the shameful oppression of the Transvaal by British imperialism.[78]

Plans were now afoot both in Liverpool and London for grand celebrations at the end of the year to honour Gladstone on his seventieth birthday. Gladstone took steps promptly to prohibit any such manifestation. There were further projects in November discountenanced by Adam. The event would be a strictly private, family affair at Hawarden. Public celebrations would give impulse to the swell of Liberal opinion in the country calling for Gladstone's resumption of Liberal leadership. Most of the intractable mountain of correspondence besetting him consisted of such appeals. Gladstone deprecated and denied; but it was an issue that would not go away.

Relief came with an autumn tour on the Continent. Together with Mary and Herbert, the Gladstones took the now accustomed route of calling on Helen in

Cologne on 15 September and thence on to Munich and Döllinger. With Acton as impresario the party then gathered at the Arco-Valley villa on the Tegernsee, high in the Bavarian Alps. Döllinger now was slightly deaf and less easy with his English, but 'the mind as heretofore free comprehensive and profound'. An excursion to Venice provided a delightful interlude. Acton entertained the younger Gladstones with an outline of his ambitious plan for a history of Liberty.[79] At Paris on return a reporter from *Le Gaulois* pressed Gladstone on the question of his resumption of the Liberal leadership: 'your countrymen will force you to do so'.[80] Gladstone was observed to gesture in a manner suggesting what will be will be.

The Gladstones returned to a London humming with speculation about when Beaconsfield would take the electoral plunge. It was helpful that the economy stuck obstinately in depression. For all that this puzzled him, Gladstone could present it as yet another Tory iniquity. Gladstone's reading of the situation was that the Conservatives 'intended sailing on a quiet tack'. They wanted 'all the past proceedings to be in the main "stale fish" at the elections'. Therefore, as he put it to Granville, 'we should keep the old alive and warm'. This meant 'autumn work'. Gladstone felt the odds were against a dissolution before February but in favour of its occurring before the budget in April. 'This is the meaning of my suggestion as to autumn work', he explained to Granville, 'rather than that I expect a Dissolution.' It seemed to Gladstone 'a good policy to join on the proceedings of 1876–9 by a continuous process to the Dissolution'.[81]

Autumn work meant indeed making a pilgrimage in Midlothian. Gladstone consulted Rosebery, who was to be his impresario. Gladstone set forth on 24 November, delivering harangues in passing. The journey from Liverpool was 'really more like a triumphal procession'. So was the whole Midlothian adventure. At Edinburgh the 'scene even to the West end of the City was extraordinary, both from the numbers and the enthusiasm'. At Rosebery's seat, Dalmeny, there were torches and fireworks. 'I have never gone through a more extraordinary day.' The two next days proved to be even more deliriously triumphant. At the Music Hall on the 25th Gladstone declared his hope that in the coming election the verdict of the country 'will give to Lord Granville and Lord Hartington the responsible charge of its affairs'. On the 27th he pressed on to West Calder. 'The enthusiasm, great along the road, was at the centre positively overwhelming.' Gladstone was being accorded the office of a 'charismatic "Priest-King"', prophet-protagonist of a popular theatre of politics,[82] an oracular cult-figure of mass worship of redemptive leadership.[83]

For all the charisma, theatre and *Schwärmerei*, the pith of Gladstone's rhetoric was strictly, almost comically, conservative. He denounced the government's 'innovations', its breaking of precedents, its mischievous 'newfangled' measures. This self-adopted image of being a rather old-fashioned elderly gentleman

Gladstone dressed with studied deliberation in the habit of the 1840s. As in 1868, he was retrieving a golden age, not looking to a new kind of golden future. Nothing was more characteristic of him or revealing of his purpose than his conjuring of the spirit of Peel. 'Could his valuable life have been prolonged to this moment, could he have been called upon to take part, as we are now called upon to take part, in the great struggle which is commencing in this country, Sir Robert Peel would have been found contending along with you against the principles which now specially place you in determined opposition to the government of today.'[84]

Much of what Gladstone said at Midlothian in 1879 bore on purely local and Scottish questions, carefully got up. Most of what he said otherwise was a restatement of his invective against the government since his return to the political fray in 1876. To the domestic iniquities of ministers and their most 'wanton' invasion of Afghanistan, he now added the case of the Transvaal, 'inhabited by a free, Christian, republican community', annexed against their clearly expressed will.[85]

On two matters Gladstone broke new or newish ground. The first related to the problematic and ill-defined concept of 'Home Rule', attached by now more or less indelibly to most Irish MPs. He repeated in essence his declaration in Dublin in 1877 about being friendly to local government that did nothing to weaken or compromise the authority of the Imperial Parliament. He pledged that Ireland should get nothing that could not upon equal terms be offered to Scotland.[86]

The second area of ground-breaking was in foreign policy. It was of the very essence of the occasion that Gladstone should provide for the Liberal party a post-Palmerston doctrine, 'a clear chart to sail by'. It had been long enough wanting. As an 'outside workman', Gladstone was at last free to discard the Whiggism and 'moderate' Liberalism in the parliamentary party that had impeded and harassed him in his time as leader from 1867 to 1875, and which thus far since 1875 had sustained the duumvirate in their resistance to his overtures and initiatives. Now he was in a position, at West Calder on 27 November, to offer to the nation 'the right principles of foreign policy'.

These were, first, just legislation and economy at home to foster the physical and moral elements of the nation's union and strength, and to reserve that strength for great and worthy occasions abroad. The second was to aim to preserve to the nations of the world the blessings of peace. Thirdly, policy must strive to cultivate and maintain the concert of Europe, the better to neutralize and fetter the selfish aims of each power. Into the Aberdeenish tone thus far Gladstone inserted, for the benefit of Bright and his isolationist Manchester School friends, an expediently Cobdenite note: 'you should avoid needless and entangling engagements'. His fifth principle ostensibly reverted to a mainstream line: 'to acknowledge the equal rights of all nations'. In reality it was a covert protest at Russia's being 'placed under moral suspicion of espionage', and being made 'the constant subject of invective'. The sixth principle, now at large after having been on many occasions occluded by circumstances since 1858, was that 'the foreign policy of England should always be inspired by the love of freedom'.[87]

The oddity of the six right principles of foreign policy at Midlothian was that Aberdeen's name was never mentioned. He was the victim of Gladstone's fixation on denying Beaconsfield any claim to the 'national' tradition of Palmerston. 'In the foreign policy of this country', Gladstone pronounced, 'the name of Canning will ever be honoured. The name of Russell will ever be honoured. The name of Palmerston will ever be honoured by those who recollect the erection of the Kingdom of Belgium, and the union of the disjoined provinces of Italy.' This was unblushing humbug. But it served its purpose. Privately, Gladstone never doubted that Palmerston and Beaconsfield were birds of a feather.[88] In a further refinement to his twisting of reputations and filiations, Gladstone applied to Beaconsfield and the Conservatives in return the name of Metternich's colleague at the Congress of Vienna. On the testimony of Acton, Gladstone regarded Beaconsfield as 'the worst and most immoral minister since Castlereagh'.[89]

Yet if anyone was Gladstone's true mentor in foreign policy, it was that disciple of Castlereagh, Aberdeen. The difficulty was that in 1879 Gladstone remained 'tarred with the same stick' as he had been tarred with in 1855, when he conspicuously failed to come to the wounded Aberdeen's aid: 'Russian politics'.[90] That was no longer the disability it had been in the days when his windows in Harley Street were being broken; but it was a disability still.

After thus acquitting himself in keeping 'the old alive and warm', Gladstone returned to Edinburgh where 20,000 cheering people packed in Waverley market. From further excursions – 'enthusiasm everywhere marvellous' – he headed for Glasgow. 'Fervid crowds at every station. The torch light procession at Glasgow was a subject for Turner.' By 8 December he was back at Hawarden, calculating the grand total of his auditory at 86,930.[91] Lucy Cavendish found him for the first time 'a little *personally* elated'.

~

The promise disclosed by the pivotal year 1876 was evidently on the way to plenary fulfilment, if Midlothian was to any substantial degree proxy for the nation at large. The 'party in the country' was, on that ground, his party. Was it not clearly the case that a grand design of things was beginning to reveal itself? The predicament also revealing itself was the now painful awkwardness of his relationship with the parliamentary leaders. A visit by Granville to Hawarden at Christmas of 1878 had disturbed Gladstone by indications of 'failing powers in his general mental force and especially his initiative. His nice tact and judgment remain.' What was sapping Granville's general mental force was mainly his despairing appreciation of the hollowness of his situation as *Roi fainéant* to

Gladstone's masterful Mayor of the Palace. Nor would Gladstone have eased matters when visiting Granville at Walmer bearing a copy of *Le Gaulois*. Granville related to Hartington Gladstone's repeating the eloquent gesture of response he had made at Paris: 'which looked like *Alors comme alors*'. The perplexed duumvirate exchanged notions of forcing Gladstone either to come forward or back out.[92] The other party chiefs found the whole thing impossible. They went round in futile circles. The impasse was reminiscent of the insoluble conundrum defined by Clarendon in 1867: that Gladstone was inevitably the impossible leader.

Gladstone himself later insisted that it was well understood that 'a change in his position' was involved when he took up the Midlothian constituency.[93] If the nation obliged him to become leader again, so be it. *Alors* indeed *comme alors*. Certain consequences for the Liberal party would follow ineluctably. That would be their problem, not his. It was no longer a question of his own personal wishes and intentions. He was playing a part assigned to him. 'For the last 3½ years I have been passing through a political experience which I believe is without example in our Parliamentary history. I profess to believe it has been an occasion, when the battle to be fought was a battle of justice humanity freedom law, all in their first elements from the very root, and all on a gigantic scale. The word spoken was a word for millions, and for millions who themselves cannot speak. If I really believe this then I should regard my having been forced into this work as a great and high election of God. And certainly I cannot but believe that He has given me special gifts of strength, on the late occasion especially in Scotland ... So then while I am bound to accept this election for the time, may I not be permitted to pray that the time shall be short?'[94]

~

That 1880 would provide a solution seemed the best hope. Gladstone mused on contingencies. He had to acknowledge that he was now 'not very fit for composition after 5 p.m.' On the other hand, could it be that 'the decline of mind along with body – which reaches by analogy into the vegetable creation – signifies a rest of the powers as in a fallow – with a refreshed revival to follow?'[95] His former private secretary Godley recorded Gladstone's saying to Catherine a day or two after his seventieth birthday celebrations: 'It is a solemn thought that one has reached such an age; and yet, do what I will, I *cannot* feel myself to be an old man.'[96] Gladstone even mused on the ultimate complete solution to all predicaments: 'To die in church appears to be the great *euthanasia*: but not at a time to disturb worshippers.'[97]

Disturbing news came of Helen in Cologne. Sir Thomas and Lady Louisa hastened there with William on 12 January. Helen died peacefully on the 16th. Gladstone examined her library of devotion. He concluded that she could not have submitted to the 1870 Infallibility dogma. He persuaded himself that 'she died at one with us as before'.[98]

Matters were transformed on 8 March, when it was announced that the Cabinet had decided to advise the dissolution of the 1874 Parliament on the 24th. Gladstone was summoned to confer at Devonshire House. Thence he hastened to his field headquarters at Dalmeny. 'Was obliged to address the people at every point (5) before Edinburgh – At York there were I think 6000: very quiet. At Edinburgh the wonderful scene of Nov. was exactly renewed.'[99] He launched into an exhilarating vortex of speechifying, 'enthusiasm everywhere the same'. The speeches also were much the same as in November, with certain explanatory and polemical revisions. Beaconsfield's election manifesto took the form of a letter to the Irish Viceroy, the Duke of Marlborough. Beaconsfield pointed to the danger in Ireland of the attempt there to sever the constitutional tie uniting it to Great Britain. Gladstone denounced these 'baseless' and 'terrifying insinuations' as merely an artful dodge to divert attention away from the government's failures and misdeeds. Gladstone was more concerned at the extent to which his doctrine on foreign policy was being confounded with that of the pacifist Cobdenites. He was at pains to correct that misapprehension. 'There is an allegation abroad that what is called the "Manchester School" is to rule the destinies of this country if the Liberals come to power.' No such thing, he insisted, would come to pass; 'no Government of this country could ever accede to the management and control of affairs without finding that dream of Paradise on earth was rudely dispelled by the shock of experience'.[100]

The polemical point touched on Gladstone's well-seasoned austrophobic zest. On the strength of a newspaper report that the Emperor Francis Joseph had expressed to Sir Henry Elliot his best wishes for the government, Gladstone launched out, at the Music Hall on 17 March, on a vituperate indictment climaxed with the ringing assertion: 'There is not a spot upon the whole map where you can lay your finger and say: "There Austria did good"'.[101] Hamilton thought it a deliberate riposte to Salisbury's hailing the Austro–German alliance of 1879 as 'tidings of great joy'.

The polls opened on 30 March. 'May God from heaven guide every one of them: and prosper and abuse and baffle us for His glory: lift us up, or trample us down, according as we are promoting or opposing what *He* knows to be the cause of Truth, Liberty, and Justice.' Within a day the 'doom of the Govt came into view'. On 2 April, Gladstone concluded his second series of speeches 'in which I have hammered with all my little might at the fabric of the present Tory power'. 'We cannot reckon on the wealth of the country, nor upon the rank of the country, nor upon the influence which rank and wealth usually bring … Above all these and behind all these, there is something greater than these – there is the nation itself. This great trial is proceeding before the nation … a grander and more august spectacle was never exhibited either in Westminster or in the House of Lords.'[102]

At Dalmeny Gladstone solemnly recorded: 'It seemed as if the arm of the Lord had bared itself for a work He has made his own.' The declaration of the Midlothian poll on 5 April gave Gladstone 1579 votes to Dalkeith's 1368. 'Wonderful, and nothing less, had been the disposing, guiding hand of God in this matter.' Having already been elected for Leeds, Gladstone could now bestow that seat on Herbert, who had failed to take a Middlesex division. Gladstone returned to Hawarden on the 6th. 'Travelled all night and had time to ruminate on the great hand of God so evidently displayed.' At Midlothian Gladstone had framed an indictment as he saw it not against a party or a government but against 'a whole system of Government' redolent of novel evils that he encapsulated in the word 'Beaconsfieldism'. At Hawarden he observed raptly its parliamentary fabric disintegrate. 'The triumph grows & grows: to God be the praise.' To Rosebery he gratefully exclaimed: 'the romance of politics which befell my old age in Scotland, has spread over the whole land'. To Argyll: 'The downfall of Beaconsfieldism is like the vanishing of some vast magnificent castle in an Italian romance.'[103]

~

Wolverton arrived at Hawarden on 9 April. 'He threatens a request from Granville and Hartington. Again, I am stunned, but God will provide.' Gladstone made Wolverton aware that he would not again take office other than as prime minister; and that any ministry headed by Granville and Hartington could depend on his full and cordial support. That was his current interpretation of his statement at Midlothian in 1879 that he looked to the coming election to give Lord Granville and Lord Hartington the charge of the new government. Wolverton departed to apprise the glum duumvirate of this – what it amounted to – ultimatum. By now the Liberal majority was of the order of 40 over Conservatives and Home Rulers combined. The hard fact of the matter was that Gladstone had as much cause to rejoice over the eclipse of the party of Granville and Hartington as he had to rejoice over the rejection of the party of Beaconsfield.

There was little doubt that Beaconsfield would resign on the precedents of 1868 and 1874, rather than meet the new Parliament. For the third successive time since the second Reform Act of 1867 a government had been decisively dismissed by the electorate. Quite what this meant in the longer term was a matter of debate. For the immediate term the Queen was at the Villa Hohenlohe in Baden-Baden, in tears. She had long dismissed from her mind any notion of ever again recalling Gladstone to service. Beaconsfield suited her, personally and politically, absolutely. He excelled in the arts of managing her, both as a sovereign and as a woman; at which Gladstone had been hopeless – or, rather, for which he had never conceived either the propriety or the necessity. She never could take Gladstone as her minister again, she declared in 1879, 'for I never COULD have the slightest *particle* of confidence in Mr Gladstone *after* his violent, mischievous, and dangerous conduct for the last three years'.[104]

On 5 April she denounced to her daughter Victoria Gladstone's 'mad, unpatriotic ravings' at Midlothian.[105] As the horror came upon her that she might very well be confronted by him she told her secretary, General Ponsonby, that she would 'sooner *abdicate* than send for or have anything to do with that *half-mad firebrand* who would soon ruin everything, and be a *Dictator*'. She instructed Ponsonby to inform Granville and Hartington that Gladstone was entirely unacceptable to her. Ponsonby advised the injudiciousness of such a declaration; and hoped that Lord Beaconsfield would ease the situation by advising that Gladstone be sent for. Beaconsfield, however, was not so minded.

It was not until 17 April that the Queen arrived back at Windsor from Germany. Gladstone on the 13th had put himself in a slightly more receptive position. Should Granville and Hartington 'see fit to apply to me, there is only one form and ground of application … which could seriously be entertained by me, namely their conviction, that on the ground of public policy, all things considered it was best in the actual condition of affairs that I should come out'. He departed from Hawarden to Harley Street on the 19th. 'May He who has of late wonderfully guided, guide me still in the critical days about to come.'

Beaconsfield tendered his resignation on 21 April, having advised Victoria that she send for Hartington. This was constitutionally perfectly correct. The Queen sent for Hartington on the 22nd and asked him to form a government. He demurred. From Wolverton he knew of Gladstone's ultimatum: all or nothing. Nothing would set the heather on fire all over the land. Victoria's request that he enquire of Gladstone whether he would accept office other than as prime minister Hartington could hardly refuse. Granville advised Hartington, as Ponsonby had advised the Queen, to make no statement to Gladstone indicative of any want of confidence in him. That would make Gladstone instantly withdraw his availability; and the fat would really be in the fire.

Gladstone recounted that Hartington 'enquired of me whether if he undertook the formation of a Government, I would form part of it. I at once declined. The work done had been my work: reluctantly and slowly undertaken in 1876–7, but, after it was once engaged in, persistently put forward.' The Queen, Gladstone allowed, had been quite right not to send for him, because he was, after all, as he had earlier described himself, an insignificant private individual, having no official position. In fact, Gladstone was greatly put out that she had sent for Hartington rather than Granville: 'it was to Granville that I had resigned my trust'; Granville was '*the* leader of the party'. The Queen was wrong to have passed him by.[106] The Queen of course knew nothing of this curious, perhaps significant, mental twist. No doubt she took the view that it was for the Liberal party to choose its leader. The party in 1875 had specifically entrusted her with that choice.

For the moment, Gladstone was indulgent to Hartington's predicament.[107] He, Gladstone, held that he was plainly right in refusing Hartington's overture, for had he acted otherwise he would have 'placed the facts of the case in conflict with its rights, and with the just expectations of the country'. Besides, as the head of a previous ministry, and still in full activity, 'I should have been strangely placed as the subordinate of one twenty years my junior and comparatively little tested in public life'.[108] Hartington knew that in gallantly acceding to the Queen's request he was putting himself in a false position. Both he and Granville wanted to escape from their absurd situation as quickly as possible, but not so quickly as to create a risk of Gladstone's being told, from any quarter, that he was not welcome at Windsor.

Hartington duly returned to Windsor with empty hands. He and Granville executed the painful task of persuading the Queen that she had no choice but to send for Gladstone. Gladstone expressed to them his 'sense of the high honour and patriotism with which they had acted.' He himself, he assured them in return, had acted in good faith and had only been drawn out of retirement by compulsion. Gladstone was summoned to Windsor on 23 April.

15

Grand Old Man, 1880–1883

'Looking calmly over the course of experience I do believe that the Almighty has employed me for His purposes in a manner larger and more special than before, and has strengthened and led me on accordingly ...'

Gladstone, diary entry, 20 May 1880.

At Windsor on 23 April Gladstone accepted the Queen's commission to undertake a new government. Never was such a commission more reluctantly confided. Victoria found the fact that Gladstone was once more her minister 'hardly possible to believe'. She told her daughter: 'I had felt so sure he could not return and it is a bitter trial for there is no more disagreeable Minister to have to deal with.'[1] She regained composure, but Gladstone was aware that she was being 'natural under effort', with a certain leavening of 'good-natured archness' on her part to cover her embarrassment. He suspected darkly that the 'undoubted slight to Lord Granville' was at Beaconsfield's instigation. In his own kind of innocence, Gladstone did not know the half of it. Ponsonby, the Queen's secretary, did his best to make things as smooth as possible. The Prince of Wales also helped to ease the tension with a courtesy visit on the 24th ('in the main satisfactory').

Placements for the official Whig lords were no problem. They were in any case a dwindling constituency. Granville, for all Gladstone's well-founded misgivings about his staying power, had to go back to the Foreign Office and the leadership of the Lords. Selborne returned to the Woolsack. Spencer took the lord presidency and Kimberley returned to the Colonial Office. Northbrook (a Baring, and former Governor-General of India) went to the Admiralty, and Ripon was posted to India to cut down 'Lytton's swagger'. Cowper took on the Irish lord-lieutenancy. Argyll went to the Privy Seal in aid of Granville in the Lords. Gladstone judged Cardwell unfit for office. Cardwell took a different view. It was a sad ending to an old Peelite friendship.

The Commoners were more difficult. Hartington hoped for the Exchequer, but Gladstone reserved that for himself. Hartington found himself fobbed off with the India Office. Childers went to the War Office, Harcourt to the Home Office. Bright resumed his totem role at the Duchy of Lancaster. Gladstone nursed resentment at Forster's distinctly unhelpful role over the Eastern question, and initially planned to exclude him from the Cabinet. J. G. Dodson was dimly promoted from the deputy-speakership to the Local Government Board. But with both Goschen and Stansfeld declining to serve, Gladstone was obliged eventually to slot Forster in as Cowper's Irish Chief Secretary. Goschen refused, more consistently than Ripon, to adhere to Hartington's acceptance in 1877 of the assimilation of the county and borough franchises. Like Cardwell, Lowe was also judged unfit. He too took it hard.

There remained the most awkward problem: what to do with the two most prominent of the younger generation of parliamentary Radicals, very forward in pressing claims in tandem, Dilke and Chamberlain? Gladstone was bound to temper somewhat the preponderance in Cabinet of the official Whigs, but found himself short of presentable candidates in the older and more seasoned Radical generation. Stansfeld preferred to devote himself to assisting Josephine Butler's campaign against the Contagious Diseases Acts.

Dilke and Chamberlain had entered into a compact that one of them was to be in the Cabinet. Failing that, they would both prefer to act independently. Dilke's explanation of this put Gladstone in a difficulty. They would be more dangerous outside than in. Dilke's former scandalous notoriety as a republican was with difficulty purged sufficiently to get him the under-secretaryship at the Foreign Office. That made Chamberlain the extraordinary case. An MP merely since 1876, he was without official experience. Gladstone trusted that Chamberlain would be sensible enough to temper political opinions 'which may on some points go rather beyond what I may call the general measure of the Government'.[2] Godley recalled seeing Chamberlain emerge 'radiant' from Gladstone's room with the offer of the Board of Trade.[3]

Gladstone and his colleagues proceeded to Windsor on the 28th when they were sworn in at a Council. 'I think H.M. was completely satisfied and relieved.' So Gladstone persuaded himself. In fact H.M. shared the view of many observers that the Liberal government was an unstable coalition of Whigs and Radicals that would crack apart under pressure.[4] The Court's discountenance was evident in the difficulties Gladstone had with the Household appointments. The Gladstones moved into No. 10 Downing Street, to Catherine's gratification. The secretariat, headed first by Godley and then from 1883 by Eddie Hamilton, moved into No. 11. Herbert was appointed Parliamentary Private Secretary.

That Gladstone should take on the Exchequer surprised many. But far from seeing it as a burden, Gladstone relished the prospect of demolishing in person the financial legacy of Beaconsfieldism. After a 'financial dinner' with the chief Treasury officers, Hamilton remarked that 'Finance seems quite a recreation to Mr. G.'[5] It was the second of the two great priorities that Gladstone set before himself at the outset of his second administration. 'The views with which the Government was assumed by me on this occasion were not less definite, than in 1868. First and foremost stood the foreign policy of the country.' That was to be entirely overhauled, with respect particularly to business left unfinished by the Berlin Treaty. Gladstone very early took occasion to assure the Ottoman Ambassador, Musurus Pasha, that his 'union of opinion on Foreign Affairs with Lord Granville was such that whatever Lord G. said might be considered as coming from me'.[6]

Nothing of all this had made Gladstone shift to any significant degree from the semi-detached position in which he had installed himself at the beginning of 1875. As he explained later to Bright, he had accepted his 'mission' in April 1880 'as a special and temporary mission', that he hoped he might reasonably expect to 'get over', if not 'sooner than the autumn' of 1881, at least before the end of that year.[7]

~

Gladstone was now so overwhelmingly ascendant in the country and as a consequence in the government and the party as to constitute a quite unprecedented phenomenon of popular politics. The greatest 'revenge' of which he had spoken darkly in 1865 was to be his revenge on his adopted party.[8] There would be many kinds of difficulty confronting him in these years of his second ministry, but they would not include the old ignominies the Liberal party had so often inflicted on him. One veteran Liberal MP put the matter candidly in 1882: 'I know the right hon. Gentleman (Mr Gladstone) can do anything he likes: I do not think the country could have a better man at the head of affairs; but whatever he says, whether it be right or wrong, I believe will receive support in the country.'[9] Harcourt later put it to Gladstone: 'Pray do not entertain the notion that you can say anything *personally* which does not commit and bind the party. *You are the Party* and your acts are its acts. It will never consent nor will the Nation consent to regard you as an individual ...'[10] The Duke of Bedford spoke for many a despairing Whig lord when he confessed that 'there is no use standing up against Gladstone'.[11] The soubriquet 'Grand Old Man', attributed to the parliamentary wit and muckraking journalist Henry Labouchere in April 1881, captured the public imagination by its sheer appositeness: 'the name stuck'.[12]

Gladstone's towering stature was now reflected in the diminished standing of his senior colleagues. 'Puss' Granville depended more than ever on Gladstone's countenance. His grip on the Foreign Office, never very tight, loosened to the point when Gladstone complained of having to conduct foreign policy 'almost single-handed'.[13] At the India Office, Hartington was exiled from the centre of things. Gladstone's taking the Exchequer underlined Hartington's shift to the margin. Gladstone's social relations with his colleagues dwindled in these years. That Catherine had neither taste nor competence in the arts of being a grand political hostess hardly mattered in this new dispensation. Gladstone's one new relationship of possible importance was with Rosebery. This relationship was already beginning to betray signs of the temperamental moodiness that would increasingly distinguish Rosebery's career. Rosebery declined Gladstone's offer of subordinate office in 1880. Able, vain, ambitious, popular – a great figure on the Turf – he wanted the palm without the dust; especially the dust of being seen to be in Gladstone's pocket.

There were others quite willing to slip into Gladstone's pocket. Acton by now was snugly installed, cultivating as an extra string to his courtier's bow Gladstone's intellectually prone daughter Mary, manager of the household and unofficial secretary for ecclesiastical preferments.[14] Acton could see John Morley as the coming rival for Gladstone's interest in affairs of the mind. Morley was in partnership with Chamberlain, planning, as man of thought and man of action, to transform the Liberal party into something much more uncompromising than the Whigs had so far allowed it to be. Morley was now editing the *Pall Mall Gazette* in the Liberal interest, with W. T. Stead as his assistant. It was the only paper Gladstone could be bothered to look at – 'our faithful and able ally'.[15] As Morley's political ambitions flowered – he became an MP in 1883 – he became more congenial to Gladstone: an Oxonian, a *littérateur*, a classicist, in such respects so very different from Chamberlain.

The other aspect of Gladstone's drift away from the old political world was his growing easiness with a class of wealthy men of business, unproblematic and undemanding, who took pride in cultivating the great man in the coming years by subsidising his times of leisure and relaxation, especially on shipboard and at Continental wintering resorts. Donald Currie of the Castle shipping line was an early specimen of this genus: it was his yacht on which Gladstone had cruised in the Channel in 1877.

~

That the Queen had declared herself 'not thinking fit to be personally present' at the opening of the new Parliament was a matter Gladstone now brushed aside. He had prepared a slew of domestic measures to reward or placate interests made eligible by their honourable part in the question of the East. His budget would set the tone. With a bravura flourish of expertise, he abolished an old bugbear of the farming interest, the excise duty on malt and revenged himself on the Trade by a compensating increase of the beer duty. The Nonconformists were to have remedy for their grievance about burial in parish churchyards.[16] The trade unions were to be mollified in the matter of employers' liability in industrial accidents. The tenant farmers were to be assuaged in the matter of landlords' privileges as to ground game.

Gladstone recorded going down with Herbert to the Commons at the commencement of the business session on 20 May. 'It almost overpowered me as I thought by what deep and hidden agencies I have been brought back into the vortex of political action and contention.' He was vividly aware of a 'new access of strength' administered to him in his old age: and of the 'remarkable manner in which Holy Scripture has been inwardly applied' to him for 'admonition and comfort'. Looking calmly over the course of experience 'I do believe that the Almighty has employed me for His purposes in a manner larger or more special than before, and has strengthened me and led me on accordingly'.[17]

The sessional thrust was to be devoted primarily to exorcising 'Beaconsfieldism' in the external spheres. In her preliminary negotiations with Gladstone, the Queen, on the advice of Granville and Hartington, had stipulated that as far as foreign and colonial affairs were concerned, Gladstone must accept the '*facts*' as accomplished by the Beaconsfield regime. There was the question also of having given offence in certain quarters. Gladstone made no difficulty over expressing prompt regret to the Austrian Ambassador for the 'polemical language' he had used 'individually' at Midlothian, 'when in a position of greater freedom and less responsibility'.[18] As far as the '*facts*' were concerned, Gladstone recognized that the Treaty of Berlin was public law and beyond his reach. Rather more reluctantly, he accepted that the status quo would apply also to the Anglo-Turkish Convention. He would have liked to repudiate it and transfer the administration of Cyprus from the Foreign to the Colonial Office; but thought it prudent, in view of his ambitions to resuscitate the European Concert, not to compromise his government's strict adherence to diplomatic correctness. He steadily resisted pressures from the Liberal backbenches led by Peter Rylands to apply the Ionian precedent, buy out Turkish interests, and allow *enosis*.

Gladstone's strategy in resuscitating the Concert was to use the Treaty of Berlin as a fulcrum upon which the Turks could be levered into compliance with the provisions relating to frontier 'rectifications' favourable to Greece and Montenegro. He started laying the ground for this by removing Austen Layard from Constantinople and replacing him with Goschen. He impressed upon the Ottoman Ambassador in London that the idea that 'in the last resort the Ottoman Power is a British interest to be sustained by our arms does *not* form the basis or any part of our policy'.[19] The Continental chancelleries were made aware of Britain's determination to give this lead and sustain it. Peter Saburov, Russian Ambassador in Berlin, declared only half mockingly in May 1880: 'Behold at long last, the realization of the philosophers' dream. The Concert of Europe is established.'[20]

Granville and Goschen prepared the way as best they could, to the bemusement and wonder of the statesmen of Europe, who echoed Saburov's pronouncement, usually in somewhat more mocking tones. The Turks proved adept at procrastination and fertile in evasion. Gladstone fumed at the Sultan Abdul Hamid, 'the greatest of all liars on earth', 'a bottomless pit of fraud and falsehood'.[21] It would not be until October that Gladstone could see daylight in the affair.

~

When, meanwhile, it came to the '*facts*' of Afghanistan and South Africa, Gladstone was rather more guardedly reluctant than in the Turkish case. His assigned mission was 'special'; and its 'peculiarity' was that it mainly related to overseas questions.[22] Getting out of Afghanistan was a relatively simple, almost purely military, matter. South Africa was much more complex.

Among the keenest observers of the fall of Beaconsfieldism were the Afrikaner 'Boers' of the annexed Transvaal Republic and the smaller Orange Free State. They had been studious hitherto to keep their case for retrocession before Gladstone's eyes. They read eagerly his words at Midlothian lamenting their Beaconsfieldian captivity. Now that Gladstone had come triumphantly to power, they were prompt to ask deliverance at his hands. This their deputies Kruger and Joubert formally did on 10 May 1880. Given their natural expectations, Gladstone's refusal came as a dismaying rebuff. Gladstone regretted that so many settlers of Dutch stock should want to repudiate the boons of government under the British Crown. 'We have to deal with a state of things which has existed for a considerable period, during which obligations have been contracted, especially, though not exclusively, towards the native population, which cannot be set aside.'

The annexations of 1877, after all, had been effected by Lord Carnarvon. Having reconciled French and British Canadians within the federal Dominion in the 1860s, Carnarvon's ideal was to reconcile Afrikaners and British within a South African Confederation. Taking a broader view, perhaps, than was applicable at Midlothian, this was not an unworthy aim. Gladstone assured the Afrikaners that, consistently with the maintenance of the Crown's sovereignty, 'we desire that the white inhabitants of the Transvaal should without prejudice to the rest of the population enjoy the fullest liberty to manage their local affairs'; which liberty would most easily and promptly be conceded 'to the Transvaal as a member of a South African confederation'.[23]

Apart from the annexation's being the 'fact' of the case, Gladstone was impressed by the Colonial Office argument that there was a positive balance of benefits for all concerned in going ahead with the existing scheme of a confederation, and that Bartle Frere, Governor of the Cape and proconsular strongman, should have his tenure extended to achieve it. That seemed to be that. All that was now required was for Frere and the Governor of Natal, Major-General Sir George Colley, to coax or intimidate the Afrikaners into compliance. All this caused restiveness in the Liberal ranks at Westminster. There too there was dismay at Gladstone's turnabout on the Transvaalers struggling to be free. They wanted Frere to be sacked and the Transvaal restored forthwith to freedom in the same spirit as the liberation of the Afghans struggling to be free. For Gladstone there was the strategically residual political 'fact' that he could get away with one renunciation of imperial power, but not two. Hartington was spokesman for restive Liberals of a different stamp.

The Transvaal and Afghanistan were far away. A swell of Irish expectations was uncomfortably near. The very fact of Gladstone's coming to power at the head of a Liberal government in itself guaranteed a recurrence of the tide of hopes and expectations of 1868. Justin McCarthy, one of the more prominent younger Home Rulers, explained that the Irish people 'usually look to a Liberal Government for relief from their grievances'. The new Prime Minister, after all, 'was the first English Minister who had ever risked his reputation on the introduction of great and statesmanlike legislation for the benefit of Ireland'. Would not Mr Gladstone, who had extolled the tradition of Fox, recognise Fox's doctrine that Ireland should be governed 'in accordance with Irish ideas'?[24] At Dublin in 1877, Gladstone had, seemingly, applied that doctrine quite decidedly to the question of landlordism and tenancy-purchase; and he had endorsed that attitude quite unequivocally in the Commons in 1879.

The question of how to respond to the Irish problem was raised quite early and quite specifically. In April William Rathbone, the Liverpool notable, put the point to Gladstone that by far the greatest hope for the Liberal future was 'the work of constructing an efficient system of local government for Ireland and Great Britain – which would not only satisfy all that is reasonable in the Home Rule demand but also regenerate local government in this country'. As for the question of tackling the land question in Ireland, Rathbone assumed that Shaw-Lefevre's 1879 report on tenant-purchase would be the nub of it, and suggested accordingly that Shaw-Lefevre and another radical exponent of a fresh start on Irish land, the O'Conor Don, be made under-secretaries at the Irish Office.[25]

Rathbone's initiative can be judged in retrospect as the most tellingly significant document bearing on the domestic fortunes of Gladstone's second ministry. It set out the essentials both for Ireland and Britain of what might most beneficially have been done. The most tellingly significant aspect of it therefore was that Gladstone snubbed it. He dismissively shunted Shaw-Lefevre off to the Board of Works and ignored the O'Conor Don.

Why was this so? It was of course the case that Gladstone's being in Dublin in 1877 was at a time of greater freedom and less responsibility. And for Gladstone, back in the Treasury, things would in 1880 to some extent necessarily take on a different aspect from those more spacious days. But such considerations hardly amount to a convincing explanation of the reasons behind his decision to snub Rathbone's initiative in 1880, and to snub every similar initiative thereafter from within both the Liberal party and the Conservative Opposition for the term of his second ministry.

What soon becomes evident in 1880 was that for Gladstone the great 'fact' of the Irish case remained his heroic Land Act of 1870. Does explanatory cogency consist in the very heroism of that measure? Looking at large at this new phase of Gladstone's career it is not difficult to detect much of what his colleagues had already detected: that he was ill-attuned to politics other than on a scale of grandeur. The psychic impact of his experiences in the grand drama of the Eastern question immensely reinforced this predisposition. How could God's instrument trouble himself with county councils and sale and purchase of tenancies?

His instinct now in any case was to cling to the Land Act as a life-raft amid the storms and surges of the Irish swell. The energy and impulse within that swell was generated by the impact of immediate and critical agricultural depression. As agricultural returns declined, Irish landlords lacked as a rule the margins often available in England for reducing or remitting rents. Incidence of eviction for non-payment of rent mounted horrendously from 1877. In 1879 at Westport an Irish Land League was formed, inspired mainly by the land nationalization advocate Michael Davitt, adopting a programme for the abolition of landlordism root and branch as alien to Irish custom, history and nationhood.

Present at Westport was the young MP (since 1875) for County Meath, Charles Stewart Parnell, a Protestant Wicklow gentleman of family who had made his name as the destroyer of Isaac Butt's leadership of the Home Rule movement. Parnell now was sessional chairman of the 35 'Mountain' or 'Jacobin' faction of Home Rule MPs who sat on Opposition benches, by contrast to the 30 'Girondins' led by William Shaw on the Liberal side of the Commons. It was Parnell's genius to understand that something was now possible in Ireland that hitherto had not been possible: a union of middle-class, urban nationalism with organized agrarian agitation. Three essential components of a great new Irish question were now in place: an extensive Irish grievance, Parnell's and Davitt's inspirational leadership and Gladstone's presence at the head of a Liberal government.

By mid-June of 1880 Gladstone belatedly realized that he had on his hands a first-class crisis compounded of a disturbing force of old Irish hopes and expectations augmented by new styles of organized agitation. Forster's and Cowper's reports from Dublin were dark with prognostications of great evil and civil tumult unless immediate remedial measures were taken to stem the incidence of evictions. Gladstone was dismayed to be made aware that there had long been urgent cause for concern about matters that did not come within the confines of the assigned mission with which he had taken office.

Forster proposed legislation to discourage or inhibit evictions for a temporary period in certain circumstances in restricted areas. This Compensation for Disturbance Bill raised a ruckus in Cabinet. It challenged 'English ideas'. Gladstone had much ado persuading Argyll not to resign. But Hartington's Under-secretary at the India Office, Lansdowne, did resign; the first pebble in what threatened to prove a Whig avalanche. Gladstone summoned Rosebery to fill the gap; and defended Forster's bill as being in the 'nature of a promise or engagement to the poorest part of the population of Ireland, now suffering heavily under a severe visitation of Providence'.[26]

After furious wrangling, the Compensation Bill was rammed through the Commons. Fifty Liberals abstained on the second reading, and twenty voted against. It was promptly thrown out by the Lords on 3 August. Gladstone's memory of the affair retained a vivid touch of bitterness in 1897. 'I was unhappily blind to the magnitude of the coming difficulties in Ireland; blind to them in part owing to the favourable picture which until recently the working of the Land Act of 1870 had presented, in part to the absorbing nature of the foreign questions in which I had been so long engaged, and with which I had to deal almost single-handed.' A 'wild excess of landlordism' in the 'disastrous' rejection of the Compensation Bill by the Lords then led to a 'rapid and vast extension of agrarian disturbance' that forced the government to resort to coercive legislation.[27]

~

Even as Gladstone became aware of dismaying Irish revelations, it was borne in upon him that his assumptions about South Africa were also unravelling. Apologetic though he might have been to the Liberal party in the Commons, he remained unapologetic to the Transvaalers.[28] This converted the swell of disappointed Afrikaner anticipations of deliverance into a whirlpool of bitterness and exasperation. Disorders in South Africa began to take on what contemporaries could not fail to interpret as a sinister Irish analogy: British power was being challenged equally by Boers in the Bogs and Fenians on the Veldt. Before the end of June Kimberley advised Gladstone that the confederation policy had 'completely broken down'. There was no longer any good reason for not recalling Frere.[29]

The fact that Frere was emblematically the last of the grand proconsular exponents of the imperial idea only made the mass of Liberals the more eager for his head to roll. The Queen protested in vain. The Palmerstonians, led by Hartington, still smarting from the Compensation for Disturbance affair, found it a sore point. Great satisfaction was thus given to most Liberals and to the Transvaal Afrikaners. Logically, this should have prepared the way for a resumption of the spirit of Midlothian and a swift turnabout of policy in South Africa.

This did not happen. By the end of July Gladstone was reduced to a state of near collapse. He realized now that he had taken on the responsibilities of government in April in serious unawareness of what he would have to contend with. Beset in front with big questions of policy, he was being constantly harassed in the rear by the 'intrusion of irritating topics'. Parnell's Irish were fast perfecting the arts of parliamentary obstruction. The attempt by a 'Freethought' MP for Northampton,

Charles Bradlaugh, to take his oath by affirmation was fumbled by Speaker Brand, who let the issue get loose in the House. Lord Randolph Churchill, at the head of a 'Fourth Party' of Tory critics of the Conservative 'Old Gang', exploited the issue cleverly to incite a fractiously Christian Commons into uproar and further obstruction through sessions to come. For many Liberals it was their only way of baiting the G.O.M. At the end of July Gladstone was seized with 'chill and nausea'. He retreated to Wellesley's Deanery at Windsor to recuperate.

The Queen, already sardonic about 'the People's William', observed rather hopefully that 'Merry Pebble' was 'not what he was – he is *très baissé* and really a little crazy'. 'I doubt (and fervently hope) he won't be able to go through another session'.[30] For the present, Gladstone managed to return to both Cabinet and Commons before the prorogation on 7 September. He spoke on the Treaty of Berlin and his intention that the Turks should bow to Europe's will in the matter of the Greek and Montenegrin frontiers. That would be his set piece for the autumn recess.

In the interval he recruited health and spirits with a cruise on Donald Currie's steamer *Grantully Castle*. Hamilton found Currie, Liberal MP for Perthshire, a 'fawning and troublesome man'.[31] He seems to have suited Gladstone well enough. He got a knighthood in 1881 for his trouble. Accompanied by a large family party, Gladstone cruised westward, getting so far, in fact, as Dublin. There the party arrived 'in time to land suddenly and go to Christ Church. The congregation all agog. Out of doors an enthusiastic extempore reception.' Back at Hawarden, refreshed, Gladstone was gratified to be given reason to hope that, in spite of the 'recent short-sighted action of the House of Lords', and Parnell's incitement to Irish popular revenge for it, Ireland might yet compose itself into a healthier mood. He thanked Captain William O'Shea, late of the 18th Hussars and an MP for County Clare, for his thoughtful reports on the 'warmth of Irish feeling' for Gladstone, exhibiting the 'union of the people and their pastors in opposition to extreme and subversive schemes'.[32]

Gladstone would not have been aware that O'Shea's wife Katharine (née Wood, niece of former Lord Chancellor Hatherley and sister of the future Field Marshal Sir Evelyn Wood) had become very intimate with Parnell; and in fact within a month of her husband's letter to Gladstone she and Parnell were lovers. That was a purely private affair, but had possible implications for the future. But an event with huge implications for the present was that a few days after O'Shea's letter the murdered body of Lord Mountmorres was found on his Galway estate.

~

What nonetheless was already exercising Gladstone's mind was redeeming the foremost of his Midlothian pledges in bringing Sultan Abdul Hamid to heel in the matter of the frontier rectifications for Greece and Montenegro stipulated in the Treaty of Berlin. His larger ambition was to use the treaty as a fulcrum upon which a resuscitated Concert of Europe could be levered into being, in hopes that it would establish itself as the habitual frame of reference for the diplomatic relations of the powers. For Gladstone, Bismarck's alliance with Austria in 1879 posed a threatening precedent: the possibility of a counter-alliance dividing Europe into rival armed camps.[33]

He admitted to Acton that he was as yet not quite sure of his capacity 'for a long and hard day's head work'.[34] But he could not afford to delay longer. He set about the tiresome attrition of stubborn Turkish resistance. A project to intimidate the Turks with a squadron of European warships dissolved into farce when it was disclosed that the Austrian and German contingents were under orders not to fire a shot. The ensuing storm of ridicule did severe damage to Gladstone's higher European ambitions. He got much better results from his project to occupy the Turkish Aegean port of Smyrna and sequestrate a considerable part of the Ottoman customs revenues. Bismarck fumed at what he judged Gladstone's reckless irresponsibility. What was a merit in a comrade in the *Kulturkampf* was highly undesirable in the fragile state of post-Berlin Europe. Bismarck recalled Palmerston's prediction that Gladstone would die in a madhouse.[35] Northcote relayed his fears to Beaconsfield of the dangers of Gladstone's thinking a European war as 'a less evil than European ridicule, and that he would try to cut his way out of the mess by some insane exploit'.[36]

The Smyrna exploit might well have turned into something like that; but in the end it was unnecessary. The Turks were made aware of the threat hanging over them. On 12 October they gave way. Thus it was that duly in 1881 the Greeks rejoiced at the accession of Epirus and Thessaly, and the Montenegrins at access to the Adriatic. All that was gratifying for Gladstone. But it was not to be the fulcrum of levering Europe into a new Concert frame of reference. Gladstone lacked the weight in Europe to keep the lever in place.

In any case the wearying realities of the domestic and Irish and South African scenes soon imposed themselves as unforgivingly as ever. By now in Ireland Forster was proposing a stringent new bout of coercion. The shock of Mountmorres's murder sent forth ripples of panic. The shunning of Captain Boycott, Lord Erne's agent in County Mayo, added a new word to the language. Forster demanded the suspension of *Habeas corpus* – imprisonment, in short, without trial. Gladstone resisted. He was overborne by his colleagues, even Bright and Chamberlain in the end. He never forgave Forster in his 'odious task'.[37] He determined on a counterweight grand remedial measure. The vital powers of 1868 would be revived. The thrust of his legislative centrepiece for 1881 would be a bravura Irish land measure.

After much wrestling through the autumn and winter months of 1880 with masses of Royal Commission and other material, Gladstone by December decided to take a stubbornly optimistic view of the working of his 1870 Act by persuading himself of its being 'one of general success, partial, and we may almost say, local, failure'. The thing to do was mark the causes of such failures and proceed accordingly. In this there was more than a reminiscent whiff of his sticking adamantly to his text in the reform debates of 1866 and 1867. His 'Treasury mind' would not readily contemplate funding an Irish agrarian revolution. The great remedial measure for Ireland in 1881 would be an improved version of the 1870 Land Act. The most extraordinary feature of Gladstone's preparation of it was his deliberate exclusion, even more marked than in 1870, of 'Irish ideas', as if they were a kind of contamination. He made no attempt to obtain consent and support in Ireland. Irish MPs were not consulted. Shaw withdrew from the Home Rule party. The Irish were almost forced into holding themselves aloof. Shaw-Lefevre considered this the most regrettable aspect of his procedure.[38]

It was also in December of 1880 that Kimberley broke the news to Gladstone that the Transvaal situation was deteriorating rapidly. Gladstone's unwillingness to follow the logic of that situation was now having consequences. Colley was uneasy at the likelihood of Boer disaffection deteriorating into an insurrection.[39] The Irish Office, itself in receipt of bad news about the arrest and indictment of Parnell and others for threatening violent resistance by the Land League to Forster's regime, had less reason than the Colonial Office to be 'stunned'. Colley was confident of restoring control. He himself was beyond control by a distracted Cabinet and a bewildered Colonial Office.

Amid all this, Godley and Hamilton presented Gladstone on his 71st birthday with a 'Gladstone Bag', with which 'he seemed to be much pleased'.[40] But for the first time in many years of office he was obliged to see the old year out at Downing Street. There would be need of procedural reforms to baffle obstruction. A Cabinet on the 30th left Gladstone 'too tired and distracted' to attend midnight service on the 31st. Thus Gladstone took farewell of 1880, which had opened with such golden promise: 'in the hand of God I plunge forward into the new'.

~

To the 1881 session in January Gladstone presented a 'further development of the principles of the 1870 Land Act' to meet the 'special needs of landlord and tenant', with provisions for giving a larger proportion of the people by purchase a 'permanent proprietary interest in the soil'. Additionally, there would be a 'measure for County Government in Ireland, founded upon representative principles', calculated to form 'habits of local self-government' and 'popular control over expenditure'.[41] Forster rammed his coercion measure past sticklers for the rule of law and frantic Irish obstruction. He could point to the fact that a Dublin jury had failed conspicuously to convict Parnell. The Lords pushed it through with exemplary dispatch and it was law by the beginning of March. In the background the 'advanced' Liberal benches were restive at the government's failure to put an end to the 'miserable Transvaal war'.

On 23 February, a slip on snow-powdered steps put Gladstone in bed for four days. On the day he was about to rise he was stunned by news of the reckless Colley's catastrophe at Majuba Hill at the hands of the insurgent Boers. Colley was dead and all his force either killed or captured. Gladstone 'slumped back in bed'. Was this the 'Hand of Judgment'?

'The work and pressure of Parliament', Gladstone told a Liberal MP, 'have nearly reduced me to inanition.'[42] On the following day, the background of events, already sombre enough, was darkened by news of the assassination of the Emperor Alexander II of Russia. There was a 'tumultuary' Cabinet on 22 March on the Transvaal over the Queen's objecting to the terms of the peace being arranged with the Boers by Sir Evelyn Wood. Gladstone could rejoice that demands for the vindication of British honour were fended off. It was fortunate that withdrawal from Afghanistan could be accomplished under cover of a brilliant feat of arms by Sir Frederick Roberts.

The dismal month of March culminated appropriately on the 31st with the resignation of the Duke of Argyll. He had been a Cabinet colleague of Gladstone since Aberdeen's ministry in 1852, and he counted as a close personal friend.[43] Argyll decided to go when the shape of the new Irish Land Bill became clear. He objected that it had never been part of the Midlothian programme. He deplored its being brought forth under terror. But his substantial criticism was that it was pointless to try again to prop up Irish landlords by depriving them of the last prerogatives of landed social authority and reducing them to mere collectors of shrunken rents.

Gladstone pressed on regardless. He was pretty much immune now to resignations. He called on Carlingford to fill the gap, much to Rosebery's annoyance. On the eve of the Easter recess he introduced his great set piece of the session, the Land Law (Ireland) Bill. It was a bravura performance in the old style of theatrical politics, displaying 'unequalled mastery of legislative skill and power'.[44] The measure took on the appearance of heroism in terms both of the luridly dramatic backdrop of the 'revolution' in Ireland and of its extraordinary complexity and voluminousness as a masterwork of legislative construction. It was a text expressive of Gladstone's personal authority. But it was hollow at the heart. Much play was made of its embodying the famed 'Three Fs' of Ulster tenant custom: fixity of tenure, freedom of sale of tenure and fair rent for tenure. They sounded impressive but in practice would make little difference. They represented the ultimate dead end of a futile policy. The Parnellites gained great credit from abstaining at the second reading; the loyal moderates gained nothing.

Of much greater consequence was the fate of the provisions for purchase of tenancies. Shaw-Lefevre hoped that these would be made into the substantive core of the measure.[45] He had to watch helplessly as Gladstone, driving the debates with astonishing 'mastery of detail', 'tact, judgment, good temper', 'outbursts of eloquence', and 'extraordinary physical power' through 32 nights in committee, whittled them down, much as he had done to Bright's clauses in 1870. By the time he pushed the bill through the Commons and negotiated his way imperiously through the Lords' amendments, the purchase provisions, in the words of another strong advocate of them, Salisbury, had 'shrunk and shrunk in the emphasis and importance given to them', until they were 'nothing but a tribute to the personal position of Mr Bright'.[46]

That this was perfectly deliberate on Gladstone's part is evident from his activities in the 1882 and 1883 sessions when he blocked and baffled all attempts to resuscitate the purchase clauses. Ultimately, in 1883, in the course of condemning as 'dangerous and impolitic' a new-fangled Conservative attempt to amend the 1881 Land Act to encourage tenant purchase, Gladstone contended with consummate deviousness that there was no point in revising the provisions for tenant purchase 'except with the introduction of a local authority'.[47] The trick, of course, was first to get your Irish Local Authority. For another measure that Gladstone made sure was whittled and shrunk in 1881 was the Irish Local Government Bill. By 11 July he lamented in the House that the press of business made any hope of 'Local Government Boards in Ireland' vanish 'into thin air'.[48] And that was precisely where, to the end of the 1880 Parliament, all such Irish local government initiatives vanished.

What was he up to? It is impossible not to speculate on what course the history of the Irish land question, and with it the Irish question at large, might have taken had Gladstone launched in 1881 a comprehensive tenancy purchase policy along the lines he sketched at Dublin in 1877. This was the land policy advocated by Irish opinion. Could Gladstone have made it, along with local government reform, as many Liberals such as Rathbone urged, a credible version of autonomy? Would the moderate Home Rulers have been thus munitioned against the Parnellites? Was a historic opportunity missed? Did he *want* that kind of credible version of autonomy?

As it was, he scored a brilliant parliamentary triumph against both Irish obstruction and the general lack of enthusiasm in the Liberal ranks, who had little grip on what he was about. Salisbury's efforts to rally Conservative resistance in the Lords crumbled. The House of Lords would not in the end resist any bill the Irish landlords were prepared to swallow. The Irish landlords were in a state of funk. Phillimore recorded Gladstone in July as 'radiant' at his victorious progress. 'It is either the government bill or the Land League now ... My bill is really a landlord's bill.' It was indeed a landlord's bill, but for a landlordism gutted of all point and purpose. To the Irish it remained, like the 1870 Act, an alien imposition, largely irrelevant, and accordingly compromised as a remedial measure.

~

On 31 August Eddie Hamilton looked back over the session whose labours had exceeded those of any other legislature in the world, dominated by the 'Great Man', 'standing head and shoulders and likewise body, over everybody else'.[49] Beaconsfield's death, on 19 April, removed the only rival contender. It was not unexpected. Knowing the Queen's feelings – she had been sending the dying man cheering bouquets of primroses – Gladstone immediately 'sent to tender a public funeral'. This was gratefully declined by Beaconsfield's executors. He had stipulated to be buried beside Mary Anne at Hughenden.

In reporting to Harry in Calcutta, Gladstone gathered his thoughts about the noble deceased, 'whose rival some call me, much against my will, for I am not and never was his rival, as far as it depended on my will or intention'. He felt there was 'something very touching' in Beaconsfield's 'determination to be buried by the side of his wife. His devoted and grateful attachment to her was I think the brightest spot in his whole life.' Gladstone held also that he had been 'most widely and sharply severed' from Beaconsfield by 'something totally different from personal hatred'; and he was 'bound to say' he did not think Beaconsfield 'felt any hatred' towards himself.[50] It was undoubtedly true that Gladstone's personal feelings were in some recondite sense different from personal hatred, though it would take an attentive student both of Gladstone's psychic energies of combativeness and his special kind of Butlerian Christianity to delineate precisely that distinction.

Like Palmerston, Beaconsfield was much more conventionally resentful at what, uncomprehendingly, they both felt to be a vindictive persecution. Beaconsfield cultivated something of an obsession about Gladstone's 'vindictiveness'. Cardinal Manning had once told him that he thought Gladstone 'the most revengeful man he ever knew'.[51] All such accusations have to be considered in the light of Gladstone's devotion to Butler's doctrines about the Christian duties of statesmen 'in that conflict between virtue and vice, which incessantly prevails in the world'.[52] It is open to be considered that, just as he sublimated sexuality by an office of rescue, so Gladstone sublimated innate combativeness by an office of distributing marks of justice in the world. Such devotion does not necessarily refute Beaconsfield (or Manning), though it goes far to explain Gladstone.

Because of prior engagements Gladstone found it impossible to attend the funeral at Hughenden. Perhaps it was the widespread observation visited on Gladstone for his absence that provoked his much less generous remarks to Hamilton about Beaconsfield's 'pose' of simplicity in choosing the Hughenden parish graveyard. Beaconsfield's most striking characteristic, exacerbated by his Judaic feeling, Gladstone thought, was 'the utter absence of any love of liberty'.[53] For Gladstone it was seriously a 'great difficulty' to deliver a parliamentary tribute without dissembling. In the end he pulled it off quite handsomely, choosing to enlarge on Beaconsfield's 'great parliamentary courage'. The Queen expressed herself 'much gratified'.[54]

Perhaps it was Beaconsfield's passing that quickened Gladstone's 'brooding upon the desire, scarcely yet a hope', as he put it to Harry, of escaping from politics. 'But I do not know when or how God will open the door for me. Last year I used to say it would be this year, and this year I am beginning to say it will be next year.'[55] It was Morley's opinion that Gladstone 'should have retired in 1881'.[56] Already, in 1881, it had become clear to Gladstone's colleagues that his oft-repeated yearnings to receive his order of release were creating a sense of unease. It had become a contingency ever hanging in the Cabinet air, inhibiting a settled capacity to look ahead, causing uncertainty, allowing Gladstone to indulge himself even more than had been his wont in matters congenial and to put off matters uncongenial. Granville complained apropos of Gladstone's incessant talk of retirement that he complicated the situation 'by insisting on discussing all Cabinet arrangements on the hypothesis that he might again shortly repeat the *coup de tête* of 1875'.[57] A mood of improvisation infected the governmental process.

A good part of the problem was that Gladstone continued astonishingly active, a ready fund of 'vital force' being ever in reserve. He revived quickly after heavy expenditures of energy. Although there were political problems enough, he was no longer oppressed by being a leader at odds with his own party. He combined a commanding new position of leadership with plausible hopes of being soon able to divest himself, at convenience, of leadership. In the autumn and winter of 1881 there were complaints about the 'indecency' of lack of Cabinets while he canvassed colleagues on his imminent retirement, 'subject to the condition that the calls to special exigency should cease'.[58] Phillimore guessed that he would retire in May 1882.[59] Catherine, entirely symbiotic with his public career, devoted herself to dissuading him.[60]

Eddie Hamilton sceptically observed Gladstone's mind continuing to work on the 'question of disentangling himself from office'. Hamilton's own belief was that it was 'impossible for him to desert the helm so long as Ireland remains in this critical state'; and Ireland would take much longer to settle down than Gladstone, 'with too sanguine expectations, reckons'.[61] Indeed, Gladstone had already confessed to Bright that, while the questions of Ireland and the Transvaal hung in the balance, his 'mission' of April 1880 could not be regarded as having been fulfilled. 'From neither of them can I run away.'[62]

~

The Transvaal question was to be resolved by the British Crown's annulment of the 1877 annexations and replacing full sovereignty with a suzerainty comprising control of the external relations of the republics and a Resident representing the Crown who would salve the Liberal conscience in the matter of the native black inhabitants. That the Convention cobbled together at Pretoria in August 1881 was eventually ratified sullenly by the *Volksraad* was all that Gladstone for the moment needed. But Kruger would no more accept the Convention as an adequate or ultimate 'wise and courageous concession' than would Parnell accept the Land Act.

For Parnell and the Land League the Land Act functioned primarily as a convenient target. By all means let it be a landlords' measure: Parnell demanded that the Irish rental be reduced from £17 million to £2 or 3 million per annum. Forster, having scooped up hundreds of suspects in his coercive net, wanted now a special session to legislate for the suppression of the Land League, with its 'No Rent' slogan. He also disconcerted Gladstone with intelligence that Parnell was preparing a campaign of deliberate provocation. Gladstone's hopes of emulating the 'wise and courageous concessions' to the Boers by commencing the release of Forster's captives were dashed. At Dublin in September Parnell led a torchlight parade, halting outside the old Irish Parliament and pointing silently at it, to rapturous applause. Gladstone countered with an even bigger torchlight parade at Leeds, and the resonant threat that the 'resources of civilisation were not exhausted'. Parnell retorted at Wexford with calculated insolence. Gladstone's riposte at the Guildhall in London on 13 October was to announce Parnell's arrest and imprisonment and the suppression of the Land League, to rapturous applause.

To Forster Gladstone confided his hopes that by these drastic measures 'a more intelligent & less impassioned body of opinion' might be formed and extended in Ireland. For if that country remained divided between 'Orangemen & law-haters' 'our task is hopeless', 'for if we are at war with a nation we cannot win'.[63] Shaw-Lefevre had some relevant thoughts about the Irish nation and opportunity missed. 'Had they listened to the demand for Land Reform put forward by the Irish constituencies, the present crisis might have been averted, and the programme of the Land League defeated.'[64]

As it was, the resources of civilization were to be severely tested by escalating 'outrages' and disaffection. And there were indications that they might soon be needed elsewhere. The Afrikaners were demanding a renegotiation of the Pretoria Convention. Gladstone agreed with Kimberley that 'we need only to hold our ground' and wear them down.[65] Signs were gathering also of another nation beginning to be troublesome. The problem of Egypt began to emerge. Under the strain of devoting most of its revenue to servicing the debt as administered by the Anglo-French Control, the khedival regime was starting to crack. In this case Gladstone had a resource not available to him in the Bogs or on the Veldt: there was 'Europe'. He and Granville agreed that, with French and Turkish assistance, the status quo could be maintained.

Indeed, what struck Hamilton most vividly in these last months of 1881 was Gladstone's extraordinary animation and vivacity, 'in wonderful force', never 'looking better or more cheery'. His parting words as Hamilton returned to London in November were about retirement – 'on which he is continually harping, and on which he harps too much'. There were important consequences. Uncertainty about future policy or arrangements of business created incoherence in Cabinet and administration generally. Paradoxically, the more Gladstone harped, the more he became the one figure of coherence in his government. His immense, enveloping presence, redolent of the invulnerability conferred upon him by his messianic repute in the country, had the effect of licensing his colleagues to loosen their own sense of obligation to cohere for the sake of the party.

There were important consequences also for the party. Throughout 1882 and 1883 indications became increasingly observable of divergences between Gladstone's Liberalism and 'Gladstonian Liberalism'. With the coming of the 1882 session, came pleadings from Gladstonian Liberals that the party and the government realize Liberalism's manifest vocation to see through a great historic measure to reform local government in Britain and Ireland and the government of London on an elective and efficient basis. The old order of traditional Quarter Sessions appointed by lords-lieutenant in the counties and the intricate muddle of London government were no longer tolerable. Consistently, throughout these sessions Gladstone offered grandiloquent phrases but avoided effective commitment. He promised legislation of 'free and large decentralisation' for local government in the three kingdoms. This would stand 'in the very first rank when Parliament is enabled to resume the work of general legislation'; the set-piece for 1882.[66] Somehow, nothing came of it. To Harcourt at the Home Office, Gladstone doubted that dealing with the government of London would be feasible in any case in 1882. Plans for Irish local government reform were dropped even before the commencement of the session.

By 1883 the Gladstonian Liberals were getting seriously rattled. The Irish 'Girondins', damned unwittingly by Gladstone with faint praise as 'nominal' Home Rulers, had given up the fight. Liberals were baffled at the disappearance of the very promising devolutionary national 'Grand Committees' that had been started up to relieve the Commons of burdens. Harcourt thought that 'critical questions were shunted or evaded in the November Cabinets'. Illness drove Gladstone to take refuge in Wolverton's villa at Cannes for nearly six weeks in the new year. Hartington deplored 'our unprepared condition'.[67] In May the London Municipal Bill was abandoned. Gladstone made noises of regret, but his point was that it would be difficult to find room for it in any future sessions of the 1880 Parliament.[68] Here he spoke as a semi-detached outsider, almost an onlooker. The incoherences this permitted developed into quarrels. Gladstone became a peacemaker, having no energizing dynamism to offer. Soon Gladstone preferred not calling Cabinets, leaving important decisions to informal 'Cabals'.[69]

There were protests in the party that told of deep Liberal dismay. Rathbone, oppressed more than ever with the loss of Ireland's precious time, put the case to Gladstone that local government could safely be extended to Ireland. 'I do not see how we can settle Ireland without Local Govt reform & yet how to do this I do not see except by passing a Bill for England which ... the Irish would ask to be extended to Ireland.' Whitbread had had a bill drawn for himself and Rathbone that 'would apply even more easily for Ireland than England & no party there would venture to oppose a measure which would give much relief'. Rathbone pleaded that Gladstone ensure the carrying of such a bill in the 1884 session.[70] Assimilation of the county franchise, due in 1884, while of course desirable and essential, was a matter of electoral mechanics, not nutritious legislative substance. London MPs pleaded in vain that the London Municipal Bill be saved. Popular opinion favoured it. The time was opportune. Squabbles about details should not be allowed to hinder. It was 'a noble conception nobly worked out'. The feeling of the party in the Commons was that 'it should be made the test of the legislative power of the party'.[71]

Rathbone duly drew for Gladstone the moral of the tale about testing the legislative power of the party. 'But what I would ask you kindly to consider is whether this is not the time when, if the Party is vigorously pulled together, this Parliament may yet be led to accomplish what is reasonably expected from it and the fearful danger be avoided of a bitter sense of want of confidence in the House of Commons becoming rooted in the mind of the thinking part of all classes.' Either, urged Rathbone, 'the Party should go to their leaders, or the leaders should appeal to the party publicly to declare that it is not safe any longer to allow the labour of the House of Commons to be so barren of results'. MPs like Whitbread wanted the party called together soon 'to secure a reasonable amount of legislation', even if as a 'diminished programme'. Rathbone quite understood that Gladstone had been under a 'tremendous strain'. So why not let Hartington take over while Gladstone recruited his strength and kept his 'leadership of the nation'? The 'Liberal Party would be on honour to work all the more loyally and better for fear lest any failure on their part should bring you back from your needed repose'.[72]

This backbench desperation cut very close to Gladstone's bone. In a way Rathbone had divined the very essence of Gladstone's noxiously semi-detached leadership since 1875. In another way he was making a devastatingly accurate critique of how Gladstone's 'leadership of the nation' nullified the parliamentary Liberal party. And if there was one lesson that experience over the years as leader of the Liberal party had taught Gladstone, it was to have as few meetings of the party as possible. In any case, Rathbone's pleadings achieved nothing more substantial in 1883 than the Corrupt Practices Act. This item of 'electoral mechanics' was successful at suppressing excessive and corrupt electoral expenditure. It was intended, like the Ballot, to hurt the Conservatives. Like the Ballot, it failed to do so. It had the unintended consequence of stimulating the brilliantly effective system of unpaid activism on behalf of the Conservative party in the massively popular memorial to Beaconsfield, the Primrose League.

~

Dismay among Liberals like Rathbone, Whitbread and others in 1883 at the lack of nutritiously substantive legislation reflected the nature of Gladstone's most dramatic exploits in 1882. The first, early in May, was to release Parnell and other of Forster's captives from Kilmainham jail and to end coercion and clear arrears of tenants' debt in return for understandings relating to the cooling of agitation generally and the dropping of the 'No Rent' campaign against the Land Act in particular. The second exploit was to invade and occupy Egypt in September in order to rescue the Khedive and his regime from an insurrection led by Colonel Arabi Bey. Both these operations were immensely controversial. Gladstone saw them as episodes within his Midlothian frame of reference. He was promoting Parnell as another sort of Kruger and the 'Kilmainham Treaty' – a term he much deplored – as another sort of Pretoria Convention. He invaded and occupied Egypt in the name of Europe and under its authority. The Arabists he identified in effect as the Land Leaguers and law-haters of Egypt.

Chamberlain and Morley had run a campaign in the *Pall Mall Gazette* to get Parnell released as a preliminary to a deal. They wanted Forster and his coercive apparatus to be dumped. Chamberlain conveyed – and 'leaked' – information to Cabinet conveyed to him by Captain O'Shea as emissary from Parnell. Gladstone himself was favoured with intelligence from Mrs O'Shea. Her achievement was to convince Gladstone that Parnell 'was a much altered man after Kilmainham', and that he showed 'evident conservative proclivities' that Gladstone would 'do his utmost to encourage'.[73] At a Cabinet on 1 May Gladstone noted: 'There has been no negotiation. But we have obtained information. The moment is golden.' He made his ministerial statement in the astonished and bewildered Commons on 2 May.

Forster would not accept the deal and resigned. Cowper was in any case intending to retire. Spencer, already primed, slotted smoothly into his place. Who to replace Forster? Chamberlain in many ways was the obvious choice. A Liberal MP put the case to Gladstone: 'Many of the Irish Parliamentary party have spoken to me today about the Chief Secretary ... They say that Mr Chamberlain is the only man who is strong enough for the post. They would respect his determination.'[74] It seems clear in any case that Gladstone did not want a Chief Secretary who had an independent standing in Cabinet. Dilke refused his offer outside the Cabinet. Gladstone offered it to his family favourite, 'the son of his right hand', Lord Frederick Cavendish, a kind of substitute Willy, eminently supervisable.

Lord Frederick accordingly crossed over to Dublin Castle to acquaint himself with the Irish administration. On Saturday, 6 May, while walking in the sunshine in Phoenix Park within sight of the Viceregal Lodge, Lord Frederick and his companion, Burke, the Under-secretary at the Castle, were cut to death by the knives of a Fenian gang.

The shock broke the Gladstones down completely but briefly. They went at once to Lady Frederick at Carlton House Terrace. 'This grief lay heavy and stunning upon us', Gladstone recorded, 'but with much to do and think of as to Parliament, Ireland, and many things and persons.' Phillimore saw him on the 8th at Carlton House Terrace, 'quite crushed'. That day, as he told Hartington, 'I was reluctant to go to the House for fear I should give way and make a scene: but it was thought requisite.' There Gladstone managed to get through 'the most painful task that ever devolved on me when standing at this Table'. Parnell declared his abhorrence of the atrocious deed and dissociated himself and his party from its perpetrators. On 10 May there was a 'stiff Cabinet of four hours on the Prevention of Crime Bill – a good spirit on both sides has carried us through'. At the Chatsworth funeral on the 11th the mourners were near 30,000.

The Phoenix Park tragedy and that 'good spirit' certainly blunted the edge of what otherwise might have been very sharp divisions within the Liberal party. Forster's refusal to be party to a policy of appeasing terrorists attracted much indignant sympathy and support. On 15 May Gladstone introduced an Arrears of Rent (Ireland) Bill, costed not to exceed £2 million. This was contentious. The Irish Church surplus would be brought to bear. Gladstone trimmed the Liberal ship with a further turn of the coercion screw, renewing suspension of *Habeas corpus* and juries and enlarging powers of search and repression of intimidation and secret societies. It was left to the Conservatives to articulate indignation. Balfour declared of the 'Kilmainham Treaty' that he did not believe that 'any such transaction could be quoted from the annals of our political and parliamentary history'; it 'stood alone in its infamy'.[75] This, coming from one whom he had coupled with Frederick Cavendish as 'the flower of rising manhood in the land', grieved Gladstone sorely.

But he, and the Liberal government, survived it. Salisbury's set to against the Arrears Bill in the Lords crumbled much as had his earlier set to against the Land Act. For Gladstone now it was a matter of hanging on and waiting for Irish affairs to settle down. Was not Parnell an 'altered man'? And were there not encourageable 'proclivities' to be developed from that great fact? Before long there were reports of Gladstone's dinner-table conversation to the effect that the events of April and May 'had completely changed, as by religious conversion, the character and views of the Irish leader'.[76] This faith that Parnell really had been converted into something better than a Kruger, into no less than a second O'Connell, remained the prime bearing of Gladstone's Irish compass. It gave him hope that, whatever the distortions and obscurities incidental to the contours of the political terrain in the short view, in the long view his reading of the course and direction was true. He appointed the superviseable G. O. Trevelyan to succeed Cavendish in Ireland.

Thus in the aftermath of horrific tragedy Gladstone did not despond. It seemed, however, that Colonel Arabi in Egypt was not a man producible to be another Parnell. The Khedive attempted a coup against him. It misfired, and Arabi emerged stronger than ever. There were those, such as the Byronic adventurer Wilfrid Blunt, who had set himself up as tribune of Egyptian liberty, and Sir William Gregory, former Irish MP and Governor of Ceylon, who tried to convince Gladstone that Arabi was Egypt's best hope. Gregory discerned the danger of Egypt's being reduced to a 'coupon-paying machine directed by European Controllers and administered solely for European Employees'.[77] A rally of non-interventionists appealed to Gladstone not to commit a great wrong 'of a kind which you have denounced with special force for the sake of the bondholders'.[78]

Gladstone refused to be impressed. He was, after all, an extensive bondholder himself. His holding of £19,400 of the Egyptian Tribute Loan made up 37 per cent of his portfolio. Its value would increase enormously. But he knew perfectly well he was not acting in his own interest. He insisted that Arabi represented 'military violence and nothing else'.[79] While protesting that he stood by all his Midlothian sentiments as to 'Egypt for the Egyptians' as the best solution for the 'Egyptian Question', Gladstone thought Blunt had been 'a good deal humbugged by Arabi Bey'.[80] Riots and massacres of Europeans in Alexandria in June confirmed Gladstone in his opinion. He reacted indignantly to any suggestion that he was playing the bondholders' game, or that things were 'drifting into war'. A conference of interested parties at Constantinople proved barren of expedients. The Turks demanded too high a price for any exertions. The French, to whom most of the money was owed, seemed willing to intervene, but that would depend on volatile politics in the Chamber.

Things became intense. There were 'stormy' Cabinets as the Arrears Bill stuck in the Lords. Dilke observed 'Mr Gladstone mixing Ireland and Egypt together, broke out in the House of Commons on July 7th, and afterwards told his colleagues that he intended to resign!' Dilke witnessed 'Mr G's Homeric rage – and – defeat'. Granville felt obliged to beg his colleagues 'to remember who Mr Gladstone was, and not to press him too hard in discussion'. In other words, as Dilke decoded, 'told them to remember they were dealing with a magnificent lunatic'. Gladstone's rage, Dilke was sure, had much to do with the fact that he was being overborne by the merest subordinates: 'he looks upon us as clerks and boys – clerks like Northbrook and Childers, and naughty boys like Hartington, Chamberlain and myself'.[81]

Hartington had come to the point of insisting that for the security of the Suez Canal intervention could not be avoided; and he much preferred that it be without Turks or French. Harassed by the Arrears crisis, Gladstone's grip on the Egyptian crisis loosened. Gladstone, reported Granville to Hartington, admitted to him 'for the first time that we were bound to protect the Suez Canal.'[82] Under pressure from the forward party Gladstone too had got to the point of conceding the possibility of single-handed intervention – he always found the French embarrassingly obsessed with the bondholding aspect – but in any case would not act apart from 'the authority of Europe'.[83]

On 11 July the signal was sent to Admiral Seymour to bombard and reduce the fortifications of Alexandria. Harcourt jested sardonically: 'At last we have done something popular.' Bright resigned in disgust, declaring that it was worse than anything Dizzy ever did. Gladstone insisted that 'in being party to this work, I have been a labourer in the cause of peace'.[84] On 29 July Freycinet's ministry fell in the French Chamber and with it any last chance of French partnership in intervention. A vote of credit was arranged. Britain alone would exercise the will of Europe.[85]

Sir Garnet Wolseley was appointed to command an expedition to rescue the people of Egypt from Arabi and restore the legitimate authority of the Khedive. To Henry Richard's agonized protest on behalf of the Peace Society, Gladstone responded that he was not conscious of any change in his own standard of action, or in that of his colleagues, 'since the day when, after three military miscarriages, we tried severely the temper of this nation by declining to shed the blood of the Boers of the Transvaal, and afford them peace'.[86]

In August Gladstone achieved his Arrears Act to fulfil his bargain with Parnell, with the bonus of humiliating the House of Lords and Lord Salisbury. Good news of Wolseley's progress began to come through in September. On the 13th Wolseley presented him with a splendid victory over Arabi's army at Tel-el-Kebir. Arabi was a captive. The way was open for a swift occupation of Cairo. Gladstone was master of the Nile, the Canal, the crossroads of the world.

~

With his legislative barrenness in the 1880 Parliament, Gladstone was the wrecker of Gladstonian Liberalism. With his invasion and occupation of Egypt he wrecked Gladstonian Liberalism's international morale. The gap yawned between Gladstone's Liberalism and Gladstonian Liberalism. For the time all was obscured by extraneous circumstance. As to barrenness, there was always the consideration that with the assimilation of the county franchise Conservatism would be dealt a permanently crippling electoral blow, and thus Liberalism's habitual contract with the people, restored in 1880, had a prospect before it of virtually guaranteed golden promise. As to international morale, Gladstone devoted inordinate attention to arranging triumphant ringing of bells and booming of guns. He summed it all up to Madame Novikov. 'We and the whole country are in a state of rejoicing, and I hope of thankfulness to God Almighty, who has prospered us in what I feel and know to be an honest undertaking ... we certainly ought to be in a good humour, for we are pleased with our army, our navy, our admirals, our generals, & our organisation. Matters were not so conducted in the days of the Crimea.'[87]

In a general way, despite protests from the Midlothian faithful, it did little harm to Gladstone to be laurelled with Egyptian victories. The Conservatives, having not quite known whether to hope for the best or the worst, had to concede that ministers had done their duty to the national interest. Ireland now seemed to be settling down to something closer to 'normal' disaffection. Egypt looked to be definitively settled, subject to later arrangements for withdrawal once the Khedive's regime was secure. True, the Transvaal Boers were still restless. As Gladstone later put it to Ponsonby, the 1881 Convention was 'not a measure embodying a sound and perfect system of relations but an expedient, the best which the difficult circumstances permitted, and which was to be tried by its working and results'.[88] For Gladstone, these events confirmed his confidence in the workings of a benign providential order within which his own inspired role took its assigned place. 'I too have my "Grammar of Assent"', he observed in allusion to Newman. 'The frame and constitution of things wherein we live teach me to believe in an Author of unbound intelligence who works towards justice truth and mercy.'[89]

This was not, however, the view taken of things by much of the Liberal public of the Midlothian ethos. They were shocked and disillusioned. It was a characteristic Liberal of that anxiously idealistic stamp who asked for reassurance from Gladstone that the Egyptian affair was not as bad as it looked. Surely the debt could have been compounded? The whole business looked dismally like 'a war of bondholders against the Egyptian peasants'.[90] That remained for Gladstone their problem, not his.

With Egypt thus marginalized and Ireland and the Transvaal simmering difficulties rather than critical problems, Gladstone was freer to look about him. On the face of things retirement looked to be an optimum opportunity. It was Gladstone's political jubilee: what more appropriate time to go? Yet as ever it was not a matter for his own decision. His obsessive harping about it, like his obsessive talk of grand initiatives in local government, rang curiously false. He achieved at last his pointless ambition to lure Derby into the Cabinet, at the Colonial Office. 'We took a slight survey of public affairs. It was altogether hearty and satisfactory.'[91] If it was Derby's job to deal with Kruger, then surely was it not Gladstone's to deal with Parnell? Before the end of October 1882 he had booked himself up pretty much for the 1883 session at least. He hoped that by Easter he might have relinquished the Exchequer.

The whole question of retirement, having become something of a comedy, now veered between tragedy and farce. It was always in the air, but notably in 1883 he harped less on it. He did at last divest himself of the Exchequer. This should have been Hartington's moment. Gladstone snubbed him by preferring Childers. Gladstone compounded the snub by shunting Hartington off to replace Childers at the War Office, which had been his first Cabinet post under Russell. The Queen was indignant about Derby. She was indignant also at Dilke's promotion to the Cabinet to replace Dodson at the Local Government Board. The great difficulty was sulky Rosebery. Gladstone thought him 'a most singular case of strong self-delusion: a vein of foreign matter which runs across a clear and vigorous intellect, and a high-toned character'.[92]

For much of the 1883 session Gladstone continued in desultory mode, leaving the session to look after itself. He humbugged his way through the abolition of the Contagious Diseases Acts, claiming not to recall his own part in their origins. Rosebery made his own comment in 1883 on the barrenness of the government's record by resigning his office and setting out on a tour to explore the resources of empire. By the end of the 1883 session what now possessed Gladstone was not so much the opportunity for retirement but rather the best opportunity he had known for plenary engagement on his own terms. Gladstone was now poised so advantageously that the old formula of 'intense anxiety to escape' now became an important component of his advantages, especially as he was careful never to suggest that he would resign his seat in the Commons. He could wield a threat to 'bolt' as a ready weapon.

As ever, the coherence he supplied from above was a licence to incoherence below. The fractiousness of the Cabinet, polarized between Hartington at one end and Chamberlain at the other, had become a prop and stay to his position. All factions preferred his staying on to the likely shape of things were he to go. Chamberlain needed more time to consolidate and prepare the way for his planned Radical Programme. He was now stirring things by making provocative speeches in the country. The Queen demanded that Gladstone put curbs on him.[93] Hartington was clear that 'if any other leader should attempt to lead, I do not think that the tie – already strained – which unites the moderate section with the party would hold for a moment'.[94] The rest straggled between these two poles, trimming as occasion suggested. Gladstone's leadership was unchallenged and, for all practical and foreseeable purposes, unchallengeable. The Almighty was telling him not that his time was fulfilled and the door of escape opened to him, but that the great good times were yet to come.

Something of this sense of a new kind of freedom opening up for Gladstone found expression in his 'escapade', as the Queen scathingly described it, of another cruise in one of Currie's steamers, *Pembroke Castle*. This post-sessional September recreation, with the lions of the party being Tennyson and Gladstone, started off as a navigation in the West Highland islands. It ended up, to Gladstone's embarrassment, as he had to scramble to get the Queen's permission to leave territorial waters, as an expedition to Norway and Denmark, culminating in brilliant junketings in Copenhagen with Danish, Greek and Russian royalties. A more substantial, if equally agreeable, aspect of the cruise, was the happy opportunity it provided Gladstone to make known to Tennyson that the Queen and he were agreed on a peerage for the Laureate. Tennyson professed himself touched to be 'the first *thus* publicly to proclaim the position which Literature ought to hold in the world's work'.[95]

It did not seem at all necessary to Gladstone to arrange a series of autumn planning Cabinets to arrange work for the 1884 session, despite despairing pleas from activist MPs. He hardly now even pretended to take an interest in what the Liberal party itself wanted in the way of 'practical' legislation. On the other hand, he had a genuine interest in extending the electoral power of the 'great mass'. Once the 'nation' was fully armed politically, really big things would become possible. 'My position is a strange one', Gladstone recorded in bidding farewell to 1883. 'A strong man in me wrestles for retirement: a stronger one stands at the gate of exit, and forbids.'

16

Such a Supreme Moment, 1884–1886

'It seems difficult ... to deny that we seem to have hold of something like a political axiom when we say that the adoption of a legislative project into the Creed of the Liberal party at large is a sure prelude to its accomplishment.'

Gladstone to Queen Victoria, 19 August 1884

The coming of 1884 was marked with what by now were rituals of habit. The activist wing of the parliamentary Liberal party, in the persons of W. S. Caine, George Melly, as well as the indefatigable Rathbone, put forward their pleas that the Liberal party be allowed some practical, substantial Liberal legislation. It appeared to them that 'we are in danger of destroying the improved position of the Liberal party if as some seem to advocate we go to the country with no more practical legislation than we have yet passed'. There must be 'some substantial good work next session'. It would be necessary to satisfy the 'great practical mass of the Liberal party who will certainly not be satisfied with nothing but County Franchise'.[1] To ritual pleas there would be the ritual response. Bills for Local Government and London Government would be solemnly introduced and then regretfully withdrawn. Gladstone pleaded that he no longer had strength for a session full of 'practical legislation'.[2] Gladstone had much bigger matters about the masses to attend to. The Liberal party was indeed going to be satisfied whether it liked it or not with 'nothing but County Franchise'.

It was a question ripe for legislating. The difficulty about it was the way it got entangled with Ireland. Extending the borough franchise of 1867 to the counties was a measure much approved of in the Liberal party, not least because of the damage to be inflicted on the traditional Conservative ascendancy in the agricultural constituencies when for the first heady time the rural and mining working classes marked their secret ballots. It was the application to Ireland that gave pause. Gladstone had pledged himself absolutely to a uniform United Kingdom basis for the legislation. It would not be a matter of supplementary Scottish and Irish Bills following on the English–Welsh primary model. There would be no opportunity to differentiate Reform in Britain from Reform in Ireland.

Conservatives in Britain were frightened by the county franchise. But, since it was going to happen, they kept publicly quiet about it. The pattern of recent events had indicated that there was not much the House of Lords could do about it. And there was nothing to be gained by insulting some millions of future new voters. Ireland was another matter. Reform in the Irish boroughs in 1868 had made little impact in thinly urbanized Ireland. What would happen in Ireland when the small farmers and cottiers cast their votes was a matter of lively speculation. Would they simply hand Ireland to Parnell? What was to stay them? The 'Girondins', with nothing to offer but the irrelevant Land Act, were a spent force.

Then there was the question of Redistribution of constituencies. The 1860s measures had done little about that. A Redistribution on a more comprehensive scale was now unavoidable in a situation where something like three-quarters of MPs were elected by one quarter of the voters. There was need for Gladstone to move circumspectly in bringing on the county franchise question in November and December 1883. He had painful memories of the way Redistribution had been used as a weapon against Reform in 1866. Gladstone was in an incomparably stronger position vis-à-vis the parliamentary Liberal party now than he had been then. On the other hand, it would be important to carry Hartington with him in Cabinet, where his grip was looser.

Gladstone assured the fretful Whig that the 'effect of the altered franchise in augmenting the power of Parnellism' was greatly over-estimated. The new labourer vote in Ireland, he felt sure, was '*quite* as likely to establish a dual current in the constituencies, as to increase the volume of that single force which now carries all before it'. To refuse equality to Ireland *would* be a blow to Unionism and the Empire. He dangled before Hartington the prospect of his imminent and definitive abdication.[3] To Hartington's threats of resignation he responded with a counter-threat: the government would fall, Hartington would have to form another, with Reform postponed, and with Gladstone forced into alliance with the Radicals, with a dissolution in the offing and the Liberal party split into two camps.[4]

On the Redistribution side of the case Gladstone deprecated false alarms. Hartington and the 'Whigs and moderates', he insisted, had no need to fear the effect of mere 'numbers' or 'population' swamping the constituencies at the expense of property and educated political leadership. Gladstone's own views on the matter were quite conservative. He envisaged a modest Redistribution, respectful of history and tradition, very much a supplement to the grandeurs of Reform. He explained to Harcourt that his faith was in the 'nation', and he could not say it would be shaken whatever way the country was 'district-ed'. But he was against 'all changes which distract or disturb, and which are not called for by any motives of necessity'.[5] He mocked Hartington's fears: 'one of the phantoms which has been scaring Hartington's usually manly mind, is that of Electoral districts; and he probably suspects me of looking to a plan on this basis'.[6]

There were further squalls with Hartington after Gladstone returned to London in the new year, in which Gladstone dilated on 'ruin to the party' and the 'fearful evil of branding Ireland with political inequality'. He could conveniently brush awkward problems under the carpet of his ever-impending retirement. But not quite yet.

By 3 January Gladstone could declare 'our little crisis' 'virtually over'; 'a great mercy, though in one sense I have to pay the piper by an extended engagement'. A 'very harmonious and satisfactory' Cabinet agreed to go ahead with the Franchise Bill without linkage to Redistribution. That would be settled later but within the present Parliament. Gladstone applied further balm to Hartington's wounds. He asked the Whip, Lord Richard Grosvenor, to find 'any *convenient* occasion' of letting Hartington know 'in a quiet way' the negative view that Parnell was said to take on the 'effect of the extended franchise on the interests of his party'. But Grosvenor was not to let Hartington suspect that he had been 'coquetting with these worthies'.[7]

~

Behind these preparations lay certain assumptions about the nature of the electoral system in Great Britain. In 1870 Gladstone had made the point to the Queen about the 'steady and permanent judgment of the country which on every occasion since 1830 except one has returned a Liberal majority'.[8] That confidence had been dented in 1874 by what Liberals generally dismissed as an 'untoward' Conservative majority. Gladstone's storming back in 1880 was interpreted widely as a correction of an anomalous electoral mishap. Things were now back on the rails. Normal Liberal service would resume. The further assumption prevalent in 1884 was that assimilation of the county vote with the borough vote would reinforce the natural Liberal electoral hegemony. From this viewpoint, Redistribution seemed equally unproblematic. Given a general equitability of arrangements, it was difficult to conceive how making votes more or less of equal value could do other than benefit the party of the nation. This was certainly Gladstone's view, and the view of the man he selected to look after the Redistributive aspect of things, Dilke.

Much of this attitude was shared by the despondent Conservatives. That their ascendancy in their heartland county constituencies would be seriously damaged by 'Hodge', the archetypical smocked agricultural labourer, seemed inevitable. Since 1832, Conservatism had of necessity to be concerned much more than Liberalism with effective electoral organization. Certain Conservatives, imbued with that kind of mental habit, could discern amid the gloom of 1884 some glimmers of light. Salisbury was one of the more prominent of these new-fangled psephologists. Careful study of the 1880 election returns indicated that a great many Liberal majorities in small boroughs were thin. Indicated also was the fact that the Conservative vote was actually increasing in urban, and especially suburban, areas. Since 1868 the Conservatives had made inroads into formerly Liberal strongholds in both the Lancashire manufacturing boroughs and the big centres of Manchester and Liverpool. The other area of Conservative advance was London and the Home Counties. The Lancashire–London Conservative axis had suffered from the Liberal revival in 1880, but it remained substantially intact.

To Salisbury and his friends it was becoming clear that Conservatism's only hope of escaping disaster was to look very carefully at what might be done with Redistribution in the way of maximizing urban and especially suburban constituencies. Hitherto, cities in general had been vastly underrepresented in the traditional electoral pattern. That had been accepted as perfectly natural. There was a big chance now of converting the old-fashioned electoral system into a reflection of the demographic realities of modern British population distribution. The key mechanism would be to shift the old pattern of multiple county and borough representation on to a new pattern of 'districted' single-member constituencies.

The Conservatives could do nothing with the franchise in the House of Commons. But it would be of the utmost consequence to them to make sure that they kept a firm grip on the negotiations relating to Redistribution. That meant keeping Reform and Redistribution, though in separate measures, in as near to parallel alignment as possible. Gladstone must not be allowed to treat Redistribution as a mere tidying-up operation to be settled at some time after the passing of Reform, which is what he had in mind. Conservatives in the Commons could not stipulate such a procedure. But in the Lords they could. The Lords could accept the Franchise Bill but refuse to pass it until an equitable deal had been done on Redistribution and a bill to that effect was in being and ready also to be guaranteed passage in the Commons. If Gladstone refused to be thus blackmailed, he could dissolve the 1880 Parliament on the existing registers and ask the country to decide which party was being unreasonable. It was all rather a desperate recourse. But for the Conservatives, desperate times called for desperate remedies.

~

Redistribution on the comprehensive lines envisaged by Salisbury would transform fundamentally the terrain and contours of politics. For Gladstone in many ways it would be a strangely unaccustomed world. His world remained one of custom and habit. Retrieval of the past became a central feature in the pattern of Gladstone's politics. The critical question of the union of the autonomous Bulgaria and the semi-autonomous Eastern Rumelia created at Berlin in 1878 was by now claiming Europe's attention. Gladstone was in the gratifying position of being able to point out to the Queen that his speech in 1858 on the union of the Danubian Principalities and the making of Romania was very material to the case. His words then were highly applicable to the Bulgarian case now. The principle of self-determination involved in either case was one of vital consequence. He made sure of Granville's application to the present case of the Midlothian principle that Britain's policy must ever be to promote freedom.[9]

Such 'Eastern' matters were in Gladstone's mind when he and Catherine visited the Derbys at Knowsley earlier in October of 1883. Ostensibly, Gladstone was catching up with the renegotiation of the Pretoria Convention in which Derby at the Colonial Office had been grappling with Kruger since July. Kruger was getting the better of it, but Gladstone worried little about such details. Derby noted Gladstone's liking for 'long casual conversations when paying business visits'. Gladstone confessed that he now found 'much work impossible' at his age. Of 'serious desk-work' 'three hours were his usual limit, in case of necessity he could go up to five hours, but anything more exhausted him'. What he was avid for were 'long & interesting conversation with Lady D. on Lord B[eaconsfield]., H.M., D[erby].'s resignation, & other matters'.[10]

That kind of avidity for retrieval was reflected also in patronage matters. On departing from Gladstone after the Copenhagen junket, Tennyson had presented him with a copy of Professor J. R. Seeley's influential imperialist *The Expansion of England*, pointing to a future English polity founded on principles of *Realpolitik* rather than what Seeeley had denounced amid Eastern question times as 'loose notions about liberty'.[11] By now he was a figure representative of a reaction against Gladstone's demophilist populism observable among many of the Liberal intelligentsia. No doubt regretting his appointment of Seeley to the Cambridge Regius Modern History chair in 1869 on the strength then of Seeley's notions of historians as a kind of Coleridgean Christian clerisy, Gladstone hit back by blocking a knighthood for Seeley and appointing to the Oxford Regius Chair the faithful turcophobe democrat, E. A. Freeman. Retrieval applied also in the domestic scene. At Hawarden, the family 'court' of Catherine, Mary and Herbert were keepers of a kind of shrine for a pilgrimage cult with the words of Midlothian as sacred texts. Gladstone himself seemed quite easy at basking in the warmth of this adoration of the 'nation'. Willy and Gertrude had managed to escape. Stephen felt uncomfortable at being 'too closely related to what might be called the "temporal power" of the ruling family of the place' – the 'Grand Old Couple', as William and Catherine were beginning to be called in slightly mocking tone by people who shared the Blantyres' opinion of the shrinish atmosphere. Stephen had an idea of joining an Oxford University Mission at Calcutta, where he would have had Harry's company. But after talking to his father Stephen 'went off pliantly' back to the Rectory.[12]

~

There were other aspects of this instinct, as it appeared, perhaps of more moment, for retrieval of the past. Not the least significant of them was Gladstone's preoccupation, in relation to Ireland, with the example of O'Connell as model Irish tribune. One of the most pleasant incidents back in the new year of 1882 had been the gift from O'Connell's daughter-in-law of a bust of the 'Liberator', 'in grateful appreciation of the generous way in which you have spoken of him on several recent occasions'.[13] A few days later after the opening of the 1882 session a motion by one of the Nationalist Irish members, P. J. Smyth, cited the familiar Home Rule analogy of the Hungarian leader Deak's being the O'Connell of Austria-Hungary.[14] This, together with citings of Sweden-Norway, was the merest alpha and beta of O'Connellite Repeal doctrine.[15] It so happened that in his rather fraught dealings with Forster in the autumn of 1880, Gladstone had come forth in a rather startling way: 'Do not suppose that I dream of reviving the Irish Parliament; but I have been reading the Union speeches & debates, & am surprised at the narrowness of the case, upon which that Parliament was condemned. I think the unavowed motives must have been the main ones.'[16] This marks a significant point when Gladstone's readings in Irish history became an integral component in his thinking about Irish policy.

Gladstone's speech in response to Smyth certainly provoked something of the same frisson as his 'pale of the constitution' speech declaration in 1864. He began by saying that he did not think exception need be taken to calls for 'an Irish Legislative Body to deal with Irish affairs', provided the integrity of the Empire was maintained and imperial questions continued to be dealt with in the Imperial Parliament. Among the difficulties of the case was that 'neither Mr Butt before them, nor as far as I know Mr O'Connell before him, ever distinctly explained in an intelligible and practical form the manner in which the real knot of this question was to be untied'. By what authority was it to be determined that some matters were Irish and some Imperial in an Imperial Chamber in which Ireland was represented? Until the Irish Home Rulers resolved a conundrum that so far had baffled the wit of man, and laid before the House 'a plan in which they go to the very bottom of that subject and give us to understand in what manner that division of jurisdiction is to be accomplished, the practical consideration of this subject cannot really be arrived at'.[17]

A buzz of astonishment followed Gladstone's statement. At that moment Parnell was still incarcerated at Kilmainham. Mitchell Henry, one of the moderate Home Rulers, made the point that this was 'probably the first time a responsible Minister of the Crown – certainly the Prime Minister – had really shown a desire to grapple with the difficulties of the question of self-government for Ireland'.[18] Plunket, Conservative MP for Dublin University, observed that Gladstone's words could be interpreted only as 'an invitation to Irish Members ... to re-open the question of Home Rule'. To Plunket it was clear that 'whether the Prime

Minister is or is not now more in favour of Home Rule than he was in the last Parliament, it is evident he has made a speech which has been interpreted in this House and in Ireland generally to mean that he is'.[19] Gladstone, again in familiar deprecatory manner, expressed surprise at Plunket's 'sensitiveness'; and took refuge in explanations that his words were to be construed as being 'of a speculative character'. Then of course his imminent retirement had to be taken into account.[20]

The Queen took alarm. The Irish would read into his words meanings that Gladstone did not intend. Gladstone offered reassurance. Lessons had been learned in the last half-century. 'The self-government now practised in Canada, and generally viewed as safe if not wholly unexceptionable was regarded, in the first years of Mr Gladstone's Parliamentary life, as a thing fatal to the empire.' He continued even less reassuringly. There was 'a very real danger which may come above the horizon'. 'That danger will have arisen, should a decisive majority of the representatives of Ireland unitedly demand on behalf of their country the adoption of some scheme of Home Rule, which Parliament should be compelled to refuse.' The great object of imperial policy would be to prevent the formation of such a majority. There had been a risk of it at the beginning of the 1880 session when 60 to 70 Home Rulers were returned. The government had done their best to break up this potential combination; 'and they have succeeded'. However, were the government to denounce in sweeping terms 'everything that may be comprised within the name "Home Rule", they would be paving the way for its reunion'.[21] There was general agreement, he concluded, that the Parnellite contingent would be augmented at the next general election. In any case, however, Mr Gladstone's views 'must soon cease to be taken into account'. And he thought it prudent to make a final clarification: he did not mean to imply that the Canadian analogy could 'be safely or properly extended to Ireland'.[22]

Much of this was wishful thinking. The legislative barrenness that Gladstone had imposed on the Liberal party since 1880 had for its most conspicuous victims the moderate Irish Home Rulers. They were now for practical purposes extinct. Meanwhile, Gladstone attempted in the Commons to clarify and defend his position. The wise way to meet a demand from Ireland that purely Irish affairs be under Irish control is that before any such plan can be dealt with on its merits, 'we must ask those who propose it ... What are the provisions which you propose to make for the supremacy of Parliament?' Nothing could be given to Ireland that could not equally be given to Scotland, should Scotland so desire. Gladstone made a point of reminding the House of his former utterances on this matter, going back to Aberdeen in 1871; with references to his undeserved repute for 'formidable novelty' at Midlothian, 'scene of so many of my misdeeds'.[23]

What was going on here? Was Gladstone simply, as he assured the Queen, engaging in tactical manoeuvres with strategic intent? Or giving harmless explanations to the Commons? Or was there something deeper and of more moment involved? Was opinion being 'manipulated'? Was it a case of the minister hinting at doings and practical intentions with a view to eliciting a corresponding conviction wrought by them upon the public mind? Was his spoiling of all efforts in the party to provide Ireland with what Rathbone had described as local government reform that would 'satisfy all that is reasonable in the Home Rule demand' the means of keeping the way clear for a larger alternative Irish policy?[24] And what if Parnell proved indeed a new O'Connell? The Irish Land Act set the style and the heroic dimension of things. Were there cause and purpose worthy of his denying himself the escape and freedom he longed for, surely such cause and purpose must reveal itself as something on an appropriately grand and insightful level, perhaps a 'juncture' comparable to the 1853 budget, or the decision to go for Irish religious equality in 1868?

~

While momentous Irish questions hung hypothetically in the air, matters on the ground elsewhere grew no less intractable. It was turning out that Egypt was far easier to get into than to get out of. Ministerial statements promising prompt withdrawal proliferated. Gladstone himself had issued five. The great Liberal public was getting impatient. The French also were impatient. The occupying authorities were adamant that reform of the Egyptian system of government was impossible without a strong British military presence. How, in Gladstone's words, 'to plant solidly western & beneficent institutions in the soil of a Mohamedan community?'[25] One extra difficulty was the Egyptian government's itself widening the scope of the problem by persisting in holding on to its own Sudanese empire centred on Khartoum, on the upper Nile. The Egyptian attempt to restore Cairo's authority against the forces of a Muslim messiah, or 'Mahdi', came to a catastrophic end with the massacre of an army commanded by a British officer, Colonel Hicks, in November 1883.

Then there was the plan to 'wear down' the Transvaalers in the negotiations about revising the Pretoria Convention. In fact it was Derby and the British who were worn down by the end of the business in February 1884. Suzerainty and the veto over the republic's relations with foreign powers were abandoned. 'We have abstained from using the word', explained Derby, 'because it is not capable of legal definition, and because it seemed to be a word which was likely to lead to misconception and misunderstanding.' 'Derby has not got the key to the S. African question', Gladstone told Granville, 'but who has?'[26] Kruger got 'Home Rule' for the South African Republic. Britain thought it had retained imperial supremacy. Here, indeed, would be abundant scope for misconception and misunderstanding.

Britain's solution to the Sudanese problem was to pressure the Egyptians to make an 'honourable withdrawal'. The Egyptians were in a mixed state of being both unwilling and unable to do this. How to get the Egyptians out without getting the British in? The solution presented itself to baffled ministers in the form of Major-General Charles Gordon. Of Chinese fame and Sudanese experience, this charismatic officer had become by his well publicised exploits a popular hero. He was about to sign on to manage the scheme of King Leopold II of the Belgians to open up the Congo basin to beneficent trade and commerce. It was in December 1883 that Granville first enquired whether Gordon would be available for service in the Sudan. His admirers scouted the widely held notion that Gordon was 'half mad'. 'He is not at all mad', insisted an admirer, '– but he is, above all things, a man of religion.'[27]

Despite protests from people who knew him well, the idea of his employment in the Sudan took on a vivid life of its own. W. T. Stead, now Morley's successor as editor of the *Pall Mall Gazette*, made Gordon's humanitarian and Christian mission into a sensational stunt of the 'new journalism'. His appointment, as Granville put it, 'would be popular at home'. The 1884 session was at hand. The Cabinet, including Gladstone, followed the thrust of events with haphazard flaccidity. It was while resting at Hawarden that Gladstone, despite Hamilton's doubts at putting trust in a 'half-cracked fatalist', telegraphed consent to the decision of the four ministers who happened to be in London – Granville, Hartington, Northbrook and Dilke – to divert Gordon from the Congo to the Nile.

Granville said to Hartington the following day: 'We were proud of ourselves yesterday. Are you sure that we did not commit a gigantic folly?'[28] Soon Gordon was off early in 1884 to Cairo and thence to Khartoum, with instructions to evacuate all Egyptians and wind up the existing regime there. Gladstone saw in him a paladin of the Midlothian ethos. 'I have from the first regarded the rising of the Sudanese against Egypt as a justifiable and honourable revolt.' He was sending Gordon on a 'mission of peace and liberation'.[29] Gordon did indeed evacuate some 2,500 Egyptians down the Nile, but soon persuaded himself that his duty before God and man was to ignore his instructions and stand fast at Khartoum and save the Sudan from the Mahdi. Gladstone 'never understood how it was that Gordon's mission of peace became one of war'.[30]

Gordon withstood with extraordinary resource and gallantry a siege of 317 days. He made it very difficult for ministers in London to help him. Not only was Gordon a man 'who has disobeyed his instructions and changed his plan of action', his dispatches also were those, as Gladstone put it, of 'a man who is not wholly sane and who perpetually contradicts himself'.[31] As Gladstone was soon to discover, he 'takes very little notice indeed of any general questions we put to him'.[32] His legalising of slavery in order to bolster local support and his demands that the Egyptian strongman and notorious slave-hunter Zobeir Pasha be sent to help him offended both the Anglican conscience of Selborne and the

Nonconformist conscience of Chamberlain. To many Liberals he became a 'sort of Egyptian Jingo'.[33] In all his long career, Gladstone found a match only in Gordon for God-driven obstinacy.

In Gladstone Gordon found a man who could rival him for God-driven stubbornness. Gordon dared the Mahdi to come at him. He dared the government to send out a rescue expedition. Gladstone allowed his resentment too much to colour his judgement in resisting both frantic public clamour and the Queen's harassment that a knightly hero must be saved, and ministerial calculations that ultimately there was nothing for it but to bow to Gordon's blackmail and pay up for an expensive relief operation. Never were Gladstone's formidably casuistical talents more brilliantly deployed than in his twistings and turnings to deny that Gordon needed rescue. In a diatribe against Gladstone in a censure debate in May 1884, Forster famously adverted to the Prime Minister's 'wonderful powers of persuasion. He can persuade most people of most things, and, above all, he can persuade himself of almost anything.'[34]

With wonderful powers of persuasion Gladstone faced down the vote of censure. He accused his critics of trying to saddle England with the task of reconquest; 'a war of conquest against a people struggling to be free. ["No! No!"] Yes; these are people struggling to be free, and they are struggling rightly to be free.'[35] By the time Gladstone was brought around to accepting what became seen as inevitable, mainly by Hartington's dogged persistence, he had left it too late. The Mahdi got to Gordon two days before Wolseley's relief force reached Khartoum on 28 January 1885.

~

The greater part of this tragical-farcical drama was played out as exotic background to a curious kind of domestic comical-tragical drama in the matter of Reform and Redistribution. Dim drums throbbed by the Nile half-heard while at Aston the invasion of a Conservative meeting by a chair-throwing Liberal mob provided what a Tory wit called the definitive model of a redistribution of seats. The Conservatives, terrified by the county franchise and horrified by the prospect in store in Ireland, found the Gordon issue a convenient means of getting at Gladstone. They did this very effectively. Gladstone's rage against their baitings did as much as anything to reinforce his denial that Gordon, merely 'hemmed in', was in danger.

Other than making futile gestures that wording in the Representation of the People Bill be altered from 'United Kingdom' to 'Great Britain', there was nothing the Conservatives could do about Reform in the Commons. The same applied in the Lords, other than insistence that Redistribution must be proceeded with in tandem. Led resolutely by Salisbury, they took the point that their party's only hopes of surviving the county franchise even as a strong Opposition depended crucially on gaining some compensating benefits from a radical restructuring of the constituencies on the basis of equal population and single-member seats.

Liberals could not be averse to this in principle. Gladstone agreed with Chamberlain that any scheme of 'just redistribution' must *ipso facto* be beneficial to the 'nation'. In any case Liberals looked upon Redistribution as a supplementary tidying up after the great and decisive Reform measure was passed. They were shocked when Salisbury announced that the Lords would block passage of the Representation of the People Bill until they got adequate assurances that an equitable Redistribution Bill would be processed concurrently. Salisbury's message was that if the government refused a reasonable request to link an agreed Redistribution to Reform, the Lords would be entitled to throw out the Reform Bill and invite ministers to dissolve and put their case to the electorate.

What was most shocking to Liberals was this notion of the House of Lords assuming a 'referendal' function in the constitution.[36] Gladstone, immensely indignant, saw it as a wholly illegitimate species of political blackmail, worse in some ways than Gordon's blackmail. By July it was evident that Salisbury was seriously intent on putting the question to the test. Having suffered a painful series of humiliations at Gladstone's hand since he succeeded Beaconsfield as Conservative leader in the Lords in 1881, Salisbury saw his chance to deploy the Lords in a constructive role by challenging Gladstone either to negotiate or to dissolve on the old registers. Gladstone was almost as much scandalized by Tennyson's intimations that he was in much of a mind with Lord Salisbury.

Tennyson notwithstanding, Liberals felt strongly that it would be beneath the dignity of the House of Commons to submit to such blatant menaces. An honourable assurance to the Conservatives that Redistribution would be attended to before the next general election was quite as much as they should expect. The blatant menace, however, stayed on track. Gladstone could hardly believe that Salisbury would go through with his reckless gamble. He attended at the Lords on 8 July to witness the spectacle. 'What a suicidal act of the Lords!' They threw out the Representation of the People Bill by 205 not contents to 146 contents (of whom in the end Tennyson was meekly one).

The government's problem was that either way they were in difficulties. To allow the Lords to force a dissolution would be 'a precedent against liberty' worse than anything since the beginning of the reign of George III. There was the absurdity of dissolving on the obsolete registers on the eve of the creation of a new democracy. And, if it came to that, would the electorate necessarily embrace constitutional purism and agree that a stipulation by the Lords that they were perfectly willing to pass the Franchise Bill if an equitable Redistribution Bill were linked to it, was so obviously, as Gladstone put it to the Queen, 'a gross and deplorable error'?[37]

The greater part of Gladstone's sense of the grossness and deplorability of the Lords' so stipulating was that, by challenging a Liberal government, they were ipso facto challenging the 'nation'. Gladstone further put it to the Queen that he knew 'how formidable an opponent the House of Lords has habitually been, and especially for the last 30 years, to the Liberal party, which has had the nearly uniform assent of the nation'.[38] Above all, while '*class* never slumbers', it was difficult on the Liberal side to keep the public's mind 'lively and intent upon great national interests'.[39]

That was precisely Gladstone's difficulty now in 1884, as he addressed the scandalous case of the challenge of hereditary privilege to the representative principle. Beneath the ground of his notion here of renewing and reasserting Liberalism's habitual hegemony, there were, however, underlying forces that were shifting and displacing the foundations of the mid-nineteenth-century social and political order. The middle-class 'reaction' that upset Gladstone in 1874 had left its traces. These now, in the burgeoning of suburbia and crucially the emergence out of the working class of what was being identified as the 'lower middle class', with striving aspirations, were to be of crucial significance. It so happened that the redistribution of constituencies envisaged by such as Salisbury would prove to be of high explanatory power in releasing the political energy of what the Liberal satirists were to lampoon as 'Pooterland'.[40]

The Conservatives, equally, had little inkling of quite how decisively the terms of political trade were about to turn in their favour. Salisbury had made himself expert in the field of Redistribution precisely because he accepted the validity of Liberal assumptions and predictions. Nor were the Conservatives above a certain amount of nodding and winking with the Irish. Tenant purchase land policy provided an opening for mutual anti-Liberal considerations. But Salisbury also had his own retrieval mode. It was his highest hope to get politics back to the healthy pre-1865 dispensation, with blurred party lines, collusive frontbenches, and with governments deprived of the dangerous capacity for having Gladstonian means to Gladstonian ends. He thought Conservatism was at its optimum situation as a strong minority in the Commons, facing a weak Liberal government, and having the Lords in reserve. In 1897, in the wake of Conservative triumph, Salisbury, by no means comfortable in this novel prosperity, bemusedly declared that 'the history of recent times, as it will be written, is a very strange history'.[41]

~

A tense and bad-tempered confrontation clouded the next three and a half months. Gladstone would not, on principle, dissolve the 1880 Parliament at the behest of the Lords. The Lords would not give way without adequate assurances about an agreed Redistribution. Liberal activists, encouraged by Chamberlain, began to get up a 'peers versus people' and 'mend them or end them' agitation in the country. Conservatives mounted a counter-agitation in defence of the

Lords' perfectly reasonable and constitutional case. The Queen, anxious at public unrest and concerned to fend off a serious conflict between the two Houses of Parliament, offered her mediation. Gladstone's line was that, while the Lords had wantonly exposed themselves to severely punitive action from the people, he would himself do all he could to temper the popular wrath. He valued the hereditary principle and would like to help the House of Lords to save it from itself.[42]

For the Queen's guidance in providing her good offices, Gladstone gave her the benefit of his thoughts on the link between the political and constitutional components of the present crisis. His point of departure was 'the lesson taught by history'. 'It seems difficult ... to deny that we seem to have hold of something like a political axiom when we say that the adoption of a legislative project into the Creed of the Liberal party at large is a sure prelude to its accomplishment.' Defiance by the Lords of this 'political axiom' could have but one consequence: it would provoke from the Liberal party a demand for an 'organic change' in the constitution. There was still time for the Conservatives and the Lords to extricate themselves from a dangerously exposed situation. Once the Reform Bill was passed the agitation against the Lords would die away. But were it not passed, the government would come under intense pressure and there would be a great conflict on the issue 'whether the hereditary or representative majority is to prevail'.[43]

No doubt the Queen took these points with the best grace she could muster. Gladstone struck back at the Lords by announcing that there would be an autumn session in October. He observed gravely to the Queen that he much feared riots and tumult if the Lords rejected the Reform Bill a second time. For her part, Victoria felt she had cause to complain at Gladstone's 'constant speeches' at railway stations, doing nothing to help for mediation.

The Reform Bill was reintroduced in the Commons on 24 October. Conservative efforts to get guarantees as to Redistribution failed yet again. Tension mounted as the bill passed up to the Lords, where it was due for its crucial second reading on 20 November. Tennyson offered advice in irritatingly sententious verse.[44] In the background persisted distant thunders out of the Sudan. When Granville shifted the second reading forward to 18 November, Salisbury declared: 'Mark my words, Khartoum has fallen.'[45] Feeling the Sudanese heat, Gladstone began overtures to lower the temperature of the domestic fever. Already he had told Dilke that he was willing to move further on details of Redistribution 'if we could thereby effectually promote peace & get the Franchise Bill passed'. This was on the day (29 September) on which he read Salisbury's article in the *National Review* on 'The Value of Redistribution: A Note on Electoral Statistics.'

Those details had to do with what Dilke wonderingly described as 'the revolutionary criticism of Lord Salisbury', who seemed to accept that an equitably straightforward system based on simple numbers would produce an adequate proportionality as between the electorate and the representation of parties in the House of Commons. Both Dilke and Gladstone were astonished at the readiness of Salisbury and his Commons equivalent to Dilke, Hicks Beach, to go for single-member and equal-population electoral districts. Gladstone, tender to 'long usages and tradition' and 'inclined to respect individuality' in constituencies, was appalled. The 'principle of population' was to be adopted absolutely, and traditional arrangements were 'to be ripped asunder everywhere & to the uttermost'.[46] But it occurred neither to Gladstone nor to Dilke that it would be detrimental to the Liberal party if Salisbury were humoured in these directions.

Salisbury managed with difficulty to hold his party outwardly steady on the eve of the critical Lords vote. Had Gladstone held out longer, the Conservative nerve might well have cracked. But Gladstone's own nerves were near cracking under the strain of the Gordon affair. With infinite reluctance, he had unleashed Wolseley to take command at Cairo of the relief expedition. Giving Hartington the Sudan expedition made it easier to get him to swallow the Reform pill. Granville was near collapse.[47] Nor was it clear that 'the peers versus the people' campaign in the country had undermined Salisbury's stand. On 7 November Gladstone canvassed Derby on the expediency, 'with a view to an early settlement', of accepting 'the Salisbury-Beach radical scheme'.

Preliminary words with Northcote opened the way. The deadlock was broken on 17 November when Granville in the Lords and Gladstone in the Commons announced that, if the Reform measure were allowed to pass in the Lords, Redistribution would be made the subject of friendly communication with the Opposition leaders. Gladstone brushed aside Liberal complaints that the House of Commons had been 'as good as extinguished' and 'humiliated'.[48] On 19 November Salisbury and Northcote were received in Downing Street: the efficient negotiators among the map-strewn tables and sofas and carpets were Dilke and Salisbury.

So inherently strong did Gladstone and Dilke assume Liberalism would be as a consequence of the county franchise that they let Salisbury have his head. On the one point where Salisbury held out for tradition, the university seats, Gladstone overruled Dilke in support. There was no move to redress the rather gross Irish over-representation. Gladstone wanted to keep Parnell in play. Salisbury wanted the Irish to help mitigate the inevitable Liberal majority in the new Parliament. Both Scotland and Wales were in any case allowed leniency. Negotiations were concluded to general satisfaction on 26 November.

Gladstone introduced the agreed Redistribution Bill to a puzzled and fretful Commons on 1 December. The two frontbenches colluded in imposing their settlement on their followers. There was no serious resistance. The principles were evidently equitable; their consequences were too intricate to be readily comprehended. The upshot was that 170 seats were abolished and 182 seats created. Hardly any constituency was unaffected. The second reading passed without a division on 4 December. The third reading of the Reform Bill was passed by the Lords on 5 December and received the royal assent on the 6th. Nearly two million new occupier voters were to be added to the existing register of three million. Something like 60 per cent of adult males were now eligible to vote: two out of three in England and Wales, three out of five in Scotland and one out of two in Ireland.

The new electorate that Gladstone was responsible for creating in 1884 was portentous in its evocation of 'mass'. Something akin to a democracy could be said to have come into being. His motive for making the great enfranchisement was rooted in his experiences between 1876 and 1880. The Representation of the People Act was his acknowledgement that the people remained 'strong & sound'. The stain of 1874 had been expunged. It was no longer a question, as in 1868 or 1880, of replacing an unworthy Parliament. It would be a matter of replacing a good Parliament with an even better one.

Yet in certain ways the popular energies embodied in the new constituencies were constrained. There were vested electoral interests that the Conservatives and Whigs had every interest in conserving, and which Gladstone felt, conservatively, no compelling call to disturb. The criteria for possessing the franchise remained complex, with a sizeable admixture of multiple votes based on property. A vote remained very much a privilege to be applied for, not a right. The registration system remained in the hands of party agents, registration solicitors and revising barristers. This fact was to be of crucial importance in a situation that involved not only millions of newly eligible voters but millions of existing voters transferred to new registers. Apart from the anomalous and really rather accidental letting of Salisbury loose, Gladstone remained fixed in familiar habits: the nation's habitual consent, the lessons of history, the axioms of politics. He had no conception of the weight and magnitude of the electoral logic he had unwittingly set loose in the Redistribution Bill, which went up to the Lords on 15 May 1885 and received the royal assent on 25 June – two days after he had ceased to be prime minister.

That logic had at its core the immense fact that the modern geography of British politics was set in being. The great conurbations were allotted their due weight. They were broken up into multiple divisions ringed with swathes of outer suburban constituencies. Masses of traditional small boroughs were swallowed in new county divisions. The shape of future politics would be determined predominantly by the loyalties of this new civic and suburban electoral order. Metropolitan London, having comprised 22 seats, now emerged with no fewer than 64 of these single-member divisions: 'Megalopolis.' The great industrial county of Lancashire burgeoned from 35 to 65 seats. Manchester-Salford and

Liverpool each boasted nine divisions. Yorkshire swelled from 38 to 52 seats. Chamberlain's satrapy of Birmingham-West Midlands was now worth a dozen seats. What price old habits, lessons of history, axioms of politics?

~

Having cleared the deck of the lumber and tackle of Reform and Redistribution, Gladstone devoted attention to Egypt. The French were being troublesome after failing to secure British undertakings about withdrawal. The Cabinet was dividing between those led by Harcourt and Chamberlain, who wanted to declare Egyptian bankruptcy and then 'scuttle', and those led by Hartington and Northbrook, who accepted that the Palmerstonian luxury of not having to occupy Egypt was no longer available, and that the strategic imperative meant declaring a protectorate. Europe became a fig leaf to cover the nakedness of Empire. An uncomfortable by-product of quarrelling with the French was a 'navy scare' about the government's neglect to safeguard Britain's maritime supremacy. The French '*Jeune École*', observing what *Alabama* had achieved, were inspired by the idea that a war against seaborne commerce was the way of getting at the English. Forster's adopted son Hugh Arnold-Forster and Captain Jackie Fisher RN put up Stead to another of his sensational stunts in the *Pall Mall Review*. Tennyson contributed rousing verse. Gladstone and Northbrook faced the scare down.

By the end of 1884 Gladstone felt the dire pressures of 'a time of *sturm und drang*'. An attempt at a Cabinet reshuffle to bring in Rosebery was stymied by Carlingford's limpet-like tenacity. Presiding in Gladstone's absences, Granville was no improvement ('so difficult to know whether he heard what was said and intended to act according to decisions come to'. 'Evidently hates tackling Bismarck in any way.') Northbrook was particularly scathing about Granville. 'He spoke of Granville as responsible for a great deal of our mistakes – having no policy of his own – making no use as against Gladstone of his position as Foreign Minister, but being entirely ruled by Gladstone etc.'[49]

There was a growing feeling among Gladstone's colleagues that the 1880 government had reached its assigned limit. The air of Liberal politics was thick with rumours of Gladstone's going. Reform would be his great farewell legacy to the party. After a Cabinet in Gladstone's absence on 5 January, Dilke, Chamberlain and Trevelyan met 'to deliver the terms on which we would join a Hartington administration', finding Egypt the only real difficulty.[50] In the uncertainties of the situation it seemed to Chamberlain the time to pile on pressure. Reform in 1884, after all, amounted to a 'peaceful revolution', and the 'reign of democracy was about to begin'.[51] At Birmingham he demanded to know what 'ransom' the possessing classes were willing to pay for their security. Outraged demands piled upon Gladstone for Chamberlain's dismissal.

Gladstone returned from Hawarden more indispensable than ever as the point of coherence but less competent than ever to direct a coherent policy. Getting Rosebery in at last made little difference. Derby wondered at the 'careless, slipshod way in which Cabinet business is done'. And always, as Derby observed, there was the 'peculiar position of the Premier, who is always declaring himself to be on the point of retiring', and who thus 'increases the difficulty, for he is very unwilling to do anything that may bind him to stay longer in office, and we cannot act without him'.[52]

Gladstone's difficulty was that it was impossible for him, as 'leader of the nation', to struggle on absurdly as merely the mediator in quarrels that his own 'peculiar position' had in any case done so much to foment. On the other hand, the Almighty seemed not to be opening the door for his release. The Almighty seemed to be offering spacious vistas of immense opportunity. Soon, by November, once the new registers and constituency boundaries were complete, there would be the first general election embracing a true measure of the 'nation'. A grand new Parliament with grand new Liberal majority would result. What then? To leave it to the 'clerks' and the 'boys'? And for what? Some piddling measures about county government?

Then the hysterical public storm broke over the news of Gordon's martyrdom. The Queen made a point of telegraphing her shock and outrage at the delayed relief *en clair*. Gladstone responded stiffly. He persuaded himself that Gordon died not as a casualty of the Mahdi's assault but through treachery within. It mattered not, therefore, that Wolseley arrived late. With the coming of the 1885 session came a motion of censure. Northcote fumbled it and the unrepentant Gladstone got through with a majority of fourteen. 'The Almighty bore me through amidst all my weakness.' He was borne through also by Liberal loyalties being excited by a cabal of Tories and Irish. At a Cabinet the following day Gladstone put the alternatives: resignation, or carrying on. On an even vote, Gladstone cast for carrying on. He hated the idea that Gordon was his downfall. He wanted to keep a grip on damage limitation and ideas of further military operations in the Sudan and their horrendous financial implications. The Redistribution Bill still had to be seen through.

Meanwhile, playing out his absurd role as ringmaster in the Cabinet circus, it was all quite hard going. Granville and others who had hoped for release sulked. Then there came to Gladstone the sign that the Lord really was offering vistas of immense possibility. There came upon him an epiphanal moment, early in March, that bore decisively on his formulating his new 'lesson in history', his new 'axiom of politics'. He read the report of a speech by the Parnellite Irish MP William O'Brien, at Phoenix Park in Dublin, on 1 March. This was the precise moment, as Gladstone later related, when he realized 'that there was and never could be any moral obligation to the Irish nation in the Act of Union'; that he was, in short, a Home Ruler.[53]

~

Once that was the established fact, little else for the time mattered. The November elections and prospects thereafter took on an immensely enhanced significance. Episodes intervened. A collision between Afghans and Russians at Penjdeh involving some British officers gave Gladstone an opportunity to play the consummate Jingo. Acton doubted that this was a mere brazen bid to make up for the Gordon fiasco. He remarked to Dilke after observing Gladstone's shifts and adjustments in the Gordon affair: 'Cannot make up my mind whether he is not wholly unconscious when working himself up to a change of position. After watching him do it, I think that he is so. He lives completely for the moment in what he chooses to believe.'[54] It also gave Gladstone the opportunity to arrange withdrawal from the Sudan under cover of exigencies of a possible Russian war. After a bruising bout of recriminations with the Queen, he was observed in Cabinet in April exhibiting a novel aspect, 'a kind of senile cheerfulness'.[55] By 4 May Gladstone could announce in the Commons that the Afghan and Russian governments had come to terms.

The 'great event' of the quarrel and settlement with the Russians had for the while upstaged the stock familiar players. Gladstone could fairly hope that the Sudan issue was neutralized. French tiresomeness over Egypt had settled into a kind of acceptable impasse. He could discern 'reasonable likelihoods' of a 'general winding up of this Parliament & Government such as to be beyond all my most sanguine expectations'. As to Ireland, Gladstone felt he could now see his way 'with tolerable clearness'.[56]

It was now two months since the epiphanal moment early in March of O'Brien's speech. The problem was that, as he later explained, it was a question of 'subjects ripe for action'.[57] Ripeness would largely be determined by what results the Irish constituencies would return in the coming elections. Action would be a matter of Gladstone's judgement thereafter in relation to his manipulating materials to form a public opinion and direct it to his chosen end, which was evidently now some measure to restore an Irish legislature in Dublin. The essence of his problem was somehow to match Irish ripeness with British readiness to act. In the analogous case of the Irish Church, he had signalled his intentions some years before he embarked, in 1869, on action, in a context where there was plenty of ambient readiness to act. Now, in May 1885, all he had was at most six months before the elections were due and at most ten months before the 1886 session was due, in a context where it was well understood that there existed very little ambient readiness to act.

Hitherto Gladstone had kept the way clear for action in Ireland by blocking and baffling all efforts by his party to provide local government reforms that could be offered to the Irish as a reasonable answer to their Home Rule demand.

Now he was confronted with an exercise by Chamberlain in that genre. This was not a matter of restive backbenchers; here was a formidable Cabinet colleague. Chamberlain wanted to clear the Irish difficulty out of the way of serious politics in the form of his Radical Programme. His present initiative was the consequence of his intercourse with Captain O'Shea as the go-between with Parnell. Gladstone had encouraged this intercourse as the provider of valuable information. Much of this information was in fact misinformation, either as Parnell's deviousness, or as O'Shea's self-promotion as a source of high value and account, with rewards due accordingly. What Chamberlain concluded, either way, was that a '*modus vivendi*' might be found that would 'enable the Irish nationalist party to work with the Government and offer the chance of the settlement of the Irish difficulty'.[58]

Chamberlain interpreted this as an invitation to conclude a deal with Parnell whereby the coercive Prevention of Crimes Act, due for renewal later in 1885, would be softened on re-enactment, or re-enacted for a year only, in return for which Parnell would countenance a comprehensive local government measure for Ireland comprising elected provincial councils and an administrative Central Board, 'altogether independent of English government influence', with powers of taxation for strictly Irish purposes. Chamberlain also had plans for a tenant-purchase land policy.

From the information he was getting from Mrs O'Shea, Gladstone could see that on local government Chamberlain and Parnell were at cross-purposes: Parnell was hostile to local government reform designed to pre-empt his own version of Home Rule; whatever that might prove to be. Pre-emption was precisely what Chamberlain had in mind: a 'solution' that would be 'sufficient to satisfy the Irish people'. When he presented his solution to the Cabinet at the beginning of May Chamberlain was also at cross purposes to Gladstone. Chamberlain hoped to use the last months of the session to get it through the Commons at least. Gladstone made sure that would not happen. Ostensibly helpful, adopting the role as merely an '*Amicus curiae*' to whom the matter would have no personal application, he put it to his colleagues. Some were responsive and sympathetic, some hostile. But, as Carlingford noticed, Gladstone 'would not go into the argument – "quite useless"'. Gladstone promptly declared Chamberlain's scheme 'dead as mutton'.

Once the scheme was safely dead as mutton, Gladstone put on a great show of solidarity with its author: it was dead 'for the present only'; it would 'quickly rise again, & as I think in larger dimensions'.[59] Chamberlain recalled Gladstone's declaring on the first-floor landing outside the Cabinet room in Downing Street, 'These men have rejected this scheme, but if God spares their lives for five years more they will be glad to accept something infinitely stronger.'[60] This was Gladstone's way of beginning his emergence from the covert position he had been in for the past two months. He told Hartington on 30 May, still in his *amicus curiae* posture, that Chamberlain and Dilke held the 'winning position' on Irish local government. 'You will, I am convinced, have to give what they recommend; at the least what they recommend.' Gladstone was prepared, indeed, to go 'rather further than they do'.[61] He was inviting people to notice the thudding of heavy hints.

To the Queen, on 23 May, Gladstone was rather more restrained, and in his mode of one on the verge of retirement. As he glossed it to Ponsonby, he regarded it not as a proposal, but rather as a 'posthumous bequest'. It was a general review of the options relating to Irish policy. Its implication was that something needed to be done to uproot the Dublin Castle system of imposing government on Ireland from outside, and by giving local self-government to the Irish people. Gladstone indicated further that, if some timely concession were not made, he was in fear of a future dishonourable surrender to Irish demands.[62]

To Spencer, Gladstone was a little less in the 'posthumous' mode. 'Policy often determines duty', he said, 'and it is my present impression that there will be no call on me to take part in the fray which I desire and seem entitled to avoid.'[63] Here was a touch of the conditional clauses that had bedevilled matters ever since 1875. By the end of May a drive and 'much conversation' with Wolverton opened 'rather a new view as to my retirement'. That 'new view', it may reasonably be supposed, related to 'subjects ripe for action' that Gladstone had 'mentally considered', though as yet neither adopted nor rejected; subjects that Wolverton described on 18 June as 'your proposed Irish policy'.[64] By the end of June Gladstone was telling Spencer that nothing could 'withhold or suspend my retirement except the presentation of some great and critical problem in the national life, and the hope, *if* such a hope shall be, of making some special contribution towards a solution of it'.[65]

~

By that time Gladstone had resigned office. The ringmaster role had indeed become absurd (16 May: 'Very fair Cabinet today – only three resignations'). Irish budgetary grievance, collusive Conservatives and strangely unpaired Liberals brought the government down on 8 June. In the matter of honours Gladstone instituted an important modern precedent with 'arts baronetcies' for Millais and Watts. He would like to have done something for the Theatre, but accepted that it was as yet premature. A peerage for Ralph Lingen, retiring as head of the Treasury, testified again to Gladstone's partiality for Civil Service honours. And at last Nathan Meyer Rothschild became the first Jew to enter the House of Lords. Gladstone declined once more the earldom pressed on him hopefully by the Queen.

Now Gladstone was much freer for manoeuvres and stratagems. Salisbury came in as a 'caretaker' Prime Minister to complete necessary business and to arrange a dissolution when convenient. He ostentatiously did not renew the

1882 Prevention of Crimes Act. His Irish Lord Chancellor took the opportunity to legislate a pilot tenant purchase land measure for Ireland, the 'Ashbourne Act', ritually denounced by Gladstone. The Conservative leadership flirted with the Parnellites in the summer of 1885 on the principle that a drowning man will clutch at a serpent.

A post-sessional cruise on Sir Thomas Brassey's *Sunbeam* along the fiords of Norway in August gave Gladstone space to contemplate matters. He began to draft his Midlothian Address. He persuaded himself that the rustic Norwegians seemed very content in their partnership with the Swedes. It was now a question, in that light, of persuading the English to be as Swedes in relation to the Irish Norwegians.[66] The 'general development of popular principles', he was sure, 'and the long experience of Norway', and the 'altogether new experience of Austro-Hungary' required 'reconsideration of the whole position'.[67] He was ready with manipulatory cues and prompts for Knowles at the *Nineteenth Century*: 'a searching and impartial article on the history of the Union; and a careful account of the novel and critical Austro-Hungarian experiment, its terms and actual working'.[68]

For manipulating opinion on his proposed Irish policy in the latter months of 1885 and the beginning of 1886 Gladstone had available an unrivalled repertoire of manoeuvres and stratagems. At the head was the earliest and best, the promise or threat of retirement. For evasion, distraction, deception, manipulation, obfuscation, for camouflage or smokescreen, it was unbeatable. The most material point about it was that Gladstone never indicated that he would retire from his seat in the Commons.

Then there was his persuading himself that the Conservatives and the Parnellites were concocting a deal. It was indeed the case that Salisbury and Northcote were advocating that reasonable Irish demands be conciliated with sympathy and respect. There was much comradely toing and froing in these days between Randolph Churchill and Parnell. It was certainly the case that Lord Carnarvon, off to Dublin as Lord-Lieutenant, was full of ideas about doing for the Irish what he had done for the French in Canada and for what he had tried to do for the Afrikaners in South Africa, endorsed by Sir Robert Hamilton in Dublin Castle, and all within an ideal of imperial federation, guided by that eminent Irish–Australian statesman, Sir Charles Gavan Duffy. Carnarvon even took the naïve risk of a solo interview to sound out Parnell.

Gladstone had no grounds whatever for alleging that Lord Salisbury was 'nursing the idea of the same experiment' as he was.[69] Gladstone would later be reported as declaring that 'he happened to *know* as a fact that Lord Randolph, Lord Ashbourne and Lord Carnarvon had prepared a scheme of home rule'.[70] Gladstone could not possibly have '*known*' any such thing. He constructed a 'fact' out of garbled rumours and Parnell's tendentious misinformation. He persuaded himself that the Irish were being 'excited by the high biddings of Lord Randolph', and that this meant that a Central Board would no longer suffice, and that there must be a Parliament. 'This I suppose', he told an alarmed Derby, 'may mean the Repeal of the Act of Union or may mean an Austro-Hungarian scheme or may mean that Ireland is to be like a great Colony such as Canada.'

The significant point of interest here is, rather as with his observations of the contented Norwegians, that Gladstone chose to interpret these spacious schemes as constituting 'an entirely new point of departure'.[71] Northcote remarked that 'Home Rule' was a slippery 'undistributed middle term', interpretable equally as local self-government at one end or separation at the other.[72] Gladstone seems to have been willing to let Lord Randolph's alleged 'high biddings' move his own thinking in a more spaciously distributed, indeed 'colonial', direction. As he put it in an altercation with Lady Cowper, the Irish must be given 'a *great deal* or *nothing*'.[73]

Then there was his coaxing and cajoling along a path of grudging and grumbling compliance by stressing a distinction between 'more or less of opinions and ideas' that did not, nevertheless, constitute 'intentions or negotiations'.[74] This he applied particularly to Hartington, who had special weight in the party and the country. In his most headmasterly style, Gladstone trusted that Hartington and his friends 'will give the Irish case a really historical consideration'.[75] If he could keep Hartington with him, he had the battle in his grasp. Gladstone seems here to be applying to Hartington primarily, to the upper Liberal echelons secondarily, and to the nation ultimately, a political version of the theological doctrine of 'reserve'. Possibly Gladstone here took example from that master of the 'principle of economy', Newman. The 'economical method' was 'an accommodation to the feelings and prejudices of the hearer, in leading him to acceptance of a novel or unacceptable doctrine'. It involved substantial issues being 'kept in the background', to be brought forward at a time when, 'reason being proportionately developed', its presence becomes necessary. Newman's *Disciplina arcani* was a method of 'withholding the truth' with 'the tenderness or the reserve with which we are accustomed to address those who do not sympathise with us, or whom we fear to mislead or to prejudice against the truth, by precipitate disclosure of its details'.[76] In this case it was at the heart of Gladstone's manipulation of opinion.

Hartington, playing honest Kingsley to Gladstone's subtle Newman,[77] grew increasingly puzzled. Innocently, he thought Gladstone might perhaps 'consider it desirable' to have some 'meeting and discussion' with members of the late Cabinet at an early date.[78]

Here was the essence of Gladstone's next stratagem. It consisted quite simply in his having not the slightest intention of consulting either his colleagues or his party. Both colleagues and party found a deliberate procedure of non-consultation incredible. This gave Gladstone a huge advantage. It was something that might at any time happen, but never quite yet. It kept everyone else off balance, and at a disadvantage. For a long time colleagues, after being surprised, shocked or otherwise disconcerted at learning what Gladstone intended, could lull themselves into a false sense of security by taking it for granted that Gladstone would sooner or later have to consult colleagues and party, and that then there would be an end to any nonsense. Derby, for example, receiving Gladstone at Knowsley, found himself bemused. 'I listened with some surprise, for though I knew that he favoured Irish claims, I was not prepared for what in fact was a declaration in favour of Home Rule.'[79] Later, applying to Granville for a contradiction of reports that Gladstone actually intended to go ahead with his plan, Derby made the obvious points that it was impracticable, would split the party, and that in any case the party ought not to be committed without previous discussion.[80]

For his part, Hartington concluded that Gladstone was acting in a very extraordinary manner, 'and I should think will utterly smash up the party' by 'imposing upon it an Irish policy without consultation or consent'.[81] He simply could not understand how 'the policy of the party' could be agreed without a meeting of the party. 'I consider that you are the leader of the party', he told Gladstone, 'and that you are the only person who can declare the policy of the party.' The object of a party meeting would be, Hartington thought, 'to ascertain whether ... the various sections of the party can acquiesce in the policy you propose to adopt'. For all Gladstone's insistence on the unity of the empire, Hartington found his exotic references to Norway and Hungary, on top of Parnell's citings of Canada, giving him the 'greatest uneasiness', and leading him to 'fear that the return to power of the Liberal party, whether pledged or not beforehand, would involve the adoption of an Irish policy for which I at least am not prepared'. Hartington stressed once more the reasonable expectations of the party: was 'agreement possible before the party is committed?'[82] He concluded in dismay that Gladstone was beginning to express a hitherto unexpressed personal object: 'putting forward an Irish policy for which he has obtained nobody's assent'.[83]

~

The only assent Gladstone felt himself in need of was the assent of the nation. That, he felt sure, he could depend on the election to provide. The nation was sound. And as Harcourt put it, '*You are the Party*, and your acts are its acts.' This would not be the first time Gladstone had essayed to impose a policy on his party. He had failed to do so in 1866 over Reform. He had failed to do so in 1873 over Irish higher education. He was in an incomparably stronger position to do it than he had been in the 1860s and 1870s. Here again, as with renewal of the income tax in 1853 and the giving of religious equality to Ireland in 1868, was a political juncture in which a providential gift endowed Gladstone with an 'appreciation of the general situation and its result'. This was far from being 'simple acceptance of public opinion, founded upon the discernment that it has risen to a certain height needful for a given work, like a tide'. It was 'an insight into the facts of particular eras, and their relations one to another, which generates in the mind a conviction that the materials exist for forming a public opinion, and for directing it to a particular end'. His proposal of Home Rule for Ireland was for Gladstone the third in that grand series of insights.[84]

Gladstone had in mind, as he put the case to Rosebery at Dalmeny, that opinion would be formed and directed by his 'stating largely the possibility and the gravity, even the solemnity', of a fitting response to the Irish demand. In October he received Parnell's draft version of a Canadian-style constitution, with adaptations of dominion status to the Irish case. Gladstone had returned a non-commital reply conveyed by Lord Richard Grosvenor. The idea of 'constituting a legislature for Ireland, whenever seriously and responsibly proposed', would cause a 'mighty heave in the body politic' and the 'full usage of a great leverage'. Thus would opinion be moved, and with it the Liberal party, by the sheer weight of the gravity and solemnity and the energy exerted in the might required in levering the heave. All the more reason, then, for 'circumspection and reserve, for keeping the party united'.[85] To tell the party what he planned would invite disunity; doing what he planned would compel unity.

Gladstone did not doubt that he possessed that power of leverage. As Carlingford watched Gladstone progress from Hawarden to Midlothian, he was put in awe: 'What power he has! What influence over public opinion and action!'[86] But it would depend crucially on the resilience of the fulcrum on which the lever would be heaved. That fulcrum would be a Liberal majority in the forthcoming Parliament 'sufficient to maintain the independence of the House of Commons as a whole in dealing with the Irish question'. That question Gladstone circumspectly defined at Midlothian as giving Ireland, 'with a generous hand, all means of local self-government' consistent with preserving the unity of the Empire.[87] These were familiar and seemingly innocuous words. But by now Parnell was in a position to hail them as 'the most important for Ireland ever uttered by an Englishman'.[88]

The precise purport of Gladstone's words got lost amid the grandeur of his presence in the great Midlothian show, in the roar of the streets and the throngs in the halls. What came across was the majestic fact of the Grand Old Man imperiously demanding a clear majority in Parliament from the country, without needing to tell the country quite why he wanted it. If the Liberal party remained united, he declared, 'it cannot fail to be returned to the House of Commons in a majority such that it may deal independently with the Irish or any other questions'. 'This is a matter of absolute necessity.'[89]

It did not seem a matter of difficulty. In September, Lord Richard Grosvenor and the party agent, Francis Schnadhorst, estimated conservatively a Liberal return of between 370 and 380, with the Irish at 80 to 90, and the Conservatives at most at 210. Grosvenor and Schnadhorst revised their estimates: 298 Liberal seats in England and Wales, 57 in Scotland, three in Ireland, 'giving us 46 as a good working majority over all other factions'.[90] That would do.

There were, it was true, problems along the way. 'Fair Trade' protectionist sentiment was disturbingly evident in industrial centres such as Sheffield. Chamberlain tiresomely pushed his *Radical Programme*, as if the future of Britain rather than Ireland was to take centre stage. Here was a heady mix of Church disestablishment, graduated taxation, free elementary education, compulsory powers of land purchase by local authorities, taxation of urban land values, and so forth, frightening to the moderate men. 'An instinct blindly impresses me', Gladstone in heavy hinting mode informed Chamberlain, 'with the likelihood that Ireland may shoulder aside everything else.'[91]

Chamberlain's programme offended Gladstone as much in its being the manifesto of a challenger for the Liberal leadership in a post-Gladstone epoch as in its policies. Never before had Gladstone been confronted by such a phenomenon. He did not like it. For him the political process was one of continuum, not of an old order being replaced by a new. Nor did he relish an edited version of Chamberlain's programme being dubbed by Goschen the 'Unauthorised Programme' of the Liberal party, in rivalry to his own. Chamberlain for the time being proposed Kirk disestablishment in Scotland. This still gave the Conservatives a good handle for a 'Church in Danger' cry. The *Radical Programme* also gave to the dissident Liberal intellectual classes a good handle for a direct critique of the guiding text of a threatening socialistic epoch, advancing under cover of Gladstone's 'demophilic' populism.

Then T. P. O'Connor, the Parnellite Liverpool MP, announced that Irish voters in Britain would best be advised to vote against the candidates of the party that 'coerced Ireland, deluged Egypt with blood, menace religious liberty in schools, and promise to the country generally a repetition of the crimes and follies of the last Liberal Administration'.[92] Like the Conservatives, the Irish had an obvious interest in keeping the Liberal majority at an optimally low level.

Gladstone's own problem at Midlothian was that he had to keep his big idea under cover. He spent much time at Dalmeny ruminating and writing draft outlines of a measure to constitute a legislature in Dublin. These drafts bore a distinct approximation to Parnell's colonial constitution. But Gladstone could not say the big thing he wanted to say. His own manifesto was anodyne. He hardly bothered to disguise his indifference to what the party wanted. Chamberlain felt snubbed. But, to Gladstone's annoyance, Chamberlain's 'unauthorized' programme moved into the vacuum. The best Gladstone could offer was his sheer presence, formidable enough, but wanting in the inspiring power of 1879 and 1880. Wherefrom a mighty heave in the body politic? Whereto full usage of a great leverage?

This was reflected in the dispiriting election results. They turned out to be a great puzzle. In the counties the traditionally ascendant Conservatives were mauled by the new occupier voters, and came out catastrophically with a mere 98 of 231 English county divisions. They had made the mistake of mocking proposals for smallholding allotments as 'Three acres and a cow'. Their mockery was very effectively turned against them. But this success, even combined with the usual solid Scottish and Welsh returns, could not reimburse the Liberal party for its unwonted failure in the English boroughs, where the Conservatives won a small but historically unprecedented majority. By the last day of polling, on 18 December, the return of 335 Liberals was matched exactly by 249 Conservatives and 86 Parnellites.

The *causae damnae* listed by Gladstone – 'Fair Trade + Parnell + Church + Chamberlain' – were contributory components of much more spacious phenomena. Liberalism was in effect subverting itself by working its way through and out of its central Peelite–Gladstonian vocation of reconciling the mass of people to government as a beneficial agency. The new urban and suburban social forces created by prosperity now made their impact on the electoral stage. Thus a purposed political achievement of Peelite Liberalism was being transmuted into a blind social trend, of which the Conservative party had become the beneficiary.

It was in Ireland, however, that novel electoral trends most dramatically displayed themselves. Outside the Protestant redoubts in Ulster and Dublin University, the Parnellites made a clean sweep, obliterating the moderate Home Rulers who had nothing to show for their Liberal loyalties as well as the Liberal remnants. The 'very real danger' that Gladstone in 1882 had pointed to in his warning to the Queen was now fulfilled. There was in being 'a decisive majority of the representatives of Ireland' unitedly demanding on behalf of their country 'the adoption of some scheme of Home Rule'.[93]

Thus for Gladstone the 1885 result was absurdly lopsided. He predicted accurately the nature of the Irish problem he had to face, but he failed to produce the Liberal solution to it. Given his many and categorical undertakings that there would have to be 'nothing but a sheer and clear majority in Parliament' to enable 'Liberals in Government to carry a plan',[94] he was awkwardly placed. But he had two escape routes from that dilemma. One was that there was a Conservative government in being that he chose to believe was considering sympathetically some initiative similar to his own. Then there was the consideration that the showing of the Parnellites was so startling as to compel cancellation of conventional reservations as to action, especially if indications of possible violence became evident.

The immediate future would therefore be shaped by an appeal to the Conservatives to step into the breach. Failing that, the imperative of what Parnell represented meant that, somehow, Gladstone would have to be his own solution to the Irish challenge. He would have to be in himself the mighty heave and the great leverage.

~

Liberals generally felt after the election that with such a 'qualified and unstable success', there should be no delay in putting a Liberal government in place and a meeting of the party to settle its programme. 'Such a meeting would not only declare but produce unity, & it might by a decisive pronouncement of the party wh. has the majority & therefore the constitutional duty, to remove or modify the difficulties of the Irish situation.'[95] What most Liberals envisaged was some measure of generous local government reform, with elective councils, along the lines long advocated by such as Rathbone or Whitbread and not incompatible with what Gladstone had proposed at Midlothian, perhaps going as far as Chamberlain's Central Board scheme. Parnell would have to like it or lump it. But Gladstone did not. There would be no party meeting. What there would be, he trusted, was 'a healthful slow fermentation of many minds, working towards the final solution'.[96]

At that moment, Gladstone seemed to be trusting that much healthful fermentation was occurring in many Conservative minds, so that they would take up the challenge, and 'solve all these questions for me, & for us all'.[97] In no respect did Gladstone live more completely in what he chose to believe than in his persuading himself of this Conservative intention. It had the advantage also of hustling Hartington. 'So far as I can learn', Gladstone misinformed Hartington, 'Salisbury & Carnarvon are rather with Randolph, but are afraid of their colleagues & their party.'[98] Much as with the case of the Conservatives talking up Reform in 1867, Gladstone did not doubt that he could shepherd and command a Conservative Home Rule measure.

More significant was the slowness of the healthful fermentation in many Irish minds. Davitt was much in favour of thoroughgoing land purchase reform as the priority. The Parnellite MP Timothy Healy put the case to Labouchere in December 1885: 'Is it not plain that if we plunge into Home Rule plans just now before your intelligent public apply their enlightened minds to it that we shall get far less than what we should get by waiting and worrying you for a few years?'[99] Parnell, Healy and Davitt knew perfectly well that a governing Liberal party left to its own devices would take time to digest the meaning of the Irish electoral revolution and adapt itself to the notion of some kind of Irish autonomy. Immediate Liberal action would stifle healthful fermentation and cause panic and instant polarization of opinion, highly detrimental to Irish prospects.

To Spencer Gladstone confessed at the beginning of December that he had 'Ireland on the brain'. He felt also that he 'may be bound to take my turn at such a supreme moment'. 'Immediate action' was now his conviction. Healthful slow fermentation was suddenly cast aside. He declared himself 'amazed when I hear people talk of waiting games. Time is indeed most precious.' His idea of immediate Liberal action was to approach the Conservatives. It happened that Balfour was staying nearby with the Westminsters at Eaton. Gladstone walked over on 15 December to accost the astonished Balfour. For an hour Balfour was the bemused recipient of Gladstone's grim assurances of the supreme urgency of the need for the Conservative government to respond to the Irish crisis. Lord Salisbury could count on Gladstone's full support and on the benefits of his good offices with the Liberal party. He followed this up with a letter, 'writing for myself and without consultation', designed for Salisbury's edification, deploring the issue's falling into the lines of party conflict.

What most struck Balfour was Gladstone's claiming to have 'information of an authentic kind, but not from Mr Parnell, which caused him to believe that there was a power behind Mr Parnell, which, if not shortly satisfied by some substantial concession to the demands of the Irish Parliamentary Party, would take the matter into its own hands, and resort to violence and outrage'. Balfour's effort at a satirical riposte – 'In other words, we are to be blown up and stabbed if we do not grant Home Rule by the end of next Session' – fell flat. Gladstone replied gravely, 'I understand that the time is shorter than that.'[100]

Where Gladstone got this 'information of an authentic kind' from has been a puzzle. He had been getting misinformation from Frank Hill of the *Daily News* about alleged Conservative intentions that he dignified as 'astonishing disclosures'.[101] In January 1886 Gladstone persuaded himself that there was a plan by the Irish party of a 'withdrawal *en bloc*' from Westminster and setting up an Assembly in Dublin, 'by far the most formidable thing that can happen', bringing into view 'very violent alternatives',[102] with gangs of Irish Americans allegedly at the ready. There appears to be no evidence that such a plan was ever envisaged.[103] Possibly Robert Hamilton was feeding stimulating rumours from Dublin Castle. In any case it certainly stimulated Gladstone to unbox himself from the stipulations about an indispensably clear Liberal majority into which he had boxed himself at Midlothian.

That was of the essence of things once Gladstone's overture was rejected by Salisbury. The Conservative leader's purpose was to avoid adding betrayal of the Union to the grisly series of betrayals of Protestantism in 1829, Protectionism in 1846 and anti-Reform in 1867. It happened that Salisbury received Balfour's report at the agitated moment of what became known as the 'Hawarden Kite'. This was a consequence of an attempt by Herbert Gladstone to give guidance to the Liberal press, floundering in ignorance as to what was going on. Herbert, a devotedly filial Home Ruler, conveyed what was in his father's mind to the National Press Agency. What was intended as confidential guidance for Liberals fell accidentally into Conservative hands; and the London *Standard* made a sensational exposé on 17 December of 'Mr Gladstone's Plan for Ireland' and his stealthy efforts to foist it on the unsuspecting British public.

The 'Kite' thus in effect exchanged Gladstone's inaccurate self-persuasions about Salisbury with accurate information for Salisbury about Gladstone. Salisbury's blank negative was all the more withering. In due course Gladstone would be withering about the moral delinquency of the Conservative party's failure to rise to the occasion of such a supreme moment. It was possible, he told the Commons, 'that they might have made one of those Party sacrifices which seem now to have gone out of fashion, but which in other days – the days of Sir Robert Peel and the Duke of Wellington – were deemed the highest honour – namely, when they saw the opportunity to serve their country, to cast to the winds every consideration of the effect upon the Party, and to secure to the nation the benefits which they alone ... were capable of securing'.[104]

Liberals, as they heard these words on 18 February 1886, could envisage, with a variety of sinking feelings, the doom of a Peelite sacrificial future that lay before their own party. They would be offered no choice but the highest honour of benefiting the nation by the inclusion into their creed the giving to the Irish what they wanted in the way of Home Rule.

Already Hartington, Chamberlain, Harcourt and Dilke had met to 'resolve on some way to bring Mr Gladstone to book'.[105] But Gladstone had his own way of bringing his colleagues and his party to book. A party meeting, he conceded, might be held, but only on the basis of its not attempting to draw him 'on the Irish question' and of giving him what amounted to a blank cheque. Unwillingness to do that he ascribed to a 'jealousy' 'stronger than logic'. To Granville he insisted oracularly that he had 'done nothing, and shall do nothing, of myself, except what I firmly believe that those whom I speak of not only ought to, but in principle would assent to and even desire'.[106] This seems to be something relevant to the *Disciplina arcani*: the objectors would be believers, though did not yet know it. But should there be dissidence, and an unwillingness to give a 'general support of the party to a plan of duly guarded Home Rule', Gladstone would see it as his duty to 'stand aside', and give a Liberal government 'the best general support I could give it'.[107] Not a blank cheque then; but a menace of abdication.

Gladstone took care not to depart from Hawarden until the very opening of the session in January. Gladstone addressed the high proportion of debutant MPs on his intention to keep his counsel: 'and I will venture to recommend them, as an old Parliamentary hand, to do the same'.[108] On 27 January 1886 the Irish, fulfilling the logic of the situation, joined with the Liberals to defeat ministers. The vote, to add insult to Conservative injury, was on the merits of 'Three acres and a cow'. The Irish benches cheered, but the Liberal benches were forebodingly silent. Nearly a hundred Liberal MPs were missing from the division. The majority was provided by the Irish. On 1 February Gladstone became Prime Minister for the third time. Hartington, baffled, despairingly enquired of Granville: 'Did any leader ever treat a party in such a way as he has done?'[109]

17

Old Man in a Hurry, 1886

'It is to the *people*, & in the main the people only, to whom we have to look.'

Gladstone to Arnold Morley, 20 April 1886

The Queen was naturally distressed at the turn of events. After the cruel deferment of so many fervent hopes that she might at last be rid of Gladstone, it was the cruellest cut of all now to be confronted with the author of the 'posthumous bequest' rising from his grave. To his surprise, Gladstone was not immediately summoned to Osborne after his winning the vote on 27 January. There was much febrile talk at Osborne of some Conservative and 'Liberal-Unionist' combination to block Gladstone's Liberal and Irish combination. After all, there were near a hundred Liberal MPs floating somewhere in political limbo. The necessary linchpin of any such combination, Hartington, well realized, however, that his influence with his Liberal following both in the House and in the country would be compromised by close proximity at this stage to Salisbury.

Hartington was nearing the point of open rebellion at what he saw as Gladstone's brazen intention to hijack the Liberal party in a step-by-step strategy. Hartington had in mind a forthright declaration of his determination to maintain the legislative Union. Gladstone appealed for Granville's intervention to head this off. It would 'play the Tory game with a vengeance', reduce the Liberal party to chaos, and make his position impossible. Gladstone suddenly became solicitous for the party. If Hartington persisted in meditating his stroke, 'ought not the party to be previously informed?'[1]

In the interval Gladstone conferred about jobs and appointments, entertained and was entertained. In his conferrings with former colleagues he took care to avoid any collective gathering. Harcourt hoped for a 'posse comitatus' to pin him down. But now he found himself pinned down by being summoned individually for interview. As Harcourt put it to Hamilton, 'it is the Headmaster going to see his naughty boys singly'.[2] Hartington appealed to Granville, as the only one of them who had any influence with Gladstone, 'not to allow these interviews to exclude a more general collective consultation'.[3] That is precisely what Gladstone did exclude, with masterful ease.

Hamilton, again in charge of the secretariat, saw him 'much bowed down' by the difficulties of ministerial reconstruction, 'but he still maintains his pluck'.[4] Everyone observed his high spirits. There was something of a festive family atmosphere as Catherine prepared to set up house in Downing Street again. Hamilton found 'confidence prevailing that all will come round to Mr G.'[5] Mary had become engaged to Stephen's senior curate at Hawarden, Harry Drew. From Catherine's point of view the match was not entirely what she would have wished. Mary had 'bolted' to be affianced to a man much younger than herself, that would mean, moreover, leaving an awkward gap at the centre of the domestic management of the lives and comforts of the Grand Old Couple. However, there it was. Helen would have to renounce her hopes of an academic career and return home to the 'rather grim' prospect of filling the gap of 'domestic duties'.[6]

Nor was Mary the only bolter in the family scene. In musing over the Liberals missing from the division on 27 January, Gladstone could at least rejoice that Willy was not among them. Willy Gladstone had startled his father prior to the election by disclosing that he was in much of a mind with Hartington on Irish policy. Willy withdrew from politics in order to devote himself to managing his Hawarden estate.

Selborne was out and Hartington would probably be out, but Gladstone remained sure that, while damaging, their defections would not necessarily be ruinous to his prospects of forming a government. It distressed Hamilton that Gladstone's behaviour gave almost the 'appearance of a greed for power which I believe is not in him'[7] That Gladstone was tailoring his proceedings to fit the shape of the new House of Commons was widely adduced at the time as sufficient to account for his behaviour. His repudiation of the Kite as inauthentic rumours succeeded in stilling public unease. The general assumption obtained that he could not be envisaging anything outlandish, since clearly he would not be able to get away with it.

The point of substance in this is that, in the circumstances of January 1886, no one would be surprised at Gladstone's apparent greed for power. What would surprise people would be to learn exactly why he was greedy. He had not told them exactly why at Midlothian. His public talk now was for keeping his counsel. Behind that discretion was the fact that, as Hamilton glumly observed, he had 'Ireland on the brain: and thinks himself bound to make an effort, heedless of consequences, to effect a settlement'.[8] Nor was Gladstone in any doubt as to 'what seems to me the plain duty of the *party* in the event of a severance between Nationalists and Tories'.[9] That duty was so plain that consulting the party about it would be superfluous.

The Irish in particular had good reason to fear 'precipitate action' on Gladstone's part. Healy's notion in December of a 'few years' of waiting and worrying British opinion into digesting the need for an adequate response to the Irish revolution reflected their general attitude. How could Healy have dreamt that in a little over three months since his letter to Labouchere, Gladstone would be heroically presenting a far-reaching bill to the Commons? Davitt's idea of 'setting to work at once to get the *land* question out of the way' would seem indeed to be the sensible way to proceed. There was once more a rising tide of Irish expectations as Gladstone prepared to take office. The Whip, Lord Richard Grosvenor, quailed at the prospect. He hoped desperately that 'the Tory party will be forced to deal with the Irish question.'[10] Hope was now far gone of the Tory party's readiness to sacrifice itself for the higher good as defined by Gladstone. That was going to be the Liberal party's job.

There were loose ends meanwhile to be tidied up. Gladstone was now reluctantly ready to take the Irish cue about tenant purchase. But he would not have it as a preparatory introduction to a judiciously delayed exercise in 'autonomy'. He did not know if he had a 'few years' of time available to him. For Gladstone, a land measure would be a means to an end of something big on 'autonomy', as a matter of urgency.[11] Parnell wanted a colonial-style constitution. Gladstone set about giving it to him. He took Parnell's and Davitt's cues on the 'hobgoblin' threat of separation. 'It is much debated whether the Irish people are in favour of separation', he ruminated in December 1885. 'I lean to the opinion that they are not. After all, we must not presume them to be political madmen.' He put it to Derby that Grattan's words about the Channel forbidding Union and the Ocean forbidding separation were 'one of the wisest statements ever uttered by man'.[12]

Gladstone had imposed his grand Land measures on the Irish without consultation. Now he was preparing to impose a grand scheme of autonomy for Ireland on the British without consultation. Lord Richard Grosvenor resigned as Chief Whip at the end of January. Imperturbably, Gladstone replaced him with Arnold Morley. Having broken with the Conservatives, the Irish felt vulnerable to being pressured by the Liberals to moderate their demands. Gladstone made no such move. He drew up a memorandum of intent about 'autonomy' for the Queen's benefit preparatory to his attending at Osborne. He proposed 'to examine whether it is or is not practicable to comply with the desire, widely prevalent in Ireland, and justified by the return of eighty-five out of her one hundred and three representatives, for the establishment by Statute of a Legislative Body, to sit in Dublin, and to deal with Irish as distinct from Imperial affairs'. This would be done in such a manner as to be 'just to each of the three Kingdoms, equitable with reference to every class of the people of Ireland, and calculated to support and consolidate the unity of the Empire on the continued basis of Imperial authority and mutual attachment'.[13]

Thus was the Queen informed when Gladstone presented himself on 1 February at Osborne. 'I kissed hands', Gladstone recorded, '& am thereby Prime Minister for the third time. But as I trust, for a brief tenure only.' Hamilton found him that day 'in the most charming of humours and in good spirits'. The Queen noted that he 'looked very pale when he first came in, and there was a momentary pause, and he sighed deeply'. She remarked that 'he had undertaken a great deal, to which he replied he had, and felt the seriousness of it'. She thought him throughout 'dreadfully agitated and nervous'. He did his best to be tactful: 'he might fail, it was 49 to 1, that he would, but he intended to try'. In a second audience, after lunch, Victoria found Gladstone 'intensely in earnest, almost fanatically so, in his belief that he is almost sacrificing himself for Ireland'.

The Queen had already made it clear that she would not have Granville back at the Foreign Office, nor Childers in either of the Service departments. Dilke, tainted in the divorce court, she would not have in any office. Gladstone explained that Hartington, Derby, Selborne, Northbrook and Carlingford would not join him. He accepted that there was a general consensus that Granville would not be feasible as Foreign Secretary. Rosebery would take that place. Harcourt went to the Exchequer, Childers to the Home Office, Mundella to the Board of Trade. Campbell Bannerman was promoted to the War Office. Trevelyan was shunted to the new Scottish Office outside the Cabinet. Herbert Gladstone went to the War Office as Financial Secretary.

The faithful Whig lords, Ripon and Kimberley, took the Admiralty and India respectively. Spencer became Lord President. Gladstone tried to cater for the deeply afflicted Granville with a dignified precedence, perhaps even as nominal First Lord. But Granville desperately needed the salary of a first-rate working department. He moped his way back to the Colonial Office. This was awkward. Chamberlain was keen for that place. He was willing to come in as being ready to give 'an unprejudiced examination to any more extensive proposals that may be made' beyond his own central board scheme; 'with an anxious desire that the result may be more favourable' than he was then 'able to anticipate'.[14]

Chamberlain had already made it clear to Gladstone that he had no doubt that were there 'a dissolution on this question, & the Liberal party or its leader were thought to be pledged to a separate Parliament in Dublin, it is my belief that we should sustain a tremendous defeat'. The English working classes were 'distinctly hostile to Home Rule carried to this extent', and it would not be possible to convert them before a general election. He feared that 'with the expectations now raised in Ireland, it will not be possible to satisfy the Irish party with any proposals that are likely to receive the general support of English Liberals'.[15] Gladstone's riposte to this was to make withering comments on unseemly ambitions for a secretaryship of state and to shunt Chamberlain into the dim Local Government Board.[16]

For Chamberlain, insult was added to injury when Gladstone preferred John Morley, an MP only since 1883, as Irish Chief Secretary. From this point Morley passed over from being Chamberlain's partner in their Radical enterprise to being

Gladstone's favourite as his right hand at the Irish Office, a kind of semi-familial substitute for the lamented Frederick Cavendish. In Lord Aberdeen, Gladstone replaced Spencer with an agreeably pliant nonentity as Lord-Lieutenant. Chamberlain was sore also that Dilke had been excluded. Gladstone added further insult by docking the salary of Chamberlain's own faithful parliamentary right hand, Jesse Collings. Gladstone took every opportunity to wither ambitions Chamberlain might be nursing as the 'coming man' of Liberalism.

~

In preparing Morley for his new responsibilities Gladstone allowed that land had a 'logical priority', but practically it was one with the 'other great members of the trilogy, social order and autonomy'. Morley thought, 'as I have often done before', that 'he regards Parnell far too much as if he were a serious & responsible party leader of ordinary English style. This vitiates his idealism, I fear.'[17] On 2 February Gladstone played his part at Mary's wedding at St Margaret's, Westminster. It was an occasion highly inconvenient amid the bustle of ministry-building; but Gladstone 'looked as if he had nothing in the world to do but give away a daughter'.[18]

A stiff letter from the Queen on 5 February in answer to his explanatory memorandum made Gladstone 'anxious'. Dean Wellesley's death in 1882 had deprived him of expert counsel in dealing with the Queen. He called on Granville to advise. She required Gladstone to '*state explicitly what* his "examination" would lead to – for it wd not be right that the Country shld be led step by step … to approve a measure, which Mr Gladstone *knows* the Queen cannot approve'. In reply Gladstone blandly disclaimed 'the idea of leading on the country step by step to a given conclusion, as he has no such conclusion before his own mind to which to lead them'. He helpfully enclosed a copy of his Midlothian address, which 'will bind him before the world'.[19] The 'enlarged powers' for Irish self-government in the Midlothian address had so far transmuted into a possible 'Legislative Body'.

On Monday 8 February Gladstone 'worked for some hours in drawing my ideas on Ireland into the form of a plan'. What his 'Rough sketch of proposed constitution for Ireland' would lead to was very little different from the drafts he had composed at Dalmeny in November. The key point at this stage was that Irish representation in the Imperial Parliament 'might be retained or might be given up'.[20] For the time, Gladstone thus evaded the 'real knot of the problem'. Morley grappled meanwhile with the Irish Land Sale and Purchase Bill – 'some settlement of the Land question which would prevent the tenants from confiscating the property of the landlords'. James Caird, Peel's former adviser on Irish land matters, advised Gladstone to expand the purchase clauses of the 1881 Act and adapt the Conservative Ashbourne measure. Gladstone spurned such paltry expedients. He turned to Harcourt to exert '*to the uttermost*' the financial strength of the country to set up a massive fund to facilitate landlords' selling;

without which 'we cannot either establish social order, or face the question of Irish Government'.[21]

When eventually Gladstone faced the question of Irish government in introducing his Home Rule measure, he did so within a 'historical and therefore a comprehensive view of the Irish question', attained through an intensive course of self-instruction. The autumn weeks at Hawarden had been occupied in persuading himself that the historical literature supplied testimony overwhelmingly in favour of interpreting 'enlarged powers of self-government' as meaning the restoration of a Parliament in Dublin. What he also persuaded himself of, moreover, in his choice of readings of Irish history, was that the passing of the Act of Union in 1800 was an iniquitous transaction; and that indeed the whole history of the English tutelage of Ireland from the Conquest, and with particular reference to the post-Reformation Ascendancy, was an unmixed story of historical horror.

Thus, instead of approaching the matter of providing enlarged powers of self-government for Ireland on the basis of rational calculations as to what Westminster might reasonably be asked to give in relation to what the Irish might reasonably be asked to accept, Gladstone approached the issue as a passionate partisan. This episode was a signal illustration both of Argyll's diagnosis of the fanatical turn of his mind[22] and of Acton's diagnosis of his faculty for living completely in what he chose to believe.[23] A *great deal* or *nothing* was of the essence. He imported into the Irish question the moral intensities that had borne him triumphantly through the question of the East.

The effects have been described as 'cataclysmic'. 'He had Gavan Duffy's word for it that Carew's campaign in sixteenth-century Munster was the closest historical parallel to the Bulgarian atrocities.' Gladstone's reading 'dazzled' him with misconceived notions of Grattan's Parliament of 1782 – 'the respectable face of Irish nationalism'.[24] Among the cataclysmic effects, not least was Gladstone's instinctive urge to distribute the 'undistributed middle term' of Home Rule in the direction of mighty heaves and great leverages. Nor was Gladstone less imbued in the Irish question than he had been in the Eastern question with an awareness that the inner and higher prescriptions of religion were applicable to the outer and lower world of affairs and politics. Was he not seeing no less vividly the relation between his public duties 'and the primary purposes for which God made and Christ redeemed the world'? Was he not fighting the same battle for justice, humanity, freedom and law; with the word spoken 'a word for millions'? Was it not now no less a matter than then of his being summoned to a 'great and high election of God'?[25]

~

Given all this, there was nothing surprising in Gladstone's exuding, as he prepared to meet the prorogued Parliament on 18 February, the mien of a political master player exultantly in command of the political stage. As Davitt put it, 'there is only one man alive who can successfully grapple with this question'.[26] In a ministerial statement in the Commons Gladstone announced his intention to 'introduce measures of a positive and substantive character' in relation to Ireland, in which he would undertake 'the most difficult and arduous of all the questions which in 53 years of political life I have had to deal with'. Beyond that he declined to elaborate. Instead, he denounced the Conservatives for not having the nerve to brace themselves to make sacrifices, and for having nothing to offer Ireland but another bout of coercion. He made also sarcastic comments on the marked tendency of Conservative politicians to make 'pilgrimages to the North of Ireland'.[27]

The 'North of Ireland' was indeed beginning to figure notably. Unionism was spread very thinly over the most part of Ireland, mainly as a veneer of Anglican and Roman Catholic gentry and quality together with the 'commercial classes' and an admixture of Roman Catholic commonality resentful of Parnellite and clerical intimidation. But in half of Ulster it formed a majority, composed predominantly of Calvinist Protestants with no liking for the prospect of being ruled by a clerico-Nationalist regime in Dublin. They were a quarter of the population of Ireland. Already Gladstone had been made aware of how false were his assumptions about Churchill's being a Home Ruler, when Labouchere passed on a message from Lord Randolph that if Gladstone went for Home Rule, he, Churchill, would not hesitate to 'agitate Ulster even to resistance beyond constitutional limits'.[28]

Irish Nationalists early set a tone of mockery and contempt for any notions of Protestant resistance.[29] This Irish cue was the cue Gladstone would consistently take about Protestant Ulster. He rejected numerous representations from Liberals urging otherwise.[30]

Other Liberals tried to interest Gladstone in what the Liberal party wanted to do as opposed to what he wanted it to do. Dillwyn, veteran of the Irish disestablishment issue in 1865, now introduced early in March his Welsh disestablishment motion. It failed by only twelve votes. Gladstone judiciously abstained, as he did a few weeks later on a motion for Scottish disestablishment. These, along with such as local and London government reform, allotments for smallholders and free elementary schooling, were the issues of most interest to most Liberals. There was a susurrus of resentment in the party at the way Gladstone had imperiously sidelined its interests in order to impose his own interest.

Gladstone's response was that the Liberal party must concede to the larger interest of the nation. Only after it had done its duty to Ireland could it indulge itself with its own pleasures. Gladstone could not deviate from the path set for him, not by him. In the certitude of this faith was a kind of freedom. Within it, Gladstone radiated an extraordinary confidence and self-sufficiency.[31]

Self-sufficiency was most in evidence in Gladstone's keeping the Home Rule measure 'entirely in his own hands'. Apart from occasional references to Spencer and Morley, and consultations with the chief legal officers, he kept 'the monopoly of it; and he seems to monopolise the whole interest in it'.[32] He drew heavily on the British North America Act of 1867. The physical toll on the old gentleman was exacting. 'Whatever energies I possess are drawn off by the inexorable demands of my political vocation.' Gladstone was now clear in his mind that the only way out of the conundrum of Irish representation at Westminster was simply to abolish it.

The following day, 13 March, was the critical moment of Gladstone's introducing the Irish Land Purchase and Sale Bill to the Cabinet. This provided for putting up £50 million of credit in order 'to afford to the Irish landlord refuge & defence from a possible mode of Government in Ireland which he regards as fatal to him'.[33] Chamberlain led the objection that this imputation of a larcenous disposition in Dublin was hardly a recommendation for any spacious definition of Home Rule. Such considerations suggested that the measure might be difficult to sell to the party and the public.

Such were the issues seized upon by Chamberlain, who linked the implications of Land Purchase to the implications of Home Rule, and flushed Gladstone out into the open by demanding an exposition of what specifically would be involved in conceding to the Irish 'large local powers of self-government'. In this he was supported by 'Kimberley & others ditto'. Gladstone broke cover by revealing that his Government of Ireland Bill provided for an Irish executive and a unicameral legislature of two orders of indefinite powers for the peace, order and good government of Ireland, subject to a series of restrictions on those powers, comprising such matters as the Crown, foreign policy, military and naval forces, trade and navigation, coinage, establishment or endowment of religion, religious disability and setting of customs and excise duties. Ireland would contribute a proportion of Imperial financial charges. The lord-lieutenancy would continue. The Dublin Metropolitan Police and the Royal Irish Constabulary would remain under the control of the Lord-Lieutenant. The Irish legislature would have the power to create county and borough police forces. Irish representation at Westminster would cease. The Crown, in the person of the Lord-Lieutenant, would exercise the prerogative to give or withhold the assent of Her Majesty to bills passed by the Irish legislature. Gladstone had dropped earlier notions of the Westminster Parliament's retaining the right to legislate for Ireland for urgent or weighty cause, and of provision for representation of minorities.

After hearing Gladstone's exposition, Chamberlain declared that what Gladstone proposed would be 'disastrous': 'an unstable & temporary Government which would be a source of perpetual irritation & agitation'. He thought the exclusion of Irish MPs from Westminster an invitation to separation. He was sure the enormous expenditure contemplated would not secure 'closer &

more effective Union' but 'the practical separation of Ireland from England & Scotland'.[34] Chamberlain requested that his resignation be presented to the Queen.

For the first time since the Irish question emerged in its new phase in 1885, Gladstone, having to put up a practical case, had run into a serious obstacle. He adopted to Chamberlain an innocently bewildered stance. All that Chamberlain had heard were but '*ideas*' in Gladstone's head. It was Chamberlain's duty to stay on and see what substantially emerged. Chamberlain agreed to postpone resignation for two weeks. Bright was in no doubt that Chamberlain's view was 'in the main correct'.[35] Gladstone, anxious to win Bright over and bring him back into the Cabinet as a surety in the eyes of the party, grappled with him for two hours in argument 'historical in character'. He could not persuade Bright other than that his Dublin Parliament 'would work with constant friction, and would press against every barrier' proposed by Gladstone to 'keep the unity of the 3 Kingdoms'. He felt Gladstone was being far too trustful of the leaders of the 'Rebel party'.[36] Tennyson chimed in helpfully with a quotation from Pindar's Fourth Pythian Ode on the theme that it was easy to shake a city but difficult to set it back in place again.[37]

Morley observed Gladstone working indomitably on the Land Bill, 'figuring up the sums of his Irish arithmetic just like a boy at school, his grandchildren making a hideous noise on the piano in the neighbouring room, but himself all serene and cheerful'. He found Gladstone on the 23 March very confident. He was sure that the Land Bill's providing landlords a 'fair option of escape from a false position' might 'very greatly ease the passing of the entire political settlement'. By now Morley was the go-between with the Irish. Gladstone gave Parnell in confidence a draft of the Bill, with permission to show it to a few of his colleagues. Parnell was impressed by the 'thoroughness' of Gladstone's 'proposals in regard to Ireland which went really farther than he could have expected from any great English statesman & that they meant a most satisfactory solution'.[38] Having surprised Healy by his rapidity, he now surprised Parnell by his generosity.

That generosity could take radically expansive forms. Gladstone would have been 'perfectly ready to give Ireland the right to impose protective duties on British goods' – perhaps with old memories of New Zealand in mind.[39] As to foreign policy, given that Ireland was to have no voice in the Imperial Parliament, Gladstone was much taken by the way the 'foreign affairs of that United Kingdom', Sweden-Norway, were conducted by 'delegations' from their respective parliaments.[40] He dared not, in the end, incorporate such spacious notions; but they gave cues to the Irish about 'going really farther than could have been expected'.

Gladstone was to present his Home Rule Bill to the Cabinet on the 26th. On seeing Gladstone's ideas as substance, Chamberlain definitively resigned.

Trevelyan followed suit. Gladstone imperturbably replaced them with Stansfeld and Dalhousie. As one of its most formidable critics allowed, Gladstone's Government of Ireland Bill of 1886 was 'a most ingenious attempt to solve the problem of giving Ireland a Legislature which shall be at once practically independent, and theoretically dependent, upon the Parliament of Great Britain; which shall have full power to make laws and appoint an Executive for Ireland, and yet shall not use that power in a way opposed to English interests and sense of justice'.[41] This 'Gladstonian Constitution' combined federal and colonial elements. It raised deep juristic questions as to whether the envisaged Parliament of Great Britain continued to retain the sovereignty of the existing Parliament of the United Kingdom.

The more practical issues about which debate on it turned were that in the absence of Irish representation at Westminster, Ireland, though a component of the Empire, would have no voice in imperial policy. One of the points about 'instability' turned on the provision that both the two orders in the legislature – corresponding roughly to lords and commons – were to have a veto on the other. Then there was the question of the vice-regal veto. The Crown had not vetoed a bill at Westminster since Queen Anne's time. Would the Crown's representative in Ireland dare otherwise? And what of the practicability of extracting Ireland's financial contribution, or 'suzerain tribute', as it was inevitably dubbed? Control of customs and excise was a lively issue of debate. Gladstone held that if the Irish were not allowed control and collection, they would have to be retained at Westminster. Another area of controversy was the absence of securities against executive and legislative oppression; which shaded into the wider issue of Ulster Protestant objection in principle to Catholic rule from Dublin.

All these questions and problems were aired in the Liberal Cabinet and the Liberal party. Apart from its intrinsic merits of ingenuity in attempting to fit the square peg of Ireland free into the round hole of Ireland bound, its greatest advantage for Gladstone was that there was no readily available alternative. Returning to the status quo meant returning to coercion. There was little stomach for that in the Liberal party. Gladstone set about exploiting that advantage to the hilt.

He was now in a state of intense and exalted excitement. He continued confident that, if the landlords accepted his Land Sale and Purchase policy, there was 'no doubt of his being strong enough to carry it off'.[42] And if he carried that off, he would have the 'entire political settlement' in the bag. There was no doubt about the landlords accepting the land policy. The doubt was whether the Liberal party would accept it. On going to Downing Street to settle matters about the Land Bill, Morley found Gladstone 'in something like an altercation' with Spencer. 'S. very plaintive: G. vehement and masterful beyond belief.'[43]

Harcourt was plaintive about Chamberlain's departure, and the mode of it.

He warned Gladstone presciently that 'a good deal of the future' would depend on Chamberlain's 'post-resignation attitude'.[44] But Hamilton knew that 'Mr G. is not in a humour to make a compromise for Chamberlain. He has been forced too long and too hard by Chamberlain.'[45] Among other things, Gladstone never forgave the 'leaks' he felt had discredited his 1880–85 Cabinet. As later events indicated, Gladstone felt a personal distaste for 'the first gentleman of Birmingham'. Catherine might well have played her own part in this affair. 'She is not a little jealous of Chamberlain', as Hamilton observed, 'and the increased position he has lately made for himself.'[46]

It was arranged that Gladstone would introduce his Government of Ireland Bill on 8 April. 'The burden on mind & nerve becomes exceedingly heavy: heavier than I ever felt it. May God sustain his poor failing & unworthy instrument.' Mrs O'Shea's efforts at last bore fruit in a conference in Morley's room at Westminster between Gladstone and Parnell to settle contentious matters of financial arrangement. Parnell was not satisfied with Gladstone's reduction of Ireland's contribution to the Imperial Exchequer from one fourteenth to one fifteenth of overall revenue. Parnell wanted it set at not more than one twentieth.[47]

Morley recorded the occasion. Gladstone 'shook hands cordially with Mr Parnell and sat down between him and me'. It struck Morley that Parnell was sitting on the sofa 'where poor old Forster had laid his weary head many a night – he died today'. Parnell was 'very close, tenacious, & clever'. Too tenacious for Gladstone, who announced at midnight: 'I fear I must go: I can't sit late as I used to.' As Morley ushered him out, Gladstone remarked of Parnell, 'very clever, very clever'.[48]

Parnell himself, astonished at how fast Gladstone was driving, found the old man an extraordinary sight. 'I never saw him so closely before. He is such an old, old man! ... Once, when he yawned, I really thought he was dying, but he flared up again.' Later, when asked how the Home Rule Bill was going, Parnell replied: 'Badly, and going to be worse.' Justin McCarthy found him 'less optimistic than I have seen him yet during this chapter of our history. He is afraid Gladstone may be led to make concessions to English partners which might make it difficult for us to accept his scheme.'[49]

Many of Gladstone's English partners felt that Parnell protested too much. Some would have been perfectly happy for the Irish to take responsibility for rejecting what was from any objective point of view a generous proposal. Stansfeld, Chamberlain's replacement, was not all that far removed from Chamberlain's sceptical attitude on controverted issues. Behind Stansfeld were growing numbers of Liberals of the rank and file, increasingly anxious at the trend of events, offended at the way Gladstone had treated the party, bewildered at the hurtling pace he was driving, fearful of damage and possible disaster for the party in the constituencies.

Heneage, Chancellor of the Duchy, became spokesman for a variety of influential Liberal notables outside the ministry. He warned Gladstone candidly that the existence of the government would be assailed for certain and '*with success*' as soon as Gladstone proposed a statutory Parliament in Dublin, irrespective of the land purchase scheme. The grounds of Heneage's opinion were, firstly, that 'the Country will not hear of Home Rule, as you propose', and secondly, that the government as constituted had not the confidence of any party.[50] Presumably, Heneage was alluding to the nature of the Liberal vote in the confidence division two months previously. Such disaffected Liberals were beginning to look to John Bright as their fugleman. Bright much feared 'that Mr Gladstone has led himself and his Party into a difficulty which cannot be measured'.[51]

Harcourt, fulminatingly, was their heavyweight representative in Cabinet. He made furious scenes early in April over the financial provisions and Parnell's demands. Gladstone felt 'sorely tried' by Harcourt. 'Angry with myself for not bearing it better.'[52] Harcourt was sorely tried at seeing the Liberal party on the brink of tearing itself apart. Spencer dissuaded Harcourt from resigning. Bright, aware of 'great anxiety' on the Irish question 'in the House and thro' the Party', saw Gladstone again on 3 April. 'He insisted on it that there was no Cabinet difficulty, only the ordinary difficulties as to details. This I know not to be accurate.' Gladstone seemed 'obstinately determined to go on with it'.[53] Possibly Gladstone's wilfulness derived from messages from his spiritualist friend Lady Sandhurst, who certainly understood shrewdly the best way to his heart. She reported that one of her spirits had informed her, 'Daughter, there is a message from Sir Robert Peel to Mr Gladstone – it is this "Tell him to hold fast to his intentions on the Irish question. Never mind if he stands alone. Let him carry out his intention."'[54]

~

Gladstone would certainly carry out his intention. It was to be his finest Peelite moment. Peel had ever insisted on the right and duty of government to govern unencumbered by mandate. Mandates were in any case coming to Gladstone from quarters more exalted than Mrs O'Shea and Lady Sandhurst. On the fateful 8 April, at his habitual Bible-reading in his dressing room, 'The message came to me this morning: "Hold thou up my goings in thy paths that my footsteps slip not".'[55] That afternoon Gladstone introduced in the Commons his Government of Ireland Bill. Liberals learnt what was about to be added to the creed of their party as a sure prelude to its accomplishment.

There was 'never anything like the excitement'. Every seat in the chamber was bespoken hours before. Gladstone entered to a 'storm of applause'. 'Extraordinary scenes outside the House & in', noted Gladstone. 'My speech, which I sometimes have thought would never end, lasted nearly 3½ hours. Voice & strength &

freedom were granted to me in a degree beyond what I could have hoped.' Strength and freedom were indeed at the heart of Gladstone's own awareness of his heaving mightily the body politic and testing the full usage of great leverage as he tilted on the fulcrum of Parliament the ultimate great purpose of his life. He was possessed of an insight telling him that 'the great question of autonomy for Ireland had been brought to a state of ripeness for practical legislation'. He was in no doubt that the requisite popular materials were there to be formed and directed to the end he had divined.

Recalcitrance in the party and the prospect of colliding with the Lords if anything reinforced the wilfulness Bright had detected. Gladstone had dealt faithfully with the party before. He had dealt faithfully also with the Lords. There is little doubt that he would have relished a collision in 1886 and a settling of accounts. That he would conjure a majority in the Commons in 1886, however reluctant in many ways and degrees, however bewildered and resentful, he did not seriously doubt. His line consistently was that, on the analogy of Catholic Emancipation, a Commons majority was the crucial thing. Intimidating the Lords could come later. There were many tactical manoeuvres available in the course of debate and committee to give him ample play in the parliamentary struggle to come. A later Liberal admirer sorrowfully concluded that 'a man with gifts far inferior to his could have obtained a second reading for his Bill once that Bill had reached the position the Home Rule Bill reached in April 1886'.[56] It took someone of Gladstone's overweening confidence and wilfulness to create the conditions of failure.

Hamilton's view of the 'gamble' was that of a cautious Treasury officer. His analyses of the overall prospects had been acute and pessimistic. His prediction now was, on first impressions, 'from a sort of pulse-reading of the House', that 'the Bill may be and probably will be read a second time; it will be scotched and killed in Committee or undergo most radical amendment'.[57] Behind the ingenuities of Gladstone's text and the magnificence of his rhetoric and the heroism of his purpose lay much muddled thinking. Labouchere reported to Chamberlain Herbert Gladstone's comment: 'H. G. says the real *bona fide* difficulty of father is that he cannot devise a scheme.'[58]

The scheme devised by Gladstone in 1886 in all respects proclaimed itself as consistent within the great series of measures he had set forth in earlier times: Reform, Irish Church, Irish Land. It bore the stamp of Gladstone's own hand and personal authority unaided by other than higher inspiration and his own indomitable will and his assumably heroic powers of leverage. It was a text to which he would, as with the others, stick intransigently. Gladstone denied that his measure repealed the Union. His legislature would be a derivative body acting under Imperial authority. But where was Imperial authority? Perhaps the noblest aspect of Gladstone's heroic endeavour was his drive to excite a new sense of mutual trust to extinguish the mistrust that lay at the heart of the Union, to replace a Union of legislatures with a 'Union of hearts'. To that end Gladstone persuaded himself that the subordination to the Crown of the self-governing colonies was far from being a constitutional fiction. His hardest task was to persuade British opinion likewise. That opinion, moreover, could fairly ask: where was the gratitude and trust promised by the atonement of the Church Act? Or by the Land Acts?

Then Gladstone assured the Commons that there would be no return to 'co-ordinate Parliaments' as before the Union, so there would be no reason to discuss national independence, legislative independence, or 'Federal arrangements'.[59] He then invoked the precedents of Sweden–Norway and Austria–Hungary;[60] yet these were instances precisely of co-ordinate parliaments. He would have educated himself 'historically' much more usefully had he examined the way Vienna let the Poles run the Kingdom of Galicia to the detriment of Ukrainians and Ruthenians; or how the derivative Croat Diet in Zagreb operated in a state of constant friction and animosity with the Budapest Parliament, so often cited approvingly by Irish Nationalists.[61] As for the dualism of Sweden–Norway, it was already well on its way to eventual acrimonious break-up.

Nor was the conundrum 'passing the wit of man' identified by Gladstone in 1882 convincingly resolved. Either the Irish would suffer both taxation without representation and debarment from a share in imperial policy, or Britain would suffer, with Irish representation at Westminster, Irish privilege in enjoying both self-government and a share in the government of others. Nor would the Ulster question go away. The essence of it was that if Ireland had a claim against a united British Isles, did not Protestant Ulster have a claim against a united Ireland? Gladstone was on this point candidly dismissive. He could not allow that a Protestant minority was 'to rule the question at large for Ireland'. There was no justification for removing Ulster or parts of Ulster from the operation of the bill. 'That is what I have to say on the subject of Ulster.'[62]

Debate centred not on abstruse matters but around guarantees against separation and securities for the Protestant minority. The Commons as a whole was in two minds about Irish representation being withdrawn. To many it was the one feature that recommended the bill to them. At the same time it raised unwelcome implications of separation. The initial impact of the Grand Old Man's splendid performance generated a positive impetus behind the measure. Gladstone recorded himself on 13 April as '"astonied" as Holy Writ says at the strength given me in voice & tongue, after a day in which I felt to the uttermost the sum of weakness isolation and dependence'.

However, after the initial reception of dazzled wonder, the doubts, misgivings and bewilderment in general passed steadily on to complaints and criticisms in particular. The deficit of Liberal MPs at the opening of the session hung ever more ominously over the Commons scene. Heneage's resignation from the Duchy of Lancaster and Lord Morley's from the Board of Works set off a chain reaction. Gladstone held a 'conclave' on 'vacancies which thicken'. His '*mot d'ordre*' was 'to close the ranks at once'.[63]

Introduction on 16 April of the Sale and Purchase of Land (Ireland) Bill should, on all expectations, have bolstered the government's position and reinforced Gladstone's advantage in his great enterprise. Gladstone again had cause to be 'thankful for much support' from on High. Even so, the bill fell flat. Had it been put forward as preliminary to a later self-government measure it might have taken purchase. Stumping up £50 million to fund a bailing out of Irish landlords did not readily commend itself to British Liberals. They saw it as an extra impost on top of a measure that, left to themselves, they would never have embarked on.[64] Chamberlain pointed out that 'its central idea was wrong, inasmuch as it was brought in less for the advantage of the tenant of Ireland than to modify the supposed hostility of the Irish landlord'. The 'Treasury mind' in any case offended the Irish by providing for the British Receiver-General to ensure that none of the flow of funding should pass through Irish hands. The Irish denounced it as a 'transparent sham'. Far from being a buoyant float for Home Rule, the Land Bill became, in Gladstone's words, 'an albatross around its neck'. The general verdict obtained that it had caused 'a decided weakening of the Ministry'.[65]

Gladstone's credit slumped. As Gladstone went down, so Chamberlain came up. The point pressed by Harcourt about the expediency of keeping Chamberlain in some degree conformable took on a new cogency. The main sticking point for Chamberlain was the exclusion of Irish members from Westminster and the separatist implications involved. Was there no scope to ease his disquiet? Proposals that a reduced contingent of Irish MPs might remain, proportional to Ireland's financial contribution, were canvassed. So urged Arnold Morley, the Chief Whip, anxious to negotiate terms for Chamberlain's return to the Cabinet. Confident that he had made a stir in debate that marked him out as a key player in the game, Chamberlain was heard to declare 'his feelings of admiration and wonder for the power of the G.O.M. over the minds of men was greater than ever'.[66]

The G.O.M. was in no doubt about his power over the minds of men. He did not welcome rivals in the game. With John Morley now in his pocket, he made great difficulties about rehabilitating Chamberlain. Experience had shown that 'such concession is treated mainly as an acknowledgement of his superior greatness & wisdom, & as a fresh point of departure accordingly'. Gladstone declined writing 'Kootooing letters to Chamberlain & I doubt as to their effect'. Chamberlain had in him, as Gladstone remarked to Morley, 'with other notable gifts, a good deal of repulsive power'.[67] Rebuffed, Chamberlain had no option but revert to antagonism. He again alluded grimly to Gladstone's power over the minds of men. 'I don't know what I can do.' 'What can be done with a madman as leader? ... Why, he is going to destroy Ireland and we are helpless. It is all very well saying prevent this and prevent that. The mischief is already done. The evil has taken root.'[68]

~

By now resistance in the party was beginning to take shape and substance. Those who had abstained from voting on 27 January exerted by their mere existence an increasingly subversive influence. There were Liberals outside the inner loop of high political practitioners who did not accept that they were helpless, and who thought that this might be prevented or that might be prevented, and that something might be done about a madman as leader. They were the Liberals who resented bitterly having suddenly foisted on them, without consultation or discussion, an immensely controversial policy that they would never have undertaken on their own account. They were Liberals who might well have agreed with Healy that, after digesting the Irish situation for a few years, it would be incumbent on the Liberal party, the party ever looked to by the people of Ireland for redress of grievances, to respond fittingly to what Parnell represented as Irish tribune. What they saw confronting them now was the likelihood of their party in shock being split and suffering possibly irreparable damage at the next polls.

A meeting of Liberal peers at Derby House on 15 April comprised 48 attenders and 16 sending letters of support. Hartington attended. A Liberal Unionist office was established in Spring Gardens to cater for Liberal dissidents on 22 April. It was the peers who attracted Gladstone's attention. He counter-attacked on his demophilic line. He was preparing himself, if and when occasion suggested, to be virulent against the representatives of class privilege and class selfishness.[69] What Gladstone had in mind was the theme he had opened up to Arnold Morley. 'It is the *people*, & in the main the people only, to whom we have to look.'

In retreat at Hawarden for the Easter recess, Gladstone was the recipient of yet another helpful offering from Tennyson, ever resolute for Gladstone's enlightenment from the latest luminaries of the science of politics. Henry Maine's *Popular Government* was a text expressive of a growing disaffection among the Liberal intelligentsia.[70] Gladstone knew how best to get back at Tennyson. He asserted 'a strong assurance that the subject of *In Memoriam* would have been with us'. Gladstone further assured Tennyson that he would not, in his 76th year, have thrown himself into struggle without a 'clear conviction' and 'a strong sense of personal call'. 'For 42 years at least of my 54 in public life, Ireland has had rather a dominant influence over it. Which is those of my opponents that has had occasion to study it as resolutely & for the same time?'[71]

Leaving the Laureate to chew on that, Gladstone brooded about Ireland and the people. The people were much with him that Easter. The Hawarden shrine was besieged by pilgrims. Gladstone deputed Herbert to address them. He tried to keep the field clear of routine governmental distractions. He was reluctant to share Rosebery's concerns at the Foreign Office. 'Many tactical lessons are to be learned from Peel's conduct, and I recollect that in 1846, with the repeal of the Corn Law in view, he went very great lengths, perhaps even too great, in order to avoid side issues.'[72]

What Gladstone immediately had in view was drawing up an address to the Midlothian electors that would be also a manifesto calling to battle both on the renewal of the parliamentary session on 3 May and on the gathering of the National Liberal Federation at Birmingham of 5 May. It was the aim of the party managers to wrest control of the Federation from Chamberlain's 'Caucus'. In his manifesto Gladstone made a great point of asserting his leadership of the nation, by implication, against Parliament. He deplored the way the Commons occupied itself with the petty details of the Government of Ireland Bill instead of attending to the high and historical principle of Irish self-government that it embodied and was what really mattered. But the burden of his message was to accuse his opponents of representing the 'spirit and power of class'. In the great struggle to confer the boon of Home Rule on Ireland the 'adverse host', Gladstone declaimed, consisted of 'class and the dependants of class'. Gladstone here reverted to the doctrine of his *Nineteenth Century* piece in July 1878 on the moral superiority of the popular judgement to that of the higher orders.[73] The mood and tone was now that of 1878, and all which that holy time of the question of the East portended. The 'formidable army' of class was the same that had fought 'in every one of the great battles of the last sixty years', and had been defeated by 'the upright sense of the nation.'[74]

Soon there would be the matter of the second reading to confront. On Gladstone's return to London, Arnold Morley reported that 'a considerable number' of Liberal dissidents 'outside the 65 whom I consider to be certain to vote against, would be satisfied with the recognition of the principle of Irish Representation', but there were others 'whose action would more or less depend on C.'s vote, and I still think it important to secure his support'.[75] Gladstone and John Morley, however, even as their ranks thinned, remained adamant against any 'Kootooing'. On 5 May the Gladstonian forces wrested control of the Liberal Federation from Chamberlain. 'Though Chamberlain is rather in the dust', Gladstone told Rosebery, 'Hartingtonism is on its high horse, & I am sorry to say that though things are said to be moving in the right direction, & I have much faith in the country, the Parliamentary outlook at this moment is very far indeed from clear.'[76]

A rally of Liberal notables offered good offices to redeem the situation. Stansfeld advised that the Irish representation issue be left '*not quite closed*' on the second reading. He offered his own plan of 'Federation'. This brought in a simplified version of Grand Committees extendable to England, Scotland and Wales severally, with powers similar to an Irish legislature.[77] Stansfeld criticised accurately Gladstone's memorandum to the Cabinet on the handling of the second reading as 'expedients not founded on any clear principle carried to a logical conclusion'. They would 'not recommend themselves to the popular mind in or out of the House', and as 'evidences of weakness & insufficient in their character as concessions, they would damage the chances of passing the 2nd reading of the Bill'. The true principle to apply, '& I think the most popularly acceptable one, was Federation practically & simply applied'. Stansfeld did not think it possible to carry the present measure without an appeal to the country.[78]

This was candid good sense, but for that very reason inapplicable to Gladstone's wilful purposes. He would stick closely to his Home Rule text in 1886 as he had stuck to his Reform text in 1866. He opened the second reading debate on 10 May. 'The reception entirely inferior to that of the Introduction.' Gladstone offered his concessions in a manner suggesting that they would be subject to Parnell's approval. Gladstone took away with one hand what he offered in the other. The Liberal benches were left dismayed and seething. The atmosphere was now charged with Randolph Churchill's notorious tocsin, 'Ulster will fight and Ulster will be right.'[79]

From the backbenches Whitbread, coached by Bright, urged that prospects for the second reading would be materially advanced if it were made known that the government would allow time after the vote for consideration of objections raised on what was, after all, 'a subject newly presented to Parliament'. Ministers would then stand better before the country when an appeal to the constituencies had to be made, if they could show 'they had no desire to force this question on with haste'. Many voters now doubtful 'would be brought in by this course'.[80] For Gladstone, however, haste was of the essence.

Alfred Illingworth chaired a meeting of 50 Liberal MPs anxious to carry the second reading but 'painfully aware that there is a considerable number of earnest Liberals who are hesitating as to their course'. Illingworth conveyed a plea to Gladstone to summon 'a private meeting of the party if you could see your way to convene it at a very early date'.[81] Gladstone could not see his way. He had offered all that could reasonably be expected in a spirit of goodwill for the removal of difficulties felt by 'sincere friends of the principle of the Bill'. It was 'dangerous at this late stage for the Govt. to produce appendices to their own suggestions'.[82]

John Bright's vote on the second reading would be crucially influential. Gladstone hoped that he would abstain, and lead a large following to do likewise. In eloquent representations on 13 May, Bright indeed left open that possibility. He made a last plea that 'more time should be given for the consideration of the Irish question. Parliament is not ready for it.' A policy of such gravity 'cannot and ought not be thrust through the House by force of a small majority'. It was a quite different matter from Reform Bills, the Irish Church Bill and the Land Bills.[83]

A heavyweight Tyneside notable, Sir Joseph Pease, put the matter even more candidly than Stansfeld. The bill would not pass its second reading. The break-up of the party would be deplorable and would not be healed by a general election. The only thing to do was to withdraw the measure and prepare a new one for the autumn session such as 'would satisfy the reasonable wants of Ireland and have the support of the *entire Liberal* Party', and become law in 1887. Pease aimed both for the 'good of Ireland and to prevent the disintegration of the Liberal Party'.[84] To Pease Gladstone responded in headmasterly style. 'I must observe that the whole force of the dissentients *has not yet availed to tender to us a single suggestion in a practicable shape*'. What Parliament was sadly defective in would be remedied by the people. 'Meanwhile, the body of the nation, so far as we can judge, has hailed our imperfect efforts with enthusiasm, & so has the great British race throughout the world.'[85]

On 14 May Gladstone did go so far as to put before his colleagues five possible expedients as to withdrawal or holding on. 'Could there be truth in the statement', he asked Arnold Morley, 'that Hartingtondom, let alone Chamberlaindom, is ready to vote a Resolution in favour of Home Rule on the withdrawal of the Bill?'[86] There had indeed been suggestions that a resolution on the principle of Home Rule, in lieu of a second reading, might be a mode of avoiding a confrontation of Liberal with Liberal. For John Morley it was 'rather distressing to see the desperate sort of tenacity with wh. he clings to his place'.

At this juncture came Salisbury's notorious 'blazing indiscretion' at St James's Hall. Dabbling in amateur anthropology, he implied the relevance to Ireland of consideration of the eligibility of Hottentots to self-government. The Irish were rabid with offence; particularly as Salisbury barged on to advocate Irish emigration to Manitoba as preferable to Gladstone's expensive and clumsy scheme of tenant purchase. He rounded off by proclaiming that what Ireland needed was not Home Rule but twenty years of resolute government to make Ireland fit for self-rule.

This stiffened Gladstone wonderfully. He brushed aside Heneage's insistence that, with the Land Bill dead, it was necessary to withdraw the Government Bill; and in the gap thus created some of the useful measures promulgated in the Midlothian programme could be proceeded with. Gladstone conferred on the 18th with Parnell and Morley. He judged Parnell 'very noteworthy in conversation'. As Parnell departed, Gladstone remarked, 'most satisfactory man'. What was most satisfactory about Parnell was that he would have no truck with concessions to the bill's candid friends. The upshot was that Gladstone would 'stick to his guns' and neither withdraw, postpone, nor proceed by resolution on the principle.[87]

In the heroic posture of one sticking to his guns, Gladstone swatted the persistent Pease. The Tyneside MP had reiterated his feeling as to the '*intense*' desire of a great many Liberals to avoid 'an entire break-up of the party'. Such a 'disintegration would be as terrible as it would be complete'. He presumed to dispute Gladstone's opinion that an appeal to the country would succeed.[88] 'A Government', Gladstone admonished Pease, 'cannot afford to degrade itself by the confession of errors it has not committed.' He was at his most crushing in his dismissal of Pease's doubts about the healing powers of a general election. 'As regards the country, you will excuse me if (without pretending to anything like certainty) I in contemplating my *fourteenth* Dissolution – if that is to be the issue – am more confident than I should be.'[89]

~

Arnold Morley and Schnadhorst had consulted with Gladstone on 19 May about a possible dissolution. Schnadhorst did not doubt the preferability of an immediate general election if the second reading were lost. Though not without risk, it would be better than 'showing the white flag'. Gladstone cordially concurred. It appealed, as Hamilton observed, to his 'natural pluck' and partiality to a 'bold front'. The managers calculated that the Irish vote would turn some 30, perhaps 40, seats. Schnadhorst had faith in Gladstone's 'ability to carry the country with him'.[90] Labouchere advised that with the Irish retrieving at least 40 seats, the combined Opposition would face the impossible task of capturing over 100. It was as certain that Gladstone would win 'as anything can be certain in politics'.[91] Gladstone was full of analogies with the defeat of the Reform Bill in 1866, and of the mistake then made of not boldly taking the question to the people.

Nor, with such a dissolution in prospect, was Gladstone in the least apologetic to those Liberals such as Hutton of the *Spectator*, who deplored Gladstone's recourse to the rhetoric of class. 'I *do* think the common ruck of your "Unionists" from Dukes downwards are warped by the spirit of class, but that few comparatively are aware of it, & a few consequently compromise their integrity. So, among the opponents of Peel in 1846, there were some of the best men I ever knew. And the average were men worthy of respect. Am I warped by the spirit of anti-class? Perhaps – I cannot tell. My dislike of class feeling gets slowly more & more accentuated: & my case is particularly hard & irksome, because I am a thoroughgoing inequalitarian.'[92]

Sir Thomas Brassey, associated with Whitbread, Maguire, Pease and others, made a supreme effort to convince Gladstone of his party's 'one universal and anxious desire to avoid defeat on the second reading'. Hartington hitherto had held his fire. Timing his broadside well, he had come out with all guns blazing on 18 May. He made a big impression. Brassey pleaded that with Gladstone 'things may be done which would be impossible for any other statesman'. Would it not be best for the promotion of the cause in the longer term to drop the Home Rule

Bill, and replace it with an Irish Local Government measure acceptable to the party? 'Could it not be done by you without discredit?'[93]

No: relapse into what Rathbone had proposed before the opening of the 1880 session could not be done without, for Gladstone, immense discredit. But pressures on him were now too insistent to permit his resisting any longer the expedient – for him, truly desperate – of a party meeting. It was summoned for 27 May in the spacious Foreign Office, confined to Liberal MPs known to be more or less sympathetic to the principle of Home Rule. Chamberlain was not invited. Gladstone prepared himself for 'a statement of importance & extreme delicacy'. The Cabinet's view was that, after the bill's being passed through second reading, it could not be proceeded with without an autumn session and 'necessary amendments'.

A meeting of the Liberal party in that context was looked upon by Parnell as a dangerous course. Gladstone's precipitancy so far was not at all what Parnell and his friends would initially have advised. They were now vindicated in their deprecation of risky haste. Still, they had to take things as they found them. If Gladstone could pull it off, all would be well that ended well. But Parnell was not pleased at the possibility of being asked to settle for less than what Gladstone had initially and generously offered. This refractoriness disconcerted Gladstone. Parnell was now talking loudly of not voting for the second reading. That would have suited many Liberals.

The Foreign Office gathering was attended by some 260 Liberal MPs. Gladstone's line was to refuse a vote there and then on the principle, but to agree that the second reading would be treated as a vote on the principle, with particulars to be attended to later. The Land Bill was consigned to oblivion. The main issue was whether to keep the Home Rule Bill alive after passing the second reading and proceed with it in the autumn, or wind up the session and call Parliament for a new session when the bill could be reintroduced with necessary amendments. Gladstone preferred the latter course, which was agreed to.[94] 'The meeting went off well enough', Gladstone recorded, '– but I don't believe in these tactics.'

His disbelief in those tactics became explicable when in the Commons on 29 May he denied that he had undertaken to remodel the bill. 'Never, never, never', he exclaimed to the delighted Hicks Beach. This greatly disconcerted many attenders at the Foreign Office, who had understood Gladstone to provide for precisely that. More than ever, Gladstone's indefatigable twists and turns to avoid departing from his own text were reminiscent of the distressing sessions of 1866 and 1867.

The Foreign Office meeting was answered by a meeting of dissentients on 31 May summoned by Chamberlain in Committee Room 15 at Westminster. Fifty-two representatives of Hartingtondom and Chamberlaindom attended, though not Hartington in person. The dramatic climax to the occasion was Chamberlain's reading a letter from Bright in Rochdale announcing his intention of voting against the second reading, 'if Mr Gladstone is unwise enough to venture on it'. Bright was willing for dissentients to abstain if this would result in a small majority for Gladstone. That would be '*almost*' as good as a defeat, and might have the advantage of avoiding a dissolution, instead of compelling one.[95] On the main question, there were 45 votes for positively voting against the second reading.

'Great dismay in our camp', Gladstone recorded, 'on the report of Chamberlain's meeting.' Bright's letter was, in John Morley's phrase, the 'death warrant' of Gladstone's Home Rule Bill. Gladstone took a certain relish in what was to be visited on the recalcitrants by way of retribution in the fullness of time. It was in its way a revisit to that dire occasion of the party's unwillingness to rally to him in May 1877.[96] 'I think with great comfort', he told Rosebery, 'of the fact that in all human probability all connection between Chamberlain and myself is over for ever.'[97]

Throughout all the critical debates of April and May into June Gladstone radiated confidence. On 4 June he admitted to Childers that 'the *odds* are still I imagine in favour of the rejection of the Bill – In that case our *main* subject of discussion will of course be a Dissolution or a resignation – though it is just possible there may be other alternatives.' On the morning of the division, 7 June, a letter was published in *The Times* from W. E. H. Lecky, doyen of Irish historical scholarship. He was as alienated by Gladstone's twisting the Irish historical evidence as Max Müller had been by Gladstone's twisting the Homeric evidence; the worse for being all *bona fide*. 'An honest man with a dishonest mind' was Lecky's phrase for it.[98] Lecky called attention to Gladstone's remoteness from public opinion over Home Rule. 'It is, I believe, perfectly notorious that if it had not been proposed by Mr Gladstone there are not fifty English members of Parliament who would vote for it.'[99]

'At last came the Old Man's speech, as vigorous as ever and in beautiful voice, but it was a losing speech.'[100] For the first time in public, Gladstone burst out with his denunciation of the 'dreadful story of the Union' of 1800, 'unfolded in all its hideous features'. But now was 'one of the golden moments of history – one of those opportunities which may come and may go, but which rarely return, or, if they do, return at long intervals, and under circumstances which no man can forecast'. He pointed to what he saw as Ireland's previous golden moment, the abortive mission of Lord Fitzwilliam in 1795, when the cup of emancipation was dashed from Ireland's lips. 'The long periodic time has at last run out, and the star has again mounted into the heavens. What Ireland was doing for herself in 1795 we at length have done.' The forces opposed to this golden endeavour were the forces of 'class and its dependants'. 'You have power, you have wealth, you have rank, you have station, you have organization. What have we? We think we have the people's heart; we believe and we know we have the promise of the future.' On behalf of the people, Gladstone and his friends hailed Ireland's plea 'for what I call a blessed oblivion of the past. She asks also a boon for the future, and that boon ... will be borne to us in respect of honour, no less than a boon to her in respect of happiness, prosperity, and peace. Such, Sir, is her prayer. Think, I beseech you, think well, think wisely, think, not for the moment, but for the years to come, before you reject this Bill.'[101]

The magic did not work. There were many – not only Liberals – who thought that if a golden moment was being missed, it was being missed because of Gladstone's deception, wilful haste and imperial style in attempting to impose inflexibly a settlement that went too far beyond reasonably acceptable terms and caused unnecessarily bitter division of opinion. There were Liberals who found it intolerable that Gladstone was demanding the sacrifice of their party in the way Peel had demanded it of the Conservatives in 1846. They found it lamentable that, in so doing, Gladstone had wasted Liberalism's golden opportunities to legislate beneficially for the country – including Ireland – in the years since 1880.

The Government of Ireland Bill was defeated on its second reading by 341 votes to 311, the largest division thus far recorded. The missing Liberal votes of 27 January now reappeared, with devastating impact on Gladstone's fortunes. 'We are heavily beaten on the 2nd Reading ... a scene of some excitement ... one or two Irishmen lost their balance.' A Cabinet on 8 June decided on dissolution. Wolverton and Schnadhorst both recommended it decidedly. Gladstone was 'entirely composed though pallid'. He thought 'dissolution is formidable, but resignation would mean for the present juncture abandonment of the cause'.[102] 'Excellently well and full of go', Gladstone proceeded thereupon to advise the Queen to proclaim what he was later to describe as 'a people's dissolution' for 'a people's election'.

~

At Downing Street Gladstone prepared to make his progress to Edinburgh. The mood was revivalist: revival of the spirit of 1880, revival of the positive cause of 1868. It had been want of the latter that had stultified the promise of 1885. Now all the elements were in place. The power of the people would give him the means of repairing the omissions and derelictions of Parliament. Thus far they, and he, had come since his first, tentative essay in the genre of summoning the nation against its recalcitrant representatives back in the Easter recess in 1866, in Liverpool.[103]

Taking the whole perspective of Gladstone's career, this has the best claim to figure as the supreme moment. 'I am now arrived at the last of the series.' For more than twenty years he had been possessed of the idea that the 'object of the highest prize' was to 'complete the list'.[104] Ireland was the last on the list. 'The first two were the Church and the colonies. Freedom of trade the third. The discussion upon finance, the fourth. Then came the emancipation of the subject races, the fifth.'[105] 'Series' was ever one of Gladstone's keywords. In summoning the nation to his aid, Gladstone, masterful within the precinct of Christianity, would put to the proof his conviction that, just as his determination to implement Home Rule was, as Catherine put it, 'a duty owed by man to God',[106] so the people, uncontaminated by the derogations of class, must 'feel the issue of the moment as part of the eternal duel between good and evil', and take their stand accordingly.[107] This was the moment of Max Weber's insight about Gladstone's 'completely personal charisma' challenging the 'everyday power of the party', the 'Caesarist plebiscitarian' 'dictator' on the electoral battlefield.[108]

It was as exponent of 'charismatic domination' that Gladstone drew the Queen's attention to what he persuaded himself was one of the 'new elements' in the case, 'the popular enthusiasm of the liberal masses which he had never seen equalled'. Against that enthusiasm would be arrayed anti-Irish prejudice, the power of rank, station and wealth, and the influence of the established clergy.[109] Gladstone tactfully refrained, as one having no skill in such matters, from any forecast of the likely result of the contest between those forces. But the Liberal managers made no doubt that, with the Irish vote returned, the mislaid majority of 1885 would be retrieved. Chamberlain himself was shaken by the seeming 'universality and completeness' both of the passionate devotion of the British democracy to the Prime Minister and of the sentiment 'out of doors', 'which, I dare say, has taken many of us by surprise, in favour of some sort of home rule to Ireland'. He wrote, panic-stricken, to Churchill: 'I fear the G.O.M. is going to win.'[110]

The 1885 Parliament was dissolved on 26 June and the elections were to get under way from 1 July. Gladstone set out from St Pancras station with Catherine (and Willy in tow) on the now familiar way to Dalmeny. All throughout England and Scotland were 'wonderful demonstrations all along the road'. At Edinburgh on 18 June Gladstone proclaimed his 'doings and intentions'. 'Again God gave me voice according to the need.' At the Music Hall he declared the case to be that of a 'people's dissolution' and a 'people's election'. It was to be like Inkerman in the Crimea, a soldiers' battle. The officer class of politics had failed in their duty to give the right lead. As to Lord Salisbury's resolute remedy for Ireland in particular, Gladstone invited his audience to 'reflect in the name of Almighty God in the sanctuary of the chamber, in the sanctuary of your heart and Soul', what it was, in that year of 1886, after nearly a century of continual coercion, to propose such a remedy 'as an alternative to the policy of local government for Ireland!' He invited the people to join him 'in that happy, I may almost say that Holy, effort'.[111]

There were protests against the blasphemy of public invocation of the Almighty for partisan political purposes. One of the protesters, Lord Randolph Churchill, added to denunciation of Gladstone's 'audacious profanity' the explanation of his frenetic proceedings: 'an old man in a hurry'[112] Feted at Midlothian, the indomitable old man was at the centre of 'a crush which was trying & might have been dangerous': quite in the spirit and manner of 1879 and 1880, the 'whole scene a triumph'. Uncontested at Midlothian, Gladstone progressed through Glasgow, Manchester and Liverpool on the return to Hawarden. He was gratified at Guinness Rogers's assurance that the Nonconformists were as sound as ever.[113] As he remained unapologetic about invoking God, so he refused to retract his invocations against class. To Hengler's Circus in Liverpool, on 28 June, Gladstone 'went in bitterness, in the heat of the spirit: but the hand of the Lord was strong on me'. That hand made him declare: 'All the world over, I will back the masses against the classes.'

'Now begins the great struggle', Gladstone supplicated as polling began at the beginning of July. 'Govern it, O most High.' Notwithstanding the most High, the elections soon revealed themselves as a disaster. Schnadhorst was taking a 'gloomy view' as early as the second day. Given that the 1885 poll was hardly more than six months since, a great many constituencies were uncontested. Liberal Unionists and Conservatives had the benefit of a greater number of these seats. There were many arrangements to avoid splitting the Unionist vote. The agricultural labourer vote that had done such execution against the Conservatives in the counties in 1885 collapsed. 'Poor Hodge, another of our allies', Gladstone grieved, 'I fear may lose heart.'[114] He had every reason to. Liberal candidates had no answer to the accusation that Gladstone, having gained office on the 'Three acres and a cow' allotments policy, 'threw aside the interests of the agricultural labourer and insisted on forcing Irish affairs to the front'.[115] The much-touted Irish vote proved a will-o'-the-wisp. Probably as many Irish voters in Britain voted for Conservative policy on religious education as for Home Rule.

The most damaging blow struck at Gladstone was by Bright. Up until the start of polling he had kept public silence. He had told Whitbread that if Gladstone dissolved the Parliament, he 'would be responsible for the greatest wound the Party has received since it was a Party'.[116] Every word in his unforgiving speech at Birmingham, in John Morley's phrase, 'seemed to weigh a pound'.[117] The gravamen of his indictment was that Gladstone had deceived the electorate in 1885 by concealing his conversion to Home Rule. Gladstone found this difficult to rebut convincingly. The paths of Home Rule were proving slippery footing indeed.

Bright's attack struck a responsive chord in the British public mind. The general election of 1886 was a most intensely fought contest. Anti-Catholic sentiment, stimulated by the very effective 'Home Rule means Rome Rule' jingle, flared up. The 'slumbering genius of Empire' also was awoken. Memories of Gordon at

Khartoum mingled with Ulster's war-cry of 'No Surrender'. Guinness Rogers was not an accurate prognosticator of Nonconformist steadiness. Liberal abstentions rather than Unionist advances did most of the damage. Thorold Rogers explained his loss at Bermondsey: the voters could not understand 'what they deem is an entire change of front'; and they looked to Bright as their guide.[118] As the days passed, indications accumulated analogous to Bermondsey. 'The Elections perturb me somewhat', Gladstone noted: 'but One ever sitteth above.'

Perturbation led to much wild flailing of telegrams showering over the constituencies. 'If Warwickshire does not wish Dukes & Earls to overrule the nation & wreck its fortunes', he advised the Liberals of Rugby in a typical specimen, 'she will return the Liberal candidate, not Tories nor seceders who are working with & for the Tories.'[119] In the case of George Leveson Gower, defeated in Staffordshire, Gladstone protested amazement 'at the deadness of vulgar opinion to the blackguardism and baseness (no words are strong enough) which befoul the whole history of the Union'. He advised Leveson Gower 'to take resolutely to the study of Irish history'.[120]

By 7 July Herbert had studied the returns and glumly estimated a House of Commons in which 197 Gladstonians would be confronted by no less than 315 Conservatives and 72 Liberal Unionists. The Parnellite contingent remained unaltered at 86.[121] 'The defeat is a smash', Gladstone concluded on 8 July. The supreme moment had turned into a kind of grotesque parody. Gladstone found it difficult quite to reconcile himself to the enormity of the way the most High had governed the affair. 'Everyone will be puzzled', he insisted to John Morley, 'no one happy.'[122] What remained conspicuously absent was any hint of doubt that perhaps, in the rapture of his peculiarly God-driven style of vanity, he had misread grossly the 'facts' of this political juncture; that his 'appreciation of the general situation and its result' had been manifestly awry. Not the slightest suggestion is detectable indicative of any anxious reflections about the authenticity of the 'insight' that had generated in his mind the conviction that the materials existed in 1886 for forming a public opinion and for directing it to his particular end. He remained seemingly as magnificently impervious to compunction as he had been to advice.

Should the government resign at once? Should they meet the new Parliament? Would Morley 'kindly ascertain from Parnell what he has to suggest'? Even now Gladstone was reluctant to let go his grip on the levers. He talked of a possible autumn session to test what the National Liberal Federation people called the 'so-called Liberal Unionists' with a resolution on the 'principle'.[123] His colleagues steered him back to the inevitability of summary resignation. Granville declined a marquessate. Victoria found Gladstone 'pale and nervous' at his closing audience on 30 July. He found the Queen in good spirits, 'her manner altogether pleasant. She made me sit at once.' Her single remark about him personally was that he would require some rest. She carefully avoided all political and controversial matters. She saved those for a 'I told you so' letter the following day. For his own part, Gladstone concluded that her mind and opinions had of late years become 'seriously warped'.[124] Somehow, in the stress of it all, it seemed appropriate to Gladstone to see out his third ministry with a visit to the unwarped mind of Mrs Thistlethwayte. 'I told her how glad I should be if I could be able to feel that I had been of the smallest use to her in any particular.'[125]

18

Appeal against the Verdict, 1886–1892

'O for ... insight into the true measure of my relations to Him who has done such wonders for me, and yet Who mysteriously holds me on in a life of suspicion and contention, at a time when Nature which is the voice of God calls & sighs & yearns for repose.'

Gladstone, diary entry, 29 December 1889

While extricating himself from office, Gladstone quickly recovered equanimity and composure. He remained puzzled and unhappy, and persuaded that everybody else must be also. But practical matters soon took precedence. Two things occupied his mind. The first was to settle the fact that he intended to stay on in the leadership of the party. There was no question of retirement now. He was not the man to fade away in defeat and discredit. He had come back triumphantly from disaster before, and he intended to do so again. The second was to consider the question of rebuilding the unity of the Liberal party in relation to continuing or revising the Home Rule policy embodied in the defeated Government of Ireland Bill.

Continuing in the leadership meant continuing on his own terms. There was absolutely nothing the Gladstonians could do about it. As Harcourt had put it, Gladstone *was* the party, whether the party liked it or not. Gladstone set out his terms. He wanted a 'dispensation from ordinary and habitual attendance in parliament, but should not lay down the leadership so as to force them to choose another leader, and would take an active part when occasion seemed to require it, especially on the Irish question'. Meanwhile, Liberals would be free to promote legislative plans generally in co-operation with the Dissentients, so as to allow the party to re-form itself.[1]

Thus Gladstone intended to continue as leader of the Home Rule policy rather than as leader of the Liberal party. As Hamilton put it, 'What are Land Laws and County Government to him?'[2] The former Cabinet, players in a political theatre of the absurd, swallowed these terms on 20 July, and 'all applauded'.

For Gladstone retirement had always been something of a threat as well as a promise. Now it became entirely a threat. To Harcourt, who had been offensively lukewarm about Home Rule, and who took the lead among his colleagues for moves towards reunion, Gladstone made it clear that Ireland was to have absolute priority in Liberal counsels. If that was not agreeable to Harcourt and his friends, Gladstone of course was always ready to retire to the backbenches. 'As in the case of Ireland, so in the matter of reunion, I am above all things determined not to be personally an obstacle in the way of what is good.'[3]

He promptly made clear that he would not remodel his bill to make it more palatable to the party. The question of Irish representation at Westminster had become a touchstone of sentiment about rethinking both within and without the Gladstonian fold. But, as Knowles of the *Nineteenth Century* put it, 'while he was personally so absolutely modest and diffident, he was "officially" entirely the reverse. No pope, indeed, was ever more infallibly certain and immovable than Mr Gladstone when once he had become convinced that such or such a course was right and true. It was then "borne in upon him" as a duty.'[4] On 12 July, Gladstone set out his 'official' opinion. 'Could we hope to remodel our measure, this might be ground for an endeavour to make up a majority through the union of Liberals, Seceders, & Nationalists. I, however, though I might suggest some amendments, do not at all see my way to remodelling the Bill, or presenting a new Bill.'[5] In due course, Gladstone would lay it down that 'to propose any measure, except such as Ireland could approve on the lines already laid down, would be fatuity as regards myself, and treachery to the Irish nation'.[6]

So that was that. Where the scope would be for all allowing the party to reform itself consisted entirely in assuming that reactivation of coercion by the Conservatives must so repel seceders as to impel them back to the Gladstonian ranks and, thereby, Gladstone's Home Rule policy. That remained to be seen. Meanwhile, Salisbury's minority Conservative government presented itself in August to the new Parliament to complete necessary business. Lord Randolph Churchill, as both Chancellor of the Exchequer and Leader of the Commons, stood forth as the Conservatism's 'coming man'. Hartington raised the question of seating arrangements for his Unionist section, much the larger segment of the dissident Liberals. Gladstone declared that he 'earnestly' desired, subject to the paramount exigencies of the Irish question, to 'promote in every way the reunion of the Liberal party'.[7] He urged Hartington 'not to encourage talk of a coalition with the Conservatives'. Such would mean 'extinction for the Whig party'.[8] Salisbury was quite willing to serve under Hartington. But both Hartington and Chamberlain had as yet to be careful about getting too close to Salisbury. The Liberal Unionists sat together with their Gladstonian comrades on the Opposition benches, much like the Peelites consorting with Disraeli during Russell's Whig ministry of 1846–52.

The new session gave Gladstone the opportunity to make publicly clear his position on the Home Rule issue. He gave unapologetic notice that Home Rule as he defined it remained entire and intact. Nothing that had happened 'had produced the slightest change in my convictions with regard to the basis of that policy'. He could not afford 'the slightest encouragement or the smallest ground' for any suppositions to the contrary. All that had happened, 'instead of weakening, has confirmed me in my strong belief that we did not err in the main principles of the measures we recommended to this House'. He denied that the late election result had about it anything of an 'irrevocable' verdict of the country.[9] 'Another turn of the wheel has placed us on the underside, but the turning has not ended, only begun. We, the promoters of Home Rule, continue in the certitude of our belief that the measure will and must pass. But I cannot find on the part of the opponents any corresponding certitude that it will not.'[10]

The pattern of the 'official' Liberal future stemming from the circumstances of 1886 seemed likely to resolve itself into two parallel lines of development: Gladstone's Liberalism would proceed to put his Home Rule measure of 1886 back on the political rails in readiness to be triumphantly reintroduced and passed into law when the people would come to repent of their great error in 1886. Gladstonian Liberalism meanwhile would attempt to provide itself with the political nutrients denied to it between 1880 and 1886 by Gladstone himself. That would eventually take shape and form by 1891 in what came to be known as the 'Newcastle Programme', a kind of genteel version of Chamberlain's Radical Programme of 1885.

Neither of these proceedings would be without trial and tribulation. Gladstone's Liberalism would not get the 1886 version of Home Rule back on the political rails of legislation entire and intact. The Gladstonian Liberals for their sad part had to sit back and watch their erstwhile comrades of Hartingtondom and Chamberlaindom spur on Lord Salisbury's government as it legislated the great Local Government Act of 1888 for England and Wales, the Scottish version in 1889, the epochal creation of the London County Council in 1889, the Primary Education Act of 1891, providing 'assisted', or virtually free schooling, and the vast expansion of Lord Ashbourne's Irish Land Purchase Act of 1885 in Balfour's Irish Land Purchase Act of 1891.

All that had been predictable within the frame of the dissidence not only of the Home Rule Liberals and the anti-Home Rule dissentient Liberals, but also the dissidence that had grown steadily through the 1880s between Gladstone's Liberalism and 'Gladstonian' Liberalism.

~

Gladstone's Liberalism through these years was not without its resources and its fair hopes and expectations. The Irish backlash of resentment and defiance at having been denied Gladstone's Home Rule tested Salisbury's government to its limits. Gladstone calculated his assets. 'We have Scotland, Wales, Ireland, Yorkshire & I hope the North, and we have with us the civilized world. From this cause it is probable that our cause will visibly move upwards.' Its final triumph was 'certain'. The only question was 'how much of unhappiness for Ireland, of difficulty & delay, of pain & shame for England before the consummation will be reached'.[11]

There was indeed massive evidence of support for Gladstone in the self-governing colonies and the United States. Much of this came naturally from the Irish diaspora. But much also came from colonial opinion that could see no problem in Gladstone's importing into Home Rule a 'Canadian' dimension. The practical fact was that such opinion would not have had to take responsibility for coping with the consequences ensuing from establishing in Dublin a legislature, dependent in theory but independent in reality, whose only serious point would be to pass legislation that the Imperial Parliament would not pass.

For Gladstone the immediate tasks requiring his attention were, first, explanation and justification, then a longer-term remedy for the electorate's gross misjudgement. By 19 August he launched an elaborate pamphlet, *The Irish Question, I, The History of an Idea. II, Lessons of the Election.* He declared this as having the same explanatory motive as *A Chapter of Autobiography* in 1868. The explanations had to be of quite different kinds. In the case of the Irish Church it had been a matter of accounting for a change of opinion that had already been publicly professed. With Home Rule it was a problem of explaining away what to the public seemed to be a change of opinion covertly sprung.

What he asserted, in effect, and quite accurately within what might be called a Gladstonian frame of mind, was that his progress to Home Rule had been publicly observable to the observant who followed his tracks. He passed over in silence his stipulation for a clear majority as indispensable for taking on the Home Rule case. He did not mention Ulster. He denied intrigues with Parnell. 'There was no communication of any kind between the Nationalists and myself before the fall of the Salisbury Government.' That came under Hamilton's observation about disclaimers 'savouring of an origin from Jesuitical dictionaries.'[12] He denied precipitancy. 'What antagonists call precipitancy, I call promptitude.'

Of more consequence was Gladstone's reading of the election and its implications. Toryism, he was sure, could not by its own resources win a majority, 'unless and until the temper of the British nation shall have undergone some novel and considerable change'. The pattern of the nineteenth century would again be repeated: Toryism would resist and then retreat as it had done over the Anglican Constitution in 1828–29, over Free Trade in 1846 and over Reform in 1866–67. Home Rule, he asserted, was now in the same position Free Trade had been after the 1841 election. Liberalism, when reunited, 'must again become predominant in Parliament', for it spoke for the nation against the classes. The people would come to realize how 'unspeakably criminal' had been the means of attaining the Union.

Here was indeed the big idea at the heart of Gladstone's Home Rule politics between 1886 and 1892, when Salisbury dissolved the 1886 Parliament. The explanation of what went wrong in the 1886 election was obvious. 'The people did not know the case.' The remedy was obvious. The 'whole iniquities of the Union' must be 'laid bare and become common property'.[13] Gladstone would set about teaching the nation that his Home Rule policy would put right the wrongs of 1800.

As Headmaster of the nation Gladstone would do for Home Rule what Cobden and Bright had done for Corn Law repeal, 'neither (generally) cared about or understood till Cobden illuminated it with his admirable intellect, Bright putting in the passion'.[14] To intellect and passion aroused, to fulfilling the deeper trends of the movement of the times towards restoring Liberalism's habitual ascendancy, Gladstone could, as ever, add the Butlerian credentials of fulfilling God's purposes in the never-ending struggle in the lower world between right and wrong. He had evidently misunderstood the most High's governance in 1886. There could be no misunderstanding now. He rejoiced at opportunities for 'review', for 'probing inwardly the intention, to see whether all is truly given over to the Divine will'.[15] After a speaking foray outside Birmingham in 1888, Gladstone stayed with the Philip Stanhopes at Wodehouse, Wimbourne, 8–9 November. 'I woke without a voice, and in the pouring rain, after *four* days of fair weather while we needed them. How He maketh all things in measure & number. I think there have been since 1879 not less than fifty of these fair days and not one has failed us. And I am asked to believe there is no Providence, or He is not "Knowable."'[16]

This vision of the most High attending to the state of Gladstone's vocal chords and to the microclimate of the West Midlands for the ulterior benefit of the cause of Irish Home Rule, with reference to the sanctified question of the East, is a striking illustration of the sheer cosmic faith in his assignment from on High that sustained and energized Gladstone.

There were other sustaining and energizing phenomena in the times. Irish initiatives both in Parliament and in Ireland now claimed attention. Parnell's Tenant Relief Bill of September 1886 caught the government on the hop. Had they promptly incorporated it into official policy, as Chamberlain advocated, they might have headed off the 'Plan of Campaign', inaugurated in October 1886. This was a formidable operation designed to lay siege to carefully selected estates deemed vulnerable to being reduced to surrender in the matter of evictions for non-payment of rent. A tenant, having been refused an abatement of rent, would hand over to trustees a 'fair' rent, which would go into a fund to help evicted tenants. Hicks Beach, Salisbury's strong man for Ireland, was preparing a swingeing coercive response for the 1887 session. Gladstone could well anticipate that the trickle of dissidents returning to his fold would turn into a stream.

All in all, Gladstone could see no reason to doubt his certitude in the unchanging substance of the electoral materials he saw himself forming and directing. His assumptions about the nature of politics remained fixed and rooted in the High Victorian epoch of his prime. He detected no evidence that the temper of the British nation was undergoing some novel and considerable change. Within that frame of assumptions he could assert that, looking at the Irish question 'which way we will', the 'cause of Irish self-government lives and moves, and can hardly fail to receive more life, and more propulsion' from the unwitting hands of the new government. 'It will arise, as a wounded warrior sometimes arises on the field of battle, and stabs to the heart some soldier of the victorious army, who has been exulting over him.'[17]

~

Having loosed this Parthian shot, Gladstone could retreat to Hawarden. Helen had replaced Mary at the centre of domestic management. She repined at abandoning her academic career and the prospect of the principalship of Holloway College offered her, but she accepted the legitimacy of the patriarchal manners of the time. For Gladstone himself there were changes. One of Eddie Hamilton's last services, inspired by Rosebery, was to combine with Malcolm MacColl and W. T. Stead to warn Gladstone that his 'nocturnal activities' had been of 'baneful effect' in the London constituencies. Hamilton begged Gladstone to consider the risks. He consented to confine his interest to a couple of cases he wanted to pursue further.[18] He burned old letters, 'which might in parts have suggested doubt & uneasiness'.

A visit to Döllinger enlivened the recess. This was Gladstone's last sight of him, now in his 87th year. 'My short excursion to Germany', he reported to Laura Thistlethwayte, 'was of great use. It broke the flood of correspondence, and it took me for a time entirely out of the atmosphere of contention and suspicion, for which I got in exchange free & harmonious conversation with friends on subjects of deep interest.'[19]

Back at Hawarden, the flood of correspondence did not slacken. There was a very unharmonious bout of wrangling with Hartington and Chamberlain. Deputations from Ireland bore thanks for Gladstone's exertions for Irish liberty. Gladstone was inspired to an addendum for a new edition of his *Irish Question*, expanding his critique of the 'horror' of the years 1795–1800 in Ireland. Having exposed the delinquencies of the governments of Naples and Turkey, he explained, he was morally bound to expose the like delinquencies of his own country. Opponents like Bright could not understand why these historical arguments needed to be opened up. They needed to be opened up because they exposed the 'moral invalidity' of the Union. Gladstone could only admit the irony of the fact that the only two persons 'of real historical eminence who are against us in this' – Lecky and Goldwin Smith – 'are the two men who, as historians, have said the very things which form the main foundation of our bill'.[20]

Wranglings and polemics with many other historically-minded opponents who questioned Gladstone's readings of Irish history mingled with significant literary occasions he could not let pass in acquiescent silence. Tennyson's *Locksley Hall Sixty Years After*, presented in December 1886, he dealt with faithfully. The old narrator's repudiation of the hopes and dreams of the young narrator of the original *Locksley Hall* of 1838 cut far too close to Gladstone's bone for comfort. Here was the revered Poet Laureate, the 'pre-eminent Victorian', declaring that the society of the time was rotten with greed and misery and that the politics of the time was a pit of hypocrisy and demagogy. Gladstone's vision of 1859 of a partnership in art and politics was founded on the premise of their both as young men having set out on 'the march of mind'. Just as the young Gladstone renounced the narrow vocation of political service for the Church and stepped forward into the ampler role of Christian service of the State, so the young Tennyson renounced the temptation to flee the obligations of being 'the heir of all the ages, in the foremost files of time', and embraced commitment to the 'wondrous mother-age'. Over the years Gladstone had spent time and energy keeping Tennyson steady in the yoke Gladstone had devised of an Arthurian-Peelite partnership betokening the coming of a better age. Gladstone was relentless in his attentions. He soothed Tennyson's tantrums. He humoured his distempers. Now Tennyson had broken out in an extraordinary effusion of public and political tantrums and distempers. 'When was age so crammed with menace, written, spoken lies?'

Gladstone passed over Tennyson's overt hostility to Home Rule; but he could not ignore a poetic explosion that bore so directly and invidiously before so large a public on the merits of the Peelite and Liberal record over the time between the two *Locksley Halls*. Tennyson's lines about 'leaders of realm-ruining party', 'tonguesters' leading astray the simple goodness of the people, took on an invidiously personal implication. Encouraged by Knowles of the *Nineteenth Century* – founded, after all, precisely to celebrate the coming of better times, the achievements of the Peelite–Liberal world – Gladstone rebutted Tennyson's speaking rantingly through the mask of the Old Prophet by employing every available statistic and anecdotal instance to demonstrate that the hopes of the Young Prophet 'for all the wonders that would be' were not betrayed. It had been, rather, 'a *wonderful* half-century'. In a characteristically cunning touch, Gladstone rebuked Tennyson in '*Locksley Hall* and the Jubilee' for the impropriety of commencing the Queen's Jubilee year of 1887 with so dark and pessimistic an outlook.

In the meantime, the flood of correspondence at Hawarden included many pleas that Gladstone modify his stance to reassure 'influential Liberals of various classes' who 'hold aloof from us & follow Lord Hartington'. There were pressures also from Ireland about the virtues of hastening slowly.[21] Gladstone's constant rule with all such overtures was to admit the conceivability of any amount of modifications, subject to the approval and acquiescence of the Irish party. He was greatly put out in 1887 when Archbishop Walsh of Dublin suggested that he might climb down a little from the heights of his 1886 bill. Nonplussed, Gladstone had to allow that 'if Ireland shall consider a smaller measure or a different measure of Home Rule satisfactory, (no injustice at the same time being due to Great Britain or the Empire) I shall wish it all success'.[22] To Gavan Duffy's daughter he declared himself 'far from discouraged' in his bid to 'complete the list' with the 'last of the series' of his life's vocations. 'But you do well to remind me ... that there is One above us & them who rules & overrules our poor counsels, & to whom we may fearlessly commit a cause alike beneficial to all the countries concerned in it, & to all sects & classes of the people.'[23]

Although Gladstone remained unaware of indications that the political temper of the British nation was undergoing novel and considerable change, he was acutely aware of novel and considerable changes in the temper of the cultural dimension of the nation's life. He told MacColl that he wanted 'some solid and scientific work which shall set up historical or institutional Christianity to take its chance in the melee of systems dogmatic and undogmatic, revealed or unrevealed, particularist, pagan, secular, antitheistic or other, which marks the age'.[24] Though a professed 'believer in the harmony between science and religion', he feared 'the effort to procure a greater ease in our position' would 'introduce a new element', destructive to religion's position'. His response in these years to the 'strides of science' of Darwinism was less defiant in tone than it once had been, more aware of the need to build defences. Acton and Morley both made him aware of the turning against his Liberalism of many of the eminences of the Liberal intellectual classes, led by such as Matthew Arnold and Huxley, the Diceys and Henry Sidgwick. But Gladstone's vision ever looked beyond to higher things. To Newman he declared his feeling that 'mankind is not now principally governed from within the walls of Cabinets & Parliaments – higher issues are broadly revived, & higher interests are in question, than those with which Ministers & Oppositions mainly deal'; and it was 'by subtler & less intrusive instruments that the Supreme wisdom acts upon them'.[25]

~

At the end of 1886 Gladstone found great encouragement in the astonishing event of the resignation of Lord Randolph Churchill. Any shock to the political status quo could not be interpreted as other than beneficial to the Home Rule cause. One possible far-reaching consequence might have been the break-up of Salisbury's rickety government. Again, as in July 1886, Salisbury offered to serve in a Unionist coalition under Hartington. But Hartington's Liberal following did not as yet have the stomach to swallow so indigestible a pill. Hartington, however, did provide as a kind of token of better Unionist times the person of Goschen as one entirely qualified to fill the gap left by Churchill and thereby help rescue Salisbury.

Churchill's fall left Chamberlain much at a loss. A species of entente with Churchill as the 'coming men', joint representatives of the younger generation against their respective 'Old Gangs', had been an important feature of his recent occupations in political exile. He was now prompt to declare at Birmingham that the time was ripe for Liberals to come together. After all, they agreed on nine points out of ten. Chamberlain had no doubt that 'a few representative men meeting round a table' could agree on a programme for a reunited Liberalism. An Irish land policy would be the best point of junction.[26] Gladstone sardonically observed Chamberlain's difficulties, but promised Morley that 'everything honourable should be done to conciliate and smooth Chamberlain'. 'On the whole I rejoice to think that, come what may, this affair will really effect progress in the Irish question.'[27]

There remained the difficulty that Gladstone's definition as to what was honourable in effecting progress on the Irish question was not easily reconcilable with the hopes and expectations of a multitude of Liberals anxious for concord and unity. Of the Liberal chiefs, Harcourt made the most eager acknowledgement of Chamberlain's overture. Chamberlain responded once more on the theme of '3 Liberals around a table'. Harcourt insisted to Gladstone that there was 'a solid basis for union'.[28]

Surer than ever in the strength of his position and his prospects, Gladstone imperturbably brushed aside these eager brokers of unity. He was apparently immovable and certainly irremovable. 'The tendency of the late exciting events is to stir men's minds from their moorings; & we must be on our guard.'[29] There could be no abandonment of his definition of Home Rule and replacement by a land policy and alternative schemes of local government unless such a course were acceptable not only to the Liberal majority as well as the Liberal dissentients, but equally to the representatives of Ireland. As for himself, Gladstone could not 'abandon a cause which is so evidently that of my fellow men *and* in which a particular part seems to be assigned to me'.[30]

Such delusions sustained Gladstone and wrecked any chance of success for the series of 'Round Table' negotiations that began in January 1887.[31] (There actually was a round table, provided by Harcourt's son Lewis, 'Loulu'.) Gladstone saw the negotiations as a means of allowing heretics to abjure their heresy. Time, he was convinced, was on his side. Chamberlain was isolated, without the Liberal Federation for shelter. Soon the Conservatives and the Hartingtonians would start cracking down on the Irish, exposing his isolation even more invidiously.

Goschen, as Hartington's alter ego, had gone over to Salisbury as Churchill's replacement. Where could Chamberlain go? A by-election recapture of Burnley from the Liberal Unionists in February looked very much like the beginning of a turn of the tide. Hamilton found Gladstone 'quite up in his stirrups' on the strength of it.[32]

Recriminations flared up once more between Gladstone and Chamberlain. Gladstone pointed out to restless Liberals that their hopes of reform measures for England and Scotland and Wales were being blocked by intransigent Liberal Unionists. Chamberlain countered by pointing out that the English, Scots and Welsh were being made to wait 'until Mr Parnell is satisfied and Mr Gladstone's policy adopted'. Thirty-two million people must go without much-needed legislation because three million are disloyal.[33] To the editor of the Welsh *Baptist*, who complained that law-abiding Wales was neglected while Ireland gets her way through agitation, Gladstone responded that he had been telling the country 'on every occasion that I could find, that no great political matter of any kind ... could be practically dealt with, until the Irish question which blocks the way is settled and put out of the way'. Therefore, he who wishes to have a 'great Welsh question' attended to must see that 'his own aim is to clear the road'.[34]

As the long and fraught session of 1887 wore on, Gladstone continued 'up in his stirrups'. The Gladstones were now encamped in their accustomed state of domestic incoherence at Dollis Hill in suburban Willesden, grace of the Aberdeens. His semi-detached style of leadership made this perfectly feasible. Dining there on 19 March, Hamilton noted Gladstone 'in great form – in high spirits and buoyant mentally and physically'. Gladstone was especially vivacious on 'one of his favourite topics', Sir Robert Peel – the greatest man he 'ever knew or could conceive of.' Peel was indeed 'a perfect God with Mr G.'[35]

Salisbury's ministry, although shored up by Hartington and Goschen, looked anything but convincing. Confronted with subjecting Ireland to 'resolute government', Salisbury was in difficulties. Beach's health would not stand the strain. Salisbury took a deliberate risk and replaced him with Balfour. This could plausibly be represented as an act of despair by a collapsing administration. The Criminal Law and Procedure (Ireland) Bill that Balfour took charge of was a comprehensively rigorous measure to replace temporary coercive measures with a systematic counter-attack on terrorism and intimidation. It would be rammed through by an unapologetically abrupt use of the new 'Closure' provisions to restrict debate. Gladstone denounced it as 'a Bill aimed at the Irish people', 'a Bill aimed at a nation'.[36] Chamberlain and his friends were in an agony of doubt between Gladstone and Parnell on the one side and Balfour and Hartington on the other. A trickle of dissentients came back to Gladstone, including Trevelyan. It came to Chamberlain's being received at Dollis Hill on 5 April. 'The general impression left on my mind by the interview', Chamberlain recorded, 'was that

Mr G. confidently counts on the unpopularity of coercion to bring about an early appeal to the country and to secure a decision in his favour and that under these circumstances he does not desire to proceed further in the direction of conciliation and does not believe that the party will allow him to do so.'[37]

This confidence was dented by *The Times*'s publishing on 18 April, the day of the introduction of the Crimes Bill, a sensational item in special format, the first of a projected series called 'Parnellism and Crime', designed to expose the intimate collusion of Parnell and his party and the National League with criminal terrorism. Most sensational of all were facsimiles of letters allegedly signed by Parnell, one of which stated that while the death of Lord Frederick Cavendish was regrettable, Under-secretary Burke got no more than his deserts; and that, in the circumstances of the case, Parnell had no choice but to denounce the event as atrocious and distance himself and his party from it. Parnell declared the letters to be forgeries, and requested a parliamentary committee of inquiry. Salisbury, however, sensing that he had Parnell by the throat, decided on a full-scale judicial commission designed to expose Irish Nationalism as a vast criminal conspiracy.

To Gladstone the affair was a painful jolt. There was a resurgence of Liberal demands for rethinking the 1886 policy. Randolph Churchill's accusation that Gladstone was 'Leader of the Repeal of the Union' needed convincing rebuttal. Gladstone elaborately failed to convince. Liberals observed that the Irish people thought otherwise. The issue of Irish representation at Westminster simply would not go away. There was disaffection in the Liberal ranks about Gladstone's casual and remote parliamentary leadership. Hamilton tried to persuade Acton to talk candidly to Gladstone. 'He can say things to Mr G. which hardly anyone else can say. I told him what I thought ought to be impressed upon Mr G. was the expediency of holding more frequent communication with his ex-Cabinet colleagues and occasionally with his party, and of not putting off *sine die* the consideration of some Home Rule measure, so that the difficult points might be met beforehand. Lord Acton thought Mr G. somewhat age-ing, and that a want of proportion and perspective was growing upon him.'[38]

Samuel Whitbread, ever one of the more candid of those trying to help Gladstone help himself, called attention to utterances within the party calculated to make the public 'wonder what it is that keeps the party from reuniting'. He warned Gladstone: 'the enemy will not be slow to assert that it is because you will not consider any alternative to the plan of last year'.[39] To this, Gladstone's dismissive marginal comment was: 'The Irish!'

~

Gladstone reacted instinctively: from parliamentary sulks and party resentments and Westminster heavinesses and troubles he would repair to the people, and renew strength from their touch. The Whitsun recess in 1887 offered an opportunity for an exercise in his charismatic mode. It would be a way of hitting back at Tory coercion. Wales suggested itself as the beneficiary. Its grievances about neglect were not to be disdained. Gladstone knew his Scotland and felt his position there secure. It would be a mistake to risk Welsh disaffection for want of a touch of cultivation. Gladstone took Scottish disestablishment seriously. He considered Welsh disestablishment a shallow, derivative movement without bottom, a matter of crude sectarian agitation. But there it was. The thing to do was hold it at bay while bringing Welsh opinion around to understanding that the primary duty of 'the most Protestant nation in Europe' was to help bring about a Roman Catholic government in Dublin.

An excursion from Hawarden through the heart of Wales would have Swansea as its natural terminus. The imminent descent among them of one they held in awe as 'some Grand Llama of Thibet or Vested Prophet of Khorassan', put the Welsh in high excitement.[40] The manner of Gladstone's triumphant progress, accompanied by Catherine and the Rev. Stephen, recalled the grand precedents of demophilic embracings of the masses at Tyneside and Merseyside and Midlothian: the 'charismatic priest-king' in plenary splendour. The crowds that besieged his train as it passed through Llanidloes, Newtown, Builth and Merthyr, and the Swansea throng that tried to storm the High Street Station, were converting their chapel, radical and national emotions into a hero-worshipping response to the first major British statesman who had, in turn, responded sympathetically to Welsh grievances. But Gladstone was also a stern headmaster of the nation. At Singleton Abbey, seat of Sir Hussey Vivian MP, Gladstone skated evasively around what the Welsh Liberals were seriously interested in and insisted that 'the cause of Ireland is the cause of Wales'.

That was his unspoken evangel to the great mass demonstration at Singleton on 4 June when 50,000 marchers paraded before Gladstone for four hours and 25 minutes as he took the salute, a large leek on his lapel, surrounded by the flower of Welsh Liberalism. Refreshing claret was thoughtfully provided in teacups. Just as the politicos clustered about him, such as Henry Richard and Stuart Rendel, were recharging the batteries of their prestige by public proximity to the radiances of the Grand Old Man, so Gladstone recharged his own batteries by immersion in the invigorating dynamic of the masses. The Swansea episode he could interpret as confirmation and enhancement of his credentials as the nation's leader, wielder of the people's power, harnesser of public energy, manipulator of great issues.

There were problems about the small print. It had been widely anticipated that Gladstone would use the Swansea occasion to make a revisionist move in his Home Rule doctrine. Advocates of revision scanned anxiously the reported texts of his speeches, both at Swansea and at Cardiff on his way back to London. It was difficult quite to decipher the cryptic utterances of the oracle. Gladstone returned to Westminster well pleased that he had got the better of the implicit bargain with Welsh Liberalism.

~

By now it was the Queen's Golden Jubilee season. Gladstone thought the Abbey service on 21 June 'too courtly'. That was hardly the word appropriate for his presence at the garden party at the palace on 29 June. 'Disposed of eleven royalties. Saw Abp of Canterbury – and the Pope's Nuncio.' His disposing of the greatest royalty was most entertainingly recorded by a lady-in-waiting from the testimony of the Queen's cousin, the Duke of Cambridge.

> That brute Gladstone stood in the forefront of the circle outside her tent while she had her tea, bang opposite her, hat in hand; she said to the Duke: 'Do you see Gladstone? There he has been standing hat in hand, straight opposite me this Half-hour, determined to force me to speak with him! But I am as determined *not* to speak with him!' So he continued to stand the *whole* time! But when she came out of the tent, instead of coming out in the centre, upon him, she went out at the end, and went along the line to the right, then made a circuit and took the other line to the left and most skilfully avoided him so that she neither spoke to him nor gave him her hand. But alas! The Duke heard afterwards, which is too *exasperating*, when she had so successfully and markedly avoided him, the brute contrived to get around to *inside* the house and placed himself so, that when she passed through the house to go away, at the last moment she came all suddenly *upon* him, round the corner, and was forced to give him her hand!!! Too provoking.[41]

~

Political conflict soon recommenced, centred on passionate contention over Balfour's driving of the Crimes Bill. Gladstone denounced it as marking the onset of a new and disastrous era. Seven hundred years of English mastery had resulted, he alleged, in a discredit, misery and shame more indefensible than Austria in Italy and Russia in Poland. In the bitter end Balfour got his bill through by grace of Hartington and Bright. Gladstone observed Chamberlain's agonised twistings and writhings with ever more sardonic satisfaction.

Another splendid by-election success in wresting the Nantwich division of Cheshire from the House of Grosvenor also did much for Gladstone's morale. Ever more up in his stirrups, he interpreted it as making a 'considerable addition to the evidence now approaching to a demonstrative character, that the people of England intend to do full justice to the people of Ireland'.[42] He got down to 'Electoral Facts of 1887', which came out in the September *Nineteenth Century*. This was an updated version of his skills in what he termed 'political meteorology' as to the imminent electoral success of the Home Rule cause, repairing the anomalous false step of the 1886 election and restoring Liberalism's historic and natural hegemony. That false step, he was sure, 'indicated not the conviction, but the perplexity of the country'.[43] More cogently than ever was the analogy convincing to Gladstone that Dublin Castle rule now stood exactly in the same situation that the Corn Law stood in 1841, when Peel came into power: seemingly stable and assured, but in reality ripe for demolition.

Dublin Castle, however, now had in Balfour an energetic champion. Balfour set about boldly confronting the Plan of Campaign. His first stroke under the new Crimes Act was to proclaim the Irish National League, successor to the earlier proclaimed Land League. An affray at Mitchelstown, Co. Cork, in which the Royal Irish Constabulary defended themselves from the 'Blackthorn Brigade', left many police gravely injured and one demonstrator dead and two mortally wounded. Balfour made unflinching support of the beleaguered forces of law and order the watchword of his administration. Irish Nationalists who had joked about 'Pretty Fanny' at the time of his appointment now made a great set at 'Bloody Balfour'. It caused scandal that Gladstone should have telegraphed 'Remember Mitchelstown' to a correspondent, and cited the words again in a speech at Nottingham. He insisted that never in his life had he used words 'he more rejoiced to have used'.[44]

Contention was at depths of bitterness unusual even in Gladstone's experience. What was felt to be Gladstone's ambivalent attitude to the Plan of Campaign gave particular offence.[45] Gladstone's unabashed defence of his 'Remember Mitchelstown' watchword exacerbated these fears; as did his constant harping on the theme of the illegitimate and ultimately self-defeating deployment, 'systematically and boldly', of the power of wealth and high station against his policy.[46] His giving unreserved credence to Parnell's version of the Carnarvon interview as against Carnarvon's own account appalled Hamilton, who had ever been convinced of the 'absolute untrustworthiness' of Parnell. 'Mr G. has always pinned his faith too much to Parnell.'[47]

An interlude in Florence with Catherine and Helen to set off the new year of 1888 ('a luxurious journey' all provided by Sir Edward Watkin of the South-Eastern Railway, with the best attentions of Messrs Cook's, whom Gladstone had extolled in his '*Locksley Hall* and the Jubilee' piece as one of the signal indicators of better times) was restorative of spirits. For a renewed 'life of contention' back in London, the encampment was in James Street, Buckingham Gate. Now that he was no longer secluded in remote Willesdon, Gladstone vexed Hamilton by neglecting to entertain his party. Hamilton feared that Gladstone's invulnerability made him inexpediently aloof. Gladstone continued imperturbably to see that as a problem for the party, not for him.

Ever in the background of events were the stirrings of the 'Parnellism and Crime' issue, and the setting up of the Special Commission. With difficulty Gladstone was restrained from direct assault on what he held to be a most unsavoury transaction, 'so unjust to Parnell and so disgraceful to the government and to parliament'.[48] In March 1888 Gladstone conferred with Parnell in their first review of the post-1886 Home Rule policy. As ever, Gladstone persuaded himself that Parnell's 'coolness of head appeared at every turn'; and that the 'whole of his tone' was undoubtedly 'very conservative'.[49] Parnell professed not to regard Irish representation at Westminster as a matter of much moment either way. All he had to do was say soothing things and hold Gladstone to his pledge that any revision of the 1886 bill would have to be approved by the Irish party. Gladstone's 'chief point' in these conversations was whether 'the idea of the American Union' as pushed by his admirer in America, Andrew Carnegie, offered a 'practical point of departure'. This relapse into unsurveyed constitutional terrain was reminiscent of his earlier hapless wanderings amid the *terra incognita* of Austro-Hungarian and Swedish-Norwegian dualism; especially as Gladstone volunteered lamely that he had 'not been able to obtain sufficient information'.

~

One reason for this inability was Gladstone's being at the centre of what he justifiably claimed as 'probably the largest correspondence that any human being had ever had'.[50] By the mid-1880s Hamilton calculated that Gladstone was in receipt of some 20,000 letters a year, and had retained near to 50,000 of them. Harry estimated his 'select letters' in 1888 at 60,000, including 5000 from the Queen. One of his current preoccupations was fixing a design and a site for a muniment depository to contain his extensive archive. It eventually took shape as the 'Octagon', near the north-east corner of the Castle, close to the 'Temple of Peace'.

He was engrossed also in plans for 'a building meant to be the nucleus of an institution for religion and learning'. Its 'secondary and possible' purposes would be as a home for retired clergy, a centre for occasional instruction, and an aid to the parish church. But its 'higher purpose' would be the furthering of 'Divine learning and worship'.[51] It was to be dedicated to St Deiniol, reputed first Bishop of Bangor, and established eventually outside the Castle gate in Hawarden village, adorned with statues of Aristotle, Augustine, Dante and Butler. The stimulus for this ambitious project was what he saw to be the dangerous implications for Christian belief present in the 'new lines of criticism', pressing hard and needing to be resisted. His theological library together with an endowment of £30,000 would provide its munitions.

He lived a full social life. A. E. Elmslie's painting, *Dinner Party at the Earl of Aberdeen's*, with Gladstone prominent among the guests, shown at the New Gallery in April 1890, was an agreeable image of Gladstone's social agreeableness at the time. 'I dined with Mr Knowles & afterwards witnessed the astonishing performance of Mr Eddison's [*sic*] phonograph, and by desire made a brief address to him which is to pass vocally across the Atlantic.'[52] A fellow-guest at one such dinner 'heard him hold forth on the highly uninteresting subject of *compensation to publicans*'.[53] Compensating publicans for loss of their licences was the subject Gladstone discussed with the newly-elected young Welsh MP, David Lloyd George, at a gathering hosted by Stuart Rendel to connect the Liberal leader with Rendel's fellow Liberal Welsh members.

Gladstone much enjoyed the 'refined' and 'bounteous' hospitality of the Stuart Rendels. A wealthy member of the Armstrong engineering and armaments concern, Rendel cultivated Gladstone assiduously in these latter years. Gladstone found him agreeable; though his 'kindness' was 'possibly more remarkable than his aptitudes'.[54] A sub-plot in their relationship was that Harry Gladstone, now returned from Calcutta, was soon to be engaged to Rendel's daughter Maud. It was as Rendel's guests that the Gladstone entourage saw 1888 out at the Villa Rocca Bella near Naples. Hamilton disapproved. 'I am sorry that Mr and Mrs G. should go abroad in this fashion. It gives the unkind world such ground for charging them with always *sponging* upon others: though I admit that having been done so often before it does not greatly matter if it is done once more.'[55] On his birthday, after a week in Naples, Gladstone recorded as he entered his eightieth year: 'All I can see is that I am kept in my present life of contention because I have not in the sight of God earned my dismissal.' Amid 'scenery and weather almost heavenly', Gladstone reviewed memories of 56 years before. It was in these Neapolitan evenings that he became addicted to the game of backgammon as a stimulating diversion.

Literary concerns distracted him. He kept his polemic against the Irish Union of 1800 in good repair. The question of an archival depository related to biographical projects in preparation by authors. There were lucrative proposals to Gladstone himself at this time about autobiographical writing.[56] Intrusive popular curiosity about the doings of the great was becoming a phenomenon of the age. Hamilton had already had occasion to deplore it: 'the practice of questioning the private actions of public men is an entirely modern growth'.[57] What most concerned Gladstone was that his survival and consequent seniority among the public figures of his time exposed increasingly his vulnerability to the modern tendency to biographize. He had been quite helpful in the matter of the biography of Bishop Wilberforce. But he found himself obliged to remonstrate in 1880 about certain references to him in Theodore Martin's *Life of the Prince Consort*. Edwin Hodder's *Life of Shaftesbury* in 1887 came as a vexatiously disagreeable shock. Gladstone was much concerned that material from Shaftesbury's journals 'of a profoundly painful character' would cause public mischief and be turned to account by Tory reviewers.[58] Then came the disobliging memoirs of F. Hastings Doyle, whom Gladstone assumed to be an old and loyal friend. His response was brusque: 'the silly parts might be cut out'.[59]

Consequently Gladstone was much on his guard in the matter of biographical materials. He refused permission for his letters to be published in Andrew Lang's biography of Lord Iddesleigh, the late Stafford Northcote. At first he refused permission for the biography of Manning projected by E. S. Purcell on the Cardinal's death in 1892. It would be absurd, as Hamilton approvingly remarked, to 'allow his biography to be written piecemeal'.[60] However, once he realized that Purcell had in mind something subversive to the Ultramontane party and was amenable to a degree of supervision in return for access to materials, Gladstone was prepared to be helpful.[61] Wemyss Reid's biography of Forster, in 1888, was a different case. 'I find matters which do not lend themselves to treatment satisfactory to myself', Gladstone admonished Reid, '& on which I must [resort?] to my normal expedient, a suspension of final judgment.'[62] His review in the September 1888 *Nineteenth Century* well exemplified the remark he made to Lady Rothschild at that time: 'I never write a review without some object beyond the review.'[63]

As lone surviving trustee of Aberdeen's literary estate, Gladstone was in a good position to protect his interest from what he felt were the superfluous literary ambitions of Aberdeen's deplorable younger son, Arthur Gordon. After having made himself objectionable in the Ionian mission, Gordon had made a career out of colonial governorships. He now planned to publish his father's papers. Gladstone twice vetoed the project on the grounds of indiscretions about Aberdeen's private life. Gladstone later made difficulties about Gordon's biography of Aberdeen, and about Sidney Herbert's widow's biography of her late husband.[64] But he found himself the biter bit when, in pursuing his polemic against Forster, Gladstone was refused permission by the Queen to publish extracts from his letters and memoranda to her on Parnell's release from Kilmainham in 1882. He considered her prohibition 'insulting' and 'absurd'.[65]

Above all, Gladstone now was beginning to betray some of the disabilities of an old man, with appropriate foibles remarked upon. Hamilton observed that 'Mr G. is difficult to move from London, as he is from Hawarden once he is down there'.[66] He was a great Burkean denouncer of newfangled Conservative procedural innovations.[67] Hamilton noticed that in private 'he is apt to monopolize the conversation more than formerly; and to expect more attention from those sitting within hearing distance'.[68] Rosebery feared that Gladstone was outliving his political time. 'However, Mr G. may do what he likes – his closing years may comparatively be a fiasco – but he can't change the position he must occupy in the history of this country.' Where he was blameable, Rosebery thought, was in his being 'wholly engrossed in one subject'. He 'forgets that he is … the Leader of one of the great parties of the State'.[69]

~

Politics, however, seemed meanwhile to be going well for Gladstone. By the end of the 1886 Parliament the Unionists would lose a net 25 seats. Gladstone had much ado holding his line against revisionists pressing for reinstatement of Irish representation at Westminster. The particular danger from his angle of view was that this might become a wedge opening the way for much more radical revision. This issue took on a new urgency with the activities of the South African empire-builder Cecil Rhodes. Rhodes wanted to mesh Home Rule into a scheme of imperial federation, and offered the Irish party £10,000 if they pledged themselves to retention at Westminster. This was eagerly seized upon by revisionists who wanted to capitalize on the flow of by-election successes.[70]

Gladstone counter-attacked with a foray to the Liberal Federation meeting in Birmingham under Chamberlain's nose. This was the great event of 1888. At the Town Hall he 'spoke 1h. 40m. with a voice *lent* me, as heretofore, for the occasion'. At Bingley Hall he addressed a vast audience: 'strength & voice were given me'. 'I am *baculus in manu ambulantis: sed Ille magnus est qui ambulat*.'[71] He upstaged Chamberlain by advocating the equitable principle of raising death duties on landed property to match those on personalty. He kept the door to Irish representation at Westminster sufficiently ajar to appease revisionists without further opening it. To deputations wanting measures 'parallel' to Home Rule such as one-man-one-vote, payment of MPs and labour representation, Gladstone countered with his standard proviso about the need to clear away the Irish obstacle. He held out also against the attempts of such as Labouchere to promote 'an active policy on our part' in the matter of linking to Home Rule such things as Scottish or Welsh disestablishment or 'temperance' or miners' eight-hours day measures.[72] On that latter issue he informed a deputation of colliers led by Keir Hardie that the heart of the matter 'centred around the need for maintaining the liberty of the collier'.[73]

His one concession was to abandon in effect his plan to replace Conservative policy on Irish land purchase. The pressures here were too strong to resist. A member of the Irish Land Commission begged him to 'kindly reconsider your opposition to a further grant under the Land Purchase Act', which opposition 'blighted the hopes of thousands of Irish tenants'.[74] Archbishop Walsh once again proved heretical. ('I hope there is nothing inconvenient in what I say about Lord Ashbourne's Act.')[75] So did some of the younger Liberals such as R. B. Haldane and Edward Grey.[76] Gladstone recovered strength by extolling O'Connell in the January *Nineteenth Century*: his defiant comment upon Parnell as a worthy successor to the 'Liberator'. He was rewarded early in 1889 by the dramatic vindication of Parnell from the charges being investigated by the special Commission on 'Parnellism and Crime'. The exposed forger fled to Madrid and suicide.

This put Gladstone once more up in his stirrups. He stage-managed Parnell's triumphant re-entry to the Commons on 1 March with a speech ('A poor scannel pipe indeed unless He play on it') and later a celebratory dinner. This put him in a strong position to resist an effort by Rosebery to arrange for a committee of the ex-Cabinet to revise the 1886 Home Rule Bill. Behind Rosebery were half Gladstone's former colleagues, eager to ditch the Home Rule policy altogether.[77] 'Mr G. however won't see it', as Rosebery had to conclude in exasperation.[78] Gladstone would keep the matter in his own hands, as he had done from the beginning. If there was going to be revision, it would be done by direct negotiation with Parnell alone. For that event Gladstone in August drew up a preparatory 'Prime Points of Difficulty'. It was arranged that Parnell would visit Hawarden in December.

Parnell's vindication was a heavy blow to Salisbury, for all that the Commission did indeed expose a mass of evidence about criminal activity in the Irish national movement. Salisbury also paid a heavy price for the Liberal Unionist support that saw him through his local government legislative achievements. There was much resentment on the Conservative benches at the exactions demanded by their Liberal allies for keeping the Union. Had there been coherent Liberal leadership in the 1890 session Salisbury would almost certainly have been driven to resignation. Apart from his by now quite regular semi-detached mode of leading, Gladstone had been distracted in March 1889 by the serious illness of his eldest son, Willy. This had also undoubtedly affected Gladstone's leadership in the 1889 session. The Naval Defence Bill, designed to guarantee Britain's maritime supremacy by a candid contribution to Europe's arms race, and for which Goschen provided a rolling financial programme of many millions over five years, would normally have excited Gladstone's most vehement resistance, much on the lines of his response to the 'Navy Scare' of 1884. But he was now subdued.

Behind the celebrations of the Gladstones' golden wedding in July 1889 lay the sad figure of stricken Willy. In a hectic visit to the International Exposition in Paris in September (all expenses again paid by Sir Edward Watkin, exponent of the moral beauty of international communications in the form of the Channel tunnel), Catherine was entirely overborne. She could not cope with the sensational new Eiffel Tower, at the dizzying summit of which Gladstone briefly orated. For the family it was in any case a time of some tribulation. The stroke that felled Willy was followed late in March by the death of Sir Thomas Gladstone. At the funeral at Fasque ('abundant tokens of respect') Gladstone learned of the death of John Bright.

On returning to Hawarden from Paris, Gladstone found himself at odds with Mary, who 'made a conversation which much distressed me, but may do me good'. There was a further fraught conversation on 'the subject' that evening with Lucy Cavendish.[79] The 'subject' remains mysterious. Possibly it related to the issue of Gladstone's 'rescue work', as relayed by Hamilton. More likely, it related to the side of Gladstone's life veiled from his family: the 'entwined lives' of the late Newcastle, Lady Susan Opdebeck (formerly Lady Lincoln), and Laura

Thistlethwayte (now the widow of her suicide husband). A few days later there was a further conversation with Lucy 'on detachment, & my own case which I could not make good to her satisfaction'.[80]

~

Gladstone arranged a preparatory select gathering of conformable colleagues – Ripon, Granville, Morley – at Hawarden in October 1889 to consider points to be raised with Parnell. There was reluctant agreement that Irish MPs had to be retained at Westminster. Morley argued that if the Irish were to have both a Parliament in Dublin and representation at Westminster, the competence of their Parliament and their numbers in the Commons should both be much curtailed. This equitable pragmatism would unquestionably have been sensible policy; but had no chance of getting past Parnell. Gladstone was more for a modest reduction in Irish members and for restricting their competence to imperial matters only. Granville conveyed the candid opinions of Spencer and Harcourt that Irish representation should be undiminished both in numbers and scope: the party 'shall want them for a Liberal majority'.[81]

The discussions at Hawarden on 18–19 December renewed Gladstone's conviction that Parnell was 'certainly one of the very best people to deal with that I have ever known'. He reported to his colleagues that the Irish leader was without crotchets, full of good sense and in all respects satisfactory. The essence of the matter was to know what ex-ministers might confer about 'without having reason to fear Irish dissent'.[82] On Irish sectarian issues such as the Roman Catholic university question, Gladstone warned Parnell that the 'backbone of the Liberal party lies in the Nonconformists of England and Wales, and the Presbyterians of Scotland. These men have a higher level and a stiffer rule of action than the Tory party.'[83] No commitments were exchanged. For his part Parnell reported to representatives of his party at Liverpool immediately after the interview his entire satisfaction with what Gladstone had to say.

In his birthday retrospect at the end of 1889 Gladstone recorded something of the spirit of puzzlement that had been evident in the stunning aftermath of his 1886 'smash'. 'O for … insight into the true measure of my relations to Him who has done such wonders for me, and yet Who mysteriously holds me on in a life of suspicion and contention, at a time when Nature which is the voice of God calls & sighs & yearns for repose.' Of the physical signs of age, he could identify a decline in sight, hearing and locomotion; with memory not quite consistent. 'But the trunk of the body is in all its vital operations … what it was ten years back: it seems to be sustained & upheld for the accomplishment of a work.'

Thus emboldened, Gladstone set off early in 1890 for eight immensely enjoyable days of retreat at Oxford in All Souls College. Party strife 'was hushed, and a sort of Truce of God prevailed through University and Town'.[84] For his part,

Gladstone kept a discreetly low political profile. The President of the Union, a Peel, hoped Gladstone would consent to speak there, 'the voice of the most distinguished President we have produced'.[85] To observers it appeared that Gladstone, 'quite without affectation', retained 'the views and habits of an earlier age'. All his portraits 'make him look too fierce'. It seemed that 'in many ways he was an old-fashioned Conservative'. A modern slackness in codes of dress offended him: members of the University smoking while in cap and gown; he was shocked by the 'scanty costume' of the sporting men, of the 'laxity' of undergraduates perambulating the streets in 'shorts'.[86] Harry's marriage to Maud Rendel at St Margaret's, Westminster, brought the Gladstones back to town for the new session. They encamped in 'a large but very gloomy-looking mansion' in St James's Square.

Salisbury survived until 1892 largely because Balfour's resolute government in Ireland faced down the Plan of Campaign and because the Liberal Unionists grew more comfortable in their alliance. With the free elementary education measure in 1891, Chamberlain declared that he no longer desired Liberal reunion. He had got more out of Salisbury than he could ever have hoped to get out of Gladstone. Conservatives could but ruefully agree. Then, Parnell's dramatic exposure in November 1890 as a sordid adulterer in an action for divorce brought by Captain O'Shea proved immensely sustaining for the Unionists. Parnell's defiant refusal to retire, even as a temporary expedient, split the Irish National party and compromised heavily Gladstone's position as leader of the Home Rule policy. The Nonconformist conscience in England and Wales and the Presbyterian conscience in Scotland joined with the Catholic hierarchy in Ireland to anathematize the Irish leader. Parnell retreated to Ireland to fight to the death. Gladstone's case for Home Rule never quite recovered from the affair. But still it was his 'duty of course to preserve the brightness and freshness of our hopes'.[87]

Retention of Irish MPs in any case stirred much intellectual confusion and squabbles among British Home Rulers. Retentionist 'federalists' such as Stead and the rising young MP H. H. Asquith quarrelled with anti-federalists such as John Morley and Professor Freeman. The Professor's polemical denunciations of the '"imperial" and "federal" ravings of the *Pall Mall Gazette*' set off ripples and caused disturbance in the party.[88] What hurt Gladstone was balm to his Liberal revisionist critics. Gladstonian Liberalism recruited strength against Gladstone's Liberalism.

This was reflected in renewed pressures from the Liberal backbenches. 'Is it not clear that the maximum of strength at the next general election will be attained if English reforms run abreast of Irish reforms, and the conviction spreads among Irishmen as well as Englishmen that the two go together and must be fought for and won together.'[89] This was asking Gladstone to be leader of the Liberal party rather than leader of the Home Rule policy. It was telling Gladstone also that many backbench Liberals were at one with Harcourt in wanting 'only a big county council for Ireland'.[90]

John Morley observed Gladstone having returned from Oxford looking 'old and weary', 'rather deaf and a little confused'. 'He does not see that we are less and less able to force a strong scheme, as the years go on.'[91] Even Catherine, normally resolute in inciting Gladstone's fighting instincts, was beginning, as Hamilton noticed, to have doubts. She was gradually, he thought, 'better recognising facts, and to be conscious that resumption of power is not at all a certainty, and possibly not desirable, for Mr G.' She 'evidently looks to Spencer to succeed Mr G. in the lead. "Rosebery can well afford to wait."'[92]

~

On returning to London for the 1891 session the Gladstones shifted their encampment to 18 Park Lane. The session in itself was of little concern to Gladstone. He remained a fitful and intermittent party leader. He made encouraging noises about Welsh disestablishment to help keep it in humour. Granville's death at the end of March was a heavy sorrow. As he wrote to Laura Thistlethwayte of the recent deaths 'packed' in the last eighteen months, Granville had been 'the most intimate of them all'.[93] Unhappily for Granville's surviving friends, he left them with a parlous and tangled financial legacy to unravel.[94] Then in July Willy, diagnosed eventually with a brain tumour, died after a desperate operation. 'Terribly shocked and broken down', Gladstone followed Willy to his grave, 'with its wide and inspiring outlook'.[95]

His primary public concern was to nurse the Home Rule policy back to the brightness and freshness of the hopes for it before the Parnell scandal. He assured Andrew Carnegie that the 'cruel blow struck at us by the defection of Mr Parnell' had 'not broken up or terrified the Liberal phalanx; and it marches steadily on to battle'.[96] He was at his most resilient in his third exercise in electoral meteorology, 'Electoral Facts', which came out in the September issue of the *Nineteenth Century*. The election of 1886, he declared, 'did not blind the eyes of the defeated party: for they had built their hopes, not on the humour of the moment, but on faith in the operation of principles broad and deep, and on the results of world-wide experience'. There never had been a time, Gladstone was sure, since the first Reform Act, when 'indications were so largely supplied as they now are, to aid in reckoning what was likely to be the judgment of the people in an impending General Election'. He calculated that, 'while endeavouring to rule every doubtful point against ourselves, we are landed at last in a conclusion which assigns to the Liberals at the coming election a majority, from Great Britain alone, which may probably take rank with the remarkable majorities of 1868 and 1880'. Together with his lesson of history about the inconceivability of anything like a serious Conservative challenge to Liberalism's natural hegemony, he counted on a general elimination of Liberal Unionist heresy. Gladstone referred back to his earlier psephological prediction in 1878, where he estimated modestly a Liberal majority for the coming general election of between 56 and 76. His method thus was not one of mere sanguine temper. His 'probably too low' prediction for a British majority in 1892 was 97 seats.[97] That would give him the adequate legitimization he had failed to get in 1885.

All Gladstone's immense reserves of resilience were taxed to the full by the great political event of 1891, his speech at the National Conference of the Liberal Federation at Newcastle at the beginning of October. He did not assume that his role at Newcastle would be as reluctant hostage to the party's demands for English reforms to run abreast of Irish reforms. If he got the majority he wanted there would be no question of his power to command the parliamentary agenda. Home Rule was no longer a startling novelty. The big problem for Gladstone would be the House of Lords; and he had ready keenly forged arguments that resistance by the Lords to a clearly expressed will of the nation would be immensely to the advantage of the Radical movement.

Thus, while the tilt of Gladstone's reading of the situation remained that 'under any circumstances we must wait upon Ireland', and that 'we can take no fresh cargo aboard till that is discharged',[98] his approach to the Liberal Federation also remained very much what it had been at the time of his assistance at its inauguration in 1877. He never lost sight of the view he had of it then: representing, however imperfectly, but in some authentic sense, through the Liberal party 'out of doors', the 'nation' at large; and the nation very decidedly against the parliamentary party. His impresario at Newcastle was John Morley, on his political home ground, anxious lest Gladstone's obsession with Home Rule might be exploited to let loose 'the *fads* that infest the air like midges'.[99]

After limbering up with a tour of Scotland taking in both Glenalmond and Fasque, the Gladstones arrived on Tyneside on 1 October. Gladstone reviewed a list of items that became known immediately as the 'Newcastle Programme'. It included the 'local option' to vote for the closing of public houses on Sundays, payment of MPs, registration reform and one-man-one-vote, elective parish councils, land reform, and disestablishment in Scotland and Wales. He did not ratify them as a programme; and indeed entirely ignored Nonconformist demands on elementary education because of their hostility to denominational schools. He largely pleased himself in picking and choosing. He ignored 'labour' questions. He ignored female suffrage.[100]

The keynote at Newcastle was Gladstone's informing the Liberal delegates of their primary duty. 'As to the title of Ireland to the precedence, there is no question about it at all – it is a matter fixed and determined and settled long ago, upon reasons which in my opinion – and, what is much more, in the opinion of the people – cannot be refuted, cannot even be contested.' Guinness Rogers, the Nonconformist eminence, who remembered the great days on the Tyne in 1862, congratulated Gladstone for putting the big show on the road once more. 'You have given a new inspiration to the country.'[101] In truth, Gladstone gave an old inspiration to the country; nor was it entirely clear that Home Rule was at the heart of it.

Retreating promptly to Hawarden, Gladstone reflected on the news of Parnell's death on 6 October, disowned miserably in Ireland amid recrimination and vituperation against Gladstone. He could hope that the 'healing process' in Ireland might now 'advance without a break'. Newcastle seemingly confirmed for Gladstone that things generally prospered. 'We have reached a point in the course of this long struggle, at which we are almost compelled to contemplate for the next Parliament a Liberal and Home Rule majority ...' 'As far as I know, matters continue, in Great Britain, to move in the right direction, and rather with an accelerated than a backward force.' 'I have myself once known a majority too large for the longevity of a Government: but no majority can be too large for securing the success of a Home Rule Bill. We must not make light of a single seat that can be kept or gained.'[102] To representatives of the 'Labour' interest who resented Gladstone's ignoring their concerns at Newcastle, he unapologetically drew attention to the record of Liberalism in its engagement 'in the great task of procuring an act of justice for the fellow-labourers of the British workmen in Ireland'.[103]

A gathering at Althorp early in December of Gladstone, Morley, Harcourt and their host Spencer laid preparations for the new session. They were hardly of high moment, since Salisbury's only purpose was to dissolve once necessary public business was transacted. Rosebery, despondent at the recent death of Lady Rosebery, consented eventually to attend with great reluctance. Gladstone rejoiced on 8 December: 'Political confabulation & survey: good.' But behind the façade of social amenities both Rosebery and Morley shared a premonition of Gladstone's fading into political limbo. The prospect of a new Liberal government with the octogenarian Gladstone at the helm dismayed them. At Mentmore earlier they had speculated on the conceivability of Gladstone's handing over the premiership to Spencer and taking office without portfolio, purely to frame and introduce a Home Rule Bill.

By now Gladstone had persuaded himself balefully of Hartington's bad faith in 1880: '*to my certain knowledge*', he tried to form a government. 'This statement is in all points beyond contradiction.'[104] Rosebery had been shocked recently at Hawarden at Gladstone's losing control of himself ('for the third time in my experience') in speaking of the Irish rebellion of 1798. For his own literary part, Rosebery was much occupied with his *William Pitt*, in which he gave an interpretive twist to the Act of Union somewhat different from Gladstone's. (Gladstone recorded reading *Pitt* 'with sighs at important points').[105] Morley had misgivings about the whole business. He could discern little evidence after the Newcastle rally that Home Rule commanded the attention of the British electorate. He confided to Rosebery and Hamilton that he doubted 'if Mr G. will reoccupy the conspicuous nitch in history that his admirers now accord him: he will never get over the *spills* he has given his party in 1874 and 1886'.[106]

From Althorp the Gladstones paused at Mentmore en route to London. Gladstone tried to put a stop to the widower Rosebery's talk of retirement: 'when one had attained to a certain point in politics it was impossible to retire'.[107] Back in London they were lodged 'luxuriously' by Rendel in Carlton Gardens before proceeding to Paris accompanied by Helen and Morley. On this occasion their generous host was George Armitstead, 'Russia merchant', and former Liberal MP for Dundee, another of the wealthy men of business who delighted in paying the Gladstones' bills. 'Everything most comfortable', as Gladstone remarked, 'but too sumptuous.'[108] Thence they were 'personally *conducted* by Mr Armitstead' to the Grand Hotel, Biarritz. Gladstone rejoiced in the bracing ambience and the Atlantic breakers. There was bracing conversation. Morley was startled in a 'long morning conversation on Locke'. It was 'a tremendous tussle, for Mr G. is of the same mind, and perhaps for the same sort of reason, as Joseph de Maistre, that contempt for Locke is the beginning of knowledge'. This insight into the ulterior values of a Peelite High Churchman shook Morley profoundly. 'All very well for de Maistre, but not for a man in line with European Liberalism.'[109] On the completion of his 82nd birthday Gladstone mused on his 'singular lot'. He was not permitted the release he longed for. 'But I am called to walk as Abraham walked, not knowing whither he went. What an honour.' At Rendel's villa at Valescure, near Saint-Raphael, Gladstone was cheered by the 'splendid report' of the capture of the Rossendale division of Lancashire, vacated by Hartington on his succeeding to the Devonshire dukedom.

Further cheering electoral news greeted Gladstone shortly after his return. The London County Council elections had gone well for the Liberals. The Deputy Chairman of the Council congratulated Gladstone 'because of its immediate significance in respect of the coming General Election in London'.[110] Breaking the Conservative hold on the metropolis would be an indispensable prerequisite for the big majority Gladstone would need to validate Home Rule and overawe the House of Lords. As he put it to Catherine, 'my desire is for three figures'.[111] A visit to Hawarden by the Carnegies offered yet more tantalising prospects of electoral largesse from the 'giant millionaire'.[112] The Liberal war-chest, indeed, with the departure of many wealthy Liberal Unionists, was much in need of replenishment. Gladstone had allowed himself in 1891 to be persuaded by Arnold Morley and Schnadhorst that it would be expedient to exchange promises of peerages to 'two insignificant but wealthy' Liberal MPs for 'substantial contributions to the Liberal party funds'.[113]

Complaint by Gladstone at Goschen's budget centred on what by now had become one of his most characteristic themes: the rudely radical manner with which the Conservative government dealt with old customs of procedure.[114] Another new-fangled Conservative initiative to be resisted was the inconvenient and, in Gladstone's opinion, precipitate promotion by Salisbury and Balfour (now Leader of the Commons) of female suffrage. He broke cover by loosing *Female Suffrage: A Letter from the Right Hon. W. E. Gladstone to Samuel Smith, MP* (11 April 1892). In this he concluded on the dangers confronting the sex: 'The fear I have is, lest we should invite her unwillingly to trespass upon the delicacy, the purity, the refinement, the elevation of her own nature, which are the present sources of her power.' Gladstone found himself voting against the Women's Suffrage Bill 'in an uncomfortably small majority of 23'.[115] Lady Florence Dixie indignantly denounced him as a 'Grand Old Humbug'.[116] An attendant embarrassment was that Catherine was President of the Women's Liberal Federation, the council of which had voted to support female suffrage. Catherine eventually resigned in 1893.

Compared with this problem, nimble evasion of such as the deputation from the London Trades Council on 'labour' questions was a matter of old habit. The new and worrying twist was the Council's threat to wreak electoral damage at the coming elections. Gladstone's 'dishonest evasion' revealed him as 'blind to industrial life'.[117] Gladstone would have been much more impressed by the electoral menaces of the Rev. Hugh Price Hughes, the Methodist leader, who stipulated that the Methodist vote would depend on *full* Irish representation at Westminster and the Dublin Parliament's being made really and effectively subordinate to the Westminster Parliament.[118] Gladstone confessed to Hamilton, believing a Liberal majority to be 'unavoidable', his anxieties not only about physical infirmities, particularly sight and hearing, but even more, the depressing immanence of the problem passing the wit of man he had defined in 1882: how to have the Irish both at Westminster and Dublin. It was 'impossible now to make a clean job of it'.[119]

~

It was to be a truncated session: a June dissolution and a July election. A Gladstonian majority in Britain was universally predicted. The Conservative Chief Whip estimated it at 28 to 30. But Conservative Central Office was nervous. Many Liberals were known to be preparing to vote for Gladstone and the Newcastle programme, yet trusting to the Lords to do their plain duty with respect to Gladstone's plan for Irish Home Rule. There was always the chance that Gladstone might get his majority by accident or default. It was known that Gladstone would be content 'with nothing less than three figures'.[120] The Conservative *Standard* claimed that he had fixed his calculation at 154.[121] The

Queen enquired hopefully of Cranbrook that she 'understood that Mr Gladstone said he *must* have 100 majority. How was he to obtain such a change?'[122]

Already the Unionist majority of 1886 had been whittled down by by-elections and defections from 116 to 66. But to overturn decisively the verdict of 1886 would still require in England a heave of the body politic of seismic proportions. Nothing of this penetrated Gladstone's fixed certitude that there should stand ultimately no obstacle to his political will as sanctified by his instrumentality to the divine will. The final triumph, as he had predicted in 1886, was certain. It was a case indeed of '*Now* is the time, or never'. A recurrence of the interest he had shown in 1876 in the proverbial tag *Vox populi vox dei* is curiously suggestive.[123] This was at the time he was working on *Special Aspects of the Irish Question: A Series of Reflections in and since 1886*, published in 1892 as his culminating contribution to the literary war he had waged for Ireland.

Gladstone was in hopes once more that another 1876 would lead to another 1880. He had endeavoured to convince the English public that the whole history of the English empire in Ireland had been a story of oppression and atrocity sufficiently analogous to justify a response analogous to the dismissal of Beaconsfieldism in 1880. His explanation of failure in 1886 was that the people did not know the case. He had now, over six years, as the Headmaster on the nation, explained the case. The nation was no longer puzzled. He issued his electoral address on 24 June. He put the case for Home Rule 'on the outlines of the proposal for which the Liberal party has unitedly contended for the last six years'. Liberal Unionism he thus brushed aside as an irrelevance. He was concerned particularly to rebut objections that the Imperial Parliament's supremacy over the self-governing colonies was a constitutional fiction. He added a judicious selection of items from the Newcastle programme. He concluded with a ritual denunciation of 'these leisured classes, these educated classes, these wealthy classes, these titled classes'.

He set out from Hawarden for Midlothian on the 25th. At Chester a 'middle-aged bony woman', replete with 'spite and energy' – an early version of a 'suffragette'? – flung with 'force and skill' a 'hardbaked little gingerbread say 1½ inches across' striking Gladstone's left and most serviceable eye. This sent him back to Hawarden to bed and dark for four days before he could set forth again on the 29th to 'hospitable Dalmeny once more', 'dark spectacles' all the way. Dalmeny in fact was not all that hospitable. Rosebery continued to mourn, determined not to take office in a new Liberal government and unresponsive to Gladstone's talk about men and policies. Hamilton received reports from Rosebery. 'Evidently things have been very unpleasant at Dalmeny. R. says he has had a terrible week of it. It is evident that Mr and Mrs G. have got on his nerves, which are not in the best of conditions, and they have been more than usually tactless.'[124]

The pattern of the campaign was seemingly much as it had been in 1879,

1880, 1885 and 1886. 'Vast & enthusiastic masses in our two street processions.' At Edinburgh Gladstone urged his audience to 'go forward in the good work we have in hand and let us put our trust not in squires and peers – and not in titles and acres. I will go further and say not in man as such, but in the Almighty God, who is the God of justice, and who has ordained the principle of right, of equity, and of freedom to be the guides and masters of our life.'[125] There were protests about 'sacred names and holy words' being dragged into the political arena. Gladstone himself faced a contest for the Midlothian seat.

The first results appeared on 4 July. 'At first they were even too rosy: afterwards turned down but the general result satisfactory, pointing to a gain in Britain of 80 seats. This may be exceeded.' It was not. In the following days the prospect faded dismally. Soon the majority looked nearer 50 than 80. Gladstone reflected gloomily: 'the burden on me is serious: a small Liberal majority being the heaviest weight I can well be called on to bear'. By 13 July the Liberal managers were down to estimating a mere 30 majority. Gladstone trusted, accurately, that it might be nearer 40. The Unionist alliance had not crumbled. The Conservative Metropolitan–Lancashire axis, though battered, was not broken. The Liberal Unionists preserved, with near 50 seats, their integrity as a major political player.

John Morley, demoted to second place in the Newcastle poll, arrived to find Dalmeny a scene of desolation. His gloomy host was unable to 'contain his weariness <and almost loathing> of the interior situation. They had passed a horrid week of dejection and dismay, the telegrams of the polls coming to the house all day long, and smashing to atoms the illusions of many months.' 'It was really tragic', Morley recorded, as Rosebery 'cried out in bitter intensity of repugnance to it all. "Oh, my dear M., as I sit with him half-deaf & three parts blind", and see him "feverishly clutching at straws here and straws there, a downright horror comes over me."'

The culminating horror was Gladstone's own poll at Midlothian, on 13 July. The party waited anxiously in what Morley described as a 'fevered atmosphere', with a 'horrid pall of physical decline hanging over all, slowly immersing the scene and its great actor in dreary light'. In 1885 his majority had been near 4000. Then came the shattering news: 'not 4,000, not 3, not 2, but 690!!' Gladstone's chagrin at this personal humiliation was undoubtedly intense, but he put a brave face on it.[126] Rosebery recalled his saying, a 'great trial of this kind throws one back upon oneself, and makes one examine oneself, and now I see how for the last six years I have been buoyed up with the belief that we should have a great majority and that the Irish business would be a very short business.'[127] The mystery of the governance of the most High was even more of a puzzle than in 1886.

Bizarre twists heightened the scene of desolation. In the background was the homely presence of Armitstead – in Gladstone's phrase, 'old shoe, and tame cat'– deputed to remove the Gladstones to Braemar for a change of air.[128] Even more bizarrely, Acton pressed Morley, plainly asking 'would Mr Gladstone put him in the Cabinet?'

The Gladstones set off on the afternoon of 13 July for Aberdeen, under Armitstead's convoy, with Acton tenaciously in attendance. It was beyond doubt that the appeal against the verdict of 1886 would be dismissed by the new Parliament. A decisive aspect of the novel and considerable change being undergone in the political temper of the British nation was that Gladstone's grand doctrine of 1856 no longer applied. His doings and intentions as the nation's headmaster failed to take purchase in forging a corresponding conviction in the public mind. As the events of 1876 suggested, ironically, the public was capable of making up its own mind. It was, in the nature of the case, asking much of that public that the Irish horrors as depicted by Gladstone should make the same moral impact as the Bulgarian horrors. Gladstone's fanatical partisanship seemed to many both out of time and out of place. 'The difficulty is', as one observer noted, 'that the English rural constituencies are sick of the Home Rule question.' It was notorious in the mining divisions, as another observer reported, that 'Home Rule had no more to do with the result of the elections than rival theories as to the personality of Shakespeare'.[129] Rosebery's instinct was sound: Gladstone had outlived his time. What price, indeed, old habits, lessons of history, axioms of politics?

19

Appeal Dismissed, 1892–1893

'The Almighty & not any counsel of mine brought it about: surely He will provide for it.'

Gladstone, diary entry, 31 July 1892

Salisbury prepared to meet the new Parliament for a short sitting early in August. His one purpose was to extricate himself promptly from office. He and the other members of the Unionist 'Quadruple', Balfour, Devonshire and Chamberlain, could feel well pleased with their solid showing in the English constituencies. Gladstone's overall majority came from the 'Celtic fringe' of the British Isles, the 'outlying extremities of the body politic – from the places where the vital force is low and the pulse beats slowly'.[1] Gladstone had as much reason as Salisbury to conclude that 'the history of recent times as it will be written is a very strange history'.[2]

Reinvigorated by the Highland air, Gladstone geared himself up for battle. As spokesman for the *vox populi*, he protested at the 'pointless delay' of Salisbury's going through the motions of awaiting the formal verdict of the House of Commons. On returning to Hawarden on 21 July, Gladstone's line was to cast the balance fairly between English and Irish claims, to anticipate mischief from the Lords, and therefore, as he put it to Harcourt, to open up against that House 'as many *bouches à feu* as possible', looking for issues that could be 'concisely handled' in bills.[3] For Gladstone, being 'bold to the Lords' was ever an attractive prospect. A Cabinet minute on Home Rule would be framed as a resolution both in the Commons and the Lords as a basis for possible future legislation.

By 27 July the Gladstones were back with Rendel at Carlton Gardens, preparing to move into Downing Street. There were lurking fears that the Queen might turn awkward. It was known that Victoria was alarmed and despondent at the prospect of Gladstone yet again, even with claws drawn, and was talking of asking Rosebery to take over. This was the same danger she had risked in 1880 in her determined effort to install Hartington. At the Rothschild chateau at Waddesdon, Hamilton concerted with Ponsonby and the Prince of Wales's private secretary, Francis Knollys, to keep the Queen on a straight track.[4]

In a 'stiff conversation' with Spencer and Morley, Gladstone's proposal to be content with a resolution on the principle of Home Rule was rebuffed. The Irish simply would not have it.[5] Harcourt was 'much shocked at the physical & mental change for the worse in Mr G. since he left the H. of C. in June. He thinks him confused & feeble.'[6] Possibly Harcourt's shock was much induced by his exasperation at Home Rule's coming back to life again. Yet Gladstone himself had recorded on 15 July: 'from the condition (*now*) of my senses, I am no longer fit for public life: yet bidden to walk in it. "Lead Thou me on."' Cataracts were starting to form over his eyes; his deafness would be a very practical problem in Cabinet. He fortified himself with the theme of deep and hidden agencies. 'Now is the time for the thoughts that wander through eternity. When I look at the task apparently before me, and at the equipment of spirit and sense with which I am furnished I cast up my eyes to heaven abashed and dismayed. A reply came from thence. My grace is sufficient for thee. O thou of little faith wherefore dost thou doubt … The Almighty & not any counsel of mine brought it about: surely He will provide for it.'[7]

Getting an administration on paper ready to present to the Queen was becoming an urgent requirement. Rosebery put everything in doubt by his temperamental moodiness. Gladstone was under the impression that he had settled with Rosebery at Dalmeny about the Foreign Office and the leadership of the Lords. Rosebery now refused the Lords leadership and fled abroad to Paris. Gladstone complained that he had 'never been treated so ill by any colleagues before'.

Hamilton found more than the usual amount of confusion and fuss reigning in Carlton Gardens. 'Mrs G. and Helen waylaying everybody, scheming this and scheming that, intercepting letters, and almost listening at keyholes. I pity poor Algy West, who naturally complains with some bitterness.'[8] Loulou Harcourt gathered from Mrs Gladstone and Mrs Drew and Helen that Gladstone's voice 'was hoarse from arguing with people', and they were protecting him from them.[9] Catherine's earlier doubts were now quite extinguished. Hamilton observed her 'as keen herself as ever to return to Downing Street'. She was as sensitive as ever, as with the case of Chamberlain, to any notions of a rival successor in waiting. She did not allow that Rosebery had any grounds for complaint: it would be 'monstrous' of him, after all Mr G.'s kindnesses, to make difficulties.[10]

The difficulties of getting Rosebery in were compounded by difficulties in keeping others out. Labouchere accused Gladstone of being an accessory to 'royal ostracism' when his claim for the Washington Legation and a privy councillorship was refused: yet another case, he felt, of the G.O.M.'s 'perpetually bringing an ace down his sleeve, even when he only has to play fair to win the trick'.[11] Acton was more troublesome. He was believed to have said that 'at this crisis he is going to govern England through Gladstone'. He talked openly of being in the Cabinet. He 'gave the impression of grasping at office'. There was a rally of Acton's enemies to block the 'court favourite, upstart, busybody, intruder, flatterer'. John Morley, Acton's rival for Gladstone's intimacy and confidence, was the 'chief enemy'. Acton, for his part, was free with his opinion that Morley was 'not, in the supreme sense of the word, quite a gentleman'. Eddie Hamilton inveighed against Acton's '*meddlesomeness*'. Spencer, for whom Acton had been useless in the Lords, dismissed his pretensions. Gladstone still talked of him as a Cabinet possibility on 1 August. 'Morley is recorded as saying he *put his foot on this at once*.' Gladstone was coerced into sending Welby, the Treasury Secretary, to tell Acton not to appear at Carlton Gardens. Acton ended up rather absurdly with a lordship in waiting, where his expertise in the pedigrees of the German princely families stood him in good stead.[12]

At the opening of the session on 8 August Gladstone menaced the Lords with the wrath of the people should it transgress its proper bounds. He insisted that Irish votes were not only as good as any other votes in the Commons, but were, as testimonies to a decided opinion on a matter of capital Irish concern, in a way even better. He discoursed on the felicitous example of the Melbourne ministry, coming in with a majority hardly touching 30 in 1835, and staying on for six and a half years. He warned England that it had 'a giant's strength, but must not use it like a giant'.[13] Balfour, with reference to 'Mr Parnell's Bill of 1886', took the opportunity to quote Gladstone's statements at Edinburgh in 1885 on the very great problem of a Liberal government dependent on Irish votes. 'By a happy prescience the right hon. Gentleman foresaw the exact situation in which he would find himself in the year of 1892.'[14] On 11 August the amendment to the Address, for which Gladstone put forward two notable 'new men', Asquith and Thomas Burt, came to a huge division: the Salisbury government was defeated 350–310. As Salisbury went off to Osborne Hamilton observed Gladstone 'rather depressed and looking tired', but 'quite calm and unexcited'.[15] The Queen announced pointedly that she had accepted Salisbury's resignation 'with much regret'.

After tiresome difficulties Gladstone eventually wrested consent from Rosebery to allow his name to be placed before H. M. Gladstone thought it 'very trying & rather sad'. Rosebery's adhesion was generally judged indispensable to sustain the new administration. Rosebery thought Gladstone 'a splendid ruin'.[16] Possibly Rosebery capitulated to Harcourt's comradely appeal: without you we would be ridiculous; with you merely impossible. That was very much the spirit of Harcourt's contribution to a 'conclave' summoned by Gladstone on 14 August. 'A storm. I am sorry to record that Harcourt has used me in such a way since my return to town that the addition of another Harcourt would have gone far to make my task impossible.' The exchanges were 'as unpleasant as anyone could remember, with Harcourt brutally rude to Gladstone, and Gladstone pouring reproaches on Morley's head for backing Harcourt'. Gladstone 'became a chairman instead of a commander'.[17]

At Osborne the following day Gladstone found the Queen 'cautiously polite'.

She enquired after Catherine 'with evident sincerity, and perhaps a touch of warmth'. Gladstone sat nearer to her than usual on account of deafness.[18] The Queen confided in her daughter the Empress Frederick that with the 'half crazy and half silly' 'O. M.' it was 'quite idle to attempt to have any influence with him. He listens to no one and won't hear any contradiction or discussion.'[19]

In one respect, Victoria was helpful. She was eager to have Rosebery back at the Foreign Office, and Gladstone could use this to hold Rosebery steady. Appropriate offices were approved for the regular Whig peers: Kimberley for India and as Lord President, with the lead in the Lords; Ripon for the Colonies, Spencer at the Admiralty. Herschell returned to the Woolsack. Harcourt returned to the Exchequer, Morley to the Irish Office and Campbell-Bannerman to the War Office. The appointments that made a stir were Asquith, direct from the backbenches to the Home Office, and the working-class Burt as Secretary to the Board of Trade, to boost the Labour Bureau. Otherwise Cabinet places were distributed to Mundella, Henry Fowler, A. H. D. Acland, Trevelyan, Bryce, Shaw-Lefevre, and Arnold Morley, replaced as Whip by Edward Marjoribanks. Gladstone slotted in Herbert as Asquith's Under-secretary, and Rosebery got the man he wanted, Edward Grey, as his spokesman in the Commons.

A Cabinet of 17 Gladstone thought 'outrageous', but excused himself as being 'beset right and left'. He had thus included 'more than one man insufficient in experience or in force'. In retrospect he came to realize that his more important mistakes were 'in the persons of men whose title to Cabinet office was indisputable, and whom by my very own fault I misplaced'. In Rosebery Gladstone hoped to get another malleable Granville. In Spencer he hoped to get a man who would face down the admirals.[20] These were to be his most grievous disappointments as far as collegiality was concerned. His new Cabinet met for the first time on 19 August at Rendel's house in Carlton Gardens. This incongruous setting somehow seemed to be in character. Rosebery declared: 'I thought I was at a public meeting, and nearly moved Mr Gladstone into the chair.'[21] Gladstone decreed a new arrangement of Cabinets to get around the problem of his deafness. He alone would sit at a table, with Rosebery at his right hand; all the others would sit as near as possible on whatever seating was convenient.

Gladstone 'showed little or no trace of the worry or difficulties'. He was, thought Hamilton, 'a very marvel, and certainly shows no signs of being a "ruin"'.[22] Even so, Andrew Carnegie's grandiloquent salute to 'the People's "William the Fourth"' was hardly appropriate to Gladstone's straitened political circumstances. Carnegie's 'fervent wish is now that you will be spared to strengthen the United Kingdom by giving to Ireland the rights of an American State', by giving self-government to Scotland through a Grand Committee, and 'justice in religious matters' to Wales.[23]

~

Commencement of the Hawarden season was enlivened for Gladstone by a life-threatening encounter with a wild heifer in the park.[24] Stiffness and soreness did not long stem his literary energies. In Scotland he had taken up a translation of Horace's *Odes* on the ground that no English version satisfactorily represented their terseness and economy. He became immersed in preparing the inaugural lecture on the Romanes foundation at Oxford. Having originally declined the invitation of Vice-Chancellor Boyd on the ground of pressing public duties, Gladstone now devoted inordinate amounts of time at the expense of public duties to distilling his academic love affair with Oxford into lecture form. In the June *Nineteenth Century* he disclosed the wish that fathered his thoughts: 'Did Dante Study at Oxford?'

He drafted also a 'Preliminary outline of Work' for the 1893 session, headed by a 'Bill for the Government of Ireland' together with a series of *bouches à feu*. He contemplated while a guest at Edward Watkin's Snowdonian chalet a memorandum for the Queen on the theme of the dangers to the constitution that would be occasioned by the Lords blocking the coming Home Rule Bill. As well as beginning 'Mem. for H.M. a serious business', Gladstone composed also 'Mem. on Uganda'.

The Ugandan question inaugurated serious politics for Gladstone's fourth ministry. It was a problem inherited by Rosebery from Salisbury. After replacing Iddesleigh at the Foreign Office in 1887, Salisbury had declared that he would continue the policy of Rosebery. This broke the pattern of contention and disruption that had marked successive changes at the Foreign Office since the days of Pitt and Fox, Castlereagh and Canning, Palmerston and Aberdeen, culminating in the epochal confrontation of Beaconsfield against Gladstone. Now, in 1892, Rosebery returned Salisbury's compliment.

'Continuity' with Salisbury meant continuing the policy of the 1887 Mediterranean Agreements, secret arrangements whereby Britain linked through Italy to the Austro-German alliance in order to preserve the status quo in the Near East from being subverted by the Franco-Russian combination. The Agreements were Salisbury's recourse after his failure in 1887 to clinch a deal with the French about withdrawing from Egypt on terms allowing for re-occupation if necessary. The French were known to entertain ambitions to winkle the British out of Egypt by getting in from the Congo at the Sudanese back door. By 1887, under pressure from the admirals, Salisbury had abandoned all realistic hopes that the 'Great Game' with Russia could be played in Beaconsfieldian rules of engagement at Constantinople. Alexandria in Egypt was the fall-back position. It had to be secured. The Naval Defence Act of 1889 was the main part of that security against the French and the Russians. It would become renewable after five years' time.

The point about Uganda was that it was the western part of British East Africa linking to the Indian Ocean and in itself the link with the Sudan, and therefore to Egypt.

Thus, behind the mundane question whether or not Britain should take over responsibility for Uganda from the insolvent British East Africa Company and the agitation of the missionary interest, loomed immense strategic implications. Rosebery wholly accepted Salisbury's reading of them. This put him in direct conflict with Gladstone's declared determination to withdraw from Egypt. Behind the scenes they fought a battle quite as epochal in its way as was the Gladstone–Beaconsfield confrontation. As Gladstone was ultimately to conclude, the 'fatal element' in his appointment of Rosebery to the Foreign Office in 1892 was Rosebery's 'total gross misconception of the relative position of the two offices we respectively held and secondly his really outrageous assumption of power apart from the First Minister and from the Cabinet'.[25]

Although the Mediterranean Agreements were not an alliance and did not involve Britain strictly in obligations of belligerency, they came as close to it as the 'ententes' before 1914. Indiscretions in Italy led to questions being asked in Britain. Rosebery soothed Gladstone's suspicions as to 'tangible' support or adhesion. Rosebery's problem was that he could not explain why he wanted to stick in Uganda in order to stick in Egypt without blowing up the Liberal government. His strength, on the other hand, was that he was held to be indispensable to the Liberal government. By September tussles between the two led to steps being taken to avoid the 'scandal and mischief of patent differences between Foreign Sec. and Prime Minister'.

'Rosebery has I think', Gladstone told Spencer, 'been carried quite off his legs by the Jingoes at the Foreign Office and its agents', in what Gladstone reckoned 'as one of the strangest occurrences' of his life of 60 years in the House of Commons.[26] A critical point was reached in October when Rosebery, with only Fowler and Mundella in support, defied Gladstone and the Cabinet majority. There was a furious row. Gladstone was observed as never having been seen 'more excited and more determined than he was about this Uganda business; and it took a good many plain words to make him realise that on the decision which might be taken depended a very serious Ministerial crisis'.[27] Rosebery's indispensability told. He had the Queen solidly in support. The crisis was averted by a postponement and a Commission. Rosebery colluded with Lord Cromer (erstwhile Evelyn Baring) in Cairo to rig the Commission. As he put it, 'Mr Gladstone's hair would stand on end if he knew what was going on there.'[28] What was going on there was, substantially, fulfilment of Gladstone's misdirected prophecy of 1877 in relation to 'Beaconsfieldism'. 'Our first site in Egypt, be it by larceny or be it by emption, will be the almost certain egg of a North African Empire, that will grow and grow until another Victoria and another Albert, titles of the Lake-sources of the White Nile, come within our borders.'[29]

The Uganda episode was an instructive paradigm of Gladstone's last Cabinet. For all that he commanded a majority on the issue, Gladstone could not make his will prevail. He no longer had the weight his cohering role had given him in the 1880–85 government. Partly this was because of the 'spills' he had given the Liberal party. Mainly it was because of his oft-proclaimed insistence, as he had again stated at the opening of the 1892 session, that the 'question of Ireland' 'is almost, if not altogether, my sole link with public life. It has been for the last seven years my primary and absorbing interest, and so will continue to be.'[30] As Hamilton observed, Cabinets came to be conducted 'on "prize-fight" principles'. The heavyweights – Rosebery, Harcourt, Morley, along with Gladstone himself – were 'sparring in the middle of the ring', with the rest looking on.[31] Rosebery could often get his way because of the violent antipathy that had grown between Harcourt and Morley (known to Harcourt as 'Priscilla'). The Cabinet did not '*pull* together enough', with so little in common between its members. Relics of Palmerston's last ministry mingling with a generation who would come to the fore in the next century made up one of the most uncollegiate of Cabinets. Rosebery recorded one occasion when Gladstone walked between himself and Harcourt with 'bewildered colleagues in a knot all round'.[32]

~

His resentments simmering, Gladstone found relief in his Romanes preparations. West complained that the Prime Minister neglected attending to the Home Rule issue, 'which don't seem to progress at all'.[33] Then came the stillness on the impact of Tennyson's death. At a reading of *Maud* earlier in 1892 Gladstone recanted the severe criticisms he had made in 1859. Hallam Tennyson was gratified to be able to tell Gladstone of his father's comment: 'No one but a noble-minded man could have done that.'[34] Gladstone, nonetheless, found it impossible to accept the honour of being a pall-bearer in the Abbey because of Romanes pressures. Possibly the *Locksley Hall Sixty Years After* wound never quite healed. His long relationship with Tennyson ended rather as it had begun: a somewhat prickly, defensive, quasi-friendship, carefully sustained as to forms on both sides but increasingly empty of the warmth of real intimacy. Difficulties in finding a replacement for the laureateship, with Swinburne an alcoholic, erotomaniacal republican, led Gladstone and the Queen to agreeing that it would be for the best to leave the place for the present unfilled.[35]

Then came the great day, 24 October, for the inaugural Romanes Lecture at Oxford. The Sheldonian Theatre presented an 'impressive scene – the intolerable crush without, the silent crowd within, the red-gowned figure of Oxford's greatest son as he illustrated with loyal and eloquent erudition the proud saying: *Universitatis Oxoniensis aemula Parisiensis*'.[36] Many undergraduates, victims of proctorial mismanagement, fainted in the 'fearful crush' on the stairs. A good deal of the erudition of *An Academic Sketch* was cribbed from the Rev Mr Hastings Rashdall's generously provided typescript and proofs of his forthcoming *Universities of Europe in the Middle Ages*, and its accuracy owed much also to Acton. In his peroration his voice vibrated with emotion. His last words remained unspoken as 'he bowed his head in a storm of enthusiasm'.[37]

As the time approached for preparatory autumnal Cabinets, the Gladstones settled in at 10 Downing Street. Hamilton wonderingly observed them 'I am afraid very cramped in the old house; but then they don't mind living in a sort of hugger-mugger style'. The main thing occupying Gladstone's mind was the 'serious business' of the memorandum for the Queen. This had something about it of the character of the 'posthumous bequest' he had presented to her in May 1885 on the theme of 'some great and critical problem in the national life'. Then it had been the question of Irish self-government as entangled with the contingency of a Parnellite sweep of the Irish constituencies. Now, in more Cassandra-like tones, it was the question of Irish self-government as entangled with the House of Lords and what Gladstone alleged to be 'the widening of that gap, or chasm, in opinion, which more largely than heretofore separates the upper and more powerful from the numerous classes of the community'.

The controversy surrounding Home Rule for Ireland, Gladstone argued, raised issues going far beyond it, issues inconvenient, maybe even injurious, to a safe and stable working of the constitution. Two points in particular he stressed. The first was that the widening of the chasm was aggravated by the prolongation and intensity of the Home Rule controversy. The second was that for the last 60 years the direction in which the Liberal party moved was sooner or later the direction in which the country at large moved; and the longer the struggle continued, the more the Liberal party 'will move towards democratic opinion', a movement that would greatly be enhanced by a conflict with the House of Lords. The fault for widening the chasm of opinion and laying open the working of the constitution to inconvenience and even injury lay wholly therefore with those upper and more powerful classes who wilfully misapprehended the truly 'Conservative' nature of his proposal to resolve the Irish question by the bill he presented in 1886, and the bill he proposed to present in the next session, in 1893.[38]

Possibly Victoria might have been tempted to make some pungent comments on what she described to Ponsonby as this 'curious' document, especially had she considered it side by side with its earlier counterpart of 1885. Then, the focus of Gladstone's memorandum had been Chamberlain's 'Central Board' local government scheme. Perhaps, she might have suggested, the saddest fact in the whole business of Irish self-government was that the Liberal party had not been given the opportunity to consider any such scheme of autonomy to put in due course before the country as a reasonable response to the Irish constituencies.

She might have contrasted that possibility with Gladstone's suddenly intervening and imposing without consultation on the startled Liberal party a scheme going further than even the Nationalist leadership envisaged, which the Liberal party, left to itself, would never have countenanced, and which the country at large had refused to accept.

That very imperious imposition, in itself, she might have continued, split the Liberal party in such a degree that reunion was now out of the question, and consequently the role of proxy for the nation at large that Gladstone still claimed for it, was, on the evidence of recent general elections, obsolete. Gladstone's heroic intervention had polarized what had been a largely unformed and malleable mass of opinion. He, it seemed, for whatever reason, had miscalculated grossly his capacity to command the shape of events. And as for the 'chasm' formed by the Irish issue between the classes and the masses – a chasm that Gladstone himself had done his best to deepen – where was the evidence?[39] It was perfectly well understood that the Lords were going to throw out the forthcoming Home Rule Bill. Where was the excitement? Where was the agitation? If anything, the nation was bored. The Lords in fact had every reason to assume that their denial would be endorsed by the electorate. And even did such a crisis exist, it was brazen on Gladstone's part, having thus imperiously taken the responsibility for opening that alleged chasm in opinion, then to complain in a kind of blackmailing manner at the failure of opponents to surrender to him quickly enough to restore his definition of a safe and stable working of the constitution. It was an egregious specimen of the 'heads I win, tails you lose' style of argument.

Then, on the constitutional point, she might have drawn attention to the notorious fact that there was nothing safe and stable about the working of Sweden–Norway's dualism, which was on the brink of breaking apart in bitter recrimination. And who could take seriously Gladstone's repeated assertions that imperial supremacy over the self-governing colonies was a practical and working reality?[40] Back in 1882 he had reassured her that the Canadian analogy could not safely be applied to Ireland.[41] Both the Commons and the country in 1886 had agreed that indeed it could not be safely applied. Was it no less risky now? The Queen, however, contented herself with requesting Ponsonby to acknowledge and confined her own response to a polite intimation that she appreciated Gladstone's motives in so addressing her.

For his part, Salisbury was making ready for the coming work of the Lords. His 'Constitutional Revision' in the November issue of the *National Review* was a preparatory essay in scene-setting. The British constitution, lacking the resource of a United States Supreme Court, or yet of precedent for recourse to a referendum, at least had a House of Lords that could be equipped with a doctrine, as adumbrated by Salisbury in 1884, of referendal 'revision' by way of inviting an appeal to the electorate.

~

Pre-sessional Cabinets got under way late in October. Gladstone's colleagues expected to hear something of his plans for the Home Rule Bill. They heard nothing. 'Mr G. seems hardly to have given a thought to his Home Rule Bill', grumbled Hamilton. Fowler soon discovered that Gladstone had not a glimmer of interest in the Parish Councils Bill. By November, Hamilton found Morley 'very depressed politically as usual'. Gladstone wanted to put off consideration of the Home Rule Bill till January. 'He sees he can't pass a measure and so does not exert himself to no purpose.' At this the Cabinet rebelled. Gladstone agreed at least to allow Spencer and Morley to produce heads for discussion in December. Rosebery thought these proceedings 'rather pitiful'.

At tea with Granville's widow in Kensington, Gladstone 'told her of *my* infinite loss in her husband'. Granville's emollient tact and disarming deftness of personal touch were much missed, especially in a situation where Rosebery felt that Gladstone was 'more active than necessary' in foreign affairs. A squall over Egypt erupted in January 1893. Cromer in Cairo, apprehending possible trouble over the succession to the khedivate, requested reinforcements. Rosebery readily consented. This put Gladstone in 'a very excited state', denouncing the demands from Cairo and the Foreign Office as 'appalling' and 'preposterous'. 'With such pistols presented at my head', he protested, 'my life is a perfect burden to me. I would as soon put a torch to Westminster Abbey as send additional troops to Egypt.' He could see 'nothing for it but for Rosebery to resign'. But it was Rosebery who won the trick. He held the stronger hand in Cabinet. Cromer got his reinforcements. Britain's grip on Egypt was tightened another notch. All Gladstone could do was deprecate the sending of warships to Alexandria as 're-awakening the memory of the bombardment'.[42]

John Morley was the nearest thing Gladstone had to another Granville. 'He is on the whole from great readiness, joined with other qualities, about the best stay I have.' He was especially useful as 'Envoy to Rosebery'; but his effectiveness was limited when it came to the case of Harcourt. Cabinet on 11 November: 'One person outrageous.' Rosebery also threatened resignation. At a Cabinet on Home Rule on 21 November Rosebery and Harcourt sat ostentatiously aloof on a sofa, waving Spencer away with 'Oh no, this is the *English* bench.' Two days later it was for Rosebery a 'Rembrandt *Monte Carlo* scene wh. Asquith & I viewed from a side table. Excited men round table – pale old croupier in midst with passion seething in his face – a memorable and painful scene.'[43] Gladstone formed an Irish Cabinet Committee to shut Harcourt out.

Gladstone was now in a position to apprise the Queen that the new Home Rule Bill would retain Irish members at Westminster, 'according to the apparent public desire'.[44] The difficulty on the financial side, as Hamilton discerned, would be 'to persuade Mr G. to throw over his own cherished scheme of 1886'. Retention of Irish members made it redundant. 'The more one goes into the provisions generally ... the more insurmountable do the difficulties appear to me to be', declared Hamilton. He was beginning to think that Home Rule 'may be killed by its inherent difficulties'. Gladstone himself, hating to have his hand forced in the matter of Irish representation, hated all the more having to grapple with the financial difficulties of it.

Restiveness in the party began to manifest itself. There were demands for a Scottish Grand Committee to deal with accumulated arrears of legislation. Chamberlain was well placed to mock the Liberal party's legislative barrenness. He could assert plausibly that 'in social questions the Tories have almost always been more progressive than the Liberals'.[45] Gladstone's humiliation in the Midlothian poll in 1892 had certainly concentrated his mind on the need to bear Kirk disestablishment and Scottish autonomy in mind. The question for the 1893 session was now urgent as to 'what satisfaction we can give to other wants, English, Welsh, and Scotch'.

With so much to do by the beginning of the session, fixed for 31 January, and so little done, ministers and officials were unnerved by Gladstone's decision to hold a Cabinet or two early in December and then retreat to Biarritz under Armitstead's convoy for a winter season. Gladstone's last public appearance in 1892 was to receive the Freedom of the City of Liverpool, his birthplace. There, amid the classic pomp of St George's Hall, he delivered as the living embodiment of the faith of Free Trade a confident assertion of the triumph of Liverpool in the next century as the centre of world commerce.[46] The closing Cabinets Rosebery thought largely a waste of time. 'Words, words, words, and very unnecessary.'

At Biarritz Gladstone wonderingly contemplated his 83rd birthday and the year's end. 'For me in some ways a tremendous year. A too bright vision dispelled. An increased responsibility undertaken, with diminished means.' 'Lead me through duty into rest.' Back on duty at Downing Street by 12 January, Gladstone was observed by Hamilton as looking well, and in 'one of his jaunty humours, entirely eschewing shop. He will avoid touching on Irish finance as long as he can. He knows I don't agree with his plan; and he has become much less tolerant of opinion differing from his own than he used to be.' Morley too found Gladstone 'certainly more imperious and less open to reason than he was'. If the Irish did not like his proposals, Gladstone declared, 'they must *lump* them.'[47] Harcourt thought the whole business 'merely *pour rire*: it is ludicrous and impossible'. At a Cabinet on the 16th 'Sir W. H. pursued his line in his usual way.' Gladstone was persuaded to abandon his plan for a sliding scale quota and accept the scheme proposed by Hamilton and Alfred Milner at the Inland Revenue Board. Ireland was to have full control of stamps and taxes and to be credited with excise proceeds; but the imperial government would take customs, for good or ill, as Ireland's contribution to the imperial charges.

Gladstone relented on the matter of his social obligations to the extent of offering an 'Official dinner & evening party' on the eve of the opening of the session. 'I feel, what? much troubled & tossed about: in marked contrast with the inner attitude on former like occasions.' After Sunday service at the Chapel Royal he returned from the sacred precincts feeling 'both depression & worry'. Old nagging worries about Egypt revived, with dismal memories of the 1880s on top of the deplorable Uganda affair. These worries would soon stimulate an initiative to stipulate a definite date for withdrawal from Egypt by allowing two years for time and space to dispense with Britain's 'insidious though in the circumstances necessary powers'. Gladstone's move to revive an entente with the French to this end was bitterly resented and resisted by Rosebery. After nine years dealing as Prime Minister with the pliant Granville, Gladstone was mortified to find himself now yet again overborne by his Foreign Secretary.[48]

Another occasion of depression and worry was 'the tendency there was to embark on the perilous course of socialistic legislation', with which Gladstone 'was thankful that he neither would nor could have anything to do'. The impulse for such legislation came 'mainly from the party that pleases to call themselves Conservative'. The issue pressing on him that he disliked immensely was payment of MPs. He had been pushed into accepting it for the sessional programme very reluctantly; but he would not accept 'indiscriminate payment'. He wanted money to be available only to members who really needed it, so as to preserve the honour of unpaid service.[49] He was to be overborne also on this point by the party's and his colleagues' unwillingness to accept the invidious implications of this. Harcourt warned that the Radical section could 'break up the united action of the party' unless they were appeased on this question.

Otherwise, to pacify 'English' sentiment, Fowler had his Parish Councils and Asquith his Employers' Liability. The Newcastle Programme was honourably represented: local option, one-man-one-vote, shorter Parliaments, prevention of new vested interests in the Kirk and Welsh ecclesiastical establishments. But Gladstone rejoiced early in the session when Keir Hardie's amendment to the Address about unemployment and trade depression was heavily defeated. 'An anxious day', he recorded, 'but with a good ending.'[50]

~

Apart from the Kirk issue, Gladstone scarcely bothered to conceal his lack of interest in anything but his Government of Ireland measure, the details of which he kept very close to his chest. Asquith wrote to Rosebery on a drily mocking note on Friday, 10 February: 'I understand that on Monday a Bill (to "amend the provision" for the Government of Ireland) which neither you nor I have seen, is to be introduced into the House of Commons. I send you word of this, as you may possibly like to be present, and hear what Her Majesty's Government have to propose.'[51]

That Monday, 13 February, was the occasion of Gladstone's last performance in the heroic parliamentary mode he had first established with his assault on Disraeli in 1852, his budgets in 1853 and 1860, which he brought to a peak with his Irish measures of 1869 and 1870; and which he sustained with decreasing effect in 1881 and 1886. Hamilton saw Gladstone that morning 'quite calm and collected, free from all excitement'. In the afternoon all the standard props of the drama were in place amid the atmosphere of parliamentary theatre so relished by Gladstone: the cheers as he entered the packed House, the waving hats and handkerchiefs 'amidst the loudest of renewed cheers'. But it was no longer the Gladstone of 1869 or even of 1886. The issue of Home Rule was now threadbare. There was an artificiality about the drama of the occasion. Everyone knew how the plot of the play was to unfold.

Hamilton found the exposition 'not quite as clear as it usually is'. The speech was received 'somewhat coldly, at any rate without any real enthusiasm on the part of Mr G.'s followers or any pronounced outcries on the part of the Unionists'. Gladstone made 'his very solemn appeal and impressive as well as beautiful peroration'. But it was 'not a speech that carried one away as one has been so often carried away before'. Rosebery thought the Commons' scene 'most pathetic, if not tragic'.[52] Gladstone himself recorded: 'Spoke 2½ h on Introduction of Irish Bill. I felt very weak having heard every hour (or all but one) strike in the night. I seemed to lie at the foot of the Cross, and to get my arm around it. The House was most kind: and I was borne through.'

In Selborne's opinion the second Home Rule Bill was a much better piece of legislative '*workmanship*' than the 1886 version, but the proposal to retain Irish representation had little of the effect it might have had in 1886. Ireland would undergo the Redistribution it had been spared in 1884, and return 80 members instead of 103. In any case, it simply shifted the location of the logically insoluble conundrum of Irish legislative privilege and British legislative penalty within the wider conundrum of fitting the square peg of Ireland free into the round hole of Ireland bound. Edward Clarke's powerful response on the part of the Unionists confirmed a general verdict that the whole subject was stale.

The anomaly of Irish representation was, as Gladstone admitted, serious. Irish MPs were to be restricted to voting on matters deemed 'imperial', but they were not to be excluded from votes of confidence. Gladstone made no mention of Ulster other than to insist that Ulster Protestants would in time come to see no harm in being governed from Dublin. The essence of his appeal was that, despite anomalies, the scheme would work in practice because of the sheer necessity of its so doing. This necessity of a new trust within a 'Union of Hearts' would constitute a great act of indemnity and oblivion. 'Cast behind you every recollection of bygone evils', pleaded Gladstone; 'let the dead bury the dead' under a 'living union for power and for happiness'.[53]

The Unionist strategy was for the Conservatives to fight the bill in the Commons and leave the Liberal Unionist peers led by Devonshire to administer the *coup de grâce* in the Lords. Balfour's lead was that Gladstone's analogy of imperial supremacy over Canada or the Australian colonies was a barren and empty gesture. 'Supremacy is nothing unless it is supremacy over the unwilling as well as the willing.'[54] But Chamberlain thrust himself forward to steal the Unionist show in the Commons and, as a kind of Disraeli to Gladstone's Peel, became a hero to the Conservative backbenches. The thrust of his critique of the bill was that it satisfied the criteria neither of logical federalism nor of subordinate devolution. He led the Unionist attack with grim pertinacity. 'I have never *known* such an opposition', Gladstone declared, 'one so detached from the merits & from rule. But it is probably suicidal.' Then: 'Spoke at the dinner hour for 30m against Chamberlain. Is it fanatical to say I seemed to be held up by a strength not my own?'[55]

Rosebery had by now, ironically, come round to thinking that the ultimate solution to the Irish difficulty would possibly be 'the establishment of the 4 Provincial Councils as projected in 1885 by Chamberlain'.[56] That scheme had the merit of simplicity. As Hamilton now had occasion to remark of Gladstone's complex measure, great legislation ultimately lives or dies in the details. By 21 March Morley was gloomy on the financial aspect. Gladstone was in great difficulty, and he 'would not appreciate or face the situation', which could well result in the bill's being wrecked in committee, which was an 'ugly confession' for him to make. 'In short, Ireland was a d----d fool to wish for Home Rule.' The Liberal party should never have embarked on it. 'We have no Parnell to deal with; and Ulster will give us more trouble than we ever had reason to expect. But, however insoluble may be the problem, I must fight it out.'[57]

That certainly was Gladstone's intention. For all his disabilities, the old Gladstone remained incomparably the greatest parliamentary performer. He was no longer a commanding wielder of Cabinets or a sure constructer of intricate or epochal measures. But he still had no trouble declaiming publicly on his feet. Though half blind and half deaf, the voice was still there and the mind as ready as ever in debate. He recorded for 8 April: 'Spoke I fear near one hour on compulsion. Never in my life more despondent: never more helped. I never rose with less knowledge or idea of what I should say; and it seemed to bubble up.' Some of his colleagues felt he was only too ready and too copious in debate. 'It must be rather heart-breaking for you', Asquith told Morley. 'It's brutal to put into words, but really, if Mr G. stood aside more, we might get on better.'[58]

~

The Easter recess gave an opportunity to recruit at Brighton under Armitstead's hospitable care, with occasional excursions back to London or to Rosebery at The Durdans. At Brighton Gladstone found 'Pier & salt air to perfection'. An odd occurrence towards the end of the stay was the affair of an 'intruder', one MacCurran.[59] In the following year Gladstone wrote to Mme Sadi-Carnot, widow of the assassinated French President: 'I have been the less able to remain altogether silent, because last year, when I was minister, an individual now in confinement, made his way unimpeded to the window of my Brougham, with a loaded pistol, for the purpose of dispatching me, but at the last moment relented, & abstained on account of observing, or thinking he observed in me, a likeness to his father.'[60] As with the 'mad cow' episode, Gladstone seems to have taken this threatening incident without trauma.

He was much more affected by the Queen's menaces. To Catherine he commented on the 'formal and menacing character' of his audience' on 10 March. Victoria had in fact expressed candidly her anxiety and apprehension that the Home Rule measure would 'tend towards the disruption of her Empire and the establishment of an impracticable form of Government'.[61] She seems to have been as embarrassed as Gladstone about the nullity of their meetings. She told her daughter the Empress Frederick of them: 'It is very difficult [to know] what to talk of, as Ireland is impossible and I was particularly warned by Lord Rosebery (who is my support and very open towards and much devoted to me) not to mention Uganda, so that one's political conversation was very restricted, but we talked of other things.'[62]

For all its vulnerabilities, the Home Rule Bill got through to its second reading debate in fair shape. Gladstone addressed a rally of the party at the Foreign Office on 28 March. His lengthy harangue seems to have elicited unanimity and a degree of enthusiasm. 'Speeches seem to be no effort to him at all, even at his age', Hamilton observed. 'It is administrative work only at which he shies.'[63] He moved the second reading on 6 April, on his return from Brighton, 'spritely and radiant'. He won the division on the 21st, with a majority of 43. But there was 'nothing like the same excitement there was in 1886'. Hamilton noted an 'absence of all real enthusiasm even among the Irishmen'.[64]

It was in the committee stage that the bill ran into serious trouble. The elaborate provision for restricting the procedural scope of the Irish members did not long survive. This reopened the old problem of Irish legislative privilege. 'In 1893 Mr Gladstone and his colleagues thought themselves compelled to change clause 9 of the new bill', as Morley recalled, 'just as they had thought themselves forced to drop clause 24 of the old bill.' Each plan, therefore, 'ended in a paradox': the Irish were either to be taxed without representation, or to be privileged 'to meddle in our affairs, while we were no longer to meddle in theirs'.[65]

At the Treasury, Hamilton knew all too well the weaknesses of the financial provisions; and he knew also Gladstone's 'delusions' about getting round them. Gladstone took no trouble to rally his Cabinet. By 28 April there had been no Cabinets for five weeks; nor would there be another until 5 May. Hamilton watched in dismay as the financial clauses crumbled. 'Mr G. won't take the trouble: Harcourt declines the task, partly from laziness and partly from pique: J. Morley can hardly be expected to get the subject up.'[66] Gladstone took comfort in the 'continuing boon which seems the boon for me' of the fellowship of the Holy Ghost, perhaps in its special vocation as comforter and enemy of evil spirits: Chamberlain's 'able though almost rabid opposition to the Conservative measure of Home Rule'.[67] At the end of May, after a 'very anxious & *rather* barren morning on Irish Finance', Gladstone delphically recorded: 'My present position as a whole seems peculiar: but of this it is unheroic either to speak or think.' Hamilton was shocked to hear Gladstone refer to 'that confounded Bill'.[68]

~

Amid the heavy pounding Gladstone took relief in a regular series of excursions and country house visits as well as retreating to Hawarden for the Whitsun recess. Deference accorded to ancient eminence combined with inveterate loquacity and readiness in conversation made him increasingly a social star turn. Lady Monkswell observed him after dinner at the Ripons': the 'body so old', the 'mind burning with the fires of youth – & *those terrible eyes*'.[69]

Whatever the *terribilità* of the eyes to the outward view, for Gladstone they were now a critical problem. He had startled Morley at Dalmeny with confidences about their deterioration. His Chester oculist examined them and reported hopefully about eventual cataract operations. There were encouraging experiments with a speaking trumpet 'of a clever kind'. Writing he found much less difficult than reading. The Horace translation ('which I find almost as fascinating as it is difficult') was a comforting and companionable task. There was little enough of literature feasible anyway at this fraught time. The irritating problems of biographers had arisen again in the case of Arthur Gordon's biography of his father, Aberdeen, published in 1893, which Gladstone deemed injurious to himself in particulars relating to his grudging attitude to Reform in the 1850s. Gordon trounced him with relevant quotations. Gladstone was distressed to learn from Purcell that Manning's 'Anglican' letters to him were lost, presumably destroyed by Manning after the exchange of correspondence in 1862.[70] On the other hand, having twice gone through with Lord Rothschild Disraeli's correspondence with his benefactress Mrs Brydges Willyams, Gladstone thought it prudent to burn his box of Laura Thistlethwayte's 'older' letters to him. 'They would lead to misapprehension: it was in the main a one-sided correspondence: not easy to understand.'[71]

Much more congenial was the distraction from his 'life of contention' of brooding fondly over his St Deiniol's foundation. Wilfrid Scawen Blunt was of a party who visited the temporary 'terrible building of corrugated iron' in 1892. Blunt observed Gladstone talking about his books 'in the absorbed way he has, going on, without paying the least attention to the person he is speaking to, especially if it is his wife and she ventures to interpose a remark'.[72] Stephen, now, like all the Gladstone sons, a late marrier, and having enjoyed a tour as Rural Dean of Mold, was again restless in his cure at Hawarden. Gladstone's solution was that Stephen exchange his Hawarden Rectorship for the Wardenship of St Deiniol's, with his father's assurances of 'sweet Counsel'. As Hamilton had remarked, the Gladstones' ideas of tact were peculiar to themselves.

~

But Gladstone's life of contention was never far away. By the beginning of July 30 nights had been devoted to the committee stage of the Government of Ireland Bill. Gladstone accepted an amendment explicitly asserting Westminster's supremacy over the proposed Dublin legislature. By this he hoped to bolster his claim that 'the supremacy of the Imperial Parliament is visible from one extremity of the Empire to another'.[73] The effect, however, was to put the issue all the more in doubt. Hamilton saw that Gladstone's gladiatorial sparrings with Chamberlain were 'a real delight to him: they possibly infuse fresh life into him'.[74] But they did not infuse fresh life into the bill, which Chamberlain mauled relentlessly.

The very fact that the doom of the Home Rule Bill was sealed in the Lords made it necessary for the Unionists to persecute it intransigently in the Commons. Gladstone in return was obliged to resort equally intransigently to the 'guillotine' of closure of debate. Balfour on 26 July could quite plausibly damn it, after Chamberlain's savaging, as 'defunct' and a 'corpse'. Amid the heats and humidities of high summer, after no less than nine exhausting divisions on 27 July, frayed tempers broke loose. Chamberlain sneered at the Gladstonians: 'never since the time of Herod has there been such slavish adulation'. This provoked from the Irish benches cries of 'Judas!' Instantly there was a scrimmage of 40 or so members swinging fists in front of the Clerks' Table: 'a sad scene never to be forgotten'. Gladstone and Balfour smoothly arranged for necessary apologies from guilty principals and 'got the wretched incident to a close' on the 31st.

Gladstone moved the third reading on 30 August. He rehearsed old themes. One of those themes was what he persuaded himself was the beneficial relevance of the Sweden–Norway relationship. He had requested the Foreign Office to prepare a précis of material bearing on the question. 'He refused to believe that this union was not a success; he sympathised with the Norwegian point of view, and he desired Sweden to be warned against coercing Norway.'[75] Gladstone was aware of what he called a 'race of folly' and a threat of civil war between these Scandinavian parties, but seemingly could not envisage any such race within his own Home Rule provisions. By the time of the final division on 2 September 82 sittings had been devoted to the bill, 'entirely in excess of anything that has ever before happened'.[76] He got his third reading with a majority of 34. There were conscientious Liberal abstentions, Rathbone among them, on the ground that the amended privileged position of the Irish members was unacceptable to British opinion.

It was Gladstone's last achievement in the House of Commons. 'This is a great step', he recorded. He knew it would soon be cancelled by the Lords. But it remained something that the principle of Home Rule had been accepted by the Commons. He would not wait to see his old colleague Devonshire lead the Lords to do their execution. On 4 September he moved an 'astringent' resolution that the business of the session, obstructed for so long by the Home Rule question, be resumed in the autumn, making it the longest session on record. He then departed for the Scottish Highlands.

When the Lords did their execution early in the morning of 9 September by the devastating margin of 419 to 41, the Gladstones were relaxing as Armitstead's guests at Black Craig, Perthshire. It was as well Gladstone did not witness the scene outside Parliament, with the crowd singing 'Rule Britannia' and setting off fireworks as the lords emerged after their second exercise in referendal mode. Their claim that they were better exponents of the 'will of the people' than 80 Irish MPs would soon enough be put to the test in the constituencies. Frank Burnand, the editor of *Punch*, sent Gladstone the 'capital cartoon' John Tenniel had drawn, 'Over the hills and far away', with Gladstone in tartan trews and cap, watched over by a friendly stag, taking a nap with a copy of Homer by his side.

20

Resignation, 1893–1894

'There were two things especially conspicuous about [Peel]. One was his overriding sense of public duty ... The other thing was his sense of measure ... and of the relation in which the leaders of his party stood to their followers.'

Gladstone, 29 January 1894, in Lionel Tollemache, Talks with Mr Gladstone *(1903), 116.*

After a brief stop at Edinburgh, where Gladstone caused a stir by hinting that the Home Rule Bill might be reintroduced in the Lords in 1894,[1] he and Catherine were back at Hawarden for a long October season before returning to London on the eve of the reassembly of Parliament on 2 November. Labouchere, a bitter enemy since Gladstone refused his application for preferment in 1892, told Dilke apropos of the Edinburgh hint: 'We are in the hands of an aged fetish thinking of nothing but Home Rule, senilely anxious to retain power, & fancying he can do so by tricking and dodging everyone.'[2] In fact, at Hawarden Gladstone was much more concerned with getting the Octagon into order. Making Kosmos out of Chaos was his phrase for it. Among the comings and goings of family and guests he worked at the Queen's personal request, relayed by Ponsonby, on the financial complications of the Duke of Edinburgh's succeeding to the duchy of Saxe-Coburg-Gotha. He worked also on his Horace translation but stopped short in Ode IV, i ('To Venus') in 'sheer disgust' at the pederastic final eight lines.[3] Reading was now a tiresome difficulty. And having to replace – 'after what a course of years!' of fitting into 'the nooks & crannies of one's life' – his veteran but alcoholic valet, Zadok Outram, was a distressing episode.[4]

Among the guests was the new Home Secretary, the great 'find' of his fourth Cabinet. 'Long conversation with Mr Asquith', Gladstone noted on 28 October. 'He will rise.' As the affianced of Margot Tennant, sister of the lamented Laura, Asquith, a widower, had already risen near to becoming a member of the extended family. At the moment, Asquith was deeply concerned with the distressing incident at the Featherstone colliery near Wakefield, where two striking miners had been killed by soldiers. When Gladstone rejoined his colleagues back in London for the renewed session, to Hamilton he 'looked younger and more vigorous than ever'. There was no question of retirement. He was evidently in one of his 'staying humours'. He would go when duly given his leave to go, not when his colleagues wanted him to go. He disliked the idea in any case of going merely on grounds of sight or hearing. He proposed to 'take things very easily'.[5]

So easily did he take things that his colleagues were soon complaining of lack of Cabinets, administrative incoherence, and 'Government by Departments'. Gladstone had no interest in his government's surviving items of legislation – Employers' Liability, Parish Councils, Local Government, Welsh Disestablishment and so on – other than in their prospective fortunes in the House of Lords. As the resumed session ploughed its way on through November and December Gladstone intervened little in the Commons and consulted little in Cabinet. He was restless and irritated and bored. He became increasingly detached from day-to-day affairs. 'I have repeatedly expressed my strong sense', as he put it to a Liberal MP, 'of the disadvantage at which the Liberal party is placed by my necessarily growing physical debilities.'[6] But it was clear also that, apart from anything else, Gladstone was unwilling to retire on a low note of failure and defeat.

Rosebery rather felt that Gladstone's staying on to see the government out would be for the best. It would 'avoid the horrible scrimmage which will inevitably ensue over his political carcase'. Gladstone's inclination in December 1893 was that the problem about his eyesight should be known. Catherine, however, as Hamilton recorded, 'won't hear of it: so of course the matter will be kept dark. She said in effect that Mr G. with hardly any eyes is worth more than anyone else with two pairs of sound eyes – characteristic of her, and another instance of his being so much under her thumb and that of the sons and daughters.'[7]

The optimum strategy for 1894 and after would be to re-establish the Liberal party on a footing enabling it to confront a dissolution of the 1892 Parliament with some credit and fair prospects, and to make the dissolution the fitting and proper occasion for Gladstone's departure. But how? Where was the 'cry'? Gladstone had flown his own 'kite' at Edinburgh about resuscitating Home Rule. 'Circumstances *point* to the reintroduction of the Bill in the House of Lords', he wrote cajolingly to Asquith, 'at the beginning of the session'; but it was as yet premature to decide this, and improper to indicate it.[8] If Gladstone hoped for a warmly supportive response, he was disappointed. Most of his colleagues wanted Home Rule to slide quietly out of sight and out of mind. There was always Employers' Liability and the rest of it. But, as ever since 1880, what were such trifles to the Grand Old Man? Then, later in November, a new prospect of possibilities began to take shape.

~

Lord George Hamilton, Salisbury's former First Lord of the Admiralty, raised in the Commons on 17 November the question of the 'Naval Policy of the

Government'. Gladstone responded, much in the manner of his facing down the 'Navy scare' of 1884, that the House need not have 'the smallest apprehension as to the maintenance of the distinct naval supremacy of Great Britain'. Beyond these bland formulae lurked a series of critical issues linking and entangling matters of foreign policy, with special reference to the Mediterranean Agreements and the Franco-Russian alliance, relating to specific points of abrasion with British interests in the Straits and Egypt (and the Sudan), and the extent to which French and Russian naval construction programmes raised hazardous questions for Britain.

It had been Lord George's proud achievement to get the 'two-power standard' – the powers being in fact France and Russia – of British naval supremacy embodied in his Naval Defence Act of 1889. That act gave the admirals ten battleships, 42 cruisers and 18 torpedo boats of the latest approved designs. At that time Gladstone was disabled from direct challenge to either the policy or the huge expenditure involved in a new-fangled rolling procedure over five years.[9] The matter of the second tranche of the money envisaged in 1889 would arise in 1894. Hence Hamilton's intervention. The immediate critical point for Gladstone was that Spencer at the Admiralty seemed in no doubt that the admirals had a compelling case.

Gladstone was well aware of the larger implications involved. 'The proceedings of the French', he expostulated to Rosebery, 'conceived in a spirit of aggressive shabbiness, have given me extreme pain: for I retain from my youth a feeling for the old idea of French alliance, within due limits, which was so cherished by the Grey Government, & that of Peel.'[10] Within the frame of that 'aggressive shabbiness' were the emerging outlines of the collapse of Salisbury's Straits policy against the Russians in 1896 and the consequent dangerous Fashoda crisis of 1898, when the French made their attempt from the Congo at the Sudanese back door of Egypt. But for Gladstone now the matter never got beyond that mood of regretful reminiscence. A series of such moods began to take the form of needing to retrieve memories of conflicts with Palmerston and of conflicts with Beaconsfield and the 'Jingoes'. So too with evocations of his 'European' reputation as the challenger of Bismarck and the embodiment of peace, the Concert, and resister of militarism.

If he had failed to give a lead against the admirals in 1889, Gladstone recurred now all the more emphatically, as if in apology, to the spirit of his rebuke to Lord Clarence Paget in 1866, on the theme of Britain's being deeply responsible to the world if we continued to set other countries the example that our enormous naval expenditure placed before them.[11] The more Gladstone came under pressure – there was a major debate on 19 November, followed up by an intervention from the Queen on 7 December – the more stubbornly he stood his ground.[12] The country, he declared, could depend on the government's making fitting proposals in due time and measure. There was no state of danger or emergency in the present or the foreseeable future. The present agitation was wholly unwarranted and founded on fallacious arguments. To the Queen Gladstone enlarged on the 'premature' nature of demands that subverted established procedures as to estimates in relation to annual expenditures. She had the benefit of his views on 'immature' proposals, views which had 'varied little from those which were entertained by the leaders of both parties at the time when he had first had the honour of becoming one of Your Majesty's Advisers under Sir Robert Peel'.[13]

It was Gladstone's presumption that resistance to the navalist Jingoes would be the natural stance of his party and his colleagues in accordance with the hallowed principles of Liberalism. Had he not after his brush with Paget armed Childers at the Admiralty in 1868 to dislodge the Sea Lords from their seats of professional interest and assert the supremacy of the First Lord? Spencer, it would be reasonable to assume, would accept revised estimates on a proper annual expenditure basis once the arguments were removed from too close proximity to the admirals. As he told Morley, Gladstone looked on a political battle with the alarmists as 'good for us from a party point of view'. A Cabinet on 14 December disillusioned him. The First Lord was in accord with the Sea Lords. He took it hard. 'The situation almost hopeless when a large minority allows itself to panic and joining hands with the professional elements works on the susceptibilities of a portion of the people to alarm.'[14] Morley was away in Ireland, and Harcourt, who on all past form Gladstone should have been able to count upon, seemed strangely to have capitulated to the Jingoes.

Gladstone found it particularly alarming that the expertise of the 'professional elements' was now, in effect, usurping the prerogative of responsible ministers. It had long been a rule with him that, when the experts 'charge their so-called professional opinions with political elements', they 'thus give authority to very worthless doctrine'.[15] Now it was a question of proclaiming to Europe that Britain proposed to ratchet an acceleration to the armaments race.

The new year of 1894 opened with Gladstone's summoning Eddie Hamilton for explanations about the present state of naval expenditure and about the charges that the envisaged construction programme would entail. His position was that 1889 was a special case and not a benchmark for the future. The proposed programme would initiate a 'race for Europe of huge armaments'. Had the nation gone mad?[16] Gladstone worked on the figures: 'they seem but too conclusive'. At the Exchequer, however, Harcourt revealed himself as 'rather severe'. There seemed no prospect of accommodation with Spencer. Gladstone felt himself 'rather hard hit from a combination of circumstances. I seem to stand alone though Morley is sympathetic: my sleep is a good deal disturbed: but "it is the Lord: let him do what seemeth him good"'.

What semethed him good was that Gladstone should retreat once more to

Biarritz to repair his sleep and escape the 'savage weather'. Harcourt was under the impression that Gladstone's family were in favour of his retirement; but Hamilton had his doubts: 'it is Mrs G. who has most power with him; and I doubt if she will concur in his making his bow'. Harcourt turned very severe indeed. 'Mr G. has already twice brought the Liberal party to grief – first in 1874 and afterwards in 1886.' Mr G, declared Harcourt, 'does not care a rush for the party. So long as the party suits his purpose, he uses it. The moment the question of his own personal convenience turns up, or he finds himself out of touch with the party, he is ready to discard it regardless of consequences.'[17]

Hamilton judged by 5 January that 'the fat was in the ministerial fire with a vengeance'. Gladstone could not see how he could go on with a policy that amounted to 'a sort of challenge to France and Russia'. Harcourt thought it best that Gladstone should retire. On the 7th Gladstone had 'a little conversation with C. and Mary on the sore subject'. To Morley he protested: 'I think the proposal a most alarming one. It will not be the last. It is not the largest piece of militarism in Europe, but it is one of the most virulent.'[18] Morley suffered 'one of the most uncomfortable & painful' hours of his life on 8 January when he was detained by Gladstone in a kind of Ancient Mariner mode. 'This is no ordinary occasion for me', declared Gladstone. 'It is not a question of a million here or a million there. It is a question of a man resisting something wh. is a total denegation of his whole past self.' He continued with 'suppressed passion'. 'More than that, I seem to hear, if I may so say, I seem to hear voices from the dead encouraging me.' 'With a gesture pointing to a distant corner of the darkened room.'[19]

A Cabinet was summoned for the 9th when Gladstone intended to reassert his control. He prepared voluminous memoranda. He harangued his colleagues for 50 minutes. Morley recorded that Gladstone's voice was 'clear, grave, and steady, and he spoke slowly, without anything like heavy solemnity or anything of the sepulchral, with a sort of composed authority, that was in the highest degree impressive'. He was admirable 'in simplicity, sincerity, and the pathos of tragic reality'. Nothing could have struck 'more absolutely true'. Morley thought his most telling stroke 'was when he sd., "I cd. not help you. I cd. not be of use to you. I cd. not speak for the plan. *I shd. sit by, a silent and dishonoured man.*"'[20]

For all the pathos, Gladstone made no impression. 'H., and in some degree R., pursued a remarkable course: different, however. In the end the matter stood over but without a ray of hope against this mad & mischievous scheme.' Harcourt's remarkable course was to accept the argument that the Navy needed the money in a speech of which Morley used the words violent, spiteful, obnoxious, forced, irrelevant, ill-natured, superfluous, ungracious, malicious, and profoundly detestable. In reply, Gladstone simply 'turned and said, "Of course I can go at once if you wish it". (Sensation.) Then silence, and after a pause Rosebery, supported by Asquith, asked for a decision. Gladstone would not declare himself, but urged his ministers to continue to talk informally among themselves.'[21] Four days hence, Gladstone announced, he would be going to Biarritz and would take the opportunity to retire after his return. He indicated that his family, 'within *viva voce*, are made aware'.[22] Rosebery hinted at the convenience to all of immediate retirement, but Gladstone was determined on first going to Biarritz. He stipulated that there should be no Cabinets in his absence. Withdrawal of Cabinets had ever been one of his weapons against recalcitrant colleagues.[23]

'Am I Athanasius contra mundum? Or am I Thersites, alone in the Achaian Assembly?'[24] He could not get over the enormity of it all. 'Three only of the sixteen were in sympathy with me on the *merits* of the scheme. Thirteen against me!'[25] He identified Harcourt as the chief villain. By the 11th he was slightly calmer. 'I am now like the sea in swell after a storm, bodily affected, but mentally pretty well anchored. It is bad: but oh how infinitely better than to be implicated in that plan!' There was much manoeuvring in the background to prepare the way for Gladstone's making his decision either to agree or go. Mary Drew, who wanted him to go, pulled Acton into the plot. She told Loulou Harcourt who sped to see Acton at the Athenaeum to rehearse his role. Acton would accompany Gladstone to Biarritz.[26] Catherine was prepared for what was impending. 'Poor Mrs G. is much broken down. After her talk last night with John Morley, she realizes for the first time the real picture of affairs.'[27]

~

Gladstone went off to Biarritz under 'friendly convoy of Mr Armitstead', with Catherine, Mary Drew and her daughter, Herbert, Acton and Algernon West in attendance. In a flourish of nepotism before departure he made his son-in-law Wickham Dean of Lincoln. He simmered with resentment both at his colleagues' failure to fall in with his views and their evident readiness to see him go. For all that he had incessantly begged for release ever since taking office in 1880, Gladstone had never imagined or foreseen the dispiriting circumstances now confronting him. Surely this could not, in the end, be the way of the Lord's opening the door for him? Hamilton recorded on 11 January: 'There is an ingenious theory, founded mainly on surmise, that Mr G., finding to his surprise that his speech to the Cabinet made no converts, is reconsidering the position of affairs and casting about for some excuse to withdraw his threat to resign.' Hamilton thought there was something 'decidedly comic and ludicrous in this'. Morley thought 'Mr G. should never have taken office at all'.[28]

Life at Biarritz was Horace, backgammon and gloomy talk about iniquitous Navy estimates. For agreeable and entertaining conversation there were the Lionel Tollemaches, a couple Gladstone had earlier met wintering at the Grand Hotel in 1892. The Tollemaches were Cheshire neighbours. An avowed student of human nature, Tollemache set out to 'Boswellize' Gladstone. Possibly the most telling indication of Gladstone's animus against his colleagues was his remark to Tollemache about Peel's two most conspicuous attributes as a statesman: his sense of public duty and his sense of measure. For the latter Gladstone instanced 'his concept of the relations between the leader of a party and his followers'.[29]

That opinion would have come as something of a shock to anyone acquainted with the story of Peel and his party.[30] Given that Gladstone's own sense of measure in January 1894 was so attuned, his party had reason for foreboding. West reported to Hamilton that there was 'such an atmosphere of moodiness and excitement about him', and that he 'never got a civil word out of Mr G., who either fulminated against everybody as if they were all criminals or treated everything with the utmost levity'. It was a case of 'the old, very old, man'.[31] Acton reported that Gladstone still believed the others would give way. 'He was loud, unreasoning, inurbane, in proclaiming his own fixity.' Acton found Gladstone 'different at different times. Generally, he was wild, violent, inaccurate, sophistical, evidently governed by resentment. Now and then, for a moment, he collected himself, and was full of force – but never full of light, or able to see any argument but his own.'[32]

West escaped and returned to London for a brief respite to tell Hamilton on 25 January that Gladstone 'intended to preserve his complete freedom of action as regards the future – he might indeed continue to retain his seat in Parliament; and not only that, he might express his own views and disclose the real cause of his resignation in one way or another, perhaps in the House of Commons, perhaps by an appeal to his constituents, perhaps by a letter to the *Times*!' Hamilton was stunned. 'Could anything be worse? Mr G. is evidently quite beside himself.' It was what Hamilton 'always feared – that senility would show itself in some form or another'. Rosebery feared the fulfilment of Palmerston's prophecy that Gladstone would ruin the Liberal party and die in a madhouse.[33]

Weary of Gladstone's obstinacy, Acton fled the scene of desolation. He did so 'by way of conveying to him that I was losing my time, and thought him a little below his own level, and he quite understood, and resented it'. To Acton it was all a 'tragic and sinister catastrophe', in which 'pure reason had lost its way'.[34] He made on his return to London 'an uncomfortable report of the state of things' at Biarritz. He told Harcourt how irritable the old man grew, of his 'brusqueness and rudeness'. Acton also warned that Gladstone was clutching at straws, such as the idea that one or two of his colleagues (meaning Lefevre and Trevelyan) were still with him'. Rosebery was convinced that Gladstone's 'natural impulse' was to quit but that 'the "petticoats" around him won't let him give up power'.[35]

~

A critical turning point came when Gladstone decided that Biarritz was a kind of quasi-abdication, in the mode of 1874–75, preliminary to a counter-attack and capture in the mode of 1877–80. That point can be identified as 31 January, when Gladstone 'found West in a great state' with a telegram from London quoting a *Pall Mall Gazette* announcement that 'I had determined on resigning almost immediately'. Gladstone 'framed a contradiction, rather a tough business, in terms carefully weighed', and read it 'again & again to West & Herbert: we got it shortened & then despatched in West's name, on my behalf'. The toughness of the business consisted in the fact that the press report was accurate. Gladstone's denial – 'pure Gladstonese', as Hamilton put it, 'sailing very dangerously to the wind of veracity' – took the form of: 'The statement that Mr Gladstone has definitely decided, or has decided at all, on resigning office is untrue. It is true that for many months past his age, and the condition of his sight and hearing have, in his judgment, made relief from public cares desirable.'[36]

'Poor dear old man!' was Hamilton's comment. The news came also at this moment that the House of Lords had re-amended the Employers' Liability Bill in defiance of the House of Commons. Though ever one to menace the Lords with *bouches à feu* and to relish the notion of punitive dissolutions, Gladstone had been so obsessed with the Navy estimates issue that only now did a denial of his intention to resign click together with a spacious new vista of possibility. West volunteered that the Parish Councils Bill was also at peril. A kind of epiphany now came down upon Gladstone. He was much more cheerful after dinner. There was no further allusion to the Navy estimates.

Another jolt at this time helping to expedite Gladstone's revised outlook on matters was a letter from Marjoribanks, the Whip. Reflecting the dismay widespread in the party at the reports West had brought back about Gladstone's threatening public disclosure of the cause of his resignation, Marjoribanks wrote suggesting the desirability of Gladstone's retiring from the House of Commons at the same time as his resignation of office and the leadership.[37] This impertinence stimulated Gladstone wonderfully. More and more the pattern of counter-attack as leader of the nation against the parliamentary party as in 1877–80 suggested itself. Acton had told Mary Drew that Gladstone's colleagues were unanimous in hoping that he would repudiate them on the Navy estimates. It was clear that, far from being intimidated by Gladstone's withdrawal of his countenance, his colleagues were accustoming themselves to his absence quite comfortably.[38] Gladstone would turn the tables on them by setting aside the naval problem and by using the wickedness of the House of Lords against his party as he had once used the Eastern question. A grand insight had come upon him, reaching far beyond the petty issues of the time. It was a little awkward that, unlike his situation at the time of the Eastern question, he was in office as Prime Minister. The difficulty would be persuading his colleagues to acquiesce in a *coup de tête* against themselves.

The early days of February 1894 saw Gladstone galvanized into activity. He wrote to Welby at the Treasury enquiring what were the necessary number of days between dissolving a Parliament and assembling a new one, and what were the minimum number of days required after assembling a new Parliament before votes could be proposed for estimates. To Morley and Harcourt he fleshed out his new approach. 'I am looking with deep interest and anxiety at the proceedings in the Lords. Until Friday or Saturday's news came here they had not assumed the character which it now seems possible they may bear – that of a virtual destruction of the entire year's work of the Commons. If they do this it seems to raise a hard & very large question indeed: possible [*sic*] one large enough to carry us for the *moment* into some new current.'[39] He prepared Mundella for a change of front. 'The Lords *may* raise for us another not less urgent question crossing the scent. The unforeseen often does much in politics.'[40] He alerted his Midlothian committee chairman with a gloss on his forthcoming resignation statement: it would not be a decision 'irrespective of circumstances & fixing a time'.[41]

To West, Gladstone announced that 'the situation has now changed'. It depended on whether the House of Lords had completed its 'tale of iniquities'. If so, Gladstone would obtain a provisional vote for Army and Navy estimates first, 'and then ask the country to judge of him by the past – not the future – and to give a commission to the new Government to deal with the House of Lords'. West observed Gladstone 'brilliant at dejeuner, being full of his new idea, saying he had strength enough, and physique enough for the fight. But pointing to his eyes.'[42]

Rumours seeped back to London of an astonishing and dramatic turn of events at the Grand Hotel, Biarritz. Hamilton speculated on 5 February: could it be that Mr G contemplates a dissolution? A last desperate throw of the political dice? Surely his colleagues would never agree? Surely it would be political suicide? Mary Drew seemed to indicate that some volte-face on her father's part was possible, ostensibly on the grounds of the Lords' cruelty to the Parish Councils Bill.[43] The rumours were confirmed by telegraph from Algernon West. Gladstone proposed to dissolve the 1892 Parliament on the grounds of its representation of the people being thwarted by the Lords. It was a case of now or never to get the benefit of Gladstone's leadership of the nation.

Gladstone's second *coup de tête* died a mercifully quick death. Harcourt thought it 'the act of a selfish lunatic': '"Heads I win and tails you lose."' He telegraphed back to West that the Biarritz proposal was 'absolutely insane'.[44] Even Morley dismissed the idea as 'impossible and preposterous'. Rosebery was sure that what was 'actuating Mr G. now' was 'malevolence towards his colleagues'. Asquith was discouraging: there was too much yet to do. Marjoribanks stressed that the party was not ready for an election. In any case the Lords had not yet gone far enough for a convincing case to be made against them.[45] Kimberley deemed it impossible to abandon the government's present measures and to 'attack the House of Lords in its present aspect'. As Leader in the Lords he summarized his colleagues' responses and telegraphed that they were 'strongly and unanimously against proposal to dissolve'. Hamilton concluded that 'Mr G. has lost his sense of balance altogether, and is not really fitted to continue to be Prime Minister even in the most nominal and ornamental capacity. It is a very distressing state of things.'[46]

~

Was this the Great Refusal of Liberalism? Was a golden opportunity let slip to retrieve the party's fortunes after the failure of the second Home Rule Bill? Gladstone ever after, rather naturally, insisted so. A brilliant insight had come upon him, comparable, in his view, to his insight in August 1876 into the 'virtuous passion' of the masses about the question of the East. Indeed, Gladstone would go further. His insight in 1894 was not, as was the case in 1876, simply a discernment that public opinion had risen to a certain height needful for a given work. It was something much more profound, to be ranked along with his insights as to the 1853 budget, the Irish Church question in 1868, and Home Rule for Ireland in 1886. For Gladstone the 'desire for a dissolution of Parliament in the beginning of 1894, and the immediate determination of the issue then raised between the two Houses of Parliament' was elevated into the fourth of the series of supreme moments of political juncture in his career, when his providentially inspired appreciation of the general situation and its result, and his insight into the facts of particular eras, generated in his mind a conviction that the materials existed for forming a public opinion and directing it to a particular end.[47]

It was in such a bitterly frustrated frame of mind – that supremely high stakes were there to be played for, and that his colleagues were too stunted and narrow in outlook to share even a glimpse of his insights and appreciations and convictions to have the wit to play for them – that Gladstone returned to London on 10 February. His sense of frustration and bitterness was as fresh in 1896 as it was in 1894. 'Had I not had cataract entailing early disability: had I not been eighty-three years old: had I not had vital controversy with my colleagues on the estimates, such as to break up or dislocate our whole relations, I might have come to London and proved the question of dissolution. But in view of the actual state of facts, and the very small amount of desire (except so far as kind feeling was concerned) the Cabinet had shown to avert my resignation, it was out of the question.'[48]

He would have endorsed Morley's words: 'Not the right end of a life of such power & long and sweeping triumph.'[49] He thus returned in worse situation than that in which he had left, doubly rejected by his colleagues and bereft of a cry. The Navy estimates issue now moved back to the centre of concern. At the first Cabinet, on the 12th, normal business about the Lords amendments was discussed. There were expectations that the matter of resignation would be clarified, but Gladstone said nothing. 'Out we trouped', Morley recalled, 'like schoolboys dismissed from their hour of class. Never was a dramatic surprise more perfect.' Harcourt afterwards was 'in fits of laughter'. It had indeed been 'an hour of dupery, and the Old Man left in the Cabinet room, as he surveyed the confusion of the 16 empty chairs might have been forgiven if he chuckled over the thought of the confusion of the 16 equally empty gentlemen who had just left them'. Nothing was said about the Navy estimates, ostensibly the chief question before the Cabinet. Morley suspected a ruse on Gladstone's part to enable him to deny that a decision had been taken. 'This wd. be a very characteristic bit of Gladstonian subtlety as it is called – childish duplicity is what it ought to be called.'[50]

At Downing Street that evening Gladstone recorded a 'family conversation on the question'. Hamilton had talked to Catherine and the daughters. They complained that Gladstone's colleagues had never tried to meet him half-way. They did not mind his 'leaving a little early', but resented his going 'on a lie'. Hamilton feared that they were 'almost sure themselves to let the real reason be known before long, or else encourage him to allow himself to be drawn. Indeed, Helen Gladstone said that out of office her father would be uncontrolled and (by implication) a dangerous power.' Hamilton felt more sorry than he could say for Catherine. 'She feels the situation acutely; but kept on saying "My husband never has and never will sacrifice his conscience for the retention of power, for keeping the party together, or even for the sake of Ireland; and so nothing now will make him acquiesce to what he considers to be dangerous proposals".'[51]

On the 17th Gladstone told Hamilton: 'You see I am angry; and though I may use strong language, I am quite calm.' Gladstone exercised his peevish humour by retaliation and prolonging the difficulty. That night he offered a Cabinet dinner. There was naturally intense speculation among his guests. Towards the end, Rosbery hinted promptingly that it would be well to close the doors. 'I believe it was expected that I should say something', recorded the nonchalant Gladstone. 'But from my point of view there is nothing to be said.' All he did say on this occasion – at which he 'regularly sold his colleagues' – was that he was quite prepared to listen to anything anybody else had to say. Asquith's exasperated record of the 'dreaded dinner' was '*Rien!*'[52]

The Lords amendments to the Employers' Liability Bill did eventually persuade Asquith to abandon it. Gladstone made the announcement to the Commons on 20 February. Doubtless he did so with inner reflections on the worse case of the Parish Councils Bill, and on the way he 'lay fettered if not hamstrung by the difficulties of which the most formidable lay in the disposition, and in the wants of disposition, prevailing among his immediate friends'.[53] At a Cabinet on the 23rd he 'alluded to his own position; but only at the end of the sitting just as everybody was leaving. So no one had a chance of saying anything and his words were received in silence …'[54] As Gladstone wrote in one of his biographical fragments later in 1894, 'Politics are like a labyrinth, from the ironic intricacies of which it is even more difficult to find a way of escape, than it was to find away into them.'[55] One of the twists of the labyrinth was getting the Queen to promise strict confidentiality in view of the delicacy of transactions in the Lords. Gladstone wrote a 'preliminary intimation' on 27 February of his intention to resign 'on physical grounds', and was received in audience the following day, 'doubtless my last in an official capacity'. Victoria thought he looked 'very old and deaf'. They had 'much difficulty in finding topics for an adequate prolongation: but fog and rain and the coming journey to Italy all did their duty and helped'. He thought he never saw her looking better. 'She was at the highest point of her cheerfulness. Her manner was personally kind throughout.' She said she was 'sorry *for the cause*' that had brought about his resignation.

The only part of the audience of any importance was the impression made on Gladstone that she had in mind keeping on a reconstructed Liberal government rather than turning to Salisbury; and 'further that she will not ask any advice from me as to the head, and further still that she will send for Rosebery'. He very much wanted to advise that Lord Spencer be sent for, but it was not politic to venture an initiative on a point so sensitive to the prerogative.[56]

A final Cabinet met on Thursday, 1 March. 'A really moving scene.' Kimberley started by trying to say a few words, but broke down. Then Harcourt drew out a voluminous manuscript and read, sobbing, to the company an embarrassingly pompous *éloge*, 'which was felt', as Gladstone himself put it, 'to be nine-tenths buncrum'.[57] Morley's words for it were horrid, grotesque, nauseous, almost obscene.[58] At his last Cabinet Council, 'when some Ministers were in tears, he gave no sign of feeling & even discouraged anything of the sort in others'.[59] He would afterwards refer to it as the 'blubbering Cabinet'. He was unforgiving to the last. Morley recalled Gladstone's going 'slowly out of one door; while we with downcast looks and depressed hearts filed out by the other; much as men walk away from the grave-side'.[60]

Gladstone made his last speech in the Commons that afternoon. His colleagues wanted him to unloose 'a dose of very bad language' against the House of Lords. 'I tried to follow the wish of the Cabinet: with a good conscience. The House showed feeling: but of course I made no outward sign.' The Commons were quite unaware that this was to be Gladstone's last appearance in their chamber, after 61 years. He acquiesced, under protest, to the Lords amendments to the Local Government (England and Wales) Bill. Gladstone stressed that it had become an 'intolerable' situation with the passing of the age of 'reserve and circumspection' in the Upper House. He cited the cases of Wellington, Aberdeen and others in point. Some solution had to be found for this 'tremendous contrariety and incessant conflict upon matters of high importance between the Representatives of the people and those who fill a nominated or non-elective chamber'. Gladstone declared that his duty terminated by calling the attention of the House to the fact that 'a question enormously large, a question which has become profoundly acute', will demand a settlement from the highest authority, an authority higher than the authority of the House of Commons. 'It is the authority of the nation which must in the last resort decide.'[61]

Thus, in Asquith's words, his legacy to his party.[62] At the time, quite apart from the pathos of his circumstances, there was a hollowness in his protestations. No one doubted that the Lords would be endorsed by the 'authority of the nation' in the coming general election. Gladstone departed quietly from the arena in which so often he had heard roars of acclamation. 'He took up his little box, & walked out, & gave us no sign of emotion. The old man seemed to have *steeled* himself for all those last days.'[63]

At Windsor the following day the Gladstones dined and slept. 'The Queen, long & courteous, but of little meaning on "fundamentals".' On his way to St George's Chapel the following morning Gladstone fell in with Ponsonby, who was 'much impressed with the movement among a body of members of Parliament against having any peer for Prime Minister'. Gladstone 'signified briefly' that he did not think there should be 'too ready submission to such a movement'. On seeing Ponsonby again after chapel Gladstone repeated the point, adding that there was advantage in strengthening the small Liberal minority in the Lords with the weight of office.[64] Thus was Harcourt paid back, with interest.

It was arranged that Gladstone would have his final audience of the Queen later that morning. 'I carried with me a box containing my letter of resignation.' The 'only incident of any interest in this, perhaps rather memorable audience', which closed a service near to 53 years since Gladstone himself had been sworn as Privy Councillor in September 1841, was that when he came near 'to take the seat she has now for some time courteously commanded, I did think she was going to "break down".' She kept her emotions under control, and conducted a conversation that was neither here nor there: 'not one syllable on the past', except reiterated gratitude for his services in the matter of the Duke of Saxe-Coburg's affairs. There were kind remarks about Catherine, whom she had previously seen in a sobbing state. 'There was no touch on the subject of the last Ponsonby conversation.'

Gladstone reported to Catherine that it was 'thought there had been some suggestion from the Queen' of a peerage in her own right for Catherine. The offer was 'politely declined'.[65] Perhaps the Gladstones did not relish the Beaconsfieldian precedent. Gladstone in any case dissuaded Catherine. He worried that he had been 'wrong in not tending orally my best wishes'. He was 'afraid that anything said by me should have the appearance of *touting*'. He felt also that there seemed 'some little mystery as to my own case with her: I saw no sign of embarrassment or preoccupation'. No doubt the saddest feature of Gladstone's thinking there was 'some little mystery' as to his own case with Victoria was his failing in awareness of the enormous difficulty she had, as a person of naturally transparent candour, of dissembling her honest detestation of him. Particularly was this the case when his failing in awareness reached the unintendedly comical level of his being himself virtuously 'conscious without mistrust of having invariably rendered her the best service that I could'.[66]

Arthur Balfour replied to Gladstone's intimation as to what was about to happen with words that represented accurately the feelings of every one of his fellow members: 'I can hardly realise what the House of Commons will be without you.'[67] Gladstone himself remained in a deeply equivocal state of mind about the circumstances of his resignation. He cherished, so to speak, an 'official version'. This held that the state of his sight did most towards his exchanging his 'imperious public obligations' for what seemed to him to be 'a free place on "the breezy common of humanity."' Thus, the 'operation of retirement, long ago attempted, now at length effected', must he thought 'be considered among the chief momenta' of his life. 'And like those other chief momenta which have been numerous, they have been set in motion by no agency of mine, and have all along borne upon them the marks of Providential ordination.'[68]

An unofficial version possibly exudes a more ample aura of explanatory power. On 22 February he spoke to Harcourt of retirement. To Harcourt's polite response that it would be a 'calamity', Gladstone 'bowed, and said "Yes; that may be; but it is a retirement not voluntarily effected, but compelled by others."'[69] Such ultimately was the consummation of fourteen years of striving to be free of the toils of leadership. Such was the manner ultimately of the Lord's opening the door and giving leave. And such was the compulsion of having to be pushed through it.

21

Last Years, 1894–1898

'Say what you will, I am a survival – a survival from the time of Sir Robert Peel – think of what that means.'

Gladstone in conversation with Lady Aberdeen at Pitlochry, 3 July 1894

There was much to do in receiving and acknowledging visits and messages of condolence and tribute and good wishes. There was a peerage for Reginald Welby, whose parsimony at the Treasury had ever recommended him to Gladstone. There was a peerage also for Stuart Rendel, in gratitude for 'infinite personal kindness, I might indeed say tenderness which you have shown me since the first opportunity for it was afforded in these last years: & which has had a real warming & cheering influence on my public as well as private life'.[1] His former private secretaries gave him a dinner at Brooks's Club. His effects were removed from Downing Street to Dollis Hill. A sharp attack of bronchial hoarseness prevented dining with the Duke and Duchess of York.[2] Catherine attended alone.

But always there was the rankling sense that his farewell from the Queen was not as it should have been. He was put in mind of the manner of his leave-taking from the mule that had borne him uncomplainingly but uncomfortably around Sicily in 1838. He complained that her response to his formal letter of resignation was in the manner of 'settling a tradesman's bill'.[3] He told Ponsonby candidly that the circumstances of his departing from Windsor required him to harden his heart 'into a flint'.[4] He was greatly upset when Rosebery, who sat by Catherine at the Yorks' dinner, pressed her about her husband: 'he hates the Queen, doesn't he?'

This provoked Gladstone into making a 'clean breast' of his feelings on the matter. 'I am as I hope loyal to the Throne.' He admired the 'many fine qualities' possessed by the Queen. But he used to admire her more than he did now: 'frankly I do not see that the Queen has improved in the last twenty years'. Taking her relations to himself 'since 1844, as a whole, there is in them something of a mystery, which I have not been able to fathom, and probably never shall'.[5]

Stiffly inflexible in this respect, as in almost every other respect throughout his career, Gladstone simply lacked imaginative sympathy with and psychological insight into the workings of other minds adequate to comprehending that the Queen might not see it her duty to 'improve' herself conformably to his requirements. Gladstone had a way of docketing people after conversation as 'satisfactory' or some variant of satisfactoriness as showing or failing to show evidence of having attained to a standard of outlook or opinion rather severely pre-ordained by himself. When Victoria remarked on Acton's agreeableness as a lord-in-waiting, she was undoubtedly making a point for Gladstone to chew on. 'He does not *force* his great learning and knowledge upon anyone', which 'makes him particularly pleasant in society.'[6] The famed complaint attributed to her that he 'speaks to Me as if I was a public meeting' partly explains the 'mystery', but clearly the fathoming of it needs a deeper reach.[7] Gladstone could account for the 'signs perfectly unequivocal if partly negative' in the Queen's attitude to him only in some defect of understanding and response on her part. Yet at the same time he was aware of the likely influence of rumours widely circulating in the public world concerning his 'rescue' work and his notorious association with Mrs Thistlethwayte. 'I do not speak lightly, when I state my conviction that the circumstances of my farewell, which I think were altogether without parallel, had serious causes, beyond the operation of political disagreements, which no doubt went for something, but which were insufficient to explain them. Statements, whether true or false must have been carried to her ears which in her view required (and not merely allowed) the mode of proceeding which was actually adopted.'[8]

He brooded resentfully also on what he felt was the Queen's shabby treatment of Catherine. 'What a fine opportunity of conveying by language or token to this wife herself some voluntary offering, which would have been so well merited and appropriate, and would have furnished a conclusive answer to any criticism which might have been suggested by the cold negation of her conduct to me.'[9] Either he had forgotten the offer to Catherine of a peerage or he did not consider it adequate to the occasion. In 1896 he added a note to his now sporadic diary, placing on record 'my strong desire that after my decease my family shall be most careful to keep in the background all information respecting the personal relations of the Queen and myself during these later years, down to 1894 when they died a kind of natural death: relations rather sad in themselves though absolutely unattended with the smallest ruffle on the surface'.[10]

~

Otherwise, retirement to the 'breezy common of humanity' gave Gladstone little cause for regret. By September he could declare himself 'thoroughly content'. 'I cast no lingering look behind.' He saw plenty of work before him, 'peaceful work, and work directed to the supreme, i.e. the spiritual, cultivation of mankind, if it please God to give me time and vision to perform it'.[11] Within days of his resignation he was looking into Butler with a view to resuming his plan to assert

Butler's theological greatness and restore his reputation as Christianity's most potent apologist at a time when new lines of criticism were pressing hard on belief. But to undertake an edition with accompanying commentary would be a heavy call on eyesight. Consultations in Wimpole Street established that apart from the cataracts the eyes were sound and operations would be feasible in due course. Gladstone had every reason to hope that the fog closing in on him would be dispersed.

Hamilton came upon the 'great man' on 22 March turning out his effects in Downing Street and heard him declaim against the Navy estimates, professing himself 'astonished' at how 'quietly' those 'mad or drunk' proposals were being accepted by the public. 'I dread the effect which the proposals may have on Europe.'[12] Rosebery never consulted him. The secretaries knew well how 'horrified' Gladstone would be to learn that the new prime minister was to install 'the Electric Light in Downing St'.[13] 'Rosebery has been under no obligation to give me his confidence, and he has entirely withheld it as to inner matters, while retaining unimpaired all his personal friendliness. He does not owe his position to me, and has no sort of debt to pay.' It was true, of course, that Gladstone's bringing Rosebery to the front at the Foreign Office in 1886 'was indeed an immense advancement'; but it was done 'with a belief, not sustained by subsequent experience, in his competency and wisdom'.[14]

Rosebery did not endear himself to his colleagues or his party when he inaugurated his premiership by echoing quite gratuitously Salisbury's pronouncement defending the Lords' veto on the Home Rule Bill. Salisbury asserted that no great constitutional change could be made without the consent of the 'deciding judge' of the United Kingdoms, England. Rosebery declared his 'entire accord'. As the predominant partner, England would have to be convinced of its justice and equity.[15] From Gladstone's point of view Rosebery thus represented a Liberalism ready to go ahead with the 'outrageous mischief' of the naval programme while consigning the Home Rule policy to political limbo.

In general Gladstone found little satisfaction in the way Rosebery and Harcourt were conducting the Liberal government. All this was much in accordance with his Peelite nostalgia. 'In some & some very important respects, I yearn for the impossible revival of the men and the ideas of my first 20 years which immediately followed the first Reform Act.'[16] But then, as he allowed, it was not his purpose 'to arraign the politics or politicians of the day'. His immediate purpose was to assist at the celebrations of the marriage of Asquith to Margot Tennant at St George's, Hanover Square. Margot was a 'forward' young woman of whom Gladstone did not entirely approve. 'She has very fine qualities & capacities. I should be glad were she to add to them more of humility and dependence. He has a great future.'[17] (Margot thought Catherine an 'interfering hen'.)[18]

Gladstone was one of the four past, present and future prime ministers who signed the register, the others being Rosebery, Balfour and Asquith himself. Arthur Benson, the Archbishop's son, observed Gladstone, 'very toothless and hairless', talking at length to Arthur Balfour on the vestry stairs, 'with the pathetic reverence of old age for youth and success'.[19] At the reception at Grosvenor Square Gladstone proposed the toast to the bride and groom (though not standing on a chair, as he had in 1885 when performing the same office on the occasion of Margot's sister Laura's wedding to Alfred Lyttelton). Balfour would say that while he found Gladstone's oratory for the most part dull, he did two things to perfection: speaking on a point of procedure in the Commons, and proposing the toast at a wedding breakfast.

On that brilliant occasion Gladstone's pathos was perhaps partly explained by the fact that he was shortly to undergo his operation for cataract. That operation, on 24 May at Dollis Hill, went well. But thus it was that he made no record of the death, on 30 May, of Laura Thistlethwayte, at Woodbine Cottage, Hampstead. The operation gave Gladstone also 'a good opportunity for breaking off the commonly dry daily journal, or ledger as it might be called, in which for seventy years I have recorded the chief details of my outward life'.[20] Relieved from the 'small grind of the Daily Journal', he would henceforward note only 'principal events or occupations'. There was immense relief also in the 'great revolution' in the incidence of correspondence, which had been 'for many years a serious burden, and at times one almost intolerable.'[21]

A summer excursion to Pitlochry in Scotland, again under Armitstead's care, was made agreeable by a visit from Lady Aberdeen, on leave from helping her husband to be Governor-General of Canada, a posting advised by Gladstone in 1893. She was surprised to find both Gladstones 'looking so well'. Gladstone now had 'considerable colour in his cheeks, instead of the extreme pallor of last year'. He was vehement in criticism of her brother-in-law, Arthur Gordon, now Lord Stanmore; but generally he was cheerful and 'very playful most of the time'. His mind often dwelt on the past. 'Say what you will, I am a survival – a survival from the time of Sir Robert Peel – think of what that means. My colleagues were very good to me but they felt this – they were all men twenty, thirty, forty years younger than myself. Could I break with all the associations of my middle life and of the men I then served with and under? It *could* not be and the others felt the time had come when I was best away. I cannot sympathise with much of the talk of the present day and they knew it.'

Gladstone assured Lady Aberdeen that he had never felt the dispensations of Providence 'more clear in any of the events of my life than in these last four months'. It had 'forced an overdriven man to understand something of what meditation may mean'. She observed how 'Kemble's farewell and how the line "a period between the theatre and the grave" runs in his head'.[22]

~

The great world intruded from time to time. An American Invitation Committee, in consideration of Gladstone's 'far-reaching and beneficent influence upon our common race of your long and brilliant course', offered to arrange an autumn tour of the United States in 1894.[23] Gladstone contented himself with having provided a proxy in the form of an axe exhibited in the Forestry Building at the Chicago World's Fair.[24] The great world intruded also in ways much less congenial. Extensive massacres of Armenian Christians by the Turks in that autumn of 1894 set off an agitation of moral outrage in British public opinion reminiscent of the Bulgarians and 1876. Naturally Gladstone's name was much invoked. A deputation of Armenian bishops presented a chalice for use in the parish church and heard him urge the need for Europe to intervene with deeds as well as words.

Winter came cruelly to Hawarden in 1894. Fierce gales toppled Gladstone's favourite beech trees. It was a bitter blow when Alfred Lyttelton, the most brilliant scion of his clan, came to Gladstone to declare his Unionist allegiance.[25] Mary Drew shared her parents' 'utter misery' at Alfred's defection, preparatory to his standing, successfully, as a Unionist candidate at the coming elections.[26]

Escape to Rendel's hospitable Chateau de Thorenc, or 'palazzetto', near Cannes, suggested itself. They varied Rendel's hospitality with excursions to Cannes and to Cap Martin at Menton. It was while there that a discreditable episode from his past caught up with Gladstone. The parties who had purchased promises of peerages in 1891 now demanded that the undertakings be honoured. Rosebery was disconcerted thus to be importuned. He 'naturally demurred until he had received a written request from Gladstone'. Arnold Morley, the original broker, was deputed to communicate with Gladstone, putting to him the necessity of writing to Rosebery to confirm the undertakings and accept responsibility for enriching the House of Lords with the baronies of Ashton and Wandsworth.[27]

After a detour to visit Wickham and Agnes in their decanal splendour at Lincoln, the Gladstones were back at Hawarden by the beginning of April. Having got his Horace translation off his hands and with eyesight tolerably restored, Gladstone settled down to completing his edition of the *Analogy*, with an appended volume of *Studies Subsidiary to the Works of Bishop Butler*, would be his intellectual valediction to a world that, in Gladstone's estimation, stood greatly in need of being reminded of Butler's supreme value and utility as a remedy for its spiritual distempers.

Acton had always been an irritation in this matter. Gladstone was unimpressed with Acton's opinion that Butler had been superseded by Kant. 'Kant is the macrocosm of Butler', insisted Acton. 'He is Butler writ very large.'[28] For his part, Gladstone never receded from his low opinion in general of the utility of German metaphysics to the spiritual needs of man.[29] It was precisely the Englishness of Butler, his stress on probability and the primacy of 'reason and the common sense which we rightly accept as our guide', as opposed to the absolutism of Germanic 'right reason'. Compared to Kant, Butler seemed to Gladstone a 'great moral discoverer'. 'I want to know', he demanded of Acton, 'when did Time produce a greater – perhaps not so great – a teacher on the laws of moral action as between God & Man?'[30]

~

The 1892 Parliament had come to its end. Gladstone played no part in the session other than to make Liberals nervous about his attitude to the Welsh Church Disestablishment Bill. This nervousness compromised Rosebery's government and contributed to its collapse in a footling division on 21 June. Ministers decided on resigning rather than dissolving. That would be the quickest way of extracting themselves from further embarrassment over the Welsh Bill. Rosebery resigned immediately. One signal thing from Gladstone's point of view he did: he appointed Acton to succeed Seeley in the Cambridge Regius Chair of Modern History.[31] Rosebery called on Gladstone on 24 June. He found Gladstone 'old and cold'. However, that evening they dined. Mary Drew described them as being 'merry as boys out of school'.[32]

Caught on the hop by Rosebery's rapidity, Salisbury scraped together a coalition government of Conservatives and Liberal Unionists. Devonshire was now Lord President. Chamberlain chose the Colonial Office. Already Gladstone was anticipating the dissolution by writing to his Midlothian chairman, bringing to 'final form the prospective farewell I addressed last year to the Midlothian constituency'.[33] For the first time since the general election of 1832, Gladstone was not a candidate. There was a general presumption that the Conservatives and Liberal Unionists would emerge with a majority. The best guess was that they would capture 30 or so Liberal seats, reversing in effect the Liberal-Irish majority of 1892. 'How foreign to all minds', as the *National Review* put it, 'was the notion of the utter smash-up of the Home Rule Party.'[34]

An utter smash-up indeed it turned out to be. The Liberal party lost a net 73 seats to Conservatives and a net 23 to Liberal Unionists. A mere 177 Liberals were returned to Westminster. The Conservative party, for the first time since 1874, now had an overall majority, slender but distinct. Astonished at the Liberal collapse, Gladstone could only console himself with the thought that 'should the Tories obtain a majority really heavy, how Chamberlain will shake in his shoes!'[35] This was wishful thinking on Gladstone's part. Chamberlain's partnership with Balfour would see Gladstone out.

Gladstone seems to have made at the time no recorded comment on these electoral phenomena finally expunging all the lessons of history and axioms of politics and the nation's habitual assent to Liberalism that had been at the foundations of his public career for nearly 40 years. Evidence that there had indeed been a novel and considerable change in the political temper of the British nation was now hardly disputable. Ever since Dalmeny in 1892 he had been making desultory notes under Acton's urging with a view to eventual autobiographical publication and the money to be made from it, as urged by Carnegie. Gladstone could hope that the debt encumbering the Hawarden estate might be extinguished. Once he had got the Butler edition and commentaries off his hands, he could get on with that enterprise.

Otherwise there was no lack of occupation. There was an address at Chester in aid of the Armenians. The Duke of Westminster was in the chair, and Gladstone was gratified that Eaton and Hawarden were back on terms. There were the St Deiniol Trust arrangements to complete. Harry Drew, after a spell in South Africa, returned to take up the management. Stephen, having declined ecclesiastical preferment from Rosebery, devoted his filial energies to the Grand Old Couple. On 21 November Gladstone made over to Harry and the financial Trustees of St Deiniol's all his bondholdings supplemented by other stocks together with the library and furniture. 'I am now nearly 40m poorer than this day week. All right: & may God prosper the work.'[36]

Various threads were snapped. Lord de Lisle and Dudley much regretted Gladstone's resignation as a Trustee of the National Portrait Gallery. He was helpful to R. Barry O'Brien with his biography of Parnell, setting Parnell next to O'Connell, and judging him a more masculine character than Grattan.[37] Rosebery called, 'finding his host very well, and ready to talk till midnight'.[38] Sir Walter and Lady Phillimore visited Hawarden in November 1895. 'The G.O.M. is just as energetic as ever ... He spoke for four hours one day much as usual.' They noted however that Catherine showed signs of failing; she did 'not seem to thirst after active life in the way she used'. Margot Asquith found the Gladstones 'demanding and crotchety' when they visited Glen. 'Everything had to be just as it was at home, and Margot was worn out protecting the servants.'[39]

It was in December of 1895 that the Armenian question began to impinge seriously. It was not a question, as in 1876, of confronting an errant government. Salisbury was entirely in accord with Gladstone. The problem was that of 1876 turned upside down. It was the European concert of France, Germany and Russia that sustained the Sultan. In such circumstances Britain could do little. Public opinion, however, was not content with helpless explanations. Gladstone was greatly in demand to put himself at the head of another moral crusade. Dr Clifford wanted him to say a few words at the City Temple. The Bishop of Hereford wanted him to say a few words at St James's Hall.

Having, with some reluctance, been pushed out of the life of contention, Gladstone was now reluctant to be pulled back into it. In any case, with winter setting in, swift retreat once more to Cannes was in order. Once enfolded in the warm luxury of Rendel's palazzetto, Gladstone looked forward to imminent publication of his Butler edition. Of intimate concerns he recorded himself 'out of the wild', his 'temptations' 'more inward', but as he hoped, 'losing somewhat of their force'.[40]

A copy of Purcell's *Manning* arrived, with the author's profuse thanks for Gladstone's 'invaluable aid'. Gladstone had complaint to make about the treatment of his stance in the Gorham affair, but in all other respects was perfectly satisfied with the damaging impact it made on the English Catholic hierarchy. 'The Purcell storm still rages in England', he observed gleefully at Cannes, 'and will rage. But his position is essentially strong and unassailable. The book is a real fact in Church History & in psychology.'[41]

Rather less gratifying were the questions raised in 'Bishop Butler's Apologist' in the January 1896 *Nineteenth Century* by Leslie Stephen as to the strength and unassailability of Bishop Butler's arguments and Gladstone's fervent endorsement of them. A scholar of eighteenth-century rationalism, Stephen represented a younger infidel Victorian generation sceptical of claims that Christian belief could be founded convincingly on grounds of reason. For Stephen, Butler was, like Gladstone, 'a man of powerful intellect working within the shackles of a preconceived system'. 'In spite of what I take to be his fallacies', Stephen allowed to Gladstone, 'I can understand why his argument should be treated with a respect more than proportioned to its logical merits, especially among gentlemen who have had the advantage of an Oxford education.' Famously an embodiment of the 'Cambridge ethos', Stephen addressed both Butler and Gladstone in his ultimate dismissal: 'your whole elaborate structure, with its perfectly good deity, who appears to act unjustly, and the omnipotent being who appears to be unable to make a satisfactory system, is so much waste of labour'.[42]

Hardened of old, Gladstone was immune to hostile reviews.[43] Besides, there were matters enough to occupy him at Cannes and later at Hawarden that season. Hirsch of *Le Figaro* wanted his comments on the sharp deterioration in Anglo-French relations following Edward Grey's sensational statement in the Commons on behalf of the Foreign Office that French penetration from central Africa into the Upper Nile would be regarded as an 'unfriendly act'. Gladstone reiterated the views he had held for over 40 years, redolent of the '*entente cordiale*' days of Grey and Aberdeen.[44] Back at Hawarden to enjoy the coming of spring, Gladstone rejoiced that his 'general health, the health of my trunk, is excellent'. The marriage of the Waleses' daughter Maud to Prince Charles of Denmark brought the Gladstone's briefly into the ambience of the Court. They were to be King and Queen of newly independent Norway in 1904. The Waleses were particularly attentive. Gladstone could not suppress a suspicion that 'they do so much towards us from a sense of the Queen's deficiencies'.[45]

A matter much exercising Gladstone in these days was the question of the Roman Church's view of the validity of Anglican Orders. Pope Leo XIII set up a commission in 1895 to examine the case. High Anglican ecumenical aspirations having thus been encouraged, Gladstone was foremost in hoping for a better frame of mind in the Vatican. He wrote to the Archbishop of York in May 1896 a letter which, with Gladstone's approval, the Archbishop made public. 'Your letter on Anglican Orders', Purcell assured him, 'goes to the root of the vital question – the necessity of closer relations, of cordial co-operation between the Mother Church and the Church of England in defence of Christianity against the common enemy.'[46]

Yet it was curiously appropriate that one of the foremost embodiments of the 'common enemy', Herbert Spencer, should at this moment appear as comrade-in-arms with Gladstone as exponent of High Victorian cultural and intellectual values. Divided deeply on every crucial issue of their times other than defence of the ideal of the minimal ant-imperial state, Spencer and Gladstone found themselves together by the 1890s survivors in terrain where the familiar contours and landmarks were shifting and dissolving. They were both under fire from exponents of a 'modern' sensibility that could find no solace in grand systems of human hope, whether of divine providence or social evolution. Spencer had received from Huxley, in the second Romanes Lecture in 1893, 'Evolution and Ethics', much the same kind of dismissal that Gladstone had just received from Stephen. Thus their exchange of books in 1896 was more than merely an occasion of polite literary amenity. It was almost a solemn joint profession of defiant faith in the validity of quintessential Victorian values. Spencer thanked Gladstone for his valedictory *Studies Subsidiary to the Works of Bishop Butler*; and arranged to send in return the forthcoming third volume of *The Principles of Sociology*, 'with the completion of which my life-long task will be ended'.[47]

~

Gladstone was now under pressure to make some signal public intervention in the Armenian case. He resisted on the grounds that 1876 could not be repeated. He was now a private individual without any authority due to special knowledge. There was the difficulty of discerning clearly the line of duty; but the mode of proceeding 'à la 1876' was 'beyond and distinct from this'. A step into the arena of contention could not be a single step. Contention at least had the merit of bringing Argyll back on terms. In a letter to the *Daily Chronicle* on 13 September Gladstone put it to the public that there was a conspiracy of the powers, led by Russia, at the expense of the Armenians. Gladstone much wanted Lord Salisbury to be encouraged to break through the diplomatic obstacles.[48] It was a curious reversion to his encouragement at the Eastern Question Conference in 1876 to Salisbury's mission to Constantinople.[49]

Eventually Gladstone was enticed as far as Hengler's Circus, Liverpool, the scene of his dramatic declaration in 1886 that he would, all the world over, back the masses against the classes. Now, in what was to prove his last grand public appearance, on 24 September, he denounced the 'moral infamy' of the Sultan and the Turks in an echo of the evangelical spirit and *Bulgarian Horrors* of 1876.

Rosebery eagerly seized on the occasion to resign the Liberal leadership on the grounds of his not being willing to play the Granville role to the rampant 'leader of the nation'. Rosebery's petulance flattered Gladstone more than a little. Gladstone decided, at Penmaenmawr, that there would be no harm in causing more turmoil with a letter to the Bishop of Rochester, to be read out at a big meeting at St James's Hall on 19 October. As one who 'cannot escape or disclaim the moral responsibility of one who, for a period of forty-five years from the year 1850, frequently had an active concern in the foreign affairs of this country', Gladstone again denounced the Sultan Abdul Hamid as the 'Great Assassin' and fomenter of systematic massacre. He called on the meeting to strengthen the hand of Lord Salisbury.[50]

But for Gladstone in any case attention to the Armenian case was diverted by the shock of Leo XIII's encyclical *Apostolicae curae*, issued on 13 September, which condemned Anglican Orders as invalid through defect both of form and intent. This insult set off an immense furore reminiscent of the 'Papal Aggression' of 1850, and triggered a 'Protestant' anti-ritualist and anti-popery frenzy that lasted beyond the end of the century. Gladstone shared fully the sense of smarting disappointment among High Churchmen at what they felt to be a failure of ecumenical spirit at the Vatican and a retrogression to the narrowest sacerdotalism of the time of Pius IX.

Lady Sybil Grosvenor, President of the League of Mercy, was present at Hawarden on 10 October when the Archbishop of Canterbury and Mrs Benson arrived for tea on their way back from an Irish tour. She observed Gladstone plunge straight away into the Pope's 'Bull'. 'I had never heard him so excited; what with Armenia, Lord Rosebery and most of all the Pope, all in one moment, the Archbishop sat with his teacup in his hand, I suppose for three-quarters of an hour, waiting to drink.' Gladstone felt he had been deceived. 'He was very hot on it', as Mrs Benson noted, 'and talked most delightfully.'[51]

The following morning, at service in Hawarden parish church, the Archbishop slumped dead. His body was carried down to the Rectory. Later, his coffin in the church was draped in a 'magnificent white embroidered pall', which would be used for the same purpose at the lying-in-state and funeral of Gladstone himself. The shock left Gladstone white-faced as the funeral train pulled out of Sandycroft station.

The complex matter of drawing up a new will was not finally completed until the Gladstones had returned to their 'old haunt' at Penmaenmawr to 'fortify ourselves against the coming winter'.[52] It was between returning to Hawarden late in November and departing for Cannes in January 1897 that Gladstone drew up the statement later known as his 'Declaration', signed and dated 7 December. 'With reference to rumours which I believe were at one time afloat, though I know not with what degree of currency: and also with reference to the times when I shall not be here to answer for myself, I desire to record my solemn declaration and assurance, as in the sight of God and before His Judgment Seat, that at no period of my life have I been guilty of the act which is known as that of infidelity to the marriage bed. I limit myself to this negation, and I record it with my dear son Stephen, both as the eldest surviving of our sons, and as my pastor. It will be for him to retain or use it, confidentially unless necessity should require more, which is unlikely: and in any case making it known to his brothers.'[53]

Gladstone placed this in an envelope which he sealed and addressed to Stephen, adding his initials and the instruction '*Only to be opened after my death.*' Gladstone was never an approver of auricular confession.

~

'My long and tangled life', Gladstone recorded on 29 December, 'this day concludes its 87th year.' He was making progress with 'Olympian Religion' and on a new series of 'Gleanings', or reprinted pieces, to match the set he had published in 1879. He had got St Deiniol's 'very near its launch'. He would not enter upon 'interior matters. It is easy to write, but to write honestly nearly impossible.' 'Adieu old year. Lord have mercy.'

This was Gladstone's last diary entry.

Perhaps one of the most significant features of it was that Gladstone made no mention of work on his autobiography. 'The influence of your name, your ideas, your career', Acton had assured Gladstone, 'will be the greatest force sustaining and guiding the Liberal party in the next generation.' At intervals between 1892 and 1897 Gladstone wrote a considerable amount of material, but it remained fragmentary and disjointed. Acton's hopes for revelations of 'secret history', 'secret biography of eminent men' locked in Gladstone's *intimo pectoris*, went sadly unrealized. Likewise, his editors lament that his grandest transactions, such as his launching his epochal Home Rule policy for Ireland, are untreated.[54] His only reference to it in these last years was his defiant listing of 'The proposal of Home Rule for Ireland' in his 'General Retrospect' of 1896 or 1897, in which he claimed for it an origin in a providentially assigned 'insight' that linked it in a grand series passing from the renewal of the income tax in 1853 to the 'proposal of religious equality for Ireland' in 1868 through ultimately to his proposal to dissolve in 1894 and challenge the House of Lords. Gladstone added that he intended 'to consider these four junctures severally'; but he got no further than that statement of intent.[55]

Dealing with the great '*knot*' of his career would indeed have been a fraught enterprise. Perhaps what applied to 'interior matters' applied also here: 'It is easy to write, but to write honestly nearly impossible.' Within the frame of his conviction about the governance of the most High and his assurance that all was truly given over to the divine will, how to account for what went wrong in 1885, went catastrophically wrong in 1886, and then was not repaired between 1886 and 1893? Was it all simply a matter of incorrigible self-delusion?

Beyond that lay a further knot of considerations about the possible alternative approaches to the question of Irish autonomy that might have offered plausible prospects of resolving it, within, say, the kind of timetable suggested by Timothy Healy.[56] These stretched from Rathbone's ideas in the early 1880s about linking Irish autonomy to a general policy of local government reform 'which would satisfy all that is reasonable in the Home Rule demand',[57] through to Chamberlain's Central Board scheme in 1885, then on to Whitbread's advice for less haste and Stansfeld's notions in 1886 of logical federation, and then to the pleadings of Pease for withdrawing the Home Rule Bill and replacing it with a measure that 'would satisfy the reasonable wants of Ireland and have the support of the *entire Liberal* Party';[58] and then the pleadings of Brassey that a thing might be done by Gladstone that would be impossible for any other statesman – abandoning the Home Rule Bill in favour of an Irish Local Government measure acceptable to the party.[59] And beyond all that, again, were considerations about the beneficial expediency of Gladstone's sticking to his 1877 Dublin text about tenant land purchase policy, perhaps linked to Caird's recommendations about expanding the 'Bright' clauses of the 1881 Land Act and adapting Lord Ashbourne's 1885 Act[60] rather than launching out on the heroically misconceived 1881 Land Act.

The crucial counterfactual questions that suggest themselves in relation to all these considerations are in essence simple. The question whether early work on land and local government by Gladstone from 1880 would have pre-empted a Parnellite sweep in 1885 has already been asked.[61] Beyond that, would the Irish National Party, equipped with something along these alternative lines both as to autonomy and land, have been able to avoid the obliteration later visited upon it by Sinn Fein? This approach to counterfactual questioning exerts much more explanatory power than the conventional line of lamenting 'what fools we were, not to have accepted Gladstone's Home Rule Bill.'[62] Not accepting Gladstone's far-reaching proposals in 1886 or 1893 was far from being foolish, since his schemes involved fundamental instabilities of either invidious Irish representative deprivation or unacceptable Irish legislative privilege, and depended ultimately on a suspension of disbelief as to an imperial authority that for all practical purposes was more a fiction than a reality. Kruger, it should be remembered, got 'home rule' for Transvaal in 1884. The British government thought it retained something called 'imperial supremacy'. It took a serious war to try to sort that out.

The likeliest explanation for Gladstone's silence about the great knot remains simply his reluctance to scrutinize so painfully intractable an enigma. Nothing in his autobiographical writings confronts the issue of inspiration. The tendency of his mind seems rather to have moved in the direction of disclaiming personal responsibility. 'The Almighty and not any counsel of mine brought it about: surely He will provide for it.' One of his most characteristic fragments dates from 1894: 'There is a Providence that shapes our ends/ Rough-hew them how we may. I think that no one can be more deeply penetrated with these words than I am or ought to be. The whole of my public and exoteric life has been shaped as to its ends for me, scarcely rough-hewn by me.'[63]

~

The new year of 1897 opened with touching evidence that Gladstone's name and reputation counted still with a young Liberal generation. F. W. Hirst, writing on behalf of five other young Oxford graduates who were projecting a volume of essays on themes of individual freedom versus collectivism, Home Rule for Ireland and a more democratic conception of foreign policy, requested a few words of preface.[64] The Gladstones left for Cannes at the end of January, heading once more for the palazzetto of Lord Rendel. He was glad to be of service to Bodley's Librarian in the matter of pressing for money from Carnegie.[65] He was glad also to be of service to the Greeks in their war with the Turks. 'God help your efforts', he telegraphed in an old and broken hand, 'to stop all coercion against Greece and so avert disgrace from England.'[66]

It was the Greek question that as it happened made a firm connection between Gladstone and the Queen's daughter, Princess Louise, Marchioness of Lorne. Gladstone told the Princess that he scrupled to discuss the Greek and Cretan subject 'because my opinions were so violent'. It soon became clear that her own opinions were no less so. The Queen and her party were wintering at Cimiez outside Nice; and there were what Gladstone called 'a batch of Hanoverian Royalties' at the Hotel du Parc in the English quarter of Cannes. The Princess was instrumental, after complicated negotiations in which Gladstone was concerned to do 'nothing which could possibly wear the appearance of an endeavour to lay myself in the Queen's way or to force myself upon her', in arranging that the Queen and the Gladstones should appear for tea at the Hotel du Parc.

'We were shown into a room tolerably but not brilliantly lighted, much of which was populated by a copious supply of Hanoverian Royalties including the Queen of Hanover, the Duke of Cumberland, and others. *The* Queen was in the inner part of the room, and behind her stood or sat the Prince of Wales with the Duke of Cambridge.' Gladstone found the Queen's manner entirely lacking in her old and usual vitality. Ten minutes' entirely desultory conversation convinced him that she had become more feeble and constitutionally 'now more nearly a cypher'. He found the Prince of Wales 'had become a more substantial personage, so to speak, in her presence'. He predicted, in fact, that he was witnessing 'forethought and preparation for an abdication', and for 'the beginning of the reign of Edward VII'.[67]

For much of the rest of 1897 Gladstone's 'ordinary life from day to day, though of diminished power', suffered no interruption. There were now fewer incursions from the great world. A visit in May from the Prince and Princess of Wales, up at Eaton for the Chester Races, escorted by the Duke and Duchess of Westminster, was for Gladstone a doubly gratifying occasion. H. W. Massingham of the *Daily Chronicle* wanted Gladstone's opinion of the Canadian proposal of imperial preference at Chamberlain's Colonial Conference.[68] Indeed, Gladstone received the Colonial premiers, escorted by the Prince of Wales, at Hawarden in July.[69]

In August, Arthur Benson, then a housemaster at Eton and writing the biography of his late father the Archbishop, dined at Hawarden with a family party. As he came in, he saw Gladstone and Catherine 'sitting on a sofa, side by side, hand in hand, like two lovers'. There was a 'slight jostling for places at the dinner table', with Gladstone insisting that Benson be at his right hand – '"My left ear is useless", he said, touching it.' Gladstone talked much of Eton and Hallam. '"The story of M. Gaskell's friendship with Hallam was curious; you know" – with a smile – "people fell in love very easily in those days".' Perhaps Benson took the point of this rather coy displacement allusion; in any case he made no comment. 'He was most animated and talked the *whole* of dinner. They told me it needed a *visitor* and a *topic*.'[70]

~

It was early in September of 1897 that the pangs of the cancer that was to kill Gladstone came upon him.

It was a matter at first of a numbness in the cheek on the left side of his face, thought to be an attack of catarrh, leading to neuralgic pains in the nose and cheekbone. By 17 September laudanum was being freely administered. At Butterstone, in Perthshire, under Armitstead's care once more, Gladstone complained of excruciating pains in his eye, but seemed otherwise hale and loquacious. George Curzon, then Salisbury's Under-secretary at the Foreign Office, fishing on the Tay, drove over to visit. He found Gladstone 'immensely old and a good deal bent', with both hearing and eyesight failing him. 'He talked, however, with perfectly clear and resonant voice', descanting on a wide variety of subjects. 'He wished me all success in fishing; but betrayed not the faintest interest in my public life or career.'[71]

By November it seemed that Gladstone's symptoms were abating, and the balms of the Riviera climate would once more be resorted to. On their way south the Gladstones stopped over at Bishop Talbot of Rochester's house at Kennington. Eddie Hamilton and Arnold Morley went down to wish them well. 'His voice was strong, and he was quite ready to talk. What is now uppermost in his mind is what he calls the spirit of Jingoism under the name of Imperialism which is now so prevalent.' 'It was enough', Gladstone declared, 'to make Peel and Cobden turn in their graves.'[72]

The Gladstones stayed at Rendel's Chateau Thorenc from the end of November 1897 to 16 February 1898. Gladstone's condition worsened steadily. Paroxysms of agony – 'the roaring pains', as Gladstone called them – attacked frequently and ever more severely. He and Catherine drove out occasionally when the weather was fine. But the decline was remorseless. Rendel's daughter Daphne recalled how 'music was almost his only pleasure & how dreadful it was, poor old Mrs Gladstone being at times almost off her head, indeed had it not been for Miss Phillimore, who looked after her almost entirely, I really don't know what they would have done'.[73] Something of Gladstone's old pertinacity yet survived. He was not ready to let the Tennysons' low view of Arthur Hallam's poetical talents go unchallenged. In a long article in the *Daily Telegraph* of 5 January 1898 he offered on behalf of Hallam one last public exercise in making distinctions.

Even the fondest old memories, if perhaps a solace, could not heal. It was decided to return to England. Hawarden was ruled out as unsuitable in winter conditions. Bournemouth was fixed upon: a kind of reversion to that nomadic life in southern resorts that Gladstone's father had imposed upon his family when Gladstone was at Eton and Oxford. It was at Bournemouth that cancer of the palate was diagnosed: inoperable and mortal. A public announcement was made and Gladstone determined to return to Hawarden to die. The sentence of death was for him a promise of blessed release.

On 22 March he left Bournemouth, speaking a few words to the crowd at the station: his last public utterance. At Hawarden the blessed release was agonizingly long in coming. His body, the 'health of his trunk', remained too strong to allow a quick and merciful death. He chanted his favourite biblical passages and hymns, especially Newman's 'Praise to the Holiest in the height'. To the condolences of the University of Oxford he replied: 'There is no expression of Christian sympathy that I value more than that of the ancient University of Oxford, the God-fearing and God-sustaining University of Oxford. I served her perhaps mistakenly, but to the best of my ability. My earnest prayers are hers to the uttermost and to the last.' After 9 April he was no longer able to walk outside the Castle. After 18 April he was no longer able to come downstairs. For much of the time he was in drugged semi-consciousness, or unconsciousness. Rosebery and John Morley called to pay their respects.

The end came early on Ascension Day, Thursday, 19 May. He was perfectly calm, having ceased to feel pain for the while. He had made his farewells. Shortly before five o'clock that morning, Stephen read to him his favourite hymns and offered a prayer; all the family kneeling round the bed. At the end of the prayer Gladstone was, so the official family version had it, heard to 'murmur a distinct "Amen!"' At ten minutes to five his breathing ceased.[74]

~

Gladstone's remains were laid out in his Oxford doctoral robes in the 'Temple of Peace'. He had not ruled out a public funeral, providing Catherine could eventually be interred beside him. The case of Beaconsfield, a widower, was not analogous. In the Commons, Balfour moved an adjournment and gave notice of an Address to the Queen praying for a public funeral in Westminster Abbey. 'We felt it very much', recorded Lady Monkswell, 'for he has been in the background to our entire lives. There is no loss we shall ever feel so much as this, except when the good old Queen goes. When I read of his peaceful blessed death I could not help shedding tears. How glad I feel that I have talked to him & often shaken hands with him.'[75] This testimony spoke eloquently. Lady Monkswell, unlike her husband, was hostile to Home Rule. Her feelings, quite transcending the old bitterness of party, were very representative of the general public response to the passing of someone iconic for the century. Tributes in both Houses of Parliament reflected this sense of a dispensation from anything like conventional sentiments.

Herbert Gladstone, speaking for the family, gratefully accepted Parliament's offer to pay honour to its grandest figure. Harry Gladstone negotiated with the Dean of Westminster. It was the 'good old Queen', the only person who shared with Gladstone that iconic status, and who could thus choose honestly not to share the common sentiments attached to it, who was inclined to be captious. She could not agree with her daughter the Empress Frederick that Gladstone was 'a great Englishman'. She allowed that he was a 'clever man, full of talent', and a 'good and very religious man'.[76] She took the Prince of Wales to task, along with his son the Duke of York, for agreeing, without precedent, to serve as pall-bearers at the Abbey. The Prince answered that the circumstances were unprecedented.[77] Although the Queen's respect for truth was too intense to allow her to make a hypocritical announcement in the *Court Circular*, she sent a gracious telegram to Catherine.

After a communion service in Hawarden church in the presence of Gladstone's coffin, his remains passed from Broughton Hall station, pulled by the locomotive 'Gladstone', to Willesden, where they were transferred on the London Underground to Westminster station, and thence to Westminster Hall. Although it was a state funeral, there was no long procession in state. The family wanted something prompt and on a simple scale. Gladstone's remains lay in state for an unprecedented two days, 26–27 May, while more than a quarter of a million mourners filed through Westminster Hall.

The funeral at the Abbey on 28 May was 'a most wonderful sight'. 'It was more than wonderful', thought Mary Monkswell, 'it was quite unique. Never again ... will such violent, new, painful & extraordinary emotions go thro' and thro' me, giving me strength to go through it at the time, & letting me down to a pretty low place when it was all over.' A figure in deepest mourning came slowly up the aisle. 'A sort of murmur ran through the crowd, & then it dawned on me that here was poor dear old Mrs Gladstone. I think she was leaning on Mr Drew's arm as close behind her came Mrs Drew & the charming little Dorothy.' 'To see that erect pathetic figure with her expression half dreaming & half wild but triumphant, & to remember her immense age, 86, & what she had gone through & what she had lost – & then close behind her the charming jolly child (aged about 8) whose mourning could not look anything but smart & pretty, with her beautiful curly hair hanging round her, & positively *tripping* down the aisle.'

The ten pall-bearers were the Prince of Wales and the Duke of York, Rosebery, Harcourt (then leader of the Liberal party), Salisbury, Balfour, Kimberley, Rutland (the former Lord John Manners, standing in for Argyll, who could not be present), and Gladstone's steadfast 'old shoes', Rendel and Armitstead. The music Mary Monkswell thought most beautiful, 'a multitude of voices singing very softly' 'Rock of Ages', the old edition with four verses. 'When the coffin was removed from under the Lantern to where it will be throughout the ages in the N. transept we could only catch the sound of the last two prayers. While the coffin was put into the grave we sang the hymn from Cardinal Newman's "Dream of Gerontius" – "Praise to the Holiest in the height" a hymn which is quite beyond me but which I will love for his sake.' The service finished with Stainer's 'fourfold Amen, & the hymn "*O God our help in Ages Past*", Ps XC in which we joined like the voice of many waters. We all stood reverently while the "*Dead March*" was played, & then it was all over.'[78]

At the close of the service, Catherine rested for a few minutes in a chair provided, having hitherto preferred to stand or kneel. She expressed a wish to Harry that she might shake hands with the pall-bearers. 'The most striking and touching of all the features of the ceremony', thought Hamilton, 'was the presence of Mrs G. I am truly glad she lived to see the day. It was far more striking than all the tributes of love [and] veneration paid to Mr G. when alive; and it is doubtful whether any public man ever had so great a tribute paid to his memory.'[79]

Notes

Notes to Introduction

1 R. T. Shannon, 'Matthew's Gladstone', *Parliamentary History*, 15/2, 1996, 249.

2 R. H. Jenkins, *Gladstone* (1995).

3 R. T. Shannon, 'Peel, Gladstone and Party', *Parliamentary History*, 18/3, 1999.

4 See p. 278.

5 See pp. 425, 454, 519 n. 109.

6 See J. Powell, *Art, Truth and High Politic: A Bibliographic Study of the Official Lives of Queen Victoria's Ministers in Cabinet, 1843–1969* (1996); M. R. D. Foot, 'Morley's Gladstone: A Reappraisal', *Bulletin of the John Rylands Library*, 1969; D. M. Schreuder, 'Morley and Knaplund as "Monumental Masons"' in B. Kinzer (ed.), *The Gladstonian Turn of Mind* (1985). There is shrewd comment on Morley and Gladstone also in G. M. Young, 'Mr Gladstone' in *Victorian Essays* (1962). See also D. A. Hamer, *John Morley: Liberal Intellectual in Politics* (1968).

7 D. C. Lathbury attended to that side: *Correspondence on Church and Religion of William Ewart Gladstone*, 2 vols. (1910).

8 See p. 126.

9 Morley, I, 631; see also p. 127.

10 See p. 126.

11 Jenkins, *op. cit.*, 144; see also p. 127.

12 See p. 105.

13 See p. 183.

14 Morley, I, 269.

15 See pp. 87–8.

16 Morley, II, 241–2.

17 See pp. 306–7.

18 See p. 312.

19 Morley, III, 1, 2.

20 See pp. 22–3.

21 See p. 425.

22 Morley, III, 3.

23 See pp. 390–3.

24 See pp. 297, 308.

25 See p. 102.

26 See p. 360.
27 See p. 323.
28 See p. 519 n. 109.
29 H. C. G. Matthew, *Gladstone, 1875–1898* (1995), 332.
30 Ib., 50, 92.
31 Ib., 53.
32 Ib., 234.
33 Ib., 238.
34 Ib., 339.
35 Ib., 33–4.
36 Ib., 81.
37 Ib., 255.
38 Ib., 224–5.
39 Ib., 326.
40 Jenkins, *op. cit.*, 241.
41 See p. 218.
42 Jenkins, *op. cit.*, 486.
43 Matthew, *op. cit.*, 310.
44 Ib., 390.
45 See p. 420. In fact none of the Parliaments of 1885, 1892 and 1910 gave Liberal governments promoting Home Rule a majority clear of the Irish.
46 Matthew, 387.

Notes to Chapter 1: Early Years, 1809–1831

1 See pp. 194–5, 397, 441, 472.
2 Morley, I, 192.
3 £2,791,000 in 2002 values on retail price index basis.
4 See p. 285.
5 GP, 44790, 23.
6 Morley, I, 34.
7 GP, 44790, 18.
8 Ib., 1.
9 GP, 44790, 24.
10 GP, 44790, 84.
11 GP, 44790, 84.
12 D, 29 December 1832.
13 D, 29 December, 18–19.
14 GP, 44352, 130.
15 D, 26 June 1831.
16 D, 24 March 1830.
17 D, 26 June 1831.
18 On this theme generally, see A. Isba, *Gladstone and Women* (2006).

19 GP, 44981, 2. D. C. Lathbury, *Correspondence on Church and Religion of W. E. Gladstone* (1910), I, x.
20 D, 12 January 1831.
21 PMP, I, 145, 148.
22 D, 29 December 1830.
23 D, 8 October 1831.

Notes to Chapter 2: Church and State, 1832–1841

1 PMP, I, 220–9.
2 D, 5 February 1832.
3 GP, 44790, 17.
4 D, 22 April 1832.
5 GP, 44791, 1.
6 GP, 44722, 4.
7 D, 31 July–4 August 1832.
8 H, xviii, 330–7. T. Pinney (ed.), *The Letters of Thomas Babington Macaulay* (1974), II, 25.
9 P. Butler, *Gladstone: Church, State and Tractarianism, 1809–1859* (1982), 42
10 G to Manning, 5 April 1835. GP, 44247, 3.
11 GP, 44247, 13.
12 GP, 44726, 21.
13 O. Chadwick, 'Young Gladstone and Italy', *Journal of Ecclesiastical History*, 1979, 250. G, *The State in its Relations with the Church* (fourth ed., 1841), I, 190. John Locke (1632–1704), empiricist philosopher; William Paley (1743–1805), theological exponent of intelligent design in nature as evidence of deity; Francis Bacon (1561–1626), Lord Chancellor and scientific pioneer.
14 Samuel Taylor Coleridge (1772–1834), poet and philosopher.
15 G, *State*, 115, 149, 167.
16 D, 14 April 1834.
17 G to Manning, 18 February 1838. GP, 44247, 38.
18 GP, 44723, 207.
19 D, 8 January 1838. D, 9 May 1854.
20 D, 21 March 1841. See B. Hilton, 'Gladstone's Theological Politics', M. Bentley and J. Stevens (eds), *High and Low Politics in Modern Britain* (1983), 46.
21 Ib., 22.
22 D, 23 July 1838.
23 GP, 44247, 13.
24 R. Blake, *Disraeli* (1966), 123.
25 R. B. Martin, *Tennyson* (1980), 232. Hallam was engaged to Alfred's sister Emily.
26 H, XLIV, 817.
27 Information from M. R. D. Foot.
28 H. Maxwell, *Clarendon* (1913), II, 224.
29 D, 11 November 1838.

30 S. Birkenhead, *Illustrious Friends* (1965), 108–9.
31 See R. Shannon, 'Gladstone, the Roman Church, and Italy', in M. Bentley (ed.), *Public and Private Doctrine* (1993).
32 Pinney, *Macaulay*, III, 276.
33 *Notes and Queries*, 7 series (1888), VI, 'Does Mr Gladstone Speak with a Provincial Accent?', 124–5, 153, 178, 210. H. M. and M. Swartz (eds), *Disraeli's Reminiscences* (1975), 93.
34 F. E. Hamer (ed.), *The Personal Papers of Lord Rendel* (1931), 134.
35 GP, 44729, 107.
36 G. I. T. Machin, *Politics and the Churches in Great Britain, 1832–1868* (1977), 84–6; Butler, 87–9; D. C. Lathbury, *Correspondence on Church and Religion of W. E. Gladstone* (1910), I, 17–18, 46.
37 D, 23 July 1838.
38 GP, 44247, 13.
39 H, XXXVII, 95–6.
40 T. W. Reid, *Life of Lord Houghton* (1890), I, 316.
41 F. E. Mineka & D. N. Lindley, *The Earlier Letters of John Stuart Mill (1812–1848)* (1963), II, 416.
42 PMP, II, 137.
43 GP, 44819, 50.

Notes to Chapter 3: Politician and Churchman, 1841–1846

1 Peel Papers, BL, Add. Mss. 40489, 393–4.
2 *Morning Advertiser*, 16 September 1841.
3 D, 9 May 1841.
4 D. C. Lathbury, *Correspondence on Church and Religion of W. E. Gladstone* (1910), I, 60.
5 G to Manning, 14 August 1843. GP, 44247, 166.
6 D, 27 March 1842.
7 Ib.
8 Sir Thomas Dyke Acland (1787–1871), 10th Baronet; Sir Thomas Dyke Acland (1809–1898), 11th Baronet. All Saints was a proprietary chapel within the parish of St Marylebone. When the new church designed by Butterfield was consecrated by Bishop Tait in 1859, the parish of All Saints was established. The incumbent from 1839 to 1845 was Frederick Oakeley. See P. Galloway, *A Passionate Humility: Frederick Oakeley and the Oxford Movement* (1999).
9 Lathbury, I, 259; A. Godley (ed.), *Reminiscences of Lord Kilbracken* (1931), 123.
10 PMP, I, 74.
11 G to Peel, 16 November 1841. GP, 44527, 50.
12 GP, 44819, 77–9.
13 Lathbury, *op. cit.*, II, 25.
14 F. W. Hirst, *Galdstone as Financier and Economist* (1931), 42–3.
15 D, 15 March 1842.
16 N. Gash, *Sir Robert Peel* (1972), 476; R. T. Shannon, 'Peel, Gladstone and Party', *Parliamentary History*, 18/3, 1999, 318.

17 GP, 44819, 96.
18 H, LXIX, 1476–1479.
19 D, 8 December 1842; Gash, *op. cit.*, 429–30.
20 G to Peel, 26 July 1844. GP, 44527, 185.
21 Gash, 421.
22 GP, 44777, 119–23. See D. Kerr, *Peel, Priests and Politic: Sir Robert Peel's Administration and the Roman Catholic Church in Ireland, 1841–1846* (1982).
23 PMP, II, 237.
24 Ib., 238–41.
25 G to Hope, 20 August 1844. GP, 44214, 256; GP, 44777, 186.
26 R. Stewart, 'The Ten Hours and Sugar Crises and the House of Commons in the Age of Reform', *Historical Journal*, 1969, 46.
27 G to Hope, 20 August 1844. GP, 44214, 256.
28 PMP, II, 268.
29 Ib., 127–8.
30 D, 8 July 1844.
31 G. Battiscombe, *Mrs Gladstone* (1956), 43.
32 [George, 4th Lord Lyttelton], *Contributions Towards a Glossary of the Glynne Language* (1851).
33 G to CG, 13 January 1844. GGP, 28/2.
34 Ib., 31 October and 2 November 1844. Ib.
35 For G's utmost tribute to the Free Kirk, see R. T. Shannon, 'Gladstone, the Roman Church and Italy', in M. Bentley (ed.), *Public and Private Doctrine* (1993), 123. S. J. Brown, 'Gladstone, Chalmers and the Disruption of the Church of Scotland', *Gladstone Centenary Essays*, eds. D. Bebbington & R. Swift (2000).
36 See p. 66.
37 G to Manning, 24 October 1843. GP, 44274, 177; 30 October, 179.
38 PMP, II, 268.
39 Gash, 457.
40 G to Newcastle, 30 January 1845. GP, 44528, 7–8.
41 Lord Broughton, *Recollections of a Long Life*, VI (1911), 135, 136, 140.
42 D, III, xxxii.
43 G to Manning, 8 March 1846. GP, 44247, 289.
44 Gash, 673.
45 G to Manners, 30 January 1845. GP, 44528, 8–9.
46 PMP, I, 128.
47 G to CG, 24 November 1844. GGP, 28/2.
48 R. Ormsby, *Memoirs of James Robert Hope-Scott* (1884), II, 62.
49 GP, 44731, 66–120 (undated, and catalogued as of 1842; but almost certainly the fruit of G's delving into Butler in the summer of 1845). Joseph Butler (1692–1752), Bishop of Bristol, Dean of St Paul's, Bishop of Durham.
50 Morley, I, 874.
51 Döllinger, John Joseph Ignatius von (1799–1890). Professor at Munich, 1826–1873. Excommunicated 1871.

52 PMP, III, 11–13.
53 Ib., 14–19.
54 Ib.
55 G to CG, 20 December 1845. GGP, 28/2.
56 D, 22 December 1845; P. Butler, *Church, State and Tractarianism, 1809–1859* (1982), 117, 131–2.
57 G to J. Stephen, 8 April 1846. GP, 44528, 35.
58 H, CIV, 354–5.
59 P. Knaplund, 'Extracts from Gladstone's Private Diary Touching Canadian Questions in 1840', *Canadian Historical Review*, 1939, 195–6.
60 H, CIII, 422–3. It is fair to add that G substantially modified his views as to maintaining the 'connection between British colonies and British crime'. He hoped for relief (temporarily) of the burden on Australia by spreading transportation to Nova Scotia, New Brunswick, Gibraltar, Bermuda, the Ionian Islands and the Cape. See GP, 44735, 191–4, 264–79.
61 K. Fitzpatrick, 'Mr Gladstone and the Governor', *Historical Studies, Australia and New Zealand*, 1940, 31–45.
62 G to Harris, 15 June 1846. GP, 44528, 61.
63 G to Harris, 7 July 1846. GP, 44528, 73.

Notes to Chapter 4: A New Vocation, 1846–1852

1 PMP, III, 19.
2 G, *A Chapter of Autobiography* (1868), 36.
3 P. Butler, *Church, State and Tractarianism* (1982), 207.
4 G. Finlayson, *Shaftesbury* (1981), 261. Ashley succeeded as 7th Earl of Shaftesbury in 1851.
5 D, 5 January 1853, 9 May 1854. J. B. Conacher, 'Mr Gladstone Seeks a Seat', *Canadian Historical Association Annual Report* (1962).
6 PMP, III, 32–4.
7 Ib., 34–5.
8 H, XCV, 1282–87. The Jewish Disabilities Bill, consequent on Lionel de Rothschild's election for the City of London in 1847, was passed by the Commons but rejected by the Lords. Two further measures in 1849 and 1851 suffered the same fate. The point was not gained until 1858. When G took his honorary degree at the Sheldonian in 1848, he was greeted with cries of 'Jew Bill'.
9 H, XCIX, 256.
10 D, 6 December 1848.
11 G, *Gentleman's Magazine*, July 1856, 41–55.
12 H, XCVII, 458–9.
13 D, 3, 21 May 1845.
14 G to CG, 12 October 1845. GGP, 28/2. Bassett, 63–5.
15 D. C. Lathbury, *Correspondence on Church and Religion of W. E. Gladstone* (1910), II, 274.

16 G, *Studies Subsidiary to the Works of Bishop Butler* (1896), 2, 8–9, 15, 16, 46, 76, 84, 86–7, 104. 335.
17 D, 22 November 1850.
18 G, 'The Courses of Religious Thought' (1876), *Gleanings*, III, 101.
19 GGP, Secret Account Book, 3–5; S. G. Checkland, *The Gladstones, 1764–1851* (1971), 368, 375, 416.
20 A converted workhouse in Rose St (since 1895 Manette St, evoking Dickens' character in *A Tale of Two Cities*). See p. 146.
21 PMP, III, 35–6.
22 Ib., 38–9, 46–7.
23 D, 21 March, 4 May 1850.
24 D, 28 July 1850.
25 D, 11 June 1848.
26 J. Marlow, *Mr and Mrs Gladstone* (1977), 51–2.
27 D, 22 April 1849.
28 H, CXII, 547–90, 649–52.
29 D, 18 November 1850.
30 Butler *op. cit.*, 162.
31 GP, 44738, 214–15.
32 DDCP, 45–8.
33 PMP, III, 71–3. In 1851 Stanley succeeded as 14th Earl of Derby. Died 1869.
34 D, 7 April 1851.
35 R. Ornsby, *Memoirs of James Robert Hope-Scott* (1884), II, 88–9.
36 G to Hope-Scott, 1 November 1868. GP, 44214, 396. Hope became Hope-Scott in 1853 on marriage to J. G. Lockhart's daughter and possession of Abbotsford.
37 D, 31 March 1851.
38 D, 9 July 1851.
39 D, 15 July 1851.
40 D, 7, 22 May 1852.
41 D, 19 August 1851.
42 E. Jones Parry (ed.), *The Correspondence of Lord Aberdeen and Princess Lieven, 1832–1854*, II (1939), 598.
43 Ib.
44 G quoted it as a proverbial Italian phrase.
45 GP, 44738, 227.
46 See on this theme H.C. G. Matthew, 'Disraeli, Gladstone, and the Politics of Mid-Victorian Budgets', *Historical Journal*, 1979.
47 H, CXVI, 58–65.
48 D, III, xxxix.
49 N. Gash, *Sir Robert Peel* (1972), 673.
50 See p. 105.
51 See pp. 87–8.
52 Lord Broughton, *Recollections of a Long Life* (1911), VI, 292–3; J. Prest, *Lord John Russell* (1972), 338.

53 Morley, I, 416–17.
54 PMP, III, 103.
55 Ib., 104–11.

Notes to Chapter 5: Peace and War, 1852–1855

1 D, 27 March 1852.
2 D, 12 February 1852. GGP, 94/11. Rough Book A (Accounts), 171.
3 D, 1 March 1852.
4 R. Blake, *Disraeli* (1966), 328.
5 H, CXXIII, 97.
6 Ib.
7 J. B. Conacher, *The Aberdeen Coalition, 1852–1855* (1968), 48.
8 PMP, III, 129–30.
9 GP, 44745, 173–222.
10 Ib., 181, 184, 190, 192, 195.
11 G. O. Trevelyan, *Life and Letters of Lord Macaulay* (1876), ii, 330.
12 W. F. Monypenny & G. E. Buckle, *Life of Benjamin Disraeli, Earl of Beaconsfield* (2 vol. ed., 1929), I, 1262.
13 Morley, I, 438. H, CXXIII, 1665–6.
14 H, CXXIII, 1666.
15 DDCP, 89–90.
16 Morley, I, 438.
17 G to Hope, 18 Oct. 1859. GP, 44530, 96.
18 F. W. Hirst, *Mr Gladstone as Financier and Economist* (1931), 130.
19 DDCP, 90.
20 Conacher, 47–8.
21 DDCP, 92; *Times*, 23 December 1852, 5.
22 D, 16 January 1846.
23 Hirst, 301.
24 D, 29 Dec. 1853.
25 A. West, *Recollections 1832–1886* (1899), I, 346; Hamilton, *op. cit.*, I, li.
26 H, CXXV, 634–5.
27 R. J. Moore, 'The Abolition of Patronage in the Indian Civil Service', *Historical Journal*, 1964.
28 H. C. G. Matthew, 'Mid-Victorian Budgets', *Historical Journal*, 1979, 630.
29 DDCP, 106.
30 Morley, I, 469.
31 H, CXXV, 1350–1422.
32 GP, 44791, 51. The three others were the granting of 'religious equality' to Ireland in 1868, the offer of Home Rule to Ireland in 1886, and his proposal of dissolution and election in 1894 over the obstructions of the House of Lords.
33 L. Strachey & R. Fulford (eds), *The Greville Memoirs, 1814–1860* (1938), VI, 419.

34 Ib., 422.
35 A. L. Kennedy (ed.), *My Dear Duchess* (1956), 90.
36 D, 10 May 1853.
37 Conacher, *op. cit.*, 322.
38 Morley, I, 511.
39 Stafford House is now Lancaster House.
40 G later told W. T. Stead that the advantage of tree-felling was that it *forced* one to relax one's mind by making it so dangerous to think of anything other than where the axe would next fall. D, I, xlvi, fn.
41 D, 17 July 1852.
42 D, 13 October 1853.
43 *Times*, 12 October 1853, 5; 13 October 1853, 7.
44 H, CXXXI, 357–89.
45 G to Robertson G, 29 March 1854. GP, 44529, 72–3.
46 G to Robertson G, 29 March 1854. GP, ib. Another of G's grievances was that Disraeli had refused to hand over the Chancellor's robes in the belief – probably mistaken – that they had been worn by the Younger Pitt. They are now displayed by the National Trust at Hughenden.
47 GP, 44529, 190.
48 Ib., 603.
49 H, CXXXII, 298.
50 G to Delane, 28 November 1854. GP, 44529, 182–3.
51 H, CXXXVI, 1180, 1205–1206. G to Wilson, 4 January 1855. GP, 44530, 7. G was already under parliamentary attack over the Kennedy affair.
52 D, 31 March 1857.
53 DDCP, 131.
54 J. R. Jones, 'The Conservative Party and Gladstone in 1855', *English Historical Review*, 1962, 95–8; DDCP, 132–3.
55 PMP, I, 131.
56 Ib., 167–8.
57 PMP, III, 175.
58 Ib., 179.
59 H, CXXXVI, 1823–41.
60 G to Marriot, 27 February 1855. GP, 44530, 32.
61 PMP, III, 190–2.

Notes to Chapter 6: Becoming a Kind of Liberal, 1855–1859

1 Eventually G published a polite version in the *Quarterly* for September 1856 as 'The Declining Efficiency of Parliament'.
2 PMP, III, 190. G to Northcote, 5 March 1855. GP, 44530, 36.
3 GP, 44745, 199, 200, 215, 188.
4 GP, 44745, 188, 184, 190, 217, 194. 'Philosophical government': here presumably G was

thinking of J. S. Mill and the Benthamite Utilitarian tradition; or perhaps exponents of the 'science of politics' such as Goldwin Smith or J. R. Seeley.

5 Argyll, 8th Duke of, *Autobiography and Memoirs* (1906), II, 2.
6 Ib., 193.
7 G to Brougham, 2 March 1855. GP, 44530, 34.
8 H, CXXXVII, 794. *The History of* The Times: *The Tradition Established, 1841–1884* (1939), 207–12.
9 Ib., 1086.
10 *Quarterly*, June 1855, 41–70.
11 G. B. Henderson, 'Lord Palmerston and the Secret Service Fund', *English Historical Review*,1938, 485–7.
12 E. Miller, *The Prince of Librarians* (1967), ch 13.
13 H, CXXXVIII, 1055, 1046, 1057–60.
14 Ib., 1810–25.
15 Argyll, *op. cit.*, I, 561.
16 J. R. Vincent, 'The Parliamentary Dimension of the Crimean War', *Transactions of the Royal Historical Society*, 1981, 44, 47.
17 A. R. Ashwell & R. G. Wilberforce, *Samuel Wilberforce* (1881), II, 349.
18 K. G. Robbins, 'Palmerston, Bright and Gladstone in North Wales', *Transactions of the Caernarvonshire Historical Society*, 1980.
19 D, 27 September 1855.
20 Ib.
21 D, 15 February 1856.
22 D, 20 February 1856.
23 PMP, III, 195–8.
24 Ib., 199–200.
25 J. Prest, *Lord John Russell* (1972), 378; T. W. Reid (ed.), *Life of William Ewart Gladstone* (1899), 388. H, CXLI, 1422.
26 H, CXLII, 94–8; D, 30 July 1856.
27 H, CXLVI, 142, 175.
28 *Quarterly*, September 1856, 558, 562, 564.
29 Morley, I, 553.
30 D, V, 176, fn 2; 2 December 1856.
31 PMP, III, 210.
32 *Wilberforce*, II, 335–6.
33 Aberdeen to G, 5 December 1856. GP, 43071, 332–4.
34 *Quarterly*, January 1857, 246–84.
35 PMP, III, 216.
36 D, 19 February 1857.
37 Argyll, II, 72–3.
38 DDCP, 216.
39 Ib., 149–50.
40 L. Strachey & R. Fulford (eds), *The Greville Memoirs, 1814–1860* (1938), VII, 273.
41 H, CXLIV, 985–7, 999, 1000, 1015.

42 GP, 44747, 53–81.
43 D, 6 March 1857.
44 PMP, III, 220–21.
45 Ib., 221.
46 Argyll, II, 75.
47 D, 31 March 1857.
48 Aberdeen to G, 3 April 1857. GP, 43071, 364.
49 *Quarterly*, April 1857, 541–73.
50 DDCP, 152; H, CXLVII, 858–9; QR, ib., 529–30; *Times*, 6 August 1857, 11; H, ib., 1691–1693.
51 H, ib., 364–5, 660.
52 Ib., 1667–1670.
53 D, 18 August 1857.
54 A. T. Bassett (ed.), *Gladstone to his Wife* (1936), 120.
55 D, 21 February 1858.
56 *Quarterly*, 'The Past and Present Administrations', October 1858, 543–4, 546.
57 D, 19 February 1858.
58 See p. 105.
59 PMP, III, 206.
60 *Quarterly*, ib., 515–41.
61 Ib., April 1858, 571–2.
62 *Times Literary Supplement*, 3 January 1975, 16.
63 D, 2 July 1858.
64 Republished by Freeman in *Historical Essays*, 2nd series (1873), 67–92.
65 Morley, I, 579; O. W. Hewett, *Strawberry Fair* (1956), 137.
66 H, CL, 44–66.
67 PMP, III, 222–4.
68 W. F. Monypenny & G. E. Buckle, *Life of Benjamin Disraeli* (1929), I, 1559.
69 D, 29, 31 December 1858.
70 J. K. Chapman, *The Career of Arthur Hamilton Gordon, First Lord Stanmore* (1964), 12–13.
71 Morley, I, 613.
72 D, V, 372, fn 2; 25 February 1859.
73 D, 5 March 1859.
74 1834–1902, 8th baronet.
75 More particularly in Arthur Gordon's biography of his father, Aberdeen. See p. 446.
76 T. A. Jenkins (ed.), *The Parliamentary Diaries of Sir John Trelawny, 1858–1865* (1990), 77.
77 H, CLIII, 1882–1883.
78 Morley, I, 624.
79 C. S. Parker, *Sir James Graham* (1907), II, 388.
80 D. Beales, *England and Italy, 185 –1860* (1961), 87–91.
81 Morley, I, 624.
82 Heir to the 7th Duke of Devonshire.
83 D, 13 June 1859.

Notes to Chapter 7: A Peelite in Liberal Guise, 1859–1862

1 Morley, I, 624
2 Lord Stanmore, *Sidney Herbert* (1906), II, 197.
3 E. Hodder, *Shaftesbury* (1887), III, 187–8.
4 G to Mill, 5 July 1859. GP, 44530, 44.
5 F. E. Mineka and D. N. Lindley (eds), *The Later Letters of John Stuart Mill, 1849–1873* (1972), II, 626–7.
6 W. Bagehot, *Biographical Studies* (ed. R. H. Hutton, 1860), 94, 112.
7 G, *Studies on Homer and the Homeric Age* (1858), III, 107.
8 Bagehot, ib., 95.
9 A. Vidler, *The Orb and the Cross* (1947), 147.
10 Goldwin Smith, *My Memory of Gladstone* (1904), 37.
11 Morley, II, 29. Phillimore: Admiralty Judge; baronet 1883.
12 Smith, 37–9, 28.
13 Morley, I, 631. A. R. J. Turgot (1727–81), great but thwarted reformer of the French *ancien régime*.
14 B. Hilton, 'Peel: a Reappraisal', *Historical Journal*, 1979, 614.
15 G to Bedford, 17 December 1884. GP, 44488, 277.
16 G, *Speeches and Addresses Delivered at the Election of 1865*, 19.
17 G to Damaschino, 8 July 1859. GP, 44530, 46.
18 Verona, Mantua, Peschiera, Legnago. The bloodiness at Solferino was witnessed by J. H. Dunant (1828–1910) and led to the International Red Cross.
19 D, 30 June 1859. D. Beales, *England and Italy, 1859–1860* (1961), 96; R. T. Shannon, 'Gladstone, the Roman Church and Italy', M. Bentley (ed.) *Public and Private Doctrine* (1992), 116–19.
20 G to Robertson G, 2 August 1859. GP, 44530, 57.
21 H, CLV, 183–7.
22 A. T. Bassett, *Gladstone to his Wife* (1936), 125.
23 G to Brougham, 23 August and 11 October 1859. GP, 44530, 41–2, 64. Peter, Lord Brougham, Lord Chancellor, 1830–34.
24 D, 30 July, 16 September 1859. *Victorian Studies*, XIX, 1975, 93; GP, 44392, 111. The portrait is also reproduced in the *Diaries*, v.
25 D, 18 July 1859.
26 See p. 437.
27 G, *Gleanings of Past Years* (1879), II, 145.
28 G to CG, 11 August 1859. GGP, 28/6.
29 R. T. Shannon, 'Tennyson and Gladstone', *Times Literary Supplement*, 2 October 1992.
30 J. Morley, *Cobden* (1881), 720–21.
31 D, 19 September 1859.
32 G to Lewis, 17 October 1859. GP, 44530, 95.
33 D, 27 November 1859.
34 Beales, *England and Italy*, 118–19; K. Bourne, *The Foreign Policy of Victorian England, 1830–1902* (1971), 347– 59.

35 Bourne, 354; D, 7 January 1860.
36 Beales, 124.
37 H, CLXI, 1565–1579; CLXVI, 933–50.
38 PMP, I, 86.
39 D, V, 457, fn 1; 16 January 1860.
40 G to Brougham, 18 January 1860. GP, 44530, 146.
41 Argyll, 8th Duke of, *Autobiography and Memoirs* (1906), II, 154.
42 D, V, 458, fn 1; 19 January 1860.
43 T. A. Jenkins (ed.), *The Parliamentary Diaries of Sir John Trelawny, 1858–1865* (1990), 105.
44 H. Maxwell, *Clarendon* (1913), II, 208.
45 *The Times*, 6 February 1860.
46 H, CLVI, 812–72.
47 L. Strachey & R. Fulford (eds), *The Greville Memoirs, 1814–1860* (1938), VII, 460.
48 *Trelawny*, *op. cit.*, 98.
49 H, CLVII, 420–21.
50 PMP, III, 230.
51 D, V, 487.
52 *Greville op. cit.*, VII, 462.
53 *Trelawny op. cit.*, 122.
54 J. Ridley, *Lord Palmerston* (1970), 497.
55 G to Robertson, 15 May 1860. GP, 44531, 4.
56 G to Bright, 17 August 1860. GP, 44531, 38.
57 D, 2 June 1860.
58 D, V, 494, fn 1; 6 June 1860.
59 See J. Giuseppe, *The Bank of England* (1966), 117.
60 Ib., 496.
61 H, CLIX, 1430–1431.
62 D, 7 July 1860.
63 D, V, 506, fn 8; 21 July 1860.
64 LQV, 2 series, III, 429.
65 Maxwell, *Clarendon*, *op. cit.*, II, 220.
66 B. Connell, *Regina v Palmerston* (1962), 321.
67 G to CG, 4, 5, 7 October 1859. GGP 28/6.
68 Marlow, *Mr and Mrs Gladstone*, *op. cit.*, 78.
69 J. B. Conacher, 'A Visit to the Gladstones in 1894', *Victorian Studies*, 1958, 157.
70 PMP, I, 86.
71 G & P, 166–7.
72 G to CG, 22 January 1861. GGP, 28/6.
73 S. J. Bailey (ed.), *The Diary of Lady Frederick Cavendish* (1927), I, 115.
74 *Quarterly*, July 1861, 'Democracy on its Trial', 285–6.
75 Bright to G, 1 January 1861. GP, 44112, 24.
76 Froude to G, 6 February 1861. GP, 44395, 146. Historian and man of letters (1819–94).
77 G to Froude, 16 February 1861. GP, 44351, 120.

78 Hunt to G, 2 Aug. 1861. GP, 44397, 3. Hunt a son of the writer Leigh Hunt.
79 G to Brougham, 15 March 1861. Ib., 129.
80 G to Rogers, 22 January 1861. Ib., 111. J. E. T. Rogers, political economist: Drummond Professor at Oxford.
81 PMP, I, 156. Later, G was misinformed that M had destroyed the letters, and felt that he had been duped into helping M obliterate his Anglican traces. They were in fact rediscovered during the Second World War. See Butler, *op. cit.*, 70n.
82 G to Keble, 27 Feb. 1861. Ib., 122.
83 D, 1 April 1861. Herbert suffered from diabetes and probably also renal disease, baffling to his doctors. F. B. Smith, *Florence Nightingale* (1982), 112n.
84 *The Times*, 20 March 1861, 5; 28 March, 10; 2 April, 4.
85 D, VI, 23, fn 1; 10 April 1861.
86 A. R. Ashwell & R. G. Wilberforce, *Life of Samuel Wilberforce* (1881), III, 46.
87 H, CLXIV, 1682–1689.
88 'I delivered a brief … abstract of my American article, to the astonishment and admiration of … especially the ignorant Gladstone.' J. L. Altholz *et al* (eds), *Correspondence of Lord Acton and Richard Simpson* (1971–75), II, 159.
89 G to Dss of Sutherland, 29 May 1861. GP, 44531, 167.
90 D, 28 November 1861.
91 G to CG, 29 July 1862. GGP, 29/1.
92 H, CLVIII, 632, 642–3.
93 G, *Gleanings of Past Years* (1879), I, 1, 2, 20.
94 G & P, 210–14.
95 H, CLXVI, 460–91.
96 D, 3 August 1861.
97 The House of St Barnabas-in-Soho and its chapel still continue the redemptive work of their founders. The former Rose Street is now Manette Street.
98 G to C. G. Gordon, 22 September 1862. GP, 44533, 25.
99 G to Argyll, 29 August 1862. GP, 44533, 14.
100 Ib., 233–6.
101 G to Gordon, 22 September 1862. GP, 44533, 25. Gordon, now Governor of New Brunswick, had been rebuffed again in 1861 in his suit to marry Agnes. D, VI, 64.

Notes to Chapter 8: Embracing the Millions: Lancashire and the Tyne, 1862–1864

1 *The Times*, 7 October 1862, 8.
2 T. W. Reid (ed.), *Gladstone* (1899), 435.
3 *The Times*, 9 October 1862, 7.
4 *The Times*, 8 October 1862, 7.
5 G. J. Holyoake, *Bygones Worth Remembering* (1905), I, 292–3.
6 N. Longmate, *The Hungry Mills: The Story of the Lancashire Cotton Famine, 1861–65* (1978), ch 19; M. Ellison, *Support for Secession: Lancashire and the American Civil War* (1972).
7 K. G. Robbins, *John Bright* (1979), 164.

8 F. E. Mineka & D. N. Lindley (eds), *Later Letters of John Stuart Mill, 1849–1873* (1972), II, 803.
9 PMP, I, 132.
10 G to Russell, 17 October 1862. GP, 44292, 82.
11 *The Times*, 9 October 1862, 8.
12 DDCP, 191.
13 *The Times*, 14 October 1862, 4.
14 G & P, 239–47.
15 D, 30 July 1862.
16 DDCP, 192.
17 G to Dss of Sutherland, 17 November 1862. GP, 44533, 45.
18 G to Hall, 2 February 1863. Ib., 87.
19 G to Moffatt, 24 November 1862. Ib., 52.
20 D, 29 November 1862.
21 G to Argyll, 19 December 1862. GP, 44533, 64–6.
22 D, 27 December 1862.
23 G, *An Address delivered at the Saturday Evening Assembly of the Working Men of Chester, December 27, 1862*, 9.
24 Longmate, *Hungry Mills, op. cit.*, 244.
25 G & P, 248–50.
26 G to Wilson, 5 January 1863. GP, 44533, 75. The National Reform Union was a middle-class body founded in 1864 by Lancashire merchants and manufacturers with a ratepayer franchise in view.
27 See p. 129.
28 It was while enjoying the Washington production of this play at Ford's Theatre that President Lincoln was assassinated in April 1865.
29 A. T. Bassett, *Gladstone to his Wife* (1936), 144. Acton, 5 March 1863: 'A long and charming talk with Gladstone today. We have materials for demolishing Kinglake', J. L. Altholz *et al* (eds), *Correspondence of Lord Acton and Richard Simpson* (1971–75), III, 91.
30 1855–1945; 4th baronet 1926. In 1945 the baronetcy passed to William's line.
31 G to Paget, 18 February 1863. GP, 44533, 90.
32 P. F. McHugh, *Prostitution and Victorian Social Reform* (1980), 42.
33 H, CLXXVII, 455.
34 H, CLXX, 150–3.
35 T. A. Jenkins (ed.), *The Parliamentary Diaries of Sir John Trelawny, 1858–1865* (1990), 228.
36 Ib., 243.
37 G to Phillimore, 20 April 1863. GP, 44533, 118.
38 G to Nightingale, 15 April 1863. GP, 44533, 116. The Ripon concerned was the 2nd Earl and 1st Marquis (1827–1909), son of 'Prosperity Fred' Robinson.
39 *Trelawny, op. cit.*, 240.
40 H, CLXX, 205–7.
41 H, CLXX, 391.
42 D, 16 April 1863.

43 H, CLXXI, 625.
44 See p. 153.
45 H, CLXXI, 835.
46 DDCP, 190.
47 G, *A Chapter of Autobiography* (1868), 40.
48 G to C. W. Russell, 8 September 1863. GP, 44533, 164.
49 G, 'General Retrospect', 1896–97. GP, 44791, 51. See above regarding income tax renewal, 1853, pp. 87–8.
50 G & P, 166–7.
51 *Trelawny*, *op. cit.*, 253.
52 H, CLXXI, 1801–12.
53 G to Phipps, 25 August 1863. GP, 44533, 160.
54 G to W. F. Cowper, 25 August 1863. GP, 44533, 159.
55 G to Argyll, 8 & 13 September 1863. GP, 44533, 163, 165.
56 Ib., 13 September, 165.
57 G to Sumner, 5 November 1863. GP, 44533, 187.
58 PMP, III, 238–44.
59 *Gleanings*, *op. cit.*, I, 2; Q & G, I, 123, 125.
60 Bassett, 146–52; D, VI, 227–9; G & P, 267.
61 D, 20 October 1863.
62 Ib., 168; G & P, 269–70.
63 D, 7 January 1864.
64 H. M. & M. Swartz (eds), *Disraeli's Reminiscences* (1975), 121.
65 G to Cowper, 26 January 1864. GP, 44534, 33.

Notes to Chapter 9: Embracing the Millions: Reform and Ireland, 1864–1865

1 G to Robertson G, 20 February 1864. GP, 44534, 44.
2 *Quarterly*, July 1864, 529.
3 G & P, 279–80.
4 H, CLXXV, 312–27.
5 *Quarterly*, ib., 260.
6 *Speech by the Chancellor of the Exchequer on the Bill for the Extension of the Suffrage in Towns, May 11th, 1864*, 3–4.
7 D, 11 May 1864.
8 T. A. Jenkins (ed.), *The Parliamentary Diaries of Sir John Trelawny, 1858–1865* (1990), 278.
9 DDCP, 215–16.
10 LQV, 2 series, I, 189–90.
11 G & P, 281–3.
12 DDCP, 216.
13 *Telegraph*, 13 May 1864.
14 G to Robertson G, 17 May 1864. GP, 44534, 79–80.

15 DDCP, 219–20.
16 G to Robertson G, 20 February 1864. GP, 44534, 44.
17 J. Morley, *Cobden* (1881), 868.
18 H, CLXXI, 140–7.
19 G to Panizzi, 11 January 1863. GP, 44533, 77. DDCP, 193.
20 G to Russell, 22 February 1864. GP, 44534, 45.
21 G & P, 279.
22 DDCP, 214.
23 H, CLXXIV, 1423–1425.
24 H, CLXXII, 1095–1102.
25 LQV, 2 ser, I, 168.
26 Ib., 220–21.
27 D, 8 July 1864.
28 PMP, I, 91.
29 D. Hudson, *Munby, Man of Two Worlds* (1972), 200.
30 G to Melly, 8 August 1864. GP, 44534, 111.
31 DDCP, 221.
32 Ib., 222–3.
33 On this theme see M. D. Stephens, 'Gladstone and the Composition of the Final Court in Ecclesiastical Causes, 1850–1873', *Historical Journal*, 1966. See also J. B. Atlay, *The Victorian Chancellors*, II (1908), 264. Lord Chancellor Westbury 'dismissed Hell with costs,' and deprived Anglicans of 'their last hope of everlasting damnation!'
34 D, 24 March, 2 April 1864.
35 A. T. Bassett, *Gladstone to his Wife* (1936), 161–3.
36 J. Prest, 'Gladstone and Russell', *Transactions of the Royal Historical Society*, 1966, 53.
37 M. Cowling, *1867: Disraeli, Gladstone and Revolution* (1967), 31.
38 G to Baines, 28 December 1864. GP, 44534, 175.
39 D, 14 October 1864.
40 D, 22 October 1864.
41 D, 19 October 1864.
42 Ib., 164.
43 LQV, 2 series, I, 243–4.
44 GGP, 29/1.
45 D, 15 November 1864.
46 G to Manning, 26 December 1864. GP, 44534, 174–5.
47 G to Argyll, 20 December 1864. GP, 44534, 172.
48 D, 10 December 1864. See V. Surtees, *The Beckford Inheritance: The Lady Lincoln Scandal* (1977), 131–4.
49 Auctoritate M. R. D. Foot.
50 D, V, lxii, fn. 1.
51 Bassett, *op. cit.*, 165.
52 G & P, 320–2.
53 DDCP, 228.
54 G to Cobden, 10 February 1865. GP, 44535, 14.

55 DDCP, 220–30.
56 G. M. Trevelyan, *Life of John Bright* (1913), 331.
57 Ib., 230.
58 Ib.
59 Morley, II, 133.
60 DDCP, 230.
61 See Anne Isba, *Gladstone and Women* (2000), ch 8.
62 DDCP, 229.
63 H, CLXXVIII, 421–34.
64 G, *A Chapter of Autobiography*, 45.
65 Ib., 42–3. Hannah to G, 8 June 1865. GP, 44406, 272–4. G to Hannah, 8 June 1865. Ib., 276–7.
66 H, CLXXVIII, 1086–1120.
67 H, CLXXIX, 473; CLXXX, 789.
68 H, CLXXX, 566.
69 G to Gordon, 11 July 1865. GP, 44535, 84.
70 Hudson, *Munby*, 226.
71 D, 8 July 1865.
72 E. Hodder, *Shaftesbury* (1887), III, 188.
73 D, 25 August 1865.
74 *Trelawny*, *op. cit.*, 327. G had extended the franchise thoughtfully in Flintshire by a conveyance making Stephy a freeholder, and thereby a useful 'faggot' voter.
75 G, *Speeches and Addresses delivered at the Elections of 1865*, 38–9.
76 Ib., 1, 4, 11, 14.
77 Ib., 17–19.
78 G to Thomas G, 19 July 1865. GP, 44535, 87.
79 G & P, 341.
80 DDCP, 233.
81 D, 25 July 1865.
82 DDCP, 233.
83 G to Manning, 21 July 1865. GP, 44535, 89.
84 G to Heathcote, 21 July 1865. Ib., 88.
85 G to Wilberforce, 21 July 1865. Ib., 88–9.
86 P. Magnus, *Gladstone* (1954), 174.
87 DDCP, 233.
88 G to Sumner, 25 August 1865. GP, 44535, 116.
89 DDCP, 233.
90 Bassett, 166; D, 18 October 1865.
91 Hodder, *Shaftesbury*, III, 187.

Notes to Chapter 10: Reform, 1865–1868

1 S. Walpole, *Lord John Russell* (1891), II, 422.
2 DDCP, 237.

3 W. Bagehot, *Biographical Studies*, ed. R. H. Hutton (1860), 101.
4 DDCP, 238.
5 Ib., 238–9.
6 G to Crossley, 25 July 1865. GP, 44535, 94.
7 G to Beales, 10 August 1865. Ib.,107.
8 G to Russell, 2 September 1865. GP, 44292, 164.
9 W. E. Monypenny & G. E. Buckle, *Disraeli* (1929), II, 158.
10 J. Prest, *Russell* (1972), 403.
11 Bright to Hargreaves, 23 October 1865. BL, 62079, 83.
12 Delane to G, 1 December 1865. GP, 44409, 86.
13 Gibson to G, 3 October 1865. GP, 44408, 5.
14 See p. 132.
15 G. M. Trevelyan, *Bright* (1913), 359.
16 G to Rathbone, 12 January 1866. GP, 44409, 62.
17 G to Rathbone, 17 January 1866. Ib., 96.
18 G to Paget, 21 January 1866. GP, 44409, 26.
19 *Annual Register*, 1866, 102.
20 H, CLXXXII, 22–59.
21 Earl of Selborne, *Memorials*, Part II, *Personal and Political, 1865–1895* (1898), I, 56.
22 1 Sam. 22.1–2, referring to the enemies of King Saul who gathered around David.
23 Ib., 873
24 *Telegraph*, 6 April 1866, 3.
25 Ib., 7 April 1866, 2.
26 Ib., 2089–2090.
27 G to Bruce, 26 April 1866. GP, 44410, 102.
28 G, 'Place of Ancient Greece in the Providential Order', *Gleanings* (1879), VII, 33.
29 H, CLXXXIII, 113–51.
30 G. Barnett Smith, *Gladstone* (1883), 344.
31 Ib., 344–5.
32 Ib., 1341.
33 Ib., 1488.
34 Ib., 1525–1526.
35 R. B. Wilson (ed.), *Sir Daniel Gooch* (1972), 112.
36 F. B. Smith, *Second Reform Bill* (1966), 114.
37 Ib.
38 H, CLXXXIV, 1144–1145.
39 Smith, op. cit. 133.
40 Prest, *Russell, op. cit.*, 415.
41 F.W. Hirst, 'Mr Gladstone as Leader of the House and Reformer, 1865–68', in T. W. Reid (ed.), *Gladstone* (1899), 491.
42 Smith, *op. cit.*, 165.
43 Monypenny & Buckle, *Disraeli, op. cit.*, II, 218.
44 H, CLXXXI, 1519; Bratiano to G, 19 March 1866. GP, 44409, 26. G to Bratiano, 16 May 1866. GP, 44410, 186 (draft).

45 H, CLXXXV, 69, 441–3.
46 Paget to G, 10 March 1867. GP, 44412, 116; Canning to G, 13 March 1867. Ib., 123.
47 H, CLXXXV, 486–7.
48 H, CLXXXV, 982, 988–9.
49 Ib., 1358.
50 G to Elcho, 7 March 1867. GP, 44412, 109.
51 H, CLXXXVI, 6–16.
52 Ib., 53–7.
53 Ib., 45.
54 Monypenny & Buckle, *op. cit.*, II, 256.
55 H, CLXXXVI, 377.
56 Ib., 664.
57 Smith, *op. cit.*, 172.
58 Smith, *op. cit.*, 174; M. Cowling, *Disraeli, Gladstone and Revolution* (1967), 195.
59 Morley, I, 866.
60 Morley, II, 232.
61 D, 12 April 1867.
62 Temple to G, 17 April 1867. GP, 44412, 217.
63 Hughes to G, 13 April 1867. Ib., 209.
64 Denman to G, 1 May 1867. Ib., 259.
65 D, 1 May 1867. Baron C. C. J. Bunsen, Prussian Ambassador to London 1841–54; admired for a time by G for his ecumenical Protestantism.
66 H, CLXXXVII, 715.
67 G, 'The Session and its Sequel', *Edinburgh Review*, October 1867, 565.
68 H, CLXXXVII, 719.
69 Ib.
70 Smith, *op. cit.*, 197, 201; Cowling, 235.
71 G, *Ed. Rev*, *op. cit.*, 554.
72 H, CLXXXVII, 738, 756.
73 D, 28 May 1867.
74 Ib., 1271.
75 Morley, II, 234.
76 H, CLXXXVIII, 1549.
77 Bright to Hargreaves, 19 August 1867. BL, 62079, 111.
78 D, 8 August 1867.
79 H, CLXXXVII, 121, 130.
80 G, *Ed. Rev.*, Oct. 1867, 543, 577, 581, 584.
81 H. C. G. Matthew, 'Gladstone, Vaticanism and the Question of the East', *Studies in Church History*, XV (1978), ed. D. Baker, 420.
82 G to Disraeli, 16 December 1865. GP, 44408, 219.
83 Disraeli to G, 20 November 1867. GP, 44413, 242.
84 Hirst, in Reid, *Gladstone*, *op. cit.*, 596–7.
85 Walpole, *Russell*, *op. cit.*, II, 446–7.
86 Lord E. Fitzmaurice, *Granville* (1905), I, 518–19.

Notes to Chapter 11: Strenuous Government, 1868–1871

1 R. T. Shannon, *The Age of Disraeli, 1868–1881* (1992), 37.
2 H, CLXXXX, 1288–1289.
3 Earl of Selborne, *Memorials, Personal & Political, 1865–95* (1898), I, 93.
4 Lord E. Fitzmaurice, *Granville* (1905), I, 254.
5 H, CLXXXX, 1758, 1759, 1767.
6 Ib., 1771.
7 Shannon, *Disraeli, op. cit.*, 41.
8 H, CLXXXXI, 474.
9 G to Cook, 10 May 1868. GP, 44415, 62.
10 N. E. Johnson (ed.), *The Diary of Gathorne Hardy, later Lord Cranbrook, 1866–1892* (1981), 72.
11 Shannon, *Disraeli, op. cit.*, 45.
12 O. Anderson, 'Gladstone's Abolition of Compulsory Church Rates: a Minor Political Myth and its Historical Career', *Journal of Ecclesiastical History*, 1974.
13 GP, 44415, 306.
14 H. Maxwell, *Clarendon* (1913), II, 346.
15 Ib., 351.
16 Gibson to G, 19 November 1868. GP, 44416, 206.
17 Maxwell, ib., 351–2.
18 G to Disraeli, 6 December 1868. GP, 44416, 315.
19 E. Ashley, *National Review*, June 1898, 536.
20 G to Delane, 6 December 1868. Ib., 313.
21 The title confusingly adopted in 1859 by G. F. S. Robinson, also 2nd Earl, and later 1st Marquess of Ripon.
22 J. Parry, 'Gladstone and Liberalism', in D. Bebbington & R. Swift (eds), *Gladstone Centenary Essays*, 103. See G to Paget, p. 192.
23 J. Winter, *Robert Lowe* (1976), 244–5.
24 J. Parry, *The Rise and Fall of Liberal Government in Victorian Britain* (1993), 229.
25 Butler to G, 19 December 1868. GP, 44416, 74.
26 D, 13 December 1868.
27 G to Trench, 14 December 1868. GP, 44417, 138.
28 G to Lady Salisbury, 16 December 1868. Ib., 161.
29 G to Mrs Stonor, 24 December 1868. Ib., 245.
30 G, 'The Session and its Sequel', *Edinburgh Review*, October 1867, 576.
31 A. E. West, *Recollections, 1832–1886* (1899), I, 331.
32 O. Chadwick, *Acton and Gladstone* (1976), 18.
33 G to Disraeli, 18 February 1869. GP, 44419, 89.
34 G to Sullivan, 11 January 1869. Ib., 127.
35 G & G, I, i,11.
36 Gloucester to G, 8 March 1869. GP, ib., 179.
37 Ib., 347.
38 H, CXCIV, 412–24., 458–62, 465–6.

39 Cullen to G, 18 March 1869. GP, 44419, 198.
40 H, CXCV, 2009–17.
41 D, 30 April 1869.
42 H, CXCV, 2022–2027.
43 Ib., 364, 365.
44 G & G, I, i, 29.
45 D, 12 July 1869.
46 D, 17 July 1869.
47 Derby Diaries (15th Earl), Liverpool Record Office, 16 July 1869.
48 G & G, 1, i, 74.
49 Granville, in financial straits and without a country house, had been made Warden in succession to Palmerston in 1865, by Russell.
50 R. Fulford (ed.), *Your Dear Letter: Private Correspondence of Queen Victoria and the Crown Princess of Prussia, 1865–1871* (1971), 248.
51 GP, 44422, 5.
52 D, 23 November 1869.
53 G & G, 1, i, 56–7; Q & G, i, 195–7.
54 D. W. R. Bahlman, 'The Queen, Mr Gladstone, and Church Patronage', *Victorian Studies*, 1959–60, 357.
55 D, 28 August 1869.
56 G to Döllinger, 25 March 1870. GP, 44426, 15; D, 1 December 1869. H. Jenkins, 'The Irish Dimension of the British Kulturkampf, 1870–75', *Journal of Ecclesiastical History*, 1979.
57 D, 21 October 1869.
58 M. J. Winstanley, *Ireland and the Land Question, 1800–1922* (1984); E. D. Steele, *Irish Land and British Politic: Tenant-Right and Nationality, 1865–1870* (1974).
59 D, 23 October 1869. He purchased at this time the nearby Dundas estate for £57,000.
60 D, 17 September 1869.
61 For the fullest story we are likely to get, see Isba, *Gladstone and Women* (2005), ch 8.
62 D, VIII, 575–6.
63 H, CC, 996, 1714, 1716.
64 C. S. Parker, *Graham* (1907), II, 295.
65 T. A. Jenkins (ed.), *The Parliamentary Diaries of Sir John Trelawny, 1868–1873* (1994), 414.
66 Selborne, *Memorials*, I, 147–8, 153
67 Steele, 305.
68 D, 16 April 1870.
69 H, CC, 292–3; Parry, *Rise and Fall of Liberal Government*, 262.
70 D, 24 March 1870.
71 G to Mrs Cardwell, 22 April 1870. GP, 44426, 149.
72 *Trelawny*, *op. cit*, 388.
73 Ib., 374, 389.
74 H, CCIII, 745–8.
75 *Trelawny*, *op. cit.*, 397.
76 G & G, 1, i, 89.

77 H, CC, 1901.
78 G & G, 1, i, 73.
79 D, 10 February 1870.
80 Strictly, the North German Confederation, established in 1867. The south German states also joined in the war against France. The German Empire was proclaimed at Versailles in January 1871.
81 H, CCX, 1178.
82 H, CCIII, 1576–1577.
83 G & G, 1, i, 130.
84 D, 30 September 1870.
85 G & G, 1, i., 137, 140.
86 'Germany, France and England', *Edinburgh Review*, October 1870; D. Schreuder, 'Gladstone as Troublemaker', *Journal of British Studies*, 1977–78.
87 Fulford, *Your Dear Letter*, 320.
88 P. Knaplund, *Gladstone's Foreign Policy* (1935), 61.
89 G & G, 1, i, 166.
90 H, CC, 1817.
91 G & G, 1, i, 170–1.
92 Shannon, *Disraeli*, 104.
93 *Trelawny*, *op. cit.*, 419.
94 Ib., 420, 422.
95 Shannon, *op. cit.*, 107.
96 H, CCV, 148.
97 *Trelawny*, *op. cit.*, 428.
98 Ib., 429.
99 Derby Diaries, 27 April 1871.
100 Ib., 29 April 1871.
101 *Trelawny*, *op. cit.* 431.
102 Ib., 433.
103 Ib., 434.
104 Ib., 439.
105 D, 15 July 1871.
106 H, CCVII, 1069.
107 D, 23 August 1871.
108 *Trelawny*, *op. cit.*, 441.

Notes to Chapter 12: Defeat and Abdication, 1871–1875

1 Derby Diaries, 14 June 1871.
2 D, 23 August 1871.
3 G & G, 1, ii, 256.
4 T. W. Reid, *Life of Richard Monckton Milnes, Lord Houghton* (1891), II, 253; D, 13 September 1871.

5 *Annual Register*, 1871, 106.
6 G & G, 1, ii, 274–5; D, 19 October 1871.
7 G & G, ib., 258.
8 *Letters of ... Henry Austin Bruce, Lord Aberdare* (1902), I, 318–19.
9 Tenterden to G, 20 December 1871. GP, 44432, 294.
10 D, 16 May 1871.
11 D, 29 Dec. 1871.
12 D. M. Schreuder, *Gladstone and Kruger: Liberal Government and Colonial 'Home Rule', 1880–1885* (1969), 49.
13 G & G, 1, ii, 291; D, 21 December 1871.
14 T. A. Jenkins (ed.), *Parliamentary Diaries of Sir John Trelawny, 1868–1873* (1992), 448, 449.
15 Derby Diaries, 29 April 1872.
16 Tennyson to G, 5 February 1872. GP, 44433, 130.
17 Q & G, I, 332.
18 Ellis to G, 25 January 1872: *Memorandum on Employment for the Prince of Wales*. GP, 44433, 90–103.
19 D, 9 March 1872.
20 F. Harcourt, 'Gladstone, Monarchism and the "New Imperialism", 1868–1874', *Journal of Imperial and Commonwealth History*, 1985–86, 21.
21 R. Fulford (ed.), *Darling Child: Private Correspondence of Queen Victoria and the German Crown Princess, 1871–1878* (1976), 29.
22 Derby Diaries, 29 Jan. 1872.
23 R. T. Shannon, *Disraeli* (1992), 143.
24 D, 6 July 1872.
25 Bright to Hargreaves, 7 December 1872. BL, 62079, 157.
26 Morley, II, 390.
27 D, XII, 454–5.
28 G & G, I, ii, 306.
29 F. W. Hirst, 'Mr Gladstone's First Premiership', in T. W. Reid (ed.), *Gladstone* (1899), 582.
30 H, CCXI, 912.
31 R. Robinson, J. Gallacher and A. Kenny, *Africa and the Victorians: The Official Mind of Imperialism* (1963), 30.
32 G & G, 1, ii, 340, 342.
33 H, CCXVIII, 76–7, 82.
34 D, 21 Aug. 1872.
35 Derby Diaries, 13 August 1872.
36 Wickham (1834–1910) was Headmaster of Wellington College, 1873–93. G thought him a 'superior man', though perhaps his appearance did not do him justice. G made him Dean of Lincoln in 1894.
37 D, 17 January 1872.
38 R. MacLeod, 'The Ayrton Incident: a Commentary on the Relations of Science and Government in England, 1870–73', in A. Thackray and E. Mendelsohn (eds), *Science and Values* (1974), 47.

39 John Tyndall (1820–93), physicist; first to propose explanation of why sky is blue. T. H. Huxley (1825–95); biologist and palaeontologist; famed for collision at Oxford in 1860 defending Darwin against Bishop Samuel Wilberforce, declaring that he had rather be descended from an ape than a man such as the bishop. Sir John Lubbock (1834–1913); Liberal MP 1870–86; Lib. Unionist 1886–1900; legislated bank holidays 1871; researched on primitive man and bees and ants; member with Huxley of X Club, conspiring to replace ecclesiastical establishment with a scientific one.
40 D, 24 September 1872.
41 D, 16 February 1873. Coleridge always remained a special 'English' case in this respect.
42 G to Vance Smith, 28 June 1874. GP, 44443, 319.
43 Balfour to G, 20 January 1875. GP, 44446, 102. Sidgwick (1838–1900), philosopher, resigned his Fellowship at Trinity, Cambridge, in 1869 on conscientious grounds. Balfour's brother-in-law.
44 O'Dell to G, 16 February 1875. GP, 44446, 198.
45 Spencer to G, 4 December 1873; G to Spencer, 12 January 1874; Spencer to G, 14 January 1874. GP, 44441, 171; 44442, 35, 43.
46 G to Jevons, 10 May 1874. GP, 44443, 229. R. D. Collinson Black (ed.), *Papers and Correspondence of William Stanley Jevons*, IV (1977), 38.
47 Cairns to G, 19 February 1870. GP, 44425, 15–19.
48 Cullen to G, 25 February 1872. GP, 44433, 287.
49 J. P. Parry, *Democracy and Religion. Gladstone and the Liberal Party 1867–1875* (1986), 353.
50 D, 8 February 1873.
51 H, CCXIV, 416.
52 Ib., 1240, 1254–1255.
53 *Trelawny*, *op. cit.*, 478.
54 Q & G, I, 363.
55 D, 8 March 1873.
56 D, 13 March 1873.
57 E. Drus (ed.), *A Journal of Events during the Gladstone Ministry, 1868–74, by John, First Earl of Kimberley* (1958), 37.
58 D, 19 May 1873.
59 Peel to G, 26 August 1873. GP, 44270, 289.
60 Derby Diaries, 23 September 1873.
61 *Trelawny*, *op. cit.*, 491–2, 499, 500.
62 D, 19, 20 July 1873.
63 Derby Diaries, 23 September 1873.
64 Q & G, I, 424.
65 D, 15 August 1873.
66 M. R. Temmel, 'Gladstone's Resignation of the Liberal Leadership', *Journal of British Studies*, 1976, 162.
67 G & G, 1, ii, 397; D, 29 August 1873.
68 D, 11 August 1873.
69 D, 27 August 1873.

70 D, 30 October 1873.

71 J. Vaio, 'Schliemann and Gladstone. New Light from Unpublished Documents', in *Heinrich Schliemann. Grundlagen und Ergibnisse moderner Archaologie 100 Jahre nach Schliemanns Tod*, ed. J. Herrmann (1992), 74. Newton to G, 9 October 1873. GP, 44440, 176.

72 D, 3 January 1874.

73 G & G, 1, ii, 438.

74 D, 3 January 1874.

75 D, 19 January 1874.

76 D, 18 January 1874.

77 D, 20 January 1874. Godley, one of G's assistant secretaries at the time, was in no doubt that another point bearing on G's decision was his embarrassment about the Greenwich seat. (A. Godley (ed.), *Reminiscences of Lord Kilbracken* (1931), 98). Selborne (Palmer) never doubted this as the 'determining cause' (Hirst, in Reid, *op. cit.*, *Gladstone*, 589).

78 G & G, 1, ii, 445.

79 F. Harrison, 'The Conservative Reaction', *Fortnightly Review*, March 1874, 296. Harrison was a leading Positivist doctrinaire.

80 Derby Diaries, 24 January 1874.

81 G & G, 1, ii, 441.

82 D, 28 January 1874.

83 H, CCXVIII, 84.

84 D, 23 February 1874.

85 G to Peel, 26 February 1874. GP, 44270, 297.

86 D, 6 February 1874. 'Next to this comes Education ... with the Nonconformists and Irish voters.'

87 Q & G, I, 446.

88 *Aberdare*, I, 361–2.

89 Ib. 362.

90 D, 19 February 1874.

91 D, 20 February 1874.

92 D, 23 February 1874.

Notes to Chapter 13: The Question of the East, 1875–1877

1 G to Fielden, 26 February 1874. GP, 44443, 37.

2 D, 25 February 1874.

3 G, memo, 7 March 1874. GP, 44762, 37.

4 D, 13 March 1874.

5 G & G, 1, ii, 449–50. For a psycho-historical interpretation of G's 'strategy of withdrawal', see T. L. Crosby, *The Two Mr Gladstones. A Study in Psychology and History* (1997), 145, 150.

6 D, 21 April 1874.

7 Peel to G, 30 April 1874. GP, 44270, 361.

8 M. R. Temmel, 'Gladstone's Resignation of the Liberal Leadership', *Journal of British Studies*, 1976, 156.

9 H, CCXVIII, 42–3, 46.
10 Ib., 82–3.
11 Ib., 130.
12 Ib., 90, 1101–1121.
13 H, CCXVIII, 1285–1287.
14 A. Godley (ed.), *Reminiscences of Lord Kilbracken* (1931), 84.
15 D, 3 March, 1874.
16 D, 12 May, 1874.
17 Martin to G, 24 December 1874. GP, 44445, 264.
18 D, 18 June 1874.
19 H, CCXX, 1372–1391.
20 G & G, 1, ii, 457.
21 Earl of Selborne, *Memorials* (1898), I, 334.
22 Ly Ripon to CG, 20 August 1874. GP, 44444, 219.
23 G to Ly Ripon, 21 August 1874. Ib., 222.
24 D, 13 September 1874; G, 'Ritualism and Ritual', *Contemporary Review*, October 1874, 674. *Semper eadem*; 'ever the same'.
25 G, *Vatican Decrees*, 21.
26 G to Mazzari, 11 December 1873. GP, 44441, 215.
27 G & G, I, ii, 458.
28 R. Fulford, *Darling Child, 1871–78*, 162.
29 Münster to G, 25 November 1874. GP, 44445.
30 Shannon, 'Gladstone, the Roman Church and Italy', in M. Bentley (ed.), *Public and Private Doctrine* (1992).
31 Bismarck to G, 1 March 1875. GP, 44445, 293.
32 G & G, I, ii, 458–9.
33 G to Bismarck, 5 March 1875. GP, 44445, 294.
34 Emly to G, 3 October [1874]. GP, 44152, 235; Emly to G, 10 October [1874]. Ib., 241.
35 H. Jenkins, 'The Irish Dimension of the British Kulturkampf: Vaticanism and Civil Allegiance, 1870–1875', *Journal of Ecclesiastical History*, 1979, 358–60.
36 G, *Vatican Decrees*, 46.
37 Bassett, 208.
38 G & G, I, ii, 460–2.
39 Ib., 465.
40 GP, 44762, 148.
41 G & G, I, ii, 464–5.
42 GP, 44762, 169. ('Ab F 12').
43 Mundella to Leader, 1 March 1875. Mundella Papers, Sheffield City Library.
44 See p. 315, for G's taking it much amiss that in 1880 the Queen did not share this presumption.
45 Lord E. Fitzmaurice, *Granville* (1905), II, 149.
46 Ib. Disraeli in 1868 became Conservative leader in that manner.
47 Ib., 154.
48 Ib., 153.

49 Mundella to Leader, 19 March 1875. Mundella Papers.
50 H, CCXXIV, 297–8.
51 Caird to G, 31 December 1875. GP, 44448, 357. To soften the blow G became a trustee.
52 *The Life and Letters of … Friedrich Max Müller*, edited by his Wife (1902), I, 417.
53 D, 25 November 1875. From 1874 to 1889 Harry worked for the East India House of his grandfather and uncle, Gillanders, Arbuthnot & Co, Calcutta.
54 See pp. 116–17.
55 See p. 169.
56 See p. 94.
57 See pp. 201–2.
58 Farley to G, 19 August 1875. GP, 44447, 364.
59 R. T. Shannon, *Gladstone and the Bulgarian Agitation, 1876* (1963), 92. (Henceforth, GBA).
60 Ib.
61 G & G, 1, ii, 473–4.
62 Disraeli to Barrington, 29 November 1875. BL, 58210, 43.
63 Levy to G, 29 November 1875. GP, 44448, 257.
64 G & G, 1, ii, 476.
65 Count Julius Andrassy was the Austro-Hungarian Foreign Minister.
66 P. Magnus, *Gladstone* (1954), 229.
67 D, 23 March 1876; H, CCXXVII, 734.
68 H, CCXXVII, 102–4.
69 GBA, 92.
70 D, 14 May 1876. On the question of the status of Lyttelton's life assurance policy, see Talbot of the Guardian Assurance office to G, 3 May 1876. GP, 44450, 14.
71 GBA, 93.
72 See p. 168.
73 Stratford to G, 29 June 1876. GP, 44450, 219. It should be remembered that until 1878 no such country as modern 'Bulgaria' officially existed.
74 G to Granville, 27 June 1876. PRO, 30/29/29.
75 GBA, 46–7.
76 The League was founded in December 1875 by J. Lewis Farley, disillusioned former officer of the Ottoman Bank. See GBA, 250–51.
77 GP, 44790, 112–14.
78 GBA, 94–5.
79 G to Granville, 27 July 1876. Ib.
80 H, CCXXXI, 174–203.
81 GBA, 41–2.
82 GP, 44790, 112–14.
83 Ib.
84 H, CCXXXI, 215, 1146. That was Disraeli's last speech in the Commons. It was announced the following day that he was to go to the House of Lords as Earl of Beaconsfield.
85 GBA, 59.
86 G to Granville, 7 August 1876. PRO, 30/29/29A.

87 D, XII, 517.
88 R. T. Shannon, *Disraeli* (1992), 282–6.
89 GBA, 86.
90 Ib.
91 GP, 44790, 112–14. Morley's version: *Gladstone*, ii, 158.
92 G to Broadhurst, 20 Sept. 1896. Broadhurst Papers, LSE, V,i.
93 GP, 44790, 112–14.
94 In 1879 he docketed them in pencil: 'From this I was called away to write on Bulgaria.' GP, 44698, 367.
95 D, 19 August 1876.
96 GBA, 100.
97 G & G, 2, i, 1.
98 Ib.
99 GBA, 106.
100 G & G, 2, i, 3.
101 G to Elliot, 3 September 1876. GP, 44451, 116.
102 GBA, 112.
103 There is no definite article at the beginning of the title, despite innumerable authoritative suppositions to the contrary. Granville advised against dedicating it to Russell: 'It is too late.'
104 G & G, 2, i, 26; G to Acton, 16 October 1876. GP, 44093, 192.
105 GBA, 108.
106 D, 27 April 1877.
107 W. F. Monypenny & G. E. Buckle, *Disraeli* (1929), II, 933.
108 GBA, 109.
109 See R. W. Seton-Watson, *Britain in Europe, 1789–1914* (1937), 102, 520; S. Lane-Poole, *Stratford de Redcliffe* (1888), I, 307.
110 Beaconsfield to Barrington, 11 Sept. 1876. BL, 58210, 60: 'None of the howlers have [*sic*] any proposal, practical or precise. Gladstone, more absurd than any of them. He writes a fiery pamphlet to prove, for ethnological reasons, that the Turks, as a race, shd. be expelled from Europe, & then finding what a fool he has made of himself, even before his speech [at Blackheath, 9 September], the only point of wh. was to show how this was to be done – he writes a letter to the "Times" to say he did not mean the expulsion of the Turkish nation, only the Turkish ministers. No doubt, he meant only the expulsion of the ministers, but I doubt whether they were Turks. His pamphlet is really a "Bulgarian atrocity".'
111 Derby Diaries, 7 September 1876.
112 Magnus, 242.
113 GBA, 108.
114 Monypenny & Buckle, II, 929.
115 Morley, II, 548.
116 The formulae of 1856 and 1896.
117 GBA, 90.
118 Magnus, 239.
119 GBA, 113.

120 Ib., 116–17.
121 Ib., 117–29.
122 Ib., 130.
123 Fulford, *Darling Child*, 222–3.
124 D, 23 September 1876.
125 GBA, 136.
126 Ib.
127 G, *Gleanings*, IV, 277, 302.
128 G & G, 2, i, 18.
129 GBA, 200.
130 W. E. H. Lecky, eminent Irish historian, author of *Democracy and Liberty* (1896), asserting their incompatibility.
131 Historian, democrat, author of *A Short History of the English People* (1874).
132 Idealist philosopher.
133 James Bryce, Professor of Civil Law at Oxford; advocate of rights of Armenian people.
134 Henry Fawcett, blind political economist, MP for Hackney. Husband of feminist Millicent Fawcett.
135 D, 8 December 1876.
136 GBA, 260.
137 G to Bryce, 29 January 1877. Bryce Papers, Bodleian, Oxford, E.6.
138 G to Schuyler, 30 January 1877. GP, 44453, 62.
139 G to Novikov, 6 February 1877. GP, 44268, 148.
140 D. Hudson, *Munby* (1972), 389.
141 Parliamentary Papers, XC, *Turkey* (1877), No. 221.
142 G & G, 2, i, 31.
143 H, CCXXXII, 111, 113, 118, 554–5.
144 D, 19 March 1877.
145 H, CCXXXIII, 605; G & G, 2, i, 34. Elliot was transferred to Vienna, and replaced by Austen Layard.
146 F. W. Hirst in T. W. Reid (ed.), *Gladstone* (1899), 622.
147 Morley, II, 548.
148 D, XII, 482.

Notes to Chapter 14: A Great and High Election of God, 1877–1880

1 See p. 321.
2 G & G, 2, i, 29.
3 Ib., 38.
4 R. T. Shannon, *Gladstone and the Bulgarian Agitation, 1876* (1963), 120.
5 Ib., 120–21.
6 Ib., 269–70.
7 G & G, 2, i, 42.
8 Ib.

9 D, 31 May 1877.
10 Morley, II, 570, fn 1.
11 G & G, 2, i, 44.
12 Hartington to Devonshire, 28 June 1877. Devonshire Papers, Chatsworth, 8th Duke, 340/695.
13 G, 'Aggression in Egypt and Freedom in the East', *Nineteenth Century*, August 1877. *Gleanings* (1879), IV, 357.
14 G had to make do with the Miltonic efforts of one Oscar Wilde, in Dublin.
15 G to Hill, 11 August 1877. GP, 44454, 322.
16 See p. 338.
17 Shannon, *op. cit.*, 162–4.
18 *The Times*, 21 August 1877, 7.
19 H, CCLIV, 1287.
20 G to Bryce, 6 October 1877. Bryce Papers, Bodleian Library, Oxford, E. 6. See A. Austin to G, 2 June 1877. Gp, 44454, 295. For regrets at the break between G and the *Telegraph*, Lawson to G, 20 June [1877]. GP, 44454, 207.
21 Shannon, *op. cit.*, 277.
22 G & G, 2, i, 54.
23 G & G, 2, i, 54.
24 Shannon, *op. cit.*, 275.
25 Ib., 160. For his part, Butt was decidedly pro-government on the question.
26 Shannon, *op. cit.*, 277.
27 G to Errington, 14 September 1877. GP, 44455, 49.
28 D, 18 October 1877.
29 G to Novikov, 31 October 1877. GP, 44268, 169.
30 The Shaw-Lefevre committee's scheme provided for the Land Commission to purchase estates and resell to tenants assisted by state-funded loans.
31 *Daily Express* (Dublin), 18 November 1877.
32 H, CCXLV, 1622–1628.
33 G to Novikov, ib.
34 G & G, 2, i, 65.
35 Rogers to G, 27 December 1877. Ib., 350.
36 Rogers to G, 3 January 1877. GP, 44456, 4.
37 D, I, xxxix. L. March-Phillips and B. Christian (eds), *Some Hawarden Letters* (1917), 21.
38 G & G, 2, i, 66–7.
39 D, 17 January 1878.
40 D, 26 January 1878.
41 *The Times*, 31 January 1878, 10–11.
42 Shannon, 213.
43 D, 5 February 1878.
44 H, CCXXXVII, 933–4, 938–9.
45 D, 10 February 1878.
46 *Annual Register*, 1878, 15.
47 D, 4 March 1878.

48 D, 10 March 1878.
49 H, CCXXXIX, 871.
50 G & G, 2, i, 70–71.
51 H, CCXL, 1069–1070, 1616.
52 P. Metcalf, *James Knowles, Victorian Editor and Architect* (1980), 282.
53 Barrington to Beaconsfield, 11 July 1878. Hughenden Papers, Bodleian Library, Oxford, B/xx/Ba/67.
54 D, 21 July 1878.
55 *Annual Register*, 1878, 96.
56 H, CCXLII, 672, 693, 716.
57 G, 'England's Mission', *Nineteenth Century*, August 1878, 562.
58 Metcalf, *Knowles, op. cit.*, 282.
59 Morley, II, 582.
60 G contributed to it on 67 occasions between March 1877 and October 1896.
61 G, 'Postscriptum on the County Franchise', *Gleanings*, I, 199–202.
62 G & G, 2, i, 29.
63 Ib., 78.
64 Ib. 'Electoral Facts' appeared in the November *Nineteenth Century*.
65 H, XXCLIII, 904.
66 Beaconsfield to Barrington, 30 November 1878. BL, 58210, 94.
67 D, III, 92. See p. 24.
68 See p. 24.
69 See p. 21.
70 See pp. 23–4.
71 R. T. Shannon, *Gladstone: Peel's Inheritor, 1809–1865* (1982), 166.
72 G to McCormick, 12 August 1894. GP, 44519, 9.
73 D, 29 December 1878.
74 Rosebery to G, 9 January 1879. GP, 56444; Adam to G, 10 January 1879. Ib.
75 G to Adam, 11 January 1879. Ib.
76 H, CCLXV, 1596, 1622.
77 D, 26 Jan. 1878. G was hoping to get Irving a knighthood.
78 GP, 44461, 72; 253.
79 O. Chadwick, *Acton and Gladstone* (1976), 11.
80 Lord E. Fitzmaurice, *Granville* (1905), II, 182.
81 G & G, 2, i, 99.
82 C. Harvie, 'Gladstonianism, the Provinces, and Popular Political Culture, 1860–1906', in R. Bellamy (ed.), *Victorian Liberalism, Nineteenth-century Political Thought and Practice* (1990), 170.
83 E. F. Biagini, *Liberty, Retrenchment and Reform: Popular Liberalism in the Age of Gladstone, 1860–1880* (1992), 369ff.
84 M. R. D. Foot (ed.), *Midlothian Speeches, 1879. W. E. Gladstone* (1971), 27–8, 32.
85 Ib., 48.
86 Ib., 86, 88.
87 Foot, *op. cit.*, 115–17.

88 Morley, II, 551.
89 H. Paul (ed.), *Letters of Lord Acton to Mary Gladstone* (1904), 202.
90 D, 25 July 1854.
91 D, 11 December 1879.
92 Fitzmaurice, *Granville*, II, 182–3.
93 G to Reid, 1 February 1892. GP, 56445.
94 D, 28 December 1879.
95 GP, 44763, 152.
96 A. Godley (ed.), *Reminiscences of Lord Kilbracken* (1931), 108.
97 D, 28 December 1879.
98 D, 18 January 1880.
99 D, 16 March 1880.
100 G, *Political Speeches in Scotland, March and April 1880* (1880), I, 30.
101 *Annual Register*, 1880, 47. Salisbury told Northcote: 'My impression is that the Emperor did say to Elliot something about wishing that we should succeed. I don't think he mentioned Gladstone's name.' Salisbury to Northcote, 20 March 1880. BL, Iddesleigh, 50020, 1.
102 Morley, II, 610, 613.
103 Ib., 615.
104 Q & G, II, 16.
105 R. Fulford (ed.), *Beloved Mama, 1878–85* (1981), 73.
106 See p. 268.
107 For his later withdrawal of indulgence, see p. 424.
108 G to Reid, 1 February 1892. GP, 56445.

Notes to Chapter 15: Grand Old Man, 1880–1883

1 R. Fulford (ed.), *Beloved Mama, 1878–85* (1981), 75.
2 D, 27 April 1880.
3 A. Godley (ed.), *Reminiscences of Lord Kilbracken* (1931), 19.
4 R. T. Shannon, *Disraeli* (1992), 400.
5 Hamilton, I, 3.
6 G memo, 14 May 1880. GP, 56445.
7 D, 29 Sept, 1881.
8 See p. 185.
9 H, CCLXIX, 1713 (Sir Wilfrid Lawson).
10 D, 16 June 1885.
11 Shannon, *Disraeli*, *op. cit.*, 406–07.
12 A. L. Thorold, *Life of Henry Labouchere* (1913), 144. See also A. G. Gardiner, *Harcourt* (1923), I, 457. The Queen made satirical reference to it: Fulford, *Beloved Mama*, *op. cit.*, 148.
13 GP, 56445.
14 G. Battiscombe, *Mrs Gladstone* (1956), 181.
15 D, 22 October 1880.

16 D. Wiggins, 'The Burial Act of 1880, The Liberation Society and George Osborne Morgan', *Parliamentary History* (1996), 173–89.
17 D, 20 May 1880.
18 Karolyi to G, 1 May 1880; G to Karolyi, 4 May 1880. GP, 44464, 48, 50.
19 G, memo, 14 May 1880. GP, 56445.
20 W. N. Medlicott, *Bismarck, Gladstone, and the Concert of Europe* (1956), 1.
21 D, 10, 19 September 1880.
22 D, 14 June 1880; 16 March 1882.
23 D. M. Schreuder, *Gladstone and Kruger* (1969), 66–8; C. F. Goodfellow, *Great Britain and South African Confederation, 1870–1881* (1966), 188–9.
24 H, CCLII, 150, 157.
25 Rathbone to G, 17 April 1880. GP, 44463, 142. The O'Conor Don, former Liberal MP for Roscommon, advocated large-scale purchase and resale of Irish land by the state.
26 H, CCLIII, 1652, 1656; CCLIV, 1437.
27 G, 'Second Cabinet of 1880–5'. GP, 56445.
28 D, 15 June 1880.
29 D, 29 June 1880.
30 Fulford, *op. cit.*, *Beloved Mama*, 84, 88.
31 Hamilton, I, 37, 39. 'I presume Donald Currie aspires at least to a baronetcy.'
32 D, 18 September 1880.
33 See p. 313.
34 D, 19 September 1880.
35 R. T. Shannon, 'Gladstone and the Hellenic Factor in the Eastern Question', *Actes du Symposium Historique International, 'La Dernière Phase de la Crise Orientale et l'Hellénisme (1878–1881)'* (1983), 440.
36 Northcote to Beaconsfield, 7 October 1880. BL, Iddesleigh, 50018, 230.
37 G, 'Second Cabinet of 1880–5'. GP, 56445.
38 Lord Eversley (G. Shaw-Lefevre), *Gladstone and Ireland* (1912), 147.
39 Schreuder, *op. cit.*, 88–9.
40 Hamilton, I, 94. *Shorter Oxford English Dictionary*: 'a light kind of travelling bag, 1882'. A specimen displayed at the National Liberal Club is surprisingly small: 12 ins. by 3 ins. at the base.
41 H, CCLVII, 3–7.
42 D, 12 March 1881.
43 Hamilton, I, 125. 'The Duke is the only man in the Cabinet to whom Mr G. subscribes himself "affectly".'
44 Morley, II, 293.
45 D, 25 May 1881. G. Shaw-Lefevre, 'The Duke of Argyll and the Irish Land Bill', *Nineteenth Century*, June 1881, 1044–1045.
46 H, CCLXIV, 267. See also Lansdowne's comments, ib., 279–80.
47 H, CCLXXX, 446–54.
48 H, CCLXIII, 594.
49 Hamillton, I, 162.
50 D, 21 April 1881.

51 Shannon, *Disraeli*, *op. cit.*, 402–3.
52 See p. 62.
53 P. Magnus, *Gladstone* (1954), 280–81.
54 D, 10 May 1881.
55 D, 21 April 1881.
56 Hamilton, I, 61, n5.
57 Lord E. Fitzmaurice, *Granville* (1905), II, 301.
58 D, 11 November 1881.
59 D, 13 November 1881.
60 D, 21 November 1881.
61 Hamilton, I, 187.
62 D, 29 September 1881.
63 D, 13 October 1881.
64 *Annual Register*, 1881, 196. *Berkshire Chronicle*, 29 October 1881, 5. Shaw-Lefevre took care to blame the Conservative members of the Irish Land Commission, set up by the Conservative government; but the general point holds.
65 D, 19 October 1881.
66 D, 4 November 1881; 18 January 1882.
67 Schreuder, *op. cit.*, 369.
68 D, 18, 23 May 1883.
69 T. A. Jenkins, *Gladstone, Whiggery and the Liberal Party, 1874–1886* (1988), 234–5.
70 Rathbone to G, 16 April 1883. GP, 44480, 192.
71 Firth to G, 13 April 1883. Ib., 157.
72 Rathbone to G, 9 May 1883. Ib., 309.
73 Hamilton, II, 138.
74 Cross to G, 3 May 1882. GP, 44475, 89.
75 H, CCLXIX, 836.
76 B. Holland, *Devonshire* (1911), I, 356.
77 Gregory to G, 8 June 1882. GP, 56450. Of Coole Park in Co. Galway, Gregory was the husband of Lady Gregory, after his death patroness of the Irish cultural revival and of W. B. Yeats.
78 Harrison to G, 5 July 1882. GP, 44476, 10. The largest item in G's bond portfolio (one third) was £19,400 of Egyptian Tribute Loan. See H. C. G. Matthew, *Gladstone, 1875–1898* (1975), 375.
79 G to Gregory, 9 June 1882. GP, 56450.
80 G & G, 2, i, 348.
81 S. Gwynn and G. M. Tuckwell, *Life of … Sir Charles Dilke* (1917), I, 446–7.
82 R. Robinson *et al.*, *Africa and the Victorians* (1963), 111.
83 G & G, 2, i, 380.
84 D, 14 July 1882.
85 G memo, 14 September 1882. GP, 46450.
86 G to Richard, 31 August 1882. Ib.
87 D, 16 September 1882.
88 Q & G, II, 236.

89 D, 14 August 1882.
90 Abbott to G, 16 September 1882. GP, 56450.
91 D, 30 November 1882. Derby was the only man who was a Cabinet colleague of both Disraeli and Gladstone.
92 D, 28 December 1882.
93 Q & G, II, 233–4; D, 22 June 1883.
94 Jenkins, *op. cit.*, 183.
95 Tennyson to G, 2 October 1883. GP, 44483, 188.

Notes to Chapter 16: Such a Supreme Moment, 1884–1886

1 Rathbone to G, 23 Oct. 1883. GP, 44483, 266.
2 Ib.
3 T. A. Jenkins, *Gladstone, Whiggery and Liberal Party* (1988), 236–7; D, 29 December 1883.
4 G & G, 2, ii, 130; Jenkins, *op. cit.*, 181–2.
5 D, 23 October, 26 December 1883.
6 Ib.
7 D, 18 January 1884.
8 See p. 223.
9 Eastern Rumelia (capital Philippopolis, or Plovdiv) was duly united with Bulgaria in 1885.
10 D, 10 October 1883.
11 D, 27 December 1883. See R. T. Shannon, 'John Robert Seeley and the Idea of a National Church', in R. Robbson (ed.), *Ideas and Institutions of Victorian Britain* (1967), & D. Wormall, *Sir John Seeley and the Uses of History* (1980). G had read Seeley's *Life and Times of Stein* (1878), a text implying the impolicy both of Disraeli's Palmerstonian atavism and G's sentimental populism.
12 D, 11 September 1882.
13 Ellen O'Connell to G, 27 January 1882. GP, 44474, 97. No such bust is known now at Hawarden.
14 Franz Deak, 1803–76, restored Hungary's constitution in 1867 as preliminary to Austro-Hungarian Dual Monarchy.
15 H, CCLXVI, 203.
16 D, 25 October 1880.
17 H, CCLXVI, 260–3.
18 H, CCLXVI, 266.
19 Ib., 273, 521.
20 Ib., 865.
21 Q & G, II, 176, 176–7.
22 Ib.
23 H, CClXVI, 866. For Aberdeen in 1871, see p. 240 above.
24 See p. 323.

25 D, 15 November 1883.
26 G & G, 2, ii, 84.
27 Verney to G, 24, 30 April 1881. GP, 44469, 164, 211.
28 Granville to G, 11 March 1888. GP, 56452.
29 Hamilton, II, 825.
30 G, memo, 9 April 1885. GP, 56452.
31 Hamilton, II, 611.
32 D, 13 April 1884.
33 H, CCLXXXIII, 672–3; CCXCIV, 1765.
34 Ib., 216.
35 Ib., 55.
36 C. C. Weston, 'Salisbury and the Lords, 1868–1895', *Historical Journal*, 1995; R. T. Shannon, *The Age of Salisbury* (1999), 14.
37 Q & G, II, 283.
38 Ib., 284.
39 D, 14 August 1882.
40 G. & G. Grossmith, father and son, *The Diary of a Nobody* (1894), featuring the Pooter family.
41 Shannon, *Salisbury*, 107.
42 Hamilton, I, xvix. G, 'Hereditary Principle', 1884. GP, 44768, 117.
43 G, 'The Franchise Bill and the Present Situation', *Secret*, 19 August 1884. GP, 44768, 93–107.
44 'Steersman, be not precipitate in thine act
of steering, for the river here, my friend
parts in two channels moving to one end
This goes straight forward to the cataract –
That streams about the bend:
But though the cataract seems the nearer way,
Whate'er the crowd on either bank may say,
Take thou the "bend", 'twill save thee many a day.'
'To Miss Gladstone', 5 November 1884.
GP, 44488, 31.
45 Shannon, *Salisbury*, *op. cit.*, 94.
46 Q & G, II, 311. Even Dilke's Redistribution scheme, as G sorrowfully informed the Queen, involved 'more extensive changes than Mr Gladstone would have thought necessary or desirable'.
47 R. Fulford, *Beloved Mama* (1981), 158, 168.
48 H, CCXCIV, 157.
49 A. B. Cooke and J. Vincent (eds), *Lord Carlingford's Journal* (1971), 49–50, 60.
50 S. Gwynn and G. M. Tuckwell, *Dilke* (1917), II, 97.
51 J. Chamberlain, *Political Memoir, 1880–1892*, ed. C. H. D. Howard (1953), 109.
52 Jenkins, *op. cit.*, 235–6.
53 M. MacDonagh, *The Life of William O'Brien* (1928), 81–2. *The Times*, 9 October 1913, 8; *Freeman's Journal*, 2 March 1885.

54 Gwynn and Tuckwell, *op. cit.*, II, 62.
55 *Carlingford*, 89.
56 D, 2 May 1885.
57 G, *The Irish Question* (1886), 7–8.
58 Chamberlain, *op. cit.*, 136.
59 D, 9 May 1885.
60 Chamberlain, *op. cit.*, 149.
61 Morley, III, 194, 197.
62 Q & G, II, 354–8.
63 D, 9 May 1885.
64 D, 18 June 1885.
65 D, 30 June 1885.
66 The British Minister in Stockholm concluded in 1885: 'There is little now to prevent the United Kingdoms from drifting asunder.' *British views on Norwegian-Swedish Problems, 1880–1895. Selections from Diplomatic Correspondence*, ed. P. Knaplund (1952), 227.
67 B. Holland, *Devonshire* (1911), II, 82–3.
68 D, 5 August 1885.
69 Shannon, *Salisbury*, *op. cit.*, 161.
70 Ib., 157.
71 D, 17 July 1885.
72 Shannon, *Salisbury*, *op. cit.*, 156.
73 A. B. Cooke and J.Vincent, *Governing Passion* (1974), 53.
74 Holland, *Devonshire*, *op. cit.*, II, 99.
75 Ib, 42–3.
76 I. Ker, *John Henry Newman* (1988), 51.
77 Newman's *Apologia pro Vita Sua* of 1864 was a riposte to Kingsley's accusation that Newman did not consider truth a necessary virtue.
78 D, 29 August 1885,
79 D, 10 October 1885.
80 G & G, II, 415.
81 Holland, ib., 101.
82 Ib., 83–5.
83 Holland, ib., 99.
84 PMP, I, 136.
85 Morley, III, 240.
86 *Carlingford*, *op. cit.*, 134.
87 *Annual Register*, 1885, 176
88 *Carlingford*, *op. cit.*, 141.
89 *The Times*, 10 November 1885, 7.
90 D, 18 November 1885. Schnadhorst had originally been one of Chamberlain's Birmingham apparat. Retired 1893.
91 D, 25 October 1885.
92 *Annual Register*, 1885, 180.
93 See p. 349.

94 D, 11, 18 October 1885.
95 Channing to G, 15 December 1885. GP, 44493, 225.
96 G to Granville, 9 December 1885. GP, 56446.
97 D, 30 June 1885.
98 D, 15 December 1885.
99 J. Loughlin, *Gladstone, Home Rule, and the Ulster Question, 1882–93* (1986), 33, 45.
100 A. J. Balfour, *Chapters of Autobiography*, ed. B. Dugdale (1930), 211–12.
101 G to Hill, 15 December 1885. GP, 44493, 231. Hill was at the point of being sacked at the *Daily News* for its failure to match the rising circulation of the Conservative *Standard* and *Telegraph*.
102 G to R. Grosvenor, 7 January 1886. GP, 56447.
103 Loughlin, *op. cit.*, 41–5.
104 H, CCCII, 635–6.
105 Holland, *op. cit.*, 105.
106 G to Granville, 31 December 1885. GP, 56446.
107 G, memo, 26 December 1885. Morley, II, 510–12.
108 H, CCCII, 10–19.
109 Holland, *op. cit.*, II, 110. Hamilton recorded Morley on 31 July 1902: 'J.M. has come to the conclusion, he says, that the machinations of December 1885 strike him more and more as "the most absolutely indefensible thing in Mr G.'s career." They drive him wild. "There were", he adds, "only two honest men in the whole affair – namely, Hartington and Parnell."'

Notes to Chapter 17: Old Man in a Hurry, 1886

1 G to Granville, 18 January 1886. GP, 56447.
2 Hamilton, III, 15.
3 B. Holland, *Devonshire* (1911), II, 111.
4 Hamilton, III, 21.
5 Ib., 17.
6 She was Vice-Principal of Newnham College, Cambridge. She had been offered the principalship of Holloway College in London. P. Jalland, 'Mr Gladstone's Daughters: the Domestic Price of Victorian Politics', in B. Kinzer (ed.), *The Gladstonian Turn of Mind* (1985), 97, 116–17.
7 Ib.
8 Ib., 13.
9 G to Granville, 22 December 1885. GP, GP, 56446.
10 Grosvenor to G, 14 December 1885. GP, 56446.
11 G to K. O'Shea, 29 January 1886. GP, 56447.
12 R. F. Foster, 'History and the Irish Question', *Transactions of the Royal Historical Society*, 1983, 181.
13 G, memo, 30 January 1886. GP, 44771.
14 Chamberlain to G, 30 January 1886. GP, 44126, 132.

15 Chamberlain to G, 19 December 1885. Ib., 127.

16 Chamberlain refused the Admiralty as a mockery. It was true that he had only been ten years in Parliament, and six years in Cabinet office. But Gladstone had only been thirteen years in Parliament and less than three years in Cabinet office when he became Colonial Secretary in 1845.

17 D, 15 February 1886.

18 Hamilton, III, 23.

19 Q & G, II, 390, 391.

20 GP, 44771, 1–2.

21 D, 12 February 1886.

22 See p. 102.

23 See p. 360.

24 Foster, *op. cit.*, 181.

25 The Ulsterman Hugh Holmes was one of the few to penetrate G's inwardness in this respect, concluding after much rumination and observation that G had 'gradually come to believe that he was the man especially appointed by divine providence to make Ireland peaceful and contented'. A. B. Cooke and J. R. Vincent, 'Ireland and Party Politics, 1885–87', *Irish Historical Studies*, 1968–69, 166.

26 Davitt to Labouchere, 29 January 1886. GP, 44494, 89.

27 H, CCCII, 581–636; 1917.

28 R.T. Shannon, *Salisbury* (1999), 190–91.

29 H, CCCII, 173.

30 Salis-Schwabe to G, 6 March 1886. GP, 44495, 153. O. Browning to G, 8 March 1886. Ib., 176. J. Bryce to G, 12 March 1886. GP, 56447.

31 A. B. Cooke and J. Vincent, *Governing Passion* (1974), 54.

32 Hamilton, III, 29.

33 Chamberlain to G, 15 March 1886. GP, 44126, 154, quoting Gladstone's 'own words'.

34 Chamberlain to G, 15 March 1886. GP, 44126, 154.

35 G to Chamberlain, 15 March 1886. Ib., 160. D, 23 March 1886. R. E. J. Walling (ed.), *Diaries of John Bright* (1930), 535.

36 *Diaries of John Bright, op. cit.*, 536–7.

37 Tennyson to G, [14 March 1886]. GP, 44495, 259.

38 Evans to G, 28 November 1890. GP, 44511, 199.

39 See p. 241.

40 G to Morley, 22 March 1886. GP, 44255, 65. That was the practice also of the Austro-Hungarian Monarchy.

41 A. V. Dicey, *England's Case Against Home Rule* (1886), 226.

42 D, 25 March 1886.

43 D, 26 March 1886.

44 Harcourt to G, 26 March 1886. GP, 56445.

45 Hamilton, III, 31.

46 Ib.

47 It was eventually set at a fixed sum.

48 D, 5 April 1886.

49 F. S. L. Lyons, *Charles Stewart Parnell* (1977), 343.
50 Heneage to G, 29 March, 1886. GP, 44496, 90.
51 *Diaries of John Bright, op. cit.*, 538.
52 D, 1 April 1886.
53 *Diaries of John Bright, op. cit.*, 538.
54 Sandhurst to G, 2 April 1886. GP, 44496, 162.
55 Psalms 17.5.
56 J. L. Hammond. *Gladstone and the Irish Nation* (1938), 489.
57 Hamilton, III, 33–4.
58 J. Chamberlain, *Political Memoir*, ed. C. H. D. Howard (1953), 212.
59 H, CCCIV, 1038–1085. See J. Kendle, *Ireland and the Federal Solution, 1870–1921* (1989), 47.
60 Fischer to Primrose, 15 April 1886. GP, 44496, 251.
61 The Budapest Parliament suspended the Croat Diet in 1912.
62 H, CCCIV, 1053–1054.
63 Cooke and Vincent, *Governing Passion, op. cit.*, 403.
64 G. D. Goodlad, 'The Liberal Party and Gladstone's Land Purchase Bill of 1886', *Historical Journal*, 1989.
65 *Annual Register*, 1886, 148. Lord Eversley, *Gladstone and Ireland* (1912), 305.
66 Cooke and Vincent, *Governing Passion, op. cit.*, 403.
67 Ib., 403.
68 Ib., 410.
69 D, 20 April 1886.
70 See J. Roach, 'Liberalism and the Victorian Intelligentsia', *Cambridge Historical Journal*, 1957.
71 D, 26 April 1886.
72 D, 28 April 1886.
73 See pp. 304–5.
74 *The Times*, 4 May 1886, 7.
75 A. Morley to G, 9 May 1886. Ib.
76 D, 7 May 1886.
77 Stansfeld to G, 5 May 1886. GP, 44497, 134.
78 Same, 6 May 1886. Ib., 176.
79 He formulated this jingle in a public letter to a Liberal Unionist on 7 May 1886.
80 Whitbread to G, 11 May 1886. GP, 44497, 199.
81 Illingworth to G, 12 May 1886. Ib., 201.
82 G to Illingworth, 12 May 1886. Ib., 203.
83 Morley, II, 567–69.
84 Pease to G, 14 May 1886. GP, 44497, 223.
85 G to Pease, 15 May 1886. Ib., 231.
86 D, 14 May 1886.
87 D, 18 May 1886.
88 Pease to G, 20 May 1886. GP, 44497, 246.
89 G to Pease, 21 May, 1886. Ib., 258.

90 Hamilton, III, 37–8.
91 Labouchere to Herbert G, 20 March [1886]. GP, 56447.
92 D, 24 May 1886.
93 Brassey to G, 24 May 1886. GP, 44497, 267.
94 *Annual Register*, 1886, 194–6.
95 Chamberlain, *Memoir*, 225. Morley, III, 336.
96 See p. 289.
97 R. T. Shannon, 'Gladstone and Home Rule, 1886', *Ireland after the Union, Joint Proceedings of Royal Irish and British Academies*, 1986, 55.
98 E. D. Steele, 'Gladstone and Ireland', *Irish Historical Studies*, 1970–71, 73.
99 See D. G. Boyce, 'In the Front Rank of the Nation: Gladstone and the Unionists of Ireland', D. Bebbington & R. Swift, *Gladstone Centenary Essays*, 191–4.
100 G. P. Gooch, *Life of Lord Courtney* (1920), 259.
101 H, CCCVI, 1218–1240.
102 Morley, III, 341.
103 See pp. 194–5.
104 G to Duffy, 11 December 1886. GP, 44499, 237.
105 PMP, I, *Autobiographica*, 75.
106 Shannon, 'Gladstone and Home Rule', *op. cit.*, 53.
107 See p. 62.
108 M. Weber, 'The Nature of Charismatic Domination', in W. G. Runciman (ed.), *Max Weber: Selections in Translation* (1978), 248.
109 Q & G, II, 416.
110 P. T. Marsh, *Joseph Chamberlain* (1994), 252.
111 *The Times*, 19 June 1886, 8.
112 W. S. Churchill, *Lord Randolph Churchill* (1905), Appendix V. Shannon, 'Gladstone and Home Rule, 1886', *Ireland after the Union, op. cit.*, 52.
113 Rogers to G, 19 June [1886]. GP, 44498, 40.
114 G to A. Morley, 9 July 1886. GP, 56445.
115 Fyffe to G, 5 May 1890. GP, 56445.
116 G. M. Trevelyan, *Bright* (1913), 453.
117 Morley, III, 342.
118 Rogers to G, 6 July 1886. GP, 44498, 149. See T. W. Heyck, 'Home Rule, Radicalism, and the Liberal Party, 1886–1895', *Journal of British Studies*, 1974–75.
119 G to Bailey, 5 July 1886. GP, 44498, 131.
120 D, 10 July 1886. G. Leveson Gower, *Years of Content, 1858–1886* (1940), 248–9.
121 The final figures were 193 Gladstonian Liberals, 76 Liberal Unionists, and 316 Conservatives.
122 G to Morley, 9 July 1886. GP, 56445.
123 Ib.
124 Morley, III, 348.
125 D, 31 July 1886.

Notes to Chapter 18: Appeal against the Verdict, 1886–1892

1 G to HG, 16 July 1886. GP, 56445
2 Hamilton, III, 8.
3 D, 2 August 1886.
4 F. W. Hirst, 'Mr Gladstone and Home Rule, 1885–1892', in T. W. Reid (ed.), *Gladstone* (1899), 708.
5 G, memo, 12 July 1886. GP, 56445.
6 G, draft, 29 November 1890. GP, 56448.
7 D, 3 August 1886.
8 J. Vincent, *The Later Derby Diaries* (1981), 64–5.
9 H, CCCVIII, 106.
10 G to Hg, 16 July 1886. GP, 56445.
11 D, 9 July 1886.
12 Hamilton, III, 13–14.
13 D, 8 July 1886.
14 Ib.
15 D, 12 October 1886.
16 D, 9 November 1888. Stanhope was Liberal MP for Wednesbury, 1886.
17 G, *The Irish Question* (1886), 32–3.
18 D, 16 July 1886. G would not have welcomed Stead's role in the matter. By now he detested him, finding his sensational expose of the prostitution of young girls in 'The Maiden Tribute of Modern Babylon' especially offensive. 'He has done more harm to Journalism than any other individual ever known.' (Hamilton, III, 58.)
19 D, XII, 516. Döllinger and his friends were in fact deeply suspicious of the temper of Ultramontanism infecting Irish Roman Catholicism. The same was true of the Italian liberal Catholics extolled by G in his 'Italy and her Church'.
20 G, *The Irish Question* (new edn.), 13 October 1886, 29. See Foster's comments: 'History and the Irish Question', *Transactions of the Royal Historical Society*, 1983, 179–80, 192.
21 Kay-Shuttleworth to G, 29 November 1886. GP, 44499, 206.
22 G to Walsh, 1 June 1887. GP, 44501, 39. The parenthesis is a treasure of Gladstonese. The Archbishop was attracted to R. W. Dale's plan for 'Home Rule All Round'. See A.W.W. Dale, *Life of R.W. Dale* (1898), 459ff.
23 G to Duffy, 11 December 1886. GP, 44499, 237.
24 D, 27 March 1881.
25 G to Newman, 18 December 1881. GP, 44473, 185.
26 J. Chamberlain, *Political Memoir* (ed. C. H. D. Howard, 1953), 233–4.
27 D, 23 December 1886.
28 Chamberlain, *op. cit.*, 234–5.
29 G to Labouchere, 29 December 1886. GP, 44499, 304.
30 D, 29 December 1886.
31 M. Hurst, *Joseph Chamberlain and Liberal Reunion. The Round Table Conference, 1887* (1967).
32 Hurst, *op. cit.*, 284.

33 Chamberlain, *op. cit.*, 252–3.
34 G to *Baptist*, 23 February 1887. GP, 44500, 129.
35 Hamilton, III, 57–8.
36 H, CCCXIII, 1203.
37 Chamberlain, *op. cit.*, 268.
38 Hamilton, III, 119.
39 Whitbread to G, 20 May 1887. GP, 44501, 21.
40 R. T. Shannon, *Mr Gladstone and Swansea, 1887* (1982), 6.
41 G. St Aubyn, *The Royal George* (1963), 233–4.
42 G to Brunner, 15 August 1887. GP, 44501, 222.
43 D, 16 November 1887.
44 D, September 1887. H, CCCXXII, 755–6.
45 White to G, 23 January 1888. GP, 44503, 73.
46 E.g., H, CCCXXII, 776.
47 Hamilton, III, 1.
48 F. S. L. Lyons, *Charles Stewart Parnell* (1977), 403.
49 D, 8 March 1888.
50 G to Laing, 9 September 1888. GP, 44504, 249.
51 D, 12 November 1888.
52 D, 19 December 1888.
53 E. F. C. Collier (ed.), *A Victorian Diarist. Extracts from the Journal of Mary, Lady Monkswell, 1873–1895* (1944), 160.
54 D, 19 November 1888.
55 Hamilton, III, 85. It is fair to record that G's 'Expenditure for Charity and Religion', 1881–90, was £28,694. GGP, Secret Account Book, 94/13, 167.
56 T. W. Reid to G, 24 June 1887. GP, 44501, 95.
57 Hamilton, II, 797.
58 D, 19 March 1887. G to Hodder, 30 April 1887. GP, 44500, 273; Hodder to G, 29 April 1887. Ib., 269. G, however, was forgiving enough to agree to compose the inscription for a series of small panels to be set around the skirt of the bronze mantle on the monument to Shaftesbury eventually sited in Piccadilly Circus, with a design by Albert Gilbert for a figure of Christian Charity (or Divine Love – there has never been an authoritative designation). G's words were: 'During a public life of half a century/ he devoted the influence of his station/ the strong sympathies of his heart/ and the great powers of his mind/ to honouring God/ by serving his fellow men/ an example to his order/ a blessing to his people/ and a name to be by them/ gratefully remembered.' The monument was unveiled in 1893.
59 D, 23 January, 1 February 1888.
60 Hamilton, III, 67.
61 Purcell to G, 24 May 1887. GP, 44501, 29.
62 G to Reid, 6 July 1888. GP, 44504, 85.
63 G to Ly Rothschild, 27 October 1888. GP, 44505, 70.
64 M. E. Chamberlain, *Lord Aberdeen* (1983), 1–2.
65 Hamilton, III, 82–3.
66 Ib., 122.

67 H, CCCXL, 64.
68 Hamilton, III, 81.
69 Ib.
70 Ivory to G, 17 July 1888. GP, 44504, 118.
71 D, 7 November 1888. 'I am a stick in the hand of Him who walks: but it is He who walks that is great.'
72 G to Labouchere, 12 January 1889. GP, 44506, 21.
73 D, 8 Dec. 1888.
74 McCarthy to G, 14 July 1888. GP, 44504, 118.
75 Walsh to G, 25 October 1888. GP, 44505, 61.
76 Haldane to G, 21 November 1888. Ib., 140.
77 Hamilton, III, 94.
78 Ib., 102.
79 D, 4 October 1889.
80 Matthew, *Gladstone, op. cit.*, II, 365–6. D, 13 October 1889.
81 Lyons, *Parnell, op. cit.*, 448.
82 G, memo, 12 January 1891. GP, 56449.
83 G to Parnell, 30 August 1889. GP, 44507, 203. On the problems of getting the Liberal party to accept Catholic claims to the funding of denominational education, see Archbishop Walsh to G, 18, 20 October 1889. GP, 44508, 79, 81. For the Conservatives, Balfour was much more prone to accommodation.
84 GP, 44509, 148.
85 Peel to G, 25 January 1890. Ib., 85.
86 C. L. R. Fletcher, *Mr Gladstone at Oxford, 1890* (1908), 29–39; C. W. Oman, *Memoirs of Victorian Oxford* (1941), 140–41.
87 D, 2 December 1890.
88 Freeman to G, 14 October 1889. GP, 44508, 64.
89 Channing to G, 11 October 1889, Ib., 55.
90 D, 8 February 1890.
91 Ib.
92 Hamilton, III, 121.
93 D, XII, 526–7.
94 D, 4 June 1891.
95 A tiresome consequence of Willy's demise was that Lord Penrhyn, who had married Henry Glynne's daughter Gertrude, challenged – in the result unsuccessfully – the resettlement of the Hawarden estate on Willy's heir, William Glynne Charles Gladstone, then aged six.
96 G to Carnegie, 3 July 1891. GP, 44513, 1.
97 G, 'Electoral Facts, No. III', *Nineteenth Century*, September 1891, 330–31; 337–8; 340.
98 Caine to G, 24 September 1891. GP, 44513, 181. D. A. Hamer, *Liberal Politics in the Age of Gladstone and Rosebery* (1972), 173–4. W. S. Caine, recently Chamberlain's whip and a defector back to Gladstone, was a Temperance man above all else who could not be comfortable with the Tories and the Trade.
99 M. Barker, *Gladstone and Radicalism, 1885–1894* (1975), 160–61.
100 Ib., 162.

101 Rogers to G, 8 October 1891. GP, 44513, 202.
102 G to Labouchere, 24 November 1891. GP, 56449.
103 G to Perry, 5 December 1891. GP, 44513, 293.
104 G to T. W. Reid, 1 February 1892. GP, 44514, 50. See p. 316.
105 D, 26 November 1891. See G's comments to Rendel. F. E. Hamer (ed.), *The Personal Papers of Lord Rendel* (1931), 93–4.
106 Hamilton, III, 148.
107 D, 10 December 1891.
108 D, 15 December 1891. H. G. Hamilton (ed.), *The Private Diaries of Sir Algernon West* (1922), 23–31.
109 Morley, II, 716. Comte Joseph de Maistre (1754–1821), philosopher of the clerical reaction against the French Revolution. See p. xvii.
110 Stuart to G, 6 March 1892. GP, 44514, 114.
111 D, 1 April 1892.
112 D, 21–22 April 1892.
113 H. J. Hanham, *Elections and Party Management* (1959), 375.
114 H, III, 1170, 1672.
115 D, 27 April 1892.
116 Dixie to G, 22 April 1892. GP, 44514, 191.
117 Press clippings, June 1892. GP, 44515, 75.
118 Hughes to G, 30 April 1892. GP, 44514, 225.
119 Hamilton, III, 157.
120 PMP, I, 116.
121 *Standard*, 22 July 1892, 2.
122 R. T. Shannon, *Salisbury* (1999), 372.
123 Marsham to G, 24 June 1892. GP, 44515, 172.
124 Hamilton, III, 158–9.
125 D, McCartney, *W. E. H. Lecky. Historian and Politician* (1994), 125.
126 D, XIII, 431–3. The <> marks indicate passages deleted in Morley's diary.
127 Lord Crewe, *Rosebery* (1931), II, 391–2.
128 A. T. Bassett, *Gladstone to his Wife* (1936), 256.
129 Shannon, *Salisbury*, *op. cit.*, 372.

Notes to Chapter 19: Appeal Dismissed, 1892–1893

1 *Standard*, 22 July 1892, 2.
2 R. T. Shannon, *Salisbury* (1999), 518.
3 D, 22 July 1892.
4 Hamilton, III, 160–61.
5 D, 28 July 1892.
6 Ib.
7 D, 31 July 1892.
8 Hamilton, III, 164–5.

9 D, 28 July 1892.
10 Hamilton, III, 164.
11 A. L. Thorold, *Labouchere* (1913), 375. The other version of 'Labby's' quip was G's trick of 'laying upon Providence the responsibility of always placing the ace of trumps up his sleeve'. Ib.
12 O. Chadwick, *Acton and Gladstone* (1976), 34–5, 37–42. Carnegie's recent purchase of Acton's library had staved off bankruptcy. Like the late Granville, he needed income from office.
13 H, VII, 199–215.
14 Ib., 218, 223.
15 Hamilton, III, 169.
16 Ib., 168.
17 Chadwick, *op. cit.*, 46.
18 D, 15 August 1892.
19 A. Ramm (ed.), *Beloved and Darling Child. Last Letters between Queen Victoria and her Eldest Daughter, 1886–1901* (1990), 146–7.
20 PMP, I, *Autobiographica*, 135.
21 R. R. James, *Rosebery* (1963), 254.
22 Hamilton, III, 172.
23 Carnegie to G, 17 August 1892. GP, 44515, 187.
24 The beast was shot, and its head mounted in the Glynne Arms public house in Hawarden. It was not long before a wreath arrived with an inscription: 'To the memory of the patriotic cow which sacrificed its life in an attempt to save Ireland from Home Rule.'
25 PMP, I, 135.
26 D, 26 September 1892.
27 Hamilton, III, 174, 176–7.
28 Ib., 272.
29 See p. 294.
30 H, VII, 212.
31 Hamilton, III, 191.
32 James, *op. cit.*, 267.
33 Hamilton, III, 177.
34 J. D. Jump, *Tennyson. The Critical Heritage* (1956), 214.
35 Q & G, II, 443.
36 F. W. Hirst, 'Mr Gladstone's Fourth Premiership and Final Retirement, 1892–1897', in T. W. Reid (ed.), *Gladstone* (1899), 724.
37 L. Masterman (ed.), *Mary Gladstone (Mrs Drew): her Diaries and Letters* (1930), 420.
38 Q & G, II, 447–50.
39 Ramm, *Beloved and Darling Child*, *op. cit.*, 150: '*He* it is who has done all he could to set class against class … and *he* only.'
40 See p. 241.
41 See p. 349.
42 Hamilton, III, 186–7. G to Campell-Bannerman, 23 January 1893. GP, 44517, 20.
43 James, *op. cit.*, 275–6.
44 Q & G, II, 458.

45 R. Jay, *Chamberlain* (1981), 171, 173.
46 See p. 1.
47 Hamilton, III, 183–4.
48 PMP, I, 135–6.
49 Hamilton, III, 185.
50 D, 7 February 1893.
51 James, *op. cit.*, 283.
52 Hamilton, III, 190–91.
53 H, VIII, 1260–1262, 1273.
54 Ib., 1412.
55 D, 8, 11 May 1893. G wrote 'it is'.
56 Hamilton, III, 197.
57 Ib., 194–5.
58 J. Spender and C. Asquith, *Life of Lord Oxford and Asquith* (1932), I, 78–9.
59 D, 5 April 1893.
60 G to Mme Sadi-Carnot, 26 June 1894. GP, 44518, 244.
61 Q & G, II, 463–4.
62 Ramm, *Beloved and Darling Child, op. cit.*, 150.
63 Hamilton, III, 195.
64 Ib., 199.
65 Morley, II, 738.
66 Hamilton, III, 204.
67 D, 23 May 1893.
68 Hamilton, III, 205.
69 E. C. F. Collier (ed.), *A Victorian Diarist. Extracts from the Journals of Mary, Lady Monkswell, 1873* (1944), 223–4.
70 See p. 142.
71 D, 25 February 1893. 'Mrs Bridges Willyams enjoyed the same sort of relationship with Disraeli with respect to money as Mrs Thistlethwayte did to Gladstone with respect to sex.' H. C. G. Matthew, *Gladstone, 1875–1898* (1995), 364–5.
72 W. S. Blunt, *My Diaries. Being a Personal Narrative of Events, 1888–1914* (1921), I, 73.
73 H, XIII, 1552.
74 Hamilton, III, 209.
75 In a curiously apposite way, a Scandinavian sub-plot ran parallel with the Westminster debate. G's assurances as to its beneficent relevance sat ill with indications otherwise. G commented to Rosebery on 30 March 1893: 'So far as I know, Norway has a strict *right*, but is making bad use of it.' Alarmed by Swedish threats of military coercion of Norway, G requested the Foreign Office to 'drop some friendly expression of deprecation'. Rosebery reported on 9 June that he had instructed the Minister in Stockholm to urge 'how suicidal would be a civil war between Sweden and Norway'. 'In the race of folly in Scandinavia', commented G, 'Sweden seems at the present moment to get ahead.' GP, 44517, 131. D, 10 May 1893. P. Knaplund, ed., *British Views on Norwegian–Swedish Problems, 1880–1895* (1952), 201.
76 H, XVI, 1458, 1463.

Notes to Chapter 20: Resignation, 1893–1894

1 D, 7 October 1893.
2 P. Stansky, *Ambitions and Strategies. The Struggle for the Leadership of the Liberal Party in the 1890s* (1964), 17.
3 In the published edition of 1894 G footnoted: 'The concluding lines of the Ode are purposely omitted.'
4 D, 10 October 1893. The tragic outcome was that Outram drowned himself in the Thames soon after.
5 Hamilton, III, 213.
6 D, 19 October 1893.
7 Hamilton, III, 213–15.
8 D, 7 October 1893.
9 See p. 419.
10 D, 18 September 1893.
11 See p. 192.
12 Q & G, II, 478.
13 Ib., 479–80.
14 D, 19 December 1893.
15 D, 18 September 1880.
16 Hamilton, III, 216.
17 Ib., 217–18.
18 D, 7 January 1894.
19 D, XIII, 434.
20 Ib., 436.
21 Stansky, *op. cit.*, 28.
22 D, 9 January 1894.
23 T. L. Crosby, *The Two Mr Gladstones* (1997), 220.
24 St Athanasius of Alexandria (296–373), indomitable champion of the Trinitarians against the Arians. Thersites, in the *Iliad*, a deformed and impudent talker among the Greeks at Troy. Dispatched by Achilles.
25 PMP, I, 122.
26 Stansky, *op. cit.*, 29.
27 Hamilton, III, 220–21.
28 Ib., 221–2.
29 R. T. Shannon, 'Peel, Gladstone and Party', *Parliamentary History*, 1999, 317. L A. Tollemache, *Talks with Mr Gladstone* (1901), 116.
30 N. Gash, *Peel* (1972), 709.
31 Hamilton, III, 226–7, 234.
32 Stansky, *op. cit.*, 30.
33 Hamilton, III, 226.
34 Stansky, *op. cit.*, 30–31.
35 Hamilton, III, 229.
36 D, 31 January 1894.

37 S. Brown, 'One Last Campaign from the G. O. M.: Gladstone and the House of Lords in 1894', in B. Kinzer (ed.), *The Gladstonian Turn of Mind* (1985), 157–8.
38 Stansky, *op. cit.*, 41–56.
39 D, 4 February 1894.
40 D, 6 February 1894.
41 D, 8 February 1894.
42 Brown, *op. cit.*, 157–8.
43 Hamilton, III, 232.
44 Ib., 233.
45 Brown, *op. cit.*, 159–60.
46 Hamilton, III, 226, 233.
47 PMP, I, 136.
48 Ib., 120.
49 D, 6 March 1894.
50 D, 12 February 1894.
51 Hamilton, III, 236.
52 Ib., 238–9; Stansky, *op. cit.*, 62–3.
53 H, XXI, 851–2; PMP, I, 120.
54 Hamilton III, 242.
55 PMP, I, 121–2.
56 Q & G, II, 491.
57 J. B. Conacher, 'A Visit to the Gladstones in 1894', *Victorian Studies*, 1958–59, 158.
58 D, 1 March 1894.
59 E. F. C. Collier (ed.), *A Victorian Diarist. Extracts from the Journal of Mary, Lady Monkswell, 1873–1895* (1944), 241.
60 D, 1 March 1894.
61 H, XXI, 1151–1152.
62 Lord Oxford and Asquith, *Fifty Years of Parliament* (1926), I, 212.
63 Collier, *op. cit.*, 241.
64 D, 3 March 1894.
65 A. T. Bassett (ed.), *Gladstone to his Wife* (1936), 260. The precedent presumably was Mary Anne Disraeli in 1868. G much preferred the idea of Catherine's regaining dormant peerages to which she was 'supposed to have a good claim'.
66 PMP, I, 136.
67 Balfour to G, 2 March 1894. GP, 44517, 65.
68 PMP, I, 121–2.
69 Hamilton, III, 241.

Notes to Chapter 21: Last Years, 1894–1898

1 D, 2 March 1894. Armitstead got his peerage eventually from the new Liberal government in 1906.
2 Later King George V (1910–1936) and Queen Mary.

3 D, 10 March 1894.
4 D, 5 March 1894.
5 D, 10, 11 March 1894. A. Isba, *Gladstone and Women* (2006), ch 9.
6 Q & G, II, 457–8.
7 G. W. E. Russell, *Collections and Recollections* (1898), ch 14. *Oxford Dictionary of Quotations* (1953), 552.
8 PMP, I, 136.
9 Ib., 169.
10 D, 2 January 1896.
11 PMP, I, 262–3.
12 Hamilton, III, 253.
13 Murray to G, 11 September 1894. GP, 44519, 68.
14 PMP, I, 164.
15 H, XXII, 22–3.
16 D, 6 March 1894.
17 D, 17 February 1894.
18 D. Bennett, *Margot* (1984), 123.
19 D. Newsome, *On the Edge of Paradise* (1980), 50.
20 PMP, I, 164. The first entry in the diary was for 16 July 1825.
21 D, 1 September 1894.
22 J. B. Conacher, 'A Visit to the Gladstones in 1894', *Victorian Studies*, 1958–59, 156–60. Lady Aberdeen was Lord Tweedmouth's sister.
23 AIC to G, 4 July 1894. GP, 44518, 265.
24 Shurick to G, 12 December 1894. GP, 44519, 272.
25 D, 24 December 1894.
26 L. Masterman, *Mary Gladstone (Mrs Drew): Her Diaries and Letters* (1930), 426.
27 R. R. James, *Rosebery* (1963), 380.
28 D, 19 September 1892.
29 See p. 247.
30 D, 26 September 1892.
31 One of the first things Rosebery did on succeeding G was to appoint Seeley K.C.M.G.
32 Lord Crewe, *Rosebery* (1931), II, 507.
33 G to Cowan, 1 July 1895. GP, 44520, 240.
34 R. T. Shannon, *Salisbury* (1999), 406.
35 Ib., 419.
36 I.e., £40,000.
37 G to O'Brien, 10 December 1895. GP, 56445.
38 Crewe, *Rosebery*, II, 515.
39 E. F. C. Collier (ed.), *Later Extracts from the Journals of Mary, Lady Monkswell, 1895–1909* (1946), 1. Bennett, *Margot*, 145.
40 D, 2 January 1896.
41 G to Webster, 3 March 1896. GP, 44522, 88.
42 As father of Virginia Woolf and Vanessa Bell, Stephen himself became an icon of the Victorian world reacted against by the 'Bloomsbury' ethos.

43 G in 1884 had read Stephen's critique of Butler in *The History of English Thought in the Eighteenth Century* (1876). J. Garnett, 'Bishop Butler and the *Zeitgeist*: Butler and the Development of Christian Moral Philosophy in Victorian Britain', in C. Cunliffe (ed.), *Joseph Butler's Moral and Religious Thought* (1922). It should be noted that *The Oxford Dictionary of the Christian Church* (ed. F. L. Cross, 1957), 47, 211, listed G's edition as the best modern edition of the *Analogy*, and his edition of the *Works* similarly.

44 G to Hirsch, 13 February 1895. GP, 44522, 65.

45 D, 27 July 1895.

46 Purcell to G, 2 June 1896. GP, 44522, 206.

47 Spencer to G, 11 August 1896. GP, 44523, 187.

48 G to *Daily Chronicle*, 13 September 1896. Ib., 264.

49 See p. 285.

50 GP, 44524, 124.

51 A. C. Benson, *The Life of Edward White Benson, Sometime Archbishop of Canterbury* (1899), II, 733.

52 D, 20 October 1896. The will was signed and dated 26 November 1896. The three sons were each to receive a share worth £37k, the three daughters a share each worth £20k.

53 D, 7 December 1896. In a legal case involving accusations against G in 1927, counsel for the Gladstone family advised that the Declaration be not cited. Matthew, *Gladstone, 1875–1898* (1995), 377–8.

54 Brooke and Sorenson, *The Prime Ministers' Papers: W. E. Gladstone*, vol. I, *Autobiographica*, 2–3. R. T. Shannon, 'Political Memoirs: Disraeli and Gladstone', in *Politische Memoiren in deutscher und britischer Perspektive*, ed. F. Bosbach and M. Brechtken, *Prinz-Albert-Studien*, v. 23 (2005), 69–74.

55 PMP, I, 136. See pp. 87–8.

56 See p. 369.

57 See p. 323.

58 See p. 391.

59 See p. 392.

60 See p. 363.

61 See p. 348.

62 H. C. G. Matthew, *Gladstone, 1875–1898*, 184, citing King George V.

63 GP, 44791, 19.

64 Hirst to G, 1 January 1897. GP, 44525. The others were J. S. Phillimore, Hilaire Belloc, P. J. McDonald, J. L. Hammond and J. A. Simon. Both Hirst and Hammond became notable journalists and Gladstone scholars. Phillimore became a Professor at Glasgow. Simon became Foreign Secretary. Belloc became Belloc.

65 G to Carnegie, 22 February 1897. GP, 44525, 103.

66 GP, 44776, 180.

67 Ib., 173–5. On G's earlier 'reckless and naïve' proneness to recommend her abdication, see Isba, *Gladstone and Women*, 185.

68 Massingham to G, 14 June 1897. GP, 44525, 256.

69 For a charmingly informal photograph of the occasion see I. March-Phillips and B. Christian (eds.), *Some Hawarden Letters, 1878–1893* (1917), 82.

70 Newsome, *On the Edge of Paradise*, 96–7.

71 Lord Ronaldshay, *Life of Lord Curzon* (1928), I, 249–50.

72 Hamilton, III, 344–5.

73 Collier, *Later Monkswell Journals*, *op. cit.*, 59.

74 F. W. Hirst, 'Mr Gladstone's Last Days', in T. W. Reid (ed.), *Gladstone* (1899), 742.

75 Collier, *Later Monkswell Journals*, *op. cit.*, 44.

76 A. Ramm (ed.), *Beloved and Darling Child, 1886–91* (1990), 215.

77 Hamilton, III, 356.

78 Collier *op. cit.*, 45–8.

79 Hamilton, III, 357. The Queen recorded that the account of the funeral 'and above all one from Mrs Gladstone was very touching'. (Ramm, 215.) Catherine joined G in the north transept on 19 June 1900.

Select Bibliography

The Royal Historical Society Bibliography (www.rhs.ac.uk) lists 646 entries concerning W. E. Gladstone. Caroline J. Dobson, *Gladstoniana: A Bibliography of Material Relating to W. E. Gladstone at St Deiniol's Library, Hawarden* (1981) contains 501 items, many of them, valuably, from obscure contemporary sources. The mass of unpublished papers is held at the British Library: *Catalogue of Additions to the Manuscripts: the Gladstone Papers, Add. Mss. 44086–44835* (1953), with further Add. Mss. 56444–56453); with another large Glynne-Gladstone deposit of personal, family, estate and miscellaneous material at Clywd Record Office, Hawarden. These two collections have been made available in microform by Research Publication International, Reading.

GENERAL COLLECTIONS

Three recent collections ranging widely over pretty well all aspects of Gladstone's life and career are: P. J. Jagger, ed., *Gladstone, Politics and Religion: A Collection of Founder's Day Lectures Delivered at St Deiniol's Library, Hawarden, 1967–83* (1985), P. J. Jagger, ed., *Gladstone* (1998) and D. W. Bebbington and R. Swift, eds, *Gladstone Centenary Essays* (2000), with a comprehensive bibliography by R. Swift.

GLADSTONE'S WRITINGS AND PUBLICATIONS

A Bibliography of Gladstone's Publications at St Deiniol's Library (1977), by Patricia M. Long, lists 348 titles of books, articles and addresses. St Deiniol's Library contains 38 volumes of Gladstone's *Speeches and Writings*, mostly press clippings. The Stationery Office published *The Prime Ministers' Papers: W. E. Gladstone* (4 vols, 1971–81), eds J. Brooke and M. Sorenson, including much autobiographica.

The most important of Gladstone's published writings are the 14 vols of *The Gladstone Diaries, with Cabinet Papers and Prime Ministerial Correspondence*, eds M. R. D. Foot and H. C. G. Matthew (1969–94). Gladstone himself collected what he considered the more significant of his numerous occasional pieces in two sets of *Gleanings*, the first in 1879, the second in 1897.

SPEECHES

There is no satisfactory edition of Gladstone's speeches. The project edited by A. W. Hutton and H. J. Cohen produced only two volumes covering the period 1892–94 (1902). A. T. Bassett's *Gladstone's Speeches: Descriptive Index and Bibliography* (1916) includes fourteen speeches between 1850 and 1886. Gladstone himself published *The Financial Statements of 1853, 1860–1863* (1863) and *Speeches on Parliamentary Reform, 1866, Speeches in South-West Lancashire, October 1868, Speeches on Great Questions of the Day* (1870), *Political Speeches in Scotland, November and December, 1879, Political Speeches in Scotland, March and April 1880*, and *Speeches on the Irish Question in 1886, Midlothian Speeches, 1879*, ed. M. R. D. Foot (1971), *Political Speeches Delivered in November 1885.*

LETTERS

Of published letters the standard collections are *The Palmerston Papers: Gladstone and Palmerston, being the Correspondence of Lord Palmerston with Mr Gladstone, 1851–1865*, ed. P. Guedalla (1928) and *The Political Correspondence of Mr Gladstone and Lord Granville, 1868–1876* (2 vols, 1952) and *1876–1886* (2 vols, 1962), ed. Agatha Ramm. P. Guedalla's edition of *The Queen and Mr Gladstone* (2 vols, 1933), traces the stages of their increasingly fraught relationship.

FAMILY

For the family the prime text is S. G. Checkland, *The Gladstones. A Family Biography, 1764–1851* (1971), complemented by P. Gladstone, *Portrait of a Family: The Gladstones, 1839–1889* (1989) and S. Gooddie, *Mary Gladstone: A Gentle Rebel* (2003), G. Battiscombe, *Mrs Gladstone* (1956), J. Marlow, *Mr and Mrs Gladston:. An Intimate Biography* (1977), and A. T. Bassett, ed., *Gladstone to his Wife* (1936), P. Jalland, 'Mr Gladstone's Daughters: The Domestic Price of Victorian Politics', in B. L. Kinzer, ed., *The Gladstonian Turn of Mind* (1985). Acton's almost familial relationship to Gladstone is examined in O. Chadwick, *Acton and Gladstone* (1976). There is much also on the family in A. Isba, *Gladstone and Women* (2006).

OTHER DIARIES, JOURNALS, MEMOIRS

Of these the most important are D. W. R. Bahlman, ed., *The Diary of Sir Edward Hamilton, 1880–1885* (2 vols, 1972), and *1885–1906* (1993), and the various editions by J. R. Vincent of the diaries of Edward Henry Stanley, 15th Earl of Derby: *Disraeli, Derby and the Conservative Party, 1849–1869* (1978), *A Selection from the Diaries of Edward Henry Stanley (1826–1893) between September 1869 and March 1878* (1994), and *The Diaries of Edward Henry Stanley, 15th Earl of Derby (1826–1893) between 1878 and 1893* (2003). Also revealing are T. A. Jenkins, ed., *The Parliamentary Diaries of Sir John Trelawny, 1858–1865* (1990) and *1868–1873* (1994), and A. B. Cooke and J. R. Vincent, eds, *Lord Carlingford's Journal: Reflections of a Cabinet Minister, 1885* (1971).

BIOGRAPHIES

J. Morley, *The Life of William Ewart Gladstone* (3 vols, 1903) brilliantly set the tone and the orthodoxy. See D. M. Schreuder, 'The making of Mr Gladstone's Posthumous Career; The Role of Morley and Knaplund as "Monumental Masons", 1903–27', in B. L. Kinzer, ed., *The Gladstonian Turn of Mind* (1985). None of E. Eyck (1938), G. M. Young (1948), P. Magnus (1954), or E. J. Feuchtwanger (1975) among the more noteworthy efforts made much impression on this orthodoxy. Nor did the 'psychological' interpretations of the 'two Mr Gladstones' theme, G. T. Garratt (1936), and T. L. Crosby (1995), nor practitioners of concision, P. Stansky (1979), A. Ramm (1989), E. F. Biagini (1999), and M. S. Partridge (2003). The challenge of R. T. Shannon in two volumes (1982 and 1999) failed to make serious impact through density and overcrowding. That leaves the formidably Morleyan volumes of H. C. G. Matthew (1986 and 1995, consolidated 1997), and Roy (Lord) Jenkins (1995), in command of the field.

POLITICS

Four studies serve as broad background: A. Sykes, *The Rise and Fall of British Liberalism, 1776–1988* (1997), J. P. Parry, *The Rise and Fall of Liberal Government in Victorian Britain* (1993), H. J. Hanham, *Elections and Party Managemen: Politics in the Time of Disraeli and Gladstone* (1978) and G. R. Searle, *The Liberal Party: Triumph and Disintegration,1886–1929* (1992). M. J. Winstanley, *Gladstone and the Liberal Party* (1990); R. T. Shannon, 'Peel, Gladstone and Party', *Parliamentary History*, 1999; H. C. G. Matthew, 'Disraeli, Gladstone and the Politics of Mid-Victorian Budgets', *Historical Journal*, 1979; J. R. Vincent, *The*

Formation of the Liberal Party, 1857–1868 (1966); F. B. Smith, *The Making of the Second Reform Bill* (1966); M. Cowling, *Disraeli, Gladstone and Revolution, 1867* (1967); E. F. Biagini, *Liberty, Retrenchment and Reform: Popular Liberalism in the Age of Gladstone, 1860–1880* (1992): C. Harvie, 'Gladstonianism, the provinces and popular political culture, 1860–1906', in R. Bellamy, ed., *Victorian Liberalism: Nineteenth-century Political Thought and Practice* (1990); T. W. Heyck, 'Home Rule, radicalism and the Liberal party', in A. O' Day, *Reactions to Irish Nationalism* (1987); P. Adelman, *Gladstone, Disraeli and Later Victorian Politics* (1970); R. Blake, *Gladstone, Disraeli and Queen Victoria* (1993); T. A. Jenkins, *Gladstone, Whiggery and the Liberal Party, 1874–1886* (1988); D. Brooks, 'Gladstone and Midlothian', *Scottish Historical Review*, 1985; W. C. Lubenow, *Parliamentary Politics and the Home Rule Crisis, 1886* (1988); D. A. Hamer, *Liberal Politics in the Age of Gladstone and Rosebery* (1972); S. Brown, 'One Last Campaign from the GOM: Gladstone and the House of Lords in 1894', in B. L. Kinzer, ed., *The Gladstonian Turn of Mind* (1985).

RELIGION AND THE CHURCH

D. Lathbury, ed., *Correspondence on the Church and Religion of W. E. Gladstone* (2 vols, 1910), tried, unsuccessfully, to fill in the dimension from which Morley was warned off. Thus was consecrated the split between Gladstone's religion and politics that has bedevilled Gladstone studies ever since. The gap left by secular interpretation following John Morley began to be filled by P. Butler, *Gladstone: Church, State and Tractarianism, 1809–1859* (1982), and D. M. Schreuder, 'Gladstone and the Conscience of the State', in P. Marsh, ed., *The Conscience of the Victorian State* (1979), B. Hilton, 'Gladstone's Theological Politics', in M. Bentley and J. Stevenson, eds, *High and Low Politics in Victorian Britain* (1983), A. Ramm, 'Gladstone's Religion', *Historical Journal*, 1985, R. J. Helmstadter, 'Conscience and Politics: Gladstone's First Book', *The Gladstonian Turn of Mind*, ed. B. L. Kinzer (1985), J. P. Parry, *Democracy and Religion: Gladstone and the Liberal Party, 1867–1875* (1986), R. T. Shannon, 'Gladstone, the Roman Church, and Italy', in M. Bentley, ed., *Public and Private Doctrine* (1993), P. J. Jagger, *Gladstone: The Making of a Christian Politician, 1809–1832* (1991), R. J. Helmstadter, 'Conscience and Politics: Gladstone's First Book', in P. J. Jagger, ed., *Gladstone, Politics and Religion* (1985) and D. Lorenzo, 'Gladstone, Religious Freedom and Practical Reasoning', *History of Political Thought*, 2005.

LITERARY AND INTELLECTUAL INTERESTS

P. Metcalf's *James Knowles, Victorian Editor and Architect* (1980), is a mine of information about Gladstone's connection with the Metaphysical Society, with the *Contemporary Review* and the *Nineteenth Century*, to both of which, especially the latter, he contributed copiously, and generally for the life of the mind in Victorian Britain. A. Ramm examines *Gladstone as Man of Letters* (1981). F. M. Turner, *The Greek Heritage in Victorian Britain* (1981), covers the ground of Gladstone's Homeric studies. See also D. W. Bebbington, 'Gladstone and Homer', in D. W. Bebbington and R. Swift, eds, *Gladstone Centenary Essays* (2000), D. W. Bebbington, *The Mind of Gladstone: Religion, Homer and Politics* (2004).

Gladstone's relationship with the ex-Carbonaro Principal Librarian of the British Museum is recorded by M. R. D. Foot, 'Gladstone and Panizzi', *British Library Journal*, 1979. For insights on Gladstone's relationship to science and scientists, see R. D. Collinson Black, ed., *Papers and Correspondence of William Stanley Jevons*, IV (1977). Gladstone's intercourse with two Victorian sages is outlined in R. T. Shannon, 'Tennyson and Gladstone', *Times Literary Supplement*, 2 October 1992, and M. Wheeler, 'Gladstone and Ruskin, in P. J. Jagger, ed., *Gladstone* (1998). P. J. Jagger examines 'Gladstone and his Library' in the same collection, in which also G. Wickham attends to 'Gladstone, Oratory and the Theatre'. J. Roach, 'Liberalism and the Victorian Intelligentsia', *Cambridge Historical Journal*, 1957, on the intellectual backlash against Gladstone's direction of Liberalism, and T. Dunne, 'La trahison des clercs: British Intellectuals and the First Home-rule Crisis', *Irish Historical Studies*, 1982.

IRELAND

The orthodox line and tone was romantically set by J. L. le B. Hammond, *Gladstone and the Irish Nation* (1938). Of more recent studies, consult D. A. Hamer, 'The Irish question and Liberal politics', *Historical Journal*, 1969, E. D. Steele, 'Gladstone and Ireland', *Irish Historical Studies*, 1970 and *Irish Land and British Politics* (1974), J. R. Vincent, 'Gladstone and Ireland', *Proceedings of the British Academy*, 1977, A. Warren, 'Gladstone, Land and Social Reconstruction in Ireland, 1881–1887', *Parliamentary History*, 1983, A. O' Day, The Irish problem', in T. R.Gourvish and A. O'Day, eds, *Later Victorian Britain* (1988), R. T. Shannon, 'Gladstone and Home Rule' in *Ireland after the Union, Proceedings of the Second Joint Meeting of the Royal Irish Academy and the British Academy* (1986), J. Loughlin, *Gladstone, Home Rule and the Ulster Question, 1882–1893* (1986), R. V. Comerford, *Gladstone's First Irish Enterprise, 1864–1870* (1989), J. Kendle, *Ireland and the Federal Solution, 1870–1921* (1989), G. D. Goodlad, 'The

Liberal Party and Gladstone's Land Purchase Bill of 1886', *Historical Journal*, 1989, A. O' Day, 'Gladstone and Irish Nationalism' and D. G. Boyce, 'In the Front Rank of the Nation: Gladstone and the Unionists of Ireland, 1868–1893', in *Gladstone Centenary Essays* ed. D. W. Bebbington (2000), D. G. Boyce, 'Gladstone and Ireland', in *Gladstone* ed. P. J. Jagger (1998), H. C. G. Matthew, 'Gladstone, O'Connell and Home Rule', in *National Questions*, eds R. V. Comerford and E. Delaney (2000).

FOREIGN POLICY

The general ground is usefully covered by M. Swartz, *The Politics of British Foreign Policy in the Era of Disraeli and Gladstone* (1985); F. R. Flournoy, 'British Liberal Theories of International Relations, 1848–1898', *Journal of the History of Ideas*, 1946, and K. A. P. Sandiford, 'Gladstone and Europe', in B. L. Kinzer, ed., *The Gladstonian Turn of Mind* (1985), and 'Gladstone and Liberal-Nationalist Movements', *Albion*, 1981. P. Knaplund, *Gladstone's Foreign Policy* (1935), J. L. le B. Hammond, 'Gladstone and the League of Nations Mind', in *Essays in Honour of Gilbert Murray*, eds J. A. K. Thomson and A. Toynbee (1936), W. N. Medlicott, *Bismarck, Gladstone and the Concert of Europe* (1956), R. W. Seton-Watson, *Disraeli, Gladstone and the Eastern Question* (1935), R. T. Shannon, *Gladstone and the Bulgarian Agitation, 1876* (1963), 'Gladstone and British Balkan Policy', in R. Melville and H.-J. Schröder, eds, *Der Berliner Kongress von 1878* (1982), and 'Gladstone and the Hellenic Factor in the Eastern Question', *Actes du Symposium Internationale (Athenes), 'La Dernière Phase de ls Crise Orientale et l'Hellénisme, 1878–1881* (1882), E. Eyck, 'Bismarck and Gladstone', *Contemporary Review*, 1946. Cf. P. W. Schroeder, 'Gladstone as Bismarck', *Canadian Journal of History*, 1980. See A. J. P. Taylor, *The Trouble Makers* (1957) and D. M. Schreuder, 'Gladstone as "troublemaker"', *Journal of British Studies*, 1978. See also P. Knaplund, ed., 'British views on Norwegian-Swedish problems', *Norsk Hist. Kjeldeskrift-Inst.*, 1952. On Italy consult D. E. D. Beales, *England and Italy, 1859–1860* (1961), D. M. Schreuder, 'Gladstone and Italian Unification, 1848–1870', *English Historical Review*, 1970. Among recent studies are R. T. Harrison, *Gladstone's Imperialism in Egypt* (1995), P. J. Parish, 'Gladstone and America', in *Gladstone*, ed. P. J. Jagger (1998), R. E. Quinault, 'Afghanistan and Gladstone's Moral Foreign Policy', *History Today*, 2002.

COLONIES AND EMPIRE

P. Knaplund, *Gladstone and Britain's Imperial Policy* (1927) still sets the scene. See also his 'Gladstone and Jamaica', *The Americas*, 1959. A. G. L. Shaw, *Gladstone at the Colonial Office, 1846* (1986) and K. Fitzpatrick, 'Mr Gladstone and the Governor', *Historical Studies, Australia and New Zealand*, 1940, examine him at the Office. A general conspectus is provided by R. Robinson, J. Gallacher and A. Denny, *Africa and the Victorians* (1961, 1981). Other aspects are: D. M. Schreuder, *Gladstone and Kruger* (1969), H. MacDonald, 'Gladstone and Imperialism', *Millennium*, 1971, F. H. Herrick, 'Gladstone and the Concept of the "English-speaking Peoples"', *Journal of British Studies*, 1972, C. C. Eldridge, *England's Mission: the Imperial Idea in the Age of Gladstone and Disraeli, 1868–1880* (1973), F. Harcourt, 'Gladstone, Monarchism and the "New Imperialism", 1868–1874', *Journal of Imperial and Commonwealth History*, 1986–86, E. F. Biagini, 'Gladstone and Britain's Imperial Role', *Journal of Liberal Democrat History*, 1998 and 'Exporting "Western & Beneficent Institutions": Gladstone and empire', *Gladstone Centenary Essays*, eds D. W. Bebbington and R. Swift (2000).

Index